BIBLIOTHECA EPHEMERIDUM THEOLOGICARUM LOVANIENSIUM

CLXVIII

WISDOM AND APOCALYPTICISM IN THE DEAD SEA SCROLLS AND IN THE BIBLICAL TRADITION

EDITED BY

F. GARCÍA MARTÍNEZ

LEUVEN
UNIVERSITY PRESS

UITGEVERIJ PEETERS
LEUVEN – PARIS – DUDLEY, MA

2003

ISBN 90-5867-337-5 (Leuven University Press)
D/2003/1869/62
ISBN 90-429-1321-5 (Peeters Leuven)
D/2003/0602/75

Library of Congress Cataloging-in Publication Data

Wisdom and apocalypticism in the Dead Sea scrolls and in the biblical tradition / edited by Florentino Garcia Martinez

p. cm. -- (Bibliotheca Ephemeridum theologicarum Lovaniensium; 168)
ISBN 90-429-1321-5

1. Dead Sea scrolls--History and criticism-- Congresses. 2. Bible. O.T.--Criticism, interpretation, etc.--Congresses. 3. Wisdom in literature--Congresses. 4. Apocalypse in literature--Congresses. I. García Martínez, Florentino. II. Series.

BM487.W56 2003
296.1'55--dc21

2003049794

Leuven University Press / Presses Universitaires de Louvain
Universitaire Pers Leuven
Blijde-Inkomststraat 5, B-3000 Leuven (Belgium)

TABLE OF CONTENTS

III

IV

INDEXES

PREFACE

The present volume contains the papers read at the 51st *Colloquium Biblicum Lovaniense* (July 31 – August 2, 2002), dedicated to the study of the theme of Wisdom and Apocalypticism, both in the Dead Sea Scrolls and in the Biblical Tradition.

The "Main papers" (with the exception of that read by Menahen Kister, which due to unforeseen circumstances was not ready on time and will be published elsewhere) and a selection of the "Offered papers" have been thematically grouped into four parts. Part I comprises three articles dealing with the relationship between Wisdom and Apocalypticism within the Dead Sea Scrolls, in comparison with the biblical tradition. Part II includes six papers which focus on specific Wisdom compositions from Qumran, such as 1Q/4QMysteries, 4QInstruction, 4QTime of Righteousness, or the "Tractate of the Two Spirits" from the *Rule of the Community*. Part III consists of nine contributions that analyse different aspects of biblical wisdom compositions (such as Qoheleth, Sirach or the Wisdom of Solomon) or of apocalyptic compositions (such as 1 Enoch or 4 Ezra) in light of Qumran Wisdom material. Part IV groups five studies together centred around several aspects of the wisdom compositions from Qumran (such as messianic ideas, ecstatic worship, the beatitudes, or the fate of the righteous) which are directly relevant for the New Testament.

The contributions are published here in the languages in which they were read: English, French, and German. The contributors to the volume are scholars of the Old Testament, of Early Judaism, of the Dead Sea Scrolls and of the New Testament.

About 130 participants enjoyed the warm and friendly welcome and hospitality offered by the President of the Paus Adrianus VI College, Prof. L. Leijssen, and his staff. They are to be thanked for their kind support in preparing the meeting. Thanks are also due to the Secretariat of the Faculty of Theology of the K.U.Leuven and its staff, particularly Annemie Dumoulin, for administrative support.

I want to express my gratitude to all who have helped me with the organisation of the *Colloquium* and with the preparation of the congress volume for publication. I am grateful to the Committee of the *Colloquium* for electing me as President of the 2002 session before my move to Leuven. I sincerely thank all the scholars who agreed to provide a "main paper" or conduct a seminar, together with all the others who offered papers and contributed to the lively discussions of the seminars and plenary sessions. It was their collective effort that transformed the *Colloquium* into a memorable event and that makes the present volume such a valuable collection. Finally, I want to express my thanks to Professors Joseph Verheyden, the secretary of the CBL, and Gilbert Van Belle, editor of the BETL, for their help during the preparation of the volume.Thanks are due also to Rita Corstjens who prepared the Indexes.

The *Colloquium* was jointly sponsored by the Katholieke Universiteit Leuven and the Université Catholique de Louvain, as well as by the National Fund for Scientific Research (FWO/FNRS, Brussels)

Florentino GARCÍA MARTÍNEZ

INTRODUCTION

The 51st session of the *Colloquium Biblicum Lovaniense*, held at the Faculty of Theology of the K.U. Leuven from July 31 to August 2, 2002, was devoted to the study of "Wisdom and Apocalypticism in the Dead Sea Scrolls and in the Biblical Traditions". The programme included ten main papers, four seminars and thirteen short papers. In the following pages the reader will find a summary presentation of the contents of the papers in the order in which they appear in the volume.

The three papers which form Part I deal with the relationship between Wisdom and Apocalypticism within the Dead Sea Scrolls and compared with the biblical tradition.

My own paper introduces the topic of the meeting and places it in the perspective of the other *Colloquia* dedicated to the study of the Dead Sea Scrolls. As early as 1957, under the presidency of Professor J. van der Ploeg, the 9th meeting of the "Journées Bibliques de Louvain" was dedicated to the study of the recently discovered Qumran manuscripts. The topic of the meeting was: "La secte de Qumrân et les origines du Christianisme", a topic which was perfectly adapted to the manuscripts as they were then known (only the manuscripts found at Cave 1 and published between 1950 and 1956 were available at the time)[1]. Nineteen years later, in 1976, a new *Colloquium*, the 27th, was dedicated once again to the study of the Qumran manuscripts under the presidency of the late Professor M. Delcor. The topic then chosen was rather general: "Qumrân: sa piété, sa théologie et son milieu"[2]. Central to this *Colloquium* were the texts that had been published in the meantime (five new volumes of the Series *Discoveries in the Judaean Desert)* and in particular the forthcoming publications by the members of the original team, which were presented at the *Colloquium* by the authors themselves. Now, twenty-six years after this second CBL dedicated to Qumran, the focus returns once more to the Dead Sea Scrolls. The sheer quantity of new material published since the previous *Colloquia* dedicated to Qumran (more than thirty volumes in the Series *Discoveries in the Judaean*

1. J. VAN DER PLOEG (ed.), *La Secte de Qumrân et les origines du Christianisme* (Recherches Bibliques, 4), Brugge, Desclée de Brouwer, 1959.

2. M. DELCOR (ed.), *Qumrân. Sa piété, sa théologie et son millieu* (BETL, 44), Paris-Gembloux-Leuven, Duculot-University Press, 1978.

Desert) rendered any suggestion of a congress that would attempt to deal with all of them in one way or another virtually impossible. A "general" Qumran congress in line with the 9th and the 27th was no longer a realistic goal. It was decided, therefore, to organise the 51st *Colloquium* according to the thematic model followed by other *Colloquia*.

The topic selected was "Wisdom and Apocalypticism in the Dead Sea Scrolls and in the Biblical Traditions". The apocalyptic component of the sectarian scrolls has been one of the key elements brought to the fore since the beginning of research into the Dead Sea Scrolls. The wisdom component of the Scrolls, on the other hand, has been the subject of only limited research, no doubt because the primary wisdom texts have only become available recently. While the quantity of sapiential texts now available in the volumes DJD 20[3] and DJD 34[4] is clearly significant, an in-depth study thereof still needs to be done and their relationship to the biblical wisdom tradition (Proverbs, Qoheleth and Ben Sira in particular) still needs to be ascertained. The combination of both lines of research (Apocalypticism and Wisdom) in a single *Colloquium* promised to be a fruitful venture. It had the potential not only to throw light on the old problem of the prophetic *versus* sapiential roots of biblical apocalypticism, but because both traditions are very much present and operative in the single concrete library of Qumran (as is attested by the recent published texts), it also had the potential to lead to a better understanding of *their mutual relationship*.

In order to introduce the topic of the meeting, my opening address (*Wisdom at Qumran: Worldly or Heavenly?*) focused on a single point of the possible relationship between Wisdom and Apocalypticism: the origin of the wisdom contained in 4QInstruction. Playing on the title of the still unpublished dissertation of M. Goff: "The Worldly and Heavenly Wisdom of 4QInstruction"[5], who asserts that the wisdom of 4QInstruction is both worldly and heavenly at the same time, my address intended to prove that, although the contents of 4QInstruction are a mix of worldly matters and heavenly mysteries, all of them are presented as revealed, and thus as heavenly.

3. T. ELGVIN *et al.*, *Qumran Cave 4. XV: Sapiential Texts, Part 1* (DJD, 20), Oxford, Clarendon, 1997.

4. J. STRUGNELL, D. HARRINGTON, T. ELGVIN, *Qumran Cave 4. XXIV: Sapiential Texts, Part 2* (DJD, 34), Oxford, Clarendon, 1999.

5. M.J. GOFF, *The Worldly and Heavenly Wisdom of 4QInstruction*. A Dissertation submitted to the Faculty of the Divinity School of the University of Chicago, March 2002. The Dissertation will be published in a revised form in the Series *Studies on the Texts of the Desert of Judah*.

The knowledge transmitted by the sage to his pupils belongs to the both sorts of wisdom. Most of the teachings concern very worldly matters and are perfect parallels to the secular wisdom transmitted in biblical wisdom books such as Qoheleth or Sirach. Our sage deals with economic matters, poverty and riches, borrowing and repaying money, how to deal with loans and securities; he instructs the one seeking understanding on how to conduct himself in his social relationships (both with superiors and inferiors), how to avoid shame, how to deal with strangers, and how to conduct himself in the case of a sudden change of fortune; he also cautions his pupils with respect to their conduct in family matters, relationships with parents and with one's wife, marriage of one's children, etc. Together with these very worldly concerns, however, the sage instructs the one seeking understanding on many other matters that pertain to the realm of heavenly wisdom. He teaches about God and God's plans, about creation, about the cosmos, about angels, about good and evil, about eschatology and afterlife, and, quite characteristically, about final judgement in which God will reward or punish the righteous and the wicked respectively. In short, the teachings of our sage concern not only worldly wisdom but also heavenly "mysteries".

This fact, in my opinion, does not mean that the wisdom we encounter in 4QInstruction is both worldly and heavenly at the same time. It is my contention that the interpretative framework provided by the beginning of the work, as preserved in 4Q416 1 and 4Q417 1, together with the continuous reference to the רז נהיה ("the mystery that is to come" in the translation of the editors), provides a "revelatory" character to the entire content of 4QInstruction, including its most worldly elements, thus making all of them "heavenly wisdom".

An analysis of 4Q416 1 as the beginning of the composition provides a theological framework for the reading of the whole composition which will follow. The topics dealt with in this introduction, as well as the vocabulary employed therein, belong to apocalyptic, not to wisdom compositions. These elements place the whole work in an apocalyptic context, which evidently functions to legitimise the corpus of instructions that are about to follow. The same strategy of legitimisation appears even more clearly in the first fragment of 4Q417, which also belongs to the theological framework of 4QInstruction and deals with the same topics, but is presented already as instructions given directly to the "understanding one". The references to the "engraved ordinances", the "vision of meditation, and the book of memorial" are more in line with the "heavenly tables" of certain apocalypses than with ordinary worldly knowledge, and they apparently have the same function within the composition. The clearest element of the strategy of legitimisation of the wisdom imparted, however, is the frequent use of the רז נהיה not only in the clearly apocalyptic sections of the composition but throughout 4QInstruction. An analysis of all the occurrences of the expression reveals that the contexts with which the use thereof is associated are by no means restricted to the apocalyptic sections of the composition. Even the most "secular" instructions are comprised within the רז נהיה.

In my view this implies that the author of 4QInstruction considered all the knowledge he transmitted, be it of an apocalyptic character or similar to traditional biblical wisdom, as the same kind of knowledge. Furthermore, by presenting his "secular" teachings as included within the רז נהיה, he provided them with the same authority he had ascribed to the other "mysteries" on which he was instructing the "one seeking understanding". He uses the same strategy of legitimisation of his authority in the whole composition, without distinguishing between heavenly wisdom and worldly wisdom. The most worldly concerns of his instruction are also presented as "revealed" wisdom.

I do not know if we can use the term of "apocalyptic wisdom" in the case of 4QInstruction. It is obvious that the composition is not an apocalypse in the formal sense with which we are used to understand the word since the paradigm of *Semeia 14*. It seems to me, however, that its author tries to present the knowledge he wanted to transmit not as simple human knowledge (as in the biblical wisdom tradition) but as "revealed" knowledge, as heavenly wisdom. I think, therefore, that we can answer the question posed in a different way to that to which Goff has responded. Qumran wisdom is not worldly *and* heavenly wisdom, it is revealed wisdom, and thus thoroughly heavenly.

The paper of Armin Lange (*Interpretation als Offenbarung: Zum Verhältnis von Schriftauslegung und Offenbarung in apokalyptischer und nichtapokalyptischer Literatur*) takes Dan 9,20-24 (in which the visionary finds the explanatory key to Jer 25,11 in the angelic vision and not in exegetical methods) as the starting point to question whether interpretation is a revelatory process and whether the interpretation itself is an act of divination. In order to answer this question Lange first discusses the hermeneutics of the *pesharim*, particularly that of 1QpHab. The basic element of the interpretative formulae of the *pesharim*, the root פשר/פתר, gives a first impression of the divinatory character of the interpretation given; in Hebrew/Aramaic literature this is always connected to the interpretation of dreams and other omens together with the explanation of authoritative texts. The analogy between *pesher* and interpretation of omens also occurs in the techniques employed in both: the elements of the dream are isolated (atomised) in the protasis, and translated to the world of the dreamer (contextualised) in the apodosis, as exemplified in Joseph's explanation of the dream of Pharaoh (Gen 41,26-32) and in 1QpHab VII 3-8. The fact that the *pesharist* understood his exegesis as revelation is stated explicitly in 1QpHab II 7-10. Dan 9 uses the same atomisation and contextualisation methods and suggests in 9,23 that exegetical insight can only be achieved by revelation. In order to prove that this way of understanding prophetic texts is not a peculiarity of ancient Judaism, be it apocalyptic or Qumranic, Lange goes on to present the Demotic Chronicle which comments on an old astrological oracle of the 3rd century BCE and the Potter's Oracle of about 130 BCE, both of which offer a perfect parallel to the *pesher* interpretation. Since there is no direct relationship or dependence between Daniel or the *pesharim* and the Egyptian texts, Lange questions whether the similarity might be explained as the reaction to a similar cultural crisis (the Persian and Ptolemaic occupation of Egypt in the case of the Demotic Chronicle, the profanation of the temple in the case of Daniel, and the strong eschatological conscience of the community of Qumran), and seeks the answer in classical Greek literature with its tradition of oracle and omen interpretation that dates back to the eight century BCE. The analysis of several parodies of oracular books and oracle interpretation by Aristophanes, particularly of the references by Herodotus to Onomakritos as compiler of the oracles of Musaios, the consultation of the oracle of Delphi by the Athenians before the battle of Salamis and the proverb of Lysistratos, provide evidence that excludes a crisis situation, be it cultural or religious, as the matrix of similar phenomena. Lange closes his argument with the analysis of Jer 23,33-40, as proof that post-exilic prophecy in the Hebrew Bible was also familiar with this revelatory hermeneutic, in which new meaning was given to old prophetic words through atomising and contextualisation.

Klaus Koch tries in his paper (*Das Geheimnis der Zeit in Weisheit und Apokalyptik um die Zeitenwende*) to unveil the understanding of the mystery of time in the Israel of the Hellenistic and Roman period by analysing how this understanding of time is expressed in four characteristic writings: Qoheleth, Sirach, 4QInstruction and Daniel. The first biblical wisdom composition to deal intensively with the problem of time is Qoheleth (in Proverbs, which represents an a-historical wisdom independent of the concept of time, the temporality of being is not yet understood as a problem, the word *'et* is used only 5 times, as against 40 times in Qoheleth and 60 times in Ben Sira). The analysis of Qoh 3 and of the three terms used therein for time (*'et, z^{e}man* and *'ôlam*) shows that the author is interested in the historicity of the individual person, but without connecting it to the history of his people or of the cultic community. In Ben Sira, on the contrary, reflection on the temporality of being takes a central part, starting with the creation of wisdom who is with God εἰς τὸν αἰῶνα. The concept of time is for him one of the fundamental principles explaining the whole of reality: the human person become conscious of the temporal dimension of things (καιρός), but also of the temporal dimension of his/her own individual life and of the temporal dimension of Israel's history as salvation history or history of doom. For Ben Sira, the different times of the changing phenomena in nature and in society and the different times of the individual life-cycles and of the history of humanity, belong to a universal temporal continuum, a time created by God and therefore with a meaning that only God can oversee but which the sage can discover. 4QInstruction, with its strong eschatological perspective, presents the meaning of the universal temporal continuum as a mystery which requires a particular revelation and meditation to be understood. This רז נהיה ("das Geheimnis des Geschehenden") as presented in 4QInstruction, includes one's own life in its family and social context, but also, in light of the use of *nihyot* in wisdom literature, the different present times and the universal temporal continuum. The fact that 4QInstruction uses the singular *(nhyh)* in order to designate this temporal universe which was crated together with the world, everything that happens in time is provided with a substantial unity, from the beginning of the universe through human history to the eschatological completion. In the apocalyptic literature it is not the historical dimension of the individual life that constitutes the object of reflection, but the epochs of the nations within the framework of the history of humanity, and especially the eschatological end of the time of the world, are the object of visions and explanations. This contrast between wisdom and apocalypticism is exemplified in the book of Daniel. In the older Aramaic sections of Daniel the problem of time is posed in terms of the four successive epochs of the world (the four kingdoms) which lead to the eschatological turnaround and introduce an epoch of peace and salvation that underscores temporality as a necessary structure of the world in which further *'almayya* are expected. The Hebrew sections that were added later exhibit a different understanding of the meaning of time in human lives: Hebrew *'et* plays a more important role than Aramaic *'iddan* and is used to indicate the final phase of world history (*'æt-qeṣ* cf. *qeṣ hayyamîn*), the *šabû'îm* express the sabbatical structure of creation, the *mô'ªdîm* the times pre-ordered by God before the end, and the Hebrew *'ôlam* (used in the singular and more comprehensive than

Aramaic *'alam*) is put in relationship with the approaching eschatological transformation in which a *ṣœdœq 'olamîm* will be imposed, and the righteous will awake to a *hayê 'ôlam*, the meaning of which is not "eternity" as transcendence of time, but a "Gesamtkontinuum von Zeit und Welt" as indicated by the use of the expression *hœy ha'ôlam* as a God's title.

Five of the six papers of Part II focus on specific Wisdom compositions from Qumran, such as 1Q-4QMysteries, 4QInstruction, 4QTime of Righteousness, or the "Tractate of the Two Spirits" from the Rule of the Community, while the sixth studies two Qumran compositions (4Q521 and 11Q13) which use elements of apocalyptic and wisdom language side by side.

Eibert Tigchelaar (*Your Wisdom and Your Folly: The Case of 1-4QMysteries*) gives an introduction to the Mysteries text of Qumran, thereby concentrating on the reconstruction of a text which is very fragmentary and fraught with problems. He questiones what Mysteries in fact is dealing with, discovering a contradiction between "hidden" wisdom and "wrong" wisdom. He also investigates whether some categories (e.g. the רז נהיה in 4Q301) are dealt with in a positive or a negative way, and makes a comparison with other Qumran texts, especially with 4QInstruction. Although there are similarities between these texts, interdependence cannot be proved. Tigchelaar also discusses the concepts of "wisdom literature", "apocalyptic literature" and "eschatology", as well as the possible links between these concepts. While elements of wisdom, apocalypticism and eschatology would appear to be present in Mysteries, it seems to be difficult nevertheless to categorise Mysteries as either apocalyptic, eschatological or wisdom literature, especially since the said categories are far from being well-defined. Tigchelaar provides a detailed analysis of the addressees of Mysteries and focuses on the function of the fragments dealing with priestly issues and concludes that "Mysteries represents an attempt to uphold the special position of Israelite culture and religion against Hellenistic and other pagan beliefs, in particular astrology. The nations, presumably in particular the Hellenistic Kingdoms, are criticized for their plundering. Their (Babylonian and Egyptian) diviners are scolded for not knowing the real secrets. At the same time the group behind Mysteries tries to safeguard the status of the Jerusalem priests as temple functionaries, judges, teachers and as sages who have real knowledge of the mysteries, including astrology".

The article by Torleif Elgvin (*The Eschatological Hope of 4QTime of Righteousness*) focuses primarily on 4QTime of Righteousness and secondarily on 4QInstruction. In the discussion of 4QTime of Righteousness it gives a new reading and structured translation of 4Q215a 1 ii. Although there is not enough text to determine the genre, it could be argued that the content is (apocalyptic) eschatology. Although written in poetic style, 4Q215a is probably not a hymnic composition as such; it is rather a didactic review of God's holy plan from creation to judgement, where the final section is clothed in poetic language similar to restoration passages in Isaiah. The closest parallels are provided by 1 Enoch and by 1-4QMysteries. With regard to the production and audience of the work, Elgvin suggests that is was probably written outside the *yahad*, containing few sectarian borders, and being more universal in its outlook, but he acknowledges that it was copied and read within the *yahad* and that authorship within the community cannot be totally excluded. If this were the case, the preserved fragments could represent the autograph, since the composition should be dated in a Maccabean or pre-Maccabean period. In any case, 4QTimes of Righteousness would easily lend itself to a sectarian reading. "It would describe the trials the elect have undergone and give meaning to their struggles which would be perceived as eschatological birth pangs". The specific contribution of 4QTimes of Righteousness, not found in the parallel passages of 1 Enoch and 1-4QMysteries, is the "kingship/kingdom of God" and the Zion theology: "Enochic" material and world view has been incorporated into a poetic rendering of the coming renewal of God's elect, the land with Zion and then all the world, under the royal leadership of the God of Israel".

Jean Duhaime examines the Instruction of the Two Spirits of the Rule of the Community. His paper entitled *Cohérence structurelle et tensions internes dans l'Instruction sur les Deux Esprits (1QS III 13 – IV 26)* offers an analysis of the structure ("analyse structurelle, non structurale") of the Instruction on the Two Spirits in three parts, each composed of two sections, and proves that in its present form it is completely coherent. He also observes tensions, irregularities and differences in meaning and in terminology of the present text, however, which proves that the present coherence is the result of a conscious work. The contents of the Instruction of 1QS pertain to different registers of cosmology, anthropology, ethics and eschatology. Some of them appear to have been taken from different sources, while others are clearly internal developments of the thought of the group. The redactional history of the Instruction of 1QS is far from being completely understood. Research has followed two paths in order to explain the present form of the Instruction of 1QS: one (followed by Osten-Sacken and formerly also by Duhaime among others) explains the tensions and irregularities on the basis of genetic and progressive developments from the same tradition; the other (followed by Collins and Tigchelaar among others) looks for the sources of the different components (creation, origin of evil, the two ways, eschatology, etc.) in related texts, be it from inside or from outside the Bible, or from other Qumranic compositions such as 4QInstruction.

Émile Puech (*Apports des textes apocalyptiques et sapientiels de Qumrân à l'eschatologie du judaïsme ancien*) gives a detailed survey of the eschatological ideas of 1-4QInstruction, 4QPseudo-Ezekiel, 4QMessianic Apocalypse, the "Tractate of the Two Spirits" of 1QCommunity Rule and the Hodayot, in order to show that all of them bear witness to the same expectation of a *post-mortem* retribution for a life of fidelity to God's precepts. The analysis of the passage concerning judgement found in 4Q416 1 7-9, one of the copies of 4QInstruction, shows that its author envisions a universal judgement for which the righteous should be prepared; the study of the eschatological diptych preserved in two copies of 4QInstruction, 4Q418 69 ii + 60 and 4Q417 5 1-5, reveals the belief that Sheol and the abyss will be transformed from the temporary residence of all the deceased into the eternal place of punishment of the impious, while the righteous will be recompensed with the eternal life that shall follow a revival from death. In 4QPseudo-Ezekiel, the vision of the dry bones of the Prophet is transformed into an affirmation of individual resurrection of the elected in the eschaton as recompense for their righteousness, clearly implying an intermediary period, the length of which can be shortened, prior to resurrection. 4QMessianic Apocalypse presents the resurrection of the righteous as a new creation, as the transformation of both the righteous deceased and the righteous living at the moment of divine judgement when the impious shall be damned, under the influence of the ideas of Iranian religion represented in the reference to the "bridge of the abyss". Although no other Qumranic texts explicitly deal with the topic, the same basic ideas are also present in the main compositions. In the "Tractate of the Two Spirits" of 1QS they are expressed in the expectation of God's visitation, which is not to be understood from the perspective of individual eschatology or belief in the immortality of the soul, but from that of a collective eschatology concerning the history of the world and human persons in which recompense and punishment can only be *post-mortem* and the reward of the righteous is the "glory of Adam", a return to Paradise in a world purified of all sin and of its consequence, death. The same understanding governs the eschatology of the Hodayot; some of them, like 1QH[a]

V 22-24 and 28-29, implying a collective eschatology with resurrection and the eternal judgement of the righteous and the eternal damnation of the impious. Others, like 1QH[a] IV 21-27 or 1QH[a] XI 20-37, envision a collective eschatology that ends with the universal conflagration which renews the universe. Still others, like 1QH[a] XIII 22–XV 8, and particularly XIV 32-39, present the faithful rising from the dead to take part in the final war and the destruction of the impious. Similar ideas are also found in other compositions, such as 1QM, CD and some of the thematic and continuous Pesharim, and are reflected in particular in the way the people of Qumran were buried in their tombs.

Claude Coulot (*L'image de Dieu dans les écrits de sagesse 1Q26, 4Q415-418, 4Q423*) analyses the main characteristics of the image of God reflected in the sapiential writings from Qumran. In a series of passages, in which the sage instructs the student on the characteristics of the God who has created the world and conducts all its affairs, two characteristics are underlined: the creator God is the God of knowledge, and the God who will judge the world is the God of truth. In another series of passages, in which the sage instructs the student on the particular relationship of God with the ones seeking understanding, the following characteristics of God are underlined: God is the one who has separated them from all perversity; God is the one who has given them their heritage and therefore should be sanctified; God is a father for them; God is the one who opens their minds; and God is the one who has given them authority.

After some introductory statements on the eschatological prophetic figures of the Qumran Library, the last paper of this section, by Géza G. Xeravits (*Wisdom Traits in the Qumranic Presentation of the Eschatological Prophet*), concentrates on two issues. It deals first with 4Q521, in which the eschatological coming of Elijah *redivivus* is described within a sapiential poem; then it turns to the eschatological prophet of 11Q13, who is described – among others – as a wisdom instructor. Besides the apocalyptic language used, the authors of 4Q521 and 11Q13 show similarity in presenting the eschatological prophet as one instructing his addressees. 11Q13 seems to specify this eschatological prophet as one connected somehow with the משכלים and, on the other hand, his message as including some metaphysical ideas that are characteristic of the thought of 4QInstruction.

The third part of the volume is formed by nine contributions that analyse different aspects of biblical wisdom compositions or of apocalyptic writings in the light of wisdom texts from Qumran.

Michael Knibb (*The Book of Enoch in the Light of the Qumran Wisdom Literature*) initially addresses the evidence within 1 Enoch and other texts belonging to the wider circle of Enochic writings for the description of Enoch as a scribe or wise man, and of his writings as a source of wisdom. He concludes that Enoch is indeed presented as a learned man, a scribe, an individual known for his wisdom and knowledge – but also as an individual who experienced an ascent to the presence of God, who was conducted around the cosmos, as one who saw everything and whose knowledge not only related to the themes of judgement and salvation, but also covered cosmological and astronomical matters. This description of Enoch as a scribe notwithstanding, the Book of Enoch is quite different in character from the books that have traditionally been regarded as belonging to the wisdom category. Secondly, Knibb examines the kind of contribution that Qumran wisdom literature might make to our understanding of Enoch. The theme of judgement, which is included within the perspective of 4QMysteries and provides a theological framework for the wisdom instruction in 4QInstruction, constitutes the leitmotif of 1 Enoch. It is announced in the prologue in chapter 1 and is constantly taken up in a variety of ways throughout the book. Perhaps of even greater relevance, however, are the themes of knowledge of the mysteries and of the secrets. Enoch knows "the mysteries of the holy ones", just as he also knows "this mystery" (103,2; 104,10) – because he has been shown the mysteries by the Lord and has read the tablets of heaven. The angel who accompanies Enoch shows him the secrets (40,2; 46,2; 71,3). Enoch sees both the secrets of the cosmos (41,1,3; 59,1-3; 71,4) and the secrets relating to the end of this era (38,3; 58,5; 61,5; 83,7). Enoch in turn passes on "the teaching of all the secrets in a book" (68,1) to Noah. In the Vision of the Animals Enoch is presented as the one who knows past and future, a point noted in Jub. 4,19a: "While he slept he saw in a vision what has happened and what will occur – how things will happen for mankind during their history until the day of judgement". This may be compared with the comment made about mankind in 4QMysteries: "But they did not know the mystery of that which was coming into being (רז נהיה), and the former things (קדמוניות) they did not consider. Nor did they know what shall befall them". The differences between the wisdom writings and the Book of Enoch must also be recognised, however. Thus while cosmology and eschatology form part of the concerns of 4QMysteries and 4QInstruction, they find expression in a way quite different from that of Enoch. In the former cosmology and eschatology provide a theological underpinning for wisdom instruction that seems to have been its main concern. In Enoch cosmology and eschatology are of primary importance and are built into the structure of the book. Again, while in the case of both 4QMysteries and 4QInstruction and in Enoch we can speak in terms of "revealed wisdom" and both contain frequent references to either the רז נהיה or to "mysteries" or "secrets", it is only in Enoch that this concern finds concrete expression in reports of visions and of journeys through the heavenly regions and around the cosmos. One should perhaps speak of a shared thought-world that finds different expression in the two kinds of writings. The final part of his paper is dedicated to the evaluation of parallels between the Book of Enoch and 4QMysteries and 4QInstruction. While J. Collins has spoken in terms of an apocalyptic influence on the wisdom writings and T. Elgvin has even spoken of the dependence of 4QInstruction on the books of Enoch, at least in the Epistle, Knibb maintains that the parallels noted tend rather to provide evidence of a shared thought-world. Although Sirach may provide evidence of a critical attitude towards the claims to the possession of esoteric knowledge made by writings like 1 Enoch, 4QMysteries and 4QInstruction present us with wisdom writings, the theological perspective of which is much closer to that of 1 Enoch. The authors of the Book of Enoch and of 4QMysteries and 4QInstruction were not so different from one another.

Pieter M. Venter (*Spatiality in Enoch's Journeys [1 Enoch 12–36]*) focuses on the three journey narratives of 1 Enoch in which God's decisions are revealed to Enoch. An analysis of these three journeys indicates that preference is given in these revelation narratives to the spatial aspect, rather than the aspect of time. Both his heavenly journey (1 Enoch 12–16) and his two earthly journeys to the ends of the earth (1 Enoch 17–36) deal with space. Trying to understand this preference, the paper investigates the macro-social world of the author(s), analysing firstly the literary context (themes in Enoch from the Bible, the Syro-Phoenician world, Pseudo Eupolemus, the Zenon Papyri, Persia and Greece are identified), and then the socio-historical context (Ptolemaic Palestine, with its history, social structure and religious groups). Adopting G. Boccaccini's division of the Judaism of the epoch in three main groups or "Judaisms" (Mosaic or Zadokite Judaism, Sapiential Judaism and Enochic Judaism), the paper offers a description of Sapiential Judaism and of Enochic Judaism and compares them as two opposing groups taking up the challenge of the third century with its Hellenistic onslaught and explosion of knowledge, in total different ways. The Enoch tradition is shown to be an early form of apocalyptic thinking influenced by wisdom literature and cosmological schemes of the world.

Leo G. Perdue (*Wisdom and Apocalyptic: The Case of Qoheleth*) focuses on the opponents with whom the sage disputes, as a way to understand the relationship of Wisdom and Apocalyptic. The epilogue in 12,9-14 describes Qoheleth as having "taught the people knowledge, weighing and studying and arranging many pleasing words, and he wrote words of truth plainly". Assuming this scribal editing is correct in its understanding of Qoheleth as a sage, the question that emerges is this, "Who are the opponents with whom Qoheleth, the sage, contends?" The various possibilities of understanding Qoheleth's opponents include fictional sages, traditional sages, mantic sages, apocalyptic seers, and apocalyptic sages. Literary fiction figures prominently in the first two chapters of Qoheleth. This being the case, one could argue that much of Qoheleth may be understood as literary fiction. Thus, the opponents of Qoheleth themselves may have been fictional characters. Perhaps the most common thesis has been that Qoheleth enters into contest with traditional, scribal wisdom, i.e. wisdom shaped within the context of a school in Jerusalem. This argument holds true in regard to most of the book. But there are elements in Qoheleth's argument that do not belong to scribal wisdom. These include references to the sage's disputation with those who contend that they have a knowledge of the totality of time (3,11), that there is hope for an eschatological judgement that will culminate in the resurrection from the dead of at least the righteous (3,19-20), and that God has revealed himself to a particular group. These affirmations first appear in full form in the wisdom tradition in the Wisdom of Solomon in the first century BCE. The third view of Qoheleth's opponents may be built on Hans-Peter Müller's thesis that von Rad was essentially correct in his argument that wisdom was the source of the development of apocalyptic. However, he modifies von Rad's thesis by adding the idea that there existed in late Israel a mantic wisdom that is illustrated by the apocalyptic stories in Daniel 1–6. A fourth view is developed by Perdue in the rest of his paper. Qoheleth's opponents included not only scribal wisdom, but also emerging apocalyptic. The most likely opponents of Qoheleth were apocalyptic sages, since the library of Qumran and some of its texts demonstrate that several originally different theological and literary traditions (wisdom, apocalyptic, and Torah) existed side by side and eventually began to influence one another and even at times to merge together. This view is built on the assumptions that Qoheleth was a sage who sought to undercut early apocalyptic arguments that a select group of seers understood the mind of God, that they could determine the time and events that God had predestined, and that there would be a final judgement in which the righteous could hope for resurrection from the dead.

Marie Maussion also deals with Qoheleth (*Qohélet et les sept refrains sur le bonheur*). Maussion summarises the results of a chapter of her doctoral dissertation on evil, good and judgement in Qoheleth. She analyses consecutively the seven refrains on the good things of life in the book (– the good things of life are a gift of God [Qoh 2,24-26]; – these good things of life should be recognised as such [3,12-14]; – because man does not know his future [3,22]; – and God reveals himself in the good things of life [5,17-19]; – Qoheleth sings the praises of these good things [8,15]; – and exhorts his reader to do the same and to enjoy them [9,7-10]; – because God will judge him according to its use [11,9–12,1]). Maussion concludes that these refrains are intended within the book of Qoheleth as the contrast and balance of the presence of evil in the world.

Jeremy Corley (*Wisdom versus Apocalyptic and Science in Sirach 1,1-10*) deals with another biblical wisdom book and concentrates on the opening poem. Trying to answer the question of how the mysteries of heaven and earth are revealed, the contemporaries of Ben Sira would be able to look in three directions. First, they could follow the sage, contenting themselves with traditional Jewish wisdom, regarded as enshrined in the Law of Moses (Sir 24,23). A second possibility would be to turn to the purported revelations contained in apocalyptic writings, particularly the early parts of 1 Enoch. A third possibility would be to investigate the inquires of Greek philosophers and scientists such as Aristotle and Eratosthenes. Corley's reading of the poem, which is a restatement of the traditional position of Hebrew wisdom and is inspired by earlier biblical texts, such as Prov 8,22-31, Job 28, or Isa 40,12, indicates that Ben Sira wishes to defend traditional Hebrew wisdom against twin challenges from Jewish apocalyptic and Greek science. In 1,1-10, Ben Sira wishes to restate the biblical presupposition that all wisdom comes as a gift from the one God. Whereas Jewish apocalypticists claimed Enoch as the revealer of the secrets of the celestial bodies and of meteorology, Ben Sira regards these matters as mysteries best left to God. Similarly, while Greek scientists attempted to calculate the number of sand grains on the seashore, or the distance of the sun from the earth, Ben Sira sees these topics as mysteries known only to God. Thus, Ben Sira directs the attention of his students, not to the "wisdom" supposedly revealed by Enoch (1 Enoch 82,2), nor to the "wisdom" claimed by Greek philosophy and science, but to the wisdom (cf. Deut 4,6-8) granted by God to those who love him, centred on the Torah given to Israel (Sir 19,20; 24,23; cf. Deut 29,28). Such wisdom forms the subject of the rest of the sage's book.

John J. Collins offers (*The Mysteries of God. Creation and Eschatology in 4QInstruction and the Wisdom of Solomon*) a comparison of several key ideas of both 4QInstruction and the Wisdom of Solomon, the novelty of the latter in terms of eschatological ideas being commonly attributed to the influence both of Greek philosophy and of Jewish apocalyptic traditions. Collins first analyses the concepts רז נהיה in 4QInstruction and μυστήρια θεοῦ in the Wisdom of Solomon and finds clear points of analogy between both. In both texts understanding the mystery is the key to right behaviour. This is so primarily because it discloses the ultimate outcome of righteous or wicked behaviour – the reward of piety and the prize of blameless souls, in the idiom of Wisdom, or "who is to inherit glory and iniquity" in the language of 4QInstruction. The author then goes on to compare hope in the afterlife of the righteous in Wisdom and in 4QInstruction. Wisdom, which does not differentiate between immortality and incorruptibility, understands the afterlife in terms of the immortality of the soul and never speaks of resurrection of the body, or even resurrection of the spirit, in such a way as to imply that life is interrupted at death. Immortality is contingent on righteousness. It constitutes the original design of the creator of all humanity and it serves thus as the hope of the righteous. 4QInstruction also entertains hope in immortality, although not in the Platonic idea of the immortality of the soul, but rather the idea that righteous humans can be elevated to share the life of the angelic host to which the righteous on earth are closely associated. 4QInstruction formulates the hope of the righteous in the language of light and everlasting glory, similar to the language of the "Tractate of the Two Spirits", but there is no indication, either in 4QInstruction or in the "Tractate of the Two Spirits", that eternal life involved a resurrected body of flesh and blood, nor does it seem to involve a resurrection, in the sense that life is suspended for a time between death and glorification. The hope of the righteous in 4QInstruction is informed by both the cultic and sapiential traditions which provide a basis for hope in immortality that does not use the more mythological language of resurrection. There are thus significant similarities between 4QInstruction and Wisdom in the hope in the afterlife. The most significant discrepancy between the two is perhaps to be found in the fact that Wisdom does not envision the punishment of the damned after death. Collins also compares the association of immortality with creation in both writings. Both writings share the view that it was the intention of the creator that humanity should be immortal. Wisdom apparently associates the immortality of the soul with Gen 1,27 and the mortality of the body with Gen 2,7. As a consequence it defends the idea that both immortality and spiritual death remain possibilities for all human beings. 4QInstruction, on the other hand, contrasts the "people of the spirit" fashioned in the image of the holy ones with the "spirit of flesh" and views the distinction of the two types of humanity as having its origin in creation, in a way similar to the "Tractate of the Two Spirits"; both types of humanity are therefore immortal. For Wisdom the wicked simply cease to exist; for 4QInstruction the wicked survive to await punishment in the hereafter.

The Wisdom of Solomon is also the topic of the article by Maurice Gilbert (*Sagesse 3,7-9; 5,15-23 et l'apocalyptique*). Gilbert concentrates on two texts from Wisdom generally considered as apocalyptic, belonging to the same eschatological section of the book, and dealing with the future destiny of the righteous. He first analyses the entire segment to which vv. 7-9 constitute the conclusion. With respect to 3,1 the author asserts that the souls of the righteous deceased survive physical death and are protected by God from every form of persecution, without telling us anything concerning the place in which these souls are. Vv. 3,2-3 contrast appearances and reality; for those who only trust their eyes the righteous have ended their earthly existence in disaster, but for the author of Wisdom the physical death of the righteous is only a "migration". They are now in peace and enjoy a serene existence. The following verses (3,4-5a) develop the same idea, going back to the existence of the righteous before death: for those who only trust appearances their death is a punishment but for our author this is only a correction in view of the blessings they are going to receive for their hope of immortality. The author explains his thoughts in three steps in the vv. 5b-6: suffering is not a punishment but a trial which has shown they are worthy of God; the trial is then compared to the fire used to refine gold; finally it is compared to a holocaust. God is thus an actor in the trial, and God's blessing of those who have sustained the trial is detailed in vv. 7-9. Such blessings will come "in the time of their visitation", a visitation which will take place in the future, in the eschaton, thus indicating a new phase for the righteous who are already dead: they will be transformed ("they shall shine"). While the author does not specify what this transformation will consist of, he indicates nevertheless that the righteous, now glorious, will participate in the destruction of the impious: as a destructive fire they will judge nations and rule over peoples, implying that the eschatological combat will take place after God's visitation and the glorification of the righteous.

The second text analysed by Gilbert (Wis 5,15-23) belongs to a series of assertions on the future destiny of the wicked which is contrasted with that of the righteous: for the former there is no hope, "the just, on the contrary, live forever" (5,15). Noting the evident symmetry with the description of the wicked in 5,14, Gilbert concludes that v. 15 may refer both to the righteous who are still alive and to the recently deceased. V. 16 deals with the eschatological future and repeats the two phases already indicated in 3,1-3 (the just are to be protected by God after death) and 3,7-9 (are to be recompensed at the time of the visitation) in different words. This means that Wis 5,14-16 simply underscores the opposite eschatological types of the two human categories living or deceased, the righteous and the wicked, preparing in this way the description of the final apocalyptic fight in which God will destroy the wicked we find in vv. 17-23. This is a textually autonomous section, which can only be understood in light of the literary structure of chapter 1–6. V. 17 announces the topic: God will take up his armour, an armour which will be detailed in vv. 18-20a (breastplate, helmet, shield, sword), and will arm creation to respond to the enemy in three sorts of assault developed on vv. 20b-23 (by celestial fire, by water and by wind), which will lay waste the earth and destroy the evildoers. The righteous do not take part in this combat and the earth suffers the consequences. Placing his description of the cosmic cataclysm at this point, the author of Wisdom left several important questions unanswered: If the apocalyptic combat can take place after the glorification of the righteous, why did they not take part in it? Why is the destruction of the wicked in the apocalyptic combat followed by the description of their judgement in the after-life of 4,20–5,13? These questions tend to show that the eschatological doctrine of Wisdom is not totally coherent and that its author uses different traditions without trying to harmonise them.

Johann Cook (*Law and Wisdom in the Dead Sea Scrolls with Reference to Hellenistic Judaism*) analyses first the role and function of the Law of Moses in several Jewish writings of the Hellenistic period: Ben Sira, Aristobulus of Alexandria, the LXX of Proverbs and the Letter of Aristeas, in order to compare this understanding of the Law of Moses with the understanding of "torah" in the Damascus Document, which is not always identical with the Law of Moses. Cook analyses two basic metaphors for the Law of Moses in CD: the Law of Moses as Wall (on CD IV 8) a metaphor also used by Aristeas and the LXX of Proverbs; and the Law of Moses as Well (on CD VI 9), which in unparalleled in Hellenistic Judaism.

The last paper of this section, by Daniel J. Harrington (*Wisdom and Apocalyptic in 4QInstruction and 4 Ezra*), consists of a comparison of 4QInstruction and 4 Ezra, intended to reveal their differences and to allow the distinctive character of each work to emerge. He first examines how 4QInstruction (which has a literary setting typical of wisdom books: a senior sage passing on wisdom to someone who seeks to understand) interweaves wisdom and apocalyptic elements in its main fragments. 4Q461 1, 4Q417 1 i-ii are the best preserved sections with apocalyptic elements, while other fragments from 4Q418, such as fragments 69, 81 and 126-27, also contain the same "eschatology-and-ethics" themes. Conventional sapiential material is represented most fully in 4Q417 2, 4Q416 2 and in some other less well preserved fragments, like 4Q418 103. 4Q416 1, considered as the first column of the work, provides a cosmological and eschatological framework for the whole composition. This theological introduction is continued in 4Q417 1 i-ii. 4Q417 1 i 1-13 introduces the main theological topic of the composition: the "mystery that is to come" which provides revelations about God, eschatology and ethics and qualifies as apocalyptic. In 4Q416 2, 4Q417 2 and other fragments, on the other hand, the sage gives advice to the *Maven* on traditional wisdom topics. Although the advice is generally set in a theological rather than secular context and contains many references to "the mystery that is to come", there is more wisdom instruction in these sections than there is apocalyptic. As a whole, therefore, 4QInstruction presents wisdom teaching in an apocalyptic framework and with motivations that include some basic concepts of apocalyptic thinking. 4 Ezra, on the contrary, is a classic apocalypse which explores the issues raised by the event of 70 CE and Israel's hopes for the future. The answers to these issues go beyond the limits of human understanding and beyond the conventional concerns of wisdom literature, to the point that the disappearance of wisdom is one of the signs that will precede the last day. The answers to the question of Ezra are placed in the future and are given in the three visions using the *raz/pesher* pattern (the angelic interpreter explains how the various elements in the vision contribute to clarify the present and forecast the future). This pattern implies that true wisdom is hidden or esoteric and accessible to the wise only through revelation; real wisdom belongs to God and humans gain access to it only through divine revelation. Although 4QInstruction and 4 Ezra have some elements in common, they are thus also very different. They differ in their settings in life (uncertain in the case of 4QInstruction, but quite clear in the case of 4 Ezra), in their approaches to wisdom and apocalyptic (traditional wisdom set in an apocalyptic context in 4QInstruction, but typically apocalyptic with dream visions and their interpretation in 4 Ezra) and in their ways of combining wisdom and apocalyptic. The latter is perhaps the most fundamental difference between the two compositions: whereas 4QInstruction presents wisdom in an apocalyptic framework, 4 Ezra presents apocalyptic or revealed wisdom.

Part IV of the volume groups five studies centred on several aspects of the wisdom compositions from Qumran (such as messianic ideas, ecstatic worship, the beatitudes, or the fate of the righteous) which are directly relevant for the New Testament.

Heinz-Josef Fabry (*Die Messiaserwartung in den Handschriften von Qumran*) traces a diachronic development of the messianic expectations of the Qumran movement, already started in the pre-history of the group and coupled to the different periods of its history. After having formulated the question, presented previous research, explained the terminology and charted the historical situations of crisis in which the messianic expectations could have been developed, Fabry arrives at the following ordering of the different manuscripts with messianic expectations: – in the pre-Essene period of opposition against Hellenisation, represented by the two Moses apocrypha (4Q374 and 4Q376) and by 4Q541 (4QApocLevi^{b}) only a single priestly messiah is expected; – in the Essene pre-Qumranic time, the difficult historical situation of cultural battle against Antiochus IV lead to the development of a collective messianology, represented by 1QM, 4Q491, 4Q471b and 4Q427, in which the pure and holy people is the decisive instrument of God in the eschatological battle; – in the early Qumranic period of the Maccabean revolt and possibly as a reaction to the fusion of the functions of High Priest and military leader by Judas Maccabeus, a dual messianic expectation was developed in the community of Qumran (1QS V 1 – IX29 and 1QSa II 11-22), although the model is already transformed in CD into the expectation of a single messianic figure with priestly and royal characteristics; – in the time of the installation at Qumran, as attested by the original text 1QS IX 11, the expectation of a triple Messiah from the house of David, from the family of Aaron and the forthcoming Prophet is developed, possibly under the influence of the *munus triplex* of Hyrcanus; – while it is possible that the Hasmoneans misused the double function of Melchizedek and the Qumran community developed the angelic dimension of Melchizedek in reaction thereto, the fact remains that the eschatological Midrash 11Q13 from the Hasmonean period presents the angelic figure of Melchizedek as a messianic figure; – at the beginning of the first century BCE a consistent Davidic messianology is expressed in CD VII 18-21, 4Q174, 4Q252, 4Q161, 1QM V 1 and 4Q285. This messianic expectation may have emerged as a reaction against the bloody High Priesthood of Janneus and of Aristobulos, but it was biblically founded and could equally be used against dominion by foreign peoples (the Romans) or non-Jewish sovereigns (Herod); – although some texts from pre-Qumranic times (like 4Q558), from Hasmonean times (e.g. 4Q521) or from the beginning of the first century BCE (e.g. 11Q13) refer to the expected prophet at the end of time, the expectation of a prophetic messianic figure develops during the high phase of apocalyptic expectations in the first century BCE (4Q174, 4Q377) and is coupled to the function of the "Dorshe haTorah" within the community; – finally, 11QPs[a] reveals a messianic transformation of the figure of David, identifying the "political messiah" of 1QSa with David *redivivus*.

Paolo Augusto de Souza Nogeira (*Ecstatic Worship in the Self-Glorification Hymn [4Q471b, 4Q427, 4Q491c]*) is interested in understanding the practice of being lifted up to the heavens during ecstatic worship in Early Christian writings, and analyses the so-called "Self-Glorification Hymn" found at Qumran in this perspective. The paper's hypothesis is that "the Self-glorification Hymn reflects the context of an ecstatic worship which involves the whole community once the speaker summons all his hearers to take part in heavenly worship. This can be deduced from the imperatives to praise and to join the celestial assembly. This hymn also presents the religious identity of the group with all its ambiguities: at the same time they are exalted among the heavenly beings, possess a distinctive discourse that differentiates them from the context, and possibly suffer some degree of persecution and poverty. Their self-identity, in terms of the suffering that they are facing and fidelity to the discourse that separates them from society, became marks required for their religious experience of ascending to the heavens, joining with the angels and – possibly – sitting on thrones".

Hermann Lichtenberger (*Makarismen in den Qumrantexten und im Neuen Testament*) discusses the relationship between the Beatitudes found (both as isolated instances or as series of blessings) in the Qumran writings (4Q185, 4Q525 2-3 ii and 1QH VI 13-16), in other texts, such as Ben Sira 25,7-11, 2 Enoch 42,6ff., 2 Enoch 52, Evg. Thomas 54. 68-69 and Acts of Paul 5-6, and in some rabbinical writings, with those found in the New Testament (Mt 5,3-11, Lk 6,20-26). While there is a clear similarity in language and content, the Beatitudes use the word

אשרי, the background of which may be found in the sapiential tradition, while the Blessings and Woes are expressed with ברוך and ארור respectively, which may have a priestly and cultic background. It is not clear, however, to what extent this hypothetical wisdom background of the Beatitude formulae has the capacity to illuminate the New Testament Beatitudes.

Jean-Marie van Cangh (*Béatitudes de Qumrân et béatitudes évangéliques. Antériorité de Matthieu sur Luc?*) also uses the Beatitudes found at Qumran, but in this case in order to solve a concrete problem: which of the two New Testament versions of the Beatitudes is the more original? The analysis of 4Q525, 1QH VI 13-16 and 1QH XXIII 13-16, as well as the use of Isaiah 61,1-3 in Lk 4,18-21 and 7,22, Matthew 11,5-6, leads van Cangh to conclude that Matthew preserves the more original reading with his expression "poor of spirit".

The last paper of the volume, by Joseph Verheyden (*The Fate of the Righteous and the Cursed at Qumran and in the Gospel of Matthew*), provides a Qumranic background for the images used in the Gospel of Matthew to describe the destiny of the righteous and of the wicked at the last judgement, where they are juxtaposed in a clear contrast. Verheyden argues that none of the texts from the OT (Dn 12,2), 1 Enoch, and Qumran that are cited in connection with Mt 25,46 offer a close parallel to this verse. He presents 4Q548, a fragmentary text that may be identified as part of the pseudepigraphical writing entitled "Visions of ʿAmram", and discusses the various reconstructions that have been proposed for the relevant verses, in particular the reconstruction that is now proposed in DJD 31. A comparison of the passage in 4Q548 with Mt 25,46 shows that the fragment offers a parallel for what are the two most characteristic features of this verse, i.e. its pointedly dualistic tendency and the use of the "plain" verb "to go" to describe the execution of the judgement. After surveying Milik's search for traces of the "Visions of ʿAmram" in later (Christian) tradition, Verheyden suggests that Origen, who according to Milik was acquainted with the work, may have been influenced by it in commenting upon Mt 25,31-46.

I think it is too early to offer a synthesis of the general results of this 51st *Colloquium* or even to delineate the general lines that emerged in the discussions. The idea was to unravel the connections between Wisdom and Apocalypticism in Qumran and in the Biblical Tradition. I think that many elements revealing a degree of continuity between both traditions have been underlined, just as many elements of discontinuity and the emergence of new elements have also been drawn to the participants' attention. While we did not succeed in establishing a label accepted by all for the new sort of Wisdom we found at Qumran, we did agree that a new sort of Wisdom was indeed present therein. Defining this sort of Wisdom is a task for the future, but this *Colloquium* has provided a solid basis for this future work.

Florentino GARCÍA MARTÍNEZ

WISDOM AT QUMRAN: WORLDLY OR HEAVENLY?

From 5-7 September 1957, under the presidency of Professor J. van der Ploeg, the 9th meeting of the "Journées Bibliques de Louvain" was dedicated for the first time to the study of the recently discovered Qumran manuscripts. The topic of the meeting was "La secte de Qumrân et les origines du Christianisme", which was perfectly suited to the manuscripts as they were then known. At the time of this meeting, though all the manuscripts had already been unearthed, the only published materials were those found in Cave 1 (all published between 1950 and 1956) and a few preliminary descriptions of materials from other finds. In Cave 1 (as would become apparent on the publication of the rest of the finds) what could be called the prototypes of "sectarian manuscripts" (the *Serek, Hodayot, Milhama* and the *Pesher Habakkuk*) were unearthed, thus providing a paradigm for comparison with other, already known, Jewish groups of that period, and particularly with early Christianity. Six lectures were given in French (van der Ploeg, Lambert, Jaubert, Barthélemy, Schmitt and Cerfaux), two in Dutch (van der Woude and Coppens) and one in German (Nötscher), but all were published in French, including a contribution written in German by O. Betz expressly for the volume of the proceedings, which appeared two years later in the "Recherches Bibliques" series under the same title as the meeting[1]. The volume was correctly described by the editor, van der Ploeg, as a "gerbe d'articles d'allure synthétique", and it was intended to "faire saisir ce qui, au terme d'une dizaine d'années de recherches, s'avère solide et digne d'être retenu"[2]. The most surprising feature of the volume was the President's decision to replace his own presidential address (on the "Holy War at Qumran")[3] with a long bibliographical article surveying the years 1952-1958[4].

Nineteen years later, in 1976, a new Colloquium, the 27th, was dedicated once again to the study of the Qumran manuscripts under the

1. J. VAN DER PLOEG (ed.), *La Secte de Qumrân et les origines du Christianisme* (Recherches Bibliques, 4), Bruges, Desclée de Brouwer, 1959.

2. *Ibid.*, pp. 9-10 (*Avant-Propos*).

3. Published in the meantime; see J. VAN DER PLOEG, *L'idée de la guerre sainte dans la Règle de la guerre*, in *Mélanges bibliques rédigés en l'honneur de A. Robert*, Paris, Bloud et Gay, 1957, pp. 326-333.

4. J. VAN DER PLOEG, *Six années d'études sur les textes du Désert de Juda. Aperçu analytique et critique*, in *La Secte de Qumrân* (n. 1), pp. 11-84.

presidency of the late Professor M. Delcor. Half of the protagonists at the first Qumranic Colloquium were also present at the second (Coppens, Jaubert, Schmitt, van der Ploeg and van der Woude), but the number of participants had dramatically increased and the number of contributions published in the volume of proceedings was 28. The topic chosen then was the rather general "Qumrân: sa piété, sa théologie et son milieu"[5]. Central to this Colloquium were the texts published since the previous one, five new volumes of the *Discoveries in the Judaean Desert* series, and many preliminary publications of fragments from Cave 4 and 11[6], and particularly the new publications by the members of the original team, which were presented at the Colloquium by the authors themselves[7]. There was a clash between Yadin and van der Ploeg, who presented some fragments of 11Q20 as "Une halakha inédite de Qumrân" which had been identified by Yadin as parts of a copy of the Temple Scroll and whose photographs he was to publish in his forthcoming edition disregarding the rights of the Dutch Royal Academy of Science, and the ensuing dispute has remained notorious in the annals of Qumran research[8].

A noticeable difference with the first Colloquium was the emphasis on Qumran as an independent entity and not as a background to Christian origins. Another was the presence of young scholars who presented the first fruits of their labours at this forum. The presidential address[9] was a thorough bibliographical survey of 25 years of Qumranic research, covering congresses, series, periodicals, books, articles, dissertations, and contributions of all sorts, country by country[10].

5. M. DELCOR (ed.), *Qumrân. Sa piété, sa théologie et son milieu* (BETL, 46), Paris-Gembloux, Duculot-Leuven, University Press, 1978.

6. The contributions by A.S. van der Woude (4QprNab), B. Jongeling (11QtgJob), H. Pabst (4Q179), H. Lichtenberger (4Q185) were dedicated to them.

7. M. Baillet presented the forthcoming DJD VII, J.T. Milik, a series of small 4QAramaic fragments on the Patriarchs, J. van der Ploeg, some fragments of the Dutch lot from Cave 11, Y. Yadin, his forthcoming edition of the Temple Scroll, and P.W. Skehan, a collation and description of all fragments of Psalms from Cave 4.

8. A faint echo of the dispute is to be found in a P.S. added by van der Ploeg to his contribution: cf. M. DELCOR, *Qumrân. Sa piété, sa théologie et son milieu* (n. 5), pp. 112-113.

9. *Ibid.*, pp. 11-46 (*Où en sont les études qumrâniens?*).

10. Even without the footnotes, it is difficult to imagine any audience listening to this long list of names and titles without falling asleep or running out of the lecture theatre. I cannot resist quoting a characteristic sentence from the section dealing with Spain, because I have discovered that even my name is mentioned there: "Le professeur A. Díez Macho nous a signalé un important travail dactilographié d'un de ses élèves Florentino García Martínez, *Corpus Qumrânico. Textos arameos de Qumrân*, Madrid 1976" (p. 42).

Now, 26 years after this second *Colloquium Biblicum Lovaniense* dedicated to Qumran, the focus has returned once more to the Dead Sea Scrolls. If the precedent set at the two previous Colloquia is to be followed, I should treat you now to a survey of Qumranic research in the form of a *status quaestionis*, which would be necessarily dry and much longer than the one provided by Delcor. During the last 25 years, the publication of the Scrolls has been virtually completed, increasing the volumes of the DJD series from the 5 available in 1976 to the 37 now at our disposal[11], and the volume of research has increased exponentially with the number of texts available. Happily, I think there is no real need today for this sort of bibliographical survey or *status quaestionis*. The study of the Dead Sea Scrolls has become an independent academic discipline and, as such, is well provided with tools for research, such as bibliographies[12], encyclopaedias[13], and a whole host of general surveys published on the occasion of the fiftieth anniversary of the discoveries[14].

Instead of a *status quaestionis*, I will first explain the reasons that led me to choose "Wisdom and Apocalypticism in the DSS and the Biblical Tradition" as the topic for the 51st Colloquium, and secondly will deal briefly with a single problem related to this topic.

I. Wisdom and Apocalypticism in the DSS and the Biblical Tradition

The sheer volume of new material published since the previous Colloquia dedicated to Qumran has rendered impossible a congress which could attempt to deal with all of them. A "general" Qumranic congress, like the two previous ones, is no longer possible. The last congress of this sort was the gigantic marathon held in Jerusalem in 1997 in order to celebrate the fiftieth anniversary of the discoveries, at which more than 130 lectures, delivered by scholars from around the world, tried to present "the state of the art"[15]. It was therefore necessary to change the

11. See E. Tov (ed.), *The Texts from the Judaean Desert. Indices and An Introduction to the* Discoveries in the Judaean Desert *Series* (DJD, 39), Oxford, Clarendon, 2002.

12. F. García Martínez and D.W. Parry, *A Bibliography of the Finds of the Desert of Judah 1970-95* (STDJ, 19), Leiden, Brill, 1996; A. Pinnick, *The Orion Center Bibliography of the Dead Sea Scrolls (1995-2000)* (STDJ, 41), Leiden, Brill, 2001, and the current Bibliography published in each issue of the *Revue de Qumran*.

13. L.H. Schiffman and J.C. VanderKam (eds.), *Encyclopedia of the Dead Sea Scrolls*, New York, Oxford University Press, 2000.

14. Among them, the two impressive volumes by P.W. Flint and J.C. VanderKam (eds.), *The Dead Sea Scrolls after Fifty Years*, Leiden, Brill, 1998, are arguably the most significant.

15. L.H. Schiffman, E. Tov, J.C. VanderKam (eds.), *The Dead Sea Scrolls: Fifty Years after Their Discovery. Proceedings of the Jerusalem Congress, July 20-25, 1997*, Jerusalem, Israel Exploration Society-Shrine of the Book, 2000.

model of the two previous Qumran Colloquia, to move from the general to the particular, and to chose a specific topic which could be of interest not only to the restricted field of Dead Sea Scrolls scholars, but also to students of both the Hebrew Bible and the New Testament alike.

When the Committee's invitation to present a proposal for the 51st Colloquium reached me in Groningen in the summer of 2000, I was reading the recently published DJD 34[16] (the volume which contains the edition of the eight preserved copies of 4QInstruction), and at the same time, putting the final touches to the edition of the proceedings of the third meeting of the IOQS, a meeting dedicated to the study of the "Sapiential, Liturgical and Poetical texts from Qumran"[17].

During the introductory speech to the Oslo meeting, I gave a rather subjective list of what I considered to be the main problems common to the three categories of texts we were dealing with, and I also added a list of each of these categories' specific problems. Concerning the sapiential texts, I indicated three areas in need of further research. I wrote in 1998:

> Specific to the wisdom texts seems to me the acute need to analyse their relationship with Biblical wisdom compositions (in terms of ideas, vocabulary, compositional techniques, literary patterns, etc.) and with the larger continuum of the Near Eastern wisdom tradition. There is also the specific problem of the historical context in which these texts originated and their function there, as well as their function in the Qumran context in which they were transmitted, in which they were almost certainly used, and to which they may have been adapted. And finally, there is the specific problem of the relationship of these texts to the Wisdom of the Rabbis and to Christian Wisdom[18].

As you can imagine, I was eager to see if those problems had been solved in the new, magnificent *editio maior* of 4QInstruction, without any doubt the largest and most important sapiential composition recovered from Qumran and published in DJD 34.

The editors had certainly tackled the first of the three problems indicated (the relationship to biblical wisdom) and had also dealt with the original *life-setting* of the work (a rather vague 'school' setting in their opinion)[19]. They paid rather less attention to the Qumran location, where

16. J. Strugnell, D. Harrington, T. Elgvin, *Qumran Cave 4. XXIV: Sapiential Texts, Part 2* (DJD, 34), Oxford, Clarendon, 1999.

17. D.K. Falk, F. García Martínez, E.M. Schuller (eds.), *Sapiential, Liturgical and Poetical Texts from Qumran. Proceedings of the Third Meeting of the International Organization for Qumran studies, Published in Memory of M. Baillet* (STDJ, 35), Leiden, Brill, 2000.

18. *Ibid.*, p. 8.

19. They envision briefly the possibility of a different life-setting, associating the work with the foundational pre-Qumranic stage of the group which later will become the Qumran community, but consider it less likely. DJD, 34, p. 21.

the work had been preserved, copied and read for a long time, which was rather surprising. They considered the idea that 4QInstruction came "neither from the Qumran sect, nor from any secular associates of the Qumran movement, nor yet from pre-sectarian groups, but rather was a general offshoot of Jewish wisdom, of uncertain date and not sectarian at all"[20] as the most likely explanation of its origins. They did acknowledge that the work was very popular in Qumran though, as proved by the number and date of the copies found, but they left to others the task of ascertaining what purpose it could have served at the location where it was preserved.

I shall illustrate the answer Strugnell and Harrington gave to the first problem, that of the relationship of 4QInstruction to biblical wisdom, with a few quotes from their "General Introduction" to the volume.

> Within these varying indications, then, it would be easiest to see in 4Q**415** ff. a true 'missing link', to be set somewhere in the history of the common (i.e. non-sectarian) Jewish wisdom tradition, datable between Proverbs and Sirach, in vocabulary and in theology being sometimes closer to the one, sometimes to the other[21].

And a little further, they add:

> In any case it represents a venerable 'missing link' in the development of 'secular' or common Israelite wisdom from Proverbs to Sirach[22].

They recognised that the sort of wisdom transmitted in 4QInstruction was not totally equivalent to the sort of wisdom transmitted in the sapiential books of the Bible, because a number of its elements are more characteristic of the apocalyptic than of the sapiential tradition. As they put it:

> Thus this sapiential work joins (though in no clear pattern) ordinary practical instructions (about loans and surety, family relations, etc.) with cosmological and theological teachings familiar from Jewish apocalypticism[23].

But, basically, assuming I have understood them correctly, they placed 4QInstruction in a *continuum* within the biblical sapiential tradition, far from the apocalyptic world-view we can perceive in some of the Qumran compositions.

> Indeed, it is only the frequent concern with רז נהיה that differentiated 4Q**415** ff. from any general Jewish sapiential work (so long as that work also had strong eschatological concerns)[24].

20. *Ibid.*, pp. 21-22.
21. *Ibid.*, p. 31.
22. *Ibid.*, p. 36.
23. *Ibid.*, p. 33.
24. *Ibid.*, p. 30

When I reflected on this answer, I had the strong impression that they have somehow downplayed the apocalyptic components of the composition. The fact is, we do not know of any other Jewish sapiential work with such strong eschatological concerns, and the only parallels to the expression רז נהיה we have come from other Qumran manuscripts which reflect the apocalyptic world-view of the community.

I started to think that, if the editors were wrong in their appreciation of the importance of the apocalyptic elements of the work, it would be possible to consider 4QInstruction as evidence of a major development in the sapiential tradition. Much as Ben Sirach represents a new development with its fusion of traditional biblical wisdom with priestly elements[25], 4QInstruction could represent a new development with its fusion of traditional biblical wisdom with apocalyptic elements. More than just taking its place in a continuum, 4QInstruction could represent a change, a new development, a new form of Jewish wisdom not previously attested to within the biblical tradition.

The problems I have outlined were thus not yet solved, it seemed to me. At least not all of them, or not in a complete satisfactory manner. It would therefore be worthwhile to examine the recently published Qumran wisdom texts, looking for clues which may illuminate their relationship to biblical wisdom and apocalyptic traditions. This was a concrete topic, but one which could be approached from different perspectives. It was a topic which would allow the presentation of discussions current among specialists of the Dead Sea Scrolls[26], while at the same

25. See J.J. COLLINS, *Jewish Wisdom in the Hellenistic Age* (The Old Testament Library) Louisville, KY, Westminster John Knox, 1997, and D. HARRINGTON, *Two Early Jewish Approaches to Wisdom. Sirach and Sapiential Work A*, in *JSPS* 16 (1997) 25-38.

26. The interest of Dead Sea Scrolls scholars in the wisdom texts preserved in the Qumran collection had burgeoned since the publication of the first DJD volume of sapiential texts, T. ELGVIN *et al.*, *Qumran Cave 4. XV: Sapiential Texts, Part 1* (DJD, 20), Oxford, Clarendon, 1997, and particularly since the publication of the synthesis by D.J. HARRINGTON, *Wisdom Texts from Qumran* (The Literature of the Dead Sea Scrolls), London, Routledge, 1996, which made the main lines and conclusions of the then unedited 4QInstruction available. For a summary description of the wisdom texts found at Qumran, see J. KAMPEN, *The Diverse Aspects of Wisdom in the Qumran Texts*, in *The Dead Sea Scrolls after Fifty Years* (n. 15), pp. 211-243. More comprehensive and detailed is the description by A. LANGE, *Die Weisheitstexte aus Qumran: Eine Einleitung*, in CH. HEMPEL, A. LANGE, H. LICHTENBERGER (eds.), *The Wisdom Texts from Qumran and the Development of Sapiential Thought* (BETL, 159), Leuven, University Press – Peeters, 2002, pp. 3-30. The bibliography in this volume, compiled by CH. HEMPEL and A. LANGE, *Literature on the Wisdom Texts from Qumran*, on pp. 445-454, is impressive, but goes only as far as the year 2000. To the titles there listed, two important monographs published in the series STDJ should be added: C. MURPHY, *Wealth in the Dead Sea Scrolls and in the Qumran Community* (STDJ, 40), Leiden, Brill, 2001 ("Wealth in Instruction", pp. 163-209), and E.J.C. TIGCHELAAR, *To Increase Learning for the Understanding Ones. Reading and Reconstructing the Fragmentary Early Jewish Sapiential Text 4QInstruction* (SDTJ, 44), Leiden, Brill, 2001. Further, the following books and articles should be

time having a certain appeal for people whose main interests are not the Dead Sea Scrolls but the Hebrew Bible or the New Testament. Since the model of the two previous Colloquia dedicated to Qumran could not be followed, why not try a thematic model, as used during other Colloquia, such as the Jubilee Meeting dedicated to the "Biblical Canons"? For these reasons I decided to propose the present topic to the committee, and I wrote the following description of its scope:

> The apocalyptic component of the sectarian scrolls has been one of the key elements brought to the fore since the beginning of DSS research. The wisdom component of the Scrolls, on the other hand, has hardly been researched, no doubt because the main wisdom texts have been available only recently. The quantity of sapiential texts now available in two DJD volumes is great, but an in-depth study still needs to be done, and their relationship to the biblical wisdom tradition (Proverbs, Qohelet and Ben Sira in particular) need to be ascertained.
> The combination of both lines of research (Apocalypticism and Wisdom) in a single Colloquium could be very fruitful. It may not only throw light on the old problem of the prophetic versus the sapiential roots of biblical apocalypticism, but because both are very much present and operative in the single concrete library of Qumran (as attested by the recent published texts), it could lead to a better understanding of *their mutual relationship.*

These were my reasons for choosing the topic which has brought us together today. I would now like to present briefly one point of possible relationship between wisdom and apocalypticism. This point is reflected in the title given to this address, and is inspired by the title of the Matthew Goff's Chicago dissertation, "The Worldly *and* Heavenly Wisdom of 4QInstruction" (my italics)[27].

II. Wisdom at Qumran: Worldly or Heavenly?

The title of Goff's dissertation apparently answers my question by asserting that in the case of 4QInstruction, the alternative is not compel-

noted: D. Hamidovič, *4Q279, 4QFour Lots, Une interprétation du Psaume 135 appartenant à 4Q421, 4QWays of Righteousness*, in *DSD* 9 (2002) 166-186; G. Ibba, *La sapienza di Qumran. Il Patto, la luce e le tenebre, l'illuminazione*, Roma, Città Nuova, 2000; D.F. Jefferies, *Wisdom at Qumran: A Form-Critical Analysis of the Admonitions in 4QInstruction*. Vol. 3 (Gorgias Dissertations: Near Eastern Studies, 3), Piscataway, NJ, Gorgias Press, 2002; J.L. Kugel, *Some Instances of Biblical Interpretation in the Hymns and Wisdom Writings of Qumran,* in Id., *Studies in Ancient Midrash*, Cambridge, MA, Harvard University Center for Jewish Studies, 2001, pp. 155-169; K.B. Larsen, *Visdom Og Apokalyptik I 'Musar Lemevin' (1Q/4QInstruction),* in *Dansk Teologisk Tidsskrift* 65 (2002) 1-14; É. Puech – A. Steudel, *Un nouveau fragment du manuscrit* 4QInstruction (XQ7 = 4Q417 *ou* 4Q418), in *RQ* 76 (2000) 623-627; D. Steinmetz, *Sefer HeHago: The Community and the Book,* in *JJS* 52 (2001) 39-58.

27. M.J. Goff, *The Worldly and Heavenly Wisdom of 4QInstruction.* A Dissertation submitted to the Faculty of the Divinity School of the University of Chicago, March 2002. The Dissertation will be published in a revised form in the Series STDJ.

ling, and that the wisdom transmitted there is both worldly and heavenly at the same time.

When considering the 4QInstruction content, Goff's reasoning seems convincing. The knowledge the sage is communicating to his pupil[28] belongs to both sorts of wisdom[29]. Most of the teachings concern very worldly matters and are perfect parallels to the secular wisdom communicated in biblical wisdom books like Qohelet or Sirach. Our sage deals with economic matters, poverty and riches, borrowing and repaying money, how to deal with loans and securities; he instructs the one seeking understanding on how to conduct himself in his social relations, both with superiors and inferiors, how to avoid shame, how to deal with strangers, and how to conduct himself in the event of a sudden change of fortune; he also admonishes the pupil on how to conduct himself in family matters, relations with parents and with his wife, the marriage of children, etc.

But juxtaposed with these very worldly concerns, the sage instructs the one seeking understanding on many other matters which pertain to the realm of heavenly wisdom. He teaches about God and God's plans, about creation, about the cosmos, about angels, about good and evil, about eschatology and the afterlife, and, quite characteristically, about the final judgement in which God will reward or punish the righteous and the wicked. In short, the teachings of our sage concern not only worldly wisdom but also heavenly "mysteries".

Although we can find parallels to some of these teachings in biblical wisdom, most of them belong to the areas which were excluded from biblical wisdom and which only appear in apocalyptic compositions (biblical or otherwise). Ben Sirach states explicitly:

> Reflect upon what you have been commanded, for what is hidden is not your concern. Do not meddle in matters that are beyond you, for more than you can understand has been shown to you (Sir 3:22-23).

The advice of our sage is exactly the opposite:

> [Gaze upon the mystery] that is to come, and comprehend the birth-times of salvation. And know who is to inherit glory and toil (4Q417 2 i 10-11).

The presence of both elements is so obvious in 4QInstruction that Torleif Elgvin has proposed understanding the origins of the composi-

28. Whoever this may be. For the problems of determining their identity, see E. TIGCHELAAR, *The Addressees of 4QInstruction*, in *Sapiential, Liturgical and Poetical Texts from Qumran* (n. 17), pp. 72-75.

29. This characteristic has been emphasised by T. ELGVIN, *Wisdom and Apocalypticism in the Early Second Century BCE: The Evidence of 4QInstruction*, in *The Dead Sea Scrolls: Fifty Years After Their Discovery* (n. 15), pp. 226-247, and ID., *Wisdom With and Without Apocalyptic*, in *Sapiential, Liturgical and Poetical Texts* (n. 17), pp. 15-38.

tion as a fusion of two different sources: a secular wisdom composition contained in what he call the "admonitions", and an apocalyptic source most clearly apparent in the "discourses"[30]. The apocalyptic redactor would have incorporated the wisdom instructions within his own framework, in a similar way to how the apocalyptic author of the Second Sibylline Oracle inserted a wisdom extract of Pseudo-Phocylides into his work[31]. But, as Goff pointed out[32], this understanding of 4QInstruction as a synthetic work is rather problematic because the fragmentary preservation of the composition reduces all discernment of strata to wild speculation. Besides, the way in which both elements are intermingled in the preserved text made their extraction impossible without some preconceived idea of what should or should not be present in a wisdom or an apocalyptic composition; or, to put it in the words of John Collins[33], without a preconceived idea of the "generic compatibility" of both elements. This, of course, does not rule out the possibility that the author or authors of the composition may have made use of traditional wisdom sayings, and traditional apocalyptic elements. But what must count as decisive is both elements being clearly present together and intermingled in the same composition.

However, in my opinion, this fact does not totally justify Goff's conclusion that the wisdom we do have in 4QInstruction is at once both worldly and heavenly. It is my contention that the interpretative cadre established by the work's beginning, as preserved both in 4Q416 1 and in 4Q417 1 i, as well as the continuous reference to the רז נהיה ("the mystery that is to come" in the translation of the editors)[34], gives a

30. T. ELGVIN, *Wisdom and Apocalypticism* (n. 29), p. 227. He produced the first comprehensive analysis of 4QInstruction in his still unpublished dissertation: *An Analysis of 4QInstruction*, Thesis submitted to the Senate of the Hebrew University of Jerusalem, 1997. It will soon appear in the Series STDJ in a thoroughly revised form.

31. Lines 5-79 of Pseudo-Phocylides have been inserted as lines 56-148 of the Second Sybilline Oracle, see P.W. VAN DER HORST, *The Sentences of Pseudo-Phocylides. With Introduction and Commentary* (SVTP, 4), Leiden, Brill, 1978, pp. 84-85

32. M.J. GOFF, *The Worldly and Heavenly Wisdom* (n. 27), p. 19.

33. J.J. COLLINS, *Wisdom, Apocalypticism and Generic Compatibility*, in L.J. PERDUE, B.B. SCOTT, W.J. WISEMAN (eds.), *In Search of Wisdom. Festschrift John G. Gammie*, Louisville, KY, Westminster John Knox, 1993, pp. 165-185; reprinted in ID., *Seers, Sibyls and Sages in Hellenistic-Roman Judaism* (JSJSup, 54), Leiden, Brill, 1997, pp. 385-404.

34. The expression has been widely discussed and several different interpretations and translations proposed since A. LANGE, *Weisheit und Prädestination. Weisheitliche Urordnung und Prädestination in den Textfunden von Qumran* (STDJ, 18), Leiden, Brill, 1995, pp. 57-61. For a summary of the opinions, see D.J. HARRINGTON, *The Raz Nihyeh in a Qumran Wisdom Text (1Q26, 4Q415-418, 423)*, in *RQ* 17 (1996) 449-453. Later, it was also discussed by J.J. COLLINS, *Wisdom Reconsidered in the Light of the Scrolls*, in *DSD* 4 (1997) 265-281, esp. p. 274, and by A. SCHOORS, *The Language of the Qumran Sapiential Works*, in *The Wisdom Texts from Qumran and the Development of Sapiential Thought* (n. 26), pp. 61-95, esp. 86-88.

"revelatory" character to all the contents of 4QInstruction, including the most worldly ones, and makes of all of them "heavenly wisdom".

(a) I think that Strugnell-Harrington were right in considering fragment one of 4Q416 as the very beginning of the composition[35], and that this fragment provides a theological framework for the reading of the whole subsequent composition. As they also noted, the language of the fragment is that of the third person narrative, with no trace of a direct address[36]. In spite of its fragmentary state, the next five lines of fragment 1 (ll. 10-15) give a feel of its tenor:

> 10. in heaven He shall pronounce judgement upon the work of wickedness, and all His faithful children will be favourably accepted by [...] 11. its end. And they shall be in terror. And all who defiled themselves in it, shall cry out. For the heavens shall fear, and the earth too shall be shaken (from its place]. 12. The [se]as and the deeps shall be in terror, and every spirit of flesh will cry out.. But the sons of heaven [... in the day of] 13. its [judg]ment, And all iniquity shall come to an end, while the period of truth will be completed [...] 14. in all periods of eternity, for He is a God of truth. And from before the years of [...] 15. to let the righteous understand (the distinction) between god and evil, to [...] every regula[tion ...] 16 [incl]ination of flesh is he/it. And from understanding (?) (4Q416 110-15)[37].

The topics dealt with in this introduction are hardly unfamiliar, though in apocalyptic works, not in wisdom compositions. For example, the judgement upon wickedness, the vindication of righteousness, the end of evil and the arrival of the epoch of truth, etc., and the same can be said of the vocabulary used: פקודה, רוח בשר, יצר בשר, קץ האמת, עבודת רשעה, etc.[38]. The context thus established by this introduction for the

35. DJD, 34, pp. 8 and 73. This was contested by Elgvin on both material and textual considerations: see T. ELGVIN, *The Reconstruction of Sapiential Work A*, in *RQ* 16 (1995), pp. 559-580, esp. 566-567. The matter has now been thoroughly dealt with by E. TIGCHELAAR, *Towards a Reconstruction of the Beginning of 4QInstruction (4Q416 Fragment 1 and Parallels)*, in *The Wisdom Texts from Qumran and the Development of Sapiential Thought* (n. 26), pp. 99-126.

36. Although E. Tigchelaar tentatively concludes, on the basis that 4Q418 238 may also have belonged to the beginning of the column, "that the third-person description of 4Q416 1 and parallels was embedded in a second person address, which admonished the addressee to contemplate" (p. 126).

37. In the translation of E.J.C. TIGCHELAAR, *To Increase Learning for the Understanding Ones* (n. 26), p. 176.

38. The vocabulary of 4QInstruction has already been extensively studied, see J. STRUGNELL, *The Sapiential Work 4Q415ff. and Pre-Qumranic Works from Qumran. Lexical Considerations*, in D.W. PARRY – E. ULRICH (eds.), *The Provo International Conference on the Dead Sea Scrolls. Technological Innovations, New Texts, and Reformulated Issues* (STDJ, 30), Leiden, Brill, 1999, pp. 595-608; E.J.C. TIGCHELAAR, *To Increase Learning for the Understanding Ones* (n. 26), 237-244; J. STRUGNELL, *The Smaller*

whole work is an apocalyptic one. Furthermore, the function of this context, it seems to me, is none other than to legitimise the corpus of instructions which follow.

(b) This strategy of legitimisation appears even more clearly in the first fragment of 4Q417, which also belongs to the theological cadre of 4QInstruction, and which deals with the same topics, but presented as instructions directly given to the "understanding one". The first five lines are very fragmentary, but lines 6-19 of 4Q417 1 i are fairly well preserved and worthy of being quoted in full[39]:

> 6. [*And* by day and by night meditate upon the mystery that is] to come, And study (*it*) continually. And then thou shalt know truth and iniquity, wisdom 7. [and foolish]ness *thou shalt* [*recognize*], *every* ac[t] in all their ways, Together with *their* punishment(s) *in* all ages everlasting, And the punishment 8. of eternity. Then thou shalt discern between *the* [goo]d and [evil according to their] deeds. For the God of knowledge is the *foundation* of truth. And *by/on* the mystery that is to come 9. He has *laid out* its (= truth's) *foundation, And its* deeds [He has *prepared with all wis*]dom And with *all* [*c*]*unning has He fashioned it,* And the domain of its *deeds* (*creatures*) 10. *with a*[*ll*] *its secrets* [has He ...] ... [...] *He* [*ex*]*pounded* for their un[der]standing every *d[ee]d/cre[atu]re* So that *man* could walk 11. in the [fashion (inclination)] of *their/his* understanding. And He will/did *expound* for *m[an...]* And *in aboundance/property/purity* of understanding *were made kn[own the se]crets* of 12. his (?man's) plan, together with how he should walk [p]erfec[t in all] his [ac]tions. These things investigate/*seek early and* continually, and gain understanding [about a]ll 13. their *outcomes.* And then thou shalt know about the glory of [*His*] *m[ight*, Toge]ther with His marvellous mysteries and the *mighty acts He has wrought.* But thou, 14 O understanding one, study (*inherit?*) thy reward, Remembering *the re[quital, for] it* comes. Engraved is the/thy ordinance/destiny, And ordained is all the punishment. 15. For engraved *is* that which is ordained by God against all the *ini[quities* of] the children of שות. *And* written in His presence *is* a book of memorial 16. of those who keep His word. And that *is* the appearance/*vision of the meditation* on a book of memorial. And *He*/שות (?) *gave* it as an inheritance to *Man/Enosh Together with* a spiritual people. F[o]r 17. according to the pattern of the Holy Ones *is his* (man's) fashioning. *But* no more *has* meditation been given to a (?) fleshy spirit, For *it* (sc. flesh) knew/knows not the difference between 18. [goo]d and evil according to the judgement of *its* [sp]irit. *Vacat* And thou, O understanding child, gaze on the mystery that is to come, And know 19. [the *paths* of] everyone that lives And the manner of his walking that is appointed for [*his*] deed[s] (4Q417 1 i 6-19).

Hebrew Wisdom Texts Found at Qumran. Variations, Resemblances, and Lines of Development, in *The Wisdom Texts from Qumran and the Development of Sapiential Thought* (n. 26), pp. 31-60; A. SCHOORS, *The Language of the Qumran Sapiential Works*, in *ibid.*, pp. 61-95, esp. 77-94.

39. In the translation by STRUGNELL- HARRINGTON, DJD, 34, pp. 154-155.

I have deliberately retained the DJD 34 translation, in spite of its old-fashioned (King James Bible) sound, instead of using our own translation (in *the Dead Sea Scrolls Study Edition*)[40] or any other available, in order to avoid discussing the many interesting, but problematic, elements of this text which are not directly pertinent to the point I want to emphasise. Specifically, this fragment of admonition shares the same theological ideas we encountered in the previous one, but makes explicit that the theological cadre is intended as a *legitimisation* of the instruction given. The wisdom here communicated can hardly be called worldly wisdom. This wisdom is contained in the "mystery that is to come" (l. 6) whose continuous meditation brings forth knowledge of truth and of iniquity together with their punishment in everlasting ages (ll. 7-8). The addressee (singular, ואתה בן מבין) is urged to gaze on the "mystery that is to come" (l. 18) in order to know "the paths of everyone that lives and the manner of his walking that is appointed for his deeds" (l. 19), and even to "get understanding about all the mysteries concerning thee" (l. 25). The result of this knowledge is nothing less than knowledge of the "glory of His (God's) might" (l. 13), which is possible because he, as one of the spiritual people, has been fashioned "according to the pattern of the Holy Ones" (l. 17).

The references to the חרות החוק{כה} "engraved ordinance" (l. 14) and to חזון ההגוי לספר זכרון the "vision of the meditation on a book of memorial" (l. 16) are more in line with the "heavenly tables" of certain apocalypses than with ordinary worldly knowledge, and they apparently have the same function within the composition[41].

(c) However, the clearest indicator of the legitimisation strategy applied to the wisdom imparted is the frequent use of the רז נהיה (whatever it may be exactly), not only in the clearly apocalyptic sections of the composition, but all over 4QInstruction. Harrington, in the most detailed study of the expression published so far, concluded:

> What is the *rz nhyh*? It seems to be a body of teaching. It could be written or oral. It appears to have some fixed form. It concerns behaviour and eschatology[42].

40. F. García Martínez – E.J.C. Tigchelaar, *The Dead Sea Scrolls. Study Edition*. Vol. 2, Grand Rapids, MI, Eerdmans–Leiden, Brill, 2000, p. 859.

41. For the legitimisation function of the heavenly tables in *Jubilees*, see F. García Martínez, *The Heavenly Tablets in the Book of Jubilees*, in M. Albany, J. Frey, A. Lange (eds.), *Studies in the Book of Jubilees*, Tübingen, Mohr, 1997, pp. 243-260, and H. Najman, *Interpretation as Primordial Writing: Jubilees and its Authority Conferring Strategies*, in *JSJ* 30 (1999) 397-410.

42. D.J. Harrington, *The Raz Nihyeh* (n. 34), p. 552.

This last phrase is most significant here. The expression occurs in the 4QInstruction about thirty times (twice without prepositions, once with the preposition *m-*, but usually with the proposition *b-*) and it is, according to Harrington, "so frequent and so regular in the work that when we find either word alone and need to fill in the lacuna, we can add the missing word with some confidence"[43].

Here is a list of all these occurrences, with indication (within brackets) of the context, insofar as this can be ascertained:

1Q26 1,1 (no context); 1, 4 (revelation).
4Q415 6, 4 (poverty); 24, 1 (spirit); 25, 1 9 (no context).
4Q416 2 i 5 (birth-times of salvation); 2 iii 9 (its origins); 2 iii 14 (ways of truth and roots of iniquity); 2 iii 18 (parents); 2 iii 21 (wife); 17, 3 (no context).
4Q417 1 i 6 (truth and iniquity); 1 i 8 (truth's foundation); 1 i 18 (the paths of all living); 1 i 21 (no context); 1 ii 3 (no context); 2 i 10-11 (birth-times of salvation).
4Q418 10,1 (parents); 43,4 (truth and iniquity); 43, 14 (the paths of all living); 43, 16 (no context); 77,2 (nature of man); 77, 4 (the weight of the times); 123 ii 4 (what God has uncovered); 172, 1 (no context); 179, 5 (no context); 184, 2 (eating and being satisfied); 190, 2 (no context).
4Q423 3, 2 (crops will multiply).

What is of interest in this list is that the contexts with which the use of the expression is associated are by no means restricted to the apocalyptic sections of the composition. Indeed, as Harrington has pointed out, they deal with eschatology as well as with behaviour. Even the most "secular" instructions are comprised within the רז נהיה. The instructions to honour father and mother (a very traditional topic in biblical wisdom) are motivated thus: "because they uncovered thy ear to the mystery that is to come" (4Q416 2 iii 18)[44]. In talking about the wife it is said: "Thou has taken a wife in thy poverty, take her offspring in thy lowly state; but take care lest thou be distracted from the mystery that is to come while thou keeps company together" (4Q416 2 iii 20-21)[45]. Many of the instances of the רז נהיה are without immediate context, but in others, such as 4Q415 6,4[46], the whole context is one of instruction on how to deal with poverty, 4Q418 184, 2[47] deals with eating and 4Q423 3,2[48] is part of instructions given to a farmer.

In my view, this implies that the author of 4QInstruction considered all the knowledge he communicated, be it of an apocalyptic nature or

43. *Ibid.*, p. 550.
44. DJD, 34, pp. 110, 113.
45. *Ibid.*, pp. 110, 113.
46. *Ibid.*, p. 51.
47. *Ibid.*, p. 408.
48. *Ibid.*, p. 514.

similar to traditional biblical wisdom, as the same kind of knowledge. By also presenting his "secular" teachings as being included within the רז נהיה, he gave them the same authority he gives to the other "mysteries" about which he instructed the "one seeking understanding". He used the same strategy of legitimisation of his authority for the whole composition, without distinguishing between heavenly and worldly wisdom. His instructions' most worldly concerns were also presented as "revealed" wisdom.

I think we may conclude that if Sirach represents "secular" Jewish wisdom, the wisdom of 4QInstruction is in every way closer to the "revealed" wisdom of a full-blown apocalypse, as in 4 Ezra. In any case, I regard 4QInstruction as the representative of a new and different sort of Jewish wisdom, a wisdom whose authority is not grounded on human knowledge but on divine revelation.

I do not know whether we can use the term "apocalyptic wisdom" in the case of 4QInstruction. It is evident that the composition is not apocalyptic in the formal sense in which we are used to understanding the word, after the paradigm of *Semeia 14*. However, in my opinion, its author tries to present the knowledge he wants to communicate not as simple human knowledge (as in the biblical wisdom tradition) but as "revealed" knowledge, as heavenly wisdom. Therefore, I think we can answer the question posed in a different way to how Goff answered it. Qumran wisdom is not worldly *and* heavenly wisdom, it is revealed wisdom, and thus thoroughly heavenly.

Allow me to finish with the same words Matthias Delcor used to close the Qumran congress 25 years ago:

> Non, Qumrân n'a pas encore dit son dernier mot. Nous avons dépassé l'époque des révélations sensationnelles qui semblaient devoir bouleverser les fondements mêmes de la tradition chrétienne; mais une nouvelle ère d'études qumrâniennes, espérons-le moins passionnées et d'autant plus fructueuses, va sans doute commencer[49].

I am not sure that the last twenty-five years of Qumranic research have been less "impassioned" than the preceding years (the controversies of the nineties were even stormier than any before), but I am sure that the last ten years have been the most fruitful for Qumranic research. All the preparatory work has been completed; all the collections are now fully published and are easily available; all the necessary tools are ready. We are indeed at the beginning of a new era in Qumranic re-

49. M. DELCOR, *Conclusions. Lignes de force du Colloquium*, in ID. (ed.), *Qumrân. Sa piété, sa théologie et son milieu* (n. 5), p. 418.

search. It is now up to you to set an example and start working on these precious texts, so that at the end of these three days we will know more of the "Wisdom and Apocalypticism in the Dead Sea Scrolls and in the Biblical Tradition" and their mutual relationship.

Groot Begijnhof 53
B-3000 Leuven

Florentino GARCÍA MARTÍNEZ

INTERPRETATION ALS OFFENBARUNG

Zum Verhältnis von Schriftauslegung und Offenbarung in apokalyptischer und nichtapokalyptischer Literatur

> (20) Und ich redete noch, betete, bekannte meine Sünde und die Sünde meines Volkes Israel und lies mein Flehen um den Berg des Heiligtums meines Gottes vor den Herrn, meinen Gott fallen, – (21) während ich also noch im Gebet redete, flog der Mann Gabriel, den ich zu Beginn in einer Vision gesehen hatte, zur Zeit des Abendopfers in raschem Flug nah zu mir heran. (22) Und er erklärte und sprach mit mir und sagte: „Daniel, jetzt bin ich herausgekommen, dir Einsicht zu geben. (23) Zu Beginn deines Flehens erging ein Wort, und ich bin gekommen es zu verkünden, denn du bist kostbar. Merke auf das Wort und erhalte Einsicht in der Vision: (24) Siebzig (Jahr)wochen sind über dein Volk und deine heilige Stadt verhängt, bis der Frevel beendet, die Sünde versiegelt und die Schuld gesühnt ist, bis ewige Gerechtigkeit gebracht, bis Vision und Prophet besiegelt und das Allerheiligste gesalbt wird. (Dan 9,20-24)

Auf diese Weise berichtet das Danielbuch davon, wie der Apokalyptiker in einer Angelophanie die Deutung der für ihn rätselhaften 70 Jahre aus Jer 25,11f. erhält. Daniel 9,23 macht es ganz deutlich: וְהָבֵן בַּמַּרְאֶה („erlange Einsicht in der Vision"). Der Schlüssel zum Text liegt für den Visionär in seiner Vision und nicht in exegetischer Methodik – sei sie antik oder modern[1].

Es ist wahrlich nichts neues, wenn ich hier auf den Zusammenhang von Auslegung und apokalyptischer Offenbarung hinweise. Und es ist ebenfalls bekannt, daß dieser Zusammenhang von Textauslegung und Offenbarung nicht auf Dan 9 beschränkt ist. An dieser Stelle mag ein Hinweis auf das henochitische Buch der Träume (1Hen 83-90) genügen: Ein Teil dieses Werkes ist eine parabiblische Erzählung, die in der symbolischen Kodierung allegorischer Träume[2] die Geschichte

1. Für anregende Diskussionen zum Thema Auslegung und Divination gilt mein Dank Frau Prof. Dr. Michaela Bauks (Montpellier).

2. In der modernen Forschung wird gerne von „message dreams" und „symbolic dreams" gesprochen: s. etwa A.L. OPPENHEIM, *The Interpretation of Dreams in the Ancient Near East. With a Translation of an Assyrian Dream-Book* (Transactions of the American Philosophical Society, 46.3), Philadelphia, PA, The American Philosophical Society, 1956, pp. 184.205-212; F.H. CRYER, *Divination in Ancient Israel and its Near Eastern Environment: A Socio-Historical Investigation* (JSOT.S, 142), Sheffield, Sheffield Academic Press, 1994, pp. 158f.268; J.-M. HUSSER, *Dreams and Dream Narratives in the Biblical World* (The Biblical Seminar, 63), Sheffield, Sheffield Academic Press, 1999, pp. 23f.; S.A.L. BUTLER, *Mesopotamian Conceptions of Dreams and Dream Rituals* (Alter Orient und Altes Testament, 258), Münster, Ugarit Verlag, 1998, pp. 15-19. Wegen ihrer größeren zeitlichen Nähe zur Sache ziehe ich demgegenüber die antike Begrifflichkeit von theorematischen und allegorischen Träumen vor (cf. ARTEMIDOR, I,1f.).

Israels referiert (s. etwa 1Hen 85,3-89,40 als Nacherzählung von Gen-Dtn).

Reflektiert die exegetische Angelophanie von Dan 9 somit ein hermeneutisches Bewußtsein, nach dem Auslegung ein revelatorischer Prozess ist, und ist Auslegung damit selbst ein divinatorischer Akt?

Um dieser Frage nachzugehen, möchte ich im folgenden verschiedene Textkomplexe aus dem näheren und weiteren Umfeld des Danielbuchs diskutieren: Eine Analyse der Pescharim und ihrer Hermeutik wird die Frage aufwerfen, inwieweit die schon in Dan 9 beobachtete revelatorische Exegese ein Proprium des antiken Judentums ist. In diesem Zusammenhang werde ich mich der spätägyptischen Literatur und Texten aus der griechischen Antike zuwenden. Am Ende meines Beitrags möchte ich dann das Phänomen der Schriftprophetie ansprechen.

1. Die Pescharim und Dan 9

Schon der Kernbegriff der Deuteformeln in den Pescharim gibt einen ersten Hinweis auf den divinatorischen Charakter ihrer Deutetechnik: Die Wurzel פתר / פשר wird in der hebräisch-aramäischen Literatur Israels nur im Zusammenhang mit der Deutung von Träumen und anderen Omenformen sowie im Zusammen mit der Auslegung von autoritativen Texten verwendet[3]. So werden z.B. die Traumdeutungen Josephs in Gen 40,8.16.22; 41,8.12f.15 als פִּתְרוֹן („Deutung“) bezeichnet (vgl. פתר in Gen 40,5.8.12.18; 41,11). Und auch das akkadische Lexem *pašāru* kann

3. In Sir 38,14 wird die Untersuchung eines Arztes zwar פשרה genannt, jedoch wird der Erfolg seiner Deutung an ein Gebet geknüpft. Die Verwendung von פשר dürfte hier den gottgegebenen Charakter der ärztlichen Diagnose unterstreichen wollen. Daß Ben Sira an dieser Stelle einen Begriff aus der Divination verwendet, ist Teil seines Bemühens, in Sir 38,1-15 die als pagan empfundene Medizin mit der jüdischen Frömmigkeit kompatibler zu machen. Zum Skopos von Sir 38,1-15 vgl. etwa P.W. Skehan - A.A. di Lella, *The Wisdom of Ben Sira: A New Translation with Introduction* (Anchor Bible, 39), New York, Doubleday, 1987, pp. 441-443; G. Sauer, *Jesus Sirach / Ben Sira* (ATD Apokryphen, 1), Göttingen, Vandenhoeck & Ruprecht, 2000, pp. 261-263. Ob פֵּשֶׁר in Qoh 8,1 eine Deutung im Stil der Omeninterpretation oder eine andere Form der Deutung bezeichnet, geht aus dem Text nicht hervor. Die Interpretation von Qoh 8,1 wird zusätzlich durch die Tatsache erschwert, daß es sich bei dem Vers wahrscheinlich um eine spätere Glosse handelt; vgl. A. Lauha, *Kohelet* (Biblischer Kommentar Altes Testament, 19), Neukirchen-Vluyn, Neukirchner Verlag, p. 144.

4. Zur Bedeutung dieses Lexems vgl. A.L. Oppenheim, *Interpretation of Dreams* (s. Anm. 2), p. 219: „the Sumerian b ú r (as well as the Akkadian *pašāru*) can be used to render (a) the reporting of one's dream to another person, (b) the interpreting of an enigmatic dream by that person, and (c) the dispelling or removing of the evil consequences of such a dream by magic means. This state of affairs shows, patently, that all these activities are functionally identical, their common purpose being cathartic. This state of affairs shows, patently, that all these activities are functionally identical, their common purpose being cathartic“.

im Sinne einer Traumdeutung verwendet werden als das hebräische Lexem, der Begriff jedoch ein wesentlich weiteres Bedeutungsspektrum hat[4]. Die Analogien zwischen Pescharim und Omendeutung sind dabei nicht auf die Terminologie beschränkt, sondern finden sich auch in der verwendeten Deutetechnik[5].

Bei der Omendeutung handelt es sich im wesentlichen um einen Übersetzungsvorgang:

> But it should be stressed that no exegetic or hermeneutic approach is involved when one speaks of interpreting dreams in the ancient Near East. The symbols of the dream-language are simply „translated" into the symbols of the language spoken by the dreaming person[6].

In der Praxis werden dabei ein oder mehrere Elemente des Traumes isoliert (Atomisierung des Omens) und in die Welt des Träumenden übertragen (Kontextualisierung). Als Beispiel mag hier ein Abschnitt aus der Demotischen Traumdeutung dienen (Pap. Carlsberg XIV a 2-4)[7].

> Wenn er süsses Bier trinkt, wird er sich freuen.
> Wenn er Bäckerei-Bier trinkt, wird [er] leben.
> Wenn er Lager-Bier trinkt, [bedeutet] es ihm Heil.

Die Omendeutung besteht jeweils aus einer Protasis, die das Omen referiert (z.B. „wenn er süsses Bier trinkt"), und einer Apodosis, die die dem Omen korrespondierende Deutung gibt (z.B. „wird er sich freuen"). Aus der Menge der Symbole und ihrer Polyvalenzen werden einzelne Elemente isoliert und in das Leben des Träumers kontextualisiert. Etwa die Süße des Bieres und die Freude des Träumers. Dieser Prozess von Atomisierung und Kontextualisierung findet sich auch in Josephs Deutungen der Träume des Pharaos (Gen 41,26-32). Die Zahl Sieben wird als sieben Jahre interpretiert, die fetten Kühe und die schönen Ähren repräsentieren Jahre der Fülle, die mageren Kühe und die leeren Ähren Jahre der Hungersnot.

5. Zum Zusammenhang von Pescharim und Omeninterpretation s. L.H. SILBERMANN, *Unriddling the Riddle: A Study in the Scripture and Language of the Habakkuk Pesher (1 Q p Hab)*, in *RQ* 3 (1961-1962) 323-364, pp. 330-335; A. FINKEL, *The Pesher of Dreams and Scriptures*, in *RQ* 4 (1963-1964) 357-370; I. RABINOWITZ, *Pesher/Pittaron: Its Biblical Meaning and Its Significance in the Qumran Literature*, in *RQ* 8 (1971-1972) 219-232, pp. 230-232; M. FISHBANE, *The Qumran Pesher and Traits of Ancient Hermeneutics*, in A. SHINAN (ed.), *Proceedings of the Sixth World Congress of Jewish Studies Held at the Hebrew University of Jerusalem 13-19 August 1973 under the Auspices of the Israel Academy of Sciences and Humanities*, Bd. 1: *Division A*, Jerusalem, World Union of Jewish Studies, 1977, pp. 97-114; H.-J. FABRY - U. DAHMEN, פֵּשֶׁר *pešær*: פָּתַר *pāṭar*, פִּתָּרוֹן / פִּתְרוֹן *pittāron/piṭrōn*, in *ThWAT* 6 (1987-1989) 810-815, p. 815.

6. OPPENHEIM, *Interpretation of Dreams* (s. Anm. 2), p. 220.

7. Zu Text und Übersetzung s. A. VOLTEN, *Demotische Traumdeutung (Pap. Carlsberg XIII und XIV verso)* (Analecta Aegyptica, 3), Kopenhagen, Einar Munksgaard, 1942, pp. 90f.

Man kann sagen, der eigentliche Akt der Offenbarung findet erst in dem Moment statt, in dem das Omen in das Leben des Omenempfängers kontextualisiert wird. In diesem Sinne findet Offenbarung erst im Akt des Hörens und Deutens statt, also in der Erstkontextualisierung eines Omens oder einer Prophetie. Wenn Joseph in Gen 40,8; 41,16 betont, die Deutung komme von Gott, spiegelt das ein Bewußtsein für diesen Sachverhalt wieder. Das Wort Erstkontextualisierung signalisiert schon, daß dieser Akt der interpretativen Offenbarung damit keinesfalls beendet oder erschöpft ist.

Die Pesharim aus der Bibliothek von Qumran gehen in ihrer Auslegung prophetischer Texte ganz ähnlich wie Joseph vor. Als Beispiel mag 1QpHab VII 3-8 dienen:

> 3 Und wenn er sagt: „*damit eilen kann, wer es liest*“ (Hab 2,2b) – 4 Seine Deutung ist auf den Lehrer der Gerechtigkeit, den Gott erkennen lies 5 alle Geheimnisse seiner Knechte, der Propheten. *Denn noch gibt es eine Vision 6 hinsichtlich der festgesetzten Zeit, sie eilt dem Ende zu und lügt nicht.* (Hab 2,3a) 7 Seine Deutung ist, daß die letzte Epoche noch lange ausbleiben wird, und zwar weit über alles hinaus, 8 was die Propheten geredet haben, denn die Geheimnisse Gottes sind wunderbar.

Ähnlich wie die Omenliste aus einer Protasis, die ein Omen beschreibt, einzelne Elemente herausgreift, und in einer Apodosis deutet, atomisiert der Pescher einzelen Elemente aus dem zitierten Lemma und rekontextualisiert sie in seiner Deutung in die eigene Gegenwart hinein.[8] Man kann Lemma und Deutung geradezu mit der Protasis und Apodosis einer Omenliste gleichsetzen. Aus dem Zitat von Hab 2,2f. in 1QpHab VI 12-16 isoliert der Pescher einzelne Textstücke (Atomisierung) und interpretiert sie auf die essenische Bewegung hin: Das Ausbleiben des herbeigesehnten Eschatons läßt in der essenischen Bewegung Zweifel an ihrer eschatologischen Propheteninterpretation aufkommen. Die Feststellung von Hab 2,3, daß die Vision nicht lüge, ist im Buch Habakuk teil der Zusicherung eines unmittelbar bevorstehenden Ereignisses („und sie wird nicht verweilen“ לֹא יְאַחֵר Hab 2,3b). In die entäuschte essenische Naherwartung hinein rekontextualisiert, kann das „und sie lügt nicht“ jedoch nur als Versicherung verstanden werden, daß das Eschaton kommen wird, wenn auch mit Verzögerung. Das Wissen um diese im prophetischen Text verborgenen Geheimnisse ist dem Lehrer der Gerechtigkeit offenbart worden – so die Auslegung von Hab 2,2b. Das im Buch Habakuk selbst wohl auf die unmittelbare Verbreitung von

8. Zu Vorgehen und Methode der Pescharim s. bes. E. OSSWALD, *Zur Hermeneutik des Habakuk-Kommentars*, in *ZAW* 68 (1956) 243-256; FISHBANE, *Qumran Pesher* (s. Anm. 5), pp. 98-100.

Habakuks Botschaft bezogenene קוֹרֵא[9] wird vom Pescher als „Leser" gedeutet, aus dem Rest des Verses isoliert und auf die dem Lehrer offenbarte Textdeutung bezogen. Der Pescher Habakuk versteht seine divinatorische Exegese damit als einen Akt der Offenbarung.

Ein weiteres Beispiel für dieses hermeneutische Bewußtsein um den Offenbarungscharakter der Prophetenauslegung ist 1QpHab II 7-10[10]:

> ... wenn sie alles hören, was k[ommen wird über] die letzte Generation aus dem Mund (8) des Priesters, in [dessen Herz] Gott [Einsi]cht gegeben hat, zu deuten alle (9)Worte seiner Knechte, der Propheten, durch die Gott verkündigt hat (10) alles, was über sein Volk und [sein Land] kommen wird.

Der beobachteten divinatorischen Methodik korrespondieren somit hermeneutische Aussagen, die die Textauslegung der Pescharim als einen revelatorischen Akt beschreiben. Für die Pescharim gibt es eine Sammlung von Texten mit prophetischer Qualität. In ihnen ist verborgen, was kommen wird. Dieses esoterische Wissen mit Hilfe divinatorischer Exegese zu erschliessen ist selbst ein Akt der Offenbarung.

Ähnlich wie in 1QpHab VII lassen sich auch in Dan 9, und zwar in der Engeldeutung des Textes Jer 25,11f., Atomisierung und Rekontextualisierung beobachten. Die 167 v. Chr. im Jerusalemer Tempel errichtete Zeusstatue zeigt dem Autor des Danielbuches, daß die nach Jer 25,11f. 70 Jahre nach der Zerstörung Jerusalems zu erwartende Heilszeit noch nicht eingetroffen ist (Rekontextualisierung). Nicht Babylon ist zur Wüste geworden, der Greuel der Verwüstung findet sich vielmehr im Herzen Jerusalems. Nicht 70 Jahre sind gemeint gewesen, sondern 70 Jahrwochen. Nicht nach der persischen Eroberung des neubabylonischen Reichs und der Rückkehr aus dem Exil, sondern erst 490 Jahre nach der Eroberung Jerusalems durch die Babylonier und etwa 70 Jahre nach der Abfassung des Danielbuches (167-165 v. Chr.) wird die angekündigte Heilszeit anbrechen. Die revelatorische Hermeneutik der Pescharim entspricht somit dem in Daniel 9 Beobachteten[10]. Und

9. F.I. ANDERSEN, *Habakkuk: A New Translation with Introduction and Commentary* (Anchor Bible, 25), New York, Doubleday, 2001, pp. 204-205.

10. So zuerst K. ELLIGER, *Studien zum Habakuk-Kommentar vom Toten Meer* (Beiträge zur historischen Theologie, 15), Tübingen, J.C.B. Mohr (Paul Siebeck), 1953, pp. 156f.; zur Sache vgl. u.a. A. SZÖRÉNYI, *Das Buch Daniel, ein kanonisierter Pescher*, in *Volume du congrès: Genève 1965* (VTS, 15), Leiden, Brill, 1966, pp. 278-294, bes. 293; FISHBANE, *Qumran Pesher* (s. Anm. 5), pp. 110f.114; K. KOCH, *Die Bedeutung der Apokalyptik für die Interpretation der Schrift*, in DERS., *Die Reiche der Welt und der kommende Menschensohn: Studien zum Danielbuch*, Neukirchen-Vluyn, Neukirchener Verlag, 1995, pp. 16-45, bes. 30f.; J.J. COLLINS, *Jewish Apocalyptic against its Hellenistic Near Eastern Environment*, in *BASOR* 220 (1975) 27-36, pp. 31-33; DERS., *Daniel: A Commentary on the Book of Daniel* (Hermeneia), Minneapolis, MN, Fortress Press, 1993, p. 359; D. DIMANT, *The Seventy Weeks Chronology (Dan 9,24-27) in the Light of New*

auch Daniel 9 suggeriert ein Bewußtsein, daß interpretatorische Einsicht nur in der Offenbarung zu erlangen ist: („erlange Einsicht in der Vision"; Dan 9,23). Der Schlüssel zum Text liegt für den Visionär in seiner Vision. Interpretation ist immer auch Offenbarung[11].

Handelt es sich bei diesem Umgang mit prophetischen Texten um eine interpretorische Eigenheit des Antiken Judentums? Ist die Applikation von Omenhermeneutik auf prophetische Texte also eine apokalyptisch-eschatologische Sonderhermeneutik der makkabäischen und postmakkabäischen Zeit, oder partizipieren die Pescharim und das Danielbuch an einem in ihrer Zeit weiter verbreiteten Textzugang? Und falls es sich in der Tat um eine apokalyptisch-essenische Sonderhermeneutik handeln sollte, spricht dies für einen apokalyptischen Ursprung und Charakter der essenischen Bewegung? Zur Beantwortung dieser Fragen erscheint mir ein Blick auf die Nachbarkulturen des antiken Judentums hilfreich, und hier insbesondere auf die spätägyptische und die antikgriechische Literatur.

2. Spätägyptische Texte[12]

Das Sammeln von Orakeln und ihre Tradierung ist nicht auf Israel oder den syro-palästinischen Raum beschränkt. Anders als etwa im vorexilischen Israel entstand in Ägypten jedoch schon in ramessidischer Zeit (1300-1100 v. Chr.) eine Art Lehrkanon, der auf ältere weisheitliche Literatur beschränkt war und aus Werken von Djedefhor, Imhotep, Neferti, Cheti, Ptah-emdjehuti, Cha-cheper-Re-seneb, Ptahhotep, und Kaires bestand[13]. Neben diesem Lehrkanon ist eine Vielzahl anderer Texte erhalten, darunter seit der Spätzeit auch Omenberichte. Als Beispiel verweise ich auf den saitischen Orakel-Papyrus aus Theben

Qumranic Texts, in A.S. van der Woude (ed.), *The Book of Daniel in the Light of New Findings* (BETL, 106), Leuven, Peeters, 1993, pp. 57-76, bes. 58f.

11. Zu Dan 9 s. u.a. M. Fishbane, *Biblical Interpretation in Ancient Israel*, Oxford, Clarendon, 1985, pp. 482-489; K. Koch, *Bedeutung* (s. Anm. 10), pp. 22-31; J. Collins, *Daniel* (s. Anm. 10), pp. 344-360; D. Dimant, *Seventy Weeks* (s. Anm. 10), passim.

12. Der exzellente von A. Blasius und B.U. Schipper herausgegebene Sammelband *Apokalyptik und Ägypten: Eine kritische Analyse der relevanten Texte aus dem griechisch-römischen Ägypten* (Orientalia Lovaniensia Analecta, 107), Leuven-Paris-Sterling, Peeters, 2001, hat mich leider so spät erreicht, daß ich ihn für die folgenden Erörterungen nicht mehr berücksichtigen konnte.

13. S. Pap. Chester Beatty IV verso 2,5-3,10; 6,11-14; zur Sache S.N. Shupak, *„Canon" and „Canonization" in Ancient Egypt*, in *Bibliotheca Orientalis* 58 (2001) 535-547. Zu Pap. Chester Beatty IV, s. A.H. Gardiner, *Hieratic Papyri in the British Museum. Third Series: Chester Beatty Gift*, London, The British Museum, 1935, pp. 38f. Taf. 18f.; M. Lichtheim, *Ancient Egyptian Literature*, Bd. 2: *The New Kingdom*, Berkeley-Los Angeles-London, University of California Press, 1976, pp. 175-178; H. Brunner, *Altägyptische Weisheit*, Darmstadt, Wissenschaftliche Buchgesellschaft, 1988, pp. 218-230.

aus dem 7. Jh. v. Chr.[14]. Er beschreibt nicht nur eines der berühmten ägyptischen Barken-Orakel mit gestellter Frage und gegebener Antwort, sondern bildet es auch ab.

Wenigstens ein Teil dieser Omenberichte wurde im Laufe ihrer Tradierung interpretationsbedürftig. Daher ist für einen dieser Texte eine Kommentierung erhalten geblieben, die sogenannte Demotische Chronik[15]. Es handelt sich um die Kommentierung eines älteren astrologischen Orakelberichts aus dem 3. Jh. v. Chr., die in Deutetechnik und Skopos den Pescharim aus Qumran sehr ähnlich ist[16]. Nach dem Ende der persischen Herrschaft über Ägypten sehnt die Demotische Chronik in ihren Auslegungen das Ende der Ptolemäerherrschaft durch einen ägyptischen Pharao aus Herakleopolis herbei. Ähnlich wie etwa in Dan 9 und den Pescharim spielt die Frage desWann in der Demotischen Chronik somit eine große Rolle. Und ähnlich wie in diesen Texten reflektiert auch die demotische Chronik eine durch die griechische Fremdherrschaft ausgelöste bzw. vertiefte Sinnkrise der ägyptischen Kultur. Ähnlich wie die Pescharim und das Danielbuch sucht auch der Verfasser der Demotischen Chronik die Antwort auf diese Sinnkrise nicht in einer neuen Offenbarung, sondern in der Interpretation des Tradierten.

In den Auslegungen der demotischen Chronik finden sich Listen von Pharaonen aus der 28.-30. Dynastie (404-343 v. Chr.). Der jeweilige Erfolg oder Mißerfolg eines Pharaos wird mit den ethischen Standards seiner Herrschaft korreliert: „It was disloyalty to the Law that accounted for the failures of the past; and the restoration of the independent national state will be under rulers beloved of God“[17].

14. R.A. PARKER, *A Saite Oracle Papyrus from Thebes* (Brown Egyptological Studies, 4), Providence, RI, Brown University Press, 1962.

15. Zur Demotischen Chronik s. W. SPIEGELBERG, *Die sogenannte Demotische Chronik: Pap. 215 der Bibliothèque Nationale zu Paris nebst den auf der Rückseite des Papyrus stehenden Texten*, Leipzig, J.C. Hinrichs'sche Buchhandlung, 1914; P. KAPLONY, *Demotische Chronik*, in W. HELCK - E. OTTO (eds.), *Lexikon der Ägyptologie*, Bd. 1, Wiesbaden, Otto Harrassowitz, 1975, pp. 1056-1060; A.B. LLOYD, *Nationalist Propaganda in Ptolemaic Egypt*, in *Historia* 31 (1982) 33-55, pp. 41-45; J.H. JOHNSON, *Demotic Chronicle*, in D.N. FREEDMAN, *The Anchor Bible Dictionary*, Bd. 2, New York, Doubleday, 1992, pp. 142-144.

16. Auf diese Ähnlichkeit hat zuerst hingewiesen F. DAUMAS, *Littérature prophétique et exégétique égyptienne et commentaires esséniens*, in A. BARUCQ (ed.), *À la rencontre de Dieu: Mémorial Albert Gelin* (Bibliothèque de la Faculté Catholique de Théologie de Lyon, 8), Le Puy, Xavier Mappus, 1961, pp. 203-221; vgl. auch FISHBANE, *Qumran Pesher* (s. Anm. 5), pp. 101.103; COLLINS, *Environment* (s. Anm. 10), p. 32; J.Z. SMITH, *Map is not Territory: Studies in the History of Religions* (Studies in Judaism in Late Antiquity, 23), Leiden, Brill, 1978, pp. 67-87.

17. J. GWYN GRIFFTHS, *Apocalyptic in the Hellenistic Era*, in D. HELLHOLM (ed.), *Apocalypticism in the Mediterranean World and the Ancient Near East: Proceedings of the International Colloquium on Apocalypticism, Uppsala, August 12-17, 1979*, Tübingen, J.C.B Mohr (Paul Siebeck), ^{2}1989, pp. 273-293, hier 282; zur Sache vgl. auch LLOYD, *Propaganda* (s. Anm. 15), p. 43.

Das interpretative Vorgehen der Demotische Chronik mag folgendes Beispiel erhellen:

> *Voll ist der erste Monatstag, der 2. Monatstag, der 3. Monatstag, der 4. Monatstag, der 5. Monatstag, der 6. Monatstag*
> *Voll ist der erste Monatstag* – das heißt Pharao Amyrtaios
> *Voll ist der zweite Monatstag* – das heißt Pharao Nepherites (I)
> *Voll ist der dritte Monatstag* – das heißt Pharao Hakoris
> *Voll ist der vierte Monatstag* – das heißt Pharao Nepherites (II)
> *Voll ist der fünfte (Monatstag)* – das heißt Pharao Nektanebos
> *Voll ist der sechste (Monatstag)* – das heißt der König Pharao Tachos
> Das, was sie gesagt haben, ist von Thoth aufgeschrieben worden, als er ihre Geschichte in Hnês (Herakleopolis) erforschte.
> *Man gibt den 7. Monatstag (dem) Ptah*
> Er meint: Der Herrscher, der nach ihnen kommt, wird die Angelegenheiten von Memphis untersuchen. Es geschieht, daß das, was er tut, untersucht wird, (nämlich) das, was er in Memphis tat (Demotische Chronik II 2-6)[18].

Das interpretierte Element ist die jeweilige Zahl der Monatstage (Atomisierung). Sie entsprechen im Lebenszusammhang des Auslegers einer Abfolge von Pharaonen, beginnend mit der 28. Dynastie und Pharao Amyrtaios (404-399 v. Chr.) und endend mit der 30. Dynastie und Pharao Teos (Irmaatenra) (362-360 v. Chr.). Der 7. Monatstag repräsentiert dann die erhoffte Reinstitutionalisierung der Eigenstaatlichkeit mit einem einheimischen Pharao.

Daß die demotische Chronik kein Einzelfall ist, zeigt das Töpferorakel aus der Zeit um 130 v. Chr[19]. Bei ihm handelt es sich zwar nicht um eine versweise Kommentierung eines älteren Orakels, jedoch verweist das Töpferorakel auf das „Übel, welches das Lamm Bakharis angekündigt hat“[20]. Gemeint ist das sogenannte Orakel des Lamms[21] und sein *vaticinium ex eventu* auf die Eroberung und kurzfristige Besetzung Ägyptens durch die Assyrer 671-669 und 667-653 v. Chr. An diese Zeit der Not schließt sich für das Orakel des Lamms eine glanzvolle Vergeltung und Wiederherstellung des ägyptischen Imperiums an. Das Töpferorakel bezieht die Zeit des Übels aus dem Orakel des Lamms entweder auf die Perser oder die Ptolemäer[22]. Leider sind beide Texte nur frag-

18. Übersetzung nach SPIEGELBERG (s. Anm. 15), p. 14.

19. Zur Datierung des Töpferorakels s. L. KOENEN, *Die Prophezeiungen des Töpfers*, in *Zeitschrift für Papyrologie und Epigraphik* 2 (1968) 178-209, pp. 186ff., und GWYN GRIFFITHS, *Apocalyptic* (s. Anm. 17), pp. 289f.

20. Papyrus Oxyrhynchus 2332 Zeile 34; zum Text s. E. LOBEL - C.H. ROBERTS, *The Oxyrhynchus Papyri, Part XXII*, London, Egypt Exploration Society, 1954, p. 95.

21. Zum Text s. K.-Th. ZAUZICH, *Das Lamm des Bokchoris*, in *Festschrift zum 100-jährigen Bestehen der Papyrussammlung der österreichischen Nationalbibliothek Papyrus Erzherzog Rainer (P. Rainer Cent.)*, Wien, Österreichische Nationalbibliothek, 1983, pp. 165-174 (Taf. 2).

22. Vgl. GWYN GRIFFITHS, *Apocalyptic* (s. Anm. 17), p. 287.

mentarisch erhalten. Daher kann nicht mehr gesagt werden, auf welche Weise das Orakel des Lamms vom Töpferorakel aufgenommen und interpretiert wurde.

Trotz der aufgezeigten Analogien zwischen der demotischen Chronik, dem Danielbuch und den Pescharim dürften die Pescharim und das Danielbuch bzw. die essensiche Bewegung und die antik-jüdische Apokalyptik kaum in direkter Abhängigkeit von ägyptischen Texten stehen. Evozieren dann also gleiche oder zumindest ähnliche Problemstellungen vergleichbare Problemlösungen? Anders gesagt: Ist die divinatorische Auslegung prophetischer Texte auf eine vergleichbare religiös-kulturelle Krise zurückzuführen, nämlich den Greuel der Verwüstung im Falle des Danielbuches, das entäuschte eschatologische Selbstverständnis im Falle der essenischen Bewegung und die persische bzw. ptolemäische Fremdherrschaft im Falle der Demotischen Chronik? An dieser Stelle kann die griechische Literatur aus der klassischen Antike eine Antwort geben, denn auch im antiken Griechenland wurde die Auslegung von Orakelsammlungen praktiziert.

3. Die Griechische Literatur aus der Antike

Die Verschriftlichung von Orakeln hat im antiken Griechenland eine lange Tradition und läßt sich bis in das 8. Jh. v. Chr. zurückverfolgen, also in jene Zeit, als die griechische Kultur begann, das phönizische Alphabet adaptierte[23]. Besonders interessant ist ein Ostrakon aus dem Heiligtum des Zeus Epikoinios in Salamis auf Zypern[24]. Auf die Anfrage, ob man einen Bach zuschütten dürfe, gibt das Orakel folgende Antwort:

> Ich liebe diesen Eifer und bin gnädig, die Feinde aber schlage ich mit Blitz.
> Ich erhalte durch die Gräben des kleinen Flusses den Rindern das süße Wasser, im Frühling die Weidekräuter zu ihrem Gedeihn.
> Ich lasse mich erbitten von dem Zweifelnden, der bittend sucht.

Die notierte Deutung lautet:

23. S. W. Burkert, *Griechische Religion der archaischen und klassischen Epoche* (Die Religionen der Menschheit, 15), Stuttgart u.a.,W. Kohlhammer, 1977, p. 190.

24. Dazu s. R. Meister, *Ein Ostrakon aus dem Heiligtum des Zeus Epikoinios im kyprischen Salamis* (Abhandlungen der philologisch historischen Klasse der königlich sächsischen Gesellschaft der Wissenschaften, 27), Leipzig, B.G. Teubner, 1909, pp. 303-332; P. Amandry, *La mantique apollinienne à Delphes: Essai sur le fonctionnement de l'Oracle* (Bibliothèque des écoles française d'Athènes et de Rome, 170), Paris, E. de Boccard, 1950, pp. 166-168; V. Rosenberger, *Griechische Orakel: Eine Kulturgeschichte*, Darmstadt, Wissenschaftliche Buchgesellschaft 2001, 173. Zur Datierung finden sich außer einem „älter als das 5. Jahrh. v. Chr." (Meister, p. 314) keine Angaben.

> Entscheidung des Gottes: Ich untersage unerbittlich die Zuschüttung des kleinen Flusses[25].

Das Orakel ist mehr oder weniger eindeutig. Die Deutung greift das entscheidene Stichwort „erhalten“ auf (kyprisch σώζω; Atomisierung), und bezieht es auf die Orakelfrage (Kontextualisierung).

Zwar hat die griechische Kultur mit den Hypomnemata ab der hellenistischen Zeit eine eigene Kommentarliteratur hervorgebracht[26], jedoch sind Kommentierungen von Omenberichten oder Orakelsammlungen ebensowenig erhalten geblieben wie die Orakelsammlungen selbst. Es kann aber kein Zweifel daran bestehen, daß es Sammlungen der Aussprüche einzelner Seher im antiken Griechenland gegeben hat. So berichtet etwa Herodot im 5. Jh. v. Chr.:

> Sie hatten Onomakritos mitgebracht, einen athenischen Weissager, der auch die Weissagungen des Musaios zusammengestellt hatte. Ihren Zwist mit ihm aber hatten sie vorher beigelegt. Onomakritos war nämlich von Hipparchos, Peisistratos’ Sohn, aus Athen ausgewiesen worden, nachdem ihn Lasos von Hermione ertappt hatte, wie er dabei war, in Musaios’ Sammlung eine Weissagung einzuschieben, daß nämlich die Inseln bei Lemnos im Meer versinken würden (Herodot VII,6)[27].

Nach diesem Bericht zu urteilen dürfte die Sammlung und Kodifizierung älterer Orakelsprüche in Griechenland wohl den Sammlungsprozessen der prophetischen Literatur in Israel geähnelt haben[28]. Im Fall des Onomakritos ist von besonderem Interesse, daß dieser Orakelredaktor von Herodot als ein Orakelkundiger bzw. Orakeldeuter (χρησμολόγος) beschrieben wird. Bei Onomakritos handelt es sich somit um einen divinatorischen Spezialisten. Daß ein solcher Mantiker mit der Edition der Orakel des Musaios beauftragt wird, weist auf den divinatorischen Charakter dieser Arbeit hin (zur Sache s.u. S. 28).

Der Bericht des Herodot über Onomakritos’ Redaktion der Musaiossammlung zeigt darüber hinaus, daß das Phänomen der Schriftprophetie wohl kein Proprium Israels gewesen ist. Es bleibt jedoch einzuschränken, daß aus Israel kein Fall bekannt ist, in dem ein Redaktor wegen redaktioneller Erweiterung bestraft worden wäre. Der Hinweis auf die Frevelhaftigkeit der von Onomakritos vorgenommenen Erweiterung und

25. Zur Übersetzung s. MEISTER, *Ostrakon* (s. Anm. 24), p. 110.

26. S. E.G. TURNER, *Greek Papyri: An Introduction*, Oxford, Clarendon, ^{2}1980, pp. 112-124.

27. Übersetzung nach W. MARG, *Herodot: Geschichten und Geschichte: Buch 5-9* (Die Bibliothek der Alten Welt), Zürich-München, 1983, p. 137.

28. Zu weiteren Hinweisen auf solche Sammlungen der Orakel verschiedener Seher s. Herodot V,90; VIII,20.77.96; IX,43; Plat. rep. 364e; Suda, s.v. Ἄβαρις.

seine harte Strafe machen des weiteren den hohen Stellenwert der fraglichen Orakeltexte deutlich.

Wie verbreitet solche Orakelsammlungen waren und welche besondere Autorität sie genossen haben, zeigt eindrucksvoll die Polemik des Aristophanes. Als Beispiel zitiere ich zwei Passagen aus den Rittern[29].

> DEMOS: Laß sehen: von wem sind die Orakel denn?
> PAPHLAGONIER: Die meinen sind von Bakis.
> DEMOS: Und die deinen?
> WURSTHÄNDLER: Von Glanis, Herr, des Bakis älterem Bruder.
> DEMOS: Sag mir, von wem sie handeln?
> PAPHLAGONIER: Von Athen,
> Von Pylos, auch von mir, von dir, von allem!
> DEMOS: Nun, und von wem die deinen?
> WURSTHÄNDLER: Von Athen,
> Von Linsen, Lakedaimon, frischen Austern,
> Von Marktbeamten, die am Mehl betrügen,
> Von dir, von mir! ...
> DEMOS: Gut denn! Lest mir die Orakel vor,
> Besonders das, das mir verheißt – (wie schön!): Ich werd' „ein Adler in den Wolken schweben" (Aristoph. Equ., 1002f.)[30].

Der Wursthändler und der im Text Kleon genannte Paphlagonier zitieren im folgenden dem Demos jeweils mehrere Orakel aus der Sammlung des Glanis und legen sie zu ihren Zwecken aus. Ein gutes Beispiel sind folgende Verse:

> PAPHLAGONIER: Hör erst noch weiter, Herr, und richte dann:
> „Einst wird gebären ein Weib im heil'gen Athen einen Löwen,
> Der für das Volk in den Kampf wird gehn mit unzähligen Mücken,
> Gleich als gält' es den eigenen Jungen: Diesen bewahre Treu und beschirm ihn mit Mauern von Holz und Türmen von Eisen!"
> DEMOS *zum Wursthändler*: Verstehst du dieses?
> WURSTHÄNDLER: Beim Apoll, kein Wort!
> PAPHLAGONIER: Der Gott gebeut, du sollst mich dir erhalten,
> Ich bin dein Kämpfer an des Löwen Stelle!
> DEMOS: Was? Löwenstellverweser bist du gar?
> WURSTHÄNDLER: Eins im Orakel hat er nicht erklärt:
> Die Eisenmauer und das Holz, worin
> Dir Loxias befiehlt ihn zu verwahren.
> DEMOS: Was meint der Gott damit?
> WURSTHÄNDLER: Du sollst in den
> Fünfmund'gen Stock, den hölzernen, ihn sperren!
> DEMOS: Der Spruch kann in Erfüllung gehn, und bald! (Aristoph. Equ., 1036-1050)[31].

29. Ähnliche Polemiken finden sich auch Aristoph. Equ., 115ff.; Av., 959f.
30. Übersetzung nach L. SEEGER, *Aristophanes: Sämtliche Komödien*, Zürich-Stuttgart, ²1968, p. 101.
31. *Ibid.*, pp. 102f.

Die erste Passage aus den Rittern (Equ., 1002f.; vgl. auch Equ., 115ff., und Av., 959f.) zeigt im Umkehrschluß, daß die von Aristophanes angegriffenen Orakelbücher eine große Popularität genossen haben und auf eine Vielfalt von Fragen des Alltags, aber auch auf Fragen größerer Tragweite angewandt wurden. Trotz dieser Prominenz haben die erwähnten Orakelsammlungen sicher nicht den Stellenwert kanonischer Sammlungen im Sinne der Hebräischen oder Griechischen Bibel gehabt. Ähnlich wie Ägypten hat das antike Griechenland keinen Kanon in diesem Sinne entwickelt. Ähnlich wie in Ägypten, jedoch erst in hellenistischer Zeit entsteht auch in Griechenland eine kanonische Liste tradierungswürdiger Autoren[32]. Das schließt aber nicht aus, daß etwa Homer oder auch die genannten Orakelsammlungen im antiken Griechenland des 6.-4. Jh. v. Chr. einen ähnlichen Stellenwert gehabt haben wie Mose oder prophetische Texte im Israel dieser Zeit.

In der Art und Weise ihrer Orakeldeutung erinnert die Parodie von Equ. 1036-1050 an die demotische Chronik oder die Pescharim. Wiederum wird ein einzelnes Element aus dem tradierten Orakel isoliert (Atomisierung) – in diesem Fall der Löwe – und in das Leben der Leser dieser Sammlung hinein übersetzt (Rekontextualisierung). Der Löwe ist Kleon. Demos soll ihn sich erhalten, sprich bezahlen. Kleons Rivale, der Wursthändler, wendet mit gleicher Deutetechnik ein, daß Eisen und Holz meinten, Demos solle Kleon ins Holz legen. Auch die antik-griechische Auslegung von Orakelsammlungen geht nach dem schon aus dem antiken Judentum und Ägypten bekannten Muster vor. Eine andere Komödie des Aristophanes macht deutlich, daß die Interpretation solcher Orakelbücher im Normalfall das Privileg eines χρησμολόγος („Orakelkundiger, Orakeldeuter") genannten Mantikers gewesen ist (Av. 959f.). Die Interpretation von Orakelsammlungen dürfte damit im antiken Griechenland selbst als ein divinatorischer Akt verstanden worden sein (zur Sache s.o. S. 26).

Daß die von Aristophanes parodierte Auslegung von Orakelsammlungen in ihrem Vorgehen nicht der literarischen Kreativität des Komödiendichters zu verdanken ist, sondern ein Vorbild im Athenischen Alltag hatte, zeigen zwei Belege bei Herodot: Als Athen im Vorfeld der Schlacht von Salamis (480 v. Chr.) vom Persischen Reich bedroht wird,

32. Zur Sache s. U. Hölscher, *Über die Kanonizität Homers* und E.A. Schmidt, *Historische Typologie der Orientierungsfunktionen von Kanon in der griechischen und römischen Literatur*, in A. Assmann - J. Assman (eds.), *Kanon und Zensur: Archäologie der literarischen Kommunikation II*, München, Wilhelm Fink Verlag, 1987, pp. 237-245 und pp. 246-258; Franco Montanari, s.v. *Kanon, III. Griechische Literatur*, in H. Cancik - H. Schneider (eds.), *Der Neue Pauly*, Bd. 3, Stuttgart-Weimar, Metzler, 1999, p. 250.

schicken die Athener um Rat an das Orakel von Delphi. Nachdem der erste Bescheid des Orakels die völlige Zerstörung Athens anzukündigen scheint, erlangt die Athenische Delegation von der delphischen Orakelpriesterin (gr. πρόμαντις) einen zweiten, milder erscheinenden Spruch.

> Nicht kann Zeus, den Olympier, erweichen Pallas Athene,
> Wie sie auch bittet und fleht und rät mit klugem Verstande.
> Dir aber sag' ich dies andere Wort, wie Eisen geschmiedet:
> Wenn das andre alles was Kekrops Grenzen umschließen,
> Und die Senken und Hänge des heil'gen Kithairon verloren,
> Schenkt der waltende Zeus der Tochter die hölzerne Mauer;
> Sie allein wird bestehn, zum Nutzen für dich und die Kinder.
> Du aber warte die Reiter nicht ab noch in Ruhe das Fußvolk,
> Das von der Veste her sich heranwälzt, sondern entweiche,
> Wende den Rücken ihm zu; einst wirst du die Stirne ihm bieten.
> Salamis, göttliches Land! Doch Söhne der Weiber vertilgst du,
> Dann wenn Demeters Frucht verstreut wird oder gesammelt (Herodot VII,141)[33].

In Athen ist die Deutung des Orakels umstritten. Zwei Interpretationen hebt Herodot besonders hervor:

> Von den Älteren sagten nicht wenige, der Gott scheine ihnen anzukünden, die Akropolis werde überleben; denn die Burg der Athener war in alter Zeit von Palisaden umgeben gewesen. Diese Leute vermuteten also, das sei die hölzerne Mauer; die anderen hingegen sagten, der Gott weise auf die Schiffe hin, und waren dafür, diese instand zu setzen und das übrige im Stich zu lassen (Herodot VII,142)[34].

Die Debatte konzentriert sich offensichtlich auf ein Element des wesentlich umfangreicheren Orakelspruchs, nämlich die hölzerne Mauer (Atomisierung). Umstritten ist, worauf sie sich bezieht (Kontextualisierung), auf die alte hölzerne Mauer der Akropolis oder die athenische Flotte. Welche Deutung sich durchgesetzt hat, ist Geschichte. Die Athener vertrauten auf ihre Schiffe und fügten den Persern bei Salamis eine entscheidende Niederlage zu.

Im Zusammenhang mit der Schlacht von Salamis verweist Herodot an anderer Stelle sogar explizit auf Orakelsammlungen und interpretiert eine von ihnen:

> Von den Trümmern aber erfaßte viele der Westwind und trieb sie an die Küste Attikas, die Kolias heißt. Und so ging alle Weissagung in Erfüllung, nicht nur das, was bei Bakis und Musaios über die Seeschlacht ausgesprochen ist, sondern des weiteren auch noch, was über die dort angetriebenen Schiffsteile schon viele Jahre vor diesen Ereignissen in einem Spruch von

33. Übersetzung nach W. MARG, *Herodot* (s. Anm. 27), p. 197.
34. *Ibid.*, p. 198.

Lysistratos, einem Athener und Wahrsager, gesagt worden und allen Hellenen entgangen ist:
„Kolias' Frauen jedoch, mit Rudern werden sie rösten."
Das sollte nach dem Abzug des Königs in Erfüllung gehen (Herodot VIII,96)[35].

Die kurze Bemerkung Herodots, daß seine Deutung des Spruchs des Lysistratos „allen Hellenen entgangen" sei, zeigt, daß das fragliche Orakel ursprünglich einen ganz anderen Bezug gehabt hat. Erst die in Folge der Schlacht von Salamis an die Kolias gespülten Schiffstrümmer veranlassen Herodot zu einer Rekontextualisierung des Orakels. Bei den Rudern (Atomisierung) handelt es sich um die besagten Schiffstrümmer.

Ähnlich wie im Danielbuch, in den Pescharim oder in der demotischen Chronik wird auch der Spruch des Lysistratos in einen sekundären historischen Kontext rekontextualisiert. Wiederum wird ein einzelnes Element des fraglichen Orakels einer Übersetzung unterzogen. Im Falle Herodots kann jedoch kaum von einer Krise im kulturellen und religiösen Selbstverständnis Athens gesprochen werden. Anders als etwa Ägypten unter den Ptolemäern strebt Athen dem Höhepunkt seiner politischen Macht entgegen. Die divinatorische Hermeneutik des Orakelkommentars reagiert somit in den verschiedenen Texten und Kulturen keinesfalls nur auf religiöse oder kulturelle (Identitäts)krisen. Anders gesagt: Revelatorische Textauslegung versucht zwar auch, aber nicht nur Antworten auf Fragen des Wie-Lange-Noch zu geben. Ferner suggerieren die griechischen Texte (Aristoph. Av. 959f.; Herodot VII,6) ein Bewußtsein für den divinatorischen Charakter solcher Orakelkommentierungen.

Es bleibt zu fragen, ob die revelatorische Auslegung prophetischer Texte in Israel ein Proprium apokalyptischer und essenischer Kreise ist.

4. Die Schriftprophetie

Es steht außer Frage, daß in Israel seit den Tagen eines Amos oder Jesaja prophetische Worte gesammelt und tradiert wurden. Der edomitische oder moabitische *marzeaḥ* Papyrus aus dem mittleren oder späten 7. Jh. v. Chr.[36] zeigt ferner, daß solche Sammlungsprozesse im syropalästinischen Raum nicht auf Israel beschränkt gewesen sind.

35. *Ibid.*, pp. 287f.

36. Zu Herkunft und Datierung s. F.M. Cross, *A Papyrus Recording a Divine Legal Decision and the Root rḥq in Biblical and Near Eastern Legal Usage*, in M.V. Fox u.a. (eds.), *Texts, Temples, and Traditions: A Tribute to Menahem Haran*, Winona Lake IN, Eisenbrauns, 1996, pp. 311-320, bes. 312-318. Zum Papyrus s. auch P. Bordreuil - D. Pardee, *Le Papyrus du marzeaḥ*, in *Semitica* 38 (1990) 49-69.

> *kh · ʾmrw · lgrʾ · lk · hmrzḥ ·whrḥyn · wh*
> *byt · wšyʿʾ · rḥq · mhm · wmlk · hšlš*
> Thus says the godhead to Geraʾ: „The *marzēḥ (symposium)*, and the millstones, and the house are thine. As for Yišʿaʾ, he is without claim on them (lit., is far from them); and Malka is the depositary“[37].

Nach allem was wir im ägyptisch-griechischen Raum beobachtet haben, kann es kaum noch verwundern, daß auch die nachexilische Schriftprophetie sich der schon vertrauten divinatorischen Hermeneutik bedient. Als Beispiel[38] möchte ich auf Jer 23,33-40 verweisen[39]:

> (33) Und wenn dieses Volk oder der Prophet oder ein Priester fragt: „Was ist die Last (מַשָּׂא) JHWHs?“, dann sollst du zu ihnen sagen: „Ihr seid die Last (מַשָּׂא) JHWHs, und ich werde euch fallen lassen – Spruch JHWHs.“ (34) Und den Propheten und den Priester und das Volk, (jeden,) der sagt „Spruch (מַשָּׂא) JHWHs“ – jenen Mann und sein Haus suche ich heim. (35) So soll ein jeder zu seinem Nächsten und seinem Bruder sagen: „Was hat JHWH geantwortet, was hat JHWH geredet?“ (36) Aber „Spruch (מַשָּׂא) JHWHs“ sollt ihr nicht mehr erwähnen – denn „Spruch“ (מַשָּׂא) ist für den Mann seines Wortes – (37) sondern: „was hat JHWH geredet?“ (38) Darum – so hat JHWH gesprochen –: Weil ihr dieses Wort, nämlich Spruch (מַשָּׂא) JHWHs, gesagt habt, obwohl ich zu euch gesandt hatte: „sagt nicht Spruch (מַשָּׂא) JHWHs“, (39) darum: Siehe, ich hebe auf und werde euch fallen lassen und die Stadt, die ich euch und euren Vätern gegeben habe, von meinem Angesicht. (40) Und ich werde ewige Schmach und ewigen Schimpf auf euch geben, die nicht vergessen werden werden.

Der Text beginnt in Jer 23,33 mit einem kurzen Prophetenwort. Es basiert auf einer Homophonie zwischen zwei Derivaten der Wurzel נשׂא, nämlich מַשָּׂא I „Last“ und מַשָּׂא II „Ausspruch“. Gegen Jeremia wird aufs sarkastischste polemisiert, was denn wohl die nächste Last JHWHs (*genitivus subjectivus*) sei, die Jeremia zu prophezeien hätte. Damit wird zum einen der negative Inhalt von Jeremias Prophetie verspottet und zum anderen geleugnet, daß es sich bei seiner Botschaft überhaupt um Prophetie handelt. Sie ist nicht prophetisches Wort (vgl. die Verwendung von מַשָּׂא II in Jes 15,1; 17,1; 19,1; 21,1.11.13; 22,1; 30,6; Ez 12,10; Nah 1,1; Sach 9,1; 12,1; Mal 1,1), sondern lediglich „Last“. Jeremia erwidert: Solche Spötter seien JHWH eine Last (*genitivus objectivus*).

37. Transkription und Übersetzung nach CROSS, *Papyrus* (s. Anm. 36), pp. 311f.

38. Knappe Hinweise auf weitere Beispiele finden sich bei FISHBANE, *Qumran Pesher* (s. Anm. 5), pp. 108-110.

39. Zur Forschungsgeschichte von Jer 23,33-40 und seiner Exegese s. meine Ausführungen in *Vom prophetischen Wort zur prophetischen Tradition: Studien zur Traditions- und Redaktionsgeschichte innerprophetischer Konflikte in der Hebräischen Bibel* (Forschungen zum Alten Testament, 34), Tübingen, J.C.B. Mohr (Paul Siebeck), 2002, pp. 278-291.

Wohl im 4. Jh. v. Chr. hat ein späterer Redaktor dieses Wort an die Sammlung „Über die Propheten" (Jer 23,9) in Jer 23,9-32 angefügt und um Jer 23,34-40 erweitert. Dieser Redaktor konzentriert sich in seiner Fortschreibung auf ein einziges Element aus V. 33 (Atomisierung): „Ihr seid die Last (מַשָּׂא) JHWHs, und ich werde euch fallen lassen". Die Rekontextualisierung von V. 33 in die Auseinandersetzung mit Jeremias prophetischen Gegnern führt in Jer 23,38 zu einer neuen Deutung von Jer 23,33b: „obwohl ich zu euch gesandt hatte: 'sagt nicht Spruch (מַשָּׂא) JHWHs'". Nach V. 36 ist diese Wendung Jeremia als dem „Mann seines Wortes" (V. 36) vorbehalten. Die Präterita der Fragen von V. 35 und 37 zeigen, daß der Text als Alternative zu der mit „Spruch JHWHs" eingeleiteten aktuellen Prophetie die Orientierung an schon ergangener und jetzt schriftlich fixierter Prophetie empfiehlt. Aus ihr soll man erschließen, was JHWH geantwortet und geredet hat.

Ähnlich wie in Herodots Deutung des Orakels des Lysistratos, ähnlich wie in der Demotischen Chronik und ähnlich wie in den Pescharim gewinnt Jeremias sarkastische Erwiderung in ihrer Rekontextualisierung eine neue Bedeutung. Sie wird in „prophetischer Prophetenauslegung" als ein Verbot aller aktuellen Prophetie zugunsten eben jener „prophetischen Prophetenauslegung" verstanden[40].

5. Auswertung

Die in der Apokalyptik und den Pescharim beobachtete divinatorische Hermeneutik ist weit über das antike Judentum hinaus verbreitet gewesen und auch innerhalb der israelitisch-jüdischen Kultur nicht auf Apokalyptik und Essenismus beschränkt gewesen. Sie findet sich im Ägypten der Spätzeit ebenso wie im klassischen Griechenland und im nachexilischen Judäa. Eine Abhängigkeit etwa der antik-jüdischen Auslegung prophetischer Texte von der Deutung ägyptischer oder griechischer Orakelsammlungen anzunehmen, erscheint mir nicht zwingend.

Die Verwendung der divinatorischen Hermeneutik in der Auslegung von Prophetentexten und Orakelsammlungen oder in Stecks Worten in der „prophetischen Prophetenauslegung" legt m.E. eine andere Erklärung nahe. Bei der divinatorischen Auslegung von Orakelsammlungen und Prophetenbüchern dürfte es sich um eine natürliche Entwicklung

40. Zur Sache und zum Begriff s. O.H. Steck, *Die Prophetenbücher und ihr theologisches Zeugnis: Wege der Nachfrage und Fährten zur Antwort*, Tübingen, J.C.B. Mohr (Paul Siebeck), 1996, pp. 125-204; s. bes. pp. 131-135 zum Danielbuch und zu den Pescharim.

handeln, die in ungebrochener Linie fortführt, was schon Jahrhunderte in der Auslegung von Orakeln und Omina praktiziert wurde. Es lag wohl mehr als nahe, verschriftlichte und gesammelte Orakel und Omina auf die gleiche Art und Weise auszulegen wie das erstmalig ergangene Wort.

Die Apokalyptik und die Pescharim applizieren somit in der kulturellen Krise des „Wie-Lange-Noch“ eine für Texte von prophetischer Qualität weitverbreitete Auslegungstechnik. Daß diese Art Deutung etwa von den Pescharim z.B. auch auf Psalmen angewendet werden konnte (s. 1QpPs; 4QpPs$^{a.b}$), erklärt sich aus der Tatsache, daß eine ganze Reihe nichtprophetischer Texte sowohl im Antiken Judentum als auch in Israel (s. etwa die dtr Vorstellung von Mose als Prophet) sekundär prophetischen Charakter angenommen haben.

Die Verwendung einer im ostmediterranen Raum weitverbreiteten Hermeneutik sowohl im Danielbuch als auch in den Pescharimvon Qumranmachen die Pescharim damit nicht notwendig zu einem apokalyptischen Phänomen.

Sowohl Dan 9,23 als auch 1QpHab II 7-10 und VII 3-5 sowie das Auslegungsprivileg der Chresmologoi im antiken Griechenland legen ein Bewußtsein für den Offenbarungscharakter der fraglichen divinatorischen Hermeutik nahe. Im antiken Judentum dokumentiert sich ein solches Bewußtsein für das Phänomen von Interpretation als Offenbarung explizit in Sir 39,6 (𝔊)[41]: Dort wird über den Ausleger von Gesetz, Propheten und weiteren Schriften gesagt[42]:

> Wenn der Herr, der Große, es will,
> wird er (scil. der Ausleger) mit dem Geist der Einsicht erfüllt werden,
> er wird heraussprudeln die Worte seiner Weisheit,
> und im Gebet wird er den Herrn preisen.

University of North Carolina
at Chapel Hill
NC 27599
USA

Armin LANGE

41. Zu Sir 39,6 im Rahmen der Frage nach der prophetischen Prophetenauslegung s. STECK, *Prophetenbücher* (s. Anm. 40), 130.

42. Zur „Kanonliste“ s. Sir (𝔊) 38,34b–39,4.

DAS GEHEIMNIS DER ZEIT IN WEISHEIT UND APOKALYPTIK UM DIE ZEITENWENDE

„Eines der tiefsten Rätsel, vor denen sich die Menschheit sieht, wenn sie zu einem tieferen Verständnis des eigenen Daseins zu gelangen sucht, ist die Frage, was eigentlich Zeit ist". So beginnt ein Beitrag über „Die Zeitanschauung des Abendlandes" des jüngst verstorbenen Heidelberger Philosophen Gadamer[1]. Bekanntlich haben seit Augustin Philosophen und Theologen in unserm Kulturkreis wieder und wieder um dieses Problem gerungen, ohne daß irgendein Konsens absehbar wäre. Dem Philosoph Martin Heidegger ist es nicht gelungen, den abschließenden zweiten Band seines Hauptwerks „Sein und Zeit" zu vollenden, und doch halten viele ihn für den größten Philosophen des vergangenen Jahrhunderts. Doch das Rätsel der Zeit hat lange vor dem Beginn der abendländischen Kultur das Denken der Menschen beunruhigt und nach befriedigenden Lösungen suchen lassen.

Das gilt auch für das alte Israel, besonders in der hellenistisch-römischen Epoche. Schon längst hatte hier in den religiösen Überlieferungen die providenziell gelenkte Volksgeschichte unter metahistorischem Blickwinkel als von Gott gelenkte Ethnogenese die Stelle eingenommen im geschichtlichen und profetischen Schrifttum, aber auch in den Psalmen, die Theogonie oder Kosmogonie in der mythologischen Umwelt eingenommen hatten[2]. Allein die weisheitlich orientierten Schulen hatten sich lang gegen eine Beschäftigung mit der Volksgeschichte als Gottesgeschichte gesperrt. Das ändert sich, soweit wir sehen können, erst seit dem 2. Jahrh.v.Chr., also in einer Epoche, in der die Geistesbeschäftigung der zeitgenössischen Apokalyptik die Volksgeschichte zu einem zentralen Thema macht, allerdings sie nunmehr einbettet in eine von der Schöpfung bis zum Eschaton nach göttlichem Plan verlaufenden Menschheitsgeschichte. Seit Ben Sira kann auch die Weisheit sich dem Thema nicht entziehen, bemüht sich jedoch weit stärker um die Zeit des individuellen Menschenlebens, in einer Weise, welche der älteren Weisheit unbekannt war und die auch bei Bibelwissen-

1. H.G. GADAMER, *Kleine Schriften IV Variationen*, Tübingen, Mohr, 1977, S. 17 ff. Zuerst veröffentlicht in *Leib Geist Geschichte, Brennpunkte anthropologischer Psychiatrie*, Heidelberg, 1977.

2. K. KOCH, *Geschichte/Geschichtsschreibung/Geschichtsphilosophie*, in *TRE* 12, S. 569-586.

schaftlern bislang wenig Beachtung gefunden hat[3]. Die vielfältigen Aspekte, die sich für das Verhältnis des Menschen zu seiner Zeit in dieser Art Schriften auftun, will ich an vier ausgewählten Beispielen aufzeigen, nämlich Qohälät, Sirach, einer in Qumran gefundenen „Instruktion für den Einsichtigen" und dem Danielbuch, um einen Eindruck von dem intensiven Diskurs über das Thema in den Jahrhunderten vor der Zeitenwende zu geben. Dabei ist mir bewußt, daß die Literatur der griechischen Diaspora (in der Sapientia Salomonis und schon in der Septuaginta) in dieser Hinsicht eigene Wege einschlägt, auf die hier nicht eingegangen wird.

Um den Stellenwert zu begreifen, den damals das Zeitverständnis bei weisheitlichen und apokalyptischen Autoren einnimmt, lohnt sich ein vorgängiger, kursorischer Vergleich unsres modernen Zeitbewußtseins mit dem, was hebräische Zeitauffassung gewesen zu sein scheint. Das tiefe Rätsel, von dem Gadamer spricht, resultiert damals wie heute daraus, daß für den menschlichen Geist Zeit nicht nur wie Luft unsichtbar, sondern mit keinem der fünf Sinne wahrnehmbar und dennoch für jedes menschliche Dasein schlechthin prägend erscheint. Die Zeit kommt aber auf das sich seiner selbst bewußte Subjekt mit verschiedenen Erstreckungen zu. Dafür einige kurze Hinweise als Vorverständnis der Untersuchung. Noch im modernen Bewußtsein spiegeln sich verschiedene Weisen der Zeiterfahrung, die in der biblischen Sprache sich wohl noch deutlicher als für uns heute voneinander abheben.

1. Es gibt die *meßbare, chronometrisch* durch Uhr und Kalender systematisierte, aber inhaltsleer und deshalb *homogen und unendlich gedachte Zeit.* Sie dominiert im gegenwärtigen Bewußtsein und beeinflußt das Durchschnittsverhalten tagtäglich. In der althebräischen Sprache wird diese Zeitart hingegen erst verhältnismäßig spät mit dem (aus dem Akkadischen oder Altpersischen entlehnten) Lehnwort *zeman* bzw. der Wendung *ʿet mezuman* (Esr 10,14; Neh 10,35) auf den Begriff gebracht. Vielleicht schon in der Priesterschrift, jedenfalls in der Apokalyptik wird sie mit dem Postulat von Zeitepochen verbunden, die durch wirkungskräftige „runde" Zahlen wie 4, 7, 12 und ihr Vielfaches strukturiert sein sollen.

2. Anders ist, was im Alltag als belangreicher Einschnitt in die gegenwärtige Zeit durch Phänomene der Umwelt, die sich in den Vordergrund

3. Bezeichnenderweise gibt es im sechsbändigen *The Anchor Bible Dictionary* (1992) keinen Artikel *Time*, in *Die Religion in Geschichte und Gegenwart. Handwörterbuch für Theologie und Religionswissenschaft* (1962), Bd. 6, nur einen Beitrag *Zeit, philosophisch* (S. 1880-1885).

schieben, empfunden wird; sie tauchen auf und treten wieder in den Hintergrund, ohne daß ein Neuentstehen oder völliges Vergehen vorauszusetzen wäre. Man könnte von *phänomenalen Zeitpunkten* sprechen; Dinge, Personen, Konstellationen „zeitigen sich“ und nötigen zu entsprechendem Verhalten. So die zentrale Bedeutung des hebräischen *ʿet*, das in der Regel syntaktisch eine Näherbestimmung bei sich hat und stets eine inhaltlich gefüllte Zeit meint, hervorgerufen durch Naturerscheinungen oder die menschliche Gesellschaft oder göttliches Eingreifen. Ein solche Zeit kommt auf den Menschen von außen zu, „für dieses Leben entscheidend und doch vom Menschen unabhängig“[4]. Nicht zu Unrecht übersetzt die Septuaginta das hebräische Nomen meist mit *kairos,* nicht mit *chronos.*

3. Das menschliche Individuum erlebt seine *je eigene Zeit* als Spannen von gelungenem oder mißlungenem Leben, mit jeweils begrenzter Frist, in der man, modern gesprochen, „Zeit hat“ oder „keine Zeit hat“, oder in der Erinnerung Stunden des Glücks von denen des Unglücks unterscheidet. Unter diesem Blickwinkel wird Zeit als endlich oft angstvoll empfunden. Im orientalischen Altertum wird eine solche Erstreckung von Zeit meist im Blick auf die vorgegebene, vom Betroffenen aber mit unklarem Ausgang belastete Lebenszeit zur Sprache gebracht, hebräisch gilt auch sie als *ʿet,* oft mit Suffix „meine Zeit“ (*ʿittî)* usw.

4. Das einzelne Dasein wird gerahmt durch die *epochale Zeit* je nach dem kulturellen Gedächtnis der ihn tragenden Gesellschaft, des Volkes, der Religion u.ä. Hebräisch wird sie unter dem Stichwort der *jamîn* eingeordnet, als „Tage der Richter/der Könige von Juda/der Könige von Israel“. Auch die dadurch ausgedrückten Epochen können als gut oder böse aufgefaßt werden, und je nach ihrer Art bestimmen sie die Tage des gewöhnlichen Bürgers.

5. Im Unterschied zum modernen verlängern sich für das altorientalische Zeitbewußtsein die Tage der Geschichte nach rückwärts wie nach vorwärts in ferne, sagenhafte Zeiträume von *Urzeit und Endzeit*, denen eine qualitativ andere und höhere Dignität und Wirkungskraft zugesprochen wird als der Jetztzeit. Dafür stehen Lexeme wie *ʿôlam* (auf einer sprachgeschichtlich frühen Stufe), *rešît, qædæm, ʾaḥ^{a}rît, u.a.* bereit.

6. Vorausgesetzt wird im Altertum eine prinzipiell *finite* Zeit, auch wenn deren Anfang und Ende nicht klar zu erfassen sind. Das führt zur

4. T. Kronholm, *TWAT*, 6, S. 478.

Auffassung von einem in sich vernetzten *Zeituniversum,* das Gott vor aller Zeit geschaffen hat und ein Weltuniversum einschließt, weil im Unterschied zur neuzeitlichen Abstraktion Zeit ohne materiellen Träger nicht gedacht werden kann (vgl. *ʿôlam* im späteren Gebrauch).

7. Jede Art der erfahrenen Zeit wird auf Gott als Weltschöpfer zurückgeführt, der deshalb in der hebräisch-aramäischen Literatur als „Herr des *ʿôlam*/*ʿalam*“ gepriesen wird und sich in bestimmten *ʿit tîm*/*ʿidannayyá* durch seine verbalen Offenbarungen manifestiert oder seinen Willen durch tatsächlichen Eingriff verwirklicht.

Soviel als ein kurzer Vorspann, um das Vorverständnis zu skizzieren, mit dem die einschlägigen hebräischen Texte untersucht werden sollen. Zuvor ein Blick zurück auf die ältere Weisheit, der das Problem der Zeit noch kein Kopfzerbrechen bereitet hatte.

Die zeitunabhängige, geschichtslose Weisheit der Proverbien

Die Zeitlichkeit des Daseins ist für die Proverbien noch kein eigenes Thema, obgleich gelegentlich Zeitbegriffe auftauchen. Die Sprüche ermahnen vielmehr den Schüler, die Lehren unabhängig von den Umständen *b^{e}kål-ʿet* zu befolgen oder stellen bei Weisen und Toren ein entgegengesetztes Verhalten *b^{e}kål-ʿet* fest. Das wird im einzelnen dahin konkretisiert, daß man sich allezeit an der Liebe seiner Frau berauschen solle (5,19) oder daran zu denken hat, daß ein Taugenichts bei jeder Gelegenheit Streit beginnt, oder ein wahrer Freund immer dem andern seine Liebe erweist, auch in Notlagen (6,14; 17,17). Was hier *(kål-)ʿet* genannt wird, faßt alle sich wandelnden Zeitlagen, die für den Beteiligten angenehm oder unangenehm sind und in ihrer Wirkung auf das Gemüt entgegengesetzt sein mögen, als für weises Verhalten irrelevant zusammen. Wer den Lehren folgt und sich dadurch als *ṣaddîq* erweist, dem wird allerdings ein Leben *l^{e}ʿôlam,* also eine alle *ʿittîm* übergreifende *ʿôlam*-Zeit versprochen (10,25.30); in Anlehnung an die Rechts- oder Psalmensprache wird damit keine Unsterblichkeit, sondern eine besonders lange Lebenszeit in Aussicht gestellt. Im Blick auf das Eigentum an Gütern wird allein *ʿôlam* (als Rechtsbegriff) verwendet: die Grenzen von Grund und Boden dürfen nicht verrückt werden, weil sie seit der *ʿôlam*-Urzeit bestehen (so 22,28; 23,10 in Anlehnung an den ägyptischen Amenemope Kap. 6); und Reichtum an Vieh bleibt nicht auf unübersehbare Dauer bestehen (27,24).

Einzig das berühmte Kap. 8 über die Chokma als Schöpfungsmittlerin legt den Ton auf eine Zeitdimension, nämlich ihre einzigartige Präexistenz, ist sie doch „von Urzeit her gewebt, am Anbeginn, in den Vorzeiten der Erde (*meʿôlam nissakti meroʾš miqadmê-ʿäräṣ, V. 23*), seitdem spielt sie unentwegt (*b^{e}kål-ʿet*) vor dem Schöpfer." Der Verweis auf einen vorzeitigen, einmaligen Schöpfungsakt soll hervorheben, daß die Weisheit über allen Zeiten unverändert waltet und unabhängig von deren möglichem Wandel Menschen zu gelingendem Leben aufruft. Wer auf sie hört, was immerzu möglich ist, darf Tag um Tag an ihren Toren wachen (V. 34).

Der den wechselnden Zeiten ausgesetzte Qohälät

Wo heutzutage nach einem biblischen Zeitverständnis gesucht wird, da wird vor allem auf Ecclesiastes verwiesen. Schon die Statistik des Wortgebrauchs in dieser weisheitlichen Schrift ist aufschlußreich; während das Lexem *ʿet* in den Proverbien 5mal auftaucht, benutzt Qohälät es 40mal! Dem entspricht die inhaltliche Gewichtung. „Zu einer Grundkategorie des theologischen Wirklichkeitsverständnisses wird der Begriff *ʿet* ... erst bei Kohelet" heißt es in einer neuen Untersuchung zur späten Weisheit[5]. Vor allem Qoh 3 ist berühmt und viel diskutiert. Das Kapitel zählt zu Beginn 2x14 antithetische, aber typische Geschehnisse auf, denen jeder Mensch zu Lebzeiten ausgesetzt ist und die er passiv zu erleiden oder in denen er – so meistens – Stellung zu beziehen hat. Als Zeitarten werden gegenübergestellt.

Zeugen/Gebären – Sterben
Pflanzen – Ausreißen von Gepflanztem
Töten – heilen
Niederreißen – Aufbauen
Weinen – Lachen
Trauern – Tanzen
Steine wegwerfen – Steine sammeln
Umarmen – Umarmung meiden
Suchen – Verloren gehen lassen
Aufbewahren – Wegwerfen
Zerreißen – Zusammennähen
Schweigen – Reden
Lieben – Hassen
Krieg – Frieden.

Als Beispiele werden nicht die rhythmisch wiederkehrenden, vorhersehbaren Zyklen des Jahreslaufs (z.B. Sommer – Winter) oder die natür-

5. U. Wicke-Reuter, *Göttliche Providenz und menschliche Verantwortung bei Ben Sira und in der frühen Stoa* (BZAW, 298), Berlin, de Gruyter, 2000, S. 103. Vgl. M.V. Fox, *A Time to Tear Down and a Time to Build Up*, Grand Rapids, MI, Eerdmans, 1999.

lichen Phasen des Lebensweges (etwa Jugend – Alter) gewählt, sondern aus dem alltäglichen Geschehen herausragende Zeitsituationen, die in der Regel unvorhersehbar dem Einzelnen begegnen und die Entscheidung zu entsprechendem Verhalten fordern. Dem wird als Quintessenz einer Zeiterfahrung der Satz vorangestellt:

> *l^ekol z^eman w^e ʿet l^ekål- ḥepäṣ taḥat šamajîm.*
> Für alles gibt es eine bemessene Zeitstrecke
> und eine herausragende Zeit für jedes Engagement unter dem Himmel.

Die beiden Ausdrücke, die für „Zeit" verwendet werden, haben unterschiedliche Konnotationen. *z^eman,* ein dem älteren Hebräisch fremdes akkadisches oder altpersisches Lehnwort[6], bedeutet eine kalendarisch festgelegte, nach Tag, Monat und Jahr berechenbare Zeiteinheit (Est 9,27.31; Sir 43,7. Vgl. *ʿet m^ezumman* Esr 10,14; Neh 10,35; ähnlich vielleicht *ḥæšbôn,* Qoh 9,10). Gemeint ist demnach ein neutrales Zeitkontinuum, das die antithetisch geprägten Zeitarten übergreift, die in der Folge erwähnt werden, das gleichsam durch sie hindurchläuft. Erst danach wird *ʿet* als inhaltlich gefüllte Erstreckung von Zeitabschnitten erwähnt, die dann im Folgenden allein noch interessiert. Geburt und Tod, Weinen und Lachen, Lieben und Hassen sind Geschehnisse, welche der Mensch nicht kalendarisch berechnen kann; ihr *z^eman*-Charakter läßt sich höchstens im Nachhinein festhalten. Sie folgen nicht unmittelbar aufeinander, sondern werden durch neutrale Phasen getrennt, bedeuten ekstatische Zeitsituationen[7]. Wer in einen *ʿet* verwickelt wird, kann ihm nicht ausweichen, sondern muß sich ihm gemäß verhalten (was wohl in 3,1 als *ḥepæṣ* gekennzeichnet wird).

Die Wendung *ʿet l^ekål-ḥepæṣ* taucht noch zweimal auf. In 3,16f. weist sie anscheinend auf den geforderten rechten Einsatz im Blick auf Gerechtigkeit oder Ungerechtigkeit in einem Gerichtsverfahren hin. In 8,5-7 bezieht sie sich auf Umstände, die ein Weiser erkennt, als eigene Möglichkeit ergreift und dadurch Böses für sich vermeidet, wie es dem gewöhnlichen Menschen zustößt. Die dem Lexem *ḥpṣ* sonst eigene emo-

6. *HAL,* S. 262. Das Lexem *zmn* wird von *THAT* wie von *TWAT* nicht als theologisch eingestuft und deshalb übergangen.

7. „Das verwendete hebräische Wort *ʿet* läßt sich mit unserem Wort ‚Zeit' nur ungefähr zur Deckung bringen. Einerseits ist es enger, weil es nach der Bedeutung ‚gesetzte Zeit', ‚rechte Zeit', ‚Zeitpunkt', ‚Zeit für' tendiert. Andererseits ist es weiter, weil der temporale Aspekt derart zurücktreten kann, daß man es u.U. geradezu mit ‚Gelegenheit zu', ‚Möglichkeit für' wiedergeben kann"; G. VON RAD, *Weisheit in Israel*, Neukirchen-Vluyn, Neukirchener Verlag, 1970, p. 184, Anm. 4 mit Verweis auf J.R. WILCH, *Time and Event An Exegtical Study of the Use of ʿet in the Old Testament in Comparison with Other Temporal Expressions in Classification of the Concept of Time*, Leiden, Brill, 1969.

tionale Bestimmtheit gilt gewiß auch hier und verweist in Verbindung mit *ʿet* auf Zeitarten, die des vollen Einsatzes wert sind[8]. Da die Zeit nicht allein als durchlaufendes Kontinuum, sondern für menschliches Erleben vor allem als Quelle meist unvorhersehbar eintretender Widerfahrnisse gegensätzlicher Art das menschliche Subjekt überfällt und zu eigenem Verhalten nötigt, bleibt es nutzlos, sich ohne Beachtung solcher Zeitekstasen angestrengt zu betätigen. So ist wohl die rhetorische Frage zu verstehen, die auf die Reihe der 14 gegensätzlichen Möglichkeiten folgt:

> Welchen Gewinn hat der Tätige, wenn er sich (unablässig) anstrengt?

Anscheinend wird ein sturer Aktionismus des *ʿamel* einem auf die günstige Zeiten blickenden *ḥepæṣ*-Verhalten gegenübergestellt. „Er hat keinen Ertrag, sofern er das ‘Risiko’ der Zeit nicht einplanen kann“[9]. Allerdings, so fährt V.10 fort, hat Gott dem Menschen eine andere Art von Mühe (*ʿinjan*) verordnet, nämlich die Suche nach Erkenntnis der Zeitsituation. Der Weise vermag seine, für ihn günstige Zeit zu erkennen und nützen; wer dazu nicht in der Lage ist, verfängt sich in böser Zeit (8,5; 9,12).

Der nächste Abschnitt 3,11ff. stellt die unterschiedlichen Zeiten *sub specie dei*. Für Gott droben ist ihr Wechsel sinnvoll und notwendig:

> (11) Das All hat er gelungen gemacht zu seiner[10] Zeit.
> Sogar den *ʿôlam* hat er in ihr[11] Herz gegeben.
> Nur daß der Mensch nicht das Werk, das Gott gemacht hat, ausfindig machen kann
> vom Anfang bis zum Ende[12].
> (14)... Alles, was Gott hervorbringt, gehört zum Zeituniversum (*ʿôlam*),
> dem läßt sich nichts hinzufügen und nichts abschneiden...
> (15) Was auch immer geschehen ist, war längst (vorbereitet),
> und was geschehen soll, ist längst (bestimmt).

Als dritter Zeitbegriff ist jetzt von *ʿôlam* die Rede, anscheinend eine Größe, die sowohl *zᵉman* wie *ʿet* in sich begreift. Bedeutet *ʿôlam* hier

8. Gemeint ist sicher nicht ein neutrales „Geschehen“, so die deutsche Einheitsübersetzung mit den meisten Kommentaren, aber auch mit BOTTERWECK, *TWAT*, 3, S. 109 z.St.

9. K. GALLING, *Das Rätsel der Zeit im Urteil Kohelets (Koh 3,1-15)*, in *ZTK* 58 (1961) 1-15, S. 2.

10. Ist die Zeit des Alls gemeint in ihrem Wandel? Oder Gottes eigene Zeit? Für das erste plädiert mit vielen andern Th. KRÜGER, *Kohelet (Prediger)* (BKAT, 19), Neukirchen-Vluyn, Neukirchener Verlag, 2000, S. 171, Anm. 6; für das zweite H.P. MÜLLER, *Wie sprach Qohälät von Gott?*, in *VT* 18 (1968) 507-521, S. 514.

11. In das ‘Herz’ der Zeiten des Alls? Zumeist wird an das Herz = Bewußtsein der Menschen gedacht. Zur Diskussion s. KRÜGER, *Kohelet* (Anm. 10), S. 165, Anm. 11a.

12. Anfang und Ende der Zeit der Schöpfung, vgl. 8,17? So durchweg die Kommentare. Oder Anfang und Ende der Lebensspanne des betroffenen Menschen?

jene Zeit der Welt, die nach 1,4 Dauer hat, während menschliche Lebenszeit schnell vergeht? „Alle ‚Kairoi' sind in den unabänderlichen Zeitablauf Gottes eingeordnet"[13]. Somit umfaßt *ʿôlam* „Anfang und Ende der als Geschehen aufgefaßten Wirklichkeit, ... das von Gott erfüllte Wirklichkeitsganze"[14]. Qohälät schließt sich einer traditionellen Lehre an, daß Gott mit einer harmonische Einheit des von der Zeit geprägten Weltlaufs seine Schöpfung ausgestattet hat. Doch das geht für ihn auf eine Ahnung zurück, die kein Mensch zu beweisen imstande ist. Damit entfernt er sich von einem Großteil israelitischer Überlieferungen, die von einer aufweisbare Providenz in der Struktur der Schöpfung und im Gefälle der Zeiten des eigenen Volkes tief überzeugt waren. Der skeptische Weise sieht sich einer unverstandenen und unverständlichen Weltgeschichte gegenüber und weiß von keiner Ausnahmestellung der eigenen Nation und ihrer Geschichte. Was erkennbar ist für den wachen Betrachter sind die Zeitabschnitte der *ʿittîm* im Umkreis der Gegenwart; sie betreffen jeden auf seine Weise, kommen von außen auf das menschliche Subjekt zu, sind also nicht aus ihm selbst entstanden, sondern haben einen gewissen „objektiven" Charakter. Dazu können auch feststehende Glücks- und Unglückstage gehören, wie 7,14 wohl in Anlehnung an außerisraelitische, astrologisch orientierte Kalender formuliert.

Bisweilen hat *ʿet* die Konnotation der je eigenen Lebensspanne, und auf sie hat der Betreffende sogar einen gewissen, allerdings oft negativ sich auswirkenden Einfluß, insofern derjenige sie sich verkürzt, der zu frevelhaft oder töricht sich verhält (7,17). Eine auf das Individuum zuge-

13. M. HENGEL, *Judentum und Hellenismus* (WUNT, 10), Tübingen, Mohr, 1969, S. 221. N. LOHFINK, *Kohelet* (NEB), Würzburg, Echter, 1980, S. 33f., übersetzt freilich: „Überdies hat er Ewigkeit in alles hineingelegt" (ähnlich die Wiedergabe in der Einheitsübersetzung und der revidierten Lutherbibel) und will das „im Sinn immer neuer Wiederkehr" verstehen (V. 15). Es fehlt leider an einer gründlichen semantischen Untersuchung des Lexems *ʿôlam* in der spätisraelitischen Literatur. Bezeichnend ist die Art, wie G. BRIN, *The Concept of Time in the Bible and the Dead Sea Scrolls* (STDJ, 39), Leiden, Brill, 2001, S. 277-293, bei der Durchsicht der Belege aus Qumran zwischen Wiedergaben wie „the very beginning of history" und komplementär dazu „eschatological significance" (283), aber auch „eternity" (284) oder bloßer Superlativ oder „cosmos" (291) schwankt, ohne nach einem semantischen Zusammenhang zu suchen. Deutlich ist, daß das Lexem auf einer früheren Sprachstufe die „fernliegende Zeit" sowohl im Blick auf die Vergangenheit wie auf die Zukunft bedeutete, während es um die Zeitenwende „Welt, Kosmos" einbegreift und das deshalb, weil es inzwischen zum Begriff für das Zeituniversum von der Schöpfung bis zum Weltende geworden war, und zwar so, daß Zeit und Welt als sich gegenseitig bedingend gedacht werden.

14. H.P. MÜLLER, *Wie sprach Qohälät von Gott?* (Anm. 10), S. 510f.; DERS., *Das Ganze und sein Teile. Anschlußerörterungen zu Wirklichkeitsverständnis Kohelets,* in *ZTK* 97 (2000) 147-163, S. 150: „‚Die Weltzeit' ist die von einem vergangenheitlichen und einem zukünftigen ‚Einst' umschlossene Zeitstrecke, die Weltgeschichte insgesamt". Zu älteren, höchst unterschiedlichen Deutungen siehe O. LORETZ, *Qohelet und der Alte Orient*, Freiburg i. Br., Herder, 1964, S. 281, Anm. 277.

schnittene, für sein Leben günstige und Freude bringende Zeitspanne nennt Qohälät *ḥelæq*, „Anteil“, und meint damit von Gott angebotene Fristen des Guten, des Glücks bis hin zu Essen, Trinken, Freude am Besitztum und Vergnügen mit der Frau (3,22; 5,17-19; 9,9), was oft gerade dann glückt, wenn einer auf Anstrengung verzichtet (*ʿamal* 2,21, vgl. 3,9). Es sind *highlights*, wie sie jeder erleben kann, der sie wahrzunehmen in der Lage ist, die aber leider immer wieder vorübergehen (2,10f.). Wie das Leben als ganzes *hæbæl*, ein Windhauch, ist (3,19; 6,12 u.ö.), so auch die Stunden des Glücks (2,1.11; 6,2; 11,10), deshalb: „genieße alle Tage deines Windhauchs“ (9,9)[15].

Was in das individuelle Dasein wieder und wieder unversehens eingreift, wird als *miqräh* ausgedrückt, als eine von Gott herrührende herausragende Widerfahrnis im Geschick des Einzelnen; besonders hart trifft es ihn durch das jäh und unvorhersehbar eintretenden Ende, den Tod. Er gilt als ein alle Wesen gleichmachendes Verhängnis: der Effekt ist derselbe bei Weisen und Toren, Gerechten wie Frevlern, ja Menschen wie Tieren (2,15; 3,19f.; 9,2). Der Tod „cuts across all moral categories“[16]. „Das ist das Übel bei allem, was unter der Sonne getan wird, daß es ein Geschick für alle gibt“ (9,3). Von Belang im Blick auf frühere israelitische Selbstverständlichkeiten ist, daß für Qohälät solche Widerfahrnisse offensichtlich nicht von einem vorgängigenVerhalten des betroffenen Subjekts abhängen. Wie kein andrer biblischer Schriftsteller vor ihm bestreitet er die Auffassung von einem Tun-Ergehen-Zusammenhang im menschlichen Leben, nach dem aus ein *ṣᵉdaqah*-Handeln notwendig ein heilvolles *ṣᵉdaqah*-Ergehen folgt[17]. Er beruft sich auf seine Erfahrung: „Es gibt *ṣaddiqîm*, die es trifft, als hätten sie gehandelt wie Frevler, und es gib Frevler, die es trifft, als hätten sie gehandelt wie *ṣaddiqîm*“ (8,14; vgl. 7,15; 9,2). Daraus folgt eine Relativierung der vorgegeben moralischen Normen: „Sei nicht allzu *ṣaddîq* und verhalte dich nicht übermäßig weise; warum willst du dich ruinieren?“ (7,16). Zwar ist rechtschaffenes Handeln nicht völlig nutzlos. „Trotz seiner im Wirken Gottes begründeten ‚Zeit-Gebundenheit‘ ist

15. Das Nomen *hæbæl* wird oft „eitel, nichtig, sinnlos“ übersetzt, heißt aber wohl „dem Zeitlauf unterworfen, vergänglich, wandelbar“, es ist resignativ, aber nicht asschließlich negativ gemeint; G. WALLIS, *Das Zeitverständnis des Predigers Salomos*, in M. WEIPPERT – S. TIMM (Hgg.), *Meilensteine*. FS H. Donner (ÄAT, 30), Wiesbaden, Harrasowitz, 1995, S. 316-323. Vgl. KRÜGER, *Kohelet* (Anm. 10), S. 101-104.

16. P. MACHINIST, *Fate,* miqreh, *and Reason. Some Reflections on Qohelet and Biblical Thought*, in Z. ZEVIT – S. GITIN – M. SOKOLOFF (Hgg.), *Solving Riddles and Untying Knots.* FS J. C. Greenfield, Winona Lake, IN, Eisenbraums, 1995, S. 159-175, 166.

17. K. KOCH, *Gibt es ein Vergeltungsdogma im Alten Testament?*, in DERS., *Spuren des hebräischen Denkens. Gesammelte Aufsätze 1*, Neukircher-Vluyn, Neukirchener Verlag, 1991, S. 65-103, zu Qohälät, S. 94f.

menschliches Handeln … nicht völlig ‚determiniert'"[18]. Andernfalls bräuchte Qohelet sein Buch nicht zu schreiben und zur Beachtung der Zeitarten aufrufen. Aber eine Anstrengung, welche „zu aller Zeit" die Normen einer Tugend und Gesetzethik pünktlich zu erfüllen sucht, läuft ins Leere. „Der einzelne Mensch … kann in seinem irdischen Leben (das besagt: unter dem Himmel) konkreten Entscheidungen niemals ausweichen"[19]. Qohälät entdeckt die Geschichtlichkeit der Existenz, wodurch der Mensch gerufen ist, wieder und wieder den rechten Augenblick zu erkennen und sich so anzueignen, daß er dadurch zu Glück und Freude gelangt, ohne daß sich seine Entscheidung aus den überlieferten Normen seiner Gesellschaft von selbst ergibt.

Unter deutschsprachigen Alttestamentlern ist die Meinung verbreitet, daß die Betonung der unterschiedlichen Manifestationen von Zeit und die damit verbundene Mahnung, das Verhalten danach einzurichten, „seit je im Zentrum der altorientalischen Weisheit stand"[20]. Gelegentlich werden astrologische Omina als Beweis herangezogen[21]. Doch die auf Grund mantischer Praktiken kalendarisch festgelegten günstigen oder ungünstigen Tage liegen auf einer andern Ebene als das individuelle Gewahr-Werden der „fallenden" Zeiten, das Qohälät beschäftigt. Auch das uralte Motto *carpe diem* bezieht sich auf den Lauf der Dinge überhaupt, nicht auf besondere Gelegenheiten. Die altorientalische Weisheit kennt in dieser Hinsicht zwar die Mahnung, für Reden und Schweigen den richtigen Augenblick zu erfassen (vgl. das Ideal des Weisen als „Schweiger" in Ägypten, vgl. auch Prov 15,23). Das aber bedeutet noch nicht, die gesamte Lebensführung auf exponierte Zeitspannen hin auszurichten. Dafür gibt es auch in der hellenistischen Literatur keine wirkliche Entsprechung; es ist bezeichnend, daß die wohl griechisch verfaßte Sapientia Salomonis das Thema nicht kennt. Hier schlägt die hebräische Weisheit einen sehr eigenen Weg ein, wie sich beim Blick auf Ben Sira bestätigen wird[22].

Qohälät interessiert sich für die Geschichtlichkeit des Einzelnen, die er mit ihren Rahmebedingungen in einer Weise zur Sprache bringt, wie

18. KRÜGER, *Kohelet* (Anm. 10), S. 173.

19. GALLING, *Rätsel der Zeit* (Anm. 9), S. 2.

20. VON RAD, *Weisheit* (Anm. 7), S. 183, aber ohne Angabe von Belegstellen. So auch E. JENNI, *THAT* II, S. 382 unter Berufung auf Von Rad und O. LORETZ, *Qohelet und der Alte Orient* (Anm. 14), S. 200, der aber nur Sirachparallen anführt.

21. KRÜGER, *Kohelet* (Anm. 10), S. 160.

22. Der in hellenistischer Zeit sich rasch ausbreitende Schicksalsglaube berührt sich zwar in der Idee vom unversehens hereinbrechendem heil- oder unheilvollen Geschehen mit Gedanken Qohäläts, sieht aber in astrologischen Berechnungen oder der eifrigen Verehrung der dafür zuständigen, meist jetzt erst Bedeutung erlangenden zuständigen Gottheiten die angemessene Art zu reagieren.

keiner vor ihm. Doch dieses Individuum wird zugleich eigentümlich geschichtslos begriffen im Blick auf die Zeiten seines Volkes oder seiner Kultgemeinschaft, auf den Wandel innen- oder außenpolitischer Verhältnisse seiner Gesellschaft.

Qohäläts Stimme ist jedoch nicht das letzte Wort zur Sache in Israel, obwohl moderne Exegeten gern um seiner vorgeblichen oder tatsächlichen Modernität willen solchen Anschein zu erwecken suchen.

WEISHEIT ALS ERKENNTNIS DER RICHTIGEN ZEIT FÜR SITUATIVES HANDELN BEI BEN SIRA

Während die ältere Weisheit dem Thema Zeit kein besonderes Gewicht beilegt, ändert sich das Bild in den weisheitlichen und apokalyptischen Schriften der letzten vorchristlichen Jahrhunderten. Ganz anders als in den Proverbien rückt bei Ben Sira die Reflexion auf die Zeitlichkeit des Daseins angesichts der bedrängenden Alternative von einem weisen und dadurch gelungenen Leben und einem törichten und deshalb mißlingenden Leben in das Zentrum der Lehre[23]. Schon das häufige Vorkommen der einschlägigen Begriffe zeigt das Gewicht, daß die Beachtung des geeigneten Zeitpunkts für Handeln und Verhalten in den Ermahnungen dieser Schrift findet: während in den Proverbien das Lexem *ʿet* fünfmal benutzt worden war, kommt in der (allein vollständig erhaltenen) griechischen Fassung des Sirach das dem hebräischem *ʿet* entsprechende *kairos* rund 60mal vor; die für das in den Proverbien sechsmal gebrauchte *ʿôlam* übliche Standardübersetzung *aiôn* wird rund 45mal in Sirach für das Zeituniversum verwendet! „Die Deutung der Wirklichkeit durch den Aspekt der Zeit gehört zu den grundlegenden Gedanken im Werk des Siraziden“[24].

1. Gleich das Eingangskapitel greift auf Prov 8 zurück und preist die Schöpfungsvermittlung durch die vor allen andern Geschöpfen präexistente Weisheit und betont noch mehr als das ältere Buch ihren überzeitlichen, den *aiôn* durchwaltenden Charakter (1,1-15*G*; vgl. 24,9 *G*):

> Alle Weisheit stammt vom Herrn, und bei ihm ist sie in „Ewigkeit“ (*eis ton aiôna).*

23. Wo der hebräische Text erhalten ist, wird er zu Grunde gelegt nach P.C. BEENTJES, *The Book of Ben Sira* (SVT, 68), Leiden, Brill, 1997. Wo nur der griechische Text vorliegt, wird er durch *G* bei Übersetzung gekennzeichnet. Zur Textproblematik: J. MARBÖCK, *Sirach/Sirachbuch*, in *TRE* 31 (2000) 307-317.

24. WICKE-REUTER, *Göttliche Providenz* (Anm. 5), S. 102. Vgl. zum Thema vor allem das Sirachkapitel bei VON RAD, *Weisheit* (Anm. 7), S. 309-336.

Den Sand des Meers und die Tropfen des Regens und die Tage der „Ewigkeit“ – wer vermag sie zu zählen?
(4) Früher als alles ist die Weisheit geschaffen, und verständige Einsicht von „Ewigkeit“ her (*ex aiônos*).
(15) Bei den Menschen hat sie ein Fundament immerwährender Dauer (*aiônos)* einnisten lassen.

Der griechische Ausdruck *aiôn* läßt noch den Doppelaspekt im früheren Gebrauch des hebräischen Begriffs *ʿôlam* hindurchschimmern, nämlich den Bezug einerseits auf die ferne, aber fundamentale Urzeit (V. 1.4) und andrerseits auf die ferne, letztlich unübersehbare Zukunft (V. 15); es dominiert aber schon die jüngere Konnotation des Zeitkontinuums, dessen Tage sich von jenem Damals her bis in ein immerwährendes Danach erstrecken (V. 2.15), was der der Bedeutung der Ewigkeit und Zeitjenseitigkeit im griechischen Äquivalent nahe zu kommen, ohne sich mit ihr völlig zu decken. (Die Übersetzung versieht deshalb „Ewigkeit“ mit Anführungszeichen.) Obwohl als erste Kreatur geschaffen, bleibt die Weisheit, das Thema des Buches, mehr als jedes andre Geschöpf in Gott selbst verwurzelt, ist aber dennoch als Wirkgröße ausgegossen über die gesamte Schöpfung und in der Menschheit wie in einem zweiten Pol verankert. Als Anfang wahrer Erkenntnis ruft sie Furcht vor dem Herrn hervor und damit die Grundlage für ein langes Leben. Sirachs Anliegen ist es, aufzuweisen, wie der Leser diese Weise sich aneignen kann.

2. Dazu gehört, wie er wieder und wieder betonen wird, die Erkenntnis der für ein gelungenes Leben entscheidenden, von außen auf den Menschen zukommenden *phänomenalen* Zeitmanifestationen. Der Mensch, der sich an seinem Ort Weisheit zu eigen macht, zeichnet sich, wie es in der Fortsetzung heißt, durch Selbstbeherrschung aus und vermeidet jähe Wutausbrüche, und das deshalb, weil er sich des steten Wechsels der Zeiten bewußt ist und die geeignete Situation für ein angemessenes Verhalten abwartet: „Bis zum *kairos* hält an sich der Geduldige, und am Ende wird ihm alles erstattet. Bis zum *kairos* wird er sein Wort zurückhalten“ (1,23f. *G*). Schon für das Eingangskapitel gehört es also zur Lebensführung nach der Weisheit, den für zutreffendes Verhalten geeigneten Zeitpunkt gewahr zu werden. Auf das, was „an der Zeit ist“, achten Menschen, die der Weisheit nachfolgen.

Der nächste Abschnitt im Buch läßt die Weisheit selbst das Wort ergreifen. Sie gibt dem Leser zwanzig konkrete Lebensregeln für den zwischenenschlichen Umgang mit „Du sollst nicht“ – Sätzen, die sich u.a. gegen Hochmut, ungerechtes Richten, doppeldeutige Rede wenden und Demut vor Gott, Reue bei Verschuldung oder Freigiebigkeit fordern. Der Reihe wird die generelle Mahnung, sich stets zeitgemäß zu verhalten, vorangeschickt (4,20):

> Mein Sohn, die Zeitsituation[25]... beachte, und fürchte dich (dadurch) vor Üblem, und mache dein Leben nicht zuschanden.

Das Nachdenken über die Art der Situation ist im alltäglichen Umgang also angesagt, was unter Umständen eine nonkonformistische Haltung bedingt und von andern als Schande beurteilt wird; doch wer unzeitig handelt, ist zu sehr auf sich selbst bedacht (V. 21f.). Andrerseits darf eine geeignete Gelegenheit nicht ungenutzt verstreichen, vor allem beim Redewechsel in der Öffentlichkeit (4,23f.):

> Nicht halte den Dabar zurück zu geeigneter Zeit[26], verbirg nicht die Weisheit!
> Denn Weisheit wird durch Sprechen erkannt und Einsicht in der Antwort der Zunge.

Schon das Proverbienbuch hatte gelegentlich gemahnt, den richtigen Augenblick für kluge Rede nicht zu verpassen (15,23). Das Thema hat bei Ben Sira ungleich größeres Gewicht (1,23f.*G*; 32[35]4 u.ö.). Die Kehrseite der Sache betrifft das Schweigen zu ungünstiger Zeit, so 20,7):

> Ein Weiser schweigt bis zur (angemessenen) Zeit, ein Tor achtet nicht auf die Zeit.

Selbst Musik wäre bei traurigen Anlässen unangemessen; nur Zucht ist zu jeder Zeit angebracht (22,6 *G*).

Im alltäglichen Verhalten wird ein Weiser stets beachten, was an der Zeit ist. Denn es gibt die Zeit des Hungers und die der Fülle, eine von Armut und eine von Reichtum; und zwar unvorhersehbar: „Vom Morgen bis zum Abend kann sich die Zeit vollkommen ändern" (18,25 *G*), Termine für das Leihen von Geld wie für die Rückzahlung werden fällig (29,1-5 *G*), oder für die Erfüllung von Gelübden (18,22 *G*); belangvoll ist die Zeit der Heilung durch einen Arzt, sogar die Zeit für das Weintrinken (38,13; 34,28). Das erfordert jeweils ein spontanes, zeitgemäßes Verhalten. Phasen der Not und Bedrängnis können als verhängnisvolles Problem aufkommen; die Sorge um die richtige Weise des Verhaltens

25. Hinter *ʿet* fügt MSS^{A} über *G* hinaus einen Genetiv *hmwn* mit unklarer Bedeutung an; dazu G. SAUER, *Jesus Sirach*, in JSHRZ, 3/5, 1981, S. 515; nach T. MIDDENDORP, *Die Stellung Jesu Ben Siras zwischen Judentum und Hellenismus*, Leiden, Brill, 1973, S. 14. P.W. SKEHAN – A.A. DILELLA, *The Wisdom of Ben Sira* (AB, 39), Garden City, NY, Doubleday, 1987, S. 175 streichen den Genetiv mit *G* und erklären zu Recht *ʿet* als „qualitative time and not quantitative". Vgl. oben Anm. 7.

26. MSS^{C} *bʿtw*, MSS^{A} ein schwer deutbares *bʿôlam*.

paart sich dann mit der Angst vor lebensfeindlichen Widerfahrnissen. Solche Phasen sollte man nicht durch vornehmes Getue andern gegenüber zu verleugnen suchen (10,26). Wo ein Freund davon betroffen wird, ist ihm unbedingt beizustehen (22,23 *G*; 29,2 *G*; 37,4), ist doch auch Gott dann bereit, sich zu erbarmen (35,26). Erfährt der Weise Erniedrigung, wird sie ihm als Zeit der Prüfung bewußt, zeigt er Geduld und erfährt danach ein „Ewigkeit" von Zufriedenheit (2,1-9 *G*). Nicht von ungefähr verweist die letzte Aufforderung im Buch zum Ausblick auf eine künftige erfüllte Zeit (51,30):

> Eure Werke vollbringt in Gemeinschaftstreue *(bṣdqh)*,
> und er (Gott) wird euch Lohn geben zu seiner Zeit.

Im Vergleich zu gewöhnlichen Menschen zeichnet also einen Weisen ein intensives Zeitgefühl und reflektiertes Zeitbewußtsein aus (27,12 *G*):

> Inmitten von Unverständigen gib acht auf den *kairos*,
> und inmitten von Verständigen sei immer (zur Wahrnehmung der Zeit) bereit.

Hinter Ben Sira und seinem Kreis steht also die Absicht, „dem Kontingenten, das ihn bedroht, zu Leibe [zu] gehen", selbst wenn die Abschätzung der Umstände „zu empfindlicher Begrenzung in seinem Leben" führen[27]. Dabei lassen sich gesellschaftliche oder natürliche Bedingungen nicht auseinander halten. Allerdings werden nirgends Kriterien angegeben, um die Tendenz eines Zeitpunkts zu ergründen. Wo es sich nicht um Termine handelt, die durch Brauchtum und Recht geregelt waren wie der Verkehr zwischen Gläubiger und Schuldner oder die Darbringung eines Gelübdes, wird offenbar auf ein sicheres Gespür vertraut.

Dieses „alles Für und Wider bedenkende, weisheitliche, Bewerten und Beurteilen" hebt sich von der (damals in andern Kreisen vertretenen Hochschätzung einer ohne Wenn und Aber gültigen „absoluten göttlichen Tora" deutlich ab. „Nicht die Weisheit gerät in den Schatten der Großmacht Tora, sondern umgekehrt sehen wir Sirach damit beschäftigt, die Tora aus dem Verstehenshorizont der Weisheit heraus zu legitimieren und zu interpretieren"[28]. Hier wird eine Geschichtlichkeit menschlicher Existenz thematisiert, für die es nicht genügt, traditionellen Normen dem Wortlaut nach jederzeit gerecht zu werden, sondern die situative Entscheidungen fordert.

3. Von den durch den Wechsel der Verhältnisse und neuen in den Vordergrund tretenden Phänomenen je anderen Situationen, also dem,

27. VON RAD, *Weisheit* (Anm. 7), S. 186f.
28. *Ibid.*, S. (314-)316.

was man phänomenale Zeit nennen mag, hebt sich die *individuelle Lebenszeit* ab. Jedem Menschen hat Gott bei seiner Erschaffung eine bestimmte Lebensspanne mit auf seinen Weg gegeben. Dem Verweis auf die Schöpfungserzählung der Genesis und die Gottebenbildlichkeit des Menschen wird hinzugefügt (17,2 *G*):

> Gezählte Tage und einen *kairon* (für gelungenes Leben?) gab er (Gott) ihnen.

Das kostbare Gut kann aber der Einzelne durch falsches Verhalten verkürzen kann (30,24):

> Neid und Kummer verkürzen die Tage, und ohne daß es an der Zeit ist (*b^{e}lô ʿet)* läßt Sorge altern.

Wer sich aber bewährt, dessen Einsicht und Name werden „für alle Zeit nicht vergessen" (39,9). Es gilt, über die jeweilige Gegenwart hinaus an ein künftiges Glück am Ende des Lebens zu achten. Gegenüber Qohäläts Bestreitung eines Tun-Ergehens-Zusammenhang hält BenSira daran fest, „daß Gott dem Menschen in der Stunde des Todes sein Tun vergelten und daß diese Todesstunde gegebenenfalls alles vorherige ungerechtfertigte Leiden oder Wohlergehen vergessen machen kann" (11,15-26)[29].

4. Obwohl Juda wie der gesamte Nahe Osten einschneidende politische Umwälzungen in jener Epoche erlebt, verwundert es, wie wenig der Sirazide *epochale Zeiten* der transsubjektiven Geschichte zur Kenntnis nimmt. Anders als Profeten und Apokalyptiker beschäftigt ihn die Weltgeschichte nicht, abgesehen von beiläufigen Bemerkungen wie 10,4: „In der Hand Gottes liegt die Herrschaft über den Erdkreis, und den rechten Mann wird er zur rechten Zeit über ihm aufstehen lassen."

Nur in 36,1-17 wird angesichts der Unterdrückung Israels durch die Völker ein Klagelied des Volkes eingeschoben. Es reflektiert nicht die Ursachen und die Dauer der Fremdherrschaft. Für die Zukunft wird jedoch eine Zeit der grundlegende Wende erwartet. Erbeten wird deshalb nicht nur: „Beuge die Gegner und stoße den Feind nieder!", sondern auch: „Beschleunige die Endzeit *(qṣ)* und achte auf eine festgesetzte Zeit *(mwʿed)*!". Doch nicht die Auslöschung der Völker wird ersehnt, sondern ihr Bekenntnis zum israelitischen Gott: „Dann werden erkennen alle Enden der Erde, daß du der Gott der Weltzeit[30] bist". Wie Ben

29. KRÜGER, *Kohelet* (Anm. 10), S. 54.
30. Übersetzungen wie „Weltall" (SAUER, JSHRZ [Anm. 25]) oder „ewig" (Einheitsübersetzung) bleiben unzureichend, da es sich um Erkenntnis aus dem Verlauf der politischen Geschichte handeln soll.

Sira die individuelle Lebenszeit des Weisen optimistisch auf eine erfüllte Zeit des Glücks zulaufen sieht, so die epochalen Zeiten seines Volkes, ja der Menschheit. Man mag das Eschatologie nennen, wenn mit dem Begriff kein kosmischer Umsturz verbunden wird. Eine solche Endzeit bringt Israel die Wiederkehr seiner Vorzeit *(qdm),* der Gottestaten des Uranfangs (*r'š*).

Nachdem im Schlußteil mit dem Lob der Schöpfungswerke eingesetzt worden war, wird allerdings die eigene Volksgeschichte breit entfaltet als „Lob der Väter des *ʿôlam*" (Kap. 44-49). Auffälligerweise werden dabei keine Angabe über Länge oder Kürze der jeweiligen Periode oder die Jahre von Königen und andern Helden gemacht. Einzig *ʿôlam* wird als übergreifender Begriff einerseits für die gesamte Geschichte von Henoch bis Nehemia verwendet, verstanden wohl im alten Sinn als vergangene, aber stiftende Urzeit im Verlauf der Ethnogenese[31]. Andererseits wird in der Fortsetzung *ʿôlam* für die noch ausstehende, aber ersehnte zukünftige Heilszeit gebraucht. *Während* des Lebens einiger dieser Väter wurden herausragende Einrichtungen geschaffen, die *ʿad ʿôlam* bestehen bleiben werden, so das Hohenpriesteramt (45,13.24), das Horn Davids (47,11), der zweite Tempel (49,12). Ein Profet wie Jesaja hat „*ʿad ʿôlam* das Geschehende (*nhyh*) kundgetan, und das Verborgene vor seinem Kommen" (48,25). Von der begrenzten Phase einer künftigen *ʿet* ist nur bei Elija die Rede, der „zugerüstet worden ist für die Zeit, um das Herz der Väter zu den Söhnen zu wenden und die Stämme Israels wiederherzustellen" (48,10).

Zum ersten Mal wird durch Ben Sira *die epochale Zeit einer kollektiven Geschichte*, nämlich die Geschichte Israels als Heils- und Unheilsgeschichte, in einer hebräischen Weisheitsschrift *neben den Zeitarten des individuellen Lebens* als *Bedingung der je eigenen Existenz* zur Sprache gebracht. Erst in dieser Schrift wird die altorientalische Weisheit endgültig israelitisiert. Doch dieser erste Versuch bleibt beschränkt. Die Väter gelten nicht als Exponenten ihres Zeitalters, sondern als Vorbilder von Tugend und Gottvertrauen, wohl in Anlehnung an die hellenistische Gattung des Enkomiums. Die für die Tradition entscheidenden Stationen und Wenden der Volksgeschichte wie das Sklavendasein in Ägypten und der Exodus oder der von Profeten geweissagte und dann tatsächlich hereingebrochene Zusammenbruch von Königtum und Kult samt folgender Exilszeit bleiben (abgesehen von einer kurzen Bemerkung 49,6) unberücksichtigt (Anders dann die Sapientia, vor allem aber die Apokalyptik).

31. Eine Übersetzung wie „of old" für *ʿôlam* (SKEHAN – DILELLA, *Wisdom* [Anm. 25], S. 499) wird der hebräischen Überschrift kaum gerecht, die *G* nicht aufnimmt, vermutlich deshalb, weil ihre Bedeutung unklar erschien.

5. Die Zeiten der sich abwechselnden natürlichen und gesellschaftlichen Phänomene, die im Lebenskreis des Menschen hervor- und zurücktreten, wie auch der Wandel im Geschick einer individuellen Lebenszeit oder der epochalen Zeiten eines Volkes treten für Ben Sira nicht unvermittelt ein, fallen nicht plötzlich auf den Menschen und seine Umwelt, sondern sie gehören zum dramatischen Ablauf eines von Gott geschaffenen und deshalb sinnvollen, doch allein für Gott überschaubarem *universalen Zeitkontinuum*. Vom Anfang (*r'š*) der Weltzeit her hat er jedem seiner Werke einen eigenen Zeitrahmen mit auf den Weg gegeben (16,26). Der Schöpfungshymnus in 39,16-25[32] setzt voraus, daß mit jeder Kreatur auch ihre je eigene Zeit geschaffen wurde und alle Arten von Zeit durch Prädestination miteinander vernetzt sind:

> Die Werke des Herrn sind alle gut, sind reichlich zuhanden zur Zeit jeden Bedarfs[33].
> (20) Von der Fernzeit (*'ôlam*) zur Fernzeit geht sein Blick, es gibt keine Zahl für seine Hilfe.
> (21) Niemand sage: „Dies ist schlechter als das!" Denn alles wird zu seiner Zeit kräftig (*jgbr*).

Es gibt also eine universale Vernetzung der Kreaturen und ihres jeweils zeitgemäßen in-Erscheinung treten. Die Zeitläufte bringen deshalb Gutes dem Guten und Böses dem Bösen. Dazu gehören Sturm als Zeit der Vernichtung, um einen Zorn Gottes zu stillen, aber auch Feuer, Hagel, Hunger, Pest, reißende Tiere und das Schwert der Rache:

> Alle diese sind zu ihrem Zweck (*ṣwrkm*) erschaffen; sie sind im Speicher aufbewahrt und warten auf die Zeit, in der sie losgelassen werden (V. 30).

Auch die Übel der Welt sind also unentbehrlich für den Fortgang der Schöpfung.

In einem weiteren Schöpfungshymnus 42,15-43,33 wird die Erkenntnis und Weisheit des Höchsten gerühmt, der „die Wechselfälle der Geschehnisse" (*ḥlypwt nhywt*; *G* interpretiert: „Er tut kund Vergangenes und Werdendes") kundtut. Sie entspringen der Macht dessen, der im Unterschied zu allen andern Wesen überzeitlich „einer ist von ferner Zeit (*'ôlam*) her, so daß nichts hinzugefügt und nichts hinweggenommen werden kann" (42,21). Das wird am Beispiel der astralen und metereologischen Erscheinungen erläutert. Die Sonne besticht zwar durch Schönheit und Herrlichkeit. Doch der Mond regelt die Wiederkehr der Zeiten, ihm kommt Herrschaft der Endzeit (? *qṣ*) zu, er ist „(dominierendes) Zeichen der Weltzeit (*'ôlam*); durch ihn werden Festzeiten wie (kalendarisch) festgelegte Zeiten (*zmny*) bestimmt" (43,6-8). Dem Preis

32. J. LIESEN, *Full of Praise. An Exegetical Study of Sir 39:12-35* (JSJS, 64), Leiden, Brill, 2000.
33. Zu *ṣwrk* M. JASTROW, *Dictionary of Talmud*, New York, 1903 (= 1950), S. 1271.

der über der Erde mächtigen Naturkräfte folgt die Rühmung der Herrlichkeit, mit der der Höchste die „Väter der Weltzeit (oder der Urzeit? *ʿôlam*) ausgestattet hat" (44,1f.); auch ihr Wirken gehört vermutlich zu den von Gott hervorgerufenen „Wechselfällen der Geschehnisse". Von einem Ende der universalen Zeit durch eine eschatologische Katastrofe und einem alles bisher gewesene übertreffenden neuen Aion ist nirgends ausdrücklich die Rede, wenn auch gelegentlich auf ein *ʾḥryt* der Zeit verwiesen wird (48,24).

Zusammenfassung. Ben Sira vermittelt seinen Lesern eine Chokma, die das von Gott an Israel gegebenen und im Pentateuch niedergelegten Gesetz einbegreift. Doch seine Aufgabe sieht er nicht in dessen strikter Auslegung; er ist in dieser Hinsicht kein Schriftgelehrter. Vielmehr schärft er über die schriftliche Überlieferung hinaus dem Schüler ein, daß zu einem moralisch rechtschaffenen Verhalten die angestrengte Reflexion auf die angemessene Situation für entsprechendes Handeln gehört. Über ältere Weisheitslehren hinaus kommt die Bedeutung der wechselnden Zeiten in Blick, die dem Weisen zugänglich wird, was ihm dann zu einem zeitgemäßen und dadurch gelingenden Leben verhilft.

Eine ähnliche Sicht von der Rolle der Zeit für menschliches Leben hatte vorher Qohälät vertreten, freilich ohne den Optimismus des Siraziden zu teilen; für ihn bleibt das Zeituniversum ein unzugängliches Geheimnis; das Gewahr-Werden der jeweiligen Zeitsituation aber bedarf gedanklicher Anstrengung, deren Gelingen das Genießen ein gottgeschenkten Anteils bedeutet[34].

Das göttliche Geheimnis der sich wandelnden Zeiten nach einer in Qumran gefundenen Instruktion

Einen weiteren aufschlußreichen Wandel in der Zeitauffassung läßt eine im Qumran gefundene Weisheitsschrift erkennen, die früher Sapiental Work A, jetzt von der offiziellen Veröffentlichung in DJD 34 *Mûsār lᵉMēvîn* „Instruktion für den Einsichtigen" (4Q415-418.423) genannt wird[35]. In Qumran ist sie durch 7-8 Handschriften aus herodia-

34. Der Eifer mancher Exegeten, die späte hebräische Weisheit durch hellenischen Einfluß geadelt zu sehen, führt dazu, auch das Ringen um das Verständnis der Zeit auf griechischen Einfluß zurückzuführen. Was MIDDENDORP, *Die Stellung Jesu Ben Siras* (Anm. 25), S. 14, dafür anzuführen vermag, ist mehr als kläglich: einen Ausspruch des Pittakos aus Lesbos aus dem 7. Jahrh. v. Chr.: „Erkenne die Zeit" und einen andern aus einer Komödie des Menandros im 4. Jahrh.: „Der rechte Zeitpunkt ist für jedes Vorhaben entscheidend".

35. J. STRUGNELL – D.J. HARRINGTON – T. ELGVIN, *Qumran Cave 4 XXIV Sapiental Texts, Part 2* (DJD, 34), Oxford, Clarendon, 1999. Vgl. A. LANGE, *Weisheit und Prädesti-*

nischer Zeit belegt, eine Zahl, die weit über die der älteren Weisheitsbücher wie Proverbien (2mal in Qumran), Qohälät (2mal) und auch Sirach (1mal) hinausgeht; für die Mitglieder des Jachad galt sie also eher als autoritativ und „kanonisch“ als die drei Vorhergenannten[36]. Dennoch war die Schrift wahrscheinlich nicht in Qumrankreisen entstanden, fehlt ihr doch die dafür bezeichnende Begrifflichkeit[37], vor allem eine auf das Gesetz ausgerichtete Frömmigkeit – der Terminus *tôrāh* taucht nirgends auf –; priesterliche Kategorien wie die Unterscheidung von Rein und Rein und Unrein spielen kaum eine Rolle; anders als auch bei Ben Sira fehlt eine national-kultische Ausrichtung auf Israel, den Zion u.ä.[38]. Von den Herausgebern des DJD-Bandes wird ihre Abfassung in die Zeit zwischen Proverbien und Sirach vermutet[39].

Wie in der älteren Weisheitsliteratur beginnen die einzelnen Teile der Schrift mit der Anrede eines anonymen Lehrers an seinen „Sohn“. Doch dazu gesellt sich, anders als früher, eine nähere Kennzeichnung des Angesprochenen als *mēvîn*, „Einsichtiger, zur Einsicht Bereiter“ (vielleicht auch „Einer, der Einsicht verbreite“?)[40]. Das klingt esoterisch und nimmt vorweg, daß der Inhalt der im Buch entfalteten Lehren oft als göttliches Geheimnis (*rāz,* ähnlich im Danielbuch) erklärt wird; Was hier niedergeschrieben wird, soll nicht wie die älteren Weisheitsschriften jedermann zugänglich sein, sondern gilt einem auserwählten Kreis. Ein auf Abgrenzung von der Masse der Menschen bedachtes elitäres Selbstbewußtsein dieser Weisen kündigt sich an.

1. Schon der mutmaßliche Anfang der nur unvollständig rekonstruierbaren und in ihrem Aufbau deshalb nicht durchsichtigen Schrift (416 1= 418 1.2[41]) läßt den Blick von der Einsetzung des Heeres des Himmels für Vorzeichen und Festzeiten bis hin zu einem künftigen Gericht über alles Werk der Frevelhaftigkeit (*ršʿh)* schweifen, von dem sich das göttliche Wohlgefallen am Geschick der „Söhne der Wahrheit“ abheben

nation (STDJ, 18), Leiden, Brill, 1995; J.J. COLLINS, *Jewish Wisdom in the Hellenistic Age* (OTL), Louisville, KY, Westminster John Knox, 1997; D.J. HARRINGTON, *Sapiental Work*, in EDSS S. 825f.; T. ELGVIN, *The Mystery to Come*, in F.H. CRYER – T.L. THOMPSON (Hgg.), *Qumran between the Old and the New Testaments* (JSOT.SS, 290), Sheffield, Sheffield Academic Press, 1998, S. 113-150; D.K. FALK, F. GARCÍA MARTÍNEZ, E.M. SCHULLER (Hgg.), *Sapiental, Liturgical and Poetical Texts from Qumran* (STDJ, 35), Leiden, Brill, 2000. Siehe auch die Beiträge von Collins, García Martínez und Harrington in diesem Band.

36. DJD, 34, S. 31.36.
37. Vgl. aber ELGVIN, *Mystery* (Anm. 35), 116-129.
38. DJD, 34, S. 21f.25-27; ELGVIN, *Mystery*, S.136f.
39. DJD, 34, S. 31.
40. DJD, 34, S. 549 s.v.
41. DJD, 34, S. 81-88; J. MAIER, *Die Qumran-Essener: Die Texte vom Toten Meer* II (UTB, 1863), München-Basel, 1995, S. 430f.

wird (Z. 10). Bereits hier reicht der zeitliche Rahmen über den von Proverbien und Sirach hinaus. Die Wahrheit als gute Weltordnung erscheint als ein wichtiger Faktor der Universalgeschichte, der zu jedem Menschen gelangt und für den sich der Mensch entscheiden kann und soll. Sie hat Anteil am göttlichen Wesen: der Gott der ʻÄmät war von der Vorzeit her *(mqdmywt)*[42] in Jahren der Weltzeit (?*ʿwlm)* tätig, um *ṣdq* aufzurichten mit der Unterscheidung von gut und böse (Z. 14f.). Die Wahrheit steht als göttliche Wirkungsgröße für diese Schrift im Vordergrund und weist die Weisheit in das zweite Glied[43]. Doch der Blick des Verfassers richtet sich vor allem auf eine endzeitliche Zukunft. Dereinst wird ein endgültiges himmlisches Urteil über das Werk des Frevels *(ršʿh)* ergehen und die (heilvolle) Endzeit der ʻÄmät sich vollenden *(šlm qṣ ʾmt)* (Z. 13f.). „The Sapiental Work differs most radically from the older wisdom teaching of Ben Sira und Qoheleth by his strong eschatological perspective"[44]. Innerhalb einer während der Jetztzeit in Wahrheit und Frevel gespaltenen Lebenswelt sucht also der Einsichtige und Weise nach Erkenntnis. Um dahin zu gelangen, hat er, wie in der Folge betont wird, auf das zu achten, was sich in der Geschichte jeweils zeitigt. Zugleich wird nach vorn geblickt, auf das himmlische Urteil über das Werk des Frevels und die endgültige Rechtfertigung der Söhne der Wahrheit.

In der Instruktion hebt eine der vermutlich ersten Ermahnungen das Achten auf Zeit und geschichtliches Geschehen als Vorbedingung jedes durch Erkenntnis gelenkten Handelns hervor:

417 1i [früher 2i] = 418 43-45[45]

(2) Blicke auf die Geheimnisse der Wunder des Gottes der Furchterregenden…
(3) Blicke auf das **Geheimnis der Geschehenden** (*rz nhyh*) und die Werke der Vorzeit (*qdm*),
was geworden und was im Werden ist…
(6) Bei Tag und Nacht meditiere das **Geheimnis des Geschehenden** und untersuche (es) beständig.
Dann erkennst du Wahrheit und Frevel/Bosheit.
Weisheit (7) und Torheit [begreifen wirst?] du,
(die Art des) Werk(es) bei all ihren Wegen,
zusammen mit ihrer (der Menschenwerke) Heimsuchung in allen Endphasen der Weltzeit (*qṣ ʿwlm*)

42. Vgl. K. Koch, *Qädäm. Heilsgeschichte als mythische Urzeit im Alten (und Neuen) Testament*, in *Spuren des hebräischen Denkens* (Anm. 17), S. 238-247.

43. Die Concordance in DJD listet 11mal *ḥokmāh* und 45mal *ʾæmæt,* S. 555.546.

44. Collins, *Jewish Wisdom* (Anm. 35), S. 127.

45. DJD, 34, S. 151-169; Übersetzungen: F. García Martínez, *The Dead Sea Scrolls Translated*, Leiden, Brill, 1994, 387; Maier, *Qumran-Essener* II (Anm. 41), S. 440f.; A. Lange, *Weisheit* (Anm. 35) S. 49-92.

und der Heimsuchung, (8) der letztendlichen (*ʿd*).
Dann erkennst du (den Unterschied) zwischen gut und böse gemäß ihren Taten.
Denn der Gott der Erkenntnis ist das Fundament der Wahrheit.
Im **Geheimnis des Geschehenden** hat er (9) herausgehoben/abgeteilt ihre Grundlagen
und ihre (der Wahrheit) Werke hat er … nach aller Weisheit
und mit aller Klugheit sie gebildet.

Der als Ziel der Erkenntnis betonte Antagonismus von Wahrheit und Frevel sowie – nachgeordnet – von Weisheit und Torheit wird in der Instruktion das zentrale Thema der Unterweisung. Um die Alternative beim eigenen Verhalten in Rechnung zu stellen, bedarf es der intensiven Besinnung auf das, was in der Welt geschieht bzw. sich als künftige Entwicklung andeutet. Insofern wird auch hier das Achten auf den Charakter der Zeit zum Kriterium weisen Verhaltens, wenngleich auf einer andern, weit weniger auf das je eigene Leben bezogenen Sicht heraus als bei Ben Sira. Was bei Qohälät für den Menschen schlechthin unerkennbar bleibt, für Sirach zwar nicht zu Tage liegt, aber dem, der über seine Erfahrungen nachdenkt, einsichtig wird, nämlich der Sinn des Zeituniversums, gilt hier als ein Geheimnis Gottes, das anscheinend einer besonderen Enthüllung und Meditation bedarf, aber dann zum Leitfaden gelungenen Lebens wird.

2. Gleich dreimal taucht im zitierten Text die Wendung *Rāz Nihyæh* auf, die ich „Geheimnis des Geschehenden" übersetzt habe. In der gesamten Instruktion taucht „almost uniquely the fixed phrase" 32mal auf, und das auch im Zusammenhang von „teachings about ethics and eschatology". Parallel dazu werden Pluralverbindungen wie „Geheimnisse der Wunder (Gottes), Geheimnisse der Erkenntnis, Geheimnisse Els" verwendet[46]. Die erstgenannte Wendung wird rund 20mal mit Imperativen verbunden, die zur Reflexion über sie auffordern: „Gewinne Einsicht über es *(bjn)*, untersuche *(drš)*, meditiere *(drš)*, begreife *(lqḥ)*, erschaue *(nb hi.)* das Geheimnis". Es wird weiter in Aussicht gestellt, daß Gott (oder die Eltern?) für es „das Ohr öffnen", es wird also verbal tradiert. Das universale Geheimnis ist nach 417 ii 13f. im Himmel schriftlich in einem „Buch der Erinnerung" als „Vision der Meditation" niedergelegt. Harrington vermutet deshalb als irdische Kopie ein „body of teaching" in fixierter Fassung, „an extrabiblical compendium"[47].

46. DJD, 34, S. 28f.32.
47. D.J. HARRINGTON, *The Raz nihyeh in a Qumran Wisdom Text*, in *RQ* 17 (1996) 549-553, S. 552.

Der Genetiv wird gegenwärtig von den Experten unterschiedlich wiedergegeben und erklärt. *nhyh* ist wohl nicht Perfekt, sondern Partizip des Niph'al von *hyh*, „werden, entstehen", vielleicht mit einer passiven Konnotation: das, *was nicht aus sich selbst heraus* sich entwickelt, *sondern* kontingent geschieht, *von anderswoher zustande gebracht* wird (vgl. 1Kön 1,27; 12,24).

Als Partizip zeigt es keine Zeitstufe eindeutig an. J. Maier bevorzugt eine präteritale Entsprechung: „das Mysterium von Gewordenem", dafür läßt sich vor allem anführen, das parallel dazu von Werken der Vorzeit die Rede ist[48]. In der DJD-Fassung übersetzen Strugnell und Harrington futurisch „the mystery that is to come", da häufig im Zusammenhang auf die endzeitliche Heimsuchung verwiesen werde und erklären es zu einem „guide for the future and for action now"[49]. Doch nicht nur Anfang oder/und Ende der Zeit scheinen gemeint zu sein, sondern auch die dazwischen ablaufende Geschichte, „das Kommen der Jahre und das Vergehen der Perioden" (418 123 iii 2-8), alle Taten, die Gott tut und getan hat (417 ii 13). García Martínez wählt eine zeitneutrale Aussage: „the mystery of existence"[50]; ähnlich A. Lange mit der Übersetzung „das Geheimnis des Werdens"; er erklärt dies dann als „das Ordnungsinstrument, mit und nach dem die Schöpfung geordnet wird", und deshalb als „Welt- und Schöpfungsordnung, die ethische und historische Komponenten enthält und sich dereinst im Eschaton erfüllt"[51].

Aufschlußreich sind einige Stellen, wo das Geheimnis des Geschehenden mit einzelnen Ereignissen verbunden und dadurch konkretisiert wird. Die Instruktion kommt dann – gemäß der Weisheit in der Art von Sira und Qohälät – auf naturhafte und gesellschaftliche Vorgänge und Verhältnisse zu sprechen, denen das Individuum ausgesetzt ist. Ein Beispiel bietet ein längeres Textstück mit der wiederholten Anrede an den Leser „Du bist arm/bedürftig"; in ihm wird das Geheimnis des Geschehenden mit individueller Lebenserfahrung so verbunden, das es nicht nur dessen prekäre ökonomische Lage als ein von Gott bestimmtes Erbteil *(naḥ^{a}lah)* bedingt hat, sondern auch die entsprechende moralischen Folgerung nahelegt: „Du sollst nicht begehren, was nicht dein Erbteil" (417 2 iii 8). Schon seine Geburt durch ein bestimmtes Elternpaar war durch das Geheimnis des Geschehenden vorherbestimmt, was wieder eine entsprechende Verpflichtung für das Kind bedeutet (416 2 iii 14-19 nach DJD, S. 110-113):

48. Ähnlich im Buch der Mysterien 4Q300 3 = 127 1 i.
49. So mit sehr knapper Begründung DJD, 34, S. 32.
50. GARCÍA MARTÍNEZ, *Dead Sea Scrolls* (Anm. 45), S. 387 u.ö.
51. LANGE, *Weisheit* (Anm. 35), S. 59f.

(14b) Das **Geheimnis des Geschehenden** untersuche,
und gewinne Einsicht in alle Wege der Wahrheit.
Und alle Wurzeln der Bosheit (15) betrachte!
Dann erkennst du, was bitter für einen Menschen und süß für einen Mann.
Ehre deinen Vater trotz deiner Bedürftigkeit, (16) und deine Mutter bei deinem ‚geringen Stand(?)'.
Denn was ‚Gott' für einen Mann ist, ist (ihm zunächst) sein Vater.
Und was Herrschaft (*'dnym*) für eine Person ist, ist (ihm) seine Mutter.
Denn (17) sie sind der Schmelztiegel deiner Zeugung[52].
Und wie er sie läßt herrschen über dich und dich gebildet gemäß der Ruach,
so diene ihnen!
Und wie (18) er[53] geöffnet dein Ohr für das **Geheimnis des Geschehenden**,
so ehre sie um deiner Ehre willen...
(19) um deines Lebens willen und der Länge der Tage.

Durch das von Gott beschlossene, allumspannende Zeituniversum erhält also das je eigene Leben seine Konturen einschließlich der sozialen Einbettung. Wo das erkannt wird, ergeben sich die ethische Folgerungen von selbst. Nicht nur als natürlicher Ursprung, sondern auch mit ihrer hierarchischen Autorität gehören die Eltern zu dem als verbindlich dem Leben vorgegebenen *nihyæh*. Ebenso wird zur Fürsorge für Weib und Kind auch bei Armut aufgerufen, aber gewarnt, sich dadurch von der Besinnung auf den *Rāz Nihyæh* ablenken zu lassen (416 20f.). Wie bei Sirach wird also die Beachtung der Zeitverhältnisse zur Voraussetzung für moralisch „gerechtes" Verhalten, wenngleich jetzt unter einem sehr viel weiteren Horizont.

Zum Lauf der Weltgeschichte äußert sich kein uns erhaltener Text der Instruktion. Immerhin gehört nach einer sehr fragmentarisch erhaltenen Zeile (418 77,2) zur Erkenntnis des Geheimnis des Geschehenden das Begreifen der *tôl^{e}dot 'adam*; die Wendung entspricht der Überschrift der „Nachkommensgeschichte Adams" als erste Epoche der Menschheitsgeschichte Gen 5,1. (Allerdings halten Strugnell – Harrington eine solche Bezugnahme für „unlikely" und übersetzen *tôl^{e}dot* gegen den üblichen Sprachgebrauch als „nature/characteristics"[54].)

52. Übersetzung nach MAIER, *Qumran-Essener* II (Anm. 41), S. 34, GARCÍA MARTÍNEZ, *Dead Sea Scrolls* (Anm. 45): „the oven of your origin"; DJD, 34, S. 113.121: „The womb that was pregnant with thee".

53. DJD, 34, S. 113.122 ändert in den Plural „they" *(glw)*.

54. Die Übersetzer von DJD, 34, S. 297f. berufen sich auf 1QS III 13. Dort wird ermahnt, die Söhne des Lichts in den *twldwt kwl bnj 'iš* und den Taten der Generationen zu unterrichten, was CHARLESWORTH, *The Dead Sea Scrolls: Rule of the Community*, Philadelphia, PA, 1996, S. 58 mit „the nature of all the sons of man" wiedergibt. GARCÍA MARTÍNEZ, *Dead Sea Scrolls* (Anm. 45), S. 6, bevorzugt „the history of all the sons of man"; dem entsprechen LANGE, *Weisheit* (Anm. 35), S. 59: „die Geschichte der Menschheit" und MAIER, *Qumran-Essener* I (Anm. 41), S. 173: „Die Werdegänge (Ursprünge, Geschichte) aller Mannessöhne", und das sind vielleicht doch für die „Sektenregel" zutreffendere Übersetzungen.

3. Der Ausdruck *Nihyæh* war wahrscheinlich ein den intendierten Lesern der Instruktion vertrauter weisheitlicher Begriff für die Abfolge von Zeitstufen mit stark wechselnden Rahmenbedingungen für menschliches Glück oder Unglück, wie sie von jedem erfahren und in ihrem Sinn undurchsichtig bleiben. In diesem Sinn verwendet auch Ben Sira den Begriff, allerdings im Plural und ohne von einem Geheimnis zu sprechen. Im Hymnus über die durch das Wort entstandenen Schöpfungswerke Gottes und das damit verbundene göttliche Walten von den Anfängen des Kosmos bis zur Gegenwart heißt es (42,18-25):

> Der Höchste erkennt, er blickt auf die kommenden Ereignisse der Weltzeit (*'tjwt ʿwlm)*,
> tut kund die Wenden[55] der geschehenden Ereignisse (*ḥlpwt nhjwt)*,
> offenbart die Erforschung des Verborgenen...
> (21) Einer ist er von ferner Zeit *(ʿwlm)* her,
> nichts kann hinzugefügt oder weggenommen werden...
> (24) Nichts unter ihnen hat er nutzlos erschaffen[56].
> (25) Das eine wechselt mit dem andern nach seinem (je besonderen) Vorzug (*ṭwb*).

Die wechselnden Nihyot sind also der Motor des Weltlaufs, die im Gefälle der Seinsgeschichte ihren verborgenen Sinn haben. Der Begriff meint also nicht die Abschnitte einer neutralen Geschehenskette, sondern deren je andere inhaltliche Füllung (analog zu Qoh 3,1-9?), mit je verborgenen und dennoch immer guten Zweck, auch wenn ihn die betroffenen Menschen gewöhnlich nicht durchschauen. Der Weise jedoch vermag ihn durch Nachforschung zuerkennen und seiner Entscheidung zu Grunde zu legen, ob hinsichtlich des ganzen *ʿwlm* oder nur der für ihn persönlich belangreichen Jetztzeit, bleibt unklar. Dazu bedarf es freilich einer Perspektive für die zukünftige Entwicklungen, wie sie profetische Offenbarungen eröffnen. Ein Beispiel bietet Jesaja (nach Sir 48,24f.):

> Mit dem Geist der Kraft erschaute er die Endzeit (*'ḥryt*)
> und tröstete die Trauenernden Zions.
> Bis zur Fernzeit (*ʿwlm)* tat er kund die (Kette der) Geschehnisse (*nhywt*)
> und die Verborgenen (Ereignisse), bevor sie eintrafen.

Schon bei Qohälät war das vorher im Hebräischen meist als eine Art Hilfsverb gebrauchte HYH bereits zu einem für das Selbstverständnis

55. *HAL*, S. 306 übersetzt hingegen: „Vergangenheit". So auch SAUER, *Jesus Sirach* (Anm. 25), S. 610, Anm. 19a, der nach einer Randlesart in MS[B] und LXX eine Kopula zwischen beiden Nomina einschiebt. Der Sprachgebrauch in 4QInstr spricht jedoch für den ursprünglichen Text von MS[B].

56. Ergänzt nach MS[M].

entscheidenden Existenz- und Energiebegriff geworden, vor allem in der 14mal auftauchenden Kombination *šæhayah/šæyihyæh*[57]. Nicht aus bloßer Wißbegierde, nicht aus einem rein musealen Interesse heraus, sondern wegen der Wirkung der Zeitabschnitte auf die eigene Existenz belastet die Unerkennbarkeit der zeitlichen Strukturen aller Wirklichkeit den Menschen (7,24; 8,7):

> Fern ist, was geschehen ist, und tief, tief, wer kann es begreifen?
> Er erkennt nicht, was (eigentlich) geschehen ist; denn – wie es geschah, wer sollte es ihm mitteilen?

Auf weisheitlichen Einfluß läßt schließen, daß auch in Schriften, die innerhalb des *Yaḥad* von Qumran entstanden sind, *Nihyæh* eine gewichtige Rolle spielt. Der Sänger der Schlußhymne der Gemeinderegel weiß zu rühmen (1QS XI 3f.18; vgl. Z.11):

> Aus der Quelle seiner (göttlichen) Erkenntnis hat er sein Licht eröffnet,
> so daß mein Auge seine Wunder schaute
> und meines Herzens Erleuchtung das **Geheimnis des Geschehenden** (*nhyh*)
> und des Seienden der Weltzeit (*whww' ʿwlm)*[58]...
> (18) Alles Geschehende (*nhyh*) entstand (*hyh*) durch sein Wohlgefallen.

Nach der Damaskusschrift fällt dem Mebaqqer in der Versammlung die Aufgabe zu, „Gottes wunderbare Großtaten und die Geschehnisse der Weltzeit (*nhywt ʿwlm*)“ feierlichvorzutragen[59]. Für die Kriegsrolle gehört auch der Verlauf der Geschichte Israels zu allem, „was geschieht und zum Geschehen gebracht wird“ (*hwwh wyhyh*). In den Schriften der Qumraniten scheint demnach der vergangenheitliche Aspekt im Vordergrund zu stehen. An Sirachs Zeitverständnis erinnern, wenn der Schlußhymnus gelobt, Gottes „Gesetz nach der Richtschnur der Zeiten (*ḥq bqw ʿittîm*)“ zu beachten (1QS X 25f.).

Auf diesem sprachgeschichtlichen Hintergrund werden die Herkunft des Begriffs und dessen neuartiger Gebrauch in den Instruktionen deutlich. Während bei Qohälät die Nipḥʿal-Verbindung von *hyh* noch nicht gebräuchlich war, obwohl die entsprechende Zeitidee schon in Ansätzen vorlag, gebrauchen Ben Sira und die Damaskusschrift den Plural Nihyot

57. 1,9.11; 2,7.18; 3,15.22; 6,3.10.24; 8,7; 10,14; 12,9; in gleicher Bedeutung durch Kombination mit *ᵃšær* 1,16; 4,16.

58. In CHARLESWORTH, *The Dead Sea Scrolls* (Anm. 54), S. 131 übersetzt H. Lichtenberger „des ewigen Werdens“. Doch der Begriff der Ewigkeit schließt ein Werden aus, und eine Paradoxie ist vom Verfasser nicht beabsichtigt.

59. CD XIII 8. Wiedergaben wie „ewige Geschehnisse“ (MAIER, *Qumran-Essener* I [Anm. 41], S. 27) oder „eternal events“ (GARCÍA MARTÍNEZ, *Dead Sea Scolls* [Anm. 45], S. 43) scheinen mir wieder einen Widerspruch in sich auszudrücken, denen man antiken Autoren nicht unterstellen sollte.

für die Abfolge der vom Schöpfer vorzeitlich geschaffenen unterschiedlichen, oft gegensätzlichen Zeitarten.

In den Instruktionen wird daraus ein Singular als Bezeichnung des mit der Welt geschaffenen und in ihr verlaufenden Zeituniversums. Demnach entspringt alles in der Zeit Geschehende (*nhyh*) einer verborgenen substanziellen Einheit, die als Prozeß abläuft, der bei Anbeginn der Welt geschaffen und festgelegt worden war und den basalen Werken der Vorzeit eine dauerhafte Grundlage und Wirkung bereitet hat, sowie alle künftige Entwicklung des menschlichen Geschicks bis zur eschatologischen Vollendung aus sich heraussetzt[60].

Das Gesamtgeschehen war in seinem Ablauf schon vor aller Zeit von Gott festgelegt. Zur anfänglichen Schöpfung gehörte bereits die Prädestination menschlichen Geschicks, allerdings mit einer Schlagseite zur *'Ämät* hin; nur deren Werke und Wirkung hat der Schöpfer von Anfang an vorherbestimmt; jede gute Tat eines Menschen ist also nicht allein sein eigenes Werk, sondern durch die universale Wirkgröße *'Ämät* vorbereitet worden. Hinsichtlich des Frevels hingegen war anscheinend nur die nachfolgende Bestrafung in den Phasen der Weltzeit und endgültig beim Jüngsten Gericht vorherbestimmt, nicht die Initiativen zum bösen Tun.

Neu ist auch in der Instruktion, daß das Geschehende in seiner Gesamtheit wie in seinen vielen Stufen als Geheimnis bezeichnet wird. Der innere Zusammenhang von Zeit und Geschichte ist letztlich nur dem Gott der Erkenntnisse deutlich und bewußt, doch die Einsichtigen vermögen durch ihr meditatives Nachdenken den Charakter dieses Geheimnisses zu entschlüsseln, wenigstens so weit das Wissen für das rechtschaffenes Verhalten unentbehrlich ist.

Als Ergebnis seiner Untersuchung des Begriffs *Rāz Nihyœh* hatte Ringgren schon 1977 festgehalten[61]: „Alles, was mit Sicherheit gesagt werden kann, ist, daß die Zusammenstellung alles, was überhaupt geschieht, bezeichnen soll. Dagegen scheint es klar zu sein, daß *hājāh* hier nicht das bloße sein oder die Existenz, sondern das Geschehen und Werden bezeichnet". Zu einem entsprechenden Ergebnis kommt wieder Collins 1997:[62] „the entire divine plan, from creation to eschatological punishment". Das hat Elgvin 1998[63] weitergeführt: „*Rāz Nihyeh* is a

60. Der Singular *nihyœh* ähnelt in seiner Zuspitzung dem deutschen Begriff „Geschichte", der früher im Plural gebräuchlich war und das, „was geschicht" zum Ausdruck brachte. Erst ab Ende des 18. Jahrh. wird der Singular zu einer „Vergangenheit, Gegenwart und Zukunft umfassenden Bewegungskategorie"; J. MEHLHAUSEN, in *TRE* 12, 1984, S. 644.

61. *TWAT* 2, S. 401f.

62. *Jewish Wisdom* (Anm. 35), S. 122.

63. ELGVIN, *Mystery* (Anm. 35), S. 135.

comprehensive word for God's mysterious plan for creation and history, his plan for man and for redemption of the elect". Dem läßt er den bedeutungsvollen Satz folgen: „It is 'salvation history' in a wider meaning". Das trifft in der Tat zu, wenn unter „Heilsgeschichte" nicht eine Geschichte völlig eigener Art, eine exklusive biblische Offenbarungsgeschichte im Gegensatz zur allgemeinen, säkularen Weltgeschichte gemeint wird, sondern die Menschheitsgeschichte insgesamt zur Heilsgeschichte erklärt wird. Eine Veranschaulichung dieser Konzeption wäre nicht im Lob der Vätergeschichte bei Ben Sira zu finden, sondern eher die Vier-Monarchien-Sukzession in der danielischen Apokalyptik. Interpretiert man das Zeitverständnis der Instruktion in dieser Weise, zeigt sich hier ein Zweig der späten Weisheit auf einem entschiedenen Weg zur Apokalyptik. Damit stellt sich die Schrift in einen deutlichen Gegensatz zu Qohälät, für den ein Mensch Anfang und Ende des göttlichen *ʿôlam* nicht nur niemals erfassen kann, sondern auch darauf keine Gedanken verschwenden soll[64].

Für die in Qumran gelesene Instruktion hingegen läuft der *ʿôlam* trotz erschreckendem Leid und Unheil einer Vollendung von Wahrheit und Gerechtigkeit zu, und alles dem Menschen so oft chaotisch erscheinende Werden ist in seinem Gefälle schon in der Schöpfung vorherbestimmt worden. Was gegenwärtig als Wirklichkeit erlebt wird, ist geprägt durch die dualistische Spaltung eines guten und eines bösen Kraftfelds, dem von Wahrheit und dem von Bosheit, die ihre Wirkung je nach der anfallenden Zeit entfalten. Doch sie wird verschwinden. Die Erwählten werden zur künftigen Vollendung gelangen, wenn sie dem geheimnisvolle Werden – in der Geschichte und wohl auch der Natur – nachspüren und es durch ihr Handeln in Wahrheit internalisieren.

Von Gott oder Menschen festgelegte Zeiten in der Sicht des Danielbuchs

Während die späten Weisheitsbücher über die Geschichtlichkeit des individuellen Lebens nachsinnen, werden in der apokalyptischen Literatur die Epochen des Volkes im Rahmen einer Menschheitsgeschichte zum Anlaß für Visionen und Deutungen, die über die epochalen Zeiten hinaus vor allem das eschatologische Ende der Weltzeit in den Blick nehmen. Die Differenz zur Weisheit hangt mit einer unterschiedlichen

64. Stärker noch ist der Widerspruch zu einem modernen Lebensgefühl, daß den steten Wandel der Verhältnisse als bedrohlich und unerwünscht empfindet, jeden Fortschritt zum Bessseren in der Weltgeschichte ablehnt, das Stigma der Vergänglichkeit als dumpfes Schicksal fürchtet und verdrängt, und den Gegensatz von Wahrheit und Frevel relativiert.

Haltung zur politischen und kultischen Zeitgeschichte zusammen, nicht zuletzt aber mit einem historischen Einschnitt durch die schwere Krise, welche die hellenisierenden Kultreform in den 60er Jahren des zweiten Jahrhunderts v. Chr. hervorgerufen hatte. Während die Weisheitslehrer der persischen und der ersten 1 1/2 Jahrhunderte der griechischen Epoche sich mit der Herrschaft ausländischer Großkönige abgefunden und mit der herrschenden priesterlichen Klasse im eigenen Volk sich arrangiert hatten, leiden die Apokalyptiker unter einer schier unerträglichen Fremdherrschaft und mißtrauen der Tempelhierarchie bis hin zum Vorwurf, daß sie den heiligen Bund verlassen hat (Dan 11,30).

Bezeichnenderweise verliert Ben Sira kein Wort über die seleukidische Oberherrschaft und glorifiziert Hohenpriester und Tempel (Sir 50), während Daniel die hellenistischen Königreiche als ein Untier erschaut, das alles frißt und zermalmt (Dan 7,7.19), und den Tempel als scheußlich entweiht beklagt[65]. Das nötigt dazu, nach der kollektiven Zeit zu fragen und von da aus nach einer entscheidenden künftigen Wende Ausschau zu halten, und erlaubt nicht mehr, individuelles Geschick und seine spezifischen zeitlichen Rahmenbedingungen in den Mittelpunkt der Botschaft zu stellen. Allerdings ist damit zu rechnen, daß in apokalyptischen Kreisen schon vorher Weichen in dieser Richtung gestellt worden waren, lassen doch schon die vormakkabäischen aramäischen Daniellegenden eine herrschaftskritische Haltung erkennen. Andrerseits gibt es nach der Makkabäerzeit weisheitliche Schriften ohne solche Absicht; die Sapientia Salomonis mahnt die Regierenden mit sehr verhaltener Kritik (Sap 6,1-21) und das erste Baruchbuch ruft ohne Bedenken zur politischen Unterordnung auf (1,11; 2,21). Das führt zu einem unterschiedlichen Urteil der Autoren über die Art der epochalen Zeiten. Für die Apokalyptiker erhält die Abfolge nicht nur der Volks-, sondern der Menschheitsgeschichte dadurch eine Sinn, daß ihr Gefälle auf eine Endzeit des Frevels zuläuft, die alles übersteigt, was vorher in der Geschichte sich ereignet hatte, die eine Katastrofe von nie dagewesenem Ausmaß durch ein göttliches Eingreifen hervorrufen wird, dem dann aber nach Auferstehung der Toten und Weltgericht ein von Heil erfüllter neuer Aion folgen wird. Das soll am Beispiel des Danielbuchs verdeutlicht werden.

1. Die nacheinander entstandenen Teile des Danielbuchs lassen ein zunehmendes Interesse an Art und Maß geschichtlicher und künftiger

65. Ebenso veranschaulicht Henoch die Diadochen als Adler und andere Raubtiere, welche den Israeliten als Schafen die Augen aushacken und ihr Fleisch fressen, und lehnt den Zweiten Tempel als von vornherein unrein ab (1Hen 89,73; 90,2-4.8.11.28).

Zeiten erkennen, und zwar im Blick auf *Epochen* der Weltgeschichte. In den älteren *aramäischen* Visionen wird die Zeit vom Untergang eines israelitisch-jüdischen Königtums bis zur eschatologischen Kehre auf vier Epochen verteilt, in denen je eine globale Supermacht beherrschend den Weltauf bestimmt; die Abfolge wird in Dan 2 als vierteiliger Metallkoloß, in Dan 7 als vier dem Völkermeer entsteigende Fabelwesen versinnbildlicht. Zwar wird das Nacheinander (*batar* 2,39f.; 7,6f.) der Großmächte erwähnt, doch ohne Angabe von Jahreszahlen. Eine solche Befristung wird bei Gott vorausgesetzt, aber sie wird an dieser Stelle selbst einem Daniel nicht offenbar (2,20-23):

> Es sei der Name des ‚großen' Gottes gesegnet von der (vergangenen) fernen Zeit (*ʿalam*) bis zur (künftigen) fernen Zeit; denn Weisheit und Stärke sind ihm eigen.
> Er aber ist es. der verschieden werden läßt die meßbare Zeit (*z^{e}man*) und die inhaltlich gefüllte Zeit (*ʿiddan*),
> absetzt Könige und einsetzt,
> verleiht Weisheit den Weisen und Erkenntnis denen, die Einsicht erkennen wollen.
> Er ist es, der enthüllt die Tiefen und die verborgenen Dinge.

Die göttliche Steuerung der Zeiten und Herrschaften war vorher von Daniel als ein Geheimnis bezeichnet worden, das ihm dann in der Folge offenbart wird, soweit es zu einem der Situation angemessenen Handeln nicht für ihn, sondern vor allem für den Großkönig zu wissen nötig ist (2,19 vgl. 27-30). Der Sinn des göttlichen Programms wird von seinem Ende her einsichtig, dem „Abschluß der Tage" (*ʾaḥ^{a}rît yômayya)*; dann wird diese Art von Herrschaft des Menschen über den Menschen verschwinden und ein andersartiges göttliches Reich wird für (unabsehbar viele) Fernzeiten (*ʿal^{e}mîn)* heraufziehen (2,28.44). Die Gesamtheit solcher „Fernzeiten" wird in Kap. 7 den Heiligen (der) Höchsten zugewiesen (V. 17); das erweckt, da neben den künftigen anscheinend eine vergangene Zeit dieser Art vorausgesetzt wird, den Anschein, daß die gesamte Menschheitsgeschichte von Adam bis zum Ende des vierten Weltreichs als ein einziger *ʿalam* angesehen wurde[66].

Innerhalb der Epoche der Weltreiche können Zeitabschnitte aufeinander folgen, die durch eine Sieben-Zahl oder ihre Hälfte aus dem üblichen Lauf der Dinge herausragen, so die Dauer des Wahnsinns Nebukadnez-

66. Wenn Nebukadnezzar nach den wunderhaften Interventionen des israelitischen Gottes diesen rühmt: „Sein Reich ist ein Reich des *ʿalam*" (3,33; vgl. 4,31) bedeutet des letzte Ausdruck in seinem Mund wohl nicht „Ewigkeit" (oder ein entsprechendes Adjektiv), sondern „everlasting" (NRSV) oder sogar „Reich der (derzeitigen) Weltzeit". Der Perser Dareios geht einen Schritt in seiner Einsicht weiter, wenn er den Gott als den preist, der „für Fernzeiten (plural) besteht" (6,27).

zars mit 7 oder die der Entweihung des Tempels mit 3 1/2 *ʿiddanîn* (4,13.20.22.29; 7,25)[67]. Solche Zeitpunkte gelten aber als kontingente göttliche Setzung, nicht als vorgegebene Teilstruktur einer Weltepoche (anders das hebräische Verständnis in 9,24-27). Sie gehen nicht in jedem Fall auf einen göttlichen Entscheid zurück, sondern können der Laune eines Großkönigs entspringen, so beim *ʿiddan* für das Erschallen der Instrumente beim großen Weiheakt Nebukadnezzars (3,5.7f.), oder wenn ein für babylonische Weise günstiger Termin angeordnet wird (2,8f.), im Fall Daniels wird bei solchem Anlaß von *z^eman* gesprochen (2,16). Wo allerdings ein König (wie Antiochos IV.) sich anheischig macht, durch die Schöpfung gesetzte *zimnîn* zu verändern, was wohl auf die Einführung eines hellenistischen Kalendersystems anspielt (und die Abschaffung eines durch die Siebenzahl ausgezeichneten 364-Tage-Jahrs?), macht er sich des schwersten Frevels schuldig (7,25). Seine Maßnahmen hindern Menschen, das Gebot der kultischen Zeiten zur rechten Gottesverehrung wahrzunehmen. Vorausgesetzt wird sicher nicht, daß Menschen keine „profane" Art von Zeit anordnen dürfen, doch es gibt heilige Zeiten, die als unverrückbar gelten.

Weitere herausragende wie auch (kalendarische?) festgelegte Zeiten werden im aramäischen Danielteil vielleicht nach der eschatologischen Wende noch erwartet, denn beim endgültigen Gottesgericht wird das vierte Weltreich vernichtet, den drei andern aber ein Fortbestehen bis *z^eman w^eʿiddan* gewährt (7,12); vor allem aber werden weitere *ʿalmayya* erwartet (2,44; 6,27; 7,18).

In den aramäischen Danielkapiteln schiebt sich also das Problem der Zeit im Blick auf die längeren Epochen und die in ihnen herausragenden situativen Ereignisse der politischen Geschichte als Rahmenbedingung menschlicher Freiheit zum Handeln in den Vordergrund, mehr aber noch die Konzeption einer alle Zeitabschnitte umgreifenden Weltzeit, deren Gefälle unabwendbar auf eine eschatologischer Kehre zuläuft. Diese wird hinüberführen zu einem unvergänglichen Friedens- und Heilsreich, das aber auf Erden sich verwirklicht und in dem sich deshalb die Zeitlichkeit als notwendige Struktur von Welt in *ʿalmayya* fortsetzen wird.

2. Während der Religionswirren in der ersten Hälfte des 2. Jahrh.s werden die *hebräischen* Danielkapitel dem aramäischen Grundstock angefügt. Sie weisen eine abgewandelte Begrifflichkeit und wohl auch ein

67. Vielleicht wird in Dan 1,1 die erste Exilierung von Judäern in das dritte Jahr Jojakims verlegt, um das Zehnfache von Sieben als Summe der Jahre bis zum Kyrosedikt 538 v.Chr. nach 2Chr 36,6f. anzusetzen; K. KOCH, *Daniel* (BKAT, 22/1), Neukirchen-Vluyn, Neukirchener Verlag, 1986, S. 29f.

verändertes Bewußtsein von der Bedeutung der Zeit im Menschenleben auf. Das hebräische Lexem *ʿet* spielt eine größere Rolle im Kontext als die aramäische Entsprechung *ʿiddan* in Dan 1-7; ein Begriff für „Endzeit" taucht auf und gewinnt große Bedeutung; dagegen tritt *ʿôlam* als umfassender Ausdruck, verglichen mit aramäisch *ʿalam,* etwas in den Hintergrund und wird fast nur als Singular verwendet.

Der Abriß der Diadochengeschichte in Kap. 11gebraucht den Plural *ʿittîm* für Zeitabschnitte, in der einzelne Herrscher regieren oder siegen oder unterliegen (11,6bis.13.24). Der Singular *ʿet* kann die lange Dauer der Verwüstung Jerusalems durch 62 Jahrsiebente bedeuten (9,25); vor allem aber verweist er auf die bevorstehende Endphase der Weltgeschichte mit den Wendungen *ʿæt-qeś* oder *ʿet hahîʾ* (8,17; 11,40; 12,1; vgl. *qeṣ hayyamîn* 12,13). In ihr wird sich ein letzter Frevelkönig erheben, dann aber durch Gottes Eingreifen jede Form irdischer Herrschaftssysteme verschwinden.

Vorausgehen werden der großen Wende (ähnlich wie im aramäischen 7,25) 3 1/2 von Gott verordnete Zeiten (*môʿadîm* 12,7) der Entweihung des Tempels und Unterdrückung des Volkes, vor allem aber Beseitigung des für den Verkehr des Bundesvolkes mit Gott unentbehrliche Tamid-Opfer um die Zeit des Morgens. Als die Hälfte eines Jahrsiebent (9,27) werden die dreieinhalb Jahre geweissagt, in denen der Gott des Jersualemer Tempels und seine Opfer mit den Riten eines Zeus Olympios verschmolzen worden waren. Wie wichtig die Zeitspanne für den Verfasser gewesen ist, zeigt sich daran, daß die Abschnitte der Entweihung an andern Stellen mit 2300 Abend-Morgen (8,14), 1290 (12,11) oder 1335 Tagen berechnet werden[68].

Ausschlaggebender als andere Zeitabschnitte sind für das hebräische Danielbuch die Siebener-Einheiten der Weltzeit. Anders als in den aramäischen Texten gehören *šabûʿîm* zur Struktur der Schöpfung. Die Uminterpretation einer Weissagung Jeremias (25,11f.; 29,10) über eine Dauer von 70 Jahren der Zerstörung Jerusalems in 9,24-27 weissagt 70 Siebente = 490 Jahre der Verwüstung der Stadt bis zur eschatologischen Umwälzung und zur Durchsetzung einer für immer andauernden „Gerechtigkeit" und unterteilt sie für die persische und hellenistische Epoche in kleinere Sieben-Einheiten; dabei wird anfangs darauf hingewiesen, daß diese Zeitspanne (von Gott) „herausgeschnitten sei"[69], doch

68. Zur Umrechnung der Tageszählungen in Monate und Jahre sowie ihr Verhältnis zu den 3 1/2 Zeiten s. zuletzt G. BOCCACCINI, *The Solar Calendars of Daniel and Enoch,* in J.J. COLLINS – P.W. FLINT (Hgg.), *The Book of Daniel* (SVT, 83), Leiden, Brill, 2001, II, S. 311-328.

69. So ist wohl das hebräische *hapax legomena* nach dem Aramäischen zu übersetzen; vgl. JASTROW, *Dictionary* (Anm. 32), S. 513.

wohl aus einem größeren Zeitkontinuum. Die Aussage findet in der sogenannten Zehn-Wochen-Apokalypse des 1.Henochbuchs eine Erklärung, wo jedem der 10 *šabûʿîm* der Weltzeit anscheinend die Dauer von 490 Jahren zugeschrieben wird[70].

Wo das hebräische Lexem *ʿôlam* im Blick auf das Geschick von Welt und Mensch gebraucht wird, bezieht es sich auf die ferne und doch nun näherrückende Zeit der eschatologischen Umwälzung. Dann wird eine heilvolle „Gerechtigkeit" für unabsehbare Zeiten (*ṣædæq ʿolamîm* 9,24) sich durchsetzen, für die Frommen ein Leben mit unendlicher Dauer und für die Frevler ein entsprechender Abscheu (*ḥayê ʿôlam, dirʾôn ʿôlam*) zu Tage treten; dagegen werden die, die andern zum guten Leben verholfen haben, wie die Sterne für immer und ewig (*leʿôlam waʿad*) leuchten (12,2f.). Einzig im Blick auf Gott wird durch den Titel „Der Lebendige des *ʿôlam*" ein größerer Bedeutungsradius angezeigt; gemeint ist wohl keine Zeittranszendenz im Sinn des modernen Begriffs Ewigkeit, sondern ein die Weltzeit kennzeichnendes und über sie hinausweisendes Zeitkontinuum von Zeit und Welt.

Abschliessende Erwägung zur Schöpfung als Einheit von Zeit und Welt

Das für das biblische Zeitverständnis zentrale Lexem *ʿôlam* hat ausweislich der untersuchten Schriften spätestens in hellenistischer Zeit eine bedeutsame Ausweitung seiner Bedeutung erfahren. Im älteren Hebräisch war es doppelpolig konnotiert, drückte eine ferne Zeit sowohl in der Vergangenheit wie in der Zukunft aus. Nunmehr wird es zum Inbegriff eines gewaltigen Zeitbogens, der die beiden Aspekte überwölbt und verbindet und den Weltenlauf als ganzes von einem Uranfang bis zu einem möglichen Ende einbegreift[71]. In dem erweiterten Bedeutungsradius spiegelt sich eine bedeutsame Wandlung im Welt- und Gottesverständnis. Durch die Konzeption eines die Geschichte des Universums durchlaufenden Zeitkontinuums wird die mythische Exklusivität einer

70. K. Koch, *Sabbatstruktur der Geschichte. Die sogenannte Zehn-Wochen-Apokalypse (1Hen 93,1-10; 91,11-17) und das Ringen um die alttestamentliche Chronologien im späten Israelitentum*, in Ders., *Vor der Wende der Zeiten. Beiträge zur apokalyptischen Literatur. Gesammelte Aufsätze 3*, Neukirchen-Vluyn, Neukirchener Verlag, 1996, S. 45-76. Die 490 Jahre von Dan 9 entsprechen vielleicht dem siebten Siebent 1Hen 93,9f. + 9,11.

71. Zu einer vergleichbaren Konzeption in Phönikien s. K. Koch, *Wind und Zeit als Konstituenten des Kosmos in phönikischer Mythologie und spätalttestamentlichen Texten*, in M. Dietrich – O. Loretz (Hgg.), *Mesopotamica – Ugaritica – Biblica* (OAT, 232), Neukirchen-Vluyn, Kevelaer, 1993, S. 59-91.

die Strukturen von Natur und Gesellschaft ein für allemal konstituierenden Urzeit, wie sie für altorientalische und frühalttestamentliche Überlieferungen selbstverständlich war, notwendig relativiert. Himmel und Erde erscheinen nicht mehr als die beiden Bereiche eines stabilen Kosmos, sondern als Teile einer von der alldurchdringenden Zeit in ihren Auffächerungen bewegten, ja vorwärtsgetriebenen Welt[72]. Sie ruft epochale Einschnitte hervor, die für Israel oder die Menschheit insgesamt bedeutsam werden, aber auch zahlreiche phänomenale Zeitspannen, in denen naturhafte oder gesellschaftliche Konstellationen kontingent in den Vordergrund schieben und, meist regional begrenzt, das menschliche Dasein bestimmen. Doch der Faktor Zeit differenziert sich im Lauf der Welt noch weiter aus bis hin zu je eigenen Zeiten des einzelnen Menschen. Die für gelungenes menschliches Leben entscheidenden Teile seines Zeit- und Geschichtsplans offenbart Gott durch die Kraft seiner Weisheit, aber auch durch beauftragte Mittler, damit die Menschen sich dem zuwenden können, was nach Gottes Willen „an der Zeit" sein wird. Dazu gehört, daß auch so alltägliche Vorgänge wie die Geburt, die soziale Stellung, selbst Geldverleihen und Kreditrückzahlung in einem Gesamtkontinuum von Zeit und Welt ihren Ort haben, einem zusammenhängenden *Nihyæh*, wie es in der 4Q-Instruktion heißt und als himmlische Geheimnis geachtet wird.

So die Theorie der untersuchten weisheitlichen und apokalyptischen Texte. Sie führen zugleich das unlösliche Miteinander von Zeit und Welt auf eine göttliche Schöpfungskraft zurück, die seit einem Uranfang kontinuierlich in der Geschichte der Natur und der Menschheit wirksam ist. Der *ʿôlam*/*ʿalam* geht auf einen Plan des „Alten an Tagen" (Dan 7,9.13.22) zurück, der als „Herr der Weltzeit" (*marê ʿalmâ*, 1Hen 9,4 u.ö.) seine Zielsetzung Schritt um Schritt verwirklichen wird.

Weit stärker als die Weisheitsschriften sind die Apokalypsen von den Ungerechtigkeiten, dem Götzendienst und den Katastrofen in der Menschheitsgeschichte beeindruckt. Sie folgern deshalb, daß der menschenfreundliche Schöpfer in Zeit und Welt noch keineswegs das Endziel erreicht hat, daß er von jeher im Sinn hatte. Zugleich meinen sie zu erkennen, daß unter den Bedingungen der gegenwärtigen Weltzeit erdenweite Gerechtigkeit und vollkommenes Heil, wie sie Gottes Absicht wirklich entsprechen, unter den Menschen nicht entstehen können. Deshalb künden sie, das bald hereinbrechende, furchtbare Ende dieses *ʿôlam*/

72. Hat im Bann einer griechischen Kosmosidee die Septuaginta an einem protologisch akzentuierten Verständnis der Schöpfung festgehalten? So jedenfalls geschieht es dann in der Geschichte der abendländischen Theologie.

ʿalam, der dann von ganz andersartigen, uneingeschränkt heilvollen *ʿal^emîn* abgelöst werden wird.

Die Idee einer durch die Schöpfung hervorgerufenen, fortlaufenden und unauflösbaren Verbindung von Zeit und Welt, die bis in die alltäglichsten Lebenssituationen hinein die Rahmenbedingungen für rechtes Verhalten und gelungener Leben bedeutet, ruft nach einem monotheistischen Gottesverständnis. Sind nämlich alle Spielarten von Zeit von derselben göttlichen Kraft verordnet, gibt es andrerseits für den Menschen kein zeitunabhängiges Verhalten, dann steht er ständig, ob es ihm bewußt wird oder nicht, diesem einen Grund aller Wirklichkeit insgeheim gegenüber. Der Polytheismus hingegen setzt voraus, daß hinter der Verschiedenheit, ja Gegensätzlichkeit der Phänomene, die dem Menschen in seinem Leben begegnen, notwendigerweise unterschiedliche numinose Kräfte zu postulieren sind. Im Weltbild der vier untersuchten Schriften bietet sich keine Möglichkeit für das Wirken anderer als der einen *prima causa.* Das jedoch läßt die Gerechtigkeit Gottes im individuellen Geschick zum Problem werden, wie es bei Qohälät deutlich hervortritt, bei Sirach in den Hintergrund gedrängt und bei Daniel mit der Auferstehungshoffnung beantwortet wird.

Universität Hamburg
Diekbarg 13a
D-22397 Hamburg

Klaus KOCH

YOUR WISDOM AND YOUR FOLLY
THE CASE OF 1-4QMYSTERIES

4Q301 Fragment 1

Who are wise and who are foolish? The first lines of 4Q301 (4QMysteries^{c}?) fragment 1 run as follows[1]:

1 א]ב֯יעה רוחי ולמיניכם א֯חלקה דברי אליכם֯[
2 מ]של וחידה וחוקרי ש֯ו֯ר֯שי בינה עם תומכי ר֯[זים
3]ה֯ו֯לכי פותי ואנשי מחשבת לכול ע֯בודת מעשי[הם/כם

1. I] will speak my mind, and according to your kinds I will apportion my words to you. [
2. par]able and riddle, and who search the roots of understanding, as well as[2] who hold fast to s[ecrets
3.] who walk in foolishness and men of thought, according to all [your/their] works [

The comments in the edition are succinct: "[t]he text begins with what appears to be a hortatory, wisdom-type formula. Several common wisdom terms occur, as the text alludes in various ways to those who possess wisdom and to those who do not"[3].

Line 1 is reminiscent of Prov 1,23. The phrase **אביעה רוחי**, "I will pour out my spirit", is found only there, and **א֯חלקה דברי אליכם֯[**, "I will apportion my words to you", is more or less parallel to **אודיעה דברי אתכם**, "I will make known my words to you". In Prov 1,20-33, the first person speaking is Wisdom (חכמות) speaking to the fools (פתים), scoffers (לצים) and stupid ones (כסילים). 4Q301 1 is a small fragment: therefore the identity of speaker and addressees is not clear[4]. In line 1, the

1. 4Q299-4Q301 have been edited by L.H. Schiffman, DJD, 20, pp. 31-123, Pls. III-IX. The transcriptions in B.Z. Wacholder & M.G. Abegg (eds.), *A Preliminary Edition of the Unpublished Dead Sea Scrolls: The Hebrew and Aramaic Texts from Cave Four. Fascicle Two*, Washington, D.C., Dead Sea Scroll Research Council & Biblical Archaeology Society, 1992, pp. 1-37, are generally of J.T. Milik. In line 2 Milik reads תומכי *[, and at the end of line 3 Schiffman omits the bracket between *yod* and *he*.

2. For **עם** in a similar sense, see Deut 32,25. One may also consider **עם**, "nation". See, for example, Ps 95,10; Dan 11,32.

3. Schiffman, DJD, 20, p. 114. The line-by-line comments consist of references to other texts.

4. Throughout this contribution I use the word "addressees" for the individuals or groups who are being addressed in the second person in the text. These "addressees" should be distinguished from the groups for whom the composition was written.

word למיניכם, "according to your kinds", is of interest: in the Hebrew Bible and in the Dead Sea Scrolls, מין, "kind, type", usually refers to different kinds of one specific natural species, such as, for example, birds, fish, or locusts[5], whereas in rabbinic texts the מינים or מינין are "sectarians". The present text may represent a missing link between the biblical and rabbinic use. On the basis of the biblical use of מין, we may infer that we have here different types of addressees. Are then the groups referred to in lines 2-3 these different kinds of addressees? In that case one should not translate "those who search", and so on, but "you who search"[6]. Even then, it remains difficult to ascertain who are being addressed. The phrase הׄוׄלכי פותי[, "who behave foolishly", reminds one of the פתים, "fools", of Prov 1,22, but should all the addressees be regarded negatively? This may perhaps be the case with the אנשי מחשבת, "men of thought", since מחשבת can have a negative meaning: "plot, scheming". But what about those "who search the roots of understanding"[7]? The fourth line of the fragment is of little help, since only two words, עמים עם "peoples with", are certain, and two other possible (עׄורׄף, "neck", and קודק]וד, "crest", "skull"). Who then are these addressees? Does the text address both those who possess wisdom and those who do not? Who are wise and who are foolish?

4Q301 AND MYSTERIES

It is disputed whether 4Q301 (4QMysteries^{c}?) is a manuscript of the composition that is called 1-4QMysteries or Book of Mysteries[8] (hence-

5. Two notable exceptions are CD IV 16-17 מיני הצדק, and 1QS III 14 לכול מיני רוחותם.

6. SCHIFFMAN, DJD, 20, p. 115, renders "those who search", "those who hold fast to", "those who behave foolishly". Similarly, E. COOK, *The Book of Secrets*, in M. WISE, M. ABEGG, Jr. & E. COOK (eds.), *The Dead Sea Scrolls. A New Translation*, New York, Harper, 1996, pp. 174-177, esp. 175. His rendering in line 1, "my various sayings", seems to have disregarded the suffix of למיניכם, "according to *your* kinds".

7. A. LANGE, *Weisheit und Prädestination. Weisheitliche Urordnung und Prädestination in den Textfunden von Qumran* (STDJ, 18), Leiden-New York-Köln, E.J. Brill, 1995, p. 102 argues that those who search the roots of understanding are viewed negatively: "eine negativ bewertete und mit Magie und Mantik in Verbindung gebrachte Gruppe". On the other hand, T. ELGVIN, *Priestly Sages? The Milieus of Origin of 4QMysteries and 4QInstruction*, in J.J. COLLINS – G. STERLING (eds.), *Sapiential Perspectives. Wisdom Literature in Light of the Dead Sea Scrolls* (forthcoming), argues that those who study the roots of understanding "may be close to the *maskilim* of Daniel".

8. The Book of Mysteries (1Q27, 4Q299, 4Q300) has nothing to do with the work published as Sepher ha-Razim. See M. MARGALIOTH, *Sepher ha-Razim. A Newly Recovered Book of Magic from the Talmudic Period. Collected from Genizah Fragments and Other Sources*, Jerusalem, Yediot Achronot, 1966. Actually, that text is not called ספר הרזים, but referred to in the introduction as ספר מספרי הרזים, "one of the books of mysteries".

forth: Mysteries)[9]. I wish to make the point that the terminological correspondences between 4Q301 and Mysteries are not incidental or arbitrary. On the contrary, the correspondences concern the terms given to the addressees in 4Q301 1 2-3, who are the same as those of Mysteries.

The first phrase is only partially preserved. One should probably restore a plural participle before מ]של וחידה. "parable and riddle". The text may, for example, have read מביני משל וחידה, "who understand parable and riddle". Apart from biblical quotations or uncertain reconstructions, משל, "parable", and חידה, "riddle", are attested in the non-biblical Dead Sea Scrolls in Mysteries and 4Q301 only[10]. The combination of the two terms is found only three or four times in the Dead Sea Scrolls: in 4Q300 1a ii-b 1; 4Q301 1 2; perhaps 4Q301 2b 1-2; and 1QpHab VIII 6, which quotes Hab 2,6[11].

The second phrase, חוקרי שורשי בינה, "who search the roots of understanding", is only attested in 4Q301 1 2[12]. שורשי בינה, "roots of understanding", is found in 4Q301 2b 1 and 4Q418 55 9; 4Q300 1a ii-b 3 has שורש חוכמה, "root of wisdom". Comparable expressions are not attested

9. J.T. MILIK, *Le travail d'édition des fragments manuscrits de Qumrân: Communication de J.T. Milik,* in *RB* 63 (1956) 60-62, p. 61, refers to two, perhaps four, Cave 4 manuscripts corresponding to 1Q27. Lange suggests that 4Q301 is a copy of *Mysteries* on the following grounds: shared terminology, such as שורשי בינה in 4Q301 and שורש חוכמה in 4Q300, as well as תומכי in 4Q299, 4Q300, and 4Q301; the shared stylistic phenomenon of sets of rhetorical questions, and the concept of hidden wisdom. See LANGE, *Weisheit und Prädestination* (n. 7), p. 93 n. 2; *Physiognomie oder Gotteslob? 4Q301 3*, in *DSD* 4 (1997) 282-296, p. 283; *In Diskussion mit dem Tempel. Zur Auseinandersetzung zwischen Kohelet und weisheitlichen Kreisen am Jerusalemer Tempel*, in A. SCHOORS (ed.), *Qohelet in the Context of Wisdom* (BETL, 136), Leuven, Peeters, 1998, pp. 113-159, esp. 131 n. 63. In all these publications the same examples are given. SCHIFFMAN, DJD, 20, pp. 31 and 113, challenges this assumption on the grounds that there would be no overlaps between 4Q301 and the Mysteries manuscripts, and that the terminology of 4Q301 would be different from that of 1Q27, 4Q299 and 4Q300: "extremely unlikely that 4Q301 … and the other manuscripts constitute witnesses to the same composition. This is despite the fact that some linguistic parallels do exist". ELGVIN, *Priestly Sages?* (n. 7), is more cautious: "At present it is an open question whether 4Q301 is a copy of 1Q/4QMysteries", but nonetheless refers to 4Q301 throughout his discussion.

10. For משל, see 4Q299 19 1; 26 1 מ̊של[; 4Q300 1a ii-b 1; 4Q301 1 2; and perhaps 4Q301 2a 2 and 2b 2. 1QpHab VIII 6 quotes Hab 2,6; 4Q175 9 quotes Num 24,15; 11QT[a] LIX 2 quotes Deut 28,37. The reconstruction יש]מח במש[ל in 4Q424 3 8 "is merely a guess; other nouns and verbs are possible" (S. TANZER, DJD, 36, p. 345). In 4Q433a 2 2 one may read either מ̊[ש]ל (thus E. SCHULLER, DJD, 29, pp. 241-242) or מ̊[ז]ל (suggested by Milik). For חידה, see 4Q299 6 ii 2 החיד̊[ה (?); 4Q300 1a ii-b 1; 4Q301 1 2; 2b 1; 1QpHab VIII 6; Aramaic אחידו is in 4Q541 2 i 7 and 4 i 4.

11. Biblical verses including both terms are Ezek 17,2; Hab 2,6; Pss 49,5; 78,2; Prov 1,6. See also Sir 47,17 and 39,3.

12. SCHIFFMAN, DJD, 20, p. 116, reads in 4Q301 2b 1 ח̊ו<ק>רי ב̇שור{ש}שי בינה, but one should read ר̇ודפ̊י שור{ש}שי בינה. For differences between my readings and the DJD ones, see E.J.C. TIGCHELAAR, *Notes on the Readings of the DJD, Editions of 1Q and 4QMysteries,* in *RQ* 81 (2003) 99-107.

in the Hebrew Bible and only rarely in contemporary Jewish literature[13]. Note the use of חקר, perhaps as the verb "search", in 1Q27 13 3.

The third phrase may be restored to תומכי ר̊]זים, "who hold fast to secrets". This phrase is attested only in Mysteries (1Q27 1 i 7; 4Q299 43 2; 4Q300 8 5) and in 4Q301 1 2. The reading ר̊]זים is plausible in view of the fact that it occurs in 4Q300 8 5, which fragment has one more unique correspondence with 4Q301 1.

The fourth phrase, הולכי פותי, "those who behave foolishly", is found only in 4Q301 1 3 and 4Q300 8 4, the same fragment that has תומכי רזים.

The fifth phrase, אנשי מחשבת, "men of thought", is found only in 4Q301 1 3 and 4Q299 1 5. It is not clear whether לכול ע̊בודת מעשי̇], "according to all works", qualifies מחשבת, "thought".

In short: three of these five phrases that mention addressees in 4Q301 1, are found exclusively in 4Q301 and Mysteries, whereas the other two phrases also exhibit close resemblance to phrases from Mysteries.

4Q301 1 1, "I] will speak my mind, and according to your kinds I will apportion my words to you", is the first line of the column, and one might speculate that it was the first line of the scroll[14]. First person singular forms are extremely rare in Mysteries, but a similar first person speech at the beginning of a new section is found in 4Q299 59+53 11-12. After a blank line the first words of a new section include יכם[אשמיע̊], for example אל]יכם אשמיע̊], "I will make known to you", and, in the next line, ונריבה ריב*], "and let us contend in dispute".

Second person plural forms are relatively rare in Mysteries and 4Q301, and in a large number of cases they are found in contexts that mention the addressees of 4Q301 1 2-3[15]. In other words, the addressees of 4Q301 1 and 2 are the same as those of Mysteries. Moreover, ונריבה ריב*], "and let us contend in dispute", in the introduction to the new section of 4Q299 59+53, is fitting as a general description of the sections with second person plural addressees. In spite of the fragmentary nature

13. See ῥίζα σοφίας in Sir 1,6.20; שורשי עולה, "roots of iniquity", in 4Q416 2 iii 14 par 4Q418 9 15; שרש רע̊, "root of evil" or "evil root", in 4Q418 243 3; ῥίζα τῆς φρονήσεως in Wis 3,15.

14. COOK, *The Book of Secrets* (n. 6), p. 175, presents 4Q301 1 as the first fragment of his translation of *Mysteries*. See also ELGVIN, *Priestly Sages?* (n. 7).

15. 4Q299 3a ii-b 9 (שמעו תומכי); 4Q299 6 ii 2, perhaps החיד̊]ה, and see line 4 תומכ̊]י; 4Q300 1a ii b and 4Q299 3c i terms חידה and משל, as well as שורש חוכמה; 4Q300 8 הולכי פתי and תומכי רזים; 4Q301 2b terms חידה and משל, as well as שור{ש}שי בינה; unknown addressees in 1Q27 1 i 5 and 8 (and parallels), but there is a reference to תומכי רזי פלא̇, and in the parallel text of 4Q299 1 to אנשי מחשבת. Other second person plural forms in fragments with less context are: 4Q299 16 2 (רוחכם); 45 2 (אמרו); 53 3 (בכם); 70 2 ([ל̊ו̊א ידעתם); 70 3 (ואת[ם); 71 2 (לכם); 77 2 (בידכם). See also Milik's join of 4Q299 13a 2 י]שראל ואתכם] and 13b 2 ([המשיל אתכם]). Uncertain is 4Q299 10 8 ([א̊תם).

of the texts, these sections can be characterized as disputations between the first person singular or plural, and the second person plural addressees.

Do these correspondences indicate that 4Q301 is another manuscript of Mysteries? There are three possible objections against the identification. First, there are no undisputable overlaps between 4Q301 and the three *Mysteries* manuscripts. Second, none of the Mysteries manuscripts has hekhalot-like fragments such as 4Q301 3-7[16]. Third, from a physical point of view, both 4Q301 1-2 and 1Q27 1 i-ii may stem from the beginning of their respective scrolls. As for the first two objections, I consider it plausible that 4Q299 9 5 ב]ארך א[פיו, "in his long-suffering", overlaps with 4Q301 3a-b 4 ונכבד אל בא[ו]רך אפיו[17]. The fact that the vocabulary of 4Q299 9 is close to that of the hekhalot-like sections of 4Q301 supports the plausibility of the overlap[18]. The third objection has not been raised up to now, but is, I think, the most incisive one. From a physical point of view it is probable that 1Q27 1 belongs to the very beginning of its scroll. On the other hand, it is tempting to speculate that 4Q301 1 preserves the very first lines of its scroll, the exordium to the composition, and that frags. 2a and 2b belong to the upper part of the next columns. It may be possible to place 4Q301 1 before 1Q27 1 i, but it is virtually impossible to place 4Q301 2a and 2b near to 1Q27 1 ii. Hence, one should either conclude that 4Q301 is different from the other *Mysteries* copies, or that the 4Q301 fragments do not derive from the beginning of the composition.

On the basis of the close terminological similarities between 4Q301 and Mysteries, including the probability of an overlap between 4Q299 9 and 4Q301 2, I suggest that 4Q301 is either a manuscript of Mysteries, or a manuscript representing a different version of Mysteries (as for example with the different War Scroll manuscripts). Therefore, for all practical purposes it is justified to regard 4Q301 as a manuscript of Mysteries.

Addressees of Mysteries and 4Q301

How do the fragments that use second person plural forms characterize the addressees? 4Q301 2b, which, like 4Q301 1, mentions החידה,

16. With regard to the first two objections, see Schiffman, DJD, 20, pp. 31 and 113.

17. See also Tigchelaar, *Notes on the Readings* (n. 12).

18. 4Q299 9 3 נכבד, honoured" (five or six times in 4Q301); הדר, "majesty" (the *nifal* נהדר, "exalted" four or five times in 4Q301); מלכות (see 4Q301 5 2). Note also Tigchelaar, *Notes on the Readings* (n. 12), reading 4Q299 9 2 שרים לי זרח א[ור]ך, "(are) singing: 'Unto me has risen your light'".

"the riddle", and מ]משל, "parable", qualifies the addressees as רודפי שור{ש}שי בינה, "who pursue the roots of understanding". In line 2, מה אדיר לכם and מה שר לכם] are probably parallel, perhaps meaning: "what is a mighty one for you", and "what is a prince [for you"[19]. Perhaps line 3, "]without strength; and may he rule over him with a whip at no cost", characterizes the rulers of line 2[20]. Line 4, מיא בכם דורש פני אור ומא], "who among you seeks the presence (?) of light and ...", may be compared to 1 Enoch 58,4 where the righteous seek light and find righteousness[21]. Yet, this strange expression may perhaps also mean "who among you investigates the appearance of light and luminaries" (reading the last word as ומא]ורות), in which case the addressees may be involved in some kind of astrology[22]. In line 5, תבנית זכר is literally "the image of a male"[23], or even "an image of the male member"[24].

The preserved phrases may perhaps be read as a dispute with those who worship other gods. In that case, line 5 refers to the image of a male god who does not exist (ללוא היה). "Mighty one" (אדיר) and "prince" (שר) are common epitheta of Syro-Palestinian gods, whereas gods like Hadad, and, in later times, Jupiter Heliopolitanus, are portrayed with a whip raised in the right hand. The word מה, "what", may have been used deliberately instead of מי, "who", in the questions מה אדיר, and מה שר, "what is a mighty one", "what is a prince". It is not clear how one should reconstruct the broken words משל[and למשׁ] in line 2. Perhaps one should read in both cases למשל, "(he will be) a byword", but it cannot be excluded that we have here forms of משל, "to rule", in which case there may be references to the purported rule of foreign gods or of planets. On the other hand, it is not clear how the two words of lines 6-7 fit within this interpretation.

19. The clause והוא למשל], may perhaps have the same meaning as in Deut 28,37. The response to the question "What is a mighty one among you?" (or: "What is one of your mighty ones?") is: "He will be (no more than) a byword". I disregard Milik's suggestion of a distant join of 4Q301 2a and 2b.

20. The terminology is used in the Hebrew Bible with regard to shepherds, which in turn is, of course, often a metaphor for rulers. See Ezek 34,4 ובחזקה רדיתם אתם; with regard to the payment of a shepherd, see Zech 11,12-13.

21. SCHIFFMAN, DJD, 20, p. 116: "discernment is likened to light or to a luminary".

22. In Jer 8,2, the sun, the moon, and all the host of heaven, are object of a series of verbs, including דרש. There, דרש has the sense of "to seek in worship".

23. Deut 4,16; see also Wis 13,13 εἰκὼν ἀνθρώπου. In both cases the reference is to idols.

24. Alternatively, but less likely, זכר can be read as "memory". Thus COOK, *The Book of Secrets* (n. 6), p. 175: "the plan of memory"; F. GARCÍA MARTÍNEZ, *DSST*, p. 401: "the model of the memorial"; F. GARCÍA MARTÍNEZ, A.S. VAN DER WOUDE, *De Rollen van de Dode Zee 1*, Kampen, Kok, 1994, p. 434: "een gestalte van gedachtenis".

4Q300 1a ii-b par 4Q299 3c i refers to "parable" and "riddle", and to the "root of wisdom"[25]. The addressees of this fragment are called חר]טמים, "magicians", and מלמדי פשע, "teachers of transgression"[26]. They are challenged to tell the parable and solve the riddle before they are told the solution[27]. The following lines refer to כסלכמה, "your folly", and enumerate their shortcoming: "the seal of the vision is sealed from you", "you have not beheld the eternal mysteries", "you have not gained insight", "you have not beheld the roots of wisdom", and "if you try to open the vision, it will be kept secret from you". The text also mentions "your wisdom", and "hidden wisdom".

The general meaning is clear: the phrases "your folly" and "your wisdom" alternate; the wisdom of the addressees is assessed as folly. Yet, there are few real clues about the identity of the addressees. In Gen 41 and Daniel, חרטמים, "magicians", are supposed to be able to interpret dreams, whereas in Exod 7–9 they use incantations. The phrase רזי עד, "eternal mysteries", twice attested in this section (4Q300 1a ii-b 2; 4Q299 3c i 5), calls to mind 1 Enoch 9,6 where Asael is accused of teaching iniquity and revealing the "eternal mysteries"[28]. One may perhaps connect the skills of the "magicians" with the mysteries enumerated in 1 Enoch 8,3 (4Q201 1 iv 2 mentions חרטמו, "sorcery") and the knowledge of Jub 8,3. The specific items of the shortcoming of the magicians are less clear. The clauses "if you try to open the vision, it will be kept secret from you" and "hidden wisdom" are reminiscent of Dan 8,26; 9,24; 12,4.9, but are not of necessity dependent on Daniel. The point is that in all these texts understanding is connected to knowing the exact length of time.

4Q300 8 refers to הולכי פתי, "who walk in simplicity", and תומכי רזים, "who hold fast to mysteries". The preceding text is very fragmen-

25. See TIGCHELAAR, *Notes on the Readings* (n. 12), for a reconstruction of the combined fragments 4Q300 1a ii-b and 4Q299 3c i.

26. Milik originally read מש]טמים, "opponents", or perhaps "enmity".]טמים could also be a defective writing of טמאים (cf. 11Q20 XIV 23), but that makes no sense here. For a recent short discussion of the חרטמים, see G.W.E. NICKELSBURG, *1 Enoch 1: A Commentary on the Book of 1 Enoch Chapters 1-36, 81-108* (Hermeneia), Philadephia, PA, Fortress Press, 2001, pp. 198-199. For מלמדי פשע, SCHIFFMAN, DJD, 20, pp. 101-103, favours the rendering "who are skilled in transgression", but translates p. 43: "who teach transgression". I prefer "teachers of transgression". 4Q300 has several defective spellings, but one rarely encounters a defectively written *pual* in the Dead Sea Scrolls. For the idea of "teaching transgression", see 1 Enoch 9,6 which tells that Asael ἐδίδαξεν πάσας τὰς ἀδικίας.

27. The DJD translation is not clear; אמרו and הגידו should be read as imperatives.

28. For a discussion of the different myths in 1 Enoch 6-11, and secondary elements in the myths see most recently NICKELSBURG, *1 Enoch* (n. 26), pp. 190-193. For the textual variants in this verse, see p. 204.

tary, but the following text includes the statement "you (?)] will know whether you have understanding and whether[". This wording is similar to that of 4Q300 1a ii-b 1, "and then you will know whether you have considered [". In both cases one expects the answer to be negative.

The speech that begins in 4Q299 3a ii-b 9 has been described as "a hortatory speech addressed to the righteous who hold fast to eternity"[29]. The address in line 9 is שמעו תומכי *[, "listen, you who hold fast to [", and the question is whether one should restore תומכי ר̊[זים, "who hold fast to mysteries", or something else[30]. The first person plural forms in line 14 may either include or exclude the addressees; it is most likely that there is an opposition between the addressees and the "we-group", and that the speech is not addressed to the righteous but to the opponents.

In 4Q299 6 ii 2, insufficiency of context makes it difficult to determine the identity of the addressees. I read in line 2 ועליכם החיד̊[ה, "and against you (is) the riddle"[31], but the meaning of אוילי כסה *[in line 3 remains obscure to me[32]. In line 4 one encounters again the motif of wisdom that is hidden from the addressees: נסתרה מכול תומכ̊[י רזים, "hidden from all who hold fast [to secrets".

The introduction in 1Q27 9 3 שמעו מלכי עמ[ים, "Listen, kings of the nations", followed by line 4 עם כול שפטי[ם, "with all judges", is perhaps comparable to Wis 6,1: "Listen, kings, and understand; learn, judges of the ends of the earth" (see also 1,1, which addresses the "judges of the earth", and 6,21). Unfortunately, the context is missing, and it is not clear why kings and judges are spoken to in Mysteries. Apart from 1Q27 9, there are no direct addresses of kings or judges, nor admonitions that are directly related to kingship.

In 1Q27 1 i and parallel texts, it is questionable whether the second person plural addressees are those referred to as כול תומכי רזי פלא, "all those who hold fast to wonderful mysteries" (1Q27 1 i 7), and אנשי מחשבת, "men of thought" (4Q299 1 5). The most straightforward reading is to identify "those who hold fast to wonderful mysteries" with those described in 1Q27 1 i 3-4, namely those who have no knowledge of the רז נהיה, "the mystery of existence", and are not able to save them-

29. SCHIFFMAN, DJD, 20, p. 42.

30. Schiffman's comment suggests he considers reading תומכי ע̊[ולם or תומכי ב̊[עולם, "who hold fast to eternity". To my knowledge, these clauses are not attested anywhere.

31. Cf. Hab 2,6 הלוא־אלה כלם עליו משל ישׂאו ומליצה חידות לו.

32. One may consider an emendation: אוילי<ם>, "fools", or אוילי <לב>, "foolhearted ones"; in that case כסה may refer to something that is covered up, that is hidden, from them. Otherwise, כסה should be a noun, perhaps related to כשׂה (Deut 32,15) "to be obstinate". The construct phrase אוילי כסה would in that case mean "obstinate fools".

selves from this "mystery of existence". That would imply that here the text has different addressees. In most cases the addressees are those of 4Q301 1 2-3, including "those who hold fast to wonderful mysteries". In 1Q27 1 i, however, this group is discussed in the third person. In view of the possibility that 1Q27 1 i preserves the introduction of the work, one may hypothesize that the second person plural addressees in this introduction are those to whom the composition as a whole is directed.

In a few fragments one may have addressees that are not identical to those of 4Q301 1. ועתה מ*], "And now", in 4Q299 62 3, seems to introduce a different kind of speech, since the following line has one of the very rare second person singular forms: שנאיכה, "your enemies"[33]. The context is insufficient to determine whether here one really has an address of one individual person, or whether שנאיכה is part of a quotation. The other two attestations of ועתה are in tiny fragments, and do not supply information on the addressees[34].

Two fragments that seem to discuss priestly issues contain second person plural forms, namely 4Q299 13a 2 י[שראל ואתכם], "Israel, and you"; 70 2 [לוׄא ידעתם, "you do not know"[35]; and perhaps 70 3 ואת]ם, "and yo[u"[36]. Both in 4Q299 13a 1 and in 70 3 the issue may be the teaching of the difference between holy and profane, one of the priestly tasks, according to Lev 10,10-11 and Ezek 44,23-24. Therefore, one should consider the possibility that in these fragments priests are the addressees.

PRIESTS

Many sapiential works have a composite character, but it is not clear to what extent this is the case with Mysteries. Therefore, we do not know whether this work had a unity of argument, or consisted of more or less unrelated sections. A series of fragments, 4Q299 3a ii-b 9ff, 4Q299 3c i par 4Q300 1a ii-b, 4Q299 6 ii, 4Q299 63 par 4Q300 8, 4Q301 1, and 4Q301 2b, seems to address "those who hold fast to wonderful mysteries". Yet, 1Q27 1 i refers to them while addressing an un-

33. Other second person singular forms are 4Q299 31 4 [בׄיׄדׄךׄ, "in your hand" (but the reading is very uncertain); 4Q299 71 3 נאצתה, "you reviled", or, alternatively, "her blasphemy" or "her humiliation". In 4Q299 85 4 read לר**] and not לך**]. In 4Q299 9 2 אׄ]ור[ךׄ, "your light", is part of a hymn.

34. 4Q299 44 3 [ועתה]; 4Q299 80 2 [ועתה פׄ], or perhaps [ועתה מׄ], in which case we may have the same addressee as in 4Q299 62 3 ועתה מ*].

35. Restore perhaps ה[לוׄא ידעתם, "do you not know?".

36. אתם is not preserved elsewhere in *Mysteries* (4Q299 10 8 [אׄתם is unlikely to be the independent pronoun) and other restorations (ואת]; ואת]כם) are also possible.

specified audience. 1Q27 9 addresses kings of the nations and judges, but little else can be said. Then there are a series of fragments dealing with priestly issues. Presumably, the second person plural forms in these fragments are spoken to these priests[37].

Perhaps these speeches are not related. Still, some of the sections with priestly issues may be read as a contrast to the other sections. The priestly fragments deal with a variety of priestly affairs, such as acts of atonement, the service of the sanctuary, offerings, impurity, profane, holy, priestly dress[38], Urim and Thummim, and perhaps to Yom Kippur[39]. Some fragments preserve text that is related to Ezek 44,23-24.

This goes for 4Q299 13a 1 חׄול בין הׄטׄמׄ]א[, "profane, between the impur[e"; 70 3 לחׄול[, "profane"; 56 2 לׄ]שׁׄופטם במשפטׄיׄ[, "to] judge them with rules of["; perhaps also 59 1 יׄקׄדׄש, "he will sanctify", and 2 בׄמשפט יריב א[, "with justice he will contend with". Ezek 44,23-24, and apparently the Mysteries fragments as well, deal with the teaching of the nation and the settling of cases in court. Hence, the text compares the priests, those who teach the Israelites to distinguish between sacred and profane, to the magicians, who are the teachers of transgression. At the same time, the priests as judges may have been contrasted to the kings of the nations and the judges.

The fragments that discuss priestly issues are quite small, whereas the large fragments of Mysteries are not concerned with priestly issues. Therefore it seems that we have only "a couple of passages referring to priestly traditions"[40]. Yet, both the variety of priestly subjects discussed in these fragments, as well as the relatively large number of these small fragments, indicate the opposite. The composition puts the priests opposite the magicians and kings of the nations, just as it places Israel against the nations.

INTERMEZZO: MYSTERIES, INSTRUCTION, AND THE DISPUTATION FORM

There are correspondences, but also differences, between Mysteries and Instruction[41]. The most important lexical correspondences are רז נהיה,

37. This may go for the second person plural forms in 4Q299 13a, 13b, 53, 70, 71 and 73.

38. See 4Q299 75 1 פ]תׄיל תכלת[, "blue cord", and 3 לפתוחׄ]י, "for the engravings of" (see Exod 39,30-31)

39. See LANGE, *Physiognomie oder Gotteslob?* (n. 9), pp. 286-287; ELGVIN, *Priestly Sages?* (n. 7).

40. ELGVIN, *Priestly Sages?* (n. 7).

41. SCHIFFMAN, DJD, 20, p. 31, states that "[t]erms such as רז נהיה, הבט, התבונן, and numerous others, tie these texts together". J. STRUGNELL, DJD, 34, pp. 2, 31, refers to the

"the mystery of existence"; בית מולדים, "horoscope" (as well as other constructions with מולדי); שורשי בינה, "roots of insight"[42]. On the other hand, some of the most distinctive terms of Instruction are missing from Mysteries[43]. What then is the relation between the works?

The term "mystery of existence" is extremely characteristic of Instruction. Outside Instruction, it is attested twice in the introduction of Mysteries (1Q27 1 i) and once in 1QS XI 3-4. Several considerations suggest that *Mysteries* did not adopt the term from Instruction. First, in 1Q27 1 i, the term is used in a different context and in combination with other verbs[44]. On the other hand, phrases that are used with "mystery of existence" in Instruction, are used with other terms in Mysteries[45]. Second, the almost exclusive preference of Instruction for רז נהיה, above other constructions with רזי, seems to be due to terminological systematization. Such a process is not apparent in Mysteries[46].

In my work on Instruction, I briefly discussed 4Q418 55 and 69 ii+60 (henceforth 69 ii). I pointed out that these sections of Instruction are stylistically and terminologically different from the rest of the composition,

relation between Mysteries and Instruction. The lexicon of Mysteries is quite close to that of Instruction: "it is appropriate to ask whether [*Instruction*] knew the *Book of Mysteries*, or was known to it"; and Mysteries "seems to rework" *Instruction*. LANGE, *In Diskussion mit dem Tempel*, argues that *Instruction*, *Mysteries*, and the *Treatise of the Two Spirits* were composed in the same temple-centered milieu. ELGVIN, *Priestly Sages?* (n. 7), not only discusses the correspondences, but also the differences: Mysteries is concerned with Israel and the nations, and is much more concerned with priestly issues than *Instruction*. He associates the two texts with different milieus: Mysteries with that of Ben Sira and Daniel; Instruction with that of the Enochic writings.

42. The phrase רב שכל is attested only in Instruction and Mysteries (4Q418 158 6, 4Q423 5 8; 4Q299 8 6). קדמוניות, "former things", is found in 4Q418 148 ii 6 (בינה לקדמוניות שים) and 1Q27 1 i 3 (ובקדמוניות לוא התבוננו). Yet, see Isa 43,18 (אל־תזכרו ראשנות וקדמניות אל־תתבננו), 4Q298 3-4 ii 10 (ובקד֯[מ]ו֯ניות תביטו לדעת), 4Q413 1-2 4 (]ר֯א֯ישונים ובינו בשני ד[ור ו]דור). רדף דעת, "to pursue knowledge, is found in 4Q418 69 ii 11; 4Q299 8 7; but also in 4Q424 3 2. רז as indirect object of הבט is found in *Instruction* (*passim* הבט ברז נהיה), 4Q300 1a ii-b 2 וברז֯י עד לא הבטתם, and 1QS XI 3 (see also 19).

43. מחסור, "poverty, need", is distinctive of Instruction, but found only once (4Q299 65 3) in Mysteries. The same goes for נחלה, "lot, fate", which is attested once in 4Q301 2a 1. The hitherto not convincingly explained term אט ("storehouse"; "kindness"; "secret"?) is typical of Instruction (see also 4Q424 1 6 אט), but not attested in Mysteries. On the other hand ישראל is attested seven times in 4Q299, but not once in Instruction (in 4Q417 24 1 the restoration]ע֯מו֯ י֯ש[ראל is uncertain).

44. In 1Q27 1 i 3, 4 ידע רז נהיה, "to know the mystery of existence", and מלט נפש מרז נהיה, "to save one's life from the mystery of existence".

45. In Instruction הביט has the indirect object רז נהיה, in 4Q300 1a ii-b 2 the רזי עד. In Instruction God opens the ear (גלה אזן) by means of the רז נהיה, in 4Q299 8 6 with רוב שכל, "great intelligence".

46. Data on the distribution of occurrences of רז in Instruction and other Dead Sea Scrolls are gathered in E.J.C. TIGCHELAAR, *To Increase Learning for the Understanding Ones. Reading and Reconstructing the Fragmentary Early Jewish Sapiential Text 4QInstruction* (STDJ, 44), Leiden, Brill, 2001, pp. 204-205.

even though they share some of the characteristic vocabulary of Instruction[47]. When I wrote that part, I focused on the relation between Instruction and the Epistle of Enoch, and overlooked the correspondences between these two Instruction sections and Mysteries[48]. The following features of 4Q418 55 and 69 ii are uncharacteristic of Instruction, but reminiscent of Mysteries: the use of first and second person plural forms, including the direct address of opponents; quotations introduced by a formula[49]; rhetorical questions with interrogative *he*, הלוא, and ומה/מה. In addition, 4Q418 55 and 69 ii contain several terminological correspondences with Mysteries. Above I referred to שורשי בינה, "roots of insight" (only in 4Q301 1 2; 2b 1; and 4Q418 55 9), and רדף דעת, "to pursue knowledge" (4Q418 69 ii 11; 4Q299 8 7; 4Q424 3 2). The expression ללוא היה, "to who does not exist", is only found in 4Q418 69 ii 5 and 4Q301 2b 5. 4Q418 69 ii 4 begins a new section with ועתה, a word that is not attested elsewhere in Instruction, but is found as the introduction of a new speech in other sapiential texts, including Mysteries (4Q299 62 3; see also 44 3 and 80 2). 4Q418 69 ii 10 בחירי אמת, "truly chosen ones", is in all likelihood equivalent to בחירי צדק, "righteous chosen ones", which phrase also should be read in 4Q299 72 2: ב]חׄירי צדק[50].

It is not possible to recover the exact relation between Mysteries and 4Q418 55 and 69 ii. It is clear, though, that both texts have the same formal features of what one might call the "*rib* (ריב) pattern" or "disputation form"[51]. These texts, as well as 1 Enoch 1-5, have several features in common, namely the address of sinners in the second person plural, as well as third person plural statements about these same addressees. 1 Enoch 2-5, as well as several other Jewish texts, "contrast nature's steadfast obedience to God's commandments with humanity's divergence from the divine statutes"[52]. The basic form consists of the description of nature's obedience, followed by an observation that mankind is

47. TIGCHELAAR, *To Increase Learning* (n. 46), pp. 208-224. STRUGNELL, DJD, 34, p. 14, observed that "[T]he reversion to second singular discourse at the end of this fragment gives the impression that these two instructions might have been originally composed (or functioned) as twin set-pieces now integrated into the instruction for the maven".

48. The only reference to Mysteries in the chapter is found in p. 218, n. 20.

49. In Mysteries in 4Q301 1a ii-b 3 א]ז[תׄאמרו ל[, "Then you will say:".

50. Palaeographically ג]בׄורי is more difficult than ב]חׄורי or ב]חׄירי. For the expression, see also 4Q215a 1 ii 3; 1QH^a VI 13 [Sukenik XIV 2 + frag.]; X 15 [Sukenik II 13]; 4Q184 1 14), and ἐκλεκτοὶ δίκαιοι, "righteous elect", in 1 Enoch 1,1.

51. See L. HARTMAN, *Asking for a Meaning. A Study of 1 Enoch 1-5* (CB NT, 12), Lund, Gleerup, 1979; B. NITZAN, DJD, 20, pp. 126-127; NICKELSBURG, *1 Enoch* (n. 26), pp. 152-154.

52. The quotation is that of NICKELSBURG, *1 Enoch* (n. 26), p. 152.

not obedient, a second person plural reproach ("but you … have not"), or a second person plural exhortation ("you therefore … too").

In 4Q418 69 ii+60, and Mysteries, the form is more complex. 4Q418 69 ii+60 3-4 describes the obedience of the waters of the seas[53], which is followed (though separated by a *vacat*) by the address of the foolish of heart. Mysteries has several sections (4Q299 3a ii-b 9ff; 5; 6 i) referring to God's creation, but the relation with the second person plural speeches is not entirely clear. In 4Q299 3a ii-b the point seems to be that God is Creator, that one should not violate one's Creator's commands, and that God has revealed the secrets of his creation to some. The thrust of 4Q299 3a ii-b may be that the addressees ("those who hold fast to [wonderful mysteries") do not know the mysteries of creation which God has revealed to the first person plural speakers.

In the complex and broken text of 4Q418 55, first, second, and third person plural forms alternate. Perhaps the first person plural forms of 4Q418 55 3-4 were part of a direct speech of which the introduction has been lost (see also 4Q418 69 ii 11 and 13). In that case 4Q418 55 5 gives the reaction ("[they said:] 'with toil we contemplate her paths' – but they have not sought understanding"). Alternatively, we may have here the members of a "we" group opposed to a "they" group (we contemplate her paths – they have not sought understanding), followed by a second person plural speech.

Both in Mysteries and in 4Q418 55 and 69 ii we have broken texts which sometimes make it difficult to determine the identity of speakers and addressees. Yet, from 4Q418 69 ii it is clear that both the "sinners" and the "elect" groups can be addressed in second person plural, whereas the "sinners" can be also be referred to, in the same context, by third person speech. If that is the case, we may conjecture that first person plural forms may refer to the "elect". In other words, in these disputation forms the perspectives of the persons change. The "sinners" may be spoken to in second and third person plural speech; the "elect" in second and first plural forms. To make things complicated: in quotations the "sinners" may use first person plural speech.

Oppositions in Mysteries

First person forms are rare in Mysteries. First person singular speech is only preserved in the introductions to new sections, in 4Q299 59+53

53. See also 1 Enoch 101,6-7, and the comments of NICKELSBURG, *1 Enoch* (n. 26), p. 508.

11 and 4Q301 1 1, and in the quotation of 4Q299 9 2. First person plural forms occur in some fragments and sections of Mysteries, but in most cases the broken clauses do not illuminate the identity of the "we" group[54]. Yet, there are a few cases where these indicate an activity of the "we" group, to wit 4Q300 8 4 par 4Q299 63 1 שְׁמְעוּ ונודיעה להולכי פתי, "listen, and we shall make known to (you) who walk in simplicity", and 4Q299 59+53 12 ונריבה ריב*], "and let us contend in dispute"[55]. These verbal activities may suggest the acts of sages who teach those without knowledge and debate with opponents. In 4Q299 8 7, immediately after a first person plural speech, we find the clause]יֹצר בינה לכול רודפי דעת, "he formed (?) understanding for all the pursuers of knowledge". It is tempting to regard this term, "pursuers of knowledge", as a self-designation of the "we" group, but because of the broken context, this is not certain.

A sharp distinction between sages and priests is not warranted. First, this would force us to distinguish first person speech of the sages and second person plural address of priests, a distinction that is not indicated in the text. Second, "teaching" is not only the task of sages, but also of priests[56], and in other texts, for example the Aramaic Levi Document, wisdom and priesthood are connected. Thirdly, it is plausible that the majority of sages were in fact of priestly descent. Hence we must conclude that the "we" group of Mysteries, are priestly sages. This also goes well with the hekhalot-like sections of 4Q301 3-7 and 4Q299 9, which should be related to the Temple service.

If the "we" group of Mysteries are priestly sages, who then are their opponents? The criticism of the opponents that is preserved best is in 4Q300 1a ii-b par 4Q299 3c i. This section states that the addressees have not beheld the eternal mysteries, even though they are magicians. Their knowledge is described both as "all your wisdom", and as "your folly" (4Q300 1a ii-b 2 and 4). In this section one of the main themes is the vision (החזון): "the seal of the vision is sealed from you"; "if you try to open the vision"; "[the vision] is kept secret from you"; "the vision ...". These phrases are similar to ones in Daniel where "the vision"

54. In some cases it is not certain whether one should read a perfect *Nifal*, or first person plural imperfect forms (4Q300 1b 1 נדבר; 4Q299 3a ii-b 2, 3 par 4Q300 5 3, 4 נקרא; 4Q299 26 2 ונספרה; 4Q300 8 3 נפתח). Other first person plural forms are found in 4Q299 3a ii-b 14 כי לבנו בחן וינחילנו]; 8 6]בינה יצר לבנ[ו] ברוב שכל גלה אוזננו ונש]מעה; 59 7 (= 59+53 12) ונריבה; 63 3 וימשילנו; 4Q300 8 1]ימינו, 4a ונודיעה.

55. Most of the other possible first person verbal forms also involve speech: נדבר, "we will say", or (*Hitpael*) "we will discuss"; נקרא, "we will call"; ונספרה, "and let us recount".

56. הודיע, "make known", is used with priests as subject in Ezek 22,26 and 44,23.

refers to things that are going to happen, and, more specifically, to the exact time things will happen[57]. The point of this fragment is that the opponents, in spite of their knowledge, are not able to specify what is going to happen and when this is going to happen.

The identity of these opponents, the so-called חרטמים, "magicians", remains unclear. The use of the term "magicians" suggests a non-Israelite identity, but within an inner-Israelite dispute such terms might have been used to denounce opponents. Yet, if the interpretation of 4Q301 2b, as suggested above, is correct, than the "magicians" may have been worshippers of a foreign god. An additional argument for the non-Israelite identity of the addressees of 4Q301 1 may be the speech to the kings of the na[tions", as well as the several mentions of these nations (עמים, לאומים, גואים). The repeated references to "Israel" and the "nations" suggest that the prime concern of the text is not an inner-Israelite dispute, but that the relation between Israel and the nations is one of its main motifs. Even though 4Q301 1 4 is badly damaged, it is clear that immediately after the enumeration of the addressees, we find a mention of the nations. Allusions to the nations are perhaps also found in the "priestly" sections[58], whereas phrases such as 4Q299 60 3 לע]ם סגולה מכול [העמים], "(his) very own [nat]ion from among all [the nations", clearly indicate the special concern for Israel. 4Q299 10 3 refers to "all the nations" and "Israel" in one line, and to a "king" and "mighty warriors" in the previous lines. I hesitate, however, to conclude from these words that these lines express the "hope for a future king who with his warriors would defeat the peoples scheming against Israel"[59].

The opposition between wicked and righteous, which is common both in sapiential and apocalyptic literature, only surfaces in a few sections, namely in the apocalyptic introduction (1Q27 1 i) and in the proverbial parts (4Q300 7). In fact, Mysteries has only few sections that refer to רשע, "wickedness", or עול and עולה, "iniquity"[60]. On the other hand, צדק, "righteousness", and צדיק, "righteous", occur somewhat more of-

57. Dan 8,26 (סתם חזון) and 9,24 (חתם חזון) use exactly the same phrases. There is no equivalent of פתח חזון, "open the vision". See also Dan 12,4.9 with regard to סתם and חתם. In Dan 8,13.17.26; 9,22-27; 12,4.8-13 the most important issue is not *what* will happen, but *when* these things will happen. See also 1QM XI 7-8 (and following): the חוזי תעודות have knowledge of the ק[צי] מלחמות ידיכה, "the times of the wars of your hands".

58. Because of their limited size it often is not clear which fragments are "priestly" fragments. See perhaps 4Q299 64 1]לֹאומים, "nations" (not]הֹשמים), where line 2 has קדו[ש; certainly 4Q299 79 8.

59. ELGVIN, *Priestly Sages?* (n. 7).

60. רשע and רשעה, three times in 1Q27 1 i 5, 6, 11; four times in other fragments, namely in 4Q299 59 4; 4Q300 7 1, 4; 4Q301 3a-b 8 (4Q301 7 3 is not certain); עול and עולה are only attested in 1Q27 1 i 5 and 9.

ten[61]. In 1Q27 1 i 8-12 "wickedness" and "iniquity" are described in general terms: nations which rob (גזל) and oppress (עשק) other nations[62]. 4Q299 53+59 also describe the future punishment of the wicked. 4Q299 53 4 ואין שם למוע]די עולם, "and shall not be there for all eternal periods", is similar to 1Q27 1 i 7 ואין שם לע]ד]. 4Q299 59 3 and 4 mention "all who violate [His] command" and "helpers of iniquity". It is not clear from the preserved text whether we have here general descriptions of "iniquity", or references to more specific transgressions. Perhaps עוזרי רשעה], "helpers of iniquity", is an allusion to Zech 1,15, where God angers against the complacent nations who have helped in doing evil (והמה עזרו לרעה). 4Q300 1a i 3-4 perhaps refers to some deed which provokes (God's?) wrath. 4Q300 2 ii preserves part of a proverbial section, and mentions a series of "evils", namely שקר, "falsehood"; קנאת מדנים, "jealous strife"; מעלו אשר מעל, "the transgression which he committed"; רעׄ, "evil". In the other proverbial sections there are some more references to evils, such as "bearing a grudge unjustly" (4Q300 7 2), in a section that opposes the wicked to the righteous.

In short, with regard to the opposition between wickedness and righteousness, one should perhaps distinguish between the proverbial sections that describe different kinds of behaviour, and the "apocalyptic" parts that refer directly (1Q27 1 i) or indirectly (4Q299 59) to the violence of the nations. The latter topic fits very well the pre-Hasmonaean period when time and again Ptolemaic and Seleucid armies oppressed and plundered Judah and Jerusalem.

4Q300 1a ii-b 1-4 preserves a series of wisdom terms, כסל, "folly"; בינה, "understanding"; חכמה, "wisdom"; ידע, "know"; השכיל, "understand"; הביט, "to gaze, examine". One expects an opposition between "wisdom" and "folly", but the text is more ambiguous: the contrast is not between "wisdom" and "folly", but between different kinds of wisdom. The distinction between wise and fool, wisdom and folly, which is typical of many sapiential works, hardly occurs in the preserved fragments of the work. 1Q27 1 i 7 describes a new era: ודעה תמלא תבל ואין שם לעׄ]ד] אולת, "knowledge will fill the earth, and folly shall be there no more". 4Q301 2a 1 perhaps also refers to the future: משפטי כסיל ונחלת חכמ]ים, "the judgments (?) of a fool, and the fate of wise [men". Apart

61. צדק and צדיק are found in 1Q27 1 i 5, 6; 4Q299 3a ii-b 3, 4; 53 5; 55 2; 72 2; 80 3; 4Q300 7 1, 3; 11 1, 2.

62. The word-pair is common in the Hebrew Bible (Lev 5,23; 19,13; Deut 28,29; Jer 21,12; Ezek 18,18; 22,29; Micah 2,2; Ps 62,11; Qoh 5,7), and also attested in 4Q299 54 2. The saying in Mysteries is very close to that of 1 Macc 2,10, and some kind of relation between the two texts is likely.

from these two clauses, references to wise and fools are scarce and without much context. Of interest may be the juxtaposition of חכם, "wise", and צדיק, "righteous", in one of the proverbial sections (4Q299 3a ii-b 4), but even there the context is insufficient. It is plausible, though, that in these two lines חכם, "wise", "a sage", is used in a positive manner. This is, however, not entirely the case with the attestations of חכמה, "wisdom", in Mysteries. In 1Q27 1 i 3 par 4Q300 3 3, as well as in 4Q300 1a ii-b, "wisdom" is the wisdom of the opponents. Twice we encounter the term חכמה נחכדת, "hidden wisdom" (4Q300 1a ii-b 4-5; 4Q300 5 5). The joined text of 4Q300 5 5 and 4Q299 3a ii-b 5 has]ה חכמה נכחדת̊ [כי] אם חוכמת עורמת רוע ומ̇[, "]hidden wisdom, [ex]cept for the wisdom of evil cunning and[". The preceding words are missing, except for ולו̊]א some words earlier on. Should one restore "and he has not acquired/seen hidden wisdom, except for"[63], or "and he does not know what hidden wisdom is apart from"[64]? This latter remark, as well as 4Q300 1a ii-b 3 כי לא הבטתם בשורש חוכמה[, "for you have not gazed upon the roots of wisdom", suggests that there are different kinds of wisdom (just as there are different kinds of רזים, "secrets"). Mysteries does not deny the wisdom of the opponents, but judges this wisdom negatively, as evil, deficient, or as folly. Perhaps because of the ambiguity of the term, "wisdom" is not used in connection with the "we" group. God allots and reveals שכל, "intelligence" (4Q299 8 2, 6, 8), He creates בניה, "understanding" (4Q299 8 6, 7), whereas דעה, "knowledge", will fill the world (1Q27 1 i 7). In short, the disputation sections of Mysteries do not distinguish between those who possess wisdom and those who do not, but opposes foreign deficient wisdom to revealed insight. Hence, the question "who are wise and who are foolish" cannot be answered straightforwardly.

The Dispute of Mysteries

The sapiential language and priestly interests indicate a priestly origin of the text. Undoubtedly these priests were connected to the Jerusalem Temple. Above I argued that the text is primarily concerned with the position of Israel versus the nations, and that this may reflect the pre-Hasmonaean period. But what is the setting of the debate with the magi-

63. ולו̊]א קנ[ה חכמה נכחדת̊] כי[אם, or רא[ה instead of קנ[ה. Yet, perhaps there should be restored more letters in the lacuna.

64. ולו̊]א ידע מ[ה חכמה נכחדת̊] כי[אם, Or, ולו̊]א ידע מה הי[ה חכמה נכחדת̊] כי[אם, or ולו̊]א ידע מה הוא[ה חכמה נכחדת̊] כי[אם, but 4Q300 has no attested long forms of הוא or היא.

cians? It has been argued that these magicians "were a group of diviners which tried to grasp the hidden order of the world by the divinatory means taught to mankind by the fallen heavenly Watchers", in particular astrological approaches of divination[65]. The only forms of divination that would have been permitted in later times by the Essenes would have been the oracle of the lot and the inspired exegesis of scripture. The question is whether this also holds for the circles behind Mysteries.

Those who seek the roots of understanding (4Q301 1 2) are scorned in 4Q300 1a ii-b 3: "you have not gazed upon the root of wisdom". The key word in 4Q300 1a ii-b 1-3 is this "gaze". The contention is, implicitly in line 1, and explicitly in lines 2 and 3, that the addressees "have not gazed" or "beheld" (הביט). They have not beheld "[the tokens (?)] and signs of heaven", "the eternal mysteries", and "the root of wisdom". The gist of these lines is: you have searched, but not beheld. One may explain this failure on the basis of 1Q27 1 i 7, which states that in the new era the earth will be filled with knowledge[66], which would imply that it is impossible for any normal human being to behold the mysteries. Yet, Instruction repeatedly admonishes the addressee to "gaze" or "behold"[67]. The objects are similar to those in 4Q300 1a ii-b: twice רז נהיה, the "mystery of existence", and once שורשי עולה, "the roots of iniquity". Compare רזי עד, "the eternal mysteries", and שורש חוכמה, "the root of wisdom" in Mysteries. In Instruction, these clauses with הבט are followed by a phrase stating "and know", or "and then you shall know", where the object of this knowledge is related to the fate of men. In spite of the different terminology, the "mystery of existence" is not essentially different from other "mysteries", such as the רזי פלא, "the wondrous mysteries", or the רזי עד, "the eternal mysteries". These "mysteries" concern both the primeval heavenly structure of all that is,

65. A. LANGE, *The Essene Position on Magic and Divination*, in M.J. BERNSTEIN, F. GARCÍA MARTÍNEZ & J. KAMPEN (eds.), *Legal Texts and Legal Issues. Proceedings of the Second Meeting of the International Organization for Qumran Studies, Published in Honour of Joseph M. Baumgarten* (STDJ, 23), Leiden, Brill, 1997, pp. 377-436, esp. 408.

66. *Ibid.*, p. 407.

67. In both 4Q417 1 i 2 and 3 (parallel text: 4Q418 43, 44, 45 i 1 and 2), the reading והבט is uncertain, and the immediate context is missing. In 4Q418 123 ii 5 the object of הביט is אלה, "these things". The three phrases of interest are 4Q417 1 i 18-19 par 4Q418 43, 44, 45 i 14 ואתה בן מבין הבט ברז נהיה ודע [ ]ת כול חי, "and you, o understanding child, gaze on the mystery of existence, and know the [ ] of every living being"; 4Q417 2 i 10-11 par 4Q416 2 i 5-6 הבט ברז נהיה וקח מולדי ישע ודע מי נוחל כבוד ועול, "gaze on the mystery of existence, and grasp the birth-times of salvation, and know who is to inherit glory and iniquity"; 4Q416 2 iii 14-15 par 4Q418 9 15-16 וכל שורשי עולה תביט ואז תדע מה מר לאיש ומה מתוק לגבר, "and gaze (on) all the roots of iniquity, and then you shall know what is bitter for a man, and what is sweet for a person". For the text of Instruction, see DJD, 34, and TIGCHELAAR, *To Increase Learning* (n. 46).

and the ethical, halakhic, and eschatological consequences of this structure. Other expressions are used for the same structure of creation: רז without a complement; סוד, "counsel"; מחשבה, "thought", "plan"[68]. How can one behold or study these structures?

The question of the "mystery of existence" should be related to that of the בית מולדים or מולדים, "horoscope", which, like the "mystery of existence", is found almost exclusively in *Mysteries* and *Instruction*. In most cases, מולדים is mentioned in the same context as the "mystery of existence", or in other clauses with רז. Thus, ברז נהיה דרוש מולד(יו) ואז תדע נחלתו should be taken to mean "in/by the mystery of existence investigate his birth time and then you will know his fate"[69]. The idea that both the "mystery of existence" and the בית מולדים are related to one"s "fate" (נחלה) is attested in the phrases that are introduced by הבט ברז נהיה, "gaze on the mystery of existence", and by 4Q418 201 1 ברז]{ל}{ נהיה הודיע אל נח]לת, "in/by the mystery of] existence God made known the fa[te of". The "mystery of existence" is not only connected to the fate of individuals, but also to periods of time, and the periodization of history. See, for example, 4Q418 77 4: וקח ברז נהיה מֿשקל קצים ומדתֿ] ימים, "and grasp, by means of the mystery of existence, the weight of times and the measure of[days"[70]. Likewise, the references to מולדי עולה (1Q27 1 i 5) and מולדי ישע (4Q417 2 i 11) are related to persons born in specific periods. The "mystery of existence", as the heavenly structure of creation, is related to בית מולדים and מולדים, "horoscope", since the "mystery of existence" includes both the creation of the luminaries, and the relation of these luminaries to the fate of individuals and the course of history.

68. LANGE, *Weisheit und Prädestination* (n. 7), pp. 103-109. On the רז נהיה see especially D.J. HARRINGTON, *The Rāz Nihyeh in a Qumran Wisdom Text (1Q26, 4Q415-418, 423)*, in *RQ* 17 (1996) 549-553. For a summary of different views on the רז נהיה, see John J. COLLINS's contribution to this volume (below pp. 287-305).

69. 4Q416 2 iii 9-10 par 4Q418 9 8-9. See M. MORGENSTERN, *The Meaning of בית מולדים in the Qumran Wisdom Texts*, in *JJS* 51 (2000) 141-144, who argued for the zodiacal interpretation of בית מולדים, but did not discuss the רז נהיה, nor all the occurrences of מולדים in these wisdom texts.

70. J. STRUGNELL & D. HARRINGTON, DJD, 34, p. 297 transcribed עֿל [מ]שֿקל, which I corrected in *To Increase Learning* (n. 46), p. 94, to ע]ל מ[שקל. When I studied the fragment in the Rockefeller Museum, I did not question the reading of *'ayin*, but it seems to me now, on the basis of the photographs, that there is not enough space for the reading ע]ל מ[שקל. Moreover, grammatically, על is problematic. Therefore, even though *mem* is palaeographically more difficult than *'ayin*, I now suggest to read the trace on the edge as the right part of *mem*. If *mem* and *shin* were written slightly larger than average in this fragment, מֿשֿקל might just fit in the available space. Note that one should perhaps slightly adjust the position between the two pieces of the fragment. The restoration ימים, "days", serves as an example, and is based on Ps 39,5.

The phrase בית מולדים is found twice in Mysteries, in 4Q299 3a ii-b 9-16, which describes the divine plan lying behind God's creation (כול רז, "every mystery"), and in 4Q299 5 5, in a section that describes celestial phenomena. In the first section we read מ]חשבת בית מולדים פתח לפ̊[, "the p]lan of the horoscope He opened befo[re"(4Q299 3a ii-b 14). The section is very damaged, but the next line includes first person plural forms. Therefore, I suggest to restore at the end of line 14 לפ̊[נינו, "before us", instead of, for example, לפ̊[ניהם[71]. The meaning of this line would be that God has disclosed the meaning of the zodiac to the "we" group of the text.

We have scattered information about the use and role of astrology in Judaism of the Hellenistic and later periods. Whereas 1 Enoch and Jubilees are critical of astrology, a series of authors ascribes the new science of astrology to Enoch or Abraham[72]. In these descriptions two aspects are of relevance for Mysteries. First, the claim that astrology is not a foreign or pagan science, but revealed or transmitted to Jews. Second, that all the heavenly rulers are in fact created by God, and subservient to his will (see, for example *Jewish Antiquities* 1.155-158). In other words, in Mysteries the dispute between priests and "magicians" does not concern the acceptance or rejection of astrology. The issue is the incorporation of astrology in the Israelite monotheistic system, and the question as to who should be regarded as specialists in the field of astrology.

Hence, Mysteries represents an attempt to uphold the special position of Israelite culture and religion against Hellenistic and other pagan beliefs, in particular astrology. The nations, presumably in particular the Hellenistic kingdoms, are criticized for their plundering. Their (Babylonian and Egyptian) diviners are scolded for not beholding the real secrets. At the same time the group behind Mysteries tries to safeguard the status of the Jerusalem priests as temple functionaries, judges, teachers, and as sages who have real knowledge of the mysteries, including astrology.

Qumran Institute
Rijksuniversiteit Groningen

Eibert TIGCHELAAR

71. For פתח לפני, "to disclose before/to", see CD III 16 where it is parallel to גלה ל־, "to reveal to", with the object נסתרות, "secrets".

72. See Pseudo-Eupolemus, Artapanus, Josephus, *Jewish Antiquities* 1.158, 167.

THE ESCHATOLOGICAL HOPE OF 4QTIME OF RIGHTEOUSNESS

While wisdom texts such as 4QInstruction and 4QMysteries have received notable attention in the scholarly debate, little attention has been given to the smaller amount of preserved material in 4QTimes of Righteousness[1]. A forthcoming article by Å. Justnes discusses the biblical passages which have influenced this text as well as related writings from the intertestamental period[2]. This paper will add some more observations on the text and suggest a diachronic sequence of related writings from the 2nd century BCE.

4Q215A 1 II, TEXT AND A STRUCTURED TRANSLATION[3]

1]]ל֯ **[ ]כ֯[ ]*ה֯ת֯ם֯? ה֯ו֯ד֯ם֯[
2]]**י֯א֯* לב אדם וג֯ם֯ פ֯עולת֯ם בעת֯[ה? יע]בורו֯ ע֯נ]י֯?
3 ו֯צרתמציק ו֯נסוי שחת ויצרופו בם ל֯בחירי צ֯דק ו֯י֯מ֯ח כ֯ו֯ל פ֯שע֯ם֯
4 בעבור חס֯ד֯יו כיא שלם קעהרשע ו֯כ֯ול ע֯ולה ת[]*יו֯ [כיא]
5 באה עת הצד֯ק ומלאה הארץ דע֯ה ו֯ת֯ה֯לת אל ב֯יפ֯[יו כיא]
6 בא קצהשל֯ו֯ם֯ וחוקי חאמת ותעודת [ה]צדק להשכיל֯[כול אנש]
7 בדרכי אלו֯ב֯גבורות מעשיו֯[ובדעתו]ע֯ד֯ עולמי ע֯ד֯ כול ל֯ש֯[ון]
8 תברכנו וכול אנש ישתחוו ל֯ו֯[ויהיה לב]ב֯ם אח[ד] כיא הוא֯ה֯[ידע]
9 פעולתם בטרם הברא֯ם ועבודת הצדק פלג ג֯בולותם[ועתם]
10 בדורותם כ֯יא בא ממשל {הצדק} הטוב וירם כסא ה[צדק]
11 ומודה גבה השכל ערמה ותושיה נבחנו במחש[ב]ת֯ ק֯ו֯ד֯ש֯[ו]
12] אנ]ש֯י֯ ע֯נ֯*ה **[

1. Preliminary publication: E.G. CHAZON, *A Case of Mistaken Identity: Testament of Naphtali (4Q215) and Time of Righteousness (4Q215ª)*, in D.W. PARRY – E. ULRICH (eds.), *The Provo International Conference on the Dead Sea Scrolls: Technological Innovations, New Texts, and Reformulated Issues* (STDJ, 30), Leiden, Brill, 1998, pp. 110-124; E.G. CHAZON – M.E. STONE, *4QTime of Righteousness (4Q215ª, olim 4QTNaphtali): A Preliminary Publication of Fragment 1 ii*, *ibid.*, pp. 124-125. *Editio major* in DJD, 36 (2000), pp. 172-184. For the relation between 4Q215 (4QTNaphtali) and 4Q215a, see DJD, 22, pp. 73-76. The plate in the Rockefeller Museum contains two minor fragments which are not included in the DJD edition, one includes the words]שמרי[]מ֯צ֯ו֯ת[.

2. Å. JUSTNES, *4Q215a (Time of Righteousness) in Context*, in J.J. COLLINS – G.E. STERLING (eds.), *Sapiential Perspectives. Wisdom Literature in Light of the Dead See Scrolls*, Leiden, Brill, 2003.

3. Readings and restorations (often different from the DJD edition) by T. Elgvin and Å. Justnes, based i.a. on examination of the original fragments in the Rockefeller Museum. For notes to the readings presented here, see T. ELGVIN and Å. JUSTNES, *Notes on 4Q215a frgs. 1, 2, 3, and 4*, in COLLINS – STERLING (eds.), *Sapiential Perspectives* (n. 2). Italic font in the translation indicates tentative restoration of the meaning of the text. For the understanding of this text, I am indebted to discussions with Årstein Justnes as well as

[1]] *make an end to* their splendour [
[2] *He knew*] the heart of man and also their recompense [*in its time*.]

[*They will pass through affliction*]
[3] and distress of (the) oppressor and trial of (the) pit.

And they shall be refined by them to become the elect of righteousness,
and all their sins will be wiped out
[4] because of His loving kindness.

For the period of wickedness has been completed
and all injustice will ha[ve an e]nd.

[For] [5] the time of righteousness has come
and the land has been filled with knowledge
and glorification of God in [His] be[auty.

For] [6] the age of peace has come
and the laws of truth and the testimony of justice,
to instruct [every man] [7] in the ways of God[
and] His mighty deeds [and knowledge of Him]forever.

Every ton[gue] [8] will bless Him
and every man will bow down to Him,
[and they will be] of on[e hea]rt.

For He [knew] [9] their recompense before they were created.
As to the deeds of righteousness, He assigned their borders[*and times*] [10] for their generations.

For the dominion of goodness has come,
the throne of [*righteousness*] has been elevated,
[11] knowledge, prudence and insight are raised high.

Tested by [His] holy pl[a]n are [12] [the elect of truth,]the men of humility, [

Frgs. 2 and 3

frg. 2

[by] [1] His holy [spirit] He established them for[
[2] He created them to strengthen[
[3] from its days, and darkness[
[4] for its set time … darkness[*He ordained the heavenly lights as signs*]
[5] for the set times before [*they were made*

frg. 3

[1]]to destroy the earth with his wrath and renew it/them[[2] s]ource of their knowledge, fo[r

the participants of the CBL seminar, among them A.Y. Collins, J.J. Collins, L. Hartman, M. Knibb, and J. Corley.

Notes on Text and Translation

Frg. 1.

L. 1. Line 1 may be a supralinear addition at the top of the column by a later hand. Justnes and I have previously read the traces of the first word חסם*[I now suggest התם*[(Hip'il of תמם) which gives a good meaning before הודם.

L. 2. פעולתם is here and in line 9 understood as "their recompense", not "their deed" (so DJD, in line 9), for which cf. e.g. Isa 62,11 (see below). The restoration בעת]ה יע[בורו] may be one letter too long for the lacuna. It presupposes a smaller space between the words, cf. the lack of space between words three times in lines 3, 6, and 7.

L. 3. DJD erroneously reads וצדתמציק "hunting of (the) oppressor". צרת מציק should be understood as "distress caused by the oppressor".

L. 3. וימח can be read as Qal "He will wipe out", or Nip'al as in this translation.

L. 4. ת[]*יו]. Justnes and I have difficulty accepting DJD's ת]עבו[ר, but do not have a better suggestion. One must fill out with a verb with a meaning close to עבר or תמם.

Ll. 5-6. I translate these perfect forms "has come", "has been filled" (DJD renders "is coming"). God's kingdom is so close at hand that it is described in the past tense, as if it had already broken in.

L. 9. פלג is understood as a verb, not a noun as in DJD ("the work of righteousness is the division of their borders").

L. 10. וירם can be read as Hip'il (DJD: "He will raise up") or a Qal consecutive imperfect as in this translation. In the context of lines 10-11 the passive meaning is preferable to introducing God as active subject. F or כסא ה]צדק] one may alternatively restore כסא ה]כבוד] or כסא ה]קודש] "the throne of Holiness."

L. 11. The structure of this line is not easy to comprehend. DJD reads ומודה גבה with the preceding line, so that the throne is "very high". This seems to provide an unnecessary repetition in the text, as line 10 already describes the raising of the throne. DJD ends its translation of the text "Insight, prudence, and sound wisdom are proved by [His] h[oly thou[ght]". The CBL seminar discussion tended to connect ומודה גבה with the following "knowledge, prudence and insight"[4], and then link the testing with the elect group mentioned in the following line. With biblical tradition as referent, men seem to be a more reasonable object for testing than insight and prudence. השכל is read as a construct infinitive.

L.12. There is exactly space to restore בחירי צדק before אנ]שי ענ*ה (cf. translation). DJD only reads]שי ע*[]ה].

Frg. 2.

Ll. 01-1. I restore ברוח] קודשו יסדם. For God's holy spirit as agent in the act of creation, cf. Gen 1,2 and 4Q422 (4QParaGenExod) I 6-7 השמים והארץ ...וכול]צבאם עשה בדברו // ...כול מלאכתו אש]ר עשה ורוח קודש]ו

L. 3. מימיו may be translated "from its days" or "its waters".

4. For the elevation of knowledge, cf. 1 Enoch 91,10 "Wisdom will arise and be given to them" (the elect).

SOME COMMENTS ON THE TEXT

Cross has characterized this hand as late Hasmonean or early Herodian (*c*.30 BCE-20 CE)[5]. The orthography points to copying in the Qumran scribal school: cf. the verbal form ויצרופו (1 3), מודה, as well as the long forms כול, כיא, and הואה. The editors call 4Q215a a "poetic eschatological work". Poetic characteristics are obvious, parallelisms and rhythmic features abound in the larger fragment, which may be hymnic in character.

Frg. 2 deals with the act of creation. The text seems to refer to the luminaries and their connections with the set times (festivals) on earth as well as God's preordination of the luminaries and their role. For this theme, cf. Gen 1,14-18; 1 Enoch 2, and the opening column of 4QInstruction, 4Q416 1 7-9. Frg. 3 sums up the author's future hope; a cosmic judgement and renewal. The "source of their knowledge" may refer to the knowledge of men, angels or fallen angels (for the latter option, cf. 1 Enoch 6-16). The larger frg. 1 opens with the testing of an elect group, and describes the subsequent renewal of the earth and mankind. A logical sequence would be to place frg. 2 before frgs. 3 and 1 – creation and the order of the luminaries precedes testing, judgement and renewal[6].

Frg. 1 opens with God's foreknowledge of man and his deeds as well as the recompense he has ordained (l. 2). Ll. 2-3 refers to suffering and trials as well as an oppressor. Through the trials (ויצרופו בם) an elect group is being refined and emerges as God's בחירי צדק. A similar process is described in 1 Enoch 10 and the Apocalypse of Weeks in 1 Enoch 93 and 91. The following stichos describe the end of the "period of wickedness", and the advent of the "time of righteousness" (= the "age of peace", "the dominion of good"). We encounter some kind of periodisation of history. The present time of wickedness is contrasted with the coming time of peace. But there is no sequence of a number of periods, such as in the Apocalypse of Weeks. The time of righteousness is characterised by a transformation of mankind according to the will of God. All men will acknowledge and praise the Lord, whose kingdom has broken in. Lines 11-12 proclaim that knowledge of God, insight and prudence will be elevated among men, and then return to the theme of testing (refining) of the elect group.

The elect will be tested by Gods "holy plan", במחשבת קודשו. While מחשבה means "plan" or "thought" in general, מחשבת קודשו may desig-

5. DJD, 36, p. 173.

6. In the opening column of 4QInstruction, 4Q416 1, the created order of the luminaries (lines 7-9) precedes the final judgement (lines 10-15).

nate a more specific part of the heavenly ordination, cf. the reference to רוח] קודשו connected to the creation in frg. 2. The related writing 4QMysteries parallels מחשבה with רז: "He decides] every mystery and preordains every plan" (4Q299 3 11)[7]. Thus, מחשבת קודשו in this text may refer to God's eschatological plan, hidden for men in general but revealed to the elect, parallel to *raz nihyeh* in 4QInstruction[8].

According to the editors, the throne of line 10 may be that of the Davidic messiah or God's at the eschatological judgement. Justnes concludes with God's throne, but mentions as argument for the Davidic option a possible allusion to Isa 52,13 (ירום ונשא וגבה מאד) in line 10-11[9]. However, I have above argued that ומודה גבה should be connected to the following, not to the throne of the preceding line. For a messianic reading one could also mention Dan 7,9-15 and Isa 11,1-10, a composite passage on the rule of the Davidic sprout which culminates in a time of peace as well as salvation for the gentiles.

The context points, however, to the throne as the end-time throne of God, designated כסא הצדק or an equivalent. God is the acting subject in lines 3-10, he is the one on the throne for whom all men will bow down and prostrate themselves (line 8). If the Messiah suddenly would have been introduced at the end of line 10, we would have expected כסא משיחו "the throne of *His* messiah", not כסא ה[משיח]. For God's throne, cf. Isa 6,1; 14,13; Dan 7,9; 4Q521 2 ii 7 "He will honour the pious from the throne of the eternal kingdom"; 1 Enoch 9,4; 4Q530 (4QEnGiants[b] ar) ii 16-17 "The ruler of the heavens came down to the earth, thrones were erected and the Great Holy One sa[t down", and the mention of God as king in the related 4Q299 (4QMyst[a]) 9. The Isaianic Zion-theology reflected in frg. 1 (see below) points in the same direction. Justnes' suggestion to restore ותהלת אל ביפ]יו "glorification of God in [His] be[auty" in line 5 creates an allusion to another verse describing God as king, Isa 33,17 (מלך ביופיו תחזינה עיניך). Lines 7-8 rephrase mankind's prostration before God's throne in Isa 45,23 כי־לי תכרע כל־ברך תשבע כל־לשון. As Philonenko has observed, our text represents a striking parallel to the gospels' proclamation that the kingdom of God has come near[10].

7. מחשבת קודשו/קודשכה is used for God's holy plan in 1QS XI 19; 1QM XIII 2; 4Q425 (4QSapiential-Didactic Work B) 4 ii 3. The Treatise of the Two Spirits (1QS IV 4-5) uses מחשבת קודש on the path of the sons of light.

8. T. ELGVIN, *The Mystery to Come: Early Essene Theology of Revelation*, in F. CRYER – Th.L. THOMPSON (eds.), *Qumran between the Old and the New Testament*, Sheffield, Sheffield Academic Press, 1998, pp. 113-150, esp. 131-139.

9. ELGVIN – JUSTNES, *Notes on 4Q215a* (n. 3).

10. M. PHILONENKO, *Marc 1,15a et 4Q215a. La préhistorie esseno-qoumranienne d'une proclamation eschatologique*, in *Revue d'Histoire et de Philosophie Religieuses* 80 (2000) 213-220.

In a 1998 paper I grouped 4Q215a among the "mixed sapiential-apocalyptic" writings from the Qumran library, and suggested that it should be counted among other presectarian works in this category that were preserved by the commune at Qumran[11]. G.W.E. Nickelsburg has noted that we should reserve the terms "apocalyptic" and "apocalypticism" for entities for which revelation is a significant component[12], and there is not much distinct revelation terminology in these fragments. 4Q215a is no apocalypse, but seems to reflect an apocalyptic eschatology. A number of themes connect this work with other early apocalyptic writings such as Daniel and the Enochic books: God's predetermination of the ways of men and the world, the present time of wickedness will come to an end at God's judgement, the era of good will follow, an elect group has a key role at the culmination of the present age, mankind and earth will be radically transformed.

Participants in the CBL asked how fitting the designation "sapiential" is. Frg. 1 demonstrates sapiential terminology (knowledge, instruct, ways of God, prudence, insight, plan), but the fragmentary character of the text leaves the question of genre open. 4Q215a is eschatological, perhaps hymnic, but is it instructional (as wisdom writings are)? Some kind of parenetic agenda can be seen in the references to the elect group in lines 2-4 and 11-12: their present trials are not the end, the trials should function as testing and refinement, God will take care of the addressees and make them the elect of righteousness. Cf. also the reference to]שמרי[]מ̊צ̊[ו]ת in frag. 5 (see note 1).

The mention of the "elect of righteousness" and "men of humility" (lines 3 and 12)[13] connected to the end-time events may cast some light on the milieu of origin. The author(s) should be sought in an elite or pious group that expected imminent judgement and saw itself as the nucleus of the renewed people of Israel and all mankind. For this group the present time in Israel is "the period of wickedness" that will give way to the time of peace. Sapiential terminology and the number of fine allusions to Isaianic passages point to a scribal author. The expected renewal is for all mankind[14] (and likely all Israel as well), not for a narrow sectarian group. Thus, in its "ecclesiology" and relation to outsiders, 4Q215 may be closer to 4QMysteries, Jubilees, and Daniel, than to

11. *Wisdom With and Without Apocalyptic*, in D. FALK, F. GARCÍA MARTÍNEZ, E. SCHULLER (eds.) *Sapiential, Liturgical and Poetical Texts from Qumran. Proceedings of the IOQS Conference, Oslo, August 1998* (STDJ, 35), Leiden, Brill, 2000, pp. 15-38.

12. *Wisdom and Apocalypticism in Early Judaism. Some Points for Discussion*, in *SBLSP* 33 (1994) 715-732, esp. p. 717.

13. Cf. the combination of God's throne and kingdom with the pious, poor and faithful in 4Q521 2 ii.

14. 4Q475Renewed Earth is another poetic text that foresees an universal renewal of the earth and all mankind.

1 Enoch, 4QInstruction and the texts of the Yahad[15]. No priestly terminology can be discerned[16].

4Q215a 1 alludes to a number of biblical verses (most of them Isaianic) centered on Zion and God's renewal of Jerusalem[17]: The advent motif related to Zion is found in Ps 102,14 (בא מועד), Isa 60,1 (בא אורך), 62,11 (ישעך בא), and Isa 40,10. The gentiles' pilgrimage to Zion and their acknowledgement of the Lord (lines 6-8) are described in Isa 2,1-4; 11,10; 66,18-24.45. For the special connection of צדק to Zion (lines 3, 5, 9), see Isa 1,21-28; 9,6; 32,16-18; 33,5-6. God's throne is also a Zion motif, Justnes' restoration ביפ]יו (line 5) relates this line to Isa 33,17. While Zion or pilgrimage are not specifically mentioned in the text, a Zion theology seems to permeate this passage.

מלאה הארץ דעה ותהלת אל (line 5) quotes Isa 11,9/Hab 2,14 and alludes to Hab 3,3 תהלתו מלאה הארץ[18]. צדק occurs twice in Isa 11,1-10, another passage which may have influenced our text. The "one heart" of line 8 refers to Ezek 11,19 ונתתי להם לב אחד[19], a passage dealing with the renewal of the people of Israel (so also its use in Acts 4,32), not mankind in general. In our text the one heart is an end-time gift to all mankind. We see that lines 4-10 are formed by biblical prophetic passages, although our author clothed his hope in later sapiential language.

Some Related Writings, a Diachronic Sequence[20]

A number of early (pre-sectarian?) texts represented in the Qumran library demonstrate striking similarities with 4Q215a, especially frg. 1.

15. On 4QMysteries and Daniel as more all-Israelite than 4QInstruction and the Enochic books, see T. Elgvin, *Priestly Sages? The Milieus of Origin of 4QMysteries and 4QInstruction*, in Collins – Sterling (eds.), *Sapiential Perspectives* (n. 2). G. Boccaccini, *Middle Judaism. Jewish Thought, 300 B.C.E. to 200 C.E.*, Minneapolis, MN, Fortress, 1991, pp. 126-160.

16. Cf. A. Lange's assertion that priestly circles in Jerusalem, in the period 200-150 BCE, subsequently produced 4QInstruction, 4QMysteries, the second edition of Qohelet, and the 2 Spirits Treatise: *In Diskussion mit dem Tempel. Zur Auseinandersetzung zwischen Kohelet und Weisheitlichen Kreisen am Jerusalemer Tempel*, in A. Schoors (ed.), *Qohelet in the Context of Wisdom* (BETL, 136), Leuven, University Press – Peeters, 1998, pp. 113-159.

17. For the following biblical references, see Å. Justnes, *4Q215a (Time of Righteousness) in Context* (note 2). For the role of Zion in Qumran texts, see T. Elgvin, *4Q475. 4QRenewed Earth*, in DJD, 36, pp. 464-473, esp. 468.

18. הארץ may be understood as 'the land (of Israel)' or 'the earth'. The Zion theology of this text suggests that הארץ here should be understood as 'the land of Israel'. I thus tend to see lines 4-5 as dealing with the renewal of Zion and the land, while lines 6-8 would widen the perspective to the earth and all mankind.

19. Alternative readings are לב חדש and לב אחר (LXX).

20. These texts are discussed by Justnes, *4Q215a (Time of Righteousness) in Context* (n. 2). To his treatment I would like to add this tentative suggestion on the relation between the various texts.

We encounter in these sources a schematic view of history encompassing wickedness and trials, the emergence of an elect group, the end of wickedness and the advent of a time of peace and harmony.

The earliest passage is found in the Book of Watchers (BW), 1 Enoch 10,16–11,2. If this poem belonged to the original Shemihazah story it could be dated to the 3rd century. I cannot see, however, that this poem is integral to the Shemihazah story and suggest that it is a later addition to chs. 6-10. This text could have been added to chs. 6-10 in the period 220-198, a war-filled period where Judea and Jerusalem experienced devastation (*Ant.* 12.129-131, 138; Dan 11,16). However, the theme of the "righteous planting" has parallels only in the 2nd century (see the texts surveyed below as well as the writings of the Yahad). I therefore propose that this text belongs to the stage of editorial inclusion of chs. 6-11 in an early Enochic testament in the period 200-170 BCE[21].

This passage uses the deluge as *typos* for the coming judgement. Among terms parallel to our text one may point to "the plant of righteousness", "deeds of righteousness", "let every wicked deed be gone" (10,16); "all the earth will be tilled in righteousness" (10,18); "all the sons of men will become righteous; and all the peoples will worship (me), and all will bless me and prostrate themselves" (10,21); "all the earth will be cleansed from all defilement" (10,22); "truth and peace will be united together for all the days of eternity" (11,2). A (present) evil period will be followed by a time of peace and righteousness, as well as a universal renewal. I suggest that this passage in BW is the "grandfather" which influenced (directly and indirectly) a number of other texts which will be reviewed. BW is certainly an influential source in 2nd century Judea.

To the time of Antiochus Epiphanes and the early Maccabeans I suggest to date three texts, the Apocalypse of Weeks (AW, 1 Enoch 93/91), 1Q/4QMysteries and 4Q215a. All these authors probably knew BW and depend upon 1 Enoch 10, literally or some other way. Whether they knew each other is an open question, but one may assert some contact between the scribal circles behind these writings in the tiny temple province of pre-Hasmonean Judea.

Also AW demonstrates close parallels to 4Q215a. One may mention "a perverse generation … all its deeds will be perverse" (93:9); "the

21. Cf. G.W.E. NICKELSBURG, *1 Enoch. 1. A Commentary on the Book of 1 Enoch, Chapters 1-36; 81-108*, Minneapolis, MN, Fortress, 2001, pp. 24-26, 169-172, 226-228. *Pace* Nickelsburg, 10,16ff need not be seen as a necessary climax to the Shemihazah story, but rather as a repetitive interpretation of 10,3.7. Further, chs. 12-16 do not repeat the themes of 10,16ff., which may indicate that these chapters represent an interpretation of chs. 6-10 without the addition of 10,16ff.

elect will be chosen, as witnesses of righteousness, from the eternal plant of righteousness, to whom will be given sevenfold wisdom" (93,9-10, Eth: "the elect of righteousness"); "they will uproot the foundations of violence" (91,11); "an eighth week of righteousness" (91,12); "righteous law", "all the deeds of wickedness will vanish from the whole earth", "all humankind will look to the path of eternal righteousness" (91,14); "they will do piety and righteousness" (91,17). The detailed periodisation of AW is not found in the other sources discussed here[22].

We then turn to 4QMysteries. Four or five passages in Mysteries deal with the (day of) judgement and the consumption of evil[23]. The theme of God who has established the universe and determined the ways of men recurs here as well[24]. A well preserved poetic passage on the flow of history is represented by 1Q27 1 i, 4Q299 1 and 4Q300 3[25]:

> When the begotten of unrighteousness are delivered up,
> and wickedness is removed from before righteousness ...
> so shall wickedness cease forever,
> and righteousness shall be revealed as the sun
> (throughout) the full measure of the world.
> And all the adherents of the mysteries of Belial will be no more.
> But knowledge shall fill the world,
> and folly shall nevermore be there. (1Q27 1 i 5-7)

We recognise the same use of Isa 11,9 as in 4Q215a. This could point to one text being dependent upon the other, but independent use of the same biblical verse cannot be excluded. 4QMysteries represent self-confident scribes opposed to other Israelite sages. The book discerns those with true insight from others who lack understanding. However, the extant fragments do not preserve terms that point towards a specific elect group within Israel, such as "plant" or "elect of truth". I have argued that 4QMysteries is more national and open towards all Israel than its "relative" 4QInstruction[26]. The connection between 4Q300 1b 2 and

22. But compare Daniel 2 and 7, the four empires and the ten horns. For a dating of AW shortly before the Maccebean revolt, see J. VANDERKAM, *Studies in the Apocalypse of Weeks (1 Enoch 93:1-10; 91:11-17)*, in *CBQ* 46 (1984) 511-523; G.W.E. NICKELSBURG, *1 Enoch* (n. 21), p. 441.

23. According to 4Q299 53, God's anger is kindled by the abominations on earth, and at the appointed time He will exact vengeance upon the ungodly. 4Q299 59 is fragmentarily preserved, but seems to contain the same motif. 4Q300 9 2 refers to יום הריב "the day of dispute" for those who did not understand the heavenly secrets. 4Q301 3 8 expects the end of the period of wickedness, בכלו]ת [קׄץ רשעה.

24. 4Q299 3a ii-b 10-16; 5 1-5.

25. See L. SCHIFFMAN's edition and translation, DJD, 20, pp. 34-38.

26. ELGVIN, *Priestly Sages?* (n. 15).

Dan 9,24 can be explained not by literal dependence upon Daniel, but by linkage between the milieus of these two writings[27]. 4QMysteries is a sapiential collection encompassing wisdom instructions, hymnic material, eschatological outlooks as well as priestly-halakhic passages[28]. The priestly material may locate 4QMysteries closer to the temple milieu than the other sources discussed here[29]. I have tentatively ascribed the work to pre-Maccabean circles who hoped for a national restoration of Israel.

As in 4Q215a, the expected renewal is for all the earth. 4QMysteries represents a cosmic dualism and knows of forces antagonistic to God. The eschatological passages represent the same eschatology and world view as that of 4Q215a and may derive from the same milieu. 4QMysteries contains priestly material, 4Q215a focuses on Zion motifs, a priestly milieu in Jerusalem could be behind both writings.

The next source, probably somewhat later than AW, Mysteries and 4Q215a, is the Treatise of Two Spirits (1QS III-IV). Lange has argued that 2 Spirits is a presectarian work, dependent upon Mysteries and 4QInstruction, to be dated *c.*150 BCE, and later incorporated into 1QS[30]. Also this document demonstrates parallels to 4Q215a[31]: "their deeds in their generations", "the times of their reward" (III 14-15); "at their appointed time, they will execute all their deeds" (III 16); "all their afflictions and their periods of grief" (III 23); "He established every deed, on their paths every labour" (III 25-26); "He has determined an end to the existence of evil, on the appointed time of visitation He will obliterate it for ever. Then truth shall rise up forever in the world, for it has been defiled in paths of wickedness during the dominion of evil ... Then God will refine, with His truth, all man's deeds" (IV18-20); "He will make

27. *Pace* LANGE, *In Diskussion mit dem Tempel* (n. 16).

28. I tend to see 4Q301 (4QMyst^{c}?) as a separate writing from the same or a related milieu. 4Q301 frg. 1 preserves the beginning of a wisdom instruction, probably the beginning of the work. 4Q301 may be classified as a hymnic composition (cf. frgs. 3, 4, 5, 6, 9) introduced by wisdom instructions (frgs. 1 and 2). Frg. 3 has close parallels in Hekhalot literature, and may place the origins of this tradition in the pre-Maccabean temple, perhaps together with 11QPs^{a}Creat and the Songs of the Sabbath Sacrifice. According to E. CHAZON, 11QPs^{a}Creat is a hekhalot psalm built upon the throne visions of Isaiah and Ezekiel: *The Use of the Bible as a Key to Meaning in Apocryphal and Pseudepigraphical Psalms* (IOQS paper 05.08.01).

29. Cf. LANGE, *In Diskussion mit dem Tempel* (n. 16).

30. A. LANGE, *Weisheit und Prädestination: Weisheitliche Urordnung und Prädestination in den Textfunden von Qumran* (STDJ, 18), Leiden, Brill, 1995, pp. 126-130, 168-170; ID., *In Diskussion mit dem Tempel* (n. 16), pp. 134, 157-158. See also E.J.C. TIGCHELAAR, *To Increase Learning for the Understanding Ones. Reading and Reconstructing the Fragmentary Early Jewish Sapiential Text 4QInstruction* (STDJ, 44), Leiden, Brill, 2001, pp. 206-207.

31. Translation adapted from the *Study Edition.*

those of perfect behaviour understand the wisdom of the sons of heaven. For these God has chosen for an everlasting covenant ... there will be no more injustice" (IV 22-23); "He knows the recompense of their deeds" (הואה ידע פעולת מעשיהן, IV 25). 2 Spirits shares the predestination theology of 4Q215a and 4QInstruction. The eschatological scheme present in the writings discussed above is here integrated in philosophic-anthropological speculation. The argument is more developed and sectarian than that of 1 Enoch 10, AW, 4Q215a, and 4QMysteries. Thus, 2 Spirits is probably penned later than all or most of these other sources.

4QInstruction is difficult to date, most scholars see it as a presectarian work to be dated somewhere in the period 200-150 BCE. God's preknowledge of history and the deeds of men is an important issue for this author (4Q416 1 7-9; 4Q417 1 i 7-12; 4Q418 126 ii 3-5; 127 5-6; 4Q423 5 3-5). The opening column, 4Q416 1, integrates a section on cosmology (creation and the preordained role of the luminaries, lines 7-9)[32] with a description of the end-time cosmic judgement (lines 10-15). Lines 10-11 describe either "the end" or "the period" of wickedness (עבודת רשעה ... קצה), to be followed by "the period of truth" (קץ האמ]ת, line 13). Aramaic קשט, frequent in 1 Enoch 10 and AW, can in Hebrew be rendered both אמת and צדק. Enochic terminology such as "week of righteousness" can be behind עת הצדק (4Q215a 1 5) and קץ האמת (4QInstruction). The elect witnesses to righteousness (1 Enoch 93,9-10) resemble בחירי צדק (4Q215a 1 3) and בחירי אמת [4Q418 (4QInstruction^d) 69 ii 10], cf. בני אמתו and נוחלי אמת (4Q416 1 10; 4Q418 55 6). "Deeds of righteousness" (1 Enoch 10,16) recur as עבודת הצדק[33] (4Q215a 1 9) and פעלות אמת (4Q418 69 ii 13).

4QInstruction presents not only a cosmic, but also an individual eschatology. The faithful, struggling not to lose courage will inherit an angelic life. But this book seems to reflect a more negative view on outsiders (those not belonging to the "truly elected ones") than 4Q215a.

4QInstruction's repeated stress on revelation of God's mysteries points to some kind of esoteric circles behind this work. I have further suggested that 4Q418 81 10-14 reflects some kind of "messianic community", with terms such as "eternal planting", "inherit the land", "sprout", "men of (God's) favour"[34]. These circles, the בחירי אמת, saw themselves as the nucleus of the coming renewal of God's people. In

32. Cp. 4Q215a frg. 2.

33. Cf. 1 Enoch 91,17 וקש[טא יעבדון (4QEn^g 1 iv 26).

34. ELGVIN, *The Mystery to Come* (n. 8). I have argued that Enochic "planting" terminology influenced 4QInstruction; ID., *An Analysis of 4QInstruction* (Ph.D. diss., The Hebrew University of Jerusalem, 1998), pp. 126-140.

4Q215a, בחירי צדק may have a similar role. 4QInstruction seems to be more or less contemporary with 4Q215a. The similarities should probably be explained by independent use of similar Enochic material rather than literary dependence between these writings. As a sapiential collection, 4QInstruction presents its general parenesis within an apocalyptic/eschatological framework. A similar combined eschatological and parenetic agenda may be perceived in 4Q215a[35].

1 Enoch 107, a later addition to the Epistle of Enoch and perhaps the latest source discussed here, also demonstrates similarities with the writings discussed above[36].

Concluding Comments

The poetic style of frg. 1 is close to that of early piyyutim. The central motif of all peoples gathering before God's throne reminds us of *Unetaneh toqef*, a piyyut from the early Byzantine period included in the Rosh Hashanah liturgy[37]. The themes of creation, judgement, renewal, and God's reign are linked to Rosh Hashanah probably as early as the 2nd century BCE[38]. 4Q215a is probably not a hymnic composition as such. The textual evidence *in toto* points more towards a didactic review of God's holy plan from creation to judgement, where the final section is clothed in poetic language similar to restoration passages in Isaiah. Early traditions connected to Rosh Hashanah may have inspired this text or sections of it. Our analysis seems to confirm the separation of 4Q215a from 4Q215Testament of Naphtali.

The writings surveyed here may suggest a Maccabean or pre-Maccabean date also for 4Q215a. If the "oppressor" of line 3 points to a specific person, it is tempting to see a reference to Antiochus Epiphanes,

35. In 4QInstruction, the longer apocalyptic/eschatological discourses may represent a later stratum than the (collections of) shorter admonitions. While the discourses use and reinterpret biblical prophetic passages, the admonitions are more indebted to sapiential tradition such as Proverbs (*Ibid.*, pp. 36-57). This may be compared with my observation that 4Q215a 1 i is heavily influenced by prophetic literature, although the language is sapiential.

36. "I have seen written in them that generation upon generation will do evil in this way, and the evil will be until there arise generations of righteousness. And evil and wickedness will end, and violence vill cease from the earth, and good things will come upon the earth to them" (1 Enoch 107,1, 4Q204 (4QEn[c] ar) 5 ii 27-29).

37. For J. Heinemann, the pre-classical style of this piyyut indicates authorship in the early Byzantine period: *Prayer in the Talmud: Forms and Patterns* (Studia Judaica, 9), Berlin and New York, De Gruyter, 1977, p. 241.

38. T. Elgvin, *Qumran and the Roots of Rosh Hashanah Liturgy*, in E. Chazon (ed.), *Liturgical Perspectives: Prayer and Poetry in Light of the Dead Sea Scrolls* (STDJ, 48), Leiden, Brill, 2003, pp. 49-67.

and the trials as Antiochus' treatment of Jews in Judea from 170 BCE onwards. However, "oppressor" may be used in a more general sense (note that מציק is undeterminated, as is the following שחת), referring to the people's experiences during more than one generation. No specifics in the text preclude a dating in the time of John Hyrcanos or Alexander Janneus, both of whom treated opposition groups harshly.

4Q215a was probably written outside the Yahad. It has few sectarian borders, and seems to be more universal in its outlook. But authorship within the Community cannot be totally excluded, a Yahad member looking forward to the renewal expected after the eschatological war could have expressed his hope in such poetic terms. In that case, the preserved fragments could represent the authograph. If 4Q215a was authored outside the Yahad (my preferred option), the Qumranic orthography demonstrates that the text was copied and read within the Yahad. The composition would easily lend itself to a sectarian reading. It would describe the trials the elect have undergone and give meaning to their struggles which would be perceived as eschatological birth pangs, cf. the self designations ענוים and ענוי רוח in Yahad documents [1QH[a] XXX (Suk V) 21; XXIII (Suk XVIII) 14-15; 1QM XIV 7]. The members would recognise God's preknowledge and plan for human history as well as the hope that through his elect God would renew Israel and all the land/earth.

Prominent in 4Q215a is the Zion theology and "kingship/kingdom of God" that penetrate the description of the coming renewal. Zion, God's throne and kingdom are not at the forefront in the other writings I have surveyed. Here lies the specific contribution of our unknown poet: "Enochic" material and world view has been incorporated into a poetic rendering of the coming renewal of God's elect, the land with Zion and then all the world, under the royal leadership of the God of Israel. This writer sees Zion and a renewed earth together as one, similar to 1 Enoch 10,16-11,2; 25,3-27,5, and Revelation 21-22.

A number of New Testament *loci* are to be found in 4Q215a: the advent of the kingdom of God and its end-time realisation, the relation between the kingdom of God and the community of the faithful, God's eschatological plan for the elect and all mankind, his foreknowledge of the deeds of the elect, the testing of the elect, an active role of God's holy spirit. Similar to 4QInstruction, 4Q215a combines eschatology and wisdom – as it is done also in the gospels[39], Paul and James. Our early

39. But not in the Gospel of Thomas and the earliest source often postulated behind the Q composition. These two Jewish sources as well as the Enochic traditions put a question mark to the clear division between sapiential and eschatological material often

Jewish text illuminates scriptures such as Mk 1,15; Phil 2,10-11[40]; Rev 5,13; 11,15-16; 15,3-4; Eph 1,4-6; 1 Cor 15,24-28; Rom 8,18-27; 1 Pet 4,12-14; Acts 4,32.

Åsterudsletta 45 Torleif ELGVIN
N–1344 Haslum
Norway

asserted in the early Jesus tradition. See, e.g., B.L. MACK, *The Lost Gospel: The Book of Q and Christian Origins*, San Francisco, CA, Harper, 1993; J.S. KLOPPENBORG, *Excavating Q: The History and Setting of the Sayings Gospel*, Edinburgh, T & T Clark, 2000, pp. 118-130, 179-213.

40. Note the christological focus in many of these NT texts, while related OT texts and 4Q215a refer to God and his kingship.

COHÉRENCE STRUCTURELLE ET TENSIONS INTERNES DANS L'INSTRUCTION SUR LES DEUX ESPRITS (1QS III 13 – IV 26)

La publication récente de plusieurs manuscrits de 4QInstruction (4Q415-418c; 4Q423; cf. 1Q26) témoigne de l'existence d'un courant de sagesse qui a intégré des éléments apocalyptiques, en particulier d'ordre eschatologique[1]. Anticipant de peu cette publication, l'étude d'A. Lange sur cette question l'a amené à réexaminer l'Instruction sur les deux esprits de la grotte 1 (1QS iii 13 – iv 26)[2]. Ce texte sapientiel présente de nombreux point de contact avec l'Instruction de la grotte 4; Lange, qui le traite comme un texte unifié, le considère comme issu du même courant. Mais l'analyse d'E. Tigchelaar démontre que les correspondances entre les deux textes se répartissent inégalement dans les différentes sections de 1QS iii 13 – iv 26, ce qui l'amène à postuler l'existence de deux niveaux de rédaction dans cette instruction[3]. Comme contribution à ce dossier, je propose ici une étude assez élaborée de la structure de l'Instruction sur les deux esprits qui démontre la cohérence du texte dans sa forme actuelle; on verra cependant, dans un deuxième temps et de façon plus schématique, que des tensions entre les contenus de différentes sections de cet ensemble permettent de soupçonner qu'il y a une histoire rédactionnelle relativement complexe derrière cette unité apparente.

1. Cohérence structurelle de l'Instruction sur les deux esprits

L'analyse structurelle

L'analyse structurelle cherche à dégager les articulations principales et secondaires d'un texte en se fondant principalement sur les rapports

1. J. Strugnell *et al.*, *Qumran Cave 4, XXIV: 4QInstruction* (DJD, 34), Oxford, Clarendon, 1999.

2. A. Lange, *Weisheit und Prädestination: Weisheit, Urordnung und Prädestination in den Textfunde von Qumran* (STDJ, 18), Leiden, Brill, 1995, pp. 120-170. Pour l'Instruction sur les deux esprits, on se reportera à l'édition d'E. Qimron, *Rule of the Community*, in J.H. Charlesworth (ed.), *The Dead Sea Scrolls. Hebrew, Aramaic, and Greek Texts with English Translations* (PTSDSSP, 1), Tübingen, J.B.C. Mohr (Paul Siebeck), pp. 1-51.

3. E.J.C. Tigchelaar, *To Increase Learning for the Understading Ones. Reading and Reconstructing the Fragmentary Early Jewish Sapiential Text 4QInstruction* (STDJ, 44), Leiden, Brill, 2001, pp. 194-207.

de mots que sont la répétition, l'utilisation de termes du même champ sémantique (synonymes, antonymes, etc.), ou la reprise d'idées ou thèmes similaires. Le postulat de base est que ces rapports, particulièrement lorsqu'ils se trouvent à distance dans le texte, ont une fonction structurante et ont été délibérément utilisés par les scribes pour la composition d'un certain nombre de textes bibliques. Telle que pratiquée par M. Girard[4], la méthode structurelle accorde la priorité aux rapports de mots sur les rapports d'idées et distingue plusieurs niveaux de structuration: la *maxi-structure*, c.-à-d. l'organisation globale d'un texte, sa division en grands ensembles (volets), la *structure* propre à chacune des sections qui en constituent les principaux développements (souvent agencées en tranches de correspondance parallèles), la *mini-structure* des unités de base (phrase, groupe de propositions constitutives des tranches de correspondance) et la *micro-structure* de leur composantes (mots ou syntagmes). Dans un récent travail, j'ai eu recours à cette approche pour analyser la structure de la partie centrale de l'Instruction sur les deux esprits[5]; je l'applique ici à l'ensemble de ce texte.

Contexte

L'instruction est connue par le manuscrit de la grotte 1 de la Règle de la communauté (1QS) daté de c. 100 à 75 av. notre ère, col. iii 13 à iv 26. Il est attesté aussi par un exemplaire contemporain de la grotte 4 (4Q257 S^{c} frg. 2) dont le texte, très fragmentaire, semble à peu près identique[6]. Dans le manuscrit de la grotte 1, l'Instruction est précédée d'un préambule à l'ensemble du document, (1QS i 1-15), d'un rituel d'entrée dans l'alliance (i 16 – ii 18) et de l'évocation du recensement annuel et des exigences d'une conversion sincère (ii 19 – iii 12); elle est suivie d'un ensemble qui se présente comme «La règle pour les membres de la communauté» (v 1). Se démarquant nettement de ce contexte immédiat, l'instruction pourrait avoir circulé de façon autonome et avoir été intégrée à la Règle à une étape de sa rédaction[7].

4. M. GIRARD, *Les Psaumes redécouverts. De la structure au sens, I-III*, Montréal, Bellarmin, 1994-1996.

5. J. DUHAIME, *Les voies des deux esprits (1QS iv 2-14). Une analyse structurelle*, in *RQ* 19 (2000) 349-369.

6. Voir P.S. ALEXANDER et G. VERMES, *Qumran Cave 4, XIX* (DJD, 26), Oxford, Clarendon Press, 1998, pp. 77-80.

7. À ce propos, voir surtout P.S. ALEXANDER, *The Redaction-History of Serekh ha-Yahad: A Proposal,* in *RQ* 17 (1996) 437-456; ALEXANDER et VERMES, *Qumran Cave 4* (n. 6), pp. 9-12; J. MURPHY-O'CONNOR, *La genèse littéraire de la Règle de la Communauté*, in *RB* 76 (1960) 528-549; S. METSO, *The Development of the Qumran Community Rule* (STDJ, 21), Leiden, Brill, 1997.

Texte et traduction

Le texte présente quelques difficultés de lecture et comporte quelques lacunes. J'adopte en général les propositions d'H. Stegemann, en particulier les suivantes[8]:

iii 19 במין אור «dans une source de lumière». La lecture במון אור «dans un séjour» est également possible à cause de la similarité du י et du ו. Le parallélisme est meilleur avec la suite, comme le signale Puech auquel je me rallie sur ce point.

iii 26 [ע]ל [משפט]יהן «sur leurs [décisions / jugements]». Au lieu de [ע]ל [סוד]יהן «et sur leurs [conseils]» proposé par Dupont-Sommer, mais considéré comme trop court par Stegemann et Puech. La restauration retenue ne modifie pas le sens de manière substantielle.

iv 1 אחת תעב מודה «l'autre il (la) déteste beaucoup». Stegemann lit מודה, une variante de מאוד au lieu de סודה, «conseil», qui ne va pas du point de vue du sens. Le מ et le ס se confondent parfois le manuscrit de 1QS.

iv 26 לדעת טוב [ורע כיא א]ל [י]פיל גורלות לכול חי לפי רוחו בו [עד מועד]הפקידה «pour la connaissance du bien [et du mal car Di]eu [fait tom]ber les lots sur tout vivant selon son esprit (mis) en lui [jusqu'au moment] de la visite», avec Stegemann, plutôt que לדעת טוב [ולדעת רע ו]ל[ה]פיל גורלות לכול חי לפי רוחו בי[ום המפשט ו]הפקודה «pour la connaissance du bien [et la connaisance du mal et] pour [faire tom]ber les lots vers tout vivant selon son esprit au [jour du jugement et] de la visite» proposé par Dupont-Sommer[9].

Par ailleurs, pour faire ressortir les correspondances structurelles, un mot hébreu est habituellement rendu par un seul équivalent français. Mais cela n'est pas toujours possible, car il y a des cas où un même terme semble avoir des significations différentes, par exemple תולדות (iii 13.19.19; iv 15) qui peut signifier «nature», «générations», «origines» (j'ai signalé deux possibilités en iii 13 et iv 15); les dérivés de la racine שׂכל ont également été rendu différemment (משׂכיל «maître» iii 13, שׂכל «perspicacité» iv 3 et «science» iv. 18, להשׂכיל «soit apprise» iv 22).

Organisation graphique et structurelle

Sur le plan graphique, le début de l'Instruction est délimité par un alinéa, un crochet marginal et un espace laissé en blanc au début de iii 13. On trouve aussi des crochets sans alinéa entre les lignes iii 18 et iii 19, et des crochets avec alinéas dans la col. iv, entre les lignes 1 et 2, 8 et 9, 14 et 15. Ces crochets suggèrent une division en cinq sections:

8. H. STEGEMANN, *Zu Textbestand und Grundgedanken von 1QS III,13 – IV,26*, in *RQ* 13 (1988) 95-131. Voir également É. PUECH, *La croyance des Esséniens en la vie future: immortalité, résurrection, vie éternelle?* (ÉB, n.s. 22), Paris, Gabalda, 1993, pp. 426-440.

9. Voir A. DUPONT-SOMMER et M. PHILONENKO, *La Bible: écrits intertestamentaires* (Bibliothèque de la Pléiade), Paris, Gallimard, 1987, p. 21.

iii 13-18 Introduction et fondement théologique
iii 18 – iv 1 Présentation des esprits
iv 2-8 La voie de lumière / vérité et sa visite
iv 9-14 La voie de ténèbres / perversité et sa visite
iv 15-26 Le partage des humains entre les esprits

Un court espace a aussi été laissé, en iv 6, entre la description de la voie de l'esprit de lumière / vérité et celle de la visite de ceux qui suivent cette voie.

Du point de vue structurel, on peut diviser le texte en trois grands ensembles (voir tableaux). Un premier volet va de iii 13 à iv 1. Le deuxième comporte les descriptions des voies et des visites (iv 2-14). Le troisième s'étend de iv 15 à 26. Cette division se justifie comme suit:

iii 13-15a sert d'introduction à l'ensemble du texte. iii 15b amorce le développement de la thématique du premier volet, celle de l'agir créateur de Dieu («Du Dieu des connaissances (vient) tout ce qui est et sera» iii 15b; «et lui a créé l'humanité» iii 17b; «et lui a créé les esprits» iii 25b). Ce volet est borné par la reprise de termes «esprit», «action», et «visite» en iii 14 et iii 25b-26a.

Le deuxième volet (iv 2-14) est introduit en iv 2 par une formule explicite: «Et voici (ou telles sont) leurs voies dans le monde»; ces voies et les visites qui leur correspondent se développent suivant un parallèle rigoureux jusqu'à iv 14.

En iv 15, le troisième volet (iv 15-26) s'amorce par une formulation synthétique qui comporte le même démonstratif qu'en iv 2: «En elles (ou en celles-ci) sont les origines de tous les fils d'homme». Cette proposition reprend presque mot à mot celle de iii 13 «pour faire comprendre et enseigner à tous les fils de lumière les origines de tous les fils d'homme». Le troisième volet est borné par la reprise de l'idée d'un partage des esprits entre les fils d'homme exprimée par les expressions «et en leurs catégories se partagent toutes leurs armées...» (iv 15) et «il les a partagés entre les fils d'homme...» (iv 26); on retrouve également ce thème iv 16-17 («car (c'est) Dieu (qui) les a placées une partie contre l'autre») et en iv 25 («car (c'est) une partie contre l'autre (que) Dieu les a placées...»).

Premier volet: Dieu, l'homme, les esprits (iii 13 – iv 1)

Le premier volet se partage en deux sections, iii 13-18c et iii 18d – iv 1, qui ont entre elles trois tranches de correspondance. La première section est délimitée par la reprise des termes «esprit» en iii 14 et 18b et «visite» en iii 14 et 18c. La seconde est introduite formellement par «Voici les esprits, la vérité et la perversion» (iii 18d-19); ces esprits sont associés à la lumière et aux ténèbres au début (iii 19b) et à la fin (iii 25b) de la section.

La première section se découpe assez nettement en trois tranches: iii 13-15a; iii 15b-16b; iii 16c-18c. La première (iii 13-15a) introduit l'ensemble. Elle précise le destinataire («au maître») et l'objet de l'instruction. Elle peut être structurée selon plusieurs possibilités. Lange suppose l'énoncé d'un seul objet d'enseignement «la nature» de tous les fils d'homme, présenté sous trois aspects complémentaires, introduits par la même préposition ל. La tranche est alors partagée en deux unités (a/a^1):

iii 13 (vacat) Au maître, pour faire comprendre
et pour enseigner à tous les fils de lumière
la nature de tous les fils d'homme

14 **quant à** toutes leurs sortes d'esprits en leurs signes
quant à leurs actions dans leurs générations
et **quant à** la visite de leurs coups 15a avec les temps de paix.

Cette façon de découper l'unité a l'avantage d'annoncer trois aspects différents qui sont mis en valeur de façon particulière dans chacun des trois volets du texte actuel: les origines des esprits (iii 13 – iv 1), les actions qui en découlent (iv 2-14) et le sort ultime de ceux qui suivent leurs voies respectives (iv 15-26). Elle est retenue pour cette raison, bien qu'elle ne soit pas assurée sur le plan syntaxique[10].

La formule de la deuxième tranche (iii 15b-16a) est celle d'un chiasme $a/b//b^1/a^1$, unifié par la récurrence du verbe être / exister (היה). Elle consiste en l'affirmation d'un dessein exclusif et immuable de Dieu. Une première proposition (a) qualifie le créateur de «Dieu des connaissances» et lui attribue «tout ce qui est et sera»; elle est suivie de trois autres énoncés coordonnés par un ו. Les deux premiers se répondent en parallèle ($b//b^1$): ils font état d'un «plan» pour les êtres, établi avant leur existence, auquel ils se conforment le moment venu. Le dernier énoncé clôt le développement (a^1); il complète l'affirmation initiale que «tout» vient de Dieu en précisant que «rien» n'est changé à son plan au cours de l'existence.

La dernière tranche de la section (iii 16c-18c) est délimitée par la présence de deux suffixes pronominaux se rapportant à Dieu («dans sa main» 16c, «sa visite» 18c). Sa formule structurelle est aussi celle d'un chiasme $a/b//b^1/a^1$. Un énoncé général (a) réaffirme le contrôle que Dieu exerce sur ses créatures et le soin qu'il en prend. Puis l'attention est centrée sur l'humanité (b), caractérisée par sa tâche de dominer le monde en se guidant sur deux esprits (b^1); les deux esprits pourraient être compris

10. On s'attendrait à ce que למעשיהם soit précédé d'un ו. Pour des alternatives à cette propositon, voir P. VON DER OSTEN-SACKEN, *Gott und Belial. Traditionsgeschichtliche Untersuchungen zum Dualismus in den Texten aus Qumran* (SUNT, 6), Göttingen, Vandenhoeck & Ruprecht, 1969, pp. 17-27; PUECH, *La croyance des Esséniens* (n. 8), p. 431.

comme l'instrument dont l'humanité a besoin pour remplir le rôle que Dieu lui a confié. Le développement est clos par une précision sur la durée de cet ordre des choses, dont le terme sera marqué par la visite (a^1). La répétition du pronom «lui» (iii 16c. 17b. 18b) lie ces unités entre elles.

Avec ses trois tranches, cette première section introduit l'ensemble de l'Instruction et situe son enseignement dans un cadre cosmologique et anthropologique global. Dieu a plan précis sur le monde et il le réalise en assignant une tâche à ses créatures, en particulier à l'humanité, pour un temps limité. Les esprits dont on va maintenant parler dépendent de Dieu et sont mis à la disposition de l'humanité pour lui permettre de «dominer le monde».

La deuxième section (iii 18d – iv 1) se divise en trois tranches correspondant à celles de la première: iii 18d-21a; iii 21b-25a; iii 25b – iv 1. La première tranche pourrait être représentée par la formule $a/b//b^{-1}$. Elle nomme les deux esprits «vérité et perversion» et indique leur origine opposée dans la lumière et les ténèbres (a). Puis deux phases construites en trois segments presque identiques ($b//b^{-1}$) établissent une nette séparation de l'humanité entre deux camps, celui des fils de justice et celui des fils de perversion qui sont placés sous l'autorité de deux figures surnaturelles, un prince de lumières et un ange de ténèbres et adoptent des conduites opposées dans les «voies de lumière» ou les «voies de ténèbres». Les esprits se voient donc attribuer ici une dimension à la fois éthique (vérité et perversion, voies…), cosmologique (lumière ténèbres) et mythologique (prince, ange).

La deuxième tranche (iii 2lb-25a) est assez élaborée et apparemment construite en forme de chiasme à pointe émergente dont le dernier élément est dédoublé ($a/b/c/b^1/a^1/a^{-1}$). La thématique principale est celle de «l'égarement des fils de justice» ou des «fils de lumière» par l'ange des ténèbres, appuyé par les «esprit de son lot» (a/a^1); cet égarement prend soit la forme de transgressions (b) qu'ils commettent soit de coups dont ils sont victimes (b^1) «sous sa domination». Leurs assauts n'échappent pourtant pas à Dieu: la pointe du texte (c) précise qu'ils font mystérieusement partie de ses plans, pour un temps limité. La finale (a^{-1}) donne aux fils de lumière l'assurance d'une aide du Dieu d'Israël et de son ange de vérité, mais ne précise pas les modalités de ce secours surnaturel; elle n'indique pas non plus s'il s'agit d'une aide présentement disponible ou d'un intervention finale qui viendrait mettre un terme définitif à l'emprise exercée temporairement par l'ange de ténèbres.

La dernière tranche de cette section (iii 25b – iv 1) se présente sous forme $a/b/b^{-1}$. Un premier énoncé rapporte à Dieu seul («lui») la création des deux esprits; ils sont identifiés ici en termes cosmiques, à la lumière et aux ténèbres, les deux sphères dans lesquelles s'enracine tout l'activité humaine et sa rétribution (a). Cette affirmation est aussitôt précisée: les deux esprits ne sont pas équivalents, mais objets de rapports contraires d'amour (b) et de haine (b^{-1}) de la part de Dieu, rapports qui se traduisent par une appréciation opposée des activités générées par chacun.

Prises dans leur ensemble, les trois tranches de cette deuxième section soulignent la dimension cosmique des deux esprits (la lumière et des ténèbres) et leur caractère éthique (vérité et perversion). On les associe également à deux figures surnaturelles (prince des lumières et ange des ténèbres) exerçant une autorité deux camps opposés définis par leur conduite (les fils de justice et les fils de perversion). Si Dieu est responsable de la création de ces esprits et en a le contrôle total, il a une nette préférence pour celui qui appartient au monde de la lumière. Pour des raisons qui relèvent de ses mystères et pour un temps limité, il permet à l'ange de ténèbres et aux «esprits de son lot» de s'en prendre aux fils de justice (ou de lumière), ce qui explique leurs égarements et leur épreuves. Mais son soutien et celui de son «ange de vérité» leur sont acquis.

Le rapport entre les deux sections de ce volet paraît être celui d'un chiasme ABC//$C^1B^1A^1$. Les tranches A et A^1 servent respectivement d'introduction et de conclusion et se correspondent par la mention des «esprits», des «actions» et de la «visite». La première les annonce comme objet de l'enseignement; la seconde souligne que toute l'activité humaine et sa rétribution s'enracinent dans les deux esprits opposés de lumière et de ténèbres, en dépendance tous deux de Dieu, mais objets l'un son amour, l'autre de sa haine. Les tranches B et B^1 spécifient que Dieu a un plan bien arrêté sur le monde et qu'il le réalise sans faille, en dépit du mystère que constituent l'égarement et les épreuves des justes; la correspondance de ces deux tranches est bien réelle, même si elle est plutôt thématique, puisque le seul terme récurrent est «Dieu». La reprise des termes «main», «domination» et «se conduire» suggère de rapprocher les tranches C et C^1. La première fait dépendre de Dieu la mission humaine de dominer le monde et situe les esprits par rapport à cette mission. La seconde les qualifie sur le plan éthique et cosmologique et les associe à des puissances surnaturelles exerçant une influence sur une humanité désormais partagée en fils de justice et en fils de perversion. Au terme de ce premier volet, on peut passer à la descripton des voies des esprits dans le monde et de leur rétribution respective.

Deuxième volet: Les voies et leurs visites (iv 2-14)

Le deuxième volet est introduit par la formule «et voici leurs voies dans le monde» (iv 2)[11]. Il comporte une liste de vertus associées à l'es-

11. Pour une analyse détaillée de ce volet, voir DUHAIME, *Les voies des deux esprits* (n. 5), dont je ne reprends ici que les points essentiels.

prit de lumière ou de vérité (iv 2b-6b) et conduisant à des bienfaits durables (iv 6c-8), puis une liste de vices associés à l'esprit de perversité (iv 9-11b) et débouchant sur des châtiments (iv llc-14). On dégage ainsi deux sections à deux tranches de correspondance. La première section est délimitée par l'inclusion que forment le verbe «illuminer» (iv 2b) et le nom «lumière» (iv 8); une division entre la voie et la visite est marquée par l'annonce de la visite (iv 6c). La section sur l'esprit de perversité s'amorce simplement par l'expression «mais pour l'esprit de perversité». La borne de la deuxième section se situe au début de iv 15: «En elles sont les origines (est la nature?) de tous les fils d'hommes»[12]. La transition entre la voie perverse et sa visite est la reprise mot pour mot de celle qui introduisait la visite des fils de vérité: «Et la visite de ceux qui se conduisent selon lui» (iv 6c et 11c-12). L'organisation de cet ensemble est très nette et sa formule structurelle est celle d'un parallélisme antithétique $AB//A^{-1}B^{-1}$.

La première tranche de la section sur la voie de lumière / vérité et sa visite (iv 2-6b) est marquée par la reprise, sous forme d'inclusion, des termes «voici / voilà» (אלה) et «monde» en iv 2a et 6b, de même que par la mention de la vérité en iv 2b («vraie») et 6ab (2x). Une première série de trois propositions parallèles commence par trois infinitifs construits avec la préposition ל: «**pour** illuminer» ... «et **pour** applanir» ... «et **pour** faire craindre (à) son cœur» ... (iv 2b); cette unité est encore délimitée par la petite inclusion que constitue la mention du «cœur» dans la première et la troisième propositions.

L'unité suivante est formée de sept qualités, coordonnées par un ו, et dont la première est l'«esprit d'humilité» (iv 3b); les six autres se laissent grouper en deux triades d'expressions apparentées qui décrivent des attitudes envers autrui, puis des qualités qui évoquent plutôt l'acuité d'esprit. Une troisième unité aligne deux propositions construites en parallèle: «De la foi en toutes les actions de Dieu et l'appui sur sa grande affection» (iv 3c-4a). Ces expressions se rattachent davantage à l'unité qui suit, dans laquelle on retrouve les termes «action» et «affection». Le מ initial suggère que ces dispositions envers Dieu constituent le fondement des comportements énumérés immédiatement après; cela suppose une construction syntaxique plutôt inhabituelle, mais tout à fait plausible.

La quatrième unité est composée d'un autre septénaire dont les expressions sont coordonnées encore une fois par un ו; la première de ces sept expressions mentionne à un nouvel esprit, l'«esprit de connaissance en tout plan d'action» (iv 4). L'existence des deux sous-groupes est con-

12. Dans la terminologie de Girard, on a ici une borne extérieure à l'unité qu'elle délimite.

firmée par la présence, en tête de chacune des deux triades des termes «action» (iv 4b) et «affection» (iv 5) mis en parallèle dans l'unité précédente. Les trois premières expressions sont unifiées par la reprise du terme «plan» de la première dans la troisième («et un plan saint dans un penchant ferme»); au centre est enchâssé le «zèle pour les justes jugements». La seconde triade est délimitée par la répétition du mot «tout» («tous les fils de vérité» iv 5a et «discernement de tout» 6a) et touche plus directement la conduite. La septième expression («et une discrétion pour la vérité des mystères de connaissance»), forme une inclusion avec l'énoncé initial (reprise du mot «connaissance») et constitue une sorte de sommet de la liste, immédiatement avant la conclusion formelle de la tranche («voilà les conseils de l'esprit aux les fils de vérité du monde» iv 6b).

Ces quatre unités s'organisent en deux groupes parallèles (ab//ab): la première (iv 2b-3a) et la troisième (iv 3c-4a) comportent en effet deux expressions synonymiques «les jugements de Dieu» et «les actions de Dieu»; la symétrie des deuxième (iv 3b) et quatrième (iv 4b-6a) unités est assurée par la reprise de la mention de l'«esprit» au début de chacune et par leur arrangement similaire en septénaire. Dans les deux groupes, le premier élément annonce le second.

La liste des bienfaits promis au moment de «la visite» (iv 6c-8) comporte dix items. Deux regroupements de cinq éléments sont signalés par deux inclusions, soit le double emploi de l'adjectif «tout» en iv 6c[13] et 7a et celui du terme «éternelle» en iv 7b et 8. On note également l'utilisation symétrique d'une même séquence de prépositions (ו/ב/ו/עם) dans chacun de ces deux regroupements, si l'on excepte la première et la dernière expression:

pour une guérison	
et une grande paix	**et** une joie éternelle
dans une longueur de jours	**dans** la vie perpétuelle
et une postérité florissante	**et** une couronne de gloire
avec toutes les bénédictions durables	**avec** un vêtement d'honneur
	dans la lumière éternelle.

La première série est centrée sur les biens liés à la «guérison», tandis que la seconde décrit l'exaltation personnelle «dans la lumière éternelle»; elles se complètent donc mutuellement. Si l'on admet la possibilité de rétribution *post mortem* pour les fils de vérité, le premier groupe envisage les bénédictions qui leur sont promises en ce monde, alors que le second pointe vers leur sort dans l'au-delà[14]. On peut parler d'un pa-

13. Il s'agit d'une nouvelle borne extérieure, qui précède cette fois l'unité délimitée.

14. Il faudrait donc distinguer ces deux dimensions davantage que ne le fait PUECH, *La croyance des Esséniens* (n. 8), pp. 434-440.

rallélisme synthétique dans lequel les deux pôles extrêmes de la rétribution servent à en désigner la totalité ($a^{\alpha}//a^{\omega}$).

La seconde section porte sur la voie de ténèbres / perversité (iv 9-11b) et sa visite (iv 11c-14). Les termes clé «perversité» (iv 9a) et «ténèbres» (iv 11b) forment une inclusion aux bornes de la première tranche, celle qui décrit la voie. L'essentiel des conseils de l'esprit de perversité est énoncé immédiatement de manière synthétique dans la première unité (iv 9a), délimitée par les termes contraires «perversité» et «justice»: il suscite «une ambition personnelle» (littéralement un «élargissement» de sa personne, iv 9a,) et un laisser-aller, un «relâchement des mains dans le service de la justice» (iv 9a). La suite du texte détaille ces énoncés.

Une première énumération (iv 9b-10a) comporte dix items agencés en quatre sous-groupes juxtaposés, soit deux diades suivies de deux triades. Dans chaque sous-groupe, les items sont coordonnées par un ו. On note également une progression numérique d'un sous-groupe à l'autre: la première diade ne comporte que deux termes, «méchanceté et mensonge», tandis que la dernière triade en aligne six, «prompte colère et grande folie et un zèle insolent».

L'unité suivante (iv 10b) comporte deux expressions à caractère général qui se rapportent directement à l'agir inspiré par la perversité et insistent particulièrement sur sa corruption; elles sont construites suivant un parallélisme rigoureux qui évoque le comportement («actions» // «voies») en le qualifiant («abominables» // «souillées») puis en indique la modalité d'exécution («dans un esprit de débauche» // «dans un service d'impureté»).

Au début de la ligne 11, une nouvelle liste énumère cinq parties du corps leur donnant des attributs négatifs: la première, «la langue blasphématoire» ou «injurieuse», est isolée, alors que les quatre autres sont groupées deux à deux: «aveuglement des yeux et dureté d'oreille» d'une part, «raideur de nuque et dureté de cœur» d'autre part; ces deux sous-groupes sont reliées par l'emploi en parallèle du terme «dureté» dans la troisième et la cinquième expression. Ce portrait évoque à la fois la résistance à toute forme d'instruction et l'entêtement dans une conduite répréhensible.

Une dernière unité (iv 11b) récapitule l'ensemble des attitudes et comportements enracinés dans la perversité: ils amènent l'individu à «se conduire selon toutes les voies de ténèbres», en déployant les perfidies de la «ruse maligne».

Les quatre premières unités de cette tranche se correspondent deux à deux: la première (iv 9a) et la troisième (iv 10b) comportent en parallèle les termes «esprit» et «service», alors que les deuxième (iv 9b-10a) et quatrième (iv 11a) comportent respectivement des énumérations de dix et de cinq expresssions; elles sont en outre rattachées par la mention du cœur (לב // לבב) dans les deux séries. La cinquième unité sert de conclusion sommative à cette tranche dont la formule structurelle serait donc ab//ab/c.

L'arrangement en parallèle des quatre premières unités laisse entendre que les dix premiers «vices» détaillent des attitudes inspirées par la perversité, l'ambition et l'insouciance pour la justice, alors les cinq derniers illustrent l'agir «abominable» auquel se livrent ceux qui se laissent conduire par un «esprit de débauche» et dont le service est «impur».

La tranche sur la visite (iv 11c-14) est délimitée par la double mention des destinataires au début et à la fin: elle concerne «tous ceux qui se conduisent selon lui [cet esprit]» (iv 12a), et aboutit à ne laisser «aucun reste ou rescapé pour eux» (iv 14). Outre son introduction (iv 11c-12a), le contenu de cet ensemble se subdivise en deux unités: la visite elle-même (iv 12b-13a) et les temps de détresse qui lui sont associés (iv 13b-14). La description de la visite comporte l'énoncé de trois châtiments introduits par la préposition ל: «**pour** un grand (nombre de) coups...» (iv 12b), «**pour** la perdition éternelle...» (iv 12b), «**pour** une terreur perpétuelle et une honte durable avec l'opprobre de l'extermination» (iv 12b-13a). Chacun des châtiments est mis en rapport avec son agent propre, introduit par la préposition ב.

La seconde unité (iv 13b-14) est signalée par la formule initiale «et tous leurs temps pour leurs générations» (iv 13b). Ces temps sont ceux qui précèdent l'extermination définitive des impies. Ils sont qualifiés par trois expressions parallèles de deux termes chacune, groupées en mini-structure concentrique à l'aide d'une séquence ב/ו/ב:

dans l'affliction douloureuse
  et le malheur amer
dans les calamités de ténèbres.

Ces malheurs sont subis par les impies «jusqu'à leur extermination pour (qu'il ne subsiste) aucun reste ou rescapé pour eux» (iv 13b-14). Avec leurs possessifs respectifs, le premier (כלותם) et le dernier (למו) membre de cette triade encadrent l'affirmation centrale: l'extermination ne laissera aucun survivant parmi les impies.

Les deux sous-groupes sont unifiés par les destinataires communs des châtiments, les fils de perversité: les quatre possessifs de la seconde unité renvoient à l'expression «tous ceux qui marchent en lui», par laquelle ils sont désignés dans la première unité. Les deux sous-groupes font également mention de l'«extermination» (iv 13a. 14a) qui constitue l'horizon ultime aussi bien des fléaux qui attendent les impies au moment de la visite que de ceux qu'ils subissent durant les temps qui, vraisemblablement, la précèdent. Enfin, tous deux font référence aux ténèbres («feu des ténèbres» iv 13a, «calamités de ténèbres» iv 13b). Il y a un rapport de complémentarité entre ces deux unités, qui présentent la totalité des châtiments en évoquant leurs deux pôles extrêmes dans une séquence temporelle inversée ($a^{\omega}//a^{\alpha}$).

Les deux sections sont articulées en un parallèle antithétique opposant chacune de leur deux tranches respectives ($AB//A^{-1}B^{-1}$). Les deux voies sont construites de manière semblable, avec deux groupes d'énoncés généraux introduisant des listes détaillées. Le terme «esprit» revient à deux reprises dans chaque tranche (iv 3b. 4b et 9a. l0b), en position stratégique. De nombreux termes se retrouvent de part et d'autre, avec des valeurs contraires, par exemple la «lenteur à la colère» (en iv 4b) qui s'oppose à la «prompte colère» (iv 10a), la «modestie de conduite avec un discernement de tout» (ערמת כול iv 5b-6a) qui contraste la conduite «selon toutes les voies de ténèbres et de ruse maligne» (ערמת רוע iv 11b).

Les visites sont constituées chacune de deux sous-groupes qui forment un chiasme: ils détaillent d'un côté les bienfaits associés à la guérison (iv 6d-7a), puis à l'exaltation ultime des fils de vérité (iv 7b-8), et de l'autre, à l'inverse, les châtiments ultimes des pervers (iv 12b-13a) et les malheurs qui les précèdent (iv 13b-14). Comme dans listes de vertus et de vices, des termes identiques se retrouvent dans les deux visites, dans des combinaisons qui leur donnent une valeur contraire. Il y a, par exemple, une «grande paix» (iv 7a) pour les fils de vérité, mais un «grand (nombre de) coups» (iv 12b) pour les enfants de la perversité. En plus de ces récurrences, les oppositions sémantiques sont également très nettes. Ainsi, la «guérison» (iv 6d) des uns fait place aux «coups» (iv 12b) pour les autres. Le sort des justes est «gloire», «honneur» et «lumière éternelle», (iv 7b-8) alors que celui des méchants n'est que «honte», «opprobre» et s'achève dans l'«extermination par le feu des ténèbres» (iv 12b-13a).

Troisième volet: Partage actuel et purification des élus (iv 15-26)

Le troisième volet peut être réparti en deux sections, iv 15-20a et iv 20b-26. Cette division permet de dégager trois tranches de correspondance, construites en chiasme. Dans la première section, la tranche initiale (iv 15-18a) est délimitée par la répétition du verbe «se conduire / aller» (iv 15. 18a) et comporte cinq unités. Les deux premières (iv 15a et iv 15b-16a) sont axées sur le partage continu de l'humanité, envisagée collectivement («ses armées pour leurs générations»), entre les «catégories» de la vérité et de la perversité, qui inspirent la conduite et l'action selon une modulation variant probablement d'un individu à l'autre «pour les temps éternels». L'unité centrale (iv 16b), attribue ce partage à Dieu et souligne que ce régime vaut «jusqu'au temps ultime». Les deux dernières unités (iv 17b et iv 17c-18a) introduisent l'idée d'un antagonisme profond, posé par Dieu également, entre vérité et perversité: elles s'opposent dans leurs «actions», leurs «chemins», et leurs «jugements». Cette tranche peut être représentée par la formule $a/a^1/b/c/c^1$.

Dans la tranche centrale (iv 18b-19a), on trouve d'abord deux énoncés parallèles qui caractérisent Dieu par «les secrets de sa science» et «la sagesse de sa gloire»; ils préparent l'affirmation que la perversité ne saurait lui échapper, puisque, sans doute dès l'origine, c'est lui qui «établi un temps» pour son existence et qui «l'éliminera» définitivement «au moment de la visite». Le parallélisme des noms («sa science», «sa gloire» iv 18b), et celui des verbes («a établi un temps», «éliminera» 18c-19a) invite à schématiser l'organisation de cet ensemble synthétique par la formule $a/a^1/b/b^1$.

La troisième tranche (iv 19b-20a) est arrangée en chiasme autour des expressions «et alors», «impiété», «perversité», «moment du jugement» ($a/b/b^1/a^1$). Elle aborde de manière concise l'une des conséquences de l'élimination de la perversité. Cela permettra de révéler «la vérité du monde», qui s'est laissé dominé par elle et qui s'est égaré «dans les voies de l'impiété». Cet égarement prendra fin avec la disparition de sa cause, «au moment du jugement décisif».

La deuxième section de ce troisième volet (iv 20b-26) reprend des thèmes similaires en séquence inverse. La première tranche (iv 20b-23a) décrit un autre type d'intervention de «Dieu» (iv 20b et 22c) au moment de la visite («et alors» iv 20b). Comme l'indique la première unité (iv 20b), son action porte cette fois sur l'être humain, dont «les œuvres» et «la bâtisse» seront épurées (iv 20b). Les deux unités suivantes présentent cette opération comme une sorte de substitution des esprits: c'est dans un «esprit de sainteté» que l'homme est purifié et qu'est écarté «l'esprit de perversité» qui habite sa chair (iv 20c-21a); le jaillissement d'un «esprit de vérité» doit par ailleurs éliminer toute trace de «corruption dans l'esprit de souillure» (iv 21b-22a). Les deux dernières unités pointent vers l'aboutissement de ces gestes et sur leur justification. Dans la quatrième, dont la micro-structure a encore une fois la forme d'un chiasme, on anticipe une sorte d'illumination des «droits» et des «parfaits de conduite» qui auront accès à une connaissance et une sagesse surnaturelle (iv 22b). La finale leur promet rien de moins qu'une part à «l'alliance éternelle» et à la «gloire d'Adam» (iv 22c-

23a). En se basant sur ces indices de contenu, on pourrait suggérer formule a/b/b¹/c/c¹ pour schématiser la structure de cet ensemble.

La seconde tranche (iv 23b) ne comporte que deux brefs énoncés parallèles (a/a¹); on revient de nouveau sur la disparition de la perversité, et on voue à la honte les «actions de tromperie», un sort qui contraste avec la gloire des élus.

La dernière tranche (iv 23c-26) comporte cinq énoncés agencés apparemment de manière concentrique (a/b/c/b¹/a¹) à l'aide des mots «esprit» (iv 23c et 26b) et «partage / partager» (iv 24b et iv 26a). Le premier évoque la lutte des esprits de vérité et de perversion, mais cette fois «dans le cœur de l'humain» (iv 23c-24a); le pluriel «ils se conduisent avec sagesse et folie» pourrait avoir pour sujet les esprits, aussi bien que l'«humain», considéré comme sujet collectif. Le deuxième (iv 24b-25a) explique en deux phrases parallèles la conduite juste ou impie d'un homme par la part qui lui est dévolue dans la «vérité» ou la «perversion», et par la haine qu'il éprouve proportionnellement à l'endroit de l'une et de l'autre. L'énoncé central (iv 25b) reprend l'idée que cette répartition relève de Dieu, et vaut jusqu'au nouvel ordre des choses. On précise ensuite qu'à cause de leur partage entre elles (vérité et perversion / perversité), les humains peuvent connaître le «bien» et le «mal» (iv 25c-26a), c.-à-d. au moins les distinguer, sinon en faire l'expérience. L'unité finale (iv 26b), telle que reconstruite par Stegemann, distingue entre le moment de l'attribution des «lots» aux vivants et celui de la visite: le lot de chacun correspond à l'esprit qui est mis en lui, probablement son partage entre vérité et perversion évoqué dans les unités précédentes, en attendant «l'agir nouveau» de la visite auquel réfère le centre de cette tranche.

Les trois tranches de chacune des deux sections se correspondent en un chiasme assez net ABC // $C^{-1}B^{1}A^{1}$. Von der Osten-Sacken avait déjà fait le rapprochement entre les tranches A (iv 15a-17c) et A¹ (23c- 26b) et signalé que les cinq éléments de la première se retrouvent en ordre inverse dans la seconde[15]. Les éléments les plus visibles de ce chiasme sont des récurrences ou reprises synonymiques: «tous les fils d'homme» iv 15a et «tout vivant» iv 26b; «le travail de leurs actions ... pour tous les temps éternels» iv 15b et 25c; «car (c'est) Dieu (qui) les a placées une partie contre l'autre» iv 16b et «car (c'est) une partie contre l'autre (que) Dieu les a placées» iv 25b; «abomination (pour) la vérité ... et abomination (pour la) perversité» iv 17b et «il hait la perversité... il déteste la vérité» iv 24b-25a»; «et (elles) ont un zèle combatif ...» iv 17c «les esprits de vérité et de perversion combattent ...» iv 23c. Les deux tranches ont donc en commun le thème du partage des humains dans la

15. VON DER OSTEN-SACKEN, *Gott und Belial* (n. 10), pp. 22-23.

vérité et la perversité et celui de la haine profonde qui les opposent, mais avec des nuances importantes, passant des «catégories» entre lesquelles se partagent les «armées» humaines (iv 15a-17c), à la lutte intérieure qui se déroule dans le «cœur» de chacun (iv 23c-26b). Leur énoncé central est formulé de manière presqu'identique, bien que la séquence des termes opère un déplacement d'accent: dans la première section, l'insistance porte sur l'attribution de ce partage à Dieu (iv 16b-17a), tandis que dans la seconde, c'est le partage lui-même qui apparaît en position initiale (iv 25b); on note également que le «temps ultime» de iv 16b-17a devient plus précisément celui «de la décision et de l'agir nouveau» en iv 25b. Les tranches B (iv 18b-19a) et B^1 (iv 23b) annoncent l'élimination complète de la perversité, tel que Dieu en a décidé. Les tranches C (iv 19b-20a) et C^{-1} (iv 20b-23a) établissent un contraste entre la «vérité» du monde, dont la «corruption» sera révélée pour être vraisemblablement sanctionnée, et la «vérité» de Dieu, qui lui servira à purifier les œuvres humaines, notamment sa «corruption dans l'esprit de souillure» (iv 21b-22a). La conjonction «car» (כיא) apparaît à six reprises dans les tranches A/A^1 et C/C^{-1} (iv 16b. 17c. 19b. 22c. 25b. [26b]); cette récurrence renforce la cohérence organisationnelle de ce volet.

Correspondances entre les volets

Une vingtaine de termes sont présents dans chacun des trois volets, souvent en position stratégique sur le plan structurel, et contribuent à unifier l'ensemble. Voici les principaux, dans la séquence de leur apparition dans le volet I. (les trois chiffres suivant immédiatement le mot indiquent leur fréquence dans les volets I/II/III):

- «fils» (בן) pour désigner les humains (sauf «les fils du ciel» iv 22b) 7/2/3: iii 13. 13. 20a. 21a. 22a. 24b. 25a / iv 5. 6b. / iv 15a. 22b. 26a.
- «esprit» (רוח) 5/5/6: iii 14. 18b. 18d. 24b. 25. / iv 3b. 4b. 6b. 9a. 10b. / iv 20c. 21a. 21b. 22a. 23c. 26b.
- «action» (מעשה) 3/3/4: iii 14. 22a. 25b. / iv 4a. 4b. 10b. / iv 16a. 20b. 23b. 25c.
- «visite» (פקודה) 3/2/2: iii 14. 18c. [26a]. / iv 6c. 11c. / iv 19a. 26b.
- «temps» (קץ) 2/1/4: iii 15a. 23a. / iv 13b. / iv 16a. 16b. 18b. 25c.
- «Dieu» (אל) 4/3/6: iii 15b. 23a. 24b. 26. / iv 3a. 4a. 12b. / iv 16b. 18b. 20b. 22c. 25b. [26b].
- «connaissance» (דעת): 1/2/2: iii 15b. / iv 4b. 6a. / iv 22b. 26a.
- «gloire» (כבוד) 1/2/2: iii 16a. / iv 5. 7b. / iv 18b. 23a.
- «jugement» (משפט) 2/2/2: iii 17a. [26a]. / iv 2b. 4b. / iv 18a. 20a.
- «monde» (תבל) 1/2/1: iii 18a. / iv 2a. 6a. / iv 19b.
- «marcher / se conduire» (הלך / יתהלך) 3/4/3: iii 18b. 20a. 20b. / iv 5. 6c. 11b. 12a. / iv 15a. 17c. 24c.
- «jusqu'à» (עד) 3/3/5: iii 18c. 23a. 26b. / iv 7a. 13a. 13b. / iv 16b. 19c. 23b. 25b. [26b].

- «vérité» (אמת) 3/4/8: iii 19a. 19b. 24b. / iv 2b. 5. 6a. 6b. / iv 17b. 17b. 19b. 20b. 21b. 23c. 24b. 25a.
- «voie» (דרך) 4/4/4: iii 20a. 2la. 26a; iv 1b. / iv 2a. 2b. 10b. 11b. / iv 15a. 17b. 19b. 22b.
- «éternel» (עולם) 1/4/4: iv 1a. / iv 3b. 7b. 8. 12b. / iv 16a. 17b. 22c. [26a].

D'autres termes apparaissent dans deux des trois volets. Cela produit un effet d'inclusion (rapports entre les volets I et III) ou de concaténation (rapports entre les volets I et II, II et III). Les principales récurrences sont les suivantes (selon la séquence de leur apparition dans le premier volet).

Entre les volets I et III

Les volets I et III ont en commun, de façon exclusive, au moins six termes:

- «origines / nature» (תלדות) 3/0/1: iii 13. 19b. 19b. / iv 15a.
- «être» (היה) 4/0/2: iii 15b. 15b. 15c. 16a. / iv 18b. 23b.
- «lui» (האוה désignant Dieu) 3/0/1: iii 17a. 17b. 25b. / iv 25c.
- «domination» (ממשלה) 5/0/1: iii 17. 20a. 21a. 22a. 24a. / iv 19c.
- «moment» (מעוד) 3/0/3: iii 18c. 23b; [iv 1]. / iv 18b. 20a. [26b].
- «perversion» (עול) 3/0/2: iii 19a. 19b. 21a. / iv 23c. 24b.

En plus de ces correspondances de vocabulaire, les volets I et III présentent a une parenté de structure et de contenu. Chacun comporte deux sections de trois tranches et on peut voir une correspondance entre plusieurs d'entre elles, notamment entre chacune de leurs premières sections. Les liens les plus évidents sont entre les deux tranches initiales des deux volets (IA / IIIA), qui ont la même expression «les origines (la nature?) de tous les fils d'homme» (iii 13 / iv 15a) et évoquent «leurs actions» (iii 14 / iv 16a), «leurs générations» (iii 14 / iv 15a), «les temps» (iii 15a / iv 16a. 17b). Les correspondances sont un peu moins nettes dans les tranches IA¹ / IIIA¹; on trouve tout de même de part et d'autre les termes «esprits» (ii 25b / iv 23c. 26b), «actions» (iii 25b / iv 25c) et «visites» (iii 26a / iv 26b), le verbe «détester» (iv 1 / iv 25a) et des expressions similaires pour désigner la durée («pour tous les [mo]ments éternels» iii 26b – iv 11 «pour tous les temps [éternel]s» iv 25c-26a). Dans deux des tranches médianes (IB¹ / IIIB), on trouve une même évocation des «secrets de Dieu» iii 23a / iv 18b) et d'une limite posée au harcèlement des fils de justice (iii 23a) ou à l'existence de la perversité (iv 18b-19a). Enfin, l'idée de «domination» est présente dans les tranches IC / IC¹ / III C: l'homme est créé pour «la domination du monde» (iii 17b-18a), mais une «domination» est aussi exercée par le «prince de lumières» et l'«ange de ténèbres» (iii 20a. 21a); c'est finalement «sous la domination de la perversité» que «le monde» s'égare dans les voies de l'impiété (iv 19c). Ces éléments renforcent l'unité du texte dans sa forme actuelle.

Entre les volets I et II

Six termes reviennent dans les volets I et II, mais sont absents du volet III:

- «lumière» (אור) 7/1/0: iii 13. 19b. 20a. 20a. 24b. 25a. 25b. / iv 8.
- «avec» (עם) 1/3/0: iii 15a. / iv 7a. 8. 13a.
- «plan» (מחשבה) 2/2/0: iii 15c. 16a. / iv 4b. 4b.
- «main» (יד) 3/2/0: iii 16c. 20a. 20b. / iv 9a. 12b.
- «ténèbres» (חושך) 5/2/0: iii 19b. 21a. 21a. 21b. 25b. / iv 11b. 13b.
- «justice» (צדק) 2/3/0: iii 20a. 21b. / iv 2b. 4b. 9a.

Entre les volets II et III

Six termes ne se trouvent que dans les volets II et III:

- «cœur» (לב / לבב) 0/4/1: iv 2b. 2b. 9b. 11a. / iv 23c.
- «grand-e / abondance (רוב) 0/6/1: iv 3b. 4a. 5. 7a. 10a. 12b / iv 16a.
- «sagesse» (חכמה) 0/1/3: iv 3b. / iv 18b. 22b. 24a.
- «souillure» (נדה) 0/2/2: iv 5. 10b. / iv 21b. 22a.
- «perversité» (עולה) 0/1/7: iv 9a. / iv.17b. 17b. 18b. 19b. 20c. 23b. 24b.
- «abomination» (תועבה) 0/1/3: iv 10b. / iv 17b. 17b. 21b.

Le fait qu'une douzaine de mots du deuxième volet se retrouvent également soit dans le premier volet, soit dans le troisième facilite l'enchaînement des trois volets et renforcent de ce fait l'unité de l'Instruction.

Pour être vraiment significatives, ces observations devraient être développées davantage. Elles fourniraient certainement un excellent point de départ à une analyse plus approfondie de la dynamique du texte. Faute de pouvoir mener cette étude ici, on peut au moins en conclure que l'Instruction sur les deux esprits se présente comme un texte cohérent sur le plan structurel et qu'il se donne à lire, dans sa forme actuelle, comme un tout unifié. Tant par son contenu que par sa structure, elle apparaît comme un enseignement dont les diverses sections touchent des aspects complémentaires d'un même sujet, celui de la nature humaine et de son rapport aux deux esprits. Le premier volet touche principalement la création de l'homme et la place des esprits dans le plan divin. Le second décrit les deux voies que les esprits proposent aux humains et leur aboutissement respectif. Le troisième insiste davantage sur la lutte qui les oppose et envisage plus en détails les modalités de la purification et de l'exaltation eschatologique des élus, dans un monde enfin débarrassé de la perversité. Une telle cohérence a déjà été notée, particulièrement par J. Licht[16]. Toutefois, en dépit des l'agencement assez habile que révèle l'analyse, on peut également repérer un certain nombre d'anomalies qui ont conduit à mettre en doute son unité de composition et à faire soupçonner qu'il y a une histoire rédactionnelle assez complexe derrière ce texte tel qu'il s'offre actuellement à ses lecteurs.

2. Tensions internes dans l'Instruction sur les deux esprits

Premier volet (iii 13 – iv 1)

Dans le premier volet, on remarque les tensions et difficultés suivantes:

- Les humains sont appelés «fils d'homme» en iii 13, mais «l'humanité» en iii 17b.
- Dieu est appelé «Dieu des connaissances» en iii 15b, mais «Dieu» en iii 23a. 26b, et «Dieu d'Israël» en iii 24b; il est désigné par le pronom «lui» (הואה) en iii 17a. 17b. 25b.
- Les deux esprits sont identifiés à «la vérité et la perversion» en iii 18d-19a; mais en iii 25b, ce sont des esprits de «lumière et ténèbres».
- Les figures du «prince des lumières» et de «l'ange de ténèbres» ont un rôle de domination de leurs groupes respectifs, les «fils de justice» et les «fils de perversion» en iii 20a-21a; ce rôle de domination contraste avec celui dévolu à l'humanité en iii 17b.
- Mais, à partir de iii 21b, l'«ange de ténèbres» harcèle les «fils de justice» pour les égarer. Un peu plus loin, il est contré par «le Dieu d'Israël et son ange de vérité»; cet ange pourrait être le prince de lumières, mais cela n'est pas évident. De plus, en iii 24a, on voit apparaître «les esprits de son lot»; le terme «esprit» est ici à l'état construit masculin pluriel (רוחי גורלו), ce qui paraît étrange après avoir annoncé «deux esprits» (שתי רוחות iii 18b).
- Les hommes qui sont sous la domination du prince de lumière sont les «fils de justice» en iii 20a. 22a; mais ce sont les «fils de lumière» en iii 24b. 25a (voir iii 13).

Ces observations n'ont pas toute la même valeur et on pourrait leur trouver des explications variées. Complétées par une analyse serrée du vocabulaire et de la syntaxe de ce premier volet, elles m'ont amené, dans des travaux antérieurs, à postuler la présence d'une double interpolation dans le texte de ce volet, correspondant en gros aux sections B^1 et C^1 (iii 18b-23a et iii 23b-25a)[17].

16. J. Licht, *An Analysis of the Treatise on the Two Spirits in DSD*, in C. Rabin et Y. Yadin (eds.), *Aspects of the Dead Sea Scrolls* (ScrHier, 4), Jerusalem, Magness Press, 1965 (1958), pp. 88-100.

17. J. Duhaime, *L'Instruction sur les deux esprits et les interpolations dualistes à Qumrân (1QS III,13 – IV,26)*, in *RB* 84 (1977) 566-594; voir aussi J. Duhaime, *Dualistic Reworking in the Scrolls from Qumran*, in *CBQ* 49 (1987) 32-56.

Deuxième volet (iv 2-14)

Le deuxième volet présente une structure très équilibrée et il est assez cohérent sur le plan interne. Son contenu pose cependant quelques problèmes quand on le compare à celui du volet précédent.

- La thématique de la lumière et des ténèbres, très importante dans la deuxième section du premier volet, joue ici un rôle plus limité. On trouve seulement le verbe «éclairer» au début de la description de la voie (iv 2) et le mot «lumière» parmi les biens eschatologiques (iv 8). Les ténèbres sont mentionnées à trois reprises: le sommaire de iv 11b évoque «les voies de ténèbres», tandis qu'on trouve «le feu des régions ténébreuses» (iv 13a) et «les calamités des ténèbres» (iv 13b) parmi les liste des châtiments dont sont menacés ceux qui ont suivi l'esprit de perversité.
- Le second volet comporte plusieurs mentions des esprits, mais pas des esprits de lumière et de ténèbres: on parle plutôt, d'un côté, d'un «esprit d'humilité» (iv 3b), d'un «esprit de connaissance en tout plan d'action» (iv 4b), de l'«esprit», sans qualification (iv 6b) et, de l'autre côté, de l'esprit de perversité (עולה iv 9a, plutôt que עול) et d'un «esprit de débauche» (iv 10b).
- Il n'est pas question ici des «fils de justice» ou des «fils de lumière»; on lui préfère l'appellation «fils de vérité» (iv 5.6b); il n'y a pas d'expression correspondante pour les impies.
- Il n'y a aucune allusion à un quelconque égarement ou harcèlement des fils de vérité. Les seules transgressions dont il soit question sont celles des impies, et elles sont décrites avec un vocabulaire différent de celui qu'on trouve dans le premier volet. Il n'est pas question non plus d'un «ange de vérité» ou d'un «ange de ténèbres», mais seulement d'«anges de destruction», comme agents des châtiments eschatologiques (iv 12a).

Ces différences supposent des rapports assez complexes entre ces deux volets. Quelques-unes pourraient s'expliquer par l'existence d'interpolations dans le premier volet, mais d'autres, notamment celles concernant les esprits, ont vraisemblablement une autre interprétation.

Troisième volet (iv 15-26)

Le troisième volet présente quelques tensions internes:

- La première section (iv 15-19), parle d'une opposition entre «vérité» et «perversité» (עולה), mais ne mentionne pas les «esprits»; le terme «esprit» n'apparaît, curieusement, que dans la deuxième section (iv 20c. 21a. 21b. 22a. 23c. 26b.).
- Les deux tranches A et A[1] se correspondent (voir plus haut), mais présentent aussi des différences. En iv 15-17c, le partage entre «vérité» et «perversité» (iv 17b) est celui de «toutes leurs armées pour leurs générations» (iv 15a), tandis qu'en iv 24b, c'est chaque humain qui est partagé entre la «vérité» et «le lot de perversion». Dans le premier cas,

l'hostilité est entre vérité et perversité (iv 17bc), mais dans le second, c'est l'être humain qui hait ou déteste la vérité ou la perversité (iv 24b-25a).

- Les esprits dont il est question dans la deuxième section ne sont pas les mêmes dans les tranches C^{-1} et A^{1}: la première parle des égarements des hommes dans l'esprit de perversité (iv 20c) et de souillure (iv 22a) et de leur purification par l'esprit de sainteté (iv 21a) et de vérité (iv 21b); la seconde parle à la fois de la lutte des esprits de vérité de perversion (רוחי אמת ועול) dans le cœur de l'homme (iv 23c) et des lots que Dieu fait tomber «vers tout vivant selon son esprit (mis) en lui».

Sur la base de ces tensions internes et de quelques indices additionnels, von der Osten-Sacken en est venu à la conclusion que iv 23c-26 est une réinterprétation anthropologique secondaire de la doctrine de iv 15-23b[18]. Par ailleurs, comme l'ensemble du troisième volet présente certaines tensions avec les deux précédents, von der Osten-Sacken estime que iv 15-23a est également un développement secondaire par rapport à iii 13 – iv 14[19].

Par rapport au premier volet, on note les éléments suivants:

- Dans le troisième volet, la haine qui existe entre vérité et perversité (iv 17bc) trouve un écho dans celle que l'homme éprouve pour l'une ou l'autre, selon son partage (iv 24b). Dans le premier volet, c'est Dieu lui-même qui aime ou déteste la lumière et les ténèbres (iii 26b – iv 1).
- La notion de partage du troisième volet (iv 15b-16b. 24b-26a) est absente du premier, qui connaît seulement les égarements ou les trébuchements des justes, à cause d'une agression de l'ange de ténèbres et des esprits de son lot.
- Le couple lumière – ténèbres est complètement absent du troisième volet.
- Le troisième volet ne connaît ni «prince de lumières» ni «ange de ténèbres».

Par rapport au deuxième volet, on observe aussi quelques tensions:

- L'eschatologie du troisième volet comporte l'élimination de la perversité et voue à la honte «les actions de tromperie» (iv 18b-19a. 23b), mais elle ne semble pas impliquer un châtiment et une destruction spécifique des impies (rien qui corresponde à iv 11c-14).
- Dans le troisième volet, le sort de l'homme est envisagé en termes de purification et d'exaltation (iv 20b-23a); il y a quelques rapprochements avec la section correspondante dans le deuxième volet (iv 6c-8), mais aussi des différences. C'est dans ce contexte eschatologique qu'il est question des esprits de vérité et de sainteté dans le troisième volet. Ces esprits sont totalement absents des bienfaits attendus en iv 6c-8. Le second volet n'anticipe pas une purification, puisque la «pureté glorieuse» fait déjà partie des qualités des justes (iv 5). Par ailleurs dans le deuxième volet, les fils de vérité font déjà preuve de «puissante sagesse» (iv 3b), tandis que les impies se montrent capables d'une

18. VON DER OSTEN-SACKEN, *Gott und Belial* (n. 10), pp. 22-26.
19. *Ibid.*, pp. 17-22.

«grande folie» (iv 9b), comme l'homme partagé au cœur duquel se battent les esprits (iv 23c); mais on n'anticipe pas que les justes partagent «la connaissance du Très-Haut» et «la sagesse des fils du ciel» (iv 22b). Dans le troisième volet, on dit que les droits et les parfaits de conduite sont choisis pour «l'alliance éternelle» (iv 22c); le deuxième volet ne connaît pas cette «alliance éternelle», mais évoque simplement la «joie» et la «lumière éternelle» qui attendent les justes (iv 7b-8). «La gloire d'Adam» (iv 23a) figure parmi les promesses eschatologiques du troisième volet, alors que, dans le second, on évoque seulement «une couronne de gloire et un vêtement d'honneur» (iv 8).

- Le troisième volet introduit aussi la notion de «connaissance du bien et du mal», absente des deux volets précédents. Il décrit la visite comme «le jugement décisif», le «temps de la décision et de l'agir nouveau», des expressions également inédites dans le reste de l'Instruction.

On a donc plusieurs raisons de croire que l'histoire rédactionnelle de ce troisième volet est particulière et que ses rapports avec les deux précédents sont plus complexes que ne le laissent supposer les affinités repérées par l'analyse structurelle.

L'ensemble des observations concernant aussi bien les tensions internes de chacun des trois volets de l'Instruction que les tensions qu'ils présentent les uns par rapport aux autres, suggère de repérer et d'isoler les principaux contenus de l'Instruction, avec leur vocabulaire propre, dans certains cas. Au risque d'une trop grande fragmentation, on pourrait distinguer les composantes suivantes dans le texte actuel:

- Le «plan de Dieu» sur les êtres et sur le déroulement de l'histoire, dont la durée est limitée (iii 15b-16b. 23a; voir iv 18b-19a. 23b).
- L'attribution d'esprits à l'homme pour jouer son rôle dans le monde (iii 15-18c).
- L'identification des esprits à la vérité et à la perversion (iii 18d; voir iv 6b? 9a. 20c. 21b. 23c).
- Un «mythe» associant les esprits à la lumière et aux ténèbres et à des figures surnaturelles (iii 19b-21a).
- L'explication «mythologique» des transgressions des justes (iii 21b-23a) et celle de leurs «coups» et «détresses» (iii 23b-24b).
- L'amour et la haine de Dieu à l'égard de la lumière et des ténèbres (iii 26b – iv 1).
- Les voies suggérées par les esprits (éthique) et les visites (eschatologie) qui y sont associées présentées comme deux mondes opposés et incompatibles (iv 2-14).
- Le partage des humains comme groupe, génération après génération, entre vérité et perversité et l'opposition qui en résulte (iv 15a-17c).
- Le partage de chaque homme, dans son cœur, entre vérité et perversion (iv 23c-26b).
- La responsabilité de Dieu dans le partage de la vérité et de la perversité chez les humains, collectivement ou individuellement (iv 16b. 25b-26b).
- La conception d'une eschatologie centrée sur la disparition de la perversité, la purification des justes, leur entrée dans «l'alliance éternelle» et «la gloire d'Adam» (iv 18b-23b).

Ces éléments appartiennent aux différents registres de la cosmologie, de l'anthropologie, de l'éthique ou de l'eschatologie. Certains proviennent éventuellement de sources ou de traditions différentes; d'autres reflètent sans doute des développements internes de la pensée d'un même groupe. Il y aurait certes un grand intérêt à pouvoir en préciser l'origine et à être en mesure de reconstituer le processus par lequel ils se sont combinés pour constituer le texte actuel.

Pour répondre à ces questions, on peut élaborer des scénarios génétiques basés sur la seule analyse interne du texte. On cherchera alors à comprendre l'agencement de ces composantes soit comme le développement progressif d'une même tradition, ainsi que von der Osten-Sacken et moi-même l'avons fait dans le passé, soit comme l'intégration de sources présumées, de provenance et de tendances différentes.

Une autre piste consisterait à chercher à retracer les sources de ces enseignements et les textes apparentés, dans la Bible ou ailleurs, en particulier ceux qui concernent la création (Gn 1–2), l'origine du mal (Gn 3; 1 Hénoch 6-11; etc.), les «voies» (Dt 30,15-20; Ps 1; 37; etc.), l'eschatologie (Dn 12,1-3), etc. J.J. Collins a apporté une contribution importante en ce sens en distinguant principalement dans l'Instruction des traditions sapientiales et apocalyptiques qu'il rapproche de textes tels que Gn 1–3; 1 Hen 6–11; Sir 15,11-20; 17,1-24; 33,10-13[20]. Il examine aussi leur rapport avec les enseignements dualistes perses (Yasna 30) et avec certains éléments de l'Instruction préservée dans la grotte 4 (4QInstruction). Tel que signalé au début de cette étude, les affinités de l'Instruction sur les deux esprits avec 4QInstruction ont aussi été analysées par A. Lange et par E. Tigchelaar[21].

Tigchelaar note que la majorité des correspondances de vocabulaire entre les deux textes se retrouve en 1QS iii 13-18c; iv 15-23b. 23c-26; elles sont plus rares en iii 18d – iv 14, et surtout en iii 18d – iv 1 (figures du prince des lumières et de l'ange des ténèbres, etc.). Sur cette base, il suggère que le niveau primitif de l'Instruction sur les deux esprits pourrait être 1QS iii 18d – iv 1, auquel iv 2-14 aurait été ajouté à un certain moment. Puis cet ensemble aurait été encadré par 1QS iii 13-18c et iv 15-26, par des auteurs ou éditeurs connaissant 4QInstruction et utilisant sa terminologie[22]. Il reconnaît toutefois que le processus pourrait avoir été plus complexe.

20. J.J. Collins, *Apocalypticism in the Dead Sea Scrolls*, London – New York, Routledge, 1997, pp. 30-51.

21. Lange, *Weisheit und Prädestination* (n. 2); Tigchelaar, *To Increase Learning for the Understanding Ones* (n. 3).

22. Tigchelaar, *To Increase Learning for the Understanding Ones* (n. 3), p. 203.

Conclusion

L'analyse de la structure de l'Instruction sur les deux esprits démontre que ce texte est doté d'une cohérence indéniable dans sa forme actuelle. Cette cohérence est largement due à l'emploi d'un vocabulaire récurrent et de procédés de structuration de petits et grands ensembles qui se laissent repérer assez aisément. Cependant la présence de tensions tout aussi repérables, soit entre les trois volets, soit entre leurs éléments internes, suggère que cette cohérence résulte d'un travail délibéré d'intégration de composantes ayant éventuellement une origine différente ou ayant connu certains développements. On doit tenir compte de ces données pour parvenir à préciser davantage les relations entre l'Instruction sur les deux esprits et des textes apparentés, notamment ceux de 4QInstruction. Pour ce faire, il faudra sans doute se livrer à une analyse détaillée des diverses conceptions engagées dans chacun de ces textes. Il paraît assez évident, par exemple, que l'eschatologie envisagée dans la section sur les «visites» de ceux qui vont dans les voies respectives de la lumière (vérité) et des ténèbres (perversion) et celle que présentent les deux sections du volet final de l'Instruction sur les deux esprits sont différentes, sans être incompatibles. Les «visites» de 1QS iv 6-9 et iv 11c-14 anticipent pour les uns des jours de bonheur et une postérité, suivis d'une «vie perpétuelle» et d'une glorification», mais pour les autres des jours de malheur suivis d'un châtiment par les anges de destruction, l'expérience de la colère de Dieu, de la honte, et d'une extermination totale. Le dernier volet (iv 15-26) est plutôt axé sur l'élimination de la perversité, d'une part, et sur la purification et l'exaltation des élus et leur participation à la connaissance et à la sagesse surnaturelle, à l'alliance éternelle et à la gloire d'Adam, d'autre part. Qu'en est-il de l'eschatologie de 4QInstruction? Ses conceptions sont-elles homogènes ou varient-elles, elles aussi, d'un passage à l'autre? Si elles présentent une certaine diversité, est-il possible d'établir une correspondance, au-delà des rapprochements de vocabulaire, entre quelques-uns de ces éléments eschatologiques et ceux qu'on a repérés dans l'Instruction sur les deux esprits? Une telle approche pourrait aussi s'appliquer aux conceptions cosmologiques, anthropologiques et éthiques relevées dans l'Instruction sur les deux esprits et dans les textes auxquels elle s'apparente.

Faculté de théologie, Université de Montréal — Jean Duhaime
C.P. 6128, Succ. Centre-Ville, Montréal Qc
Canada H3C 3J7

I. Dieu, l'homme, les esprits (1QS iii 13 – iv 1)

A	iii 13 (vacat) למשכיל להבין וללמד את כול בני אור בתולדות כול בני איש 14 לכול מיני רוחותם באותותם למעשיהם בדורותם ולפקודת נגועיהם 15a עם קצי שלומם	25b והואה ברא רוחות אור וחושך ועליהון יסד כול מעשה 26a [ע]ל [משפט]יהן כול עבודה ועל דרכיהן [כול פק]ודה 26b אחת אהב אל לכול iv 1a [מ]ועדי עולמים ובכול עלילותיה ירצה לעד 1b אחת תעב מודה וכול דרכיה שנא לנצח (vacat)	A[1]
B	15b מאל הדעות כול הויה ונהיי 15c ולפני היותם הכין כול מחשבתם 16a ובהיותם לתעודותם כמחשבת כבודו ימלאו פעולתם 16b ואין להשנות	21b ובמלאך חושך תעות 22a כול בני צדק 22b וכול חטאתם ועוונותם ואשמתם ופשעי מעשיהם בממשלתו 23a לפי רזי אל עד קצו 23b וכול נגועיהם ומועדי צרותם 24a בממשלת משטמתו 24b וכול רוחי גורלו להלשיל בני אור ואל ישראל ומלאך אמתו עזר לכול 25a בני אור	B[1]
C	16c בידו 17a משפטי כול והואה יכלכלם בכול חפציהם 17b והואה ברא אנוש לממשלת 18a תבל 18b וישם לו שתי רוחות להתהלך בם 18c עד מועד פקדתו	18d הנה רוחות 19a האמת והעול 19b במעין אור תולדות האמת וממקור חושך תולדות העול 20a וביד שר אורים ממשלת כול בני צדק בדרכי אור יתהלכו 20b וביד מלאך 21a חושך כול ממשלת בני עול בדרכי חושך יתהלכו	C[1]

I. Dieu l'homme, les esprits (1QS iii 13 – iv 1)

A	**iii** 13 (vacat) Au maître, pour faire comprendre et pour enseigner à tous les fils de lumière les origines (la nature?) de tous les fils d'homme 14 quant à toutes leurs sortes d'esprits en leurs signes quant à leurs actions dans leurs générations et quant à la visite de leurs coups 15a avec les temps de leur paix.	25b Et lui a créé les esprits, lumière et ténèbres, et sur elles il a fondé toute action, 26a [su]r leurs [jugements] tout service et sur leurs voies [tou]te [visite]. 26b L'une, Dieu l'aime pour tous **iv** 1a les [mo]ments éternels et dans toutes ses activités ils se complaira à jamais; 1b l'autre, il (la) déteste beaucoup et toutes ses voies il les hait à perpétuité. (vacat)	A^1
B	15b Du Dieu des connaissances (vient) tout ce qui est et sera; 15c et avant qu'ils n'existent il a établi tout leur plan; 16a et quand ils existent selon leurs décrets, (c'est) selon le plan de sa gloire (qu')ils accomplissent leur travail 16b sans rien y changer.	21b Et à cause de l'ange de ténèbres est l'égarement de 22a tous les fils de justice, 22b et tout leur péché et leurs iniquités et leur culpabilité et les transgressions de leurs actions (sont) sous sa domination 23a conformément aux mystères de Dieu jusqu'à son temps. 23b Et tous leurs coups et les moments de leurs détresses (sont) sous la domination de son hostilité 24a et tous les esprits de son lot (cherchent) à faire trébucher les fils de lumière. 24b Mais le Dieu d'Israël et son ange de vérité (viennent en) aide à tous 25a les fils de lumière.	B^1
C	16c Dans sa main 17a (sont) les jugements de tous et lui pourvoit à tous leurs besoins 17b et lui a créé l'humanité pour la domination 18a du monde. 18b Et il lui a mis deux esprits pour se conduire selon eux 18c jusqu'au moment de sa visite.	18d Voici les esprits: 19a la vérité et la perversion. 19b Dans une source de lumière (sont) les origines de la vérité et d'une fontaine de ténèbres (sont) les origines de la perversion. 20a Et dans la main d'un prince de lumières (est) la domination de tous les fils de justice et (c'est) selon les voies de lumière (qu')ils se conduisent 20b Et dans la main d'un ange 21a de ténèbres (est) toute domination sur les fils de perversion et (c'est) selon les voies de ténèbres (qu') ils se conduisent.	C^1

II. Les voies et leurs visites (lQS iv 2-14)

	iv 2a ואלה דרכיהן בתבל 2b להאיר בלבב איש ולישר לפניו כול דרכי צדק אמת ולפחד לבבו במשפטי 3a אל	9a ולרוח עולה רחוב נפש ושפול ידים בעבודת צדק	
	3b ורוח ענוה ואורך אפים ורוב רחמים וטוב עולמים ושכל ובינה וחכמת גבורה	9b רשע ושקר גוה ורום לבב כחש ורמיה אכזרי 10a ורוב חנף קצור אפים ורוב אולת וקנאת זדון	
A	3c מאמנת בכול 4a מעשי אל ונשענת ברוב חסדו	10b מעשי תועבה ברוח זנות ודרכי נדה בעבודת טמאה	A^{-1}
	4b ורוח דעת בכול מחשבת מעשה וקנאת משפטי צדק ומחשבת 5 ?קודש ביצר סמוך ורוב חסדים על כול בני אמת וטהרת כבוד מתעב כול גלולי נדה והצנע לכת 6a בערמת כול וחבא לאמת רזי דעת	11a ולשון גדופים עורון עינים וכבוד אוזן קושי עורף וכיבוד לב	
	6b אלה סודי רוח לבני אמת תבל	11b ללכת בכול דרכי חושך וערמת רוע	
	6c ופקודת כול הולכי בה	11c ופקודת 12a כול הולכי בה	
B	6d למרפא 7a ורוב שלום באורך ימים ופרות זרע עם כול ברכות עד	12b לרוב נגועים ביד כול מלאכי חבל לשחת עולמים באף עברת אל נקמה לזעות נצח וחרפת 13a עד עם כלמת כלה באש מחשכים	B^{-1}
	7b ושמחת עולמים בחי נצח וכליל כבוד 8 עם מדת הדר באור עלמים	13b וכול קציהם לדורותם באבל יגון ורעת מרומים בהוות חושך עד 14 כלותם לאין שרית ופליטה למו	

II. Les voies et leurs visites (1QS iv 2-14)

	iv 2a	Et voici leurs voies dans le monde:			
	2b	pour illuminer le cœur de l'homme et pour applanir devant lui toutes les voies de vraie justice et pour faire craindre (à) son cœur les jugements 3a de Dieu:	9a	Mais pour l'esprit de perversité, ambition personnelle et relâchement des mains dans le service de la justice:	
	3b	et un esprit d'humilité et de lenteur à la colère et de grande miséricorde et de bonté constante et de perspicacité et d'intelligence et de puissante sagesse.	9b	méchanceté et mensonge orgueil et hauteur de cœur, fausseté et tricherie cruelle 10a et grande hypocrisie, prompte colère et grande folie et un zèle insolent.	
A	3c	De la foi en toutes 4a les actions de Dieu et l'appui sur sa grande affection:	10b	Des actions abominables dans un esprit de débauche et des voies souillées dans un service d'impureté:	A^{-1}
	4b	et un esprit de connaissance en tout plan d'action et un zèle pour les justes jugements et un plan 5 saint dans un penchant ferme; et une grande affection pour tous les fils de vérité et une pureté glorieuse abominant toutes les idoles souillées et la modestie de conduite 6a avec discernement de tout et une discrétion pour la vérité des mystères de connaissance.	11a	et une langue blasphématoire, aveuglement des yeux et dureté d'oreille raideur de nuque et dureté de cœur,	
	6b	Voilà les conseils de l'esprit aux fils de vérité du monde.	11b	pour se conduire selon toutes les voies de ténèbres et de ruse maligne.	
	6c	Et la visite de tous ceux qui se conduisent selon lui (sera)	11c	Et la visite 12a de tous ceux qui se conduisent selon lui (sera)	
B	6d 7a	pour une guérison et une grande paix dans une longueur de jours et une postérité florissante avec toutes les bénédictions durables	12b	pour un grand (nombre de) coups par la main de tous les anges de destruction pour la perdition éternelle par l'ardeur de la colère vengeresse de Dieu pour une terreur perpétuelle et une honte 13a durable avec l'opprobre de l'extermination par le feu des ténèbres.	B^{-1}
	7b 8	et une joie éternelle dans la vie perpétuelle et une couronne de gloire avec un vêtement d'honneur dans la lumière éternelle.	13b	Et tous leurs temps pour leurs générations (s'écoulera) dans l'affliction douloureuse et le malheur amer dans les calamités de ténèbres jusqu'à 14 leur extermination pour (qu'il ne subsiste) aucun reste et aucun rescapé pour eux.	

III. Partage actuel et purification ultime des élus (lQS iv 15-26)

A	iv 15a (*vacat*) באלה תולדות כול בני איש ובמפלגיהן ינחלו כול צבאותם לדורותם ובדרכיהן יתהלכו 15b וכול פעולת 16a מעשיהם במפלגיהן לפי נחלת איש בין רוב למועט לכול קצי עולמים 16b כיא אל שמן בד בבד עד קץ 17a אחרון 17b ויתן איבת עולם בין מפלגותם תועבת אמת עלילות עולה ותועבת עולה כול דרכי אמת 17c וקנאת 18a ריב על כול משפטיהן כיא לוא יחד יתהלכו	23c עד הנה יריבו רוחי אמת ועול בלבב גבר 24a יתהלכו בחכמה ואולת 24b וכפי נחלת איש באמת יצדק וכן ישנ{ה}א עולה וכירשתו בגורל עול ירשע בו וכן 25a יתעב אמת 25b כיא בד בבד שמן אל עד קץ נחרצה ועשות חדשה 25c והואה ידע פעולת מעשיהן לכול קצי 26a [עולמי]ם וינחילן לבני איש לדעת טוב [ורע] 26b [כיא א]ל [י]פיל גורלות לכול חי לפי רוחו בו [עד מועד]הפקודה	A^1
B	18b ואל ברזי שכלו ובחכמת כבודו נתן קץ להיות עולה ובמועד 19a פקודה ישמידנה לעד	23b ואין עולה והיה לבושת כול מעשי רמיה	B^1
C	19b ואז תצא לנצח אמת תבל כיא התגוללה בדכי רשע בממשלת עולה עד 20a מועד משפט נחרצה	20b ואז יברר אל באמתו כול מעשי גבר יזקק לו מבני איש 20c להתם כול רוח עולה מתכמי 21a בשרו ולטהרו ברוח קודש מכול עלילות רשעה 21b ויז עליו רוח אמת כמי נדה מכול תועבות שקר ברוח נדה 22aוהתגולל 22b להבין ישרים בדעת עליון וחכמת בני שמים להשכיל תמימי דרך 22c כיא בם בחר אל לברית עולמים 23a ולהם כול כבוד אדם	C^{-1}

III. Partage actuel et purification ultime des élus (lQS iv 15-26)

A	**iv** 15a (vacat) En elles sont les origines (est la nature?) de tous les fils d'homme, et en leurs catégories se partagent toutes leurs armées pour leurs générations et en leurs voies ils se conduisent. 15b Et tout le travail 16a de leurs actions (se fait) en leurs catégories selon le partage de l'homme entre l'abondance et la pénurie pour tous les temps éternels. 16b Car (c'est) Dieu (qui) les a placées une partie contre l'autre jusqu'au temps 17a ultime. 17b Et il a établi une haine éternelle entre leurs catégories abomination (pour la) vérité, les actions de perversité et abomination (pour la) perversité tous les chemins de vérité. 17c Et (elles ont) un zèle 18a combatif contre tous leurs jugements, car elles ne vont pas ensemble.	23c Jusqu'à maintenant les esprits de vérité et de perversion combattent dans le cœur de l'humain: 24a ils se conduisent avec sagesse et folie. 24b Et, selon le partage d'un homme dans la vérité, il est juste, et ainsi il hait la perversité et, selon sa portion au lot de perversion, il est méchant en lui, et ainsi 25a il déteste la vérité. 25b Car (c'est) une partie contre l'autre (que) Dieu les a placées jusqu'au temps de la décision et de l'agir nouveau. 25c Et lui connaît le travail de leurs actions pour tous les temps 26a [éternel]s, et il les partagés entre les fils d'homne pour la connaissance du bien [et du mal]. 26b [Car Di]eu [fait tom]ber les lots vers tout vivant selon son esprit (mis) en lui [jusqu'au moment] de la visite	A[1]
B	18b Mais Dieu, dans les secrets de sa science et dans la sagesse de sa gloire a établi un temps pour l'existence de la perversité. Et au moment 19a de sa visite, il l'éliminera à jamais.	23b Et la perversité n'existera plus et en déshonneur (finiront) toutes les actions de tromperie.	B[1]
C	19b Et alors paraîtra pour l'éternité la vérité du monde, car il s'est corrompu dans les voies de l'impiété sous la domination de la perversité jusqu'au 20a moment du jugement décisif:	20b Et alors Dieu nettoiera dans sa vérité toutes les œuvres de l'humain, il épurera pour lui la bâtisse d'homme 20c Pour anéantir tout esprit de perversité des membres de 21a sa chair, et pour le purifier dans l'esprit de sainteté de toutes ses activités d'impiété. 21b Et il fera jaillir sur lui l'esprit de vérité, comme les eaux (purifiant la) souillure de toutes les abominations de mensonge et la corruption 22a dans l' esprit de souillure, 22b pour faire comprendre aux droits la connaissance du Très-Haut, et pour que la sagesse des fils du ciel soit apprise aux parfaits de conduite, 22c car Dieu les a choisis pour l'alliance éternelle, 23a et pour eux (sera) toute la gloire d'Adam.	C^{-1}

APPORTS DES TEXTES APOCALYPTIQUES ET SAPIENTIELS DE QUMRÂN À L'ESCHATOLOGIE DU JUDAÏSME ANCIEN

Dans sa *Théologie de l'Ancien Testament,* G. von Rad fait de la sagesse comme la mère de l'apocalyptique, puisque l'apocalyptique s'approprie les connaissances de la sagesse dans une perspective d'histoire universelle jusque dans ses dimensions eschatologiques. «On peut affirmer, écrit-il, que les écrits apocalyptiques plongent leurs racines dans les traditions sapientiales, tant en ce qui concerne leur matière qu'en ce qui concerne leur façon de poser les questions et leur argumentation.»[1] C'est dire que sur des points importants, les apocalypses ont de réelles affinités avec les écrits bibliques de sagesse qui ne s'en tiennent pas à une sagesse exclusivement proverbiale. En effet, les livres bibliques de sagesse contiennent le plus souvent une dimension eschatologique en demandant à l'homme de rechercher la sagesse pour connaître le chemin qui conduit à la vie et aux récompenses après la mort, afin d'éviter les châtiments en suivant le chemin qui mène à la perdition, au Shéol en bas; voir Pr 12,28; 14,32; 15,24; 23,17-18; 24,19-20; Ps 16,10; 17,15; 49,16; 73,16-17.24-28; Si 48,11-14[2]. Cette même démarche du sage est au cœur de ce qu'il est souvent convenu d'appeler «la grande apocalypse d'Isaïe» (Isaïe 24–27). Sans doute dans ces écrits de sagesse qui rassemblent des matériaux assez disparates, il ne faut pas s'attendre à retrouver tous les thèmes centraux des apocalypses: des révélations par un être surnaturel touchant des réalités transcendantes au sujet de ce monde à la fin des temps. Mais le thème qui est le plus souvent évoqué concerne la conduite de l'homme dans sa vie quotidienne déterminant son sort final dans l'au-delà en lien direct avec le jugement et le renouvellement de la création.

Ainsi, s'il est légitime de distinguer le genre apocalyptique du genre sapiential, il est un fait que nombre de textes de sagesse contiennent des passages didactiques ou parénétiques à finalité eschatologique qui est le propre de l'apocalyptique. Aussi en ce qui concerne les manuscrits de la

1. G. VON RAD, *Théologie de l'Ancien Testament*, Volume 2, *Théologie des traditions prophétiques d'Israël*, Paris, 1965, pp. 263-283, esp. p. 274, Voir *Theologie des Alten Testaments*, Band II, München, 1960, pp. 314-328.

2. Voir É. PUECH, *La croyance des Esséniens en la vie future: immortalité, résurrection, vie éternelle? Histoire d'une croyance dans le judaïsme ancien.* Vol. I. *La résurrection des morts et le contexte scripturaire*. Vol. II. *Les données qumraniennes et classiques* (Études bibliques NS, 21-22), Paris, 1993, pp. 46-65, 73-78.

mer Morte, les auteurs disputent l'attribution de tel passage ou fragment à l'un ou l'autre genre[3]. Mon propos n'est pas ici d'entrer dans ce débat, mais de m'attacher d'abord à la conception eschatologique de ces textes et de montrer comment ils se rattachent tous à une même tradition. Pour cela nous passerons en revue essentiellement des passages des textes de sagesse, le manuscrit intitulé Instruction (1Q26, 4Q415 à 418a, 4Q423), Pseudo-Ezéchiel (4Q385, 386, 388), l'Apocalypse messianique (4Q521), l'Instruction sur les deux Esprits de 1QS III 13-IV, et des Hymnes (1QH^{a}).

Les textes de ce nouveau corpus de sagesse transmettent dans des maximes éthiques et pragmatiques sous le couvert du «mystère à venir» (*raz nih^{e}yeh*) une croyance à un jugement divin et à une vie dans l'au-delà[4]. Mais cette littérature de sagesse qui incorpore des croyances au sujet de l'eschaton, distincte de la littérature apocalyptique tels Daniel et 1 Hénoch bien qu'influencée par cette dernière, s'inscrit dans la droite ligne de ce que les textes sacrés enseignaient déjà et que la Sagesse de Salomon transmet comme révélation des secrets divins: l'espérance d'une rémunération *post-mortem* pour une vie de sainteté, Sg 2,22.

Le manuscrit qumranien 1-4QInstruction

Nous sont parvenus des restes d'au moins sept manuscrits (1Q26, 4Q415, 416, 417, 418, 418a et 423) d'une composition de sagesse aupa-

3. Voir J.J. Collins, *Wisdom, Apocalypticism and the Dead Sea Scrolls,* in A. Diesel, R.G. Lehmann, E. Otto et A. Wagner (eds.), *«Jedes Ding hat seine Zeit...». Studien zur israelitischen und altorientalistichen Weisheit Diethelm Michel zum 65. Geburtstag* (BZAW, 241), Berlin, 1996, pp. 19-32, pp. 31-32: «The Instruction of the Two Spirits is not an apocalypse; it is not presented as a revelation. Its literary genre is, in fact, a typical wisdom genre. 4QSapiential Text A, which does not have the doctrine of the two spirits, has an eschatological perspective which we associate with apocalypticism rather than with traditional Hebrew wisdom. The Wisdom of Solomon is also informed by apocalyptic traditions about the judgement of the dead». Toutefois juste auparavant l'auteur qualifiait ainsi le passage de 1QS: «This mythological structure with its eschatological implications is phenomenologically similar to what we find in the apocalypses, even though the specific myth of the two spirits is not found in the books of Enoch or Daniel... The appeal to supernatural forces as an explanation of evil clearly separates all forms of apocalypticism from the traditional wisdom of Ben Sira. The appeal to supernatural forces, however, does not necessarily distinguish apocalypticism from all wisdom literature». Le partage est des plus flous.

4. Aussi certains rangent-ils cet ensemble dans un genre mixte «apocalyptico-sapientiel», voir T. Elgvin, *Wisdom With and Without Apocalyptic,* in D.K. Falk, F. García Martínez, E. Schuller (eds.), *Sapiential, Liturgical and Poetical Texts from Qumran. Proceedings of the Third Meeting of the International Organization for Qumran Studies Oslo 1998 Published in Memory of Maurice Baillet* (STDJ, 35), Leiden, 2000, pp. 15-38, esp. 18-20.

ravant inconnue[5]. Les éditeurs en font une composition préessénienne par l'absence de terminologie typique des compositions de la Communauté qu'ils situeraient assez bien entre Proverbes et Ben Sira[6] mais d'autres soulignent des affinités qui suggèrent un milieu d'origine commun[7]. Quoi qu'il en soit, il semble que le rouleau des Hymnes connaisse cette composition: 1QH^a XVIII 29-30 (= X 27-28) paraît citer 4Q418 55 10, et donnerait ainsi un *terminus ante quem*. En outre, puisque «le Dieu des connaissances» est le créateur de l'ordre du monde désigné par le terme *mḥšbh*, il semblerait aussi que l'Instruction ait été composée par le même cercle que celui de l'Instruction sur les Deux Esprits de 1QS et des Hymnes de 1QH^a[8], et elle les précéderait alors de peu. Soit dit en passant, il paraît recommandé d'éviter les qualificatifs «secte et sectaire», étant donné que les compositions esséniennes n'ont rien de sectaire au sens moderne du mot, pas plus que la Communauté ne s'apparente à une «secte» mais à un groupe du judaïsme orthodoxe; aussi pour être fidèle à Flavius Josèphe (*Guerre* II §162, *Ant.* XIII 171, *Vita* §10), il faudrait alors user du même terme «secte et sectaire» pour tout ce qui touche aux milieux pharisiens et sadducéens.

Cette composition didactique qui donne des conseils sur le comportement des hommes et leur relation à Dieu selon la tradition sapientiale reçue, contient des admonitions fondées sur des considérations cosmologiques et eschatologiques, sur la révélation des mystères de ce qui sera,

5. J.T. MILIK, *1Q26. Un apocryphe,* in D. BARTHÉLEMY – J.T. MILIK, *Qumran Cave I* (DJD, 1), Oxford, 1955, pp. 101-102. J. STRUGNELL et D.J. HARRINGTON, *Qumran Cave 4.XXIV. Sapiential Texts*, Part 2. *4QInstruction (Mûsar lemevîn): 4Q415ff.* (DJD, 34), Oxford, 1999.

6. Voir D.J. HARRINGTON, *Wisdom at Qumran*, in E. ULRICH and J. VANDERKAM (eds.), *The Community of the Renewed Covenant. The Notre Dame Symposium on the Dead Sea Scrolls*, Notre Dame, IN, 1994, pp. 137-152; J. STRUGNELL, *The Sapiential Work 4Q415ff and Pre-Qumranic Works from Qumran: Lexical Considerations*, in D.W. PARRY and E. ULRICH, *The Provo International Conference on the Dead Sea Scrolls. Technological Innovations, New Texts, and Reformulated Issues* (STDJ, 30), Leiden, 1999, pp. 595-608, et l'édition, DJD, 34, pp. 1-36.

7. Voir par exemple T. ELGVIN, *Admonition Texts from Qumran Cave 4*, in M.O. WISE *et alii* (eds.), *Methods of Investigation of the Dead Sea Scrolls and Khirbet Qumran Site*, New York, 1994, pp. 179-194; COLLINS, *Wisdom, Apocalypticism* (n. 3), p. 26; J.J. COLLINS, Compte-rendu de DJD, 34, in *JSS* 46 (2001) 335.

8. Bien trop d'éléments communs se retrouvent dans ces compositions pour qu'il n'y ait pas de parenté entre elles. Voir A. LANGE, *Wisdom and Predestination in the Dead Sea Scrolls*, in *DSD* 2 (1995) 340-354, p. 348. T. ELGVIN, *Wisdom and Apocalypticism in the Early Second Century BCE – The Evidence of 4QInstruction*, in L SCHIFFMAN, E. TOV, et J. VANDERKAM (eds.), *The Dead Sea Scrolls Fifty Years After their Discovery. Proceedings of the Jerusalem Congress, July 20-25, 1997*, Jerusalem, 2000, pp. 226-247, esp. p. 247, suggère que «4QInstruction reflects non-priestly circles in Judea from the early Hasmonean period and that these circles had developed a distinct community identity. Perhaps these circles later merged with the priestly group of the Righteous Teacher when the community of the *yaḥad* was formed».

de sorte que les élus sont invités à discerner entre le bien et le mal (4Q416 2 iii 8-15). Elle insiste entre autres sur la nécessité de lutter dans la poursuite d'une sagesse éclairée par une théologie de la création et de l'histoire qui renseigne sur la finalité de la condition humaine, les châtiments des insensés et les récompenses des élus fidèles lors du jugement divin.

Après avoir mentionné la création des luminaires célestes et leurs fonctions en 4Q416 1 7-9, le texte continue par le jugement, ll. 10-16 (// 418 2 2-9)[9]:

10 משמים ישפוט על עבודת רשעה וכל בני אמתו ירצו ל[פניו ותבא רשעה עד]
11 קצה ויפחדו וירועו כל אשר התגללו בה כי שמים יראו[זעפו ויחרדו מפניו]
12 [י]מים ותהמות פחדו ויתערערו כל רוח בשר ובני השמי[ם יגילו וישמחו ביום]
13 [הש]פטה וכל עולה תתם עוד ושלם קץ האמ[ת לם]
14 בכל קצי עד כי אל אמת הוא ומקדם שני[עולם הכין הכל ו (משכיל)]
15 להבין צדק בין טוב לרע לדב[ר כל משפ[ט (כי)א]
16 י]צר בשר הואה ומבינו[ת

[10]Depuis les cieux Il jugera l'œuvre d'impiété et tous Ses fils fidèles trouveront grâce de[vant Lui, *et l'impiété arrivera à*] [11]sa fin. Et seront effrayés et trembleront tous ceux qui se sont souillés par elle, car les cieux craindront [*Sa colère et devant Lui seront terrifiées*] [12]les mers et les abîmes seront effrayés. Et seront anéantis tous les esprits de chair et les fils des cieux[*se réjouiront et ils exulteront le jour* où] [13]elle[sera ju]gée et toute iniquité cessera dès que sera achevée la période de la vérit[é…] [14]dans tous les temps éternels. Car Il est le Dieu de Vérité et depuis les années[d'éternité *Il a disposé toute chose et a instruit l'oreille du* sage] [15]pour expliquer au juste la distinction entre le bien du mal, pour di[r]e tout juge[ment… car] [16]il est [une c]réature de chair, et [ses] compréhensions[…

Dans ces lignes est envisagé un jugement universel de l'impiété qui aura une fin en son temps et cela dans toutes les dimensions de la création, depuis les cieux, la terre, les mers jusqu'aux abîmes. Mais au sujet de ce mystère à venir, le Dieu de vérité a pris soin d'en avertir l'homme par une voix de sagesse pour qu'il sache dès à présent distinguer entre le bien et le mal et qu'il se prépare au jugement. Un autre fragment le rappelle à sa manière (4Q418 123 ii 3-8):

[3]tout ce qui adviendra par elle, pourquoi cela a été et ce qui sera dans[…] [4]Son temps, qu'Il a révélé à l'oreille des hommes sensés au sujet du mystère à venir[…] [5][Et] toi, homme sensé, quand tu considères toutes ces cho-

9. Notre lecture et notre restauration du passage diffèrent quelque peu de l'*editio princeps* ainsi que de celles de T. ELGVIN, *Wisdom With and Without Apocalyptic* (n. 4), p. 24. Mais il n'est pas le lieu ici de les justifier. Noter simplement que *bny ʾmtw*, à la l. 10, est une expression connue de 1QH[a], 1QS et 1QM, tout comme *ʾl ʾmt*, *qṣ hʾmt*, *yṣr bśr, rwḥ bśr, htgllw bdrky ršʿ*, *kl qṣy ʿd* et bien d'autres lexèmes. A la l. 13, le manuscrit 4Q418 lit *ʿd yšlm* et à la l. 15, *lhbyn ṣdyq*. Pour les ll. 14-15, le *lamed* demande de compléter avec 1QS III 13 *lmśky]l lhbyn*…

ses[*et que tu entreprends d'accomplir*] [6]un[trava]il, pèse tes actes en fonction de [Son] temps[...] [7][...]Il te visitera. Garde-toi surtout de[...] [8][...]Il juge[ra] l'iniquité [...

Rien de ce qu'entreprend un homme n'échappera au jugement divin, car c'est dans l'activité quotidienne que se forge la gloire future ou l'affliction, ainsi que l'enseigne encore le sage (4Q417 2 i 10-12):

Scrute le mystère] [11]à venir et considère l'enfantement du salut et sache qui doit hériter la gloire ou l'affliction. [La réjouissance] n'est-elle pas [destinée aux esprits contrits] [12]et la joie éternelle aux endeuillés?

L'issue de la vie future pour la gloire ou l'affliction est un enfantement permanent et on doit avoir sans cesse présent à l'esprit le secret du plan divin, même si on doit attendre son pardon (4Q417 2 i 15-16, voir 1QS III 6-9, CD IV 18-20, comp. Sg 12,19-22):

Car devant sa [colère] [16]personne ne tiendra, et qui sera déclaré juste quand Il va juger? Et sans pardon, comment[un] pauvre [tiendrait-il devant Lui?]

Ces points importants sont comme rassemblés dans un passage un peu mieux conservé, 4Q417 1 i 6-19 // 4Q418 43 4-14 (comp. 1QS III 13s, 1QH^a V 12 ss)[10]:

...]Et jour et nuit médite le mystère]à venir, et scrute sans cesse. Alors tu connaîtras la vérité et l'iniquité, la sagesse [7][et la fol]ie tu reconnaîtras [par leurs] œuvres dans toutes leurs voies, avec leur conséquence pour tous les temps éternels, et la Visite [8]éternelle. Alors tu discerneras entre le bien et le mal selon toutes leurs œuvres. Car le Dieu des connaissances est le fondement de vérité et dans le mystère à venir [9]Il a étendu sa fondation. Ses œuvres [Il (les) a faites] toutes [avec sage]sse, et avec adresse il les a toutes façonnées, et le pouvoir de ses œuvres, [10]pour tous c'est la rétribution, et toute connaissance, toute[...]Il a étendu(es) pour qu'ils comprennent que toute créature se conduit [11]selon l'inclination de sa compréhension. Et il a étendu à[...]tout[...]et avec une abondance de compréhensions ont été connus les secrets de [12]Son plan avec la conduite parfaite en toutes Ses œuvres. Ces choses recherche-les sans cesse et médite toutes [13]leurs issues. Alors tu connaîtras la gloire de Sa puissance avec Ses secrets mystérieux et les grandeurs de Ses œuvres. Mais toi, [14]homme sensé, aspire à ta récompense dans l'aide-mémoire de la rétribution car ton destin vient gravé et décrété(e) la totalité de ta rétribution, [15]car gravé est ce qui est décrété par Dieu au sujet de toutes les fautes des fils de la fosse et un livre aide-mé-

10. Nous corrigeons quelque peu çà et là les lectures des éditeurs, en particulier en lisant *kwl ʿ[w]n[w]t bny šyt*, l. 14, «toutes les fautes des fils de la fosse», *ḥzwn hhgwt* et *wynḥylh*, l. 16, sans aucune correction, et *hḥzwn*, l. 17, non *hgwy*. Pour *bny šyt*, voir 3Q15 (C 38), et comparer 4Q418 69 ii 6 et 1QS IX 16 et 22. Les lectures *ḥzwn hhgwt* et *ntn ḥzwn* paraissent indiscutables, ce qui explique la lecture limpide *wynḥylh*. Il n'y a certainement pas de «Vision de Hagi» dans ce passage, comme le suppose ELGVIN, *Wisdom With and Without Apocalyptic* (n. 4), p. 25.

moire est écrit devant Lui [16]en faveur de ceux qui ont gardé Sa parole. Et ceci est la vision de la méditation concernant le livre aide-mémoire et Il l'a (= la méditation) donnée en héritage à l'homme d'un peuple spirituel. Car [17]conforme au modèle des saints est son façonnage mais n'a pas encore été donnée la vision à un esprit de chair, parce qu'il ne distingue pas entre [18]le bien et le mal d'après le jugement de son esprit. *vacat*
Et toi, fils sensé, considère le mystère à venir et connais [19]les [sentier]s de tout vivant et sa conduite jugée d'après [ses] œuvres...

Malgré son état de conservation, ce passage unique est d'un grand intérêt. Le sage recommande à l'homme sensé de savoir distinguer entre les deux voies opposées, sagesse et folie, qui se présentent à lui et de fixer sa conduite en fonction du jugement éternel, car Dieu a tout créé avec sagesse et il a donné à chacun de marcher selon son inclination. Etant donné le résultat du jugement lorsque sera jugée la somme des bonnes et mauvaises actions gravées sur le livre aide-mémoire, le sensé de la vision de la méditation a un avantage certain, lui qui sait distinguer entre le bien et le mal. Il sait que «celui qui a gardé la Parole» a son nom écrit à part du livre aide-mémoire où sont gravées les fautes des fils de la fosse. Comparé à l'esprit de chair, celui qui appartient au peuple spirituel est un être façonné sur le modèle des saints. C'est là son héritage. Le sage a donc quelque avantage à méditer les mystères de la Visite éternelle, «à garder la Parole» de Dieu, expression qui doit renvoyer à la Loi, maîtresse de sagesse, comme il est habituel dans les Psaumes, les écrits de sagesse et en 4Q525 en particulier[11]. Tel est le «mystère à venir»[12], le plan de l'économie du salut que Dieu a révélé aux fils du peuple spirituel[13]. C'est pourquoi il est recommandé à l'instruit d'étudier le mystère à venir pour comprendre la voie droite qui est douce pour l'homme et pratiquer ainsi la Loi divine (4Q416 2 iii 14-16 //418 9 15-17):

Etudie le mystère à venir et comprend toutes les voies de vérité, et tu contempleras toutes [15]les racines d'iniquité. Et alors tu sauras ce qui est amer

11. Il n'y a pas d'exclusion dans ce passage comme si *rz nhyh* s'opposait à *ḥkmh* ou à *twrh*, ainsi que le suggère ELGVIN, *Wisdom and Apocalypticism* (n. 8), pp. 235, 237-238. La vraie sagesse que confère l'intelligence dans le mystère à venir est bien fondée sur la pratique de la Loi.

12. Ce sens paraît de loin préférable à «Geheimnis des Werdens», ainsi que le propose A. LANGE, *Weisheit und Prädestination: Weisheitliche Urordnung und Prädestination in den Textfunden von Qumran* (STDJ, 18), Leiden, 1995, pp. 91s, 120, à propos de ce texte principalement. Cet auteur ne voit pas de référence explicite à une dimension historique et eschatologique dans ces emplois de *rz nhyh*, tout en admettant que le renvoi aux tablettes célestes peut l'y inclure.

13. On n'est pas loin de l'emploi du mot *mysterion* des épîtres pauliniennes, Rm 11,25; 16,25; 1 Co 2,7; Col 1,26, voir R.E. BROWN, *The Semitic Background of the New Testament Mysterion*, in *Biblica* 39 (1958) 426-448.

pour un homme et ce qui est doux pour un individu. Honore ton père dans ta pauvreté [16]et ta mère dans ta misère...

Ce conseil citant explicitement un des commandements du Décalogue (Exode 20 // Deutéronome 5, voir Sira 3) rejoint le passage précédent qui demandait plus généralement de «garder la Parole». On retrouverait dans d'autres fragments des allusions à la Loi concernant l'offrande des premiers-nés et des produits de la terre, ainsi que l'observance des fêtes des récoltes aux temps fixés (4Q423 3-5 // 1Q26).

En définitive, ces quelques exemples tirés d'une composition très fragmentaire montrent que la pratique de la Loi est la vraie sagesse qui introduit au cœur du mystère à venir: l'accès à la vie, aux récompenses éternelles (comp. CD I 1 – IV 12). Telle est la conclusion à laquelle est parvenu le sage méditant la Loi de Dieu dans sa vision de l'économie divine du salut réservée à l'homme sensé et non à l'esprit de chair. Le destin de l'homme de bien, de l'esprit éclairé qui agit conformément à la Loi longuement méditée, assimilée et mise en pratique, se trouve inscrit dans le livre comme en Dn 12,1, alors que l'esprit de chair qui suit la voie d'iniquité est compté dans le livre aide-mémoire au nombre des fils de la fosse dont les fautes sont gravées avec toute leur rétribution[14].

Dans cette vision d'ensemble du mystère à venir, nous sont parvenues par chance, outre un passage assez lacuneux (4Q418 126 ii 6-9)[15], quelques lignes que le sage a consacrées plus spécifiquement à sa vision de l'eschaton.

4Q418 69 ii + 60 // 417 5 1-5[16]:

1 ב/פחכה
2]ותשכיל[(ב/ל)*עמקי תהו*]מות עם
3]ב[ע]ב[ו]דתם הלוא באמת יתהלכו
4 כול[משברי]הם ובדעה כול גליהם *vacat* ועתה אוילי לב מה טוב ללוא
5 נוצר [ומ]ה השקט ללוא היה ומה משפט ללוא נוסד ומה יאנחו מתים על כ[ול יומ]ם
6 אתם ל[שא]ול נוצרתם ולשחת עולם תשובתכם כי תקיץ לגל[ות על]חטאכמה[ויושבי]

14. Voir 1 Hénoch 90,20; 104,7, Jubilés 30,22 et Testaments des XII Patriarches, Juda 20,4 pour le livre des actes des impies, mais pour le livre de vie, voir Ex 32,32-33, Ml 3,16, Ps 69,29, Dn 12,1, 1 Hénoch 104,1, Jubilés 19,9; 30,22-23, 4Q504 1-2 vi 14, 1QM XII 3, CD XX 20,19, Ap 3,5; etc.

15. Traduction: «[6]un jugement pour venger les faiseurs d'iniquité et une ju[ste] punition[aux...] [7]et pour emprisonner les impies et relever la tête des pauvres [...] [8]dans une gloire éternelle et une paix perpétuelle, et l'esprit de vie pour séparer[...] [9]tous les fils d'Eve...».

16. Nous avons justifié les notes de lecture et les restaurations de ce passage dans *La croyance à la résurrection des justes dans un texte de sagesse: 4Q418 69 ii*, à paraître dans les *Mélanges Moshe Weinfeld*. Nous avons changé une lecture à la ligne 14: *b]l[bw]š[y* au lieu de *ʿm md]t[*.

7 מחשכיה יצרחו על ריבכם וכול נהיה עולם דורשי אמת יעורו למשפטכ[ם *ואז*]
8 ישמדו כול אוילי לב ובני עולה לוא ימצאו עוד [וכ]ול מחזיקי רשעה יבש[ו *ואז*]
9 במשפטכם יריעו מוסדי {ה}רקיע וירעמו כול צ[בא אי]ל[ים] ל[הבדי]ל אהבי[ן *צדק*]
10 *vacat* ואתם בחירי אמת ורודפי [בינה ו]משח[רי חוכמה ו]שוקד[ים]
11 על כול דעה איכה תאמרו יגענו בבינה ושקדנו לרדוף דעת ב[כול עת]או בכול מ[קום]
12 {ה}ולא עיף בכול{נ}שני עולם הלוא באמת ישעשע לעד ודעה[*לנצח*]תשרתנו וב[ני]
13 שמים אשר חיים עולם נחלתם האמור יאמרו יגענו בפעלות אמת ויעפ[נו]
14 בכול קצים הלוא באור עולם יתהל[כו *כולם* ב]ל[בו]שי כ]בוד ורוב הדר אתם[*קמים*]
15 ברקיע[קודש וב]סוד אילים כול [*ימי עולמים* *va*[*cat* ואתה בן[מבין]

^{1} ...*il*]te[*glo*]*rifiera/*]ton *filet* (?)
^{2} [...]et tu comprendras[*les profondeurs des abî*]*mes* avec ^{3}[*leurs – et tu* - – -]dans leur [œ]u[v]re. N'est-ce pas fidèlement que circulent ^{4}tous leurs[courants] et, en connaissance, toutes leurs vagues? *vacat* Et maintenant, insensés, qu'est-ce qui est bon pour qui n'a pas été ^{5}façonné?[Et q]u'est-ce que la tranquillité pour qui n'a pas existé? Et qu'est-ce qu'un décret pour qui n'a pas été établi? Et que pourraient lamenter les morts sur to[us]*leurs* [*jours*?] ^{6}Vous, vous avez été façonnés pour[le Shé]ôl, et à la Fosse éternelle est votre retour, lorsqu'il/elle s'éveillera pour expos[er]votre péché.[Et *les habitants* de] ^{7}ses antres s'insurgeront contre votre plaidoirie et tous les destinés-à-l'éternité, les chercheurs fidèles, seront réveillés pour votre jugement. [*Et alors*] ^{8}seront anéantis tous les insensés, et des fils d'iniquité on ne trouvera plus,[et to]us ceux qui s'adonnent à l'impiété se dessécher[ont. *Et alors,*] ^{9}lors de votre jugement, crieront les fondations du firmament, et tonneront toutes les ar[mées cé]lestes]pour[sépare]r ceux qui aiment[*la justice*.]
^{10} *vacat* Et vous, les élus fidèles, qui poursuivez la[compréhension, et] qui assidûment recher[chez la sagesse, et] qui veille[z] ^{11}sur toute connaissance, comment pouvez-vous dire: «Nous nous sommes épuisés à la compréhension tout en veillant à poursuivre la connaissance en[tout temps] ou en tout li[eu]?» ^{12}Mais on ne se fatigue pas pour (le prix de) toutes les années d'éternité! Ne prend-on pas plaisir à la fidélité pour toujours? Et la connaissance,[pour toujours,] ne nous sert-elle pas? Et les fi[ls des] ^{13}cieux dont la part est la vie éternelle, pourraient-ils vraiment dire: «Nous nous sommes épuisés dans les œuvres de fidélité et [nous nous]sommes fatigués ^{14}à tous moments?» N'est-ce pas dans la lumière éternelle qu'ils chemi[ne]r[ont *tous avec des*]*v*[*êtemen*]*t*[*s* de g]loire et une abondance de splendeur avec eux, [*en se tenant*] ^{15}dans les firmaments de[sainteté et dans] le conseil divin, tous [*les jours d'éternité*? *va*]*cat*
Et toi, l'in[telligent, //[...

Ce passage de l'Instruction qui suit un paragraphe à résonance cosmologique sur les abîmes, reprend les thèmes et le vocabulaire de la première colonne du rouleau où sont aussi présents les cieux, les mers et les abîmes à côté des fidèles qui trouveront grâce lors du jugement de l'iniquité par le Dieu de vérité, alors que les esprits de chair seront anéantis et que les fils des cieux se réjouiront (4Q418 1-2 // 416 1, voir ci-dessus). Ce passage qui peut difficilement être un ajout tardif[17], comporte deux sections distinctes par le *vacat*.

La première section commence par un avertissement aux insensés à l'aide de quelques questions rhétoriques à la réponse indisputable. Ainsi en est-il à présent et en sera-t-il plus tard de vous, insensés. Vous avez été créés pour le Shéol et à la Fosse éternelle est dès maintenant programmé votre retour lorsqu'elle s'éveillera pour révéler et exposer votre péché. Mais tous les destinés-à-l'éternité, les chercheurs fidèles, s'éveilleront pour votre jugement, et les habitants des antres obscurs s'insurgeront contre votre plaidoirie. Alors tous les insensés seront anéantis, il ne sera plus vu de fils d'iniquité, et les impies se dessécheront. Les fondations du firmament crieront et les armées célestes interviendront pour séparer les justes. Pour le sage, le sort éternel des impies est déjà connu et il sera définitivement fixé lors du grand jugement auquel assistera le cosmos tout entier, Shéol, abîmes et antres obscurs, firmament et armées célestes, et les justes eux-mêmes qui seront réveillés. Ceux-ci seuls ressusciteront et assisteront au jugement des impies, alors que ces derniers verront définitivement fixé leur sort dans la Fosse éternelle, toute plaidoirie sera alors inutile, il sera trop tard.

En revanche, la deuxième section s'adresse aux élus fidèles qui poursuivent sans relache leur recherche de la sagesse. Elle cherche à encourager à la fidèlité ceux qui pourraient se décourager trop facilement et qui seraient tentés d'abandonner, épuisés dans cette recherche, bien que «destinés-à-l'éternité». D'abord on ne se fatigue pas pour rien, puisque le prix à recevoir au bout du compte, c'est toutes les années d'éternité. Enfin, on trouve du plaisir dans la fidélité de tout instant d'autant que la connaissance est un bien précieux qui sert toujours et en toute circonstance. A l'appui de son exhortation, le sage invoque l'exemple des anges fidèles dont la part est la vie éternelle et qui eux ne se lassent jamais. Comme le destin du juste est de cheminer un jour dans la lumière et la gloire, éternellement, en se tenant dans les firmaments de sainteté et dans le conseil divin, il doit dès maintenant les prendre pour modèle en cherchant à les imiter dans leur fidélité dans le service divin, en observant la Parole de sagesse. Alors seulement il pourra un jour cheminer pour toujours en leur compagnie dans la gloire et la lumière. Noter que le réveil des justes est seul mentionné dans la section qui s'adresse aux insensés. Cette manière de procéder devrait aider à comprendre d'autres

17. Voir STRUGNELL – HARRINGTON, DJD, 34, p. 14, en attribuant beaucoup d'importance au passage du singulier – pluriel – singulier. Mais la première colonne du rouleau annonce déjà tous ces thèmes d'une part et, d'autre part, ces changements ne sont pas rares dans des compositions de sagesse.

compositions esséniennes en tout point comparables. Et même alors il ne sera pas égal aux anges, mais vivant en présence de Dieu et en leur compagnie, il sera comme les anges, à nouveau «im-mortel».

C'est affirmer, on ne peut plus clairement, que le juste ne participe pas encore à cette gloire ni à la pleine compagnie des anges dans le conseil divin. Il y aspire comme à une récompense attendue qu'il recevra lors de son réveil au jour du jugement général auquel participera le cosmos tout entier: les cieux avec les anges, et le Shéol qui s'ouvrira pour que le juste s'éveille et que l'impie reçoive le châtiment éternel[18]. En effet, si le juste y participait déjà un tant soit peu, il n'y aurait pas de motif de découragement ou de lassitude d'une part et, d'autre part, il ne trouverait pas dans cet exemple à suivre un encouragement, puisqu'il posséderait déjà les arrhes de ce qui sera éternel et la certitude de sa pleine réalisation à un moment ou à un autre. Or ce n'est manifestement pas le cas. Le juste marche à tâtons, dans la foi et l'espérance que se réalisera pour lui ce mystère à venir. Cela explique le dilemme et la difficulté de la persévérance au centre de ce passage d'exhortation sapientielle et éthique.

Dans ce diptyque, Shéol et Fosse ne désignent pas simplement le séjour des morts que chacun va rejoindre dans la tombe, mais aussi le lieu des châtiments et de perdition éternels où les impies seront anéantis pour toujours. A l'opposé, Dieu en retirera le juste au jour du jugement lorsque le Shéol-Fosse s'éveillera, changeant alors de signification: du lieu de séjour temporaire pour tous en un lieu de châtiments éternels pour les impies, voir 1 S 2,6. Le sage ne fait que reprendre là l'espérance des Psalmistes, Ps 16,10s; 49,15s; 17,15; 73,16s,27s; et des Proverbes, Pr 15,24[19].

Si le séjour au Shéol-Fosse de perdition éternelle devient désormais le lieu de châtiment des impies, la résurrection-réveil est l'entrée dans la vie éternelle du juste, de celui qui a été fidèle dans la recherche et la pra-

18. Nous ne partageons pas l'opinion des éditeurs, DJD, 34, p. 14: «The assumption seems to be that the righteous *can even now* participate to some degree in the eternal contemplation and happiness of the angels who dwell in the heavenly court. If they remain faithful in pursuing wisdom and righteousness, they *will eventually share in the fullness of the angelic life*» (nos italiques). C'est la même conception qu'on retrouve dans les manuscrits esséniens, les *Hymnes* en particulier. Il n'y a pas là de notion d'eschatologie réalisée. P. DAVIES, *Death, Resurrection, and Life After Death in the Qumran Scrolls*, in A. AVERY-PECK – J. NEUSNER (eds.), *Judaism in Late Antiquity*. Part Four: *Death, Life-After-Death, Resurrection and the World-to-Come in the Judaisms of Antiquity*, Leiden, 2000, pp. 189-211, esp. 198, n'a pas saisi le point essentiel de cette composition: «But whether this eternal life will follow a revival from death or promises an eternal extension of the present life is not clear».

19. Pour un aperçu général, voir *La croyance des Esséniens* (n. 2), I, pp. 47-57.

tique du bien. Sa place sera dans la lumière et la gloire, en compagnie des anges, fils des cieux, dans le conseil divin et la présence de Dieu. Divers verbes sont utilisés pour décrire cet instant ou changement d'état, l'image du réveil ici (*yʿwrw*, l. 7) comme en 1QH[a] XIV 32, ou *yqyṣw* en Is 26,19, Dn 12,2, et Ps 17,15, celle de «se tenir debout» *yʿmdw* en 4Q385 3 2, Dn 12,13 (1QH[a] VI 17) ou de «se lever» *yqwmw(n)* en Is 26,14,19, Ps 1,5, 4Q385 3 2, 4Q521 7 6, et 1QH[a] V 29, voir Sg 5,1 (τότε στήσεται), et encore celle de la «revivification» avec *yḥyw* en Is 26,14,19 et 4Q385 2 8-9, *mḥyh* en 4Q521 7 6, *yḥyh* (Si 48,11), ζωοποιεῖν (Jn 5,21, Rm 4,17; 8,11, Ep 2,5;...), et ἀναβιοῦν (2 M 7,9). Toutes ces images signifiant la vie puisque la mort est un sommeil sur une couche, veulent évoquer le changement radical d'état ou de destin des justes lors de la Visite divine, qui n'est autre que la récompense promise et attendue. La conception eschatologique est identique à celle d'Isaïe 26[20] et de Daniel 12[21], en cela que seul le juste ou l'élu fidèle est bénéficiaire de la résurrection et de la vie éternelle en compagnie des anges, alors que l'insensé impie voit pour châtiment son anéantissement dans le Shéol éternel[22]. Mais contrairement à ces deux passages, l'Instruction présente le jour du jugement avec ses récompenses et punitions dans un cadre cosmologique qui faisait auparavant apparemment défaut ou était à peine présent (Yahvé châtiera Léviathan et tuera le dragon des mers en Is 27,1). En revanche, Daniel 12 insiste sur les doctes qui ont enseigné la justice aux multitudes, demandant à Daniel de sceller ces révélations dans le livre jusqu'à la Fin (12,4 et 9), les méchants feront le

20. [14]Les morts jamais ne revivront, les ombres jamais ne ressusciteront,
car tu as puni et tu les as exterminés et tu en as fait disparaître tout souvenir.
[19]Tes morts revivront, tes cadavres ressusciteront,
réveillez-vous et réjouissez-vous, les habitants de la poussière,
car ta rosée est une rosée de lumière et la terre des ombres enfantera.

21. [1b]En ce temps-là, ton peuple sera épargné:
quiconque sera trouvé inscrit dans le livre,
[2]et beaucoup de ceux qui dorment au pays de la poussière s'éveilleront.
Les uns (seront) pour la vie éternelle, et les autres (seront) pour l'opprobre, pour l'horreur éternelle.

On a peine à suivre J.J. COLLINS, *The Afterlife in Apocalyptic Literature*, in AVERY-PECK – NEUSNER, *Judaism in Late Antiquity* (n. 18), pp. 119-139, esp. 126 et 129, qui ne veut lire qu'une résurrection de l'esprit, ainsi que dans 1 Hénoch, mais DAVIES, *Death*, p. 195: «Unlike Enoch, Daniel speaks of resurrection of bodies, not reviving of spirits». Toutefois, Daniel hébreu ne parle jamais de résurrection des impies pour les châtiments *contra* Davies: «In this respect 1QS follows Dan 12,3, in which some of the wicked were resurrected for eternal shame» (p. 199).

22. Nous ne pouvons suivre J.J. Collins qui écrit que cette composition ne parle pas de résurrection mais seulement de récompenses et de châtiments: «Moreover, the kind of eschatology presented, which does not speak of resurrection but of eschatological reward and punishment, is quite close to what we find in such sectarian texts as the Community Rule and the Damascus Document» (Compte-rendu [n. 7], p. 335).

mal et ne comprendront pas mais les doctes comprendront et un grand nombre seront lavés, blanchis et purifiés (12,10). De même Isaïe 26 a également un accent de sagesse au sujet de la route droite du juste, de l'attente des jugements et de la recherche de Dieu dans la fidélité malgré des incartades, tout en notant l'insouciance du méchant qui ne voit rien et n'apprend rien de la pédagogie divine (Is 26,7-13). C'est dans ce cadre de réflexions sur la conduite de Dieu pour le peuple que le sage présente son espérance en la résurrection des justes et au châtiment des méchants (Is 26,14-19). Dans chacun des trois textes (Isaïe, Daniel et Instruction) sagesse et eschatologie sont intimement liées.

Mais cette présentation de l'espérance eschatologique de l'Instruction suivant Isaïe 26 (hébreu et LXX)[23] qu'on retrouve en Daniel 12, n'est pas isolée. Un autre texte au fort accent apocalyptique en est un précieux témoin, 4QPseudo-Ezéchiel.

Le Pseudo-Ezéchiel (4Q385 2-4 et //)

Ont été retrouvés dans la grotte 4 de Qumrân quatre (ou cinq?) copies[24] qui supposent un *terminus ante quem* de cette composition vers le milieu du Ier siècle av. J.-C., sinon déjà le dernier quart du IIe siècle[25]. Par ailleurs le contenu de 4Q386 1 ii-iii pourrait renvoyer au règne d'Antiochus IV Epiphane. Dans ce cas, la composition serait plus ou moins contemporaine de Daniel 12, vers le milieu du IIe siècle, probablement préessénienne à cause de la présence du tétragramme[26].

La partie la mieux conservée présente la vision des ossements desséchés d'Ezéchiel 37. Si la vision du prophète pouvait être interprétée comme une représentation figurative et symbolique de restauration nationale, – mais pour être comprise la métaphore ne doit-elle pas reposer sur des éléments d'une croyance? –, cette composition en supprime

23. Voir *La croyance des Esséniens* (n. 2), I, pp. 66-73.

24. D. Dimant, *Qumran Cave 4·XXI. Parabiblical Texts, Part 4: Pseudo-Prophetic Texts* (DJD, 30), Oxford, 2001, pp. 7-9, en compte six, mais 4Q385c n'est certainement pas un manuscrit à part, ce que n'exige pas la paléographie, et l'appartenance de 4Q391 est discutée. En effet, en l'absence de recoupements, la présence des quatre points pour le tétragramme fait très fortement douter de cette appartenance. Pour 4Q385 2 et 4, voir *La croyance des Esséniens* (n. 2), II, pp. 605-616.

25. Dimant, DJD, 30, p. 16, si on compte 4Q391.

26. Mais on ne peut accepter l'argumentation de Dimant (p. 13), qui repose sur des présupposés: elle déclare les thèmes de résurrection et de *Merkabah* comme non esséniens, et exclut des compositions esséniennes tous les fragments relatifs à ce sujet. Mais comment exclure *širot ʿolat ha-šabbat* et les *hymnes* qui reprennent ces thèmes? L'auteur essaie de leur faire dire autre chose, contrairement à l'évidence, et exclut les compositions gênantes pour sa théorie.

l'ambiguïté en décodant nombre de détails du texte biblique par des additions explicatives. Elle comprend la vision comme une préfiguration de la résurrection individuelle en tant que récompense eschatologique des seuls justes d'Israël. 4Q385 2-3 et // 386 1 i // 388 7:

>]...] ils ne mourront pas[... mais ils sauront 2[1]que je suis Yahvé,] le rédempteur de mon peuple, leur donnant l'alliance.
> [2][Et je dis: Yahvé,] j'en ai vu beaucoup en Israël qui ont aimé ton nom et ont marché [3]dans les voies de[justice. Mais] quand cela arrivera-t-il? et comment seront-ils récompensés (pour) leur piété? Et Yahvé me [4]dit: Moi, je (le) ferai voir aux fils d'Israël et ils sauront que je suis Yahvé.
> [5][Et Il dit:] Fils d'homme, prophétise sur les ossements et dis: Que se rapprochent chaque os de son vis-à-vis et chaque articulation [6][de son vis-à-vis. Et il en fu]t ainsi. Et Il dit une deuxième fois: Prophétise. Que les tendons poussent sur eux et qu'ils se couvrent de peau [7][par dessus. Et il en fut ainsi.] Et Il dit encore: Prophétise aux quatre vents du ciel et qu'ils insufflent l'esprit [8][en eux, et qu'ils (re)vivent. Et il en fut ainsi.] Et reprirent vie une grande foule d'hommes et ils bénirent Yahvé Sabaoth qui [9][les a fait revivre.
> Et] je dis: Yahvé, quand cela arrivera-t-il? Et Yahvé me dit: [10][*Au jour du jugement à* la fin des j]ours un arbre se courbera et se redressera[...
>
> 3 [2]...]Yahvé, et tout le peuple se leva et ils se tinrent sur leurs[pieds pour rendre grâce... [3]et pour lou]er Yahvé Sabaoth. Et moi aussi je leur parlai[...] [4]*vacat*
> Et Yahvé me dit: Fils [d'homme, di]s leur[...
> [5]... dans]leur [tombe]au ils reposeront jusqu'à ce que[...
> [6]... de]vos [tombe]aux et du pays d'[*Egypte*...
> [7]... *les fils d'Israë*]l que le [jo]ug de l'Egyp[te...

L'image de la résurrection est ici celle d'une recréation en trois étapes: rapprochement des ossements, recouvrement de la chair et insufflation de l'esprit. Elle entend signifier par là l'identité des personnes dans la continuité d'une forme d'existence au-delà de la mort comme sujet des récompenses[27]. C'est ce que souligne aussi le «repos dans le tombeau jusqu'à ce que[» au fg. 3 5, supposant un état intermédiaire. Voilà pour la réponse au «comment seront-ils récompensés». La réponse au «quand cela arrivera-t-il» devait être dans l'image de l'arbre qui doit d'abord se courber avant de se redresser lors du jugement à la fin des jours. Et le prophète de demander à Dieu d'abréger ce temps d'épreuves et d'accélérer la venue de ce jour afin que les fils d'Israël héritent du pays (4Q385 4). Dieu ne veut pas refuser au prophète cette demande.

27. Cette identité suppose la notion d'état intermédiaire et la notion anthropologique de la survie de l'âme-*npš* après la mort qui personnalise le juste qui va ressusciter et le méchant qui sera puni, les restes «mortels» que sont les ossements, chair, etc. ne peuvent entrer seuls en ligne de compte, malgré DIMANT (p. 33). Le concept des partitions du Shéol de 1 Hénoch 22 semble présent à l'arrière-plan, même si on ne peut parler de strict dualisme en anthropologie sémitique.

Ainsi, la réponse divine à la double question du prophète renvoie clairement à la résurrection à l'eschaton et non à une restauration nationale du peuple sur sa terre. C'est la réponse de Dieu, goël de son peuple, à ceux qui ont gardé l'alliance aussi fidèlement que lui. Les seuls justes du peuple seront récompensés pour leur piété (*yštlmw ḥsdm*), exactement comme en Isaïe 26, Daniel 12[28] et l'Instruction. Par «piété», il faut entendre les actions bonnes et justes, une vie menée conformément à la Loi divine et à l'alliance. La dimension personnelle et morale est ici au cœur de l'interprétation eschatologique de la vision, tout comme en 4Q521 7, «ceux qui ont fait le bien devant le Seigneur»[29] et dans les textes de sagesse. C'est pourquoi il ne saurait être question d'une recréation en vue d'un simple retour sur la terre d'Israël, les puissances ennemies étant anéanties. Si l'état des manuscrits interdit une réponse plus précise, le contenu du passage le suppose sans aucun doute, la colère divine se répandant des quatre coins des cieux et consumant comme un feu (4Q386 1 ii 9-10). Le thème de l'accélération des jours est lui aussi une caractéristique de l'eschaton, hâter la Fin pour le temps des récompenses des justes, thèmes que l'on retrouve en Mt 24,22, Mc 13,20, *LAB* 19,13, etc. Mais «hâter la fin» suppose là encore que le juste ne reçoit pas dès la mort les récompenses dans l'au-delà. La notion d'un état intermédiaire est donc ici aussi supposée (voir fg. 3 5)

Des fragments d'un Testament de Qahat, composition certainement pré-qumranienne, ne sont pas sans rapport avec l'eschatologie. L'ancêtre Qahat exhorte ses fils à se conduire de telle sorte que reposent sur eux les bénédictions éternelles, afin d'être délivrés des châtiments réservés aux pécheurs voués à disparaître pour toujours lors du Jugement du monde (4Q542 1 ii 4-8). Une même idée se retrouve dans un passage du testament de son fils, ʿAmram, Visions de ʿAmram, daté vers 200 avant J.-C., qui oppose le sort des justes et des méchants lors du Grand Jugement: ténèbres, mort et Abaddôn pour les fils de ténèbres mais lumière, joie et paix pour les fils de lumière qui, délivrés ce jour-là des fils de ténèbres, seront dans l'illumination (4Q548 1-2 ii 12-16)[30]. La théologie des «Deux-voies» de ces textes reprend la conception d'Isaïe 26 et pré-

28. Pour Dn 12,1-3 (hébreu), voir l'étude remarquable de B. ALFRINK, *L'idée de résurrection d'après Dan XII, 1-2*, in *Biblica* 40 (1959) 355-371.

29. On ne peut accepter le jugement de DIMANT, DJD, 30, p. 34, estimant que le Pseudo-Ezéchiel est la seule composition qumranienne établissant un tel lien, ce lien est constant aussi bien en 4Q521, 4QInstruction, 4QPseudo-Ezéchiel, 1QH[a] et ailleurs, qu'en Isaïe 26, Daniel 12, les Psaumes, Proverbes, etc, 1 Hénoch 22,8-13, etc.

30. É. PUECH, *Qumrân Grotte 4·XXII. Textes araméens, Première partie 4Q529-549* (DJD, 31), Oxford, 2001: 4Q542 et 4Q548. Voir la contribution de J. Verheyden dans ce volume (pp. 427-452), mais dont je ne peux accepter les remarques paléographiques ni le compte des lettres, voir *La croyance des Esséniens* (n. 2), II, p. 562.

cède la brève formulation de Daniel 12. Leur contexte lacunaire ne permet pas de dire plus, mais il serait étonnant que ces deux compositions araméennes soient en désaccord sur ce point avec les passages bibliques et d'autres apocryphes également attestés.

A ce survol de passages bibliques et de nouveaux apocryphes, il faut encore signaler des apocryphes précédemment connus, principalement 1 Hénoch datant en gros des IIIe-IIe s. Le Livre Astronomique (72-82) proclame le bonheur de celui qui meurt juste, sans aucun méfait inscrit pour le jugement où il recevra sa récompense. Le Livre des Veilleurs (1-36) connaît la compartimentation du Shéol pour les âmes selon leur degré de justice dans l'attente du jugement et de la résurrection des justes. Le *Livre des songes* (83-91) et la Lettre d'Hénoch (92-105), plus ou moins contemporains de Daniel, attestent la croyance à la résurrection des justes et aux châtiments éternels des impies. Enfin les Paraboles (37-71), du tournant de notre ère, insistent sur la résurrection des justes sur une terre renouvelée en compagnie de l'Elu qui préside au Jugement. Dans la Lettre et les Paraboles, les justes brilleront dans des vêtements de gloire comme les luminaires du ciel dans un univers transformé. 1 Hénoch présente donc la vie éternelle du juste comme une vie dans la gloire, radicalement différente de la vie terrestre, en lien avec la résurrection au temps du jugement.

2 Maccabées

Dans cet historique des conceptions eschatologiques des livres de sagesse et apocalypses qumraniens, 2 Maccabées des débuts du Ier s. av. J.-C. devrait trouver sa place en tant qu'il cherche parallèlement, tel l'enseignement d'un sage, à édifier d'autres juifs d'un autre courant contemporain.

L'histoire-parabole des sept frères martyrs par obéissance aux lois des pères, sans doute proche dans le temps des persécutions d'Antiochus IV, partage cette croyance à la résurrection qui est une foi bien assimilée au sein d'un groupe de croyants[31]. Le martyre du vieil Éléazar enseigne qu'il est préférable d'aller «sans tarder au séjour des morts» et de laisser un exemple plutôt que d'enfreindre les lois des pères, puisque, vivant ou mort, on ne peut échapper à la justice du Tout-Puissant (2 M 6,18-31). La mort n'est donc pas la fin, mais l'entrée dans une autre vie par le jugement de Dieu.

31. Pour les questions soulevées par ce livre et ce sujet, voir *La croyance des Esséniens* (n. 2), I, pp. 85-92.

En 2 Maccabes 7 cette foi est au centre du récit. Encouragés par leur mère, les sept frères acceptent de mourir plutôt que de renier les lois des pères. Le passage de la Loi invoqué comme fondement de cette foi (Dt 32,36) fait appel à la justice de Dieu envers ses fidèles (2 M 7,5), justice qui s'exercera après la mort par la résurrection de son serviteur (*litt.* «pour une revivification éternelle de vie» 7,9, cf. Dn 12,2 – LXX). Mais le tyran n'échappera pas aux punitions divines en cette vie ou après la mort, sans espoir de résurrection pour l'impie (2 M 7,14). De même que la création et le souffle vital dépendent de Dieu qui donne et retire quand il veut, de même en sera-t-il pour la résurrection, dans la recréation du corps du juste fidèle à l'alliance «au temps de la miséricorde» (2 M 7,29).

Autrement dit, les frères et leur mère expriment chacun un aspect de la croyance à la résurrection. Le premier qui meurt sans transgresser les lois obéit fidèlement à Moïse car Dieu aura pitié de nous qui mourons pour les lois et, ajoute le second, il nous ressuscitera pour une vie éternelle. Et c'est du ciel que je tiens ces membres mais je les méprise à cause des lois puisque j'espère les recouvrer à nouveau, s'exclame le troisième. Avec les quatrième et cinquième vient un énoncé de portée plus générale: espoir de résurrection (ἐλπίδας ἀναστήσεσθαι) pour le juste seul (comme en *Daniel* 12 hébreu) et solidarité des justes dans la mort à cause des péchés mais Dieu n'abandonne pas son peuple, alors que l'impie et sa race verront les tourments dès cette vie et n'auront pas d'espoir de résurrection. Enfin, la mère confesse la foi au Dieu créateur qui «au temps de la miséricorde» rendra l'esprit et la vie, et le septième fils livre son corps et sa vie pour les lois pour que Dieu soit favorable à la nation et châtie l'impie en l'amenant à confesser le Dieu unique.

Dans son suicide, Razis professe une même foi et une même espérance. En répandant ses entrailles, il pria le Maître de la vie et de l'esprit de les lui rendre un jour (2 M 14,46). C'est dire que la résurrection est ici encore conçue de façon corporelle dans la ligne de l'anthropologie sémitique et qu'elle peut être reportée au jour du jugement.

Le songe-vision de Judas visant à encourager les fidèles, peut donner une idée de la conception de l'après-la-mort et des rapports du monde des vivants et des morts. L'entretien avec Onias et Jérémie suggèrent à première vue la conception d'une existence 'corporelle' bienheureuse de justes après leur mort, sans qu'on puisse insister sur le statut *post-mortem* du martyr (2 M 15,12-16). En revanche la croyance à l'intercession des saints (après leur mort) en faveur des enfants des hommes est ici attestée pour la première fois (voir 1 Hénoch 39,5, Philon, *De exsecrationibus* §§165s,...). Réciproquement, les vivants ont le devoir de prier pour les morts (2 M 12,38-45). Mais le sacrifice expiatoire offert pour les soldats tombés coupables d'idolatrie n'a de sens que si la croyance à la résurrection est admise et conçue comme inaugurant la récompense pour les justes martyrs (12,44s). Étant donné le lien établi entre le port des idoles et la mort des soldats (12,40), l'auteur voudrait préserver les vivants des conséquences d'une faute qui souille le peuple tout en laissant entendre que la résurrection et les récompenses sont réservées aux seuls juifs endormis dans la piété et que les autres juifs coupables devront faire face aux châtiments à moins d'un sacrifice expiatoire. Car si le sort des soldats était fixé à leur mort au combat, le sacrifice pour les morts n'aurait pas de sens. C'est là une précaution en faveur des combattants juifs pour la bonne cause dont la justice et la piété ne sont pas irréprochables. Le sacrifice expiatoire devrait leur obtenir la purification nécessaire et, implicitement, les faire changer de compartiment au Shéol en les inscrivant par la suite au nombre des justes en vue de la résurrection et des récompenses. Il ne peut nullement s'agir d'une résurrection «spirituelle» après la mort dans le cadre d'une eschatologie individuelle transcendante. La résurrection est attendue dans l'avenir.

Voulant exhorter et conforter les fidèles dans la lutte contre l'impiété, l'auteur insiste sur la justice divine qui s'exerce sur terre et après la mort: l'obéissance aux lois conduit à la vie dont l'impie sera totalement exclu. En ce sens la résurrection est conçue comme le premier acte des récompenses pour ceux qui ont mérité la justice. En outre, quelques martyrs éminents pourraient même jouir d'une faveur particulière, tels Onias et Jérémie rapprochés des cas des Patriarches, dans la ligne de l'éloge des Pères de Ben Sira[32] et des «instruits/instructeurs» (*maśkîlîm)* de *Daniel* 12.

Les Psaumes de Salomon attestent la même espérance du jugement et de la résurrection des justes pour la vie éternelle mais les châtiments éternels et la perdition dans l'Hadès pour les impies. Cette espérance était loin d'être partagée par tous les courants de pensée du peuple juif, en particulier le courant sadducéen qui refusait explicitement la foi en la résurrection (Ac 23,6-8, Mishna, Talmud, Abbot de Rabbi Nathan, targums..., qui les comparent aux figures de Caïn et Esaü). Quelle est la position du courant essénien?

32. Ben Sira n'est pas sans une idée de ce qui attend le juste après la mort, 1,13: «Pour celui qui craint le Seigneur tout finira bien, au jour de sa mort il sera béni», voir aussi 7,16-17 avec le châtiment des pécheurs.

LE COURANT ESSÉNIEN

Faut-il suivre aveuglément Flavius Josèphe qui attribue aux Esséniens une foi en l'immortalité de l'âme après la mort, le juste recevant une éternelle bénédiction tandis que le méchant se retrouve dans des tourments sans fin (*Guerre* II §§151-158, résumé dans les *Antiquités judaïques* XVIII §18)? Ou, refusant cette croyance de type néo-pythagoricien, est-il préférable d'accepter la présentation de la notice d'Hippolyte de Rome qui leur attribue une croyance dans le Jugement dernier après un état intermédiaire, la conflagration de l'univers, et pour le juste la résurrection de la chair qui deviendra immortelle mais le châtiment éternel des méchants (*Elenchos* ou *Refutatio omnium haeresium* IX §27)? Ou pour faire bref, Hippolyte a-t-il christianisé une notice de formulation plus authentiquement juive de Flavius Josèphe, la rendant ainsi sans objet pour son propos?[33] Ne serait-il pas surprenant qu'au sujet des conceptions de l'Au-delà un courant religieux juif aussi conservateur que l'essénisme se soit laissé gagner par des influences grecques qu'il combattait si vigoureusement pas ailleurs? Les manuscrits de Qumrân qui ont l'avantage de n'avoir pas été interpolés par une main extérieure, expurgés ou christianisés, devraient permettre de se faire une idée plus précise sur le sujet. Il est légitime de se poser la question de savoir si les Qumraniens qui ont copié et lu une grande variété de livres, liste bien plus ample que celle retenue ensuite comme canonique par les rabbanites, y puisant inspiration et méditation, ont été influencés par ces écrits et s'ils ont accepté les conceptions de la vie future que véhiculent ces écrits?

En effet, il est plus que probable que le mouvement essénien émergeant au milieu du deuxième siècle av. J.-C. n'était pas coupé de ses racines juives et que toute la littérature si abondamment reçue, copiée et transmise de sa riche bibliothèque, devait avoir affecté, de quelque manière, sa conception de la vie future au point d'en livrer au moins la teneur générale. Une telle conclusion devrait logiquement s'imposer dans la mesure où cette conception paraît unifiée et sans quelque point de contradiction à relever. Héritiers du mouvement hassidéen du début du IIe siècle[34], les Esséniens devraient, à moins d'indication contraire, avoir épousé sa conception de la vie après la mort, qui n'est autre que la

33. Pour un état de la question assez complet, voir *La croyance des Esséniens* (n. 2), II, pp. 703-769.

34. Nous avons montré la solidité de l'étymologie de hassidéen (en hébreu) = essénien (en araméen) avancée entre autres par E. Schürer, il y a un siècle, et écartant résolument toute autre hypothèse, voir *La croyance des Esséniens* (n. 2), I, pp. 21-24.

conception biblique telle qu'elle a été transmise dans les livres canoniques et les apocryphes ou autres, et relevée ci-dessus dans ses grandes lignes.

Paroles des Luminaires (4Q504)

La composition hébraïque des Paroles des Luminaires (4QDibrē ha-me'orôt*)* qui peut être une œuvre essénienne, écrit: «Tous ceux qui sont inscrits dans le livre de vie [- (?) et se tiendront] pour te servir et rendre grâces à[ton saint nom» (4Q504 1-2 vi 14-15)[35]. Dans ce contexte, l'inscription dans le livre de vie ne peut guère renvoyer qu'à Daniel 12 où, à côté de cette mention, il est aussi question de délivrance, de résurrection et de Jugement, de préférence à Is 4,3. Comme en Daniel, l'inscription dans le livre de vie apporte une précision: il s'agit d'une eschatologie individuelle et personnelle où entre en ligne de compte d'abord la conduite morale de chaque membre du *verus Israel.*

L'Apocalypse messianique (Q521)

Les fragments de cette unique copie, destinée elle aussi à encourager les pieux à la persévérance dans leur choix religieux, fournissent des indications très importantes sur l'eschatologie essénienne et sa conception de la vie future. Comme nous l'avons montré ailleurs, plusieurs indices appuient une datation de la composition après le livre de Daniel et une attribution essénienne, en premier lieu l'usage du substitut *'dny* comme dans les Hymnes au lieu du tétragramme encore employé en Ben Sira, Daniel et Pseudo-Ezéchiel[36]. En outre l'exhortation est fondée sur l'énu-

35. Pour ce passage, voir *La croyance des Esséniens* (n. 2), II, pp. 564-568. Noter l'absence du tétragramme, l'emploi de *'l* et la dépendance de Daniel 12. E. CHAZON, *Is Divrei Ha-Me'orot a Sectarian Prayer?*, in D. DIMANT – U. RAPPAPORT (eds.), *The Dead Sea Scrolls. Forty Years of Research*, Leiden, 1992, pp. 3-17, en fait une composition préessénienne, mais on accepte difficilement que ce texte soit antérieur à Daniel qui use encore du tétragramme (J.J. COLLINS, *Apocalypticism in the Dead Sea Scrolls*, London, 1997, p. 125).

36. É. PUECH, *Qumrân Grotte 4·XVIII. Textes hébreux (4Q521-4Q528, 4Q576-4Q579)* (DJD, 25), Oxford, 1998; voir *La croyance des Esséniens* (n. 2), II, pp. 627-692. J.J. COLLINS, *Apocalypticism in the Dead Sea Scrolls* (n. 35), pp. 89 et 128, laisse ouverte l'appartenance de cette composition au milieu essénien, spécialement à cause de la claire affirmation de la résurrection sans le vocabulaire typique des grands rouleaux esséniens. DIMANT, DJD,30, pp. 13, 34, 36s, exclut catégoriquement une telle attribution, mais on peut douter de la logique de son raisonnement biaisé d'avance. Comment des lecteurs et des copistes de textes autrement inconnus et qui ont tant médité sur ces ouvrages reçus de la tradition d'une part et qui, d'autre part, ont transmis des textes postérieurs au milieu du IIe s. inconnus par ailleurs et retrouvés dans leur bibliothèque, ne pourraient-ils en être les auteurs, même sans reprendre à chaque ligne un vocabulaire connu ailleurs pour des sujets différents?

mération des bienfaits messianiques que Dieu réalisera lui-même en faveur des pieux (*ḥsydym*), des fidèles (*'mwnym*), des justes (*ṣdyqym*) et des pauvres (*ʿnwym*), dénominations qui conviennent toutes en premier aux Esséniens, des *ḥasîdîm*. «Il les renouvellera par sa force et les honorera sur un trône royal, libérant les prisonniers, rendant la vue aux aveugles, redressant les courbés» afin que nul ne soit exclu du service divin. «Il récompensera les fruits d'une œuvre bonne et réalisera des actions glorieuses qui n'ont jamais eu lieu: Il guérira les blessés et fera revivre les morts, Il évangélisera les pauvres et comblera les miséreux, Il conduira les déracinés et enrichira les affamés» (4Q521 2 ii). Cette énumération s'inspire d'Isaïe 61 et 35, tout comme le logion de Jésus en Mt 11,3-6 et Lc 7,22-23. Après une cassure, le texte reprend avec une allusion à la venue d'Élie d'après Ml 3,23-24 et la mention du messie royal que la terre acclamera en grande liesse. Dans toutes ces actions Dieu agira par l'intermédiaire de son prophète de la fin des temps, le Nouvel Élie dont le prototype avait déjà ressuscité des morts, guéri des mortellement blessés et soulagé des indigents, et par l'intermédiaire de son/ses messie(s). Ces signes, certainement liés à la venue du royaume messianique, reprennent en plus clair ce que Si 48,10-11 attribuait déjà à Élie *redivivus*.

Dans un autre groupe de fragments (4Q521 7+5 ii), le texte décrit pour l'eschaton le Jugement dernier où Dieu créateur procédera à une nouvelle création[37]:

> 1...]voyez tout ce q[u'a fait 2le Seigneur
> la ter]re et tout ce qu'elle contient,
> les mers [et tout 3ce qu'elles contiennent]
> et tout plan d'eaux et les torrents. *vacat*
> 4[Vous vous réjouirez, vous to]us qui faites le bien devant le Seigneu[r,
> 5les bénis et no]n comme ceux-là, les maudit[s,] car ils seront pour la mort,
> [lorsque] 6le vivificateur re[ssuscitera] les morts de son peuple. *vacat*
> 7Et nous rendrons grâces et nous vous annoncerons les justices du Seigneur
> qui [*a délivré* (?)] 8les mortels et a ouvert[les tombeaux de...
> 9et a..[... / 10...]
> 11et la vallée de la mort dans[...]
> 12et le pont de l'Abî[me...]
> 13se sont figés les maudit[s dans...]
> 14et les cieux ont accueilli[les justes...
> 15et to]us les anges[...

Le passage suit, en la dépassant, la conception de Daniel 12. Dieu peut, à la suite de Pseudo-Ezéchiel, créer à nouveau en faisant justice

37. La restauration de ces lignes est indisputable, malgré DAVIES, *Death* (n. 18), p. 209. Ce genre de *credo* est fondamental dans l'affirmation de la puissance divine dans l'acte de résurrection, on le retrouve dans les Actes des Apôtres à propos de la résurrection de Jésus.

aux justes de son peuple, objets de toute l'exhortation, soit en ouvrant les tombeaux pour les ressusciter dans la gloire, soit en métamorphosant en gloire les justes encore en vie ce jour-là, tandis que les maudits seront pour la mort éternelle. Au jour du grand Jugement Dieu agira comme juge, récompensant les bénis qui ont fait le bien et châtiant les maudits qui ont commis le mal. Dans ce passage, rien ne dit que les justes vivants auront à passer par la mort pour recevoir leur récompense, bien au contraire les mortels (*litt.* «les fils de la mort» – *bn[y tm]wth*) parmi les justes vont échapper à la loi inexorable de la mort pour être changés dans la gloire du Nouvel Adam «im-mortel», tout comme il en sera pour les justes qui sortent de leurs tombeaux. Ce passage annonce de très près la scène de 1 Thes 4,16-17 à propos des morts et des vivants en Christ et celle du Jugement dernier de Mt 25,31-46 à propos du tri des bénis et des maudits, voir aussi la parabole de l'ivraie, Mt 13,24-30,36-43. On note en passant que la formule *klkm hʿwśym ʾt hṭwb lpny ʾdny* à la l. 4 est bien connue de 1QS I 2, 1QH[a] IV 36 (XVII 24) et de 11QRT LIII 7-8, LV 7-8, LIX 16-17, LXIII 8. Les lignes 9 et 10 pouvaient traiter de l'ouverture des livres ou registres célestes pour le jugement, comme il est habituel dans ce type de discours, puisque la l. 11 traite du surgissement de la vallée de la mort et que les ll. 12 et suivantes mentionnent la séparation des bénis et des maudits par l'image du Pont de l'Abîme (*gšr thwm*). Cette image, nouvelle et unique dans la littérature sémitique, est de fait un emprunt à l'eschatologie zoroastrienne et védique, le Pont du Trieur (*shinvato peretu*) dont la traversée doit séparer les bons des méchants. Les maudits se figent (*litt.* «coagulent» – *qp'w)* tels des morts dans un *refrigerium* glacé et ténébreux, tandis que les cieux/ anges vont au devant des justes pour les accueillir dans le paradis extra-terrestre de la géographie mythique de 1 Hénoch.

Ce passage sur les fins dernières qui paraît être un emprunt à la religion iranienne adapté au milieu sémitique, mais encore sans l'idée d'une résurrection universelle, ne dépare pas dans une composition essénienne. Il rejoint la conviction des autres textes esséniens affirmant que, lors du Jugement, le juste se tiendra devant Dieu en compagnie des anges. Autrement dit, comme en Daniel 12 l'état du ressuscité n'est pas un retour à la vie antérieure, embellie et heureuse, ni manifestement une immortalité de l'âme, mais une profonde transformation de la condition humaine présente du juste, vivant ou mort, pour entrer dans le service divin en compagnie des anges. Ce texte envisage un retour du juste à l'état paradisiaque d'avant la chute en compagnie du Créateur dans une terre non souillée par Bélial et le péché, comparable à la renaissance (παλιγγενεσία) de Mt 19,28 et Lc 22,30. C'est dire que l'eschatologie rejoint la protologie. Ainsi est-il plus facile de comprendre l'état du corps ou de chair de résurrection, déjà présent dans les Livres d'Hénoch que certains décrivent comme corps spirituel d'autant que la doctrine du 'corps glorieux' est connue du zoroastrisme[38]. Cette conception essénienne qui suppose manifestement la notion de terre nouvelle, de cieux nouveaux, de feu purificateur que soulignent nombre d'autres passages qumraniens, lie manifestement la notion de résurrection à celle de récompenses et châtiments *post-mortem*, comme c'est toujours le cas ailleurs.

Une conception identique se retrouve dans les rouleaux qumraniens mieux conservés et unanimement reconnus comme esséniens, quoique d'une façon plus diffuse et toujours comme en passant, puisqu'aucun d'eux, dans leur état actuel, ne traite aussi directement de ce sujet.

Instruction sur les Deux Esprits de la Règle de la Communauté (1QS III 13-IV)

Le thème de la Visite est central dans l'Instruction sur les Deux Esprits (1QS III 13 – IV) (voir la traduction en appendice I) dont la composition date de la deuxième moitié du IIe siècle. Le passage considère les récompenses des justes et les punitions des méchants lors de la Visite divine pour motiver la conduite à suivre dans le moment présent où chaque être est soumis aux influences et à la domination de deux esprits, l'esprit de lumière et l'esprit de ténèbres. Si la présence conflictuelle des deux esprits dans le cœur humain conditionne son agir, Dieu a mis un terme à la domination du Mal et à celle du méchant qui périra à jamais, et il purifiera et récompensera le fidèle devenu juste lors de la Visite et du Renouvellement de la création (IV 25). L'attente de cette Visite eschatologique (IV 20) doit déterminer la conduite de chaque membre de la Communauté vivant au milieu de pécheurs. Cette Visite est donc inscrite dans une eschatologie collective concernant l'histoire du monde et de l'homme avec ses œuvres, non dans une eschatologie purement individuelle de type «assomptionniste» ou de croyance à l'immortalité de l'âme, ainsi que certains l'ont imaginé. La description des récompenses et des châtiments qui ne peuvent être que *post-mortem* en lien avec la

38. Cette croyance qui devint un sujet important dans le zoroastrisme remonte au moins au quatrième siècle avant J.-C., voir H. CORBIN, *Terre céleste et corps de résurrection: de l'Iran mazdéen à l'Iran shi'îte*, Paris, 1960 (chap. 1); M. MOLÉ, *Culte, mythe et cosmologie de l'Iran ancien. Le problème zoroastrien et la tradition mazdéenne*, in *Annales du Musée Guimet, Bibliothèque Nationale – Paris* 69 (1963) 323-328, et A. DE JONG, *Shadow and Resurrection*, in *Bulletin of the Asia Institute*, N.S. 9 (1995) 215-224 (spéc. pp. 220-221).

Visite de Dieu, reprend des termes de Dn 12,2. La récompense suppose un retour au paradis dans un monde purifié du péché, de sa cause, Bélial, et de ses conséquences, la mort. Ainsi toute la gloire d'Adam dans l'Eden est-elle à nouveau promise au juste[39].

L'Instruction sur les Deux Esprits destinée à l'instructeur pour qu'il enseigne aux fils de lumière l'histoire des hommes au sujet des deux esprits pour que chacun puisse choisir entre le bien et le mal, et totalement centrée sur la Visite-Jugement et les récompenses et châtiments lors du renouvellement de la création, est comparable à la révélation du «mystère à venir», le *rz nhyh,* concernant les hommes droits et les impies de l'Instruction (4Q418) qu'elle connaît et reprend manifestement: «Du Dieu des connaissances vient tout ce qui est et qui sera» (1QS III 15). Elle en épouse toutes les conceptions, y compris l'attente de la résurrection pour les justes à qui est destinée toute la gloire d'Adam – c'est la guérison dans un vêtement de majesté dans la lumière éternelle (IV 6-8)[40], et l'anéantissement éternel des méchants (IV 11-14), sans qu'il soit question de jugement sitôt la mort ni d'eschatologie réalisée[41].

Les Hymnes (1QH)

Une conception identique sous-tend l'eschatologie des Hymnes (1QH[a]) à finalité théologique et didactique. Qu'ils soient attribués au Maître ou à ses premiers condisciples ou disciples, les Hymnes datent aussi de la deuxième moitié du deuxième siècle et reflètent la pensée des premières générations qumraniennes.

39. Voir *La croyance des Esséniens* (n. 2), II, pp. 426-440.

40. Paul emploiera l'image du vêtement pour décrire la résurrection-transformation en gloire: revêtu ou survêtu, 2 Co 5,1-10. DAVIES, *Death* (n. 18), pp. 199-203, finit par accepter que ces images «suggest not simply a prolongation of earthly life but a transformation into something quasi-divine, a prospect that is consistent with the outlook of 1 Enoch, Daniel and the *Damascus Document*». «The notion of a transformation of the human body is nevertheless probably the most consistent interpretation of the various statements we have so far examined. This expectation is best summed up in the phrase 'glory of Adam' that we find in both CD and 1QS as the goal of righteous humanity» (p. 202).

41. COLLINS, *Apocalypticism* (n. 35), pp. 115-118, s'accorde sur le sens de Visite-jugement dernier, mais n'exclut pas aussi celui de jugement à la mort de l'individu. Toutefois il n'est pas question de résurrection *pour* recevoir les récompenses ou les châtiments, la résurrection en gloire *est* la récompense du juste au terme fixé lors du renouvellement, alors que l'impie ne s'éveillera pas. Il n'est pas question d'un retour sur cette terre dominée par l'esprit de ténèbres, mais d'un corps de gloire qui vit éternellement dans la lumière en compagnie des saints en présence de Dieu comme le premier Adam, et ce corps de gloire ne sera revêtu que lors du jugement et du renouvellement de la création, voir aussi 1QS XI 5-9. La position de Collins est difficilement tenable.

Certains auteurs veulent ramener l'eschatologie des Hymnes à une eschatologie purement individuelle, voire même réalisée[42]. C'est totalement exclu puisque le salut des justes est promis au temps du Jugement, tout comme la destruction définitive des impies lors de la guerre eschatologique dont la notion est bien présente dans les Hymnes. Présentement la Communauté vit le temps de l'exil, des épreuves et des persécutions, avec et à la suite du Maître, même si le fidèle sait que ce n'est que pour un temps et que les récompenses éternelles promises lui reviendront par pure grâce divine. Alors seulement ce sera une vie éternelle avec Dieu dans la compagnie des anges dans la gloire, vie dont l'entrée dans la Communauté n'est que promesse. Mais il est nécessaire et indispensable de persévérer pour recevoir l'héritage promis, et certains se sont laissés séduire, car le fidèle reste faible et pécheur, «fontaine de souillure, vautré dans le péché» qui ne peut rien sans l'aide de l'Esprit Saint de Dieu. Il sait aussi qu'à la mort le corps retourne à la poussière 1QH[a] XX 27-34 (XII 24-31), XVIII 5-7 (X 3-5)...[43].

Cette présentation n'est pas inconciliable avec la mention maintes fois répétée du jour du Jugement à l'eschaton qui doit concerner les Hauteurs/ les esprits, la terre et le Shéol (1QH[a] XXV 3-16), au point de devoir retenir, ainsi que le voudraient certains, une conception nouvelle attestée nulle part ailleurs dans cette littérature: la croyance à l'immortalité de l'âme. Bien que mal conservé, ce dernier passage connaît visiblement la notion d'état intermédiaire plus amplement décrit en 1 Hénoch 22, antérieur à l'installation qumranienne et attesté parmi les manuscrits retrouvés. Comment concevoir le jugement futur où les impies recevront «malheurs, châtiments et destructions» pour leurs œuvres mauvaises, et les justes «paix, gloire éternelle, délices, joie perpétuelle, longueur de jours pour l'œuvre bonne» (1QH[a] V 22-24), Dieu «faisant disparaître ce qui est ancien et créant des nouveautés, détruisant les réalités d'autrefois et [ressu]scitant des êtres éternels» (*wl[hq]ym nhywt ʿwlm*, 1QH[a] V 28-29 = XIII 11-12), sinon dans le cadre d'une eschatologie collective avec la résurrection et le jugement des seuls justes et les châtiments éternels des impies? Sans doute la résurrection n'est-elle mentionnée qu'en passant mais elle est liée à la disparition de la création ancienne sous la domination des esprits du mal et à la création d'êtres nouveaux et éternels au jour de la Visite-Jugement. Le renouvellement y est décrit avec les termes de recréation (*brʾ*). On note que cette allusion à la résurrection-

42. Ainsi par exemple H.-W. KUHN, *Enderwartung und gegenwärtiges Heil. Untersuchungen zu den Gemeindeliedern von Qumran mit einem Anhang über Eschatologie und Gegenwart in der Verkündigung Jesu* (SUNT, 4), Göttingen, 1966.

43. Nous citons d'après notre nouvelle numérotation des hymnes suite à la restauration du rouleau 1QH[a] avec, quand c'est possible, l'équivalent de la numérotation de l'éditeur (colonnes et lignes). Voir *La croyance des Esséniens* (n. 2), II, pp. 335-419.

récompense opposée aux châtiments des impies se trouve, par heureuse une coïncidence, elle aussi dans un hymne: «Pour l'Instructeur, pour s'humilier devant Dieu, pour implorer pour ses fautes, pour comprendre les grandes œuvres de Dieu et faire comprendre aux simples ses merveilleux mystères, ... pour faire comprendre à l'homme l'instinct de chair et le conseil des esprits d'iniquité...». (1QH^{a} V 12-14, comparer 1QS III 13ss)[44]. Peut comprendre celui qui est prédisposé à connaître toute intelligence et les secrets du dessein et le principe de toute action (V 17), celui à qui Dieu a révélé ses secrets; puis viennent la révélation des deux voies selon l'esprit de chair et de vérité, et la visite définitive selon leurs œuvres, en présence de «l'armée des esprits et de la congrégation des saints», armées célestes, terre, mer, abîmes (V 19-37). Enfin sont proclamés bienheureux «les élus qui ont cherché la sagesse, les purifiés de l'épreuve, ceux qui ont attendu le jugement» où Dieu viendra juger l'univers et donner l'héritage aux justes pour qu'ils se tiennent dans le conseil de sainteté pour les générations éternelles (VI 13-19). Comme l'Instruction sur les Deux Esprits, cet hymne reprend visiblement, dans le fond et la forme, le message de l'Instruction. Il est à lui seul un témoin essénien incontestable de la croyance à la résurrection lié aux récompenses-châtiments lors du jugement dernier et du renouvellement de la création. Mais d'autres hymnes vont dans le même sens.

D'autres Hymnes connaissent une eschatologie collective qui finit avec la conflagration universelle qui renouvelle l'univers. Comment comprendre l'Incendie et le Feu dans le Shéol le plus profond en lien avec les pardon-purification du fidèle à qui Dieu léguera toute la gloire d'Adam dans l'abondance des jours, 1QH^{a} IV 21-27 (XVII 9-15)[45], sinon comme allusion à la conflagration universelle (ἐκπύρωσις) et au renouvellement de la création où le juste ressuscité ou transformé sera établi dans sa condition paradisiaque d'être «im-mortel»? Cette conflagration est à nouveau décrite en 1QH^{a} XI 20-37 (III 19-36) où modelage d'argile et mortel, le juste est appelé à vivre en compagnie des anges immortels dans une assemblée de jubilation et de louanges dans un monde enfin purifié du grand péché, allusion au péché d'Adam, 1QH^{a} XI 12 (III 11)[46]. La malédiction qui pesait sur l'humanité sera changée

44. Pour l'établissement du texte à partir de fragments, voir É. PUECH, *Un hymne essénien en partie retrouvé et les béatitudes. 1QH V 12-VI 18 (= col. XIII-XIV 7) et 4QBéat.*, in *RQ* 13 (1988) 59-88; voir aussi *La croyance de Esséniens* (n. 2), II, pp. 408-415.

45. Voir *La croyance des Esséniens* (n. 2). II, pp. 391s.

46. *Ibid.*, pp. 366-375. On ne peut pas suivre COLLINS, *Apocalypticism* (n. 35), p. 120, écrivant «which is to say that he has already experienced the resurrection predicted for the wise in Daniel 12». Il est clair que le juste n'est pas encore passé de la mort à la vie; il l'espère lors du jugement et il doit tout faire pour cela dès à présent afin de mériter cette récompense.

en bénédiction pour le fidèle qui aura ainsi de nouveau accès au Paradis et à la vie avec Dieu.

Mais le renouvellement et l'accès à la vie paradisiaque sont précédés du Jugement et de la guerre finale lorsque la Communauté, à l'abri dans sa forteresse protégée par Dieu et ses anges, sortira pour participer à la victoire définitive, ses justes, morts, se relevant de la poussière pour prendre part à l'ultime combat au Jour du Jugement et bénéficier avec les vivants des récompenses de la nouvelle création, 1QH[a] XIII 22-XV 8 (V 20-VII 5) et particulièrement XIV 32-39[47]:

> Et alors se précipitera l'épée de Dieu au temps du jugement
> et tous ses fils fidèles se réveilleront pour retrancher [tous les fils de] [33]l'impiété
> et tous les fils de culpabilité n'existeront plus.
> Et le Valeureux bandera son arc
> et il ouvrira les retranchements célestes [34]pour un élargissement sans fin
> et les portes éternelles pour faire sortir les armes de guerre,
> et ils seront vainqueurs d'un bout à l'autre.
> Des flèches [35]ils tireront et pas de délivrance pour la créature coupable,
> jusqu'à extermination on foulera aux pieds,
> et il n'y aura pas de captifs, ni d'espoir par la multitude des cadavres,
> [36]et pour tous les héros de guerre, pas de refuge.
> Car au Très-Haut appartient le Ju[gement]
> et avec le reste de tes ennemis ils sont coupables.
> [37]Et les gisants de la poussière dresseront le mât
> et les vermines des morts lèveront l'étendard au rempart
> et ils frapperont en faisant périr l'ennemi [38]dans les guerres des insolents.
> Et quand passera la coulée débordante, elle n'entrera pas dans la forteresse
> mais elle atte[indra les – –] [39]et le coup fera périr les œuvres de Bé[lia]l
> [et il en sera comme de la pierre] pour le crépi et comme de la poutre pour le feu.

Les images de la guerre finale décrivent l'intervention de l'épée de Dieu régulièrement présente dans des passages eschatologiques lors de la Visite (CD VII 9-10; XIX 10-11, etc.). Même si le langage symbolique de ces hymnes est unique, il ne peut être ignoré dans la présentation de l'eschatologie qumranienne. Par là l'auteur se place dans la perspective de la rétribution éternelle des méchants et de la récompense des justes. Mais là encore seuls les justes qui reposent dans la mort ressuscitent pour participer aux récompenses. Tout comme il n'y a ni blessé ni mort parmi les justes dans ces guerres eschatologiques, il n'y a ni captif ni d'espoir pour les cadavres dans les rangs de l'ennemi. C'est dire en clair

47. *Ibid.*, pp. 354 ss, où nous avons donné le déchiffrement de ces lignes partiellement lues précédemment.

que, pour entrer dans la gloire éternelle, les justes vivants ne meurent pas et que les justes morts ressuscitent, que les méchants ne ressuscitent pas mais qu'ils restent dans la mort et le feu de l'Abaddôn avec Bélial où les rejoignent les victimes des derniers combats (comparer 4Q521 7+5 ii)[48]. Cette présentation dépend manifestement de celle de Dn 12,1-2 (d'après l'interprétation d'Alfrink) et le passage est tout à fait parallèle à celui de l'Instruction (4Q418 69 ii 6-9). La guerre eschatologique au temps du jugement pour laquelle ses fils fidèles se réveilleront, c'est l'image du jugement auquel participent aussi les justes en voyant l'anéantissement des impies dans l'Instruction. Dans l'Hymne, le Maître tient lieu du sage à qui Dieu a révélé ses secrets (1QH^{a} XIII 27s) qui garde l'espérance des récompenses (XIV 9) et conduit la plantation dans la persévérance. Cet hymne à l'accent apocalyptique et sapientiel veut encourager les fidèles à être comptés parmi les justes qui seuls recevront les récompenses éternelles dont la résurrection est le premier acte. Le thème de réveil comme récompense éternelle du juste pour participer au jugement sous forme de bataille eschatologique sera précisément repris en Sg 5,14-23[49].

Tout en exhortant pour le présent et en invoquant une vie en communion avec les anges, les Hymnes rappellent que si l'entrée et la persévérance dans la Communauté sont nécessaires pour être compté parmi les

48. Malgré DIMANT, DJD, 30, p. 34 et n. 30. Que le passage soit poétique n'enlève rien à l'enseignement qu'il transmet ou à la conception de l'auteur, en plein accord avec les autres hymnes et textes esséniens et qumraniens, et malgré COLLINS, *Apocalypticism in the Dead Sea Scrolls* (n. 35), pp. 122-123: «A reference to resurrection is possible here, but it is not certain... It is not unreasonable to expect that this war would culminate in the resurrection of the dead. Nonetheless there is no unambiguous reference to resurrection... This does not necessarily mean that there was no place for resurrection in the eschatology of the Dead Sea Sect. But it does mean that the hopes of the sectarian community were not formulated in terms of resurrection. Rather, the focus was on sharing the angelic life within the community and thereby transcending death and continuing that life in heaven». On le voit, l'auteur est très embarrassé et ne sait comment s'en sortir pour rester fidèle aux textes et à son a priori du départ à la suite de la notice de Josèphe. Nous ne pouvons accepter une telle ambivalence. DAVIES, *Death* (n. 18). pp. 204-08, est plus explicite: «But the texts we have reviewed so far suggest that the eternal destiny of the righteous is to be enjoyed in a new or transformed body. A belief in the resurrection of dead persons is thus *a priori* quite probable» (p. 208).

49. Avec M. GILBERT, *Immortalité? Résurrection? Faut-il choisir? Témoignage du judaïsme ancien*, in PH. ABADIE – J.-P. LÉMONON (eds.), *Le judaïsme à l'aube de l'ère chrétienne. XVIIIe congrès de l'ACFEB (Lyon, septembre 1999)*, Paris, 2001, pp. 271-297, spéc. p. 293. Pour la croyance à la résurrection dans le livre de la Sagesse, voir E. PUECH, *Le livre de la Sagesse et les manuscrits de la mer Morte: un aperçu*, in A. PAZZARO – G. BELLIA (eds.), *Il libro della Sapienza. Tradizione-Redazione-Teologia, Palermo 22-23 marzo 2002*, Roma, 2003. Le raisonnement des impies y est comparable à celui des insensés de l'Instruction, voir Sg 2,22s: «Ils ignorent les secrets de Dieu, ils n'espèrent pas de rémunération pour la sainteté, ils ne croient pas à la récompense des âmes pures. Oui, Dieu a créé l'homme pour l'incorruptibilité, il en a fait une image de sa propre nature».

justes, fils de lumière, celles-ci ne sont pas pour autant la réalisation du salut qui est attendu sur une terre libérée, renouvelée et purifiée lors de la conflagration universelle et du jugement final concernant tous les êtres. Bien loin de présenter une eschatologie réalisée, les Hymnes affirment l'espérance en la résurrection des justes morts pour participer avec les vivants à la gloire d'Adam dans une vie éternelle en compagnie des anges en présence de Dieu et la damnation éternelle de Bélial et des méchants dans le Shéol infernal. Dans ce schéma d'eschatologie linéaire finissant avec le Jugement et le Renouvellement, ils connaissent aussi l'existence d'un état intermédiaire et le jugement dans les différentes sphères: les cieux, la terre et le Shéol infernal. Témoignant d'une eschatologie dans laquelle la responsabilité individuelle tient une place importante, tout comme dans l'Instruction, il n'est nulle part question d'une croyance en l'immortalité de l'âme et du seul jugement à la mort de l'individu.

Cette conclusion ferme des Hymnes, présentant une eschatologie sémitique qui est celle retenue par Hippolyte et non une eschatologie grecque des notices de Flavius Josèphe, trouverait un complément dans un petit fragment non encore localisé (fg. 53) qui semble reprendre Dn 12,3 ou un texte du type 1 Hénoch 58,2-6. Mais ces passages sont tous deux en faveur de la croyance à la résurrection[50].

Règle de la Guerre (1QM)

Dans la Règle de la Guerre (1QM), composition plus ou moins contemporaine de la Règle de la Communauté et des Hymnes, certains ont cru trouver la mention explicite de la résurrection dans un passage partiellement lacuneux. Mais au lieu de lire en XII 6 «ceux qui se lèveront de la terre lorsque se disputeront tes jugements», nous lisons «dans la guerre [contre tous les p]unis de la terre disputant tes jugements» (*[ʿl kwl n]qmy ʾrṣ*)[51].

Toutefois la lecture de cette ligne n'infirme pas la croyance à la résurrection des justes que connaît manifestement l'auteur développant le thème de la guerre finale de Daniel 10–12. Les fils de lumière seront victorieux mais aucun ennemi n'échappera à la mort et il sera livré au feu de l'Abaddôn tandis que le juste brillera à jamais. Comme en Daniel 12 le prince Michel se tient «sur les fils de ton peuple» (1QM XII 4-5, XIII 10, 15s, XIV 16, XVII 6, XVIII 1-3,10s) pour le moment choisi (XIII 14s comparer *bʿt hhyʾ* de Dn 11,40; 12,1,4) qui est le jour du grand

50. Voir *La croyance des Esséniens* (n. 2), II, pp. 415-416.
51. *Ibid.*, pp. 443-498 (spéc. p. 452).

combat (XVII 1). Les hymnes des colonnes XIII et XIV[52] présentent cette guerre eschatologique selon un schéma d'eschatologie collective montrant de grandes affinités avec la finale de *Daniel*. Telle une liturgie, la guerre d'extermination menée par les fils de lumière aidés par la main de Dieu, l'épée de Dieu et ses armées angéliques, frappera tous les impies, extirpant le mal et préparant la venue d'une ère nouvelle dans un monde transformé. Les justes dont les noms sont inscrits dans les livres célestes seront vainqueurs (XII 2-3), sans victime dans leurs rangs, alors qu'il n'y aura ni rescapé ni survivant dans les rangs ennemis. Les uns seront livrés au Feu éternel qui les dévorera, les autres brilleront et resplendiront dans la lumière, la joie et la paix éternelle. Bélial et ses esprits seront enchaînés dans les lieux ténébreux de la Perdition (XVII 17s). C'est dire le changement radical attendu dans la victoire des justes lors du jugement.

La transformation-glorification du juste et son élévation jusqu'à Dieu (1QM XIV 14) témoignent-elles en faveur d'une croyance à l'immortalité de l'âme ou, liées au Jugement dernier et à l'incendie du monde, sont-elles une des facettes de la croyance à la résurrection dans une eschatologie individuelle et collective à la fois? Malgré l'absence de vocabulaire précis à ce sujet, mais un bon tiers du rouleau a disparu, cette seconde solution s'impose comme reflétant la conception de l'auteur de la Règle de la Guerre dépendant si fortement de Daniel, tout à fait comparable à celle des Hymnes et de la Règle de la Communauté. En effet, le concept d'une guerre eschatologique n'a pas de sens dans une eschatologie invoquant la seule immortalité de l'âme ni dans une eschatologie réalisée. 1QM rejoint manifestement 1QH[a] XIV.

Document de Damas (CD)

Dans le Document de Damas dont nombre de copies ont été retrouvées dans les grottes et dont la composition doit aussi dater de la deuxième moitié – fin du IIe s. av. J.-C., l'auteur se préoccupe davantage de la conversion de ses contemporains en les exhortant à observer la Loi, que de leur sort futur. Il n'ignore pas cependant le Jour du Jugement (VIII 3-4, XIX 15), la destruction définitive des impies et la récompense des justes auxquels sont promis «une vie éternelle et toute la gloire d'Adam» (*ḥyy nṣḥ wkl kbwd ʾdm)* (III 20) ou de «vivre mille (des milliers de) générations» (VII 5-6 // XIX 1), c'est-à-dire, en clair, de retrou-

52. *Ibid.*, pp. 454-479, où nous proposons une lecture nettement améliorée de ces colonnes. On ne peut suivre COLLINS, *Apocalypticism* (n. 35), pp. 118-119. Il n'y a aucune allusion à une eschatologie réalisée ni à une vie angélique avant la mort.

ver les biens paradisiaques d'avant la chute. L'impie et l'apostat recevront leur propre rétribution lors de la Visite (VII 9 // XIX 5-6). On peut même relever des parallèles de vocabulaire entre Dn 12,1b-2: «En ce temps-là ton peuple sera épargné, ceux-ci... et ceux-là pour l'opprobre» (*wbʿt hhyʾ ymlṭ ʿmk ʾlh... ʾlh lḥrpwt...*) et CD XIX 10: «Ceux-ci seront épargnés au temps de la Visite et ceux qui resteront seront livrés au glaive» (*ʾlh ymlṭw bqṣ hpqdh whnšʾrym ymsrw lḥrb...*). Ce texte connaît l'imagerie de la guerre eschatologique et du dernier affrontement du prince de lumière et de Bélial (IV 12- V 18, XII 23 – XIII 1, XIV 18 s). Si le document ne porte pas de mention précise de la résurrection[53], il n'est pas sans importance que son eschatologie rejoigne celle des trois autres rouleaux qumraniens à la conception unifiée, dans la droite ligne des développements de la littérature biblique et aprocryphe.

Divers

Dans 11QMelkîsédeq, Melkîsédeq triomphe de Bélial au terme du dixième et dernier jubilé où le lot de Bélial est jugé et s'enfonce définitivement dans les ténèbres, tandis que le lot de Melkîsédeq triomphe dans la paix et l'exaltation, comme en Daniel 12. Cette victoire finale instaurera le renouvellement du monde et la venue d'une ère nouvelle et éternelle[54].

La conception de l'eschatologie de Daniel se retrouve dans un passage lacuneux des Périodes de la Création (4Q181 1 ii 1-6) attestant la résurrection pour la vie éternelle dans une exaltation céleste en compagnie des anges en vue du service divin[55]:

> [5]...[.. Les impies seront pour l'opprobre éternel et pour l'anéantissement dans l'Abaddôn
> [6]et les justes] pour la vie éternelle.

D'après le Pesher de Michée (1Q14 10,3-9)[56] tous ceux qui suivent l'enseignement du Maître et s'agrègent au conseil de la Communauté seront sauvés au jour du Jugement, à la fin des jours. Cela revient à suivre la voie de la conversion comme le recommande la Règle de la Communauté (1QS VIII) et donc à être inscrit dans les livres célestes en vue de la résurrection.

53. C. RABIN, *Qumran Studies* (Scripta Judaica, 2), Oxford, 1957, pp. 73-74, a cru lire la mention de la résurrection en XX 10,13, III 20 et VII 6. Voir *La croyance des Esséniens* (n. 2), II, pp. 499-514. Il n'est jamais question de récompenses-châtiments après la mort, mais au temps de la visite-Jugement, malgré COLLINS, *Apocalypticism* (n. 35), p. 118.

54. Pour plus de détails, voir *La croyance des Esséniens* (n. 2) II, pp. 515-562.

55. *Ibid.*, pp. 526-531.

56. *Ibid.*, pp. 599-600.

Plusieurs passages du Pesher des Psaumes (4Q171 1-10 ii-iv)[57] insistent sur la disparition définitive des impies, tandis que les justes «vivront mille générations dans le salut et tout l'héritage d'Adam leur appartiendra à jamais» (iii 12). Ces images considèrent le salut éternel des justes contemplant le jugement des impies à la dernière génération et recevant l'héritage de vérité comme un retour à la prospérité du paradis des origines d'où la mort et le péché étaient absents.

Le Midrash eschatologique (4Q174 + 177) qui cite explicitement Dn 11,35 et 12,10, doit avoir accepté l'eschatologie collective et individuelle de Daniel, le contraire serait pour le moins surprenant[58].

Les sépultures esséniennes

Comme données internes qumraniennes, il reste encore à confronter les résultats de cette enquête dans les textes avec la pratique des habitants dans la mesure où les restes archéologiques le permettent. Il est pour le moins logique de se demander si les auteurs, scribes et lecteurs de ces manuscrits ont traduit ou cherché à traduire leur conception de l'après-la-mort dans les pratiques funéraires.

Les 53 tombes explorées sur les 1.200 tombes environ repérées en différentes parties des cimetières permettent de se faire une idée de l'identité et de la pratique des occupants du lieu[59]. L'orientation sud-nord des tombes individuelles du cimetière central montre un dédain marqué envers Jérusalem l'impure et son temple souillé, pour regarder avantageusement vers le nord où se situaient le Paradis de Justice et la Montagne-Trône divin d'après les imageries apocalyptiques bibliques ou autres et les cosmologies de l'époque (voir Is 14,13-14, Ps 48,3, 1 Hénoch 25,4-5).

A la suite de Dt 32,43, les Esséniens attribuaient-ils aussi à la terre d'Israël le pouvoir de purification de la chair de péché et d'expiation dans l'attente de la résurrection? Étant donné l'importance de la Loi mosaïque dans leur pratique et leur constant souci de pureté, c'est fort probable. Toutes ces exigences pouvaient motiver la coutume de sépultures individuelles dans une fosse à même la terre d'autant que les occupants ne vivaient pas en familles mais en célibataires[60]. Mieux qu'une inhumation dans un cercueil à l'époque hellénistique ou une réinhuma-

57. *Ibid.*, pp. 600-603.

58. *Ibid.*, pp. 572-591.

59. Voir une présentation de l'ensemble dans *La croyance des Esséniens* (n. 2), II, pp. 693-702, ou plus développé dans E. PUECH, *The Necropolises of Khirbet Qumrân and of 'Aïn el-Ghuweir, and the Essene Belief in Afterlife*, in *BASOR* 312 (1998) 21-36.

60. Comme l'ont prouvé les dernières études sur le sujet, voir J. ZIAS, *The Cemeteries of Qumran and Celibacy: Confusion Laid to Rest?*, in *DSD* 7 (2000) 220-253.

tion dans un ossuaire à l'époque romaine dans un tombeau familial, l'usage essénien respecte les restes des défunts protégés dans un *loculus* en ne les dérangeant plus dans leur repos éternel, sauf de très rares cas de réinhumation, préservant ainsi au mieux les ossements sans contact ou souillure ultérieure. Les élus couchés sur le dos, tête au sud et regardant vers le nord, feront face au Paradis de Justice et à la Montagne de Dieu et de la Nouvelle Jérusalem vers lesquels ils se dirigeront au réveil de la résurrection ou, la tête à l'ouest, ils regarderont le Soleil de Justice et sa lumière éclatante (Ml 3,20).

Ces coutumes doivent traduire les croyances esséniennes relevées dans les textes ci-dessus et elles sont nettement en faveur de la foi en la résurrection des corps qu'ils ont lue dans les passages bibliques et les aprocryphes et qu'ils ont exprimée dans leurs propres écrits. Elles impliquent la croyance à la résurrection du corps qu'animera l'esprit se joignant à l'âme tenue en réserve dans l'état intermédiaire au Paradis de Justice et elles soulignent l'importance du corps dans l'identité personnelle du ressuscité. En contemplant leurs tombes ne croit-on pas entendre résonner la parole du prophète qu'ils avaient sûrement méditée:

> Mais toi, va au terme (de ta vie) et repose-toi
> et tu te relèveras pour (recevoir) ta part à la fin des jours (Dn 12,13).

Est-il surprenant que les pratiques funéraires soient en plein accord avec les conceptions de la vie future véhiculées dans les documents préesséniens et qumraniens retrouvés dans les grottes? Ce n'est certainement pas par un hasard et le contraire mériterait explication. En retour, ces pratiques confirment l'identification des occupants du lieu avec les Esséniens. Non seulement la croyance à l'immortalité de l'âme ne rend pas compte des textes esséniens retrouvés dans les grottes aussi bien que des textes bibliques et apocryphes présents en abondance, mais encore elle n'explique pas ce soin particulier du corps des défunts, pratique qui ne saurait être coupée de toute croyance[61], et contredirait sur ce point une des notices externes aussi digne de confiance que son parallèle.

Conclusion

Au terme de ce rapide parcours des principaux textes qumrano-esséniens touchant à l'eschatologie, il apparaît clairement que ces nouvelles

61. Malgré Collins, *Apocalypticism* (n. 35), pp. 123s. Le raisonnement ne procède pas par déduction, mais il est le seul à rendre compte des faits observables: soin pour la pureté des ossements, orientation des tombes, purification par la terre d'Israël, etc. C'est une confirmation, non une contre-indication.

compositions sapientielles et apocalyptiques se situent toutes en dépendance directe de la tradition des écrits prophétiques et sapientiaux. L'expression de cette croyance est l'œuvre de cercles religieux réfléchissant sur l'indéfectible justice divine face à la mort des justes du peuple de Dieu. Que ce soit dans les apocalypses ou les écrits de sagesse, la réponse du visionnaire ou du sage est identique: la création et le plan divin ne peuvent que réussir. Le quand et le comment dépendent du «mystère à venir». C'est en fonction de ce dernier que visionnaire et sage encouragent, chacun à sa manière, les membres du peuple à persévérer dans la fidélité à l'alliance afin d'être inscrits au nombre des élus: méditer le mystère, savoir distinguer le bien du mal, produire de bonnes œuvres, suivre l'esprit de vérité, ... Dans son admonition le sage poursuit l'idéal de sagesse populaire éclairée par la Parole de Dieu en fonction du mystère à venir, tandis que le visionnaire dresse un tableau des événements de la fin dans la préparation de laquelle les thèmes sapientiaux trouvent aussi leur place.

Si Pseudo-Ezéchiel affirme clairement la croyance à la résurrection au temps du jugement venant confirmer ce que rappelait comme en passant Daniel 12 et qu'explicitera ensuite 2 Maccabées, l'Instruction est certainement le premier texte sapientiel aussi clair et explicite sur ce point, même si l'un et l'autre ont pu trouver déjà un écho dans Isaïe 26, ou dans de courts passages de Psaumes et des Proverbes ou des apocryphes comme 1 Hénoch, Testaments de Qahat et de ʿAmram en particulier. Il n'est dès lors pas étonnant que ces réflexions des sages et des visionnaires aient servi de sources d'inspiration aux auteurs esséniens, que ce soit dans l'Apocalypse messianique ou des écrits pour l'Instructeur ou les membres de la Communauté comme l'Instruction sur les Deux Esprits, des Hymnes, 1QM, CD et quelques autres allusions qui reprennent chacune à leur manière cette même espérance, sans nulle innovation comme l'immortalité de l'âme ou les récompenses sitôt la mort ou une eschatologie réalisée.

Il y a même plus. Dans le fond et la forme, l'Instruction semble dépendre du même milieu culturel que les compositions esséniennes à moins que les auteurs de ces derniers n'aient été à tel point pétris par elle: l'image de la plantation éternelle en vue de l'héritage à la fin des jours (4Q418 81), la fontaine de connaissance cachée de l'homme et objet de révélation, l'illumination, l'habitat et les habits de gloire, la compagnie des saints, les fils des cieux, le mystère à venir, les deux voies et les deux esprits, l'instinct de chair, les hommes de Son bon plaisir, etc. Il semble que l'Instruction, si elle n'est pas essénienne mais la question peut se poser, soit plus proche des compositions esséniennes que de Proverbes et de Ben Sira. Quoi qu'il en soit, que ce soit Pseudo-Ezéchiel ou l'Instruction, ces deux compositions de genres différents constituent désormais des textes clefs dans l'histoire de la croyance à la résurrection des seuls justes lors du jugement et elles permettent de relire avec plus d'assurance les quelques compositions esséniennes relatives à ce sujet, qu'elles soient de genre apocalyptique ou sapientiel[62]. Von Rad avait assez bien vu que la sagesse est comme mère de l'apocalyptique et que les deux notions font appel l'une à l'autre dans leurs admonitions et encouragements aux croyants[63].

Héritiers des mêmes textes avant leur séparation, il n'est pas étonnant qu'Esséniens[64] et Pharisiens professent une même croyance sur ce point important, croyance déjà acceptée par le milieu hassidéen. En outre, il apparaît clairement que Daniel 12 qui ne traite que brièvement et en passant de ce sujet, n'est pas le premier et le plus ancien témoignage biblique sur cette croyance qui remonte au moins au troisième siècle ou un peu plus avant avec Isaïe 26, 1 Hénoch, Visions de ʿAmram. De son côté le Pseudo-Ezéchiel confirme une relecture ancienne d'Ezéchiel 37 en fonction de la résurrection. Ce n'est donc pas la persécution d'Antiochus IV Épiphane, comme on le dit souvent, qui est à l'origine de cette croyance en essayant de rendre compte de l'espérance des martyrs pour les lois (2 Maccabées). Au contraire, la persécution et la déportation de Nabuchodonosor en 587 qui ont tant marqué les consciences sont vraisemblablement à l'origine de ce développement, peut-être et probablement même à travers des influences iraniennes, partiellement adoptées et adaptées à la foi yahviste de cercles pieux de Jérusalem, sages, psalmistes,... L'Apocalypse messianique (4Q521) qui témoigne de cet emprunt, s'intègre parfaitement dans la conception de l'eschatologie essénienne professée par les autres compositions esséniennes, Hymnes et Règles en particulier. Sans doute donne-t-elle, malgré son état très lacuneux, davantage de précisions que ces derniers textes, mais cela ne saurait surprendre étant donné le sujet traité dans les fragments conservés: l'attente du/ des messie(s) et le jugement dernier.

La résurrection est attendue pour le jour du Jugement où Dieu manifestera sa victoire sur le Prince des ténèbres, sur le péché et en consé-

62. On ne peut suivre l'opinion de DAVIES, *Death* (n. 18), p. 209 sur ce point: «It is perhaps significant that such beliefs are nowhere stated in an unambiguous manner, explicitly in an eschatological scenario or in a hymn or wisdom discourse».

63. De là vient le difficile classement des compositions, voir COLLINS, *Wisdom, Apocalypticism and the Dead Sea Scrolls* (n. 3), p. 32.

64. Il est impensable qu'un membre de la communauté, même ex-sadducéen, n'ait pas adopté le point de vue du groupe et qu'il en soit resté à sa position antérieure, sur ce point comme pour la *halakah*, etc., malgré DAVIES, *Death* (n. 18), p. 210.

quence sur la mort (Is 25,8). Elle s'inscrit dans le cadre d'une eschatologie collective, mais elle ne concerne toujours que les justes de son peuple, voire les seuls justes esséniens dans leurs propres compositions. Cette conception est beaucoup plus unifiée qu'on ne le dit souvent dans les écrits bibliques et apocryphes anciens qui ignorent la croyance à l'immortalité de l'âme selon la conception grecque.

En conséquence, les Esséniens n'ont manifestement pas adopté une eschatologie réalisée, ainsi que certains le prétendent, ni une assomption de l'âme immortelle. Ils attendaient la venue du royaume messianique et, au terme d'une guerre eschatologique à la fin du dernier jubilé, le Jour de la Visite ou du Jugement dernier. Celui-ci devait assurer la résurrection des justes morts et la transformation des justes vivants dans la gloire d'Adam sur une terre purifiée par le feu et renouvelée, dans la compagnie des anges en présence de Dieu, mais aussi la damnation éternelle des impies vaincus et figés dans le feu éternel de l'Enfer avec Bélial et ses anges.

Il est enfin possible de répondre à la question soulevée par la confrontation des notices de Flavius Josèphe et d'Hippolyte de Rome. Les données archéologiques et manuscrites (bibliques, apocryphes et esséniennes) confirment la croyance des Esséniens dans la vie future telle que la présente (la source de) Hippolyte: immortalité de l'âme séparée du corps dans l'état intermédiaire, résurrection du corps (/de la chair) du juste essénien dans la gloire à l'image de celui d'Adam avant la chute qui revêt donc l'incorruptibilité, le Jugement dernier, la conflagration universelle et le renouvellement de la terre, et le châtiment éternel des impies. Mais elles n'appuient pas la croyance en une âme immortelle tombée dans un corps qui lui servirait de prison et dont elle se libérerait à la mort pour se réjouir et rejoindre le monde céleste au-delà de l'Océan pour le juste, ou pour tomber dans un gouffre de châtiments éternels pour l'impie. Cela est certainement étranger aux textes qumraniens et sémitiques en général qui tous insistent sur le jugement divin au terme de l'eschaton, le renouvellement et la purification de toute chose et la gloire d'Adam pour le juste. Flavius Josèphe a certainement remanié sa source en la déformant et en prêtant aux Esséniens des croyances non sémitiques en contradiction avec les données antérieures, bibliques et autres, et avec les données archéologiques. La contradiction est à chercher chez Josèphe non dans la source commune aux deux notices, assez fidèlement retenue par Hippolyte malgré l'habillage grec du langage.

Appendice

Instruction sur les deux esprits (1QS III 13-IV 26):

13Pour l'instructeur.
Pour qu'il fasse comprendre et qu'il enseigne à tous les fils de lumière l'histoire de tous les fils d'homme,
14ce qui concerne toutes les espèces de leurs esprits d'après leurs marques pour leurs œuvres durant leurs générations,
et ce qui concerne la visite de leurs malheurs,
ainsi que 15les temps de leur rétribution.

Du Dieu des connaissances vient tout ce qui est et qui sera: dès avant leur existence Il a fixé tout leur plan,
16et pendant leur existence, en fonction de leurs statuts, conformément à son plan de gloire,
ils remplissent leur tâche sans changer quoi que ce soit.
Dans Sa main 17sont les lois de tout et Lui, Il les fournit en tous leurs besoins.
Lui, Il a créé l'homme pour la domination 18du monde,
et Il lui a attribué deux esprits grâce auxquels il doit se conduire jusqu'au moment de Sa visite.

Voici les esprits 19de vérité et de perversité:
Grâce à la source de lumière, il existe des générations fidèles,
mais à cause de la fontaine de ténèbres, il existe des générations perverses.
20Et dans la main du prince des lumières est la domination de tous les fils de justice,
- dans les voies de lumière ils se conduiront-
mais dans la main de l'ange 21de ténèbres est toute la domination des fils de perversité,
- aussi dans les voies de ténèbres ils se conduiront.
Par l'ange de ténèbres s'égarent 22tous les fils de justice,
et toutes leurs fautes, leurs iniquités, leur culpabilité et les péchés de leurs œuvres sont sous son emprise
23selon les secrets de Dieu jusqu'à son terme.
Et tous les malheurs et les temps de leurs détresses sont sous l'emprise de son hostilité,
24et de tous les esprits de son lot faisant trébucher les fils de lumière.
Mais le Dieu d'Israël, ou son ange fidèle, vient en aide à tous 25les fils de lumière.

Et Lui, Il a créé les esprits de lumière et de ténèbres
et sur eux Il a fondé toute œuvre, 26sur leurs [décisions] toute activité et sur leurs voies toute visite.
L'un, Dieu l'a aimé pour tous IV 1les temps éternels, et en toutes ses actions, toujours Il se complait,
l'autre, Il l'a profondément détesté, et toutes ses voies Il hait éternellement.

[2]Et telles sont leurs voies dans le monde:
faire la lumière dans le cœur de l'homme et aplanir devant lui toutes les voies de justice authentique,
et terrifier son cœur par les jugements de [3]Dieu,
un esprit humble et longanime, surabondante miséricorde et éternelle bonté, perspicacité et intelligence,
et une solide sagesse confiante dans toutes [4]les œuvres divines et s'appuyant sur l'abondance de son amour,
un esprit de connaissance en tout projet d'action et le zèle pour les justes jugements,
et un saint [5]propos dans un caractère ferme et une abondante miséricorde envers tous les fidèles,
et une purification méritoire détestant toutes les idoles de souillure,
une humble conduite [6]avec un discernement universel et la discrétion sur la vérité des mystères de connaissance.
Tels sont les conseils de l'esprit pour les fils fidèles dans le monde.

Et la visite de tous ceux qui le suivent consistera en une guérison [7]et une grande paix dans la longueur de jours,
et une fécondité avec toutes les bénédictions perpétuelles et une joie éternelle dans une vie sans fin,
et une couronne de gloire [8]avec un vêtement de majesté dans la lumière éternelle.

[9]Mais à l'esprit de perversité appartiennent une ambition de l'âme et un relâchement dans le service de la justice,
méchanceté et mensonge, orgueil et cœur superbe, fausseté et tromperie,
cruauté [10]et abondance de scélératesse, impatience et excès de folie,
et un zèle arrogant d'actions abominables dans un esprit de débauche et des voies de souillure au service de l'impureté,
[11]une langue blasphématoire, des yeux aveugles et une oreille dure, une nuque raide et un cœur dur
pour marcher dans toutes les voies des ténèbres, et une ruse méchante.

Et la visite [12]de tous ceux qui le suivent consistera en des malheurs innombrables par l'intermédiaire de tous les anges dévastateurs,
en une corruption éternelle par l'ardente colère du Dieu des vengeances,
en un tourment perpétuel et une honte [13]éternelle avec l'opprobre de l'extermination dans le feu des antres ténébreux.
Tous leurs temps, pour leurs générations, sont dans le deuil de l'affliction,
et le malheur de l'amertume dans les calamités des ténèbres jusqu'à [14]leur anéantissement sans aucun reste ni rescapé.

[15]Par eux se fait l'histoire de tous les fils d'homme
et en leurs catégories se partageront toutes leurs armées durant leurs générations,
et dans leurs voies ils se conduiront,
et toute l'activité [16]de leurs œuvres se fera d'après leurs catégories,
selon la part de chacun, entre le plus et le moins, pour tous les temps éternels.

Car Dieu les a disposés à égalité jusqu'au temps [17]dernier et Il a mis une inimitié éternelle entre leurs catégories:
abomination de la vérité sont les actes de la perversité et abomination de la perversité toutes les voies de la vérité,
et une ardeur [18]combattive au sujet de tous leurs arrêts, car ils ne vont pas de conserve.

Mais dans les secrets de Son intelligence et dans la sagesse de Sa gloire,
Dieu a mis un terme à l'existence de la perversité,
et au temps de [19]la visite, Il la détruira pour toujours.
Alors paraîtra à jamais la fidélité du monde car elle s'était fourvoyée dans les voies de l'impiété
par la domination de la perversité jusqu'au [20]temps du jugement décisif.
Alors Dieu, dans sa fidélité, purifiera toutes les œuvres de l'homme
et Il fera pour lui l'épuration parmi les humains,
en supprimant tout esprit de perversité de ses entrailles de [21]chair
et en le purifiant par un esprit saint de tous les actes d'impiété.
Il répandra sur lui l'esprit de vérité comme des eaux lustrales
en enlevant toutes les abominations mensongères, car il s'était vautré [22]dans un esprit impur,
pour faire comprendre aux hommes droits la connaissance du Très-Haut,
et pour donner l'intelligence de la sagesse des fils des cieux aux parfaits de conduite.
Car c'est eux que Dieu a élus pour l'alliance éternelle, [23]et c'est à eux qu'est destinée toute la gloire d'Adam.
Et il n'y aura plus de perversité, toute œuvre de tromperie sera pour la honte.

Jusqu'à ce moment-là seront en conflit les esprits de fidélité et de perversité dans le cœur de l'homme,
[24]et ils (= les hommes) se conduiront dans la sagesse et la folie.
Selon la part de chacun dans la fidélité, il pratiquera la justice, et ainsi il haïra la perversité,
et selon sa participation au lot de perversité, il pratiquera l'impiété, et ainsi [25]il détestera la fidélité.
Car, à égalité, Dieu les a disposés jusqu'au Terme fixé et au Renouvellement.
Lui, Il connaît les activités de leurs œuvres pour toutes les périodes [26]des temps.
Et Il les (= esprits) a répartis aux fils d'homme pour la connaissance du bien et du mal,
ainsi Dieu fera tomber les sorts pour chaque vivant, selon son esprit, au moment [de la Rétribution] de la Visite.

CNRS – ÉBAF
Jérusalem

Émile PUECH

L'IMAGE DE DIEU DANS LES ÉCRITS DE SAGESSE 1Q26, 4Q415-418, 4Q423

Plusieurs manuscrits découverts dans la grotte 4 de Qumran (1Q26, 4Q415-418, 4Q423) reproduisent des copies variées, plus ou moins étendues, d'un important écrit sapientiel, *4QInstruction*, dans lequel un sage dispense un enseignement à un élève, et où il esquisse, au cours de son exposé, plusieurs traits de la figure de Dieu. Parmi les nombreux fragments attribués à chaque manuscrit, seuls quelques-uns présentent des développements d'une certaine ampleur. Les textes de ceux-ci, parfois lacunaires, peuvent être cependant complétés par recoupement avec d'autres copies du même passage de l'écrit si bien qu'il est possible d'en reconstituer des sections, plus ou moins longues, permettant une investigation. C'est à partir de ces textes de sagesse, pour la plupart fragmentaires, que j'ai entrepris une recherche sur l'image ou la figure de Dieu dans les écrits de la mer Morte. Il ne s'agissait pas pour moi de refaire une présentation critique ou une édition critique des passages[1], mais de déceler au fil des colonnes des divers fragments de manuscrits des traits de la figure de Dieu. Mon investigation qui a porté sur des fragments relativement bien conservés m'a d'abord permis d'observer qu'au cours de certains de ses propos, le sage fait des considérations générales sur Dieu où il ébauche quelques traits singuliers de son image. Par ailleurs,

1. Une première publication des manuscrits a été faite par B.Z. WACHOLDER et M.G. ABEGG, *A Preliminary Edition of the Unpublished Dead Sea Scrolls: The Hebrew and Aramaic Texts from Cave Four. Fascicule Two,* Washington, D.C., Dead Sea Scroll Research Council, Biblical Archaeology Society, 1992, plusieurs années avant l'édition «officielle»: J. STRUGNELL and D.J. HARRINGTON, *Qumran Cave XXIV. Sapiential Texts, Part 2. 4QInstruction (Mûsar l^eMevîn)* DJD, 34), Oxford, Clarendon, 1999. Dans un ouvrage récent, E.J.C. TIGCHELAAR, *To Increase Learning for the Understanding ones. Reading and Reconstructing the Fragmentary Early Jewish Sapiential Text 4QInstruction* (STDJ, 44), Leiden, Brill, 2001, a reconsidéré et discuté un certain nombre de transcriptions proposées dans DJD, 34. Par ailleurs certains auteurs ont proposé leur publication de tel ou tel manuscrit, voir, p.e., A. LANGE, *Weisheit und Prädestination. Weisheitliche Urordnung und Prädestination in den Textfunden von Qumran* (STDJ, 18), Leiden, Brill, 1995, pp. 45-92; T. ELGVIN, *Early Essene Eschatology: Judgment and Salvation according to Sapiental Word A,* in D.W. PARRY and S.D. RICKS (eds.), *Current Research and Technological Developments on the Dead Sea Scrolls. Conference on the Texts from the Judean Desert, Jerusalem, 30 April 1995* (STDJ, 20), Leiden, Brill, 1996, pp. 126-165. D'autres ont présenté ces textes en les accompagnant de notes de traduction et d'un petit commentaire: A. CAQUOT, *Les textes de sagesse de Qoumrân (Aperçu préliminaire),* in *RHPR* 76 (1996) 1-34; D.J. HARRINGTON, *Wisdom Texts from Qumran*, London – New York, Routledge, 1996.

en d'autres passages de son écrit, le sage rappelle à son élève qu'il bénéficie d'une attention particulière de Dieu. Là, il jette un autre regard sur Dieu. A partir de cette distinction, j'exposerai ma recherche.

I. Le Dieu créateur et juge

Dans quelques passages de son écrit où le sage fait réfléchir son élève sur Dieu qui a créé le monde pour le conduire selon son dessein et qui va le juger, il ébauche deux traits particuliers de sa figure.

1. *Le Dieu des connaissances, Dieu créateur*

Dans un extrait de 4Q417 1 I, 6-18 relativement bien conservé, mais difficile à interpréter, le sage invite son élève à bien discerner le cours des choses et l'avenir afin de comprendre le dessein de Dieu. En 4Q417 1 I, 13 et 4Q417 1 I, 18, l'expression «et toi… qui discernes» semble apparemment marquer le début d'une partie. Compte tenu de cette observation, on peut donc diviser l'extrait en deux sections: 4Q417 1 I, 6-13; 1Q417 1 I, 13-18.

En 4Q417 1 I, 6-13, lorsque le sage exhorte son élève à méditer sur le mystère de l'avenir (*rz nhyh*)[2] et à étudier sans cesse, il lui déclare qu'il connaîtra la vérité, l'iniquité, la sagesse et la folie. En considérant tout acte et les châtiments qui s'en suivront, l'adepte de la sagesse saura reconnaître le bien du mal dans toutes leurs œuvres. Le sage lui en donne la raison: «**8** Car le Dieu des connaissances est le fondement de la vérité, et dans (ou par) le mystère de l'avenir **9** il a expliqué sa fondation…». Et il poursuit[3]:

> Ses œuvres,[il les a faites en toute sag]esse et en toute[intelli]gence il l'a formée, et le pouvoir de ses œuvres **10** selon… il a expliqué selon leur intelligence, pour toutes ses[œuvres], afin de marcher **11** selon[la nature] de leur discernement et il a fait comprendre… et selon l'exactitude des discernements sont con[nus les se]crets **12** de sa pensée avec sa conduite parfaite dans toutes ses œuvres. Scrute sans cesse et discernes-en tous **13** les aboutissements. Alors tu connaîtras la gloire de sa puissance avec les secrets de ses prodiges et les grandeurs de ses œuvres…

Dans ce passage énigmatique, en désignant Dieu comme le Dieu des connaissances, le sage utilise une expression qui se retrouve en 1QS III,

2. L'expression «mystère de l'avenir» (*rz nhyh*) pourrait désigner l'ordre et l'agencement du monde et de la création, avec une dimension éthique et historique (Lange, *Weisheit und Prädestination*, pp. 57-61).

3. Pour ce passage, je reprends les propositions de lecture de Strugnell – Harrington, DJD, 34, pp. 151-155.

15-17 au début de l'instruction sur les deux esprits. Là, le rédacteur de la règle de la communauté, qui désigne Dieu comme le Dieu des connaissances, laisse entendre que Dieu est le créateur de tout être, qu'il a fixé à l'avance les activités de tout être avant qu'il existe, et que celles-ci se déploieront selon son dessein[4]. Ainsi Dieu sait tout et connaît tout. De même, en 4Q417 1 I, 6-13, lorsque le sage utilise l'expression «le Dieu des connaissances», il pense au Dieu créateur qui a créé tout être selon un dessein en fonction duquel le cours des choses et la vie des hommes vont se dérouler. Cependant par rapport à l'auteur de 1QS III, 15-17, en 4Q417 2 I, 8-13, le sage suggère que Dieu a encore donné à l'homme de percevoir ou de comprendre quel était son dessein. Dans ce but, il prend soin de souligner que Dieu a fourni les explications nécessaires pour pénétrer les mystères de la création. Ainsi, en fonction de l'exactitude de son discernement, l'homme est en mesure de connaître les secrets de la pensée de Dieu et sa conduite en toutes ses œuvres. Il revient alors à l'élève du sage de scruter afin de déceler les secrets des prodiges divins et les grandeurs des œuvres de Dieu.

Dans la seconde partie du passage en 4Q417 1 I, 13-18 où le sage poursuit l'exposé de sa pensée, il encourage son élève à méditer sur ce qui a été écrit dans un mémorandum où a été gravé tout ce que Dieu a décrété:

> Et toi **14** qui discernes, récolte le fruit de ton action dans la remémoration de [ ] qui vient. Ton décret (est) gravé, toute la visite est décrétée **15** car est gravé tout ce qui a été décrété par Dieu contre toute l'i[niquité?] des fils de Seth[5] et un mémorandum a été écrit devant lui **16** pour tous ceux qui gardent sa parole. Telle est la vision à méditer du mémorandum. Il a donné cela en héritage à un homme ainsi qu'au peuple spirituel, car **17** la nature de celui-ci est selon le modèle des saints, et de plus, il ne l'a pas donné à méditer à un esprit charnel, car celui-ci ne distingue pas **18** [le bi]en du mal selon la règle de son esprit. Et toi, fils, qui sais discerner, regarde [ ] dans le mystère de l'avenir[6]...

Dans ces lignes, le sage exploite le motif du livre écrit dans les cieux où les décisions divines sont inscrites. Le motif, connu de la littérature vétérotestamentaire (Ex 32,31-33; Ml 3,16) et de la littérature juive

4. «**15** Du Dieu des connaissances provient tout ce qui est et sera. Avant que les choses soient, il a fixé **16** leur plan et lorsqu'elles sont, selon leurs statuts, conformément à son plan glorieux, elles accomplissent leur tâche sans y rien changer. Dans sa main **16** sont les lois de tout être, et lui les soutient dans tous leurs besoins. Et il a créé l'homme pour dominer **17** le monde et il a disposé pour lui deux esprits afin de marcher en eux jusqu'au temps de sa visite...» (1QS III, 15-17).

5. Ou selon la lecture de PUECH: «*des fils de la fosse*».

6. La traduction suit presque intégralement celle de CAQUOT, *Les textes de sagesse de Qoumrân*, p. 17.

(TestLev 5, 4)[7] et repris dans d'autres écrits de Qumran (1QH I, 23-25), est un autre moyen dont dispose le sage pour parler de la prédestination. Ainsi, Dieu, le créateur, apparaît comme celui qui a décrété de la destinée des hommes.

Par ailleurs, dans le passage, l'auteur semble distinguer entre deux catégories d'hommes. Les uns dénommés les enfants de Seth en référence à Nb 24,17, selon une lecture du fragment, représentent vraisemblablement les ennemis de Dieu[8] pour lesquels un châtiment est décrété à cause de leur iniquité. Les autres, désignés comme ceux qui gardent la parole de Dieu en référence à Ml 3,16, seront inscrits dans un mémorandum. Comme le laisse entendre le prophète, on peut supposer qu'ils appartiendront à Dieu.

Dans la suite de la section, le sage précise que Dieu a donné à méditer tout cela à un homme et à un peuple spirituel dont la nature est selon le modèle des saints, et il ne l'a pas laissé à la méditation de l'esprit de chair qui ne sait pas reconnaître le bien du mal. Ici, il est difficile de percevoir qui serait évoqué sous les mots «à un homme (*'nwsh*) d'un peuple spirituel». Le mot *'nwsh* ne renvoie pas, semble-t-il, au patriarche antédiluvien Enosh. Il s'agirait plutôt d'un individu[9]. Mais de qui pourrait-il s'agir? Qui est encore le peuple spirituel dont la nature est selon le modèle des saints? Un passage du rouleau des hymnes offre peut-être un indice pour arriver à percer l'énigme. En effet, lorsqu'en 1QH XI, le psalmiste, vraisemblablement le maître de justice, rappelle que Dieu l'a instruit de son secret de vérité (1QH XI, 4), et quand il loue Dieu qui a purifié un homme (*'nwsh*) du péché (1QH XI, 10-13)[10], il mentionne clairement la communauté désignée par l'expression «tes fils de vérité», «les saints» et, probablement, il parle de lui-même en rappelant qu'un homme (*'nwsh*), a été purifié par Dieu de son péché afin d'être agrégé à la communauté. Compte tenu de cette observation, en 4Q417 1 I, 16-18, il est possible de présumer que le sage utilisant les termes «un homme», «peuple de l'esprit» et «saints» fait allusion, en employant un langage

7. Voir LANGE, *Weisheit und Prädestination*, pp. 69-79.

8. HARRINGTON, *Wisdom Texts from Qumran*, p. 55.

9. CAQUOT, *Les textes de sagesse de Qoumrân,* p. 18.

10. «C'est à cause de ta gloire que tu as purifié un homme du péché afin qu'il se sanctifie [11] pour toi de toute abomination impure et de (toute) faute d'iniquité; afin qu'il soit uni av[ec] tes fils de vérité et dans un (même) lot avec [12] tes saints; afin d'élever cette vermine qu'est l'homme de la poussière vers [ton] secret [de vérité] et de l'esprit pervers vers[ton] intelligence; [13] et afin qu'il se tienne devant toi avec l'armée éternelle et [tes] esprits de[sainteté] (1QH XI, 10-13)». Traduction d'A. DUPONT-SOMMER, *Les Écrits Esséniens découverts près de la Mer Morte,* Paris, Payot, 1959. Voir aussi 1QH III, 20-23 où le psalmiste parle de lui-même, de ceux qui sont réunis dans l'Alliance de Dieu et de l'assemblée de Saints.

crypté, au maître de justice et à la communauté sadocite appelée partager le sort des saints. Ainsi la révélation que Dieu donne à méditer est réservée à la communauté sadocite, le peuple spirituel, et au maître de justice[11]. Mais elle ne sera pas communiquée à l'esprit charnel, c'est-à-dire à l'homme impie, à l'esprit pervers, qui n'a pas été justifié par Dieu, ainsi que permet de le comprendre l'emploi de l'expression «esprit charnel» en 1QH XIII, 13-17[12].

C'est tout cela que doit appréhender l'adepte de la sagesse invité à scruter dans le mystère de l'avenir ou le cours des choses.

2. *Le Dieu juge, Dieu de Vérité*

Dans la suite endommagée du fragment, en 4Q417 1 I, 18-19, où le sage poursuit son exhortation sur le Dieu des connaissances, il mentionne la visite divine à la fin des temps. C'est alors qu'il se manifestera pour juger le monde. En 4Q417 1 I, 18-19, l'état du fragment ne permet pas d'en savoir plus, mais d'autres fragments de l'écrit, parfois mal conservés, évoquent eux aussi le jugement. Comme en 4Q 417 1, en 4Q418 127, un fragment très détérioré, le sage fait allusion au jugement divin: «*dans de justes balances, il a pesé leur disposition*» (4Q418 127, 6). En 4Q418 126, 6, dans un texte lacunaire, où vraisemblablement l'auteur célèbre la puissance de Dieu, le sage décrit le jugement comme la vengeance de Dieu à l'encontre des malfaisants. En 4Q423 5, 1-4, le sage évoque le jugement divin contre la famille de Corè relaté en Nb 16, puis il rappelle que Dieu a réparti l'héritage de tous les souverains et qu'il a façonné de sa main toute œuvre; et enfin, il annonce que Dieu jugera tous les hommes selon la vérité, et qu'il visitera les pères et les fils, les gentils ainsi que tous les indigènes.

Le manuscrit 4Q416 1, bien que lacunaire, offre, lui aussi une description brève, mais plus satisfaisante du jugement que Dieu exercera dans l'univers par l'entremise des anges:

11. Le sage qui est membre du peuple spirituel a reçu de Dieu, lui aussi, la connaissance. Dans un autre fragment lacunaire (4Q426 1 I, 4), il écrit: «... Dieu a mis dans mon cœur la connaissance et le discernement...».

12. Cf. 1QH XIII, 13-17: «[Mais qu'est-il, lu]i, l'esprit charnel, pour comprendre **14** toutes ces choses et pour avoir l'intelligence de [ton] grand secret de vérité? Et qu'est-ce que celui qui est né de la femme parmi toutes [tes œuvres] formidables? Lui **15** il n'est qu'une bâtisse de poussière et une chose pétrie avec de l'eau: [lui do]nt le conseil n'est que [souillu]re, honte ignominieuse et [ ], sur qui domine l'esprit pervers! **16** Et s'il reste dans l'impiété, il deviend[ra un objet d'effroi à] jamais et un prodige pour les générations et un objet d'épou[vante pour toute] chair! C'est seulement par ta bonté que **17** l'homme est justifié et par l'immensité de ta miséricorde...» (DUPONT-SOMMER, *Les Ecrits Esséniens*).

> [7] et l'armée des cieux, il a établie sur [ ] [8] pour leurs prodiges et les signes [ ] [9] l'un à l'autre et toute leur visite [ ] [10] des cieux il jugera toute l'œuvre d'impiété et les fils de sa vérité seront agréés par [ ] [11] sa fin et ils auront peur et ils crieront tous ceux qui se sont vautrés en elle, car les cieux auront peur [ ] [12] les mers et les abîmes seront effrayés et tous les esprits de chair seront abattus et les fils des cieux [ ] [13] son [ju]gement et toute iniquité cessera pour toujours et le temps de la vérité sera accompli [ ] [14] dans tous les temps à jamais, car il est le Dieu de vérité et dès avant les années[ ] [15] pour établir la justice entre le bien et le mal…[ ]

Dans ce récit, l'aspect catastrophique et universel du jugement est bien suggéré par l'auteur qui souligne que les cieux, les mers et les abîmes seront effrayés. En jugeant toute œuvre d'impiété, Dieu frappera les hommes souillés par leurs fautes. Seuls les «fils de sa vérité» trouveront grâce devant lui. Le jugement divin marquera la fin de l'iniquité et le triomphe du bien. Il en adviendra ainsi, car pour le sage, le Dieu qui juge est le Dieu de vérité. Il établira la justice entre le bien et le mal.

Ainsi, selon ces textes de sagesse, Dieu apparaît comme le maître de l'univers dans toute sa durée. Il est le Dieu créateur de qui vient tout ce qui est et tout ce qui sera. Il a fixé le cours des choses, et l'existence de toute créature se déroulera selon un dessein connu de lui seul. C'est vraisemblablement pour cette raison qu'il est dénommé le Dieu des connaissances. Par ailleurs, les actions des hommes, bons ou mauvais, et leurs destinées sont inscrites dans des livres célestes où ont été gravés tous les décrets divins concernant chacun. Selon le dessein de Dieu, le monde s'achemine vers une fin qui sera le temps de sa visite. Alors Dieu, qui est le Dieu de vérité, apparaîtra comme juge universel. Il détruira définitivement toute impiété pour faire paraître la vérité. Et seuls, les fils de vérité seront agréés devant lui. Ce sont tous ces traits de la figure de Dieu qui apparaissent aussi dans d'autres écrits de la mer Morte[13] que le sage entend faire découvrir à son élève en l'invitant à méditer sur le cours des choses. Il a pris soin de lui dire aussi que Dieu en a donné la faculté à ceux qui gardent sa parole.

II. Dieu et le sage

Dans d'autres fragments de l'écrit sapientiel, le sage s'adresse à son élève pour lui faire observer que Dieu lui porte une attention toute particulière. L'un de ces fragments dans lesquels le sage présente Dieu sous d'autres traits (4Q418 81) est plein d'intérêt pour la recherche entre-

13. Par exemple dans l'instruction sur les deux esprits en 1QS III, 13 – IV, 26; cf. aussi 1QH XII, 18-22; 1Q27.

prise. Il décrit, en effet, assez amplement, la sollicitude que Dieu manifeste à l'égard de l'adepte de la sagesse. Pour cette partie de mon étude, j'exposerai les résultats de ma recherche à partir de la présentation du fragment. Certains passages, plus obscurs, seront explicités à l'aide d'autres informations puisées à d'autres fragments de l'écrit sapientiel.

Dans la première partie du fragment (4Q418 81, 1-8), peu détériorée, le sage évoque le sort réservé par Dieu à l'adepte dans une suite de brèves unités. Compte tenu de l'état du manuscrit, plusieurs de celles-ci sont composées, apparemment, selon un même schéma: d'abord le sage rappelle ce que Dieu a fait pour l'adepte, puis il l'interpelle par «et toi» et enfin il lui communique comment répondre à la sollicitude divine. Dans la seconde partie du fragment (4Q418 81, 9-20), moins bien conservée, les propos du sage portent sur les dons d'intelligence et d'autorité dont l'adepte a été gratifié. La partie est composée de deux développements plus amples introduits en 4Q418 81, 9 et 15, par l'interpellation «et toi».

1. *Le Dieu qui met à part*

Au début du fragment, le sage déclare à son disciple que Dieu, qui a ouvert une fontaine, l'a séparé de tout esprit charnel:

> 1 tes lèvres, il a ouvert une fontaine pour bénir les saints, **et toi,** comme une fontaine éternelle, célèbre [ ] il t'a séparé 2 de tout esprit charnel, **et toi,** sépare-toi de tout ce qu'il hait, et abstiens-toi de toute abomination de l'âme [ ] (4Q418 81, 1-2)

L'image de la fontaine qui apparaît dans les paroles du sage se retrouve dans d'autres écrits de la mer Morte. Dans plusieurs de ceux-ci, il s'agit de la fontaine de la connaissance (1QH II, 18) de laquelle Dieu fait jaillir la lumière de sorte que le fidèle peut contempler ses merveilles et être illuminé par le secret de l'avenir. Par ailleurs, selon 1QH XVIII, 12 et 13, Dieu a ouvert une fontaine, probablement celle de la connaissance, pour amender la conduite du modelage d'argile et la culpabilité du rejeton de la femme selon ses œuvres. Ainsi, Dieu a donné la connaissance à celui qui lui est fidèle. Grâce à elle, il peut changer sa conduite.

Par ailleurs, lorsque le sage précise en 4Q418 81, 1-2 que Dieu a séparé son disciple de tout esprit charnel, c'est à dire de l'humanité impie et perverse, il l'exhorte encore à se séparer de tout ce qu'il hait et à s'abstenir de toute abomination de l'âme. En fonction des textes mentionnés plus haut, on peut comprendre les propos du sage, dans le sens suivant: Dieu a communiqué la connaissance à l'adepte de la sagesse, en ouvrant pour lui une fontaine et, ainsi, par le don de la connaissance, il a fait en sorte qu'il soit séparé de toute impiété.

2. *Le Dieu que l'on doit sanctifier*

Le sage précise ensuite à son élève que Dieu est sa part et son héritage parmi les hommes:

> C'est lui qui a tout fait [3] et il a donné son héritage à chaque homme et il est ta part et ton héritage parmi les hommes et sur son héritage, il t'a donné autorité, **et toi**, en cela [4] honore-le en te sanctifiant pour lui, de même qu'il t'a placé pour un saint des saints [ ] en tout [ ] (4Q418 81, 2-4)

Pour le sage, Dieu est le créateur qui donne à chaque homme son héritage, c'est à dire ses conditions de vie et ses moyens de subsistance. En 4Q418 81, 2-4, le sage précise encore à son élève que Dieu est sa part et son héritage et qu'il lui a donné autorité sur son héritage. Cela revient à lui dire que Dieu est celui auquel il doit se consacrer. C'est ce que le sage explicite lorsqu'il l'exhorte à honorer Dieu en se sanctifiant pour lui. Puis dans son propos, le sage déclare à son disciple que Dieu en a fait un saint des saints. L'expression est employée dans la règle de la communauté au sujet du grand prêtre. En 4Q418 81, elle caractérise l'adepte de la sagesse comme un homme très saint.

3. *Le Dieu, père*

Mis à part et consacré à Dieu, l'élève est aussi considéré par Dieu comme son fils aîné:

> [5] Il a fait tomber ton sort, et ta gloire il a grandement accru, et il t'a placé pour lui comme fils aîné [ ] [6] "Je te donnerai mon bienfait", **et toi**, n'est-elle pas pour toi sa bonté, et avec confiance en lui, marche toujours [ ] [7] tes œuvres, **et toi**, enquiers-toi de ses jugements auprès de chacun des adversaires, en tout … [ ] [8] aime-le, et avec un amour (éternel) et de la miséricorde pour tous ceux qui gardent sa parole… [ ] (4Q418 81, 5-8)

Déjà, en 4Q416 2, II, 13-14, dans un passage où le sage fait à son élève des recommandations de bonne conduite, il lui rappelle qu'il est pour Dieu «*comme un premier-né*». Il continue ses propos en disant que Dieu «*aura pour lui de la compassion comme un homme en a pour son fils unique*». Dieu apparaît ici comme un père pour le sage considéré comme son fils. En 4Q418 81, le sage redit la même chose avec des propos semblables: Dieu considère l'élève de la sagesse comme son aîné et il est pour lui comme un père qui le comble de ses bienfaits. Il reste à l'adepte de la sagesse d'avoir confiance en lui.

4. *Dieu qui ouvre l'intelligence*

Dans la suite du fragment, le sage rappelle à son disciple que Dieu, qui lui a ouvert l'intelligence, a eu d'autres largesses:

> **9 et toi**, il t'a ouvert l'intelligence, et sur son trésor il t'a donné autorité, et une mesure de vérité en recherchant [ ] **10** ils sont avec toi, et dans ta main, il y a de quoi détourner le courroux des hommes de volonté, et examiner [ ] **11** avec toi (ton peuple), avant que tu reçoives ton héritage de sa main, honore ses saints, et a[vant] **12** il a ouvert... tous les saints, et tout ce qui est appelé par son nom est saint [ ] **13** pour tous les temps sa splendeur, sa beauté pour la plantation étern[elle] **14** le monde. En lui marcheront tous ceux qui héritent de la terre, car dans les cieu[x...] (4Q418 81, 9-14)

Au début du fragment, en confiant à son élève que Dieu avait ouvert une fontaine, le sage lui suggérait qu'il lui avait fait don de la connaissance[14]. En 4Q418 81, 9-14 il lui rappelle qu'il lui a ouvert l'intelligence et qu'il lui a donné autorité sur son trésor, vraisemblablement celui de la connaissance[15], et une mesure de vérité. Puis il tient des propos obscurs: «**10** *ils sont avec toi, et dans ta main, il y a de quoi détourner le courroux des hommes de (sa) volonté...*». Il ne semble pas que ces paroles, difficiles à saisir à cause de l'état du manuscrit, sont à comprendre dans le sens que l'adepte de la sagesse a reçu de Dieu la capacité d'intercéder pour autrui[16]. Il vaut mieux interpréter les propos du sage, dans le contexte du don de la connaissance: si Dieu a communiqué la connaissance au sage, c'est pour qu'à son tour il en face don à ceux qui sont avec lui. Ceux-ci éclairés par ses paroles pourront se comporter conformément à la volonté de Dieu et, en conséquence, ils éviteront le courroux divin. Le maître de justice auquel Dieu avait donné la connaissance, avait reçu un rôle analogue (1QH IV, 23-26). Il en serait peut-être de même du sage.

5. *Le Dieu qui donne autorité*

Le fragment 4Q418 81 s'achève par un petit développement qui n'est pas clair:

> **15 Et toi,** qui discernes, s'il t'a donné autorité sur les artisans(?), sache [ ] **16** indulgence (?) pour ceux des hommes qui cheminent, et à partir de là tu chercheras ta nourriture **17** [ ] réfléchis avec soin, et auprès de tout homme qui t'instruit, augmente ta science (?) **18** exprime ton besoin à tous ceux qui cherchent ce qui est précieux et alors tu établiras [ ] **19** tu seras rempli et

14. Il lui redira de nouveau, selon 4Q423 5, 2: «... et parce qu'il a confié à ton oreille le cours de choses...».

15. STRUGNELL – HARRINGTON, DJD, 34, p. 307.

16. Comme le pense CAQUOT, *Les textes de sagesse de Qoumrân*, p. 24.

rassasié d'une abondance de biens et, par l'habileté de tes mains, [ ] 20 car Dieu a réparti l'héritage de chaque vivant et tous les sages de cœur réussiront [ ] (4Q418 81, 15-20)

Dans ce passage, l'expression «travailleur manuel» peut traduire le syntagme *hkmt ydym* en référence à Sir 9, 17 comme le suggèrent J. Strugnell et Daniel J. Harrington[17]. S'il en est ainsi le sage envisage le cas où Dieu a donné à son élève autorité sur des artisans. Cependant, il est difficile de pénétrer davantage sa pensée. Dans la suite de son propos, il y a une exhortation à s'instruire, suivie d'une promesse de réussite. On peut seulement retenir de ce passage que Dieu est celui qui donne autorité.

Un trait analogue de la figure de Dieu se retrouve dans le fragment 4Q416 2 IV, 2-8:

2 Il t'a donné autorité sur elle[ ] (à son père) 3 il n'a pas donné autorité sur elle, il l'a séparée de sa mère, mais à toi [ ] 4 avec toi elle sera une. De ta fille, pour un autre il te séparera et tes fils[ ] 5 et toi en union avec la femme de ton sein, car elle est la chair de ta nu [dité] 6 Et celui qui aurait autorité, en dehors de toi déplacerait la limite de sa vie [ ] 7 il t'a donné autorité pour qu'elle marche selon ta volonté sans multiplier vœux et offrandes.

Dans ce texte qui traite de l'autorité maritale, le sage rappelle que celle-ci provient de Dieu.

Par rapport aux fragments présentés dans la première partie de mon investigation, au fil des lignes de 4Q418 81, et dans les quelques textes mentionnés lors de son analyse, c'est un autre aspect visage de Dieu que le sage ébauche lorsqu'il s'adresse à son élève. En 4Q417 2 I, 15-17 le sage lui rappellera encore que Dieu lui pardonnera ses péchés et il souligne qu'il pourvoit à sa nourriture

14 Ne passe pas sur tes péchés. Sois comme un homme pauvre en défendant ta cause [ ] 15 prends. Et alors Dieu verra et il détournera sa colère et il passera sur tes péchés… 20 … tout a existé. Mange ce qu'il de donne en nourriture et n'y ajoute pas plus[18]…

Ainsi ce sont deux aspects, différents mais complémentaires, du visage de Dieu que le sage dépeint dans plusieurs passages de l'écrit sapientiel reproduits dans les manuscrits 1Q26, 4Q415, 4Q416, 4Q417, 4Q418, 4Q423.

Dans quelques manuscrits, il présente Dieu comme le maître de l'univers. Il est le créateur qui a fixé le cours des choses selon son dessein et qui connaît la destinée de tous les hommes. Il est le Dieu des connais-

17. Strugnell – Harrington, DJD, 34, p. 309.
18. Voir aussi 4Q416 2 I, 21-22.

sances. Ses décrets concernant les impies comme les fidèles ont été gravés. Au temps de la visite, Dieu jugera les hommes et il détruira l'impiété pour faire paraître la vérité. Alors les fils de vérité seront agréés devant lui. Tel est le dessein de Dieu. Si tout au long du manuscrit, le sage invite son élève à considérer le mystère de l'avenir, la raison en est que Dieu a permis de le pénétrer à un homme et au peuple spirituel, c'est-à-dire vraisemblablement la communauté sadocite. Regroupée autour du maître de justice et constituée de ceux qui gardent sa parole, elle méditera.

Parmi les membres de la communauté à laquelle Dieu a expliqué le mystère de l'avenir, il y a le sage et son élève. En particulier dans le fragment 4Q418 81, le sage révèle à l'élève qu'il initie à la sagesse, qu'il fait l'objet d'une attention toute particulière de Dieu. Dieu est celui qui l'a mis à part de l'humanité impie. Il en fait aussi un homme très saint. Aussi l'adepte de la sagesse doit-il le sanctifier, car Dieu est sa part héritage. Dieu est encore pour lui comme un père qui prend souci de son fils aîné. S'il lui a donné la connaissance, c'est pour qu'il communique à d'autres sa volonté afin de vivre conformément aux préceptes divins. Dieu a encore donné autorité au sage et il pardonnera ses péchés.

Ainsi, Dieu, le créateur qui jugera en temps voulu l'impie, est pour le sage le Dieu qui veille sur celui qui s'initie à la sagesse, comme un père sur son fils. Les bienfaits qui ont été énumérés et dont Dieu l'a comblé révèlent qu'il a pour lui le dessein d'en faire un homme très saint, un sage de cœur qui réussira.

1, rue Notre Dame
F-67170 Hohatzenheim

Claude COULOT

WISDOM TRAITS IN THE QUMRANIC PRESENTATION OF THE ESCHATOLOGICAL PROPHET

1. INTRODUCTION

The relationship between wisdom, prophecy and apocalyptic is a widely studied issue in contemporary scholarship. Some seek the origins of the apocalyptic thought of early Judaism in the prophetic traditions of Israel, whereas others emphasise rather its connections with the perspective of wisdom literature[1]. Instead of reviewing the huge relevant scholarly agenda, we only remind that the affinities of apocalyptic thought with particular manifestations of ancient Israel's prophetic and sapiential traditions seem to be certain[2].

The perspective of several – especially sapiential – writings of the Qumran Library (perhaps the best example is 4QInstruction) shows, that in some cases certain characteristics of wisdom and apocalyptic are found together in the same composition. In this conference – the topic of which is "Wisdom and Apocalyptic in the Dead Sea Scrolls" – this short contribution wish to investigate two writings of the Qumran Library (4Q521 and 11Q13), which provide convenient cases for the symbiosis of these particular theological perspectives. The authors of 4Q521 and 11Q13 used side by side elements of apocalyptic and sapiential language. Having worked on figures of the Qumran Library we labelled "positive eschatological protagonists", we have realised that the presentation of the eschatological prophet in these texts bears certain sapiential characteristics.

This paper proceeds as follows. After some introductory statements on the eschatological prophetic figures of the Qumran Library, we will concentrate on two issues. Firstly, we will deal with 4Q521, where the parallel presence of apocalyptic and sapiential traits recalls the manner of composition of several Qumranic wisdom texts; then we will turn to

1. For the former opinion cp. D.S. RUSSELL, *The Method and Message of Jewish Apocalyptic* (OTL), Philadelphia, PA, Westminster Press, 1964, esp. pp. 92-96 and 190-195. For the latter view see the classical contribution of G. VON RAD, *Theologie des Alten Testaments* (Einführung in die evangelische Theologie, 1), München, Chr. Kaiser, 1961^2, pp. 314-321.

2. See, for example, J.C. VANDERKAM, *The Prophetic-Sapiential Origins of Apocalyptic Thought*, repr. in *From Revelation to Canon. Studies in the Hebrew Bible and Second Temple Literature* (JSJ SS, 62), Leiden, Brill, 2000, pp. 241-254.

the eschatological prophet of 11Q13, who is described – among others – as a wisdom instructor.

2. Eschatological Prophetic Figures in the Qumran Library

There are several *loci* in the Qumran Library, where an eschatological protagonist is described with prophetic characteristics. Texts as 1QS, 4Q175 or 4Q558 clearly relate the eschatological activity of various prophetic figures.

1. The Rule of the Community evokes an eschatological figure, and describes his arrival within the same scenario as the משיחי אהרן וישראל. This figure is called הנביא, his prophetic character is thus obvious (1QS ix 11).
2. The author, or rather, collector of the Testimonia collects together biblical texts, which he seems to interpret as ones referring to eschatological personages. The third quotation is from Deut 5,28-29 and 18,18-19 (4Q175 1-8), where the arrival of a prophet like Moses is presaged.
3. In 4QVision^{b} ar God declares – following Mal 3,23 – that he will send the prophet Elijah (לכן אשלח לאליה קד[ם, 4Q558 frg. 1, 4).

In addition, in two compositions, the authors denote their eschatological prophet with the word משיח[3].

1. In the second column of frg. 2 of the so-called 4QMessianic Apocalypse משיח may denote the same figure as the Elijah *redivivus* of the following column (4Q521 2 ii 1).
2. The author of 11QMelchizedek evokes a figure called משיח הרוח, who may be characterised as Moses *redivivus*[4].

In all of these cases the main task attributed to the eschatological prophet is a precursory one. His arrival could precede the day of judgement or the appearance of some other positive eschatological protagonists[5].

3. The word משיח in the Qumran Library could refer to prophetic figures. Although in the majority of cases these prophetic figures belong to the historical past of Israel (1QM; CD ii, vi; 4Q270; 4Q287; 4Q377), these texts testify to the Qumranic use of the term משיח as denoting prophets.

4. A number of texts allow us to suppose that Moses was considered in the Qumran Library as having prophetic character.

5. For a detailed treatment of the task of the eschatological prophet see my *King, Priest, Prophet. Positive Eschatological Protagonists of the Qumran Library* (STDJ, 47), Leiden, Brill, 2002.

3. The Case of 4Q521

In 4Q521 the eschatological coming of Elijah *redivivus* is described within a sapiential poem. The author uses predominantly eschatological/ apocalyptic elements in his work, but wisdom traits may also be detected. Scholars have tried to define the genre of 4Q521 in two different ways. Émile Puech in the preliminary edition characterised the work as a "messianic apocalypse". In contrast, Florentino García Martínez characterises 4Q521 in his collected translations as a "sapiential poem"[6]. In the following, we wish to show that the work contains characteristics of both wisdom and apocalyptic, which may indicate that the proposals of Puech and García Martínez do not necessarily contradict each other.

Apocalyptic Elements

Puech thought that his characterisation of 4Q521 as an apocalypse was supported by both the thematic relationship of the composition with numerous apocalyptic texts (for example, Daniel 12, 1 Enoch, 4 Ezra, 2 Baruch) and by its eschatological and messianic accents[7]. These similarities and the apocalyptic flavour of the work are undeniable; nevertheless, we notice that labelling 4Q521 an apocalypse is somewhat problematic: preserved parts of the work lack definitive elements of the genre apocalypse[8]. We find no direct revelation obtained by someone, and the task of Elijah *redivivus* – who may be interpreted as an "otherworldly being" – is not to give revelation. In addition, when the author of the work teaches about the final state of the created world the future is an open reality for him. In this, he is in contrast to the apocalypses.

Nevertheless, the preserved fragments of 4Q521 at least display some elements that are characteristic of the mode of thought called "apocalyptic". The text contains, for example, three of the eight characteristic mo-

6. F. García Martínez, *The Dead Sea Scrolls Translated*, Leiden, Brill and Grand Rapids, MI, Eerdmans, 1996, pp. 394-395.

7. É. Puech, *Une apocalypse messianique* (4Q521), in *RQ* 60 (1992) 475-522, p. 515: "Tous ces thèmes ... aussi la dominante eschatologique et messianique inviterait-elle à ranger ce texte dans le genre 'apocalyptique' des milieux juifs du IIe siècle avant J.-C".

8. Perhaps the most widely accepted and oft-repeated definition of the genre apocalypse was published by John Collins at the end of the seventies: "A genre of revelatory literature with a narrative framework, in which a revelation is mediated by an otherworldly being to a human recipient, disclosing a transcendent reality which is both temporal, insofar as it envisages eschatological salvation, and spatial insofar as it involves another, supernatural world". We may add that the channel of the revelation can be a vision, a heavenly journey ("ecstasy"), or direct communication from a heavenly being ("angel"). Cf. J.J. Collins (ed.), *Apocalypse: The Morphology of a Genre*, in *Semeia* 14 (1979), p. 9.

tifs of apocalyptic thought collected together by Klaus Koch[9]. These motifs are as follows:

1. Angelic presence (וכו]ל מלאכים, 7+5 ii 16); note that due to the damaged state of the skin, we do not know what they do.
2. The perspective of new, paradisial salvation, which is painted in the whole remaining column ii of fragment 2.
3. The kingdom of God becomes visible on earth – through the reign of his people: God "will honour the pious upon the throne of an eternal kingdom" (כסא מלכות עד, as is testified by 4Q521 2 ii 7)[10].

In addition, the author of 4Q521 uses other motifs that may be considered as characteristic of the apocalyptic thought. These are the universalistic perspective (2 ii 1: heaven and earth; 2 iii 4: the earth; 7+5 ii 2: the earth and all that is in it), the idea of punishment of the wicked (7+5 ii 4-13), or the resurrection of the righteous (המחיה את מתי עמו: 7+5 ii 6).

These elements, and the parallels that Puech has rightly observed, provide to the work an apocalyptic background. On the other hand, however, they do not classify 4Q521 a work with the genre apocalypse.

Wisdom Elements

Beside these apocalyptic elements, the composition reveals other traits that can be interpreted as wisdom characteristics. The tone of the second fragment is exhortative/admonitory. The intention of the author is to preserve his addressees in the right path of religious life. The protagonist of the text does not give nor obtain revelation.

There are some particular elements in 4Q521, which may be interpreted against the background of some wisdom texts found at Qumran. As a preliminary note, we remind that the Qumranic corpus of wisdom compositions reveals such a sapiential perspective, which is somewhat different from the wisdom works of the Hebrew Bible. The content of the Qumranic sapiential writings covers more abstract issues than the stressed this-worldly perspective of Old Testament wisdom. It includes eschatological and quasi-metaphysical themes; furthermore, the concept of mystery in some of these compositions may have come from the realm of apocalyptic thought. In this aspect, we may also mention some passages of Ben Sira.

We mention certain common concepts of 4Q521 and some of these sapiential compositions. First, 4Q521, the Book of Ben Sira and

9. K. Koch, *The Rediscovery of Apocalyptic* (SBT, 22), London, SCM Press, 1972, pp. 28-32.

10. The theme of kingdom seems to be evoked again in frg. 12, line 2: ומ]לכ֯ו֯ת֯[.

4QInstruction are interested in the theme of covenant (cp. 4Q521 frg. 10, 2: ושמרי ברי]ת and 4Q415 2 ii: ברית קד]שו). Second, the commandments (מצוות) have an importance both in 4Q521 (2 ii 2, the somewhat enigmatic מצות קדושים) and in the 4QSapiential-Hymnic Work A (4Q426 1 i 2), and we can mention here also Ben Sira. Third, the personification of certain parts of the universe is found in some instances. In 4Q521 2 ii 1-2 the heaven and earth will listen; in 2 iii 4 the earth rejoices; and perhaps 7+5 ii 14, where the heaven is told to meet. Similar personification is present in the 4QInstruction (cp., for example, 4Q416 frg. 1: heaven, seas and abyss). From a more general perspective, the repeated use of the verb שמע in 4Q521 (1 i 2; 2 ii 1) also evokes sapiential background. In addition, we may recall that 4Q521 2 ii depends strongly upon Ps 146,5-9, a passage that begins with a *macarismus* or beatitude saying. The sapiential roots of this formula may also be admitted[11]. It is furthermore probable that the evocation of God's created world (4Q521 throughout, and esp. 7+5 ii 1-3) – which is also familiar from the realm of sapiential thought – has connections with this passage of Psalm 146[12].

Finally, one of Puech's reconstruction merits attention (4Q521 2 ii 14). Fragment 2 column ii of the work ends with a stichometrically arranged passage (lines 12-14) that enumerates in pairs the beneficiaries of the coming salvation. The entities evoked here are familiar from both prophetic and sapiential passages of the Old Testament (חללים, מתים, נתושים, רעבים and especially ענוים and דלים)[13]. The last remaining pair of this list is fragmentarily preserved, but it begins with ונב]. Émile Puech proposes to restore this fragmentarily preserved expression as ונב]ונים, a solution which is theoretically possible[14]. With this reconstruction, the list seems to include such a body which has undeniable sapiential connections: "[d]ans la Bible, נבון est souvent en parallèle à חכם 'sage'..."[15].

11. On this, cp. J. DUPONT, *Les Béatitudes, II* (EB), Paris, Gabalda, 1969, pp. 324-338; see further my contribution, *Intertestamentális modellek a Boldogmondások irodalmi formájához*, in J. ZSENGELLÉR (ed.), *Hagyomány és előzmény. Intertestamentális tanulmányok* (Acta Theologica Papensia, 2), Pápa, 1999, esp. pp. 79-83. Note that Puech reconstructs a *macarismus* even within 4Q521 (frg. 2 iii 2). This reconstruction is possible, but seeing that it is based only on a remaining initial *'ālep*, it remains hypothetical.

12. See the formulae וכל א]שר בם and וכל אשר בה in 4Q521 2 ii 2 and 7+5 ii 2, which are nearly verbatim quotations from Ps 146,6bβ.

13. Relevant Old Testament passages are collected in É. PUECH, *La croyance des Esséniens en la vie future: immortalité, résurrection, vie éternelle?* (ÉB N.S., 21-22), Paris, Gabalda, 1993, pp. 641-643 and DJD, 25, pp. 16-17.

14. "Une lecture possible, sinon probable", PUECH, *Croyance des Esséniens*, 2, p. 643; DJD, 25, p. 17.

15. *Ibid.*

Summary

The characteristics collected above may testify sufficiently the parallel presence of two different perspectives within the same composition. This poem has a strong apocalyptic flavour, however, its preserved fragments do not classify it as an apocalypse. Florentino García Martínez has right when labelling it a "sapiential poem", that we may perhaps further characterise as "an apocalyptic poem containing eschatological wisdom material".

4. The Eschatological Prophet of 11QMelchizedek

The author of 11QMelchizedek when treating the activity of Melchizedek – his angelic protagonist – brings another important figure onto the scene in 11Q13 ii 15-21[16]. The role of the protagonist of these lines is related purely as "verbal activity:" he announces (משמיע), says (אומר), comforts (לנחם), and instructs (להשכילמה), he is a messenger (מבשר)[17].

The passage that 11Q13 interprets here, Isa 52,7 speaks of a messenger (מבשר) whose feet are upon the mountains. In the biblical text, the messenger is a prophetic figure, who announces salvation to Zion, and the reign of God (Isa 527c). The author of 11Q13 emphasises the prophetic connections of the passage by specifying two aspects. First, he identifies the "mountains" (הרים) of Isa 52,7aα with "the prophets" (הנביאי[ם). Second, he classifies the messenger as "the anointed of the spirit" (משיח הרו[ח])[18]. This expression is an obvious reference to Isa 61,1a[19], a verse which is the beginning of a biblical passage that – al-

16. This figure differs in several respects from Melchizedek. He has no martial activity; this could be emphasised already by the opening sentence of the passage, which alludes perhaps to the following citation of Isa 52,7. From the Isaianic text the word שלום fits best into the available space of the lacuna. See J.T. Milik, *Milkî-ṣedeq et Milkî-reša'* *dans les anciens écrits juifs et chrétiens*, in *JJS* 23 (1972) 95-144, p. 107; É. Puech, *Notes sur le manuscrit de 11QMelkîsédeq*, in *RQ* 48 (1987) 483-513, esp. pp. 498-499; see further DJD, 23, pp. 225, 228.

17. Note that only one such "verbal activity" is connected to Melchizedek: the proclaiming of liberty (קרא).

18. This also could be an indication that he is different from Melchizedek. J. Zimmermann, *Messianische Texte aus Qumran* (WUNT, II/104), Tübingen, Mohr Siebeck, 1998, p. 410, sees the main difference between Melchizedek and this figure in that the former is a heavenly, while the latter is an earthly figure. He remarks: "Soweit erkennbar, vollzieht Melchisedek seine Handlungen im *Himmel*, während die Verkündigung des 'Gesalbten' im *irdischen* Bereich stattfindet. 'Gesalbt' bzw. 'geistbegabt' sind ferner im AT, im Frühjudentum und in Qumran Menschen, aber keine Engel".

19. רוח אדני יהוה עלי יען משח יהוה אתי .

though implicitly – seems to influence the entire material of 11Q13[20]. In its original, Isaianic context, the figure anointed by the spirit of YHWH is the prophet himself.

These characteristics of the protagonist of 11Q13 ii 15-21 indicate that he must be considered as a prophetic figure[21]. The task of this prophet is twofold. He will instruct and comfort the people by announcing salvation. In the same time, he will be the herald of Melchizedek: the message attributed to the מבשר in Isa 52,7 seems to be applied to Melchizedek in the fragmentary lines 11Q13 ii 23-25.

We have thus an eschatological prophetic figure, an anointed one, whose most proper title is the "messenger". In my view, the complex entirety of these characteristics indicates that this eschatological figure is Moses *redivivus*. Although we find various eschatological prophetic figures in the Qumran Library, and the title מבשר refers in certain instances also to different figures, only one personage bears both of these titles at the same time: Moses. In 4Q377 he is the messenger *par excellence* (מי מבש]ר [כמוהו, 4Q377 2 ii 11) and he is also anointed of God (*ibid.* line 5). We find no such coincidence of these titles and functions related to another figure in the Qumran Library[22].

11Q13 retains the view that the eschatological prophet will serve as a precursor or herald. Yet, the author of this text develops the issue in an important way: 11Q13 specifies the message of the herald. Line ii 20 of the text states:

20. See M.P. MILLER, *The Function of Isa 61,1-2 in 11 Q Melchisedek*, in *JBL* 88 (1969) 467-469; J.A. SANDERS, *The Old Testament in 11Q Melchizedek*, in *JANES* 5 (1973) 373-382; ID., *From Isaiah 61 to Luke 4*, in J. NEUSNER (ed.), *Christianity, Judaism and Other Greco-Roman Cults. Studies for Morton Smith at Sixty* (SJLA, 12), Leiden, Brill, 1975, pp. 75-106, esp. 89-92; J.J. COLLINS, *A Herald of Good Tidings. Isaiah 61:1-3 and its Actualization in the Dead Sea Scrolls*, in C.A. EVANS and Sh. TALMON (eds.), *The Quest for Context and Meaning. Studies in Biblical Intertextuality in Honor of James A. Sanders* (BIS, 28), Leiden, Brill, 1997, pp. 225-240, esp. 229-231.

21. Regarding the prophetic identification of the messenger of 11QMelchizedek, only one problem emerges, the insertion of a citation from the Book of Daniel in 11QMelch ii 18. The citation is not actually preserved, however, from the preserved context it is clear that it referred to the messenger, anointed of the spirit. We can most naturally conjecture that one of those Danielic passages that contain the word משיח was cited here (Dan 9,25 and 26). Yet, none of these passages refer to a prophetic figure. Nevertheless, Dan 9,25bβ – which was probably the biblical citation in the lacuna – without its context seems to be sufficiently vague to be interpreted as referring to the future anointed messenger.

22. We can add to this, that the very name of Moses also occurs in 11Q*Melchizedek*, although in an extremely fragmentary manner, without any context, in line i 12. In this case however, the lack of context does not allow anything certain to be said about the interpretation of this reading. Cf. DJD, 23 pp. 224; PUECH, *11QMelkîsédeq* (n. 16), p. 492.

לנח]ם ה]אבלים פשרו ל[ה]שכילמה בכול קצי העו[לם

"To comfo[rt] the [afflicted", its interpretation:] to instruct them in all the ages of the wo[rld …][23]

First, this line links Isa 61,2b (לנחם כל־אבלים) to the figure. According to this, his message consists of comforting the people of God during the turbulent events of the eschatological age. Second, the author interprets the לנחם of the biblical passage as ל[ה]שכילמה. This interpretation is important for the present perspective.

The verb שכל, especially its *Hip'îl* form belongs to the realm of sapiential language. As regards of its Hebrew Bible occurrences, the majority is provided by sapiential books: Psalms, Job and Proverbs; then by Daniel and the Chronicler. The Qumran Library uses the *Hip'îl* forms of the root שכל frequently. In finite or infinite forms, we find the word in some basic texts of the Community. It occurs in 1QS, 1QSb, 1QH. It forms part of the vocabulary of 4QInstruction, Damascus Document, the Shirot 'olat hashabbat; and 4Q381 and 4Q525 also provide several examples.

In interpreting the ל[ה]שכילמה of 11QMelchizedek, we wish to call the attention to two different works of the Hebrew Bible.

Two Traditions behind This Figure

The treatment of the eschatological prophet in 11QMelchizedek is dominated by quotations from the prophet Isaiah. The author quotes immediately at the beginning of the passage Isa 52,7 (11Q13 ii 15-16), then Isa 61,2b. In this light, we can assume that the ל[ה]שכילמה of 11Q13 ii 20 may also have Isaianic connections, and we may naturally recall Isa 52,13, where the servant of YHWH is told to ישכיל. In that context, this verb opens an independent textual unit, and appears as one characterising the overall activity of the servant. In the context of 11QMelchizedek, this Isaianic allusion may strengthen the prophetic character of the treated eschatological figure.

On the other hand, we can find another scriptural background for the ל[ה]שכילמה of 11QMelchizedek. We may underline the importance of the book of Daniel for the perspective of 11QMelchizedek. The overall tone of the Qumranic work strongly reminds the theology of – especially the Hebrew part of – Daniel. Moreover, within the treatment of the eschatological prophet, 11QMelchizedek's author once explicitly refers to Daniel[24].

23. The translation is taken from GARCÍA MARTÍNEZ, *Dead Sea Scrolls Translated* (n. 6.), p. 140.

24. כאשר אמר דנ]יאל, 11Q13 ii 18.

Daniel contains the *Hip'îl* participle of the root שכל. This word at least four times refers – as a technical term – to a particular group of contemporary Judaism[25]. Scholars generally consider these משכילים as a group of wisdom teachers, whose literary activity may be reflected by the book of Daniel itself[26]. In Daniel, we do not have explicit indication about the content and nature of the teaching of the משכילים, yet we may specify it from two directions. Their teaching might contain apocalyptic themes[27]. But, on the other hand, we may admit that the Danielic משכילים, "wise teachers" are best to be placed within a sapiential tradition, which primary interest was to instruct their addressees on how to survive – and perhaps succeed in – the actual hard political and religious situation[28].

If this connection between the משכילים of Daniel and the eschatological prophet-instructor of 11QMelchizedek can really be supposed, then the author of the Qumranic text seems to specify the teaching of the biblical book. In Daniel, the משכילים are told to instruct, but the precise content of this instruction remains in silence. 11Q13 ii 20 reads ל[ה]שכילמה בכול קצי העו]לם. Seeing that the author deals with a figure expected to arrive in the future, the complement בכול קצי העו]לם is not a temporal complement, but denotes the object of the instruction. Note that this composite expression is a recurrent phrase of 4QInstruction.

5. Conclusion

Those writings of the Qumran Library that devote more detail to the presentation of the eschatological prophet develop their material by using two characteristic traditions. Besides the used apocalyptic language,

25. Dan 11,33.35; 12,3.10. To this, add Dan 1,4, where the participle is used in a general meaning, but obviously with reference to its technical sense.

26. "[I]t is likely that there is some form of social continuity between the tradents of the tales and the authors of the visions. In chap. 1 Daniel and his companions are said to be *maskilim* in all wisdom. In chap. 11 the heroes in the time of persecution are also called *maskilim* 'wise teachers.' There is widespread agreement that the author (or authors) of the visions belonged to this group". J.J. Collins, *Daniel, Book of*, in *The Anchor Bible Dictionary*, New York, Doubleday, 1992.

27. "[T]he term denotes the apocalyptic teachers, who were instructing the ordinary people in the mysteries of the present and the future". R. Albertz, *The Social Setting of the Aramaic and Hebrew Book of Daniel*, in J.J. Collins and P.W. Flint (eds.), *The Book of Daniel. Composition and Reception* (VTS, 83; FIOTL, 2), Leiden, Brill, 2001, 1, p. 193. Or see Collins, *Daniel* (n. 26.): "It is reasonable to assume that [their instruction] corresponded to the apocalyptic revelations of the book of Daniel itself".

28. Collins, *Daniel* (n. 26.): "The common designation *maskilim* may reflect continuity with the mantic wise men of the tales", followed by Albertz, *Social Setting*, "[T]hey could resist all the temptations of the religious crisis and attain righteousness in the Last Judgement".

the authors of 4Q521 and 11Q13 show similarity in presenting the eschatological prophet as one instructing his addressees. 11Q13 seems explicitly specifying the figure of this eschatological prophet as one connected somehow with the משכילים, and, on the other hand, his message as including such – metaphysical – entities that are characteristic to the thinking of 4QInstruction.

Theological Academy
of the Reformed Church
Március 15. tér 9
H-8500 Pápa
Hungary

Géza G. XERAVITS

THE BOOK OF ENOCH IN THE LIGHT OF THE QUMRAN WISDOM LITERATURE

I

The Book of Watchers is now regarded as the earliest apocalypse that we possess, and the Book of Enoch as a whole as a prime example of the apocalyptic genre, a major source for our understanding of apocalypticism. The apocalyptic genre is, of course, traditionally regarded as representing a continuation of prophecy, and the Book of Enoch does make use of prophetic genres in a variety of ways. It is also of interest to note that the quotation of 1,9 in Jude 14-15 is introduced by the statement that Enoch "prophesied" about the heretics condemned by Jude, and that in Ethiopian tradition of a much later age Enoch is called the first of the prophets. But in the Book of Enoch itself, Enoch is described as a scribe and a wise man, and his writings as the source of wisdom, and although the book cannot in any sense be regarded as a conventional wisdom book, this inevitably raises the question of the relationship of the book to "wisdom" and the wisdom literature. Within the last decade Randall Argall and Ben Wright have attempted to answer this question by comparing 1 Enoch with Sirach. Thus in a recent monograph, *1 Enoch and Sirach: A Comparative Literary and Conceptual Analysis of the Themes of Revelation, Creation and Judgment*, Argall argued that there are similarities in the way 1 Enoch and Sirach treat the themes of revelation, creation, and judgment, and "that their respective views were formulated, at least in part, over against one another"[1]. Ben Wright has taken views like this further and has argued that Ben Sira actively took the side of the temple priests in polemical opposition against those, such as the authors of the Book of Watchers, who criticized them[2]. He, like Argall, has drawn attention to a number of passages in Sirach that he believes were directly aimed at the views represented in 1 Enoch, such as Sirach 34,1-8 or 3,21-24,

1. R.A. ARGALL, *1 Enoch and Sirach: A Comparative Literary and Conceptual Analysis of the Themes of Revelation, Creation and Judgment* (SBL Early Judaism and Its Literature, 8), Atlanta, GA, Scholars Press, 1995, p. 8.

2. B.G. WRIGHT, *"Fear the Lord and Honor the Priest". Ben Sira as Defender of the Jerusalem Priesthood*, in P.C. BEENTJES (ed.), *The Book of Ben Sira in Modern Research* (BZAW, 255), Berlin and New York, W. de Gruyter, 1997, pp. 189-222.

> Neither seek what is too difficult for you,
> nor investigate what is beyond your power.
> Reflect upon what you have been commanded,
> for what is hidden is not your concern.
> Do not meddle in matters that are beyond you,
> for more than you can understand has been shown you.
> For their conceit has led many astray,
> and wrong opinion has impaired their judgement (Sir 3,21-24, NRSV).

Boccacini has similarly spoken of a "bitter debate" being reflected in Sirach against the Apocalyptic movement[3]. It may be thought, however, that this is only part of the answer.

Since the work of von Rad[4] and, subsequently, of Müller[5], the apocalyptic genre has frequently been regarded as having its roots in mantic wisdom. In relation to the Book of Enoch, VanderKam in particular has drawn attention to parallels between the Enochic traditions and the mantic traditions of Mesopotamia. In the light of the widely accepted view that the figure of Enoch incorporates features associated with Enmeduranki of Sippar, who was initiated into the secret of the gods and was the founder of the guild of diviners (the *baru*), VanderKam argued that this hardly represented an independent development[6]. However Andreas Bedenbender has argued that although the figure of Enoch has been influenced by the traditions associated with Enmeduranki, in the case of Enoch – just as in Daniel – there is no clear resemblance to mantic wisdom. He claimed that VanderKam's analysis of the technique of the mantic sages in Babylon showed more differences than common features with Jewish apocalypticism, and he played down any connection between Babylonian mantic texts and the Jewish apocalyptic texts[7]. It is certainly right that the connection between mantic wisdom and

3. G. BOCCACCINI, *Middle Judaism: Jewish Thought, 300 B.C.E. to 200 C.E.*, Minneapolis, MN, Fortress Press, 1991, 77-125 (here p. 80). VanderKam's comment, "Ben Sira manifests a certain restraint about Enoch", perhaps better reflects the relationship between Sirach and the Book of Enoch: *Enoch, A Man for All Generations* (Studies on Personalities of the Old Testament), Columbia, SC, University of South Carolina Press, 1995, p. 107.

4. G. VON RAD, *Theologie des Alten Testaments*, Band 2, *Die Theologie der prophetischen Überlieferungen Israels*, München, Kaiser Verlag, 1960; ^{9}1987, pp. 316-338.

5. H.-P. MÜLLER, *Mantische Weisheit und Apokalyptik*, in *Congress Volume, Uppsala, 1971* (SVT, 22), Leiden, Brill, 1972, pp. 268-293.

6. J.C. VANDERKAM, *Enoch and the Growth of an Apocalyptic Tradition* (CBQMS, 16), Washington, DC, Catholic Biblical Association of America, 1995, pp. 6-8, 52-75, p. 70.

7. A. BEDENBENDER, *Jewish Apocalypticism: A Child of Mantic Wisdom?*, in *Henoch* 24 (2002) 189-196..

apocalypticism should not be overstated, and it is true that Enoch himself does not function as a mantic. But Bedenbender perhaps fails to take sufficient account of the fact that von Rad's concern was with the traditio-historical *background* of apocalyptic, and from that perspective it seems clear that mantic wisdom lies in the background of both Daniel and 1 Enoch. At the end of his paper Bedenbender expressed his support for the term "revealed wisdom", earlier proposed by Argall[8], as a better designation than "mantic wisdom" both for Enochic wisdom and for Jewish apocalypticism in general. In his recently published commentary, George Nickelsburg has similarly described 1 Enoch as embodying "divinely revealed wisdom about the workings of the cosmos and the course and end of history"[9], and this is certainly a helpful way of categorizing the book. But the difference between 1 Enoch and the wisdom writings familiar from the Hebrew Bible and the Apocrypha nonetheless remains.

The question of the relationship between Enochic wisdom and Jewish wisdom in general, between the book and the Jewish wisdom literature, has been put in a new perspective by the publication, in its entirety, of the Qumran wisdom literature. There are a number of texts within this corpus – I think particularly of 4QMysteries and 4QInstruction – that would seem to have direct relevance to the categorization of Enochic wisdom as "divinely revealed wisdom", but though mentioned by Nickelsburg in his commentary, they were perhaps not exploited by him as much as they might have been. My intention in what follows is the fairly simple one of considering the relevance of this material for our understanding of the Book of Enoch. I propose, firstly, to summarise briefly the evidence, within 1 Enoch and in other texts, for the description of him as a scribe or wise man, and of his writings as a source of wisdom; secondly, to examine the kind of contribution the Qumran wisdom literature might make to our understanding of Enoch[10]; and, thirdly, to consider some of the wisdom aspects of the Book of Enoch.

8. ARGALL, *1 Enoch and Sirach* (n. 1), p. 251.

9. G.W.E. NICKELSBURG, *1 Enoch 1. A Commentary on the Book of 1 Enoch, Chapters 1-36; 81-108* (Hermeneia), Minneapolis, MN, Fortress Press, 2001, p. 6 (similar comments appear throughout the commentary).

10. See now also L. STUCKENBRUCK, *4QInstruction and the Possible Influence of Early Enochic Traditions: An Evaluation*, in C. HEMPEL, A. LANGE, H. LICHTENBERGER (eds.), *The Wisdom Texts from Qumran and the Development of Sapiential Thought* (BETL, 159), Leuven, Peeters, pp. 245-261.

11. Cf. NICKELSBURG, *1 Enoch* (n. 9), pp. 65-67.

II

We should no doubt be cautious in making any simple transference between the formal titles given to Enoch and what is said of his role, on the one hand, and the real situation of the authors of the book, on the other, but nonetheless it is hard to believe that there is no connection between the two[11]. The only title given to Enoch is "scribe", but this does fit the character of the book. Thus Enoch is described as "scribe of righteousness" (ὁ γραμματεὺς τῆς δικαιοσύνης, 12,4) or "scribe of truth" (γραμματεὺς τῆς ἀληθείας, 15,1) – in both cases rendered in Ethiopic as "scribe of righteousness" (*ṣaḥafe ṣedeq*), and it has been thought that this designation goes back to an Aramaic original ספר קושטא. In the Book of Giants Enoch is several times given the related title ספר פרשא, (4Q203 8 4; 4Q206 2 2[12]; 4Q530 2 ii + 6 + 7 i + 8-12(?) 14[13]), perhaps best translated with Puech as "scribe of discernment"[14]. He is also described as "the wisest of men" (ח[כים אנושא, 4QEn^{g} 1 ii 23[15]) in the heading, of which only a small part has survived in Aramaic, in 1 En 92,1. The Ethiopic has a paraphrastic text and the manuscript evidence is unclear, but it appears that in the original Ethiopic text here again he was called "scribe".

In a similar way a number of headings in the Book of Enoch use wisdom terminology to describe the revelation given by Enoch, although with some differences from the wisdom writings. In chapter 37 Enoch describes the Parables that follow as a "vision of wisdom" and as "words of wisdom" (vv. 1-2). The call to attention in v. 2 is reminiscent of the frequent calls to attention that occur in wisdom literature (e.g. Prov 1,8; 4,1; Sir 6,23), but is addressed to the "men of old" and the "men of latter days", not the wisdom teacher's son. Again the phrase "the beginning of wisdom" in v. 3 is familiar from the wisdom literature, but is used here in reference to Enoch's words, not the attitude expressed in the phrase "the fear of the Lord" (see e.g. Prov 9,10; Sir 1,14). Finally Enoch states that no one before him had been given wisdom comparable to that which he had received from the Lord of Spirits (v. 4). In 82,2-3, in a testamentary context between the Astronomical

12. L. STUCKENBRUCK, *4QEnochGiants^{a} ar*, in S.J. PFANN, P. ALEXANDER, *et al.* (eds.), *Qumran Cave 4.XXVI, Cryptic Texts and Miscellanea, Part 1* (DJD, 36), Oxford, Clarendon Press, 2000, pp. 28, 44.

13. É. PUECH, *Qumrân Grotte 4.XXII, Textes araméens, Première partie, 4Q529-549* (DJD, 31), Oxford, Clarendon Press, 2001, p. 28.

14. *Ibid.*, p. 35.

15. J.T. MILIK, *The Books of Enoch, Aramaic Fragments of Qumrân Cave 4*, Oxford, Clarendon Press, 1976, p. 260.

Book and the Book of Dreams, Enoch tells Methuselah that he has given him and his children wisdom to pass on to future generations, and in v. 3 he describes this wisdom in words whose imagery may be compared with that of Sir 24,20-21:

> And those who understand it will not sleep, but will incline their ears that they may learn this wisdom, and it will be better for those who eat (from it) than good food (1 En. 82,3).
> For the memory of me is sweeter than honey,
> And the possession of me sweeter than the honeycomb.
> Those who eat of me will hunger for more,
> And those who drink of me will thirst for more (Sir 24,20-21, NRSV).

Reference may also be made to the heading in 92,1, already mentioned, of which only a small part has survived in Aramaic, but enough to recognize that in this Enoch himself is described as wise; according to the paraphrastic Ethiopic his teaching is described as wisdom.

Writings more or less contemporary with the Book of Enoch provide further support for the description of Enoch as a scribe, and his writing as the embodiment of wisdom. In Jub 4,17-25, a passage that represents perhaps the oldest stage in the reception-history of the writings attributed to Enoch, and one that is frequently used in an attempt to determine which sections of the Enochic corpus were in existence by the time Jubilees was written, Enoch is described as "the first of mankind who were born on the earth who learned (the art of) writing, instruction, and wisdom"[16]. All three are of significance within the present context. The tradition that Enoch's writings were a source of wisdom reinforces the headings that occur in 1 Enoch itself and is further reflected in 1QapGen XIX 24-25, where, in a passage referring to the visit of the Egyptian princes to Abraham, it is said, "They gave [me many presents expecting from me] goodness, wisdom and truth. I read in front of them the [book] of the words of Enoch"[17].

Enoch's role in teaching is explicitly mentioned in 1 En 81,6, where the angels bring Enoch back to earth and say to him:

> For one year we will leave you with your children, until (there is) a command again[18], that you may teach your children, and write (these things) down for them, and testify to all your children.

16. All passages from Jubilees quoted from J.C. VANDERKAM, *The Book of Jubilees* (CSCO, 511), Leuven, Peeters, 1989.

17. Translation from F. GARCÍA MARTÍNEZ and E.J.C. TIGCHELAAR, *The Dead Sea Scrolls Study Edition: Volume One, 1Q1-4Q273; Volume Two, 4Q274-11Q31*, Leiden, Brill, 1997, 1998, vol. 1, p. 41.

18. So British Library Orient. 485 EMML 1768. Other manuscripts representative of the older type of text have a similar reading.

But this role is implicit in the testamentary situation that is reflected in such passages as 82,1-2; 83,1; 91,1-3; 94,1.

Jubilees 4 also states that Enoch was the first who learnt the art of writing (v. 17) and further that he was the first to write a testimony (v. 18, cf. v.19). Writing is consistent with his role as "scribe". It is again mentioned in connection with him in v. 21 ("he wrote down everything") and v. 23 ("he is there (sc. in the garden of Eden) writing down the judgment and condemnation of the world and all the wickedness of mankind"). Writing is also mentioned frequently in the Book of Enoch in relation to Enoch. His first vision is dated to the time he "learnt the art of writing" (83,2; in contrast in 69,9 it is said that the angel Penemu'e taught men the art of writing. Enoch writes out the petition of the watchers (13,4. 6), but is also said to have written down what he had been shown (74,2; 82,1) and to have written down his prayer (83,10). Books or writings are attributed to Enoch in 14,1; 92,1; 108,1. The description of Enoch as one who wrote and testified occurs elsewhere in 4QPseudo-Jubilees^{c} 1 3-4, in a passage referring to Enoch:

> [... of the ea]rth, among the sons of men, and he testified against them all [ ] and also against the Watchers and he wrote everything[19].

However, alongside the attribution of the title "scribe" to Enoch, and the description of him and his writings in wisdom terms, there has to be set the depiction of him as a seer, and it is worth noting that "to see" is one of the most frequently used verbs in the Ethiopic Book of Enoch. The Book of Watchers describes his ascent to the presence of God (chapter 14), and in the further elaboration of this vision he not only is shown the place where God will descend for judgment, and the places where the wicked will be punished and the righteous enjoy eternal bliss, but also is conducted on a journey around the cosmos and sees everything. The Parables likewise describe Enoch's ascent to heaven (39,3), where, in a series of tableaux, he sees the judgement of the Son of Man being played out before him. In the Astronomical Book, according to the Ethiopic, he sees astronomical and cosmological phenomena, including the laws of the sun and the moon. Similarly in the Book of Dreams Enoch is depicted as seeing visions. According to Jub. 4,17-25, Enoch not only "wrote down in a book the signs of the sky" for the benefit of mankind, but also "saw in a vision what has happened and what will occur", and, while with the angels for six jubilees of years, was shown "everything on earth and in the heavens".

19. Translation from GARCÍA MARTÍNEZ – TIGCHELAAR, *The Dead Sea Scrolls Study Edition* (n. 17), vol. 1, p. 483.

The picture that thus emerges of Enoch, both from 1 Enoch and from writings belonging to the wider circle of Enochic writings, is of Enoch as a learned man, a scribe, an individual known for his wisdom and knowledge – but also as an individual who experienced an ascent to the presence of God, was conducted around the cosmos, and saw everything, and whose knowledge not only related to the themes of judgment and salvation, but also covered cosmological and astronomical matters. And it remains the case that, notwithstanding the description of Enoch as a scribe, the Book of Enoch is quite different in character from the books that have traditionally been regarded as belonging to the wisdom category.

III

The question of the relationship of the Book of Enoch, and of the apocalypses in general, to the wisdom literature has, however, been put in a new perspective by the publication, primarily in DJD 20 and 34, of the entire corpus of wisdom writings from Qumran. These writings have not only shown that Jewish wisdom literature of the Second Temple period was much more variegated than might have been suspected from the wisdom writings of the Hebrew Bible and the Apocrypha, but also, as largely pre-sectarian in origin, provided evidence of the pre-history of beliefs that appear in sectarian form in texts such as the passage on the Two Spirits in the Rule of the Community. Helpful surveys of the corpus have been provided by Daniel Harrington[20] and John Collins[21]. Here my intention is to focus on only two of these writings, 4QMysteries (1Q27, 4Q299-300[22]) and 4QInstruction (1Q26, 4Q415ff[23]), which have been seen to have particular relevance to the apocalyptic literature, and to concentrate on the themes of revelation and the content of the revelation. Amongst the numerous publications on these two writings, refer-

20. D.J. HARRINGTON, *Wisdom Texts from Qumran* (The Literature of the Dead Sea Scrolls), London and New York, Routledge, 1996.

21. J.J. COLLINS, *Jewish Wisdom in the Hellenistic Age*, Louisville, KY, Westminster John Knox Press, 1997, pp. 112-131.

22. J.T. MILIK, *Livre des Mystères*, in D. BARTHÉLEMY and J.T. MILIK (eds.), *Qumran Cave 1* (DJD, 1), Oxford, Clarendon Press, 1955, pp. 102-107; L. SCHIFFMAN, *Mysteries*, in T. ELGVIN *et al.* (eds.), *Qumran Cave 4.XV, Sapiential Texts, Part 1* (DJD, 20), Oxford, Clarendon Press, 1997, pp. 31-123.

23. MILIK, *Un Apocryphe*, in *Qumran Cave 1* (n. 22), pp. 101-102; J. STRUGNELL and D.J. HARRINGTON (eds.), *Qumran Cave 4.XXIV, Sapiential Texts, Part 2, 4QInstruction (Mûsar LeMebîn: 4Q415ff.)* (DJD, 34), Oxford, Clarendon Press, 1999.

ence should be made not only to the DJD editions, but also to the studies of Elgvin[24] and Lange[25].

4QMysteries and 4QInstruction are not apocalyptic writings, and their relevance to the Book of Enoch lies primarily in the theological ideas that undergird the wisdom teaching they contain. Within 4QMysteries, it is perhaps what is said in relation to the concept of revelation that is of greatest interest, and a number of passages bear on this topic. In one of these, which is represented by 4Q300 1a ii-b and 4Q299 3c[26] and has significant parallels in the Book of Daniel, the magicians (החר[טמים, cf. Dan 1,20; 2,2) are challenged to tell in advance the hidden meaning of the parable to show whether they have understood "the signs of the heav[ens", but it is made clear that they cannot do this. The vision is sealed up from them (חתום מכם]ח[תם החזון, cf. Dan 9,24), and even if they did open it, it would be kept secret from them. The reason for this is because they "have not considered the eternal mysteries (רזי עד)" and "have not come to understand wisdom (ובבינה לא השכלתם, cf. Dan 9, 22)", and because they "have not considered the root of wisdom (שורש חוכמה)". The links with Daniel, particularly 9,22.24, suggest that what is at issue here is the true meaning of prophecy ("the vision"), as Schiffman indicates[27], and that those addressed are being accused of having no understanding of this. But it is also of interest here that the vision is linked with the concept of the eternal mysteries and with wisdom. In contrast to the true wisdom, the wisdom of the magicians is useless.

The concepts of wisdom and of mystery also appear in a key passage that has survived in fragmentary form in 1Q27 1 i, 4Q299 1, and 4Q300 3[28]. According to this passage, man was given wisdom in order that he might understand the difference between good and evil, but despite this, men failed to understand the רז נהיה, "the mystery of that which was coming into being"[29], or "the mystery that is to come"[30], or "the mystery of existence"[31] – to mention only three of the possible translations

24. T. Elgvin, *The Mystery to Come: Early Essene Theology of Revelation*, in F.H. Cryer and T.L. Thompson (eds.), *Qumran between the Old and New Testaments* (JSOT SS, 290), Sheffield, Sheffield Academic Press, 1998, pp. 113-150.

25. A. Lange, *Weisheit und Prädestination. Weisheitliche Urordnung und Prädestination in den Textfunden von Qumran* (STDJ, 18), Leiden, Brill, 1995.

26. For the texts, see Schiffman, in *Qumran Cave 4.XV* (n. 22), pp. 43-44, 100-103.

27. Schiffman, in *Qumran Cave 4.XV* (n. 22), pp. 102.

28. For the texts, see Milik, in *Qumran Cave* 1 (n. 22), pp. 103-105; Schiffman, in *Qumran Cave 4.XV* (n. 22), pp. 34-38, 105-106.

29. Schiffman, in *Qumran Cave 4.XV* (n. 22), pp. 36-37, 105.

30. Elgvin, *The Mystery to Come* (n. 24), pp. 131-136.

31. García Martínez – Tigchelaar, *The Dead Sea Scrolls Study Edition* (n. 17), vol. 2, e.g. pp. 663, 859. Cf. Lange, *Weisheit und Prädestination* (n. 25), pp. 50-52, 62-63; Id., *Wisdom and Predestination in the Dead Sea Scrolls*, in *DSD* 2 (1995) 340-354, pp. 341-343 and n. 4: "das Geheimnis des Werdens", "the mystery of becoming".

that have been offered. The words immediately following ("the former things (קדמוניות) they did not consider, nor did they know what shall befall them (מה אשר יבוא עליהם), and they did not save their lives from the רז נהיה") give some indication of what the author understood by the רז נהיה, namely understanding of both past and future – the contrast calls to mind Isa 41,22. The passage goes on to describe the sign that the end was imminent, and to describe the judgment itself, and thus makes clear that knowledge concerning the end is included in the רז נהיה. The theme of the final judgement recurs in a number of other fragments (e.g. 4Q299 53, 55, 56, 59), all unfortunately too small for much to be made of them.

In another passage related to the above (4Q299 3a ii-b, 4Q300 5(?)[32]), a contrast is drawn between the wisdom of the wicked, which is used only for evil purposes, and the knowledge of the creator. God is presented as the one who knows every mystery and predestines everything. The mysteries of creation form the theme of two other fragments, 4Q299 5 and 6 i-ii[33] (the phrase רזי אור occurs in 4Q299 5 2), and this suggests that the theme of creation also formed part of the רז נהיה.

If mankind in general has failed to make use of the wisdom given to it by God, and if the wisdom of the magicians is of no use, nonetheless, according to 4Q299 8[34], wisdom is still available to some, described as "those whose pursue knowledge" whose ear God has opened. The author contrasts the position of mankind without understanding with that of the group that he represents. Only part of the text survives, but enough is preserved to indicate that this was part of God's predetermined plan:

>] he distributed their insight [
>]
>]
>] And how can a ma[n] understand who did not know and did not hear [
> [under]standing he formed for …; by (his) great insight he opened our ears so that
> we[
>]He formed understanding for all who pursue knowledge, and [
>] all insight is from eternity; it will not be changed (*or* He will not change)[[35]

Here knowledge is revealed by God, it is not the outcome of observation and experience, as in traditional wisdom. Whether, however, the

32. For the texts, see SCHIFFMAN, in *Qumran Cave 4.XV* (n. 22), pp. 41-43, 107.

33. *Ibid.*, pp. 44-48.

34. *Ibid.*, pp. 50-51.

35. 4Q299 8 2-8; translation adapted from GARCÍA MARTÍNEZ – TIGCHELAAR, *The Dead Sea Scrolls Study Edition* (n. 17), vol. 2, p. 661.

appeal to "special revelation" is evidence that 4QMysteries originated in a sectarian milieu, as John Collins suggests seems to me doubtful[36].

The use of the phrase גלה אוזן in 4Q299 8 6 provides an appropriate link to 4QInstruction, where it is attested in the surviving fragments six times[37] – in all cases linked with רז נהיה. Much has been written about this important document, and I confine myself to what is essential for present purposes.

First, it is of importance that the document begins with a statement (4Q416 1[38]) that describes first God's ordering of the cosmos, and then the judgement of wickedness and the reward of the faithful. It provides, as the editors observe, "a theological framework of cosmology and judgement for the wisdom instructions that follow"[39]. The theme of eschatological judgement and reward recurs throughout the document (cf. e.g. 4Q416 3; 4Q417 1 i 6-8, 13c-15a; 2 i 15-17a; 4Q418 69; 4Q418 126 ii).

Second, the concept of revelation is also of considerable importance within the document. This is frequently, but not exclusively, linked to the theme of the רז נהיה, which is mentioned more than thirty times in the surviving fragments. References to this theme are often introduced by commands to those being addressed to "gaze upon" (הבט, e.g. 4Q416 2 i 4-5 = 4Q417 2 i 10-11) or "study" (דרוש, e.g. 4Q416 2 iii 9) or "grasp" (קח, e.g. 4Q418 77 4) or "meditate on" (הגה, e.g. 4Q418 43-45 i 4) the רז נהיה, and, as the editors point out[40], the passages that occur in parallel help to clarify the meaning of the phrase. From these it is apparent that the רז נהיה includes knowledge of past, present, and future (4Q418 123 i-ii 3-4), understanding of the present order of the world ("the ways of truth ... all the roots of iniquity"; 4Q416 2 iii 14), and knowledge concerning the future judgement (4Q217 2 i 10c-11). But the רז נהיה is also that by which God "laid out" (or perhaps "expounded", פרש) the foundation of truth (4Q417 i 1 9). Elgvin concludes that the רז נהיה "is a comprehensive word for God's mysterious plan for creation and history, his plan for man and for redemption of the elect", and he is surely right in seeing its background in speculation concerning חכמה (cf. Prov 8,22-31; Job 28; Sir 24)[41]. Schiffman, in relation to 4QMysteries,

36. COLLINS, *Jewish Wisdom in the Hellenistic Age* (n. 21), p. 128.

37. 1Q26 1 4; 4Q416 2 iii 17-18; 4Q418 10a-b 1; 123 ii 4; 184 2; 190 2; cf. 4Q423 5 1.

38. For the text, see STRUGNELL – HARRINGTON (eds.), *Qumran Cave 4.XXIV* (n. 23), pp. 81-88.

39. *Ibid.*, p. 8.

40. *Ibid.*, pp. 32-33; cf. ELGVIN, *The Mystery to Come* (n. 24), pp. 131-136.

41. ELGVIN, *The Mystery to Come* (n. 24), pp. 135-136.

summed up the meaning of "mysteries" (רזים) in that composition as follows: "it refers to the mysteries of creation, i.e. the natural order of things which depends on God's wisdom, and to the mysteries of the divine role in the processes of history"[42].

It is significant also in 4QInstruction that it is God who uncovers the ears of men to the רז נהיה (e.g. 4Q418 123 ii 4; 4Q418 184 2[43]), and within these passages wisdom is revealed, not acquired by experience. But in 4Q417 1 i 14-18[44] revelation is apparently linked with two written documents, a writing engraved by God condemning the wicked and a "book of remembrance" of those who keep his word (lines 15-16a). It is not quite clear whether the writing "engraved by God" (cf. Exod 32,16) is to be identified with the Mosaic Torah, as has been suggested, but the reference to the "book of remembrance" represents an obvious allusion to Mal 3,16 and there is perhaps here the idea that knowledge of the רז נהיה is linked to the understanding of scripture[45]. The text continues with the obscure statement: "it is the vision of meditation (חזון ההגו) on (ל) the book of remembrance" (line 16). The "vision of meditation" inevitably calls to mind the "book of meditation" (ספר ההגו/י) that is mentioned elsewhere (1Q28a i 6-7; CD X 6; XIII 2; XIV 7-8). The identification of the "book of meditation", whether as the Torah or as a sectarian document, is itself disputed. In the present passage it is not clear whether the use of "vision" rather than "book" is significant; whether the vision is to be understood as some kind of written document; and if so, whether it can be identified with any particular writing[46]. But the reference to the "vision of meditation" perhaps suggests that revelation is linked to the understanding of scripture.

The relevance of this material to the Book of Enoch as a whole hardly needs to be spelled out. The theme of judgement, which is included within the perspective of 4QMysteries and provides a theological frame-

42. SCHIFFMAN, in *Qumran Cave 4.XV* (n. 22), p. 31.

43. See the full list of passages in n. 37. STRUGNELL – HARRINGTON (eds.), *Qumran Cave 4.XXIV* (n. 23), p. 122, have questioned whether God is the subject of גלה און in 4Q416 2 iii 17-18 = 4Q418 10a-b 1, but it seems to me likely that God is the subject here also.

44. For the text and a very detailed and helpful discussion, see STRUGNELL – HARRINGTON (eds.), *Qumran Cave 4.XXIV* (n. 23), pp. 151-155, 160-166. I confine myself in discussion of this important and difficult passage to what is essential for the purposes of this paper.

45. Cf. ELGVIN, *The Mystery to Come* (n. 24), p. 145.

46. For the interpretation of 4Q417 1 i 14-18, cf. e.g. LANGE, *Weisheit und Prädestination* (n. 25), pp. 50-55, 66-90; ID., *Wisdom and Predestination* (n. 31), pp. 342-343; COLLINS, *Jewish Wisdom in the Hellenistic Age* (n. 21), pp. 123-325; ELGVIN, *The Mystery to Come* (n. 24), pp. 139-347.

work for the wisdom instruction in 4QInstruction, forms the leitmotif of 1 Enoch; it is announced in the prologue in chapter 1 and is constantly taken up in a variety of ways throughout the book. But perhaps of even greater relevance are the themes of knowledge of the mysteries and of the secrets. Enoch knows "the mysteries of the holy ones" (106,19, where the Aramaic attests the occurrence of the word רז; for the plural form one might compare the references to the "wondrous mysteries" (רזי פלא) of God in 4Q417 1 i 2, 13), just as he also knows "this mystery" (103,2; 104,10) – because he has been shown the mysteries by the Lord and has read the tablets of heaven. (In the Parables the Lord of Spirits is praised by the kings and the mighty as one whose secrets are deep and without number (63,3).) There are very frequent references to "the secrets" (*ḫebu'at*). The angel who accompanies Enoch shows him the secrets (40,2; 46,2; 71,3). Enoch sees both the secrets of the cosmos (41,1, 3; 59,1-3; 71,4) and the secrets relating to the end of this era (38,3; 58,5; 61,5; 83,7). Enoch in turn passes on to Noah "the teaching of all the secrets in a book" (68,1). In the Vision of the Animals Enoch is presented as the one who knows past and future, a point noted in Jub. 4,19a,: "While he slept he saw in a vision what has happened and what will occur – how things will happen for mankind during their history until the day of judgment". With this may be compared the comment made about mankind in 4QMysteries (1Q27 i 3-4), "But they did not know the mystery of that which was coming into being (רז נהוה), and the former things (קדמוניות) they did not consider. Nor did they know what shall befall them (מה אשר יבוא עליהמה)".

However, the differences between the wisdom writings and the Book of Enoch must also be recognised. Thus while cosmology and eschatology form part of the concerns of 4QMysteries and 4QInstruction, they find expression in a way quite different from that of Enoch. In the former cosmology and eschatology provide a theological underpinning for the wisdom instruction that seems to have been its main concern. In Enoch cosmology and eschatology are of primary importance and are built into the structure of the book. Again, while in the case of both 4QMysteries and 4QInstruction and in Enoch we can speak in terms of "revealed wisdom", and in both there is frequent reference to either the רז נהיה or to "mysteries" or "secrets", it is only in 1 Enoch that this concern finds concrete expression in reports of visions and of journeys through the heavenly regions and around the cosmos. One should perhaps speak of a shared thought-world that finds different expression in the two kinds of writings, and this is a point to which we must return later.

IV

If there are connections of the kind indicated with wisdom writings, it may be asked to what extent this finds expression within the Book of Enoch. From a literary point of view it is not of course a wisdom text, and it is prophetic genres that predominate in the book, although occasionally forms that occur in wisdom texts (e.g. the woe form) are used[47]. There are references to wisdom throughout the book, and though not particularly numerous, it is perhaps significant that they are present at all. Thus wisdom is depicted as a gift of the new age in the Book of Watchers (5,8; 32,3, 6) and in the Epistle (104,12; 105,1; cf. 99,10); in contrast the lack of wisdom is a characteristic of the pre-exilic period in the Apocalypse of Weeks (93,8), just as, according to the Epistle, sinners debase wisdom in the last age (94,5; 98,3). In the Parables, where in chapter 42 there is a wisdom poem, the spirit of wisdom dwells in the Son of Man (49,3; cf. 51,3; Isa 11,2). Wisdom will be poured out in the new age (48,1; 49,1) and will characterize the worship of the new age (61,7, 11). Elsewhere wisdom is seen as being possessed by God (63,2; 84,3) and given by him to his creatures (101,8).

In his article on 4QInstruction Elgvin has suggested that "apart from early sectarian writings, the books of Enoch seem to be the closest relative of 4QInstruction". He suggests that most parallels are found in the Book of Watchers and the Epistle and argues that terminological similarities indicate some kind of dependence – he thinks in fact that 4QInstruction is dependent on Enoch[48], and to this point we must return. His listing of parallels is helpful, but one point he makes in relation to the Apocalypse of Weeks seems questionable. Thus he suggests, quite properly, that the revelation of the רז נהיה may be compared with the sevenfold teaching given to the righteous as the present age reaches its climax (1 Enoch 93,10). But he seems to me to go beyond the evidence when he argues that the Epistle was a "main source" for the compiler of 4QInstruction, and that the רז נהיה is "identical" with the sevenfold instruction[49]. Equally he seems to me to go beyond the evidence in his suggestion that the (Book of) Hagi ("book of meditation") is to be identified with a part of the Enoch literature, the Apocalypse of Weeks and/or the Animal Apocalypse[50]. From a different point of view, a concern

47. For a recent survey of the literary forms used in 1 Enoch, see NICKELSBURG, *1 Enoch* (n. 9), pp. 28-35.

48. ELGVIN, *The Mystery to Come* (n. 24), pp. 116-118, cf. pp. 135-138.

49. *Ibid.*, p. 138.

50. *Ibid.*, pp. 146-147.

for the poor is one of the central issues in both 4QInstruction and the Epistle, although it finds very different expression in the two works[51].

Quite apart from the above, I would in the final part of this paper like to suggest that concerns with wisdom and knowledge are more deeply embedded in the Book of Watchers, and to consider how it might be read in this light. It is manifestly not a wisdom text in any conventional sense, but rather a narrative text concerned above all with sin and judgement, with problems of reconciling divine foreknowledge and human suffering. It begins by announcing the coming of God to judge the sinners and to bring salvation to the righteous. It traces the origins of sin to the activity of the angels, the Watchers, who came down from heaven in the days of Jared and it announces both their punishment and that of the sprits of their offspring, the Giants, which are seen to be responsible for the continuance of sin (15,8-16,1; slightly different in 19,1). The narrative includes an account of Enoch's ascent to heaven, where he is told of the fate of the Watchers (chapter 14), and the continuation of the narrative (chapters 17-36) then describes how Enoch was taken on a journey around the cosmos which culminated in his arrival at the Garden of Righteousness in the east which contains the tree of knowledge.

However, looking more closely at this, the narrative does have certain features that give the text a sapiential character and link with the themes we have been discussing. The first point to notice is that immediately after the prologue we have, in chapters 2-5, an admonition that has a sapiential character. The admonition contrasts the orderly behaviour of nature (2,1-5,4) with the disorderly behaviour of mankind, and this in turn leads back into the theme of judgement for the wicked and salvation for the righteous already announced in chapter 1 (5,5-9). The contrast between obedient nature and disobedient humanity forms a familiar theme in the Hebrew Bible, and in Jewish and Christian literature, and commentators have drawn attention to a number of comparable passages. Although not exclusive to wisdom literature, the order and regularity of nature is a familiar theme in wisdom, for example in Sir 43 or 16,24-28 – in the latter there is an implicit contrast in chapter 17 with the behaviour of man, as Nickelsburg indicates[52]. Nickelsburg also refers to Jer 5,20-29 where there is an explicit contrast comparable to that in Enoch. Somewhat differently reference might also be made to Isa 1,3 or

51. Cf. COLLINS, *Jewish Wisdom in the Hellenistic Age* (n. 21), pp. 118-119.

52. NICKELSBURG, *1 Enoch* (n. 9), p. 153; cf. ARGALL, *1 Enoch and Sirach* (n. 1), pp. 136-137. The parallels between Sir 16,24-28 and 17,1-14 were noted by L. ALONSO SCHÖKEL, *The Vision of Man in Sirach 16:24-17:14*, in J.G. GAMMIE *et al.* (eds.), *Israelite Wisdom: Theological and Literary Essays in Honor of Samuel Terrien*, Missoula, MT, 1978, pp. 235-245. For the contrast between the obedience of nature and the disobedience of sinners, see also 1 Enoch 101,6-7.8-9.

Jer 8,7, which show clear links with wisdom[53]. In Qumran sapiential literature, Bilhah Nitzan has listed 1 Enoch 1-5 as one of the texts that, like the Admonitory Parable (4Q302), makes use of the *rib* pattern[54], although in 4Q302 the *rib* is based, in part, on a parable rather than on observation of nature. One might also compare the repeated commands to the readers in 1 Enoch 2-5 to contemplate the wonders of nature with the commands in 4QInstruction to the בן מבין to contemplate the רז נהיה.

The sapiential admonition in 1 Enoch 1-5 provides a context for what follows in chapters 6-36[55]. Undergirding the narrative, and more particularly the story of the Watchers as it is finally presented in 1 Enoch 1-36, is the theme of the revelation of secrets and of true and false knowledge. As is well known, the story of the Watchers represents a conflation of two traditions. According to one, closely based on Gen. 6-9, in which Shemihazah is the leader, the angels descend because of their lust for the daughters of men; it is the offspring born to their unions, the Giants, who bring sin and violence into the world. According to the other, in which Asael is the leader, the angels descend in order to instruct mankind, and it is the knowledge that they bring that is the source of evil. Nickelsburg, in his recent commentary, is not the first who has attempted to divide these two traditions between two distinct sources on literary-critical grounds – in fact he thinks in terms of at least three layers in chapters 6-11[56], and I am not sure that it makes sense to do so. Be that as it may, the revelation of divine mysteries to mankind is emphasised as a major cause of the introduction of sin into the world. According to the summaries given in 7,1; 8,1, and particularly 8,3, the teaching was concerned with four main topics, magic, the arts of warfare, the means of beautifying the body for the purposes of sexual allurement, and astrology/astronomy, and these topics no doubt reflected contemporary concerns. But the teaching is presented as the revelation of mysteries that belonged in heaven. Thus according to the Aramaic and the Syncellus text of 8,3, the angels revealed the mysteries (רזין, τὰ μυστήρια) to their wives and their children. In their appeal to God on behalf of

53. Cf. H. WILDBERGER, *Jesaja*, 1. Teilband, *Jesaja 1-12* (BKAT, 10/1), Neukirchen, Neukirchener Verlag, 1972, pp. 14-15; D.R. JONES, *Jeremiah* (New Century Bible Commentary), Grand Rapids, MI, Eerdmans, 1992, pp. 158-159.

54. B. NITZAN, *Admonitory Parable*, in T. ELGVIN *et al.* (eds.), *Qumran Cave 4.XV, Sapiential Texts, Part 1* (DJD, 20), Oxford, Clarendon Press, 1997, pp. 125-149, esp. 126, 136.

55. Cf. L. HARTMAN, *Asking for a Meaning: A Study of 1 Enoch 1-5* (CB NT, 12), Lund, Gleerup, 1979, pp. 138-145, for the view that, as an introduction, 1 En 1-5 "gives an important clue to the understanding of the whole Book of Watchers".

56. NICKELSBURG, *1 Enoch* (n. 9), pp. 165, 171-172.

mankind (chapter 9), the four archangels state, "You see what Asael has done, who has taught all iniquities on the earth and has revealed the eternal mysteries (τὰ μυστήρια τοῦ αἰῶνος) which (were) in heaven, which men practise (and) know" (9,6). And in God's reply (chapters 10-11), the risk that all mankind will perish is attributed to the revelation of the mystery (τὸ μυστήριον) that the Watchers taught to their sons (10,7-8). (For this theme, cf. 65,6. 11; (68,2); (69,8).) The story comes to an initial climax in the message of judgement that Enoch is commissioned by God to deliver to the Watchers (16,3-4), which according to the Ethiopic reads as follows,

> You were in heaven, but (its) secrets (*ḫebu'at*) had not yet been revealed to you and a worthless mystery (*menuna mesṭira*) you knew. This you made known to the women in the hardness of your hearts, and through this mystery the women and the men cause evil to increase on the earth. Say to them therefore, You will not have peace.

The Greek of the first sentence is corrupt, but probably had "no mystery had been revealed to you, and a worthless mystery you knew"[57]. In any event it seems clear that the knowledge revealed by the watchers is condemned as being incomplete and worthless. Comparison might be drawn with the view expressed in 4QMysteries that the wisdom of the magicians is useless[58].

The story of the Watchers comes to an initial conclusion at this point, but the narrative continues in 17-19, without any introduction or explanation, by describing Enoch's journey to the edge of the world. There is a literary seam at this point, one of a number that are visible in the Book of Watchers, but the text as it is requires explanation. From a formal point of view, the narrative continues the description of the vision that Enoch experienced, which began in chapter 14 with the account of his ascent. But it seems that the narrative functions as a revelation of the true mysteries, in contrast to the worthless mysteries that the Watchers knew. Though an account of a heavenly journey, the narrative revolves around the theme of judgement of the sinners and the blessed fate in store for the oppressed righteous, and the key places that Enoch sees are related to this theme. However, the beginning of this, in 17,1–18,5, almost seems out of place – except in so far as Enoch's journey serves to

57. Reading καὶ πᾶν μυστήριον οὐκ ἀνεκαλύφθη ὑμῖν καὶ μυστήριον ἐξουθενημένον ἔγνωτε for καὶ πᾶν μυστήριον ὃ οὐκ ἀνεκαλύφθη ὑμῖν καὶ μυστήριον τὸ ἐκ τοῦ θεοῦ γεγενημένον ἔγνωτε. Cf. R.H. CHARLES, *The Ethiopic Version of the Book of Enoch* (Anecdota Oxoniensia, Semitic Series, 11), Oxford, Clarendon Press, 1906, p. 47. Cf. the comments of Stuckenbruck on 4Q203 i 3 in *Qumran Cave 4.XXVI* (n. 12), p. 36.

58. See above, p. 200.

carry him to edge of the earth, where he sees the mountain of God and the places of punishment. But this part of the narrative does have a function; it serves to establish Enoch's credentials as one who knows the secrets of nature and thus as one – in contrast to the Watchers – whose revelation of the heavenly secrets is reliable. In this connection it seems to me important that Enoch visits some of the places that Job (chapter 38) knows he cannot. Thus, for example, in 17,6-8, it is said that Enoch reaches the great darkness and goes "where no flesh walks"[59], that he sees the place where the waters of the deep pour out, the mouths of all the rivers and the mouth of the deep. This may be compared with Job 38,16-21:

> Have you entered into the springs of the sea,
> or walked in the recesses of the deep?
> Have the gates of death been revealed to you,
> or have you seen the gates of deep darkness?
> ...
> Where is the way to the dwelling of light,
> and where is the place of darkness? (Job 38,16-17.19, NRSV)[60]

Further comparisons may be drawn between 1 En 17,2 (Enoch is led to a place of darkness) and Job 38,19b; 1 En 17, 3 (he sees the storehouses of thunder and lightning) and Job 38,25; and 1 En 18,1-5 (Enoch observes the winds) and Job 38,24[61].

Enoch then sees in rapid succession the throne of God, the place of punishment for the Watchers, and the place of punishment for the disobedient stars (18,6–19,3). Little explanation is provided of what is seen, and the detail not spelled out. It is assumed that we do not need to be told that the throne is the throne where God will descend for judgement. However, it is characteristic of the description, as of that in chapters 20-36, that it draws extensively on the Hebrew Bible for its content – not by way of direct quotation, but by incorporating and reworking material from relevant passages into the narrative. The way in which the narrative, from one point of view, represents the outcome of reflection upon, and interpretation of, scripture gives the narrative something of a learned character.

59. So the Greek; the Ethiopic has "where all flesh walks".

60. The parallel is not of course precise. Job is challenged *inter alia* as to whether he has visited the realm of death, whereas the claim made in 1 En 17,6 is that Enoch had been to a region – apparently not Sheol – inaccessible to others. Enoch reaches Sheol in 1 En 22.

61. The series of rhetorical questions in 1 En 93,11-14, which have been seen to be reminiscent of the rhetorical questions in Job 38, appear to serve a similar purpose, namely of authenticating the revelation received by Enoch on his journeys. The implied answer to all the questions in 1 En 93,11-14 is: "no one except Enoch". Cf. VANDERKAM, *Enoch, A Man for All Generations* (n. 3), p. 91.

The following passage, chapters 20-36, is perhaps best seen as a commentary on, or expansion of, chapters 17-19. In any case Enoch now visits the same places that he has just visited, but here there is dialogue between Enoch and the angel who accompanies him, and explanations are given. But the narrative is expanded to include a description of the realm of the dead and of the earthly paradise based on Jerusalem[62]. Finally Enoch goes on a circuit of the earth (chapters 33-36). This passage has some similarities with material in the Book of Astronomy and may have been added in the light of that material. But, like 17,1–18,5, it also serves to confirm Enoch's status as one who does have access to the mysteries of the universe.

How should we evaluate the parallels between the Book of Enoch and 4QMysteries and 4Instruction? Collins has spoken in terms of the influence of apocalyptic traditions on the wisdom writings[63], and Elgvin has even spoken of the dependence of 4QInstruction on the books of Enoch, at least on the Epistle[64]. They may be right in terms of the direction of influence. But it seems to me more important that the parallels provide evidence of a shared thought-world. While Sirach may provide evidence of a critical attitude towards the claims to the possession of esoteric knowledge made by writings like 1 Enoch (and indeed 4Q300 1a ii-b // 4Q299 3c may also be evidence of a hostile attitude), that is clearly not the whole story. 4QMysteries and 4Instruction do present us with wisdom writings the theological perspective of which is much closer to that of 1 Enoch. The authors of the Book of Enoch and of 4QMysteries and 4Instruction were not such different people[65].

6 Shootersway Park
Berkhamsted
Herts. HP4 3NX
Great Britain

Michael A. KNIBB

62. It is interesting to observe that this journey reaches its climax in the paradise of righteousness in the east where Enoch sees "the tree of wisdom whose fruit the holy ones eat and know great wisdom" (32,3, Greek).

63. COLLINS, *Jewish Wisdom in the Hellenistic Age* (n. 21), p. 117, cf. pp. 115-131 passim.

64. ELGVIN, *The Mystery to Come* (n. 24), pp. 116-117, 138, 146.

65. Earlier versions of this paper were given at a seminar at King's College London in December 2001 and at the meeting of the Society for Old Testament Study in January 2002. I am grateful to those present on both occasions for their helpful comments, particularly Professor George Brooke and Professor Philip Davies.

SPATIALITY IN ENOCH'S JOURNEYS (1 ENOCH 12–36)

Three journey narratives are found in the Book of the Watchers (1 Enoch 1–36). 1 Enoch 12–16 narrates Enoch's journey to heave, while 1 Enoch 17–36 contain two more journey reports, this time concerning Enoch's journeys to the ends of the earth. During each of these journeys God's decisions are revealed to Enoch. Although a temporal dimension is evident in each of these revelations, a remarkable preference is shown for the spatial aspect thereof.

In order to further investigate this unusual preference for space rather than time, the narratives will be studied at different levels. In the first instance, a narrative analysis is made of the role played by space in narrative presentations in general. The micro-social world of the narratives of Enoch's journeys is then described as consisting of heterotopian zones or ideological spaces. On the second level, the macro-social world of the story teller and the author(s) of these narratives is investigated. This includes not only an intertextual investigation into possible literary parallels to the text, but also an investigation into the social world of the narrator and the audience for whom the story was intended. In this section the social world of second temple Judaism, its different social groups and the competing ideologies of that era, are included. It is possible to conclude from this study of the micro- and macro-social worlds of the three narratives that these journey narratives are the expression of an early form of apocalyptic thinking in which sapiential traditions played a significant role. They represent a trajectory of an Enochic tradition that was continued during the second century BCE and can also found in the writings of the Dead Sea Scrolls.

The Role of Space in Narrative Presentations

Different types of space are used in narrative composition, geopolitical space (towns and regions), topographical space (earth, sea, desert) and architectural space (house, temple) tending to be the primary types being employed[1]. The narrator selects the type of space that best suits the purpose of his or her narration. The narrator of Enoch generally opts

1. Cf. E.S. Malbon, *Narrative Space and Mythic Meaning in Mark,* San Francisco, CA, Harper & Row, 1986, p. 3.

for architectural and topographical types of space in which to locate his cosmological message.

While space in a story may simply represent a necessary setting for its characters and events, in most instances it functions as focal space: "[S]ymbols used by the narrator to convey his ideological perspective / narrative point on the topographical level of the text"[2]. In the micro-social world of the narrative the carefully selected spatial dimensions symbolise and reflect the values / norms / ideas that the narrator is trying to convey to the macro-social world in which he and his listeners live.

Narrative space is used to make "ontological propositions"[3]. By using different techniques, the narrator creates an "heterotopian space" or "zone"[4] in which comments are made on the events taking place in his world. Life is viewed as an endless conflict between opposing forces. Such heterotopian space makes use of the technique of deconstruction in order to construct meaning. This type of space is also found in the Enoch narratives, where cosmological space forms the arena for the struggle between good and evil, the battle between God and his rivals. The use of space in the world of Enoch's narratives reflects the narrator's apocalyptic ideology with respect to the world in which he lives.

Enoch's Journeys

The 'fallen angels' in 1 Enoch 6–11 (with its parallel in Gen 6) has received much attention in the history of research. While Enoch's ascent into heaven (1 Enoch 12–16) is usually included in studies of Merkabah-narratives, the same kind of material is also found in the Astronomical Book (1 Enoch 72–78). Enoch's two earthly journeys (1 Enoch 17–36), however, have not tended to attract a great deal of attention.

The first of Enoch's three journeys (1 Enoch 12–16) comprises five scenes[5]. He is sent down from heaven, talks to the fallen watchers, and is petitioned by them to return to heaven and to beg God for mercy. He ascends again to heaven only to hear the previous judgment confirmed. Himmelfarb included this narrative in her study of ascent apocalypses[6]

2. E. Van Eck, *Galilee and Jerusalem in Mark's Story of Jesus: A Narratological and Social Scientific Reading* (Hervormde Teologiese Studies Sup., 7), Pretoria, 1995, p. 141.

3. B. McHale, *Postmodernist Fiction,* New York, Routledge & Methuen, 1987, p. 43.

4. *Ibid.*, p. 45.

5. Cf. P.M. Venter, *Die funksie van ruimte in die reisverhale in 1 Henog 12-36*, in *Hervormde Teologiese Studies* 56 (2000) 38-62, pp. 45-54.

6. M. Himmelfarb, *Ascent to Heaven in Jewish and Christian Apocalypses*, New York, Oxford University Press, 1993.

in which she compared it to the visions in Ezek 1,8–11,43, Isa 6 and Micha ben Himla's vision in 1 Kings 22,19-22. She interpreted it as "[A]n understanding of heaven as a temple with angels and heavenly priests"[7]. As Himmelfarb was specifically dealing with the *Gattung* of ascent into heaven, the other two journeys were excluded on account of their exclusively earthly dimension.

When Enoch visits places on earth during his first journey, his visits are restricted to locations in the northern regions of Palestine. The narrative refers *inter alia* to places such as the waters of Dan, Lebanon and Sanser. Geopolitical as well as architectural space is also used to describe Enoch's movements in this first journey. The heterotopian zones created in this first narrative, especially in chapters 12 and 13, express the apocalyptic viewpoint of the narrator that good and evil co-exist alongside one another in this world. The heavenly abode, described in chapters 14 to 16, is reserved for God and his good angels. The fallen angels are restricted from returning to this heavenly abode, being confined to the earth upon which they have brought evil. Given the fact that only certain areas are reserved for them, however, it is evident that the earth as a whole is not filled with their evil. The fallen watchers restrict themselves to Oubelseyael between Lebanon and Sanser[8]. Enoch receives his revelation at a sacred place at Dan to the west of Mount Hermon and it is from this place[9] that he ascends to heaven. Later on he will also depart from this sacred place for his two journeys to the ends of the earth to discover the different locations allocated to different beings. In the micro-social world of this first narrative and the following two journeys the macro-social rivalry between good and evil, between God and the fallen angels, is depicted.

Topographical space is used in the description of the places visited by Enoch during his two earthly journeys (1 Enoch 17–19 and 20–36). This space, however, has symbolic significance since the places Enoch visits are repeatedly interpreted to him by an angel in terms of God's judgment upon the fallen watchers. Their meaning is thus conceptualised in terms of God's decision. The various cosmological places include the prison of the stars, the place where the host of heaven is reserved until the consummation of heaven and earth in the secret year (1 Enoch 16,1; 18,15.16) and the abode of the righteous. In scene seven of the second

7. *Ibid.*, p. 4.

8. According to the translation by R. LAURENCE, *The Book of Enoch*, http://www.takeitbyforce.com/1enoch01-60.htm, s.a.

9. G.W.E. NICKELSBURG, *1 Enoch 1. A Commentary on the Book of 1 Enoch, Chapters 1–36; 81–108* (Hermeneia), Minneapolis, MN, Fortress, 2001, p. 238, refers to "a heaven–earth polarity at the sacred place".

narrative (1 Enoch 26,1–27,5) the centre of the world – according to Isaac[10] and Nickelsburg[11] this is probably Jerusalem – is a blessed place with its holy mountain and valleys adjacent to the cursed deep and dry valley in which those who blasphemed against God are held. Traditional cosmological material, as found in Job 28 and 36, is used in these narratives, but linked therein to God's judgment of evil. Every place has "eschatological significance"[12]. For Nickelsburg an example can be found here in which "cosmology undergirds eschatology"[13]. Here we have "spatial reinforcement for the temporally orientated divine oracles issued against the rebel watchers"[14].

The question remains, however, as to why the spatial aspect is used to "reinforce" the "temporally orientated" oracles. Are they really time orientated? Are they not rather space orientated with the time of consummation as a secondary addition? The revelation received by Enoch in heaven is repeated during his two earthly journeys in terms of heterotopian zones. Conceptualisation of these heterotopian zones is primarily done in terms of space. Order in the world becomes the spatial order of God's judgment on evil, dividing the world into blessed places and cursed areas where the condemned are held in suspension until the consummation of heaven and earth. This spatial conceptualisation is clearly dominant in these narratives when compared to the temporal aspect. In what follows we will first investigate this phenomenon in its literary context and second in its social-historical context.

The Macro-Social Context

1. *Literary Context*

The Book of the Watchers can be divided into three main sections: 1 Enoch 1–5, 6–11 and 12–36. Each section represents older traditions and different literary layers. The three journeys of Enoch (1 Enoch 12–36) represent a set of traditions linked to the pre-Mosaic figure of

10. E. Isaac, *(Ethiopic Apocalypse of) Enoch*, in J.H. Charlesworth (ed.), *The Old Testament Pseudepigrapha. Volume 1, Apocalyptic Literature and Testaments*, London, Darton, Longman and Todd, 1983, p. 26.

11. Nickelsburg, *1 Enoch* (n. 9), p. 68.

12. C. Rowland, *The Open Heaven. A Study of Apocalyptic in Judaism and Early Christianity*, London, SPCK, 1982, p. 125.

13. G.W.E. Nickelsburg, *The Apocalyptic Construction of Reality in 1 Enoch*, in J.J. Collins – J.H. Charlesworth (eds.), *Mysteries and Revelations. Apocalyptic Studies since the Uppsala Colloqium*, Sheffield, JSOT Press, 1991, p. 97; Nickelsburg, *1 Enoch* (n. 9), p. 39.

14. Nickelsburg, *1 Enoch* (n. 9), p. 278.

Enoch[15]. The section on the fallen watchers (1 Enoch 6–11) is related to a myth of the fallen sons of God, likewise reflected in Genesis 6. This section also represents a Semihazah and an Azazel tradition, and probably a third set of traditions as well[16]. The two sections (1 Enoch 6–11 and 12–36) are linked by a mutual concern for evil and suffering on earth[17]. The cosmological order used in Enoch's earthly journeys (1 Enoch 17–36) corresponds to the depiction of order in the first section (1 Enoch 1–5).

While each of these sections have developed from older sets of traditions, they have also been influenced by contemporary literature, oral traditions and ideas circulating in society. Parallel themes can be found in Biblical literature for the Semihazah story in Lev 16[18] and in Genesis 6–9[19]. Parallels for the cosmological material, as mentioned above, can be found in Job 28,20-28 and 36,24-33.

1 Enoch 6,6 refers to "the peak of Mount Hermon". 1 Enoch 13,9 refers to "Abel-Main which is between Lebanon and Senir". George Nickelsburg, and more recently Russell Gmirkin[20], used references to northern regions such as these to relate the tradition of the watchers to traditions from upper Galilea and also to the religion of Ba'al Sjamin in the Syro-Phoenician world. Nickelsburg[21] found evidence in 1 Enoch 12–16 of "a tradition of northern Galilean provenance which, in turn, reflects visionary activity in the area of Dan and Hermon". Having taken literary, epigraphic and archaeological evidence on the Hermon area into account, and especially the parallels between 1 Enoch 13 and Testament of Levi 2–7, Nickelsburg comes to the conclusion that these serve as an attestation "of Jewish religious, indeed, revelatory activity in this area during the Hellenistic period"[22]. This area was regarded as the abode of the gods as early as the Bronze Age. Bilingual Greek and Aramaic in-

15. M.E. STONE, *Apocalypic Literature*, in ID. (ed.), *Jewish Writings of the Second Temple Period. Apocrypha, Pseudepigrapha, Qumran Sectarian Writings, Philo, Josephus*, Philadelphia, PA, Fortress Press 1984, pp. 383-441, p. 401.

16. P.D. HANSON, *Rebellion in Heaven, Azazel and Euhemeristic Heroes in 1 Enoch 6–11*, in *JBL* 96 (1977) 195-233, p. 202.

17. C.A. NEWSOM, *The Development of 1 Enoch 6–19: Cosmology and Judgement*, in *CBQ* 42 (1980) 310-329, p. 316.

18. Cf. HANSON, *Rebellion in Heaven*, p. 224.

19. Cf. G.W.E NICKELSBURG, *The Bible Rewritten and Expanded*, in *Jewish Writings of the Second Temple Period* (n. 15), 89-156, p. 91.

20. R. GMIRKIN, Old Testament Pseudepigrapha Web Page at the Divinity School of the University of St Andrews - International Discussion Group (*OTPSEUD*) archive at http://www.st-andrew.ac.uk/ ~www_sd/otpseud.html, March 10, 2002.

21. G.W.E. NICKELSBURG, *Enoch, Levi, and Peter: Recipients of Revelation in Upper Galilee*, in *JBL* 100 (1981) 575-600, p. 586.

22. NICKELSBURG, *1 Enoch* (n. 9), p. 247. Cf. Nickelsburg's excursus on Sacred Geography in 1 Enoch 6–16, pp. 238-247.

scriptions found at Tell Dan indicate that the sacred area at Dan "was in use around the time that 1 Enoch 12–16 was written"[23]. Although religious activity and even revelatory events can be related to this area, some problems remain. It was important in at least one tradition, found in 1 Enoch 12–16, that revelation was linked specifically to the northern areas near Hermon. Can we deduce from this information that an Enochic movement as such was based in these areas? Or were revelatory traditions from Dan used by an Enochic movement actually living in Jerusalem? We shall return to this problem when we deal with the various theories related to the authorship of these narratives.

Nickelsburg is of opinion that the authors of 1 Enoch drew vocabulary and conceptual frameworks from culture and religion of Mesopotamian and Greek provenance[24]. Its cosmology and mythic geography contain many elements that are not found in extant Israelite sources. Attridge designates Pseudo-Eupolemus as a document of Samaritan origin containing a form of the Enoch tradition[25]. Gmirkin, in addition, has pointed out that the Book of the Watchers was written from an anti-astrological and anti-Samaritan point of view in reaction to Pseudo-Eupolemus. Enoch quotes from Pseudo-Eupolemus[26].

Although the Zenon papyri include information on third-century BCE Palestine and even an inventory of places Zenon visited in the region between January 259 and April 258 BCE[27], nothing appears to coincide with the Book of the Watchers. Neither Dan, Hermon, Lebanon, Sanser, nor the Eritrean Sea are referred to in Zenon's writings. The fact that places are seldom given names in Enoch's journeys because they function as symbols rather than as geographic references makes it difficult to find parallels in contemporaneous writings.

Grelot[28] and Collins[29] have indicated a Mesopotamian background for the astrological and calendrical references in the Book of the Watchers. Hanson[30] maintains that an older rebellion-in-heaven myth was devel-

23. *Ibid.*, p. 244.

24. *Ibid.*, pp. 61-62.

25. H.W. ATTRIDGE, *Historiography*, in *Jewish Writings of the Second Temple Period* (n. 15), pp. 157-184, p. 165-166.

26. GMIRKIN, *OTPSEUD*, March 10, 2002.

27. Cf. P.W. PESTMAN, *A Guide to the Zenon Archive (P.L.Bat. 21)* (Papyrologica Lugduno-Batava), Leiden, Brill, 1981, p. 504. Cf V.A. TCHERIKOVER, *Corpus Papyrorum Judaicarum. Volume 1,* Cambridge, MA, Harvard University Press, 1957, pp. 121-122.

28. P. GRELOT, *La géographie mythique d'Henoch et ses sources orientales*, in *RB* 65 (1958) 33-69.

29. J.J. COLLINS, *Cosmos and Salvation: Jewish Wisdom and Apocalyptic in the Hellenistic Age,* in *HR* 17 (1977), pp. 131-132.

30. HANSON, *Rebellion in Heaven* (n. 16).

oped in both Greek (the Prometheus myth) and Jewish culture (story of the fallen watchers). The myth of the fallen gods was also known in Greek mythology in which the cosmic battle between the Olympians and Titans led to Zeus' rise to power and to the defeat and banishment of the Titans to Tartaros far below the earth[31]. According to Nickelsburg, Leviticus 16 and the Enoch tradition were moulded together on the pattern of the Prometheus myth to form the story of the fallen angels who are restricted to specific areas on earth[32]. According to Adela Yarbro Collins, Aristobulus' philosophy of the number seven as world principle played a role in the writing of 1 Enoch 34–36. She argues that the most immediate associations are to be found in the Babylonian and the Hellenistic idea of the seven planets[33]. In his commentary on 1 Enoch Nickelsburg evaluates three possible models as prototypes for Enoch's first journey (1 Enoch 17–19)[34]. Neither the model taken from ancient Near Eastern diplomacy, in which the wealth and strength of a kingdom is shown off to visiting courtiers, nor Gilgamesh's journey provide a satisfactory explanation for the story as a whole. According to Nickelsburg, the concern of the narrator of this journey was to underscore the certainty of the sinners' judgment. The model most immediately related to this concern is the Greek Nekyia's report of post mortem punishments narrated in the form of a journey to the underworld.

Although many parallels between the narratives of Enoch's journeys and contemporaneous literature can thus be found, they do not suffice to explain the macro-social world in which and for which these narratives were written. Interesting as these parallels are, the danger of what Sandmel calls "parallellomania" clearly lurks around the corner[35]. The literary as well as the socio-historical and ideological contexts all contribute to the ultimate significance of the parallel. The meaning of the heterotopian zones in the journey narratives does not only depend on the parallel themes used in the narratives, their literary form(s), or the larger literary context of the Book of the Watchers, it also depends on its ideological setting and the socio-historical context in which it is found. We are inclined to agree with Boccaccini's basic theory[36] that documents are

31. Cf. G. BOCCACCINI, *Roots of Rabbinic Judaism. An Intellectual History from Ezekiel to Daniel*, Grand Rapids, MI, Eerdmans, 2002, p. 95.

32. G.W.E. NICKELSBURG, *Apocalyptic and Myth in 1 Enoch 6–11*, in *JBL* 96 (1977) 383-405, p. 405.

33. A.Y. COLLINS, *Cosmology and Eschatology in Jewish and Christian Apocalypticism*, Leiden, Brill, 1996, p. 136.

34. NICKELSBURG, *1 Enoch* (n. 9), pp. 279-280.

35. Cf. S. SANDMEL, *"Parallellomania"*, in *JBL* 81 (1962) 1-13.

36. Cf. BOCCACCINI, *Roots of Rabbinic Judaism* (n. 31), pp. 28-32.

intellectual property and ideological records of the thoughts of social groups who exist in competition with other groups in society. As a consequence, not only a literary comparison between the Enoch narratives and similar literature is required, but also a comparison between the groups who produced and used this literature.

2. *Socio-Historical Context*

By the time Alexander had defeated Persia at Issus in 333 BCE, Palestine had already undergone two hundred and five years of Persian rule and cultural influence. Palestine was now gradually being introduced to and indeed subjected to Hellenistic influence. Up to 198 BCE it experienced the Egyptian brand of Hellenism under Ptolemaic rule. Egypt itself had likewise been subjected to many years of Persian culture. When Alexander conquered Egypt at the end of the fourth century BCE, he tried everything he could to counterbalance Persian influence. A new god, Serapis, was created to combine Zeus with the Egyptian gods Osiris, Apis (Ptah), Amun and Re. The Ptolemaic king was hailed as son of god. Old Egyptian temples were rebuilt and the animal cult reinstated. In the newly built Alexandria the Hellenistic and Egyptian ways of life merged to create a unique Alexandrian style[37]. Every effort was made to create "eine religiöse, kulturelle und politische Synthese ägyptischer und griechischen Traditionen"[38]. Given the fact a revolt broke out after the battle of Raphia in 217 BCE and a movement began to gather pace aimed at the reinstatement of traditional Egyptian values, it is evident that Alexander's efforts were only successful for a while.

Judah constituted one of the hyparchaiai in the Ptolemaic kingdom belonging to the area of Syria-Phoenicia under the leadership of a strategos[39]. According to Grabbe, Judah remained a theocratic unit under the Ptolemies, being allowed a measure of sovereignty as well as religious freedom[40]. The high priest during this time belonged to the house of Zadok and acted as leader of the country assisted by a council of priests and other individuals. An alliance was formed with the house of Tobias, whose members were known to be the owners of the concession charged

37. Cf. D. KESSLER, *The Political History of the Ptolemies and the Imperial Roman Period in Egypt*, in R. SCHULTZ – M. SEIDEL (eds.), *Egypt. The World of the Pharaohs*, Cologne, Könemann, 1998, 291-295, p. 291.

38. J. ASSMANN, *Weisheit und Mysterium. Das Bild der Griechen von Ägypten*, München, Verlag CH Beck, 2000, p. 20.

39. Cf. I. GAFNI, *The Historical Background*, in *Jewish Writings of the Second Temple Period* (n. 15), pp. 1-31, p. 4.

40. Cf. L. GRABBE, *Judaism from Cyrus to Hadrian. Volume One: The Persian and Greek Periods*, Minneapolis, MN, Fortress Press, 1992, pp. 171-220.

with gathering taxes for the Ptolemies. The fact that the Tobiads had strong diplomatic relations with the Ptolemaic rulers implies that they also played a leading role in the politics of third century Judah.

From the outset, Ptolemeus I Soter, and later his son Ptolemeus II Philadelphus, enlisted Judah as part of their economic and military expansion. Indeed, Judah played a significant role in their wars with the Seleucids. Soldiers and administrators like Zeno, who visited the area, commerce between the two countries, and the settlement of Jews in Egypt either as slaves or mercenaries, exposed Judah towards Egyptian influence. It was a time described by Hengel as "an intellectual climate that was prepared to be stimulated and influenced in a number of ways; in particular some tendencies in the development of Jewish wisdom and also in apocalyptic"[41]. Judah was open to an encounter with Greek ideas in its Ptolemaic form. A gradual process thus commenced in which various sectors of Jewish society were influenced to different degrees by Hellenistic culture and scientific knowledge of the world.

3. *Different Groups*

Within this "universal" framework, various groups operated in Judah and Jerusalem. Vanderkam's investigation into the leaders, groups and institutions in early Judaism indicates at least two main groups during the early second temple period. There were those who "...attached great authority to the Mosaic book, others used them but appealed to wider traditions"[42]. Nickelsburg refers to these groups as "movements of ideas"[43]. Relating texts as ideological records to different thought systems and grouping texts together according to original ideological relations, Boccaccini formulates his theory that "the genus Judaism was made of various synchronic species, or Judaisms – movements in competition, diachronically influencing each other by means of dialogue or opposition, having their own distinct identity yet sharing a common sense of membership to the same religious community"[44]. According to his theory, three main groups or "Judaisms" existed during the Ptolemaic era: "Zadokite Judaism", "Sapiential Judaism" and "Enochic Judaism".

"Zadokite Judaism", in Boccaccini"s view, came into being when the second temple was built in Jerusalem. On their return from exile, priests

41. M. HENGEL, *Jews, Greeks and Barbarians. Aspects of the Hellenization of Judaism in the Pre-Christian Period,* London, SCM Press, 1980, pp. 111-112.

42. J.C. VANDERKAM, *An Introduction to Early Judaism,* Grand Rapids, MI, Eerdmans, 2001, p. 186.

43. NICKELSBURG, *1 Enoch* (n. 9), p. 57.

44. BOCCACCINI, *Roots of Rabbinic Judaism* (n. 31), p. 36.

from the house of Zadok succeeded in replacing the influence of the Davidic monarchy and the prophets and became the leaders of the community. Ezekiel 40–48, the Priestly writing, the material associated with Ezra and Nehemiah and Chronicles, form the chain of documents expressing the theology of this Zadokite Judaism. It was a covenantal theology linking God's creative order to the temple's sacrificial practice, personal responsibility and a coherent system of graded purity. In some circles of research this form of Judaism is called "Mosaic Judaism".

Boccaccini also mentions other "early opponents", such as the Samaritans, the Tobiads and the prophets[45]. His view is that these groups lost their influence and gradually disappeared from the scene, being either separated from the Jewish community or marginalised by those in power. Another "group" which probably existed was the so-called Hasidim. A. LaCocque started using this term in 1988 in his book *Daniel in His Time*, employing it to designate a group living in the time of Daniel during the second century BCE. Rowland has described the Hasidim as "a loosely defined group, possibly related to the continuation of visionary activity found in some later prophetic oracles which looked to the future as the time when the promises made by God to the prophets would be realized"[46]. Hengel, however, used the term Hasidim for a fourth-century BCE apocalyptic group who was not necessarily "in conscious opposition to Jewish wisdom or to the Temple cult"[47]. Priests, Levites as well as scribes belonged to this group. Although some references are found to the pious in 1 Enoch, Nickelsburg denies that the Enochic literature can be identified with any group who referred to themselves as "Hasidim"[48]. In any event, "Hasidim" is too vague a term to be used to designate a specific group in the Ptolemaic era. We simply do not know enough about them to be sure of their existence.

Boccaccini's proposal of three different Judaisms, or at least three parallel groups in second temple Judaism, can be used as point of departure for depicting the scenario during the Ptolemaic era. Mosaic or Zadokite Judaism represents the main group which was in control of religious and political matters. Of course, there could have been other subgroups or smaller groups attending to parallel traditions, such as the Psalms or the Zion tradition as it is found in Lamentations. On the other hand, the other two groups (the sapiential group and the Enochic group) may likewise in their turn have consisted of smaller groups loosely linked to each other such as apocalyptic groups.

45. *Ibid.*, pp. 82-89.
46. ROWLAND, *The Open Heaven* (n. 12), p. 211.
47. HENGEL, *Jews, Greeks and Barbarians* (n. 41), p. 124.
48. NICKELSBURG, *1 Enoch* (n. 9), p. 65.

4. *Sapiential Judaism*

Boccaccini has identified "sapiential Judaism" as an autonomous movement that originated in the monarchical period prior to "Zadokite Judaism"[49]. It developed independently of this other form of Judaism and was able to maintain its autonomy in Jewish society. The community of texts sharing the ideological denominator "wisdom", include Ahiqar, Proverbs, Job and Jonah from the Persian era and Qoheleth, Tobit and Ben Sira in the Ptolemaic and Seleucid era. Sapiential Judaism shared the idea of a divinely ordained and basically good universe with Zadokite Judaism. They radically differed, however, on the way in which this basic order is revealed to mankind. Wisdom, gained from experiencing God's created order by living in harmony with the cosmos and all living beings, challenged the covenant concept of order as it was revealed to Moses on Sinai and interpreted by the priests.

Although Boccaccini touches on vital aspects of wisdom, such as its long tradition, its cosmopolitan relationship with the wisdom of neighbouring countries and its lay character, he too easily reduces it to mere opposition to Zadokite Judaism. Using Aleida Assmann's[50] "Weissheits-Kompaß" as model of orientation, a much broader scope is opened up for sapiential traditions. All four aspects of paternal, sovereign, critical and mantic wisdom indicated by Assmann were present in Judaism. Paternal and sovereign wisdom already had a long history in Israel and a rich legacy.

In post exilic times a "Weisheit im Singular"[51] started to develop next to the traditional proverbial wisdom. This form of wisdom was found among minority and exclusive groups. As Hellenistic influence opened up an ever widening world with its new science and philosophy, the necessity grew for providing answers on an extending scale. To accommodate the transcendental world as well, "Weisheitsmystik"[52] became an important aspect of wisdom. Wisdom of the natural order of the world traditionally belonged to sovereign wisdom. The Ptolemaic Astrolabium was an instrument used to calculate the course of the stars. Knowledge of the constellation and a reliable system for calculating time and predicting seasonal events was an important instrument which the king could use to reign in his kingdom. In mantic wisdom this new knowledge became part of an esoteric wisdom of the universe and its hidden

49. BOCCACCINI, *Roots of Rabbinic Judaism* (n. 31), pp. 103-111.

50. A. ASSMANN, *Was ist Weisheit? Wegmarken in einen weiten Feld*, in A. ASSMANN, (ed.), *Weisheit. Archäologie der literarischen Kommunikation III*, München, Wilhelm Fink, 1990, pp. 15-44, esp. 28.

51. *Ibid.*, p. 21.

52. *Ibid.*, p. 22.

order. The sage has knowledge of God's secrets and he can even manipulate cosmic powers with this knowledge.

An interesting inclination towards mantic wisdom is found in critical wisdom. Disillusioned with the thought systems to which he was accustomed, the sage broadened his scope into a "Ganzheitskonzept"[53], trying to avoid a disappointing reductionist scheme and preferring to see reality in its totality as a matter of contrasts and oppositions. This is what Qoheleth does when he investigates the "all" and finds no final answer but only contradictions everywhere. Part of the totality of the world is nature. Nature, therefore, is included in wisdom thinking as the arena in which God's order is experienced. This cannot be explained in terms of human logic. In Job as well as Proverbs wisdom is extended from everyday experience to include the world and its order. In Job 28 and Prov 3,19-20 as well as 8,22-31, wisdom is linked to creation and the order of the world. To know wisdom is to know the secret of God's world and the hidden order of the universe.

No direct equivalent to traditional Jewish wisdom literature can be found in Egyptian literature. According to Jan Assmann, the nearest equivalents to paternal and critical wisdom in Egyptian literature are the categories "Lehren" (teaching) and "Klagen" (lamenting)[54]. Mantic wisdom is found in spell formulas, especially in hymns and didactic passages in which the secrets of heaven and earth are formulated. Assmann uses the term "Kosmotheismus" when he studies a mantic type of wisdom in Egyptian literature[55]. According to Aleida Assmann, however, "dieser detaillierten Beschreibungsliteratur gehören die ägyptischen Unterweltsbücher, die eine exakte Geographie der Unterwelt erstellen ebenso wie die gnostischen und neuplatonischen Schilderungen von Himmelsreisen, die präzis die stellaren Räume vermessen"[56]. The underworld's geography was extensively documented in pictorial maps using both text and images. Many of these guides, including the "Book of Two Ways", the "Book of Gates", the "Book of Caverns" and the "Book of the Earth God", have been preserved, according to Burkard[57], on the walls of royal tombs of the New Kingdom as well as in papyrus manuscripts and even on sarcophagi floors.

53. *Ibid.*, p. 42.

54. Cf. J. ASSMANN, *Weisheit, Schrift und Literatur im alten Ägypten,* in *Weisheit* (n. 50), pp. 475-500.

55. Cf. J. ASSMANN, *Magische Weisheit. Wissensformen im ägyptischen Kosmotheismus*, in *Weisheit,* pp. 241-257.

56. A. ASSMANN, *Was ist Weisheit?* (n. 50), p. 32.

57. Cf. G. BURKARD, *Conceptions of the Cosmos - The Universe*, in *Egypt* (n. 37), pp. 445-446.

These Egyptian underworld maps may also have served as prototypes for Enoch's journeys in addition to the Greek Nekyia literature proposed by Nickelsburg. Links with Ptolemaic Egypt, moreover, indicate that the Enoch journeys were very much influenced not only by this literature, but also by the Egyptian "Ganzheitskonzept" which saw reality in its totality as a matter of contrasts and oppositions, as arenas belonging to either the pious or the evildoers. I would propose that the possibility of Egyptian wisdom influence on Enochic thinking, at least as far as Enoch's journeys are concerned, should be given priority when it comes to looking for prototypes in which the spatial aspect is dominant.

Qoheleth offers an example of the role played by Ptolemaic influence in Judaistic thinking during the third century BCE. Boccaccini reads Qoheleth against the background of early Ptolemaic rule (first half of the third century BCE)[58]. Being a staunch supporter of the Ptolemaic political and social order, Qoheleth preaches total submission to the king and to God. The king's power resembles God's power and reveals it. Everything happens in conformity with God's will. No one understands the rationale of his will and nobody can change it. It is futile to uphold the Zadokite idea that human actions correspond to divine reactions. Covenantal theology is no longer viable under the given circumstances. Simultaneously, however, Gods ordinance of time and events guarantees divine order in the world. He will not share the Enochic idea of corruption and disorder in the world. Against "the Enochian pretentiousness to a comprehensive knowledge, Qoheleth opposes the limits of human understanding"[59]. God's work is sheer mystery for humans.

Harrison also reads Qoheleth against a Ptolemaic background. He uses "comparative sociology" rather than ideological history to understand Qoheleth within its living social totality[60]. According to Harrison's research "Third century Judea was characterized by the increasing economic differentiation, social reorganization, and ideological reformation which were prompted by Palestine's material incorporation into the Ptolemaic world empire. These disturbances resulted in the production of multiple ideological responses and a growing disorientation with regard to social allegiances and obligations"[61]. Within wisdom circles, the force of social change "swept away the foundations upon which Qoheleth's predecessors had moored the sacred canopy of Israelite wis-

58. Cf. BOCCACCINI, *Roots of Rabbinic Judaism* (n. 31), pp. 120-123.
59. *Ibid.*, p. 121.
60. C.R. HARRISON, *Qoheleth among the Sociologists*, in *Biblical Interpretation* 5 (1997) 160-180.
61. *Ibid.*, p. 178.

dom"[62]. His challenge to traditional wisdom demonstrated "Judaism's ability to subvert monolithic social orders intellectually and thus remain highly adaptive in the midst of cataclysms of social change"[63].

In broader economic, political and cultural realms, the rise of the Tobiads and a new urban *petite bourgeoisie*, the rise of what would later be labelled as semi-heterodox sects, along with the formation of the Sanhedrin, lead to power struggles and ongoing ideological conflict. Not only clashes between rival groups occurred, but also the rapprochements between Judaisms which Boccaccini[64] indicates. Alliances were also formed, however, between some of these groups. Not only ideas in opposition to the ideology of other groups developed, but also ideas in which a broad spectrum of influences played a role.

5. *Enochic Judaism*

According to Boccaccini, Enochic Judaism was found among priestly groups that were excluded from the ruling classes[65]. They based their theology on ancient myths in which Enoch was the hero and their idea of the superhuman origin of evil formed a contra narrative to the Zadokite covenant theology. The Book of the Watchers (1 Enoch 1–36) represents a trajectory of this form of Judaism.

Copies of the Book of the Watchers were found in cave 4 at Qumran (4Q201-202, 204-206), the oldest of which (4Q201), according to Vanderkam, can be dated between 200 and 150 BCE[66]. The Book of the Watchers must have existed in its final form by the time copies thereof were made between 200-150 BCE. We can thus deduce that book was compiled during the third century BCE. While the contents of the book can probably be linked to circumstances of the third century BCE, the book itself represents the merging of three sets of tradition some of which should therefore be read within a still earlier context.

The main problem involved in relating the contents of the book to its macro-social setting, however, lies in the variety of scholarly opinion on what exactly happened during the third century BCE. In 1977 Nickelsburg referred to a background of "conflict so fierce, incessant, and widespread as to lead our author to claim that the existence of the human race was threatened"[67]. His analysis of events at the end of the fourth century

62. *Ibid.*, p. 179.
63. *Ibid.*, p. 179.
64. BOCCACCINI, *Roots of Rabbinic Judaism* (n. 31), pp. 113-150.
65. *Ibid.*, pp. 89-103.
66. VANDERKAM, *An Introduction to Early Judaism* (n. 42), p. 91.
67. NICKELSBURG, *Apocalyptic and Myth* (n. 32), p. 391.

BCE lead to his theory that the book was created during the wars of the Diadochi. Hanson argues that the material represents the "speculation of a sectarian apocalyptic movement of the third century B.C.E"[68]. Boccaccini relates the material to a movement that emerged during the fourth century BCE, his argument being based on his theory of a Zadokite struggle for power in the Persian period during the fifth and fourth centuries[69]. On the one hand, he argues that although very ancient and literary traditions were used in Enochic literature[70], Enochic Judaism is not a pre-Zadokite movement. On the other hand, his analysis of the early Hellenistic period (third century BCE) shows a time of stability and order during which the aforementioned struggles were already something of the past. According to his viewpoint, it was an internal struggle for power during the fourth century which was not schismatic but merely the acts of an opposition party within the Jerusalem aristocracy. It was only to become a schismatic component with a sophisticated theological alternative after the Maccabean Revolt. The general problem with these theories is, of course, the idea that apocalyptic literature must reflect a crisis in the community itself and not only a perception of deprivation found exclusively within a group in society. Apocalyptic thinking can flourish even in the midst of a time of stability. Studies of external influence on the Judaistic community, e.g. Hellenization, are often used to indicate this supposed crisis in the community.

The ideological records of this movement can be found *inter alia* in the Book of the Watchers. Stone referred to this material as "proto-apocalyptic"[71]. Although it is apocalyptic in nature it is not predominantly eschatological. We are dealing at this juncture, rather, with "a developed 'scientific' lore about astronomy, astrology, calendar and angelology"[72]. Gmirkin comes to the conclusion that the Book of the Watchers formally belongs to revelatory literature but goes much further in its scope than mere apocalyptic interests[73].

As to the character of the movement, theories tend to depend on a variety of scholarly points of orientation. Nickelsburg deduces from the stages in which 1 Enoch developed that there must have been concrete channels of transmission, channels that must have been established by a community or communities "who believed that their possession of the

68. HANSON, *Rebellion in Heaven* (n. 16), p. 219.

69. BOCCACCINI, *Roots of Rabbinic Judaism* (n. 31), pp. 100-103.

70. *Ibid.*, pp. 95-100.

71. M.E. STONE, *The Book of Enoch and Judaism in the Third Century B.C.E.*, in *CBQ* 40 (1978) 479-492, p. 491.

72. *Ibid.*, p. 391.

73. GMIRKIN, *OTPSEUD*, March, 10, 2002.

divinely given wisdom contained in the Enochic texts constituted them as the eschatological community of the chosen, who are awaiting the judgment and the consummation of the end"[74]. Hanson takes the temple as his point of departure. In his opinion, the movement represents a "sectarian point of view....outside of the mainstream of temple praxis"[75]. Stone takes intellectual groups as his point of orientation, groups that upheld an intellectual tradition of well-educated men "associated with the traditional intellectual groups, the wise and the priests"[76]. Boccaccini describes the character of this "Enochic Judaism" in terms of opposition to his central point of "Zadokite Judaism"[77]. His theory is based on an assumption of internal conflict in priestly circles during the fifth-fourth centuries. There are four issues at stake in this conflict: the Enoch group states that the stability and order the Zadokites claim to uphold has been replaced by disorder. According to their view, a cataclysmic end awaits the world. The replacement of a pre-Aaronite priesthood by a Sinaitic Zadokite structure of power is to be blamed for the disorder in the world. The correspondence of the Zadokite cultic calender is to be questioned by the cosmic structure of the world. In summary: "Enochic Judaism was a post- and anti-Zadokite phenomenon, a reaction to their claims, made by people who viewed themselves as priests and who shared the same worldview and traditions as the Zadokites, while denouncing a present of degeneration and disorder due to the rebellion of evil usurpers which caused the collapse of the divine order"[78].

The movement clearly shows apocalyptic characteristics. Frustrated expectations and cognitive dissonance are clearly signaled in the Enochic material. What they experienced was not in agreement with their views. They express alleged deprivation. In typical apocalyptic fashion there was "evil" in the world disturbing the order they championed. In their minds their vision was identical to God's will. It was not only their symbolic universe but also God's order which was endangered.

This "evil" or threat could have taken many forms. As they were probably from priestly circles[79] or related to the temple in one way or

74. NICKELSBURG, *1 Enoch* (n. 9), p. 64.

75. HANSON, *Rebellion in Heaven* (n. 16), p. 226.

76. STONE, *The Book of Enoch* (n. 71), p. 489.

77. BOCCACCINI, *Roots of Rabbinic Judaism* (n. 31), pp. 91-93.

78. *Ibid.*, p. 100.

79. NICKELSBURG, *1 Enoch* (n. 9), p. 67, says it is possible, though not altogether certain, that at least some of the authors of the Enochic literature were as priests, indeed, disaffected members of the Jerusalem priesthood.

another, it could have been something which posed a threat to their view on cultic matters. Ezra 9–10 and Malachi 2,11 refer to the desecration of the sanctuary by priests who married the daughters of a foreign god and broke faith with the wives of their youth. According to several scholars the sexual abuse in 1 Enoch 7 refers to sexual misconduct among the Jerusalemite priesthood. Enoch's heavenly ascent during his first journey is pictured in terms of a visit to the temple[80] and does indeed refer to priestly concerns. According to Hanson, the Enochic literature is a "harsh indictment against the temple cult and its expository tradition, an indictment originating within the sectarian perspective of a highly developed apocalyptic eschatology"[81]. The way in which the cult was executed at the temple was not in line with their view and was even seen as a threat to God's cosmic order. According to Boccaccini's theory, they could have been disgusted with the way the Zadokites performed their religious duties. Ian Hutchesson's opinion[82] is that we are dealing with something which comes from within the circle of the sons of Zadok. The division of the angels into two groups or classes reflects the situation in the temple in which the sons of Zadok had direct access to God, while the sons of Aaron only performed the *tamid* in weekly shifts. David Suter agrees with Nickelsburg that the problem was related to nuptial corruption among the priests in Jerusalem. In his opinion, 12–16 serve in particular as a "polemic against the priesthood, based in part on technical language from the temple and priesthood applied to the sanctuary in heaven, and the substitution of Dan for Jerusalem as the point of access to the sanctuary of heaven"[83].

Russel Gmirkin's study of Pseudo-Epolemus leads him to conclude that we are not dealing with an inner-Jewish controversy here, but rather with anti-astrological and anti-Samaritan polemics linked to the northern regions[84]. As early as 1981, Nickelsburg expressed his idea that we are dealing here with "an apocalyptic tradition emanating from circles in upper Galilee who view the Jerusalem priesthood as defiled and therefore under the irrevocable judgment of God"[85]. They found the presence

80. Cf. HIMMELFARB, *Ascent to Heaven* (n. 6), p. 4.
81. HANSON, *Rebellion in Heaven* (n. 16), p. 226.
82. I. HUTCHESSON, Old Testament Pseudepigrapha Web Page at the Divinity School of the University of St Andrews - International discussion group (*OTPSEUD*) archive at http://www.st-andrew.ac.uk/ ~www_sd/otpseud.html, March 09, 2002.
83. D. SUTTER, Old Testament Pseudepigrapha Web Page at the Divinity School of the University of St Andrews - International discussion group (*OTPSEUD*) archive at http://www.st-andrew.ac.uk/ ~www_sd/otpseud.html, March 09, 2002.
84. GMIRKIN, *OTPSEUD*, March 10, 2002.
85. NICKELSBURG, *Enoch, Levi, and Peter* (n. 21), p. 586.

of God and his revelation at the ancient holy place of Dan. Another possibility will be to use the theory of Goulder[86] that the Korahite Levites originating from Dan joined the Jerusalem priesthood, maintaining an independent position and even opposing the Zadokites. The use of the name of Dan and Hermon indicates their independent position and opposition to what was happening among the priests in Jerusalem.

There seems to be general agreement that the problem addressed in the Book of the Watchers is the notion of evil in terms of priestly concerns. The differences are mainly linked to the matter of locality. Either Jerusalem is the locus in which different priestly factions are in conflict, or the priesthood of Jerusalem stands in conflict with northern priests living at a sanctuary in Dan. Between these two positions one can pose a third possibility that either traditions originally from Dan, or Korahite priests from Dan, are present in Jerusalem and are in conflict with local traditions or groups. Whichever of these positions is the correct one, circumstances served as a catalyst for reaction from an apocalyptic type of movement represented in the Enochic material.

In their altered state of consciousness the Enoch group needed a revelation "to reassure suffering people that God was in control and would rescue them while also punishing those who oppressed them and who had filled the world with overwhelming violence and evil"[87]. What is important is the way in which this revelation is conceptualized. In the three journey narratives the revelation formulated in spatial terms is linked to the person of Enoch. The mythical figure of Enoch was "uniquely qualified to impart wisdom about the mysteries of cosmos and history"[88]. He opens up the heavens and mediates the truth of the origin of evil and God's decision on its destiny. The fallen angels embody the presence of evil and are an explanation why things go wrong in the world. Whatever the origin of the myth(s) of Enoch and the fallen angels[89], it functions in the Enochic movement as access to the truth of God, a truth that is conceptualised in spatial terms as the paths of the stars, the storehouses of the elements and the abode of the dead. Like Enmeduranki, the seventh antediluvian king of Sippar, and Gilgamesh in

86. M.D. GOULDER, *The Psalms of the Sons of Korah* (JSOT SS, 20), Sheffield, JSOT Press, 1982, pp. 51-84.

87. VANDERKAM, *An Introduction to Early Judaism* (n. 42), p. 94.

88. J.J. COLLINS, *Pseudepigraphy and Group Formation in Second Temple Judaism*, in E.G. CHAZON – M.E. STONE (eds.), *Pseudepigraphic Perspectives: The Apogrypha and Pseudepigrapha in Light of the Dead Sea Scrolls: Proceedings of the International Symposium of the Orion Center for the Study of the Dead Sea Scrolls and Associated Literature, 12-14 January, 1997*, Leiden, Brill, 1998, 33-58, p. 40.

89. Cf. BOCCACCINI, *Roots of Rabbinic Judaism* (n. 31), pp. 96-99.

his quest for eternal life[90], Enoch, the seventh man from Adam, sets out to find wisdom in God's creation (cf. Job 28 and Prov 3 and 8). This time cosmic wisdom is the revealed truth of God's decision, his "revealed wisdom"[91].

CONCLUSION

Narratives use heterotopian zones to express the narrator's ideological viewpoint. In the three journeys of Enoch an apocalyptic viewpoint is presented on good and evil as two forces co-existing alongside one another in this world. It is revealed to Enoch that God has already set his judgment upon evil and those who have brought evil upon earth. The revelation is conceptualised in terms of allocated space on earth. In a typically sapiential way of dualistic thinking, beings are divided into either righteous beings or evil beings. Similarly, the world consists of blessed places for the righteous and cursed areas where the condemned are held in suspension until the consummation of heaven and earth. Although evil exists, God maintains order on earth by allocating specific habitats for specific beings until the final consummation.

Many interesting parallels to the Book of the Watchers from the surrounding world and its literature have been found over the years. Although themes and motifs from tradition and contemporaneous literature clearly played a role in the narratives of Enoch's journeys, the heterotopian zones also reflect the ideological setting and the socio-historical context of the narrator(s).

The third century BCE is the probable historical setting of these narratives, at least in their final form. In this socio-historical context Persian influence was present together with growing Hellenistic influence in its Egyptian form. By telling the story of the antediluvian Enoch, an apocalyptic Enochic movement expressed its views on the chaotic influence of evil in their time. In telling their story they used apocalyptic ideas presented in the form of cosmic order originating from the wisdom tradition. They made use of a form of mantic wisdom which understood this order as revealed cosmic order which indicated God's decision on evil. In presenting their view in the form of three journeys by Enoch they

90. Cf. W.P. BROWN, *Ecclesiastes* (Interpretation. A Bible Commentary for Teaching and Preaching), Louisville, KY, John Knox Press, 2000.

91. Cf. G.W.E. NICKELSBURG, *Enochic Wisdom: An Alternative to the Mosaic Torah*, in J. MAGNESS – S. GITIN, (eds.), *Hesed Ve Emet. Studies in honor of Ernest S. Frerichs*, Atlanta, GA, Scholars, 1998, pp. 123-132, esp. 124.

used the encyclopaedic scientific knowledge available in their time. To present this knowledge as revealed heterotopian zones they used, as their prototype, the Egyptian *Unterweltsbücher* available to them through their relationship with Egypt.

The attitude of this group would not necessarily have been that of enmity to other groups. They had mutual concerns mainly with sapientially orientated groups and with a Mosaic movement and they shared the idea of order with the wisdom group(s). With the Mosaic movement they shared priestly concerns. While 1 Enoch 8,1–9,1 refers to the results of the transgression of the fallen watchers in terms of warfare, sorcery and astronomy, 1 Enoch 7,1-15 refers to improper sexual conduct. Linking Enoch's journeys (1 Enoch 12–36) to this previous section on the fallen watchers (1 Enoch 6–11), it is interesting that Enoch discovers the allocated places of evildoers rather than places where specific evil practices are performed. The focus falls on places not practices.

The inclusion of specific northern geographical references in the journey to heaven indicates either a conflict between Dan and Jerusalem, Danite priests and Zadokite priests among the Jerusalemite priests, or an anti-Samaritan trend[92]. Whatever the real conflict was, it was definitely linked to a geographical matter of some kind. Some (older) northern tradition(s), however, was entwined in an apocalyptical framework in which cosmic space plays a dominant role. God's cosmic order is believed to be maintained although evil is present in the world. Every place in the world receives meaning in terms of God's judgement. To those who are faithful to God, reassurance is not only given that God is in control, but also the meaning of each place is revealed in terms of good and evil.

Department Old Testament
Faculty of Theology
University of Pretoria
South Africa

Pieter M. VENTER

92. Cf. GMIRKIN, *OTPSEUD*, March 10, 2002.

WISDOM AND APOCALYPTIC: THE CASE OF QOHELETH

INTRODUCTION

One of the most intriguing issues in the study of Qoheleth is that of the opponents with whom the sage disputes[1]. This issue is made more complex by the redaction of Qoheleth by one or more traditional sages whose presence may be detected in 12,9-14. The first part of the "Epilogue" (12,9-10) presents Qoheleth as "one who taught the people knowledge, weighing, studying, and arranging many sayings. And he sought to find pleasant words, writing with honesty words of truth". Assuming this redaction is correct in its presentation of Qoheleth as a sage who taught, wrote, and edited sapiential sayings, the question that emerges in various places of the text (2,1-26; 3,10-15.16-22; 4,1–5,19; 6,10 – 7,14; 9,1-10; and 11,1-9) is, "Who are the opponents with whom this wise man contended?". Qoheleth's responses to his opponents include:

1. "What do mortals obtain from all the toil and effort with which they toil under the sun? For all their days are full of pain, and their work is a vexation; even at night their minds do not rest. This also is vanity (2,22-23)".
2. "He (God) has made everything appropriate for its time; moreover, he has put a sense of mystery into their minds, without their discovering what he has done from the beginning until the end (3,11)".
3. "Who knows whether the human spirit goes upward while that of animals goes downward to the earth (3,21)?"
4. "As they came from their mother's womb, so there they shall go again, naked as they came; they shall take nothing for their toil which they may carry away with their hands.... Besides, all their days they eat in darkness, with much stress, sickness, and resentment (5,15-17)".
5. "Do not say, 'Why were the former days better than these?' For it is not from wisdom that you ask this (7,10)".
6. "Then I saw all the work of God, that no one can find out what is happening under the sun. However much they may toil in seeking, they will not find it out; even though those who are wise claim to know, they cannot find it out (8,17)".
7. "The living know that they will die, but the dead know nothing at all; they have no more reward, and even the memory of them is lost. Their love, their

1. A.A. FISCHER argues that this type of debate, real or fictional, is found in wisdom school settings: cf. *Kohelet und die Frühe Apokalyptik. Eine Auslegung von Koh 3, 16-21*, in A. SCHOORS (ed.), *Qohelet in the Context of Wisdom* (BETL, 136), Leuven, Peeters – University Press, 1998, pp. 339-356.

hate, and their envy have already perished; never again will they have a part in all that happens under the sun (9,5-6)".

8. "Even those who live many years should rejoice in them all; yet let them remember that the days of darkness will be many. All that comes is vanity (11,8)".

Each of Qoheleth's disputations, save for the one in 7,10, is accompanied by his thesis of human joy: "*carpe diem*" (see 2,24-26; 3,12-13; 3,22; 5,17-19; 8,14-15; 9,7-10; 11,9-10)[2]. The various possibilities of understanding Qoheleth's opponents include fictional characters, traditional scribes active in the bureaucracy, the temple, and later the temple school, practitioners of mantic wisdom, early apocalyptic seers, and apocalyptic sages[3].

Qoheleth most likely was a sage of the Hellenistic period who wrote perhaps at the time of transition from Ptolemaic rule to the Seleucid control of Palestine (circa 200 BCE following the battle of Panium); he may be known and opposed by either Ben Sirah's students or those of a similar bent (ca 200-175 BCE). The time of Hellenistic rule was one of the accumulation of wealth in the hands of the social elite, including pagan nobles and upper echelon Jews, although ultimate political power belonged to the foreign Hellenistic rulers. However, in the period of transition from the rule of the Ptolemies to that of the Seleucids (200 BCE), social and political disruption occurred that led to the repositioning and new concentration of wealth in the hands of new foreign powers. Even those Jews who were among the social elite had little control over these political developments. Qoheleth, who either was among the social elite, or at least taught their children, despaired over this lack of political control and the consequent reconfigurations of foreign and domestic wealth. This same crisis gave additional shape to early apocalyptic that emerged from the prophetic theme of future escha-

2. See R.N. WHYBRAY, *Qoheleth, Preacher of Joy?*, in *JSOT* 23 (1982) 87-98; and S. FISCHER, *Die Aufforderung zur Lebensfreude im Buch Kohelet und seine Rezeption der ägyptischen Harfnerlieder* (Wiener Alttestamentliche Studien, 2), Frankfurt, Peter Lang, 1999. In his positive review of this book, A. SCHOORS makes the important observation that "Qoheleth puts each of his recommendations to enjoy the pleasures of life after having recorded an absurdity 'under the sun.' In the end death is the fundamental absurdity.... Thus, life comes to nothing, and the thought of that should incite people to enjoy the good things of this life". Joy is a limited gift of God that counterbalances the absurdity and tragedy of the finality of death (in *BibOr* 58 [2001], p. 668).

3. Also see H.-P. MÜLLER, *Der unheimliche Gast*, in *ZTK* 84 (1987) 464; and O. KAISER, *Die Botschaft des Buches Kohelet*, in *ETL* 71 (1995) 48-70. A. LANGE has argued that Qoheleth engages in debate with the temple sages of the third century, B.C.E. (4,17–5,6; see *In Diskussion mit dem Tempel. Zur Auseinandersetzung zwischen Kohelet und Weisheitlichen Kreisen am Jerusalemer Tempel*, in *Qoheleth in the Context of Wisdom* [n. 1], pp. 113-159).

tology (proto-apocalyptic included Isaiah 24–27; 65–66; Ezekiel 38–39; Joel; Zechariah 9–14; and Malachi) and began to form during the early Hellenistic period. The "corpus propheticum" (Isaiah through Malachi) continued to be written, copied, and handed down in the second century BCE, while the Torah became the basis for social and religious life in Judah as early as the first century, BCE. Thus, Qoheleth, early apocalyptic seers, and Torah scribes offered alternative approaches to reality in a time of social and political upheaval[4]. The first responds in pessimistic overtones, stressing, however, that moments of joy are to be affirmed as God's gifts, while the second views the immanent future in eschatological hope[5]. The third brings together Torah, wisdom, individual/collective piety/worship, and salvation history that begins at creation and culminates in the founding and rituals of the temple cultus in Jerusalem (Sir 24).

The sage known only as Qoheleth set forth a world view that lamented the lack of human, especially Jewish, shaping of social and individual destiny. It was only the hidden God who determined all events and human fates. In essence, Qoheleth lost his trust in the justness and beneficence of God. James L. Crenshaw identifies five major theses in Qoheleth that spring from this loss[6]:

1. death cancels everything (4,1-3; 6,1-6; 12,1-8)
2. wisdom cannot achieve its goal, i.e. the securing of existence through knowledge (3,11; 8,1)
3. God is unknowable (8,16–9,6)
4. the world is crooked, i.e. without cosmic or moral order (1,4-9; 9,1-3)
5. pleasure commends itself (2,24-26; 3,12-13; 3,22; 5,17-19; 8,14-15; 9,7-10; and 11,9-10).

Fictional Sages

Presenting himself in the typical fashion of the day, as a pseudonymous author/speaker, Qoheleth appears in the literary guise of Solomon,

4. D. Hellholm, *The Problem of Apocalyptic Genre*, in *Semeia* 36 (1986) 13-64. Crises could be historical, social and political, and even theological. In any event, this crisis arose out of a catastrophic situation that led to disillusion about the current state of reality. Apocalyptic addressed this state of affairs by speaking of some new world that would materialize in the future, while wisdom tended either to return to its tradition, or to enter into a period of questioning past values and belief, or to look to the Torah as the basis of divine revelation that provided the basis for social life.

5. Much of apocalyptic arose out of actual historical and political distresses, ranging from the sacking of Jerusalem and the destruction of the temple to the persecution of Antiochus IV Epiphanes, 175-168 BCE, to the aftermath of the Roman destruction of Jerusalem and the temple in 70 CE.

6. J. Crenshaw, *Old Testament Wisdom*, revised and enlarged, Louisville, KY, Westminster/John Knox Press, 1988, pp. 117-128.

or at least as a "son of David". The sage chooses a fictional narrator, in this case Solomon, to serve as the primary voice that tells an autobiographical story and instructs his audience in wisdom. A second voice, consisting of one, perhaps two redactors, appears in the traditional redaction that was responsible for the titulary in 1,1, the opening statement of the narrative following the introductory poem (1,12), occasional instructions (3,17; 7,27, "says Qoheleth; 11,9c), and the Epilogue (12,9-14). It is important to note that the second voice (or perhaps even a later redactor) adds the statement that the summation of true wisdom is

> Fear God, and keep his commandments; for that is the whole duty of everyone. For God will bring every deed into judgment, including every secret thing, whether good or evil (12,13b-14).

This emphasis on the Torah and judgment is especially significant, since it suggests the redactional activity of either a colleague or early disciple of Ben Sirah, or precursors of those responsible for the Qumran community's combination of wisdom, Torah, and eschatological judgment[7].

In the writing of this testament, or first-person narrative, the implied author enables the narrator to instruct future generations in his teaching and fictional experiences. First-person narratives, real or ficitional, represent the presentation of a story teller's self-justification, that is, they attempt to find something of significance in life to declare human meaning[8]. Thus, this sapiential narrator, speaking through the mouth of the long dead Solomon, sought to find the good in human life and that of his own existence through critical reflection on his personal human experience. This, in turn, would affirm his values that he sought to teach to his students.

In this case, it is the implied Solomon[9] who sought to speak to future generations through the sage's appropriation of the royal testament, a form found especially in ancient Egypt ("The Wisdom of Imhotep"[10];

7. The redaction of Qoheleth emphasizes two major themes: the fear of God which is realized in the observation of the commandments and the certainty of an all-embracing divine judgment (LANGE, *In Diskussion mit dem Tempel* [n. 3], p. 115).

8. See W. BOOTH, *The Rhetoric of Fiction*, Chicago, IL, The University of Chicago, 1961, pp. 70-77.

9. "Nevertheless there can be no doubt that the implicit claim to be Solomon is a fiction; and indeed, the fact that it is made only indirectly, hinting at the identification but never actually naming Solomon (contrast the direct claims made in Prov. 1,1; 10,1; 25,1; and Cant. 1,1) may suggest that Qoheleth never intended his readers to take it seriously"; R.N. WHYBRAY, *Ecclesiastes* (NBC), Grand Rapids, MI, Eerdmans, 1989, p. 4.

10. His teaching has not survived, but he is mentioned in one of the Harper's songs (*ANET*, p. 567; *AEL* 1, p. 196; *LAE*, p. 306).

"The Instruction of Hardedef"[11]; "The Instruction of Kagemni"[12]; "The Instruction of Ptah-hotep"[13]; "The Instruction for King Merikare"[14]; and "The Instruction of King Amenemhet")[15]. If Qoheleth dates from the end of the Ptolemaic period and the beginning of Seleucid rule (ca 200 BCE), it is possible that the teacher was familiar with this form and perhaps even some of the classical Egyptian texts[16]. Thus, we find in Qoheleth the fiction of a dead king who instructs his audience from the tomb. Only this king does not legitimate the emerging Seleucid dynasty's rule over Palestine, but rather mourns the lost of Jewish kingship and local royal autonomy and the subsequent infusion of political and social injustice.

If we have in this Testament an autobiographical fiction that is consistently developed in the first two chapters and implied for the remainder of the Book, we could easily assume that Qoheleth's opponents would have been fictional. But, even so, it would be foolish to suggest that the opponents did not represent literary types of social categories from Qoheleth's time. These fictional opponents would have included, then, the traditional sages whose writings would have included Proverbs and, later on, the disciples of Ben Sirah, early apocalyptic seers who began to appear in the Hellenistic period, and apocalyptic sages who undoubtedly were active before the establishment of the Qumran community.

The biblical sages and Ben Sirah are normally viewed as scribes who were skilled in the arts of oratory, writing, and reading (Proverbs, Job, Qoheleth, and Jesus Ben Sirah)[17]. They were especially educated to

11. *AEL* 1, pp. 58-59; *LAE*, p.340.

12. *AEL* 1, pp. 59-61; *LAE*, pp. 177-179.

13. *ANET*, pp. 412-414; *AEL* 1, pp. 61-80; *LAE*, pp. 159-176.

14. *ANET*, pp. 414-118; *AEL* 1, pp. 97-109; *LAE*, pp. 180-192.

15. *ANET*, pp. 414-418; *AEL* 1, pp. 135-139; *LAE* pp. 193-197; also see R.J. WILLIAMS, *The Sage in Egyptian Literature*, in J.G. GAMMIE and L.G. PERDUE (eds.), *The Sage in Israel and the Ancient Near East*, Winona Lake, IN, Eisenbrauns, pp. 95-98. That the Israelite and Judahite sages were familiar with some wisdom literature from ancient Egypt is apparent in the dependence of Prov. 22, 17-24, 22 upon "The Wisdom of Amenemopet" (*ANET*, pp. 421-425; *AEL* 2, pp. 146-163; *LAE* pp. 241-265).

16. T. Krüger dates the book at the beginning of the reign of Ptolemais V Epiphanes (204-180 BCE): *Kohelet* (BKAT, 19), Neukirchen-Vluyn, Neukirchener Verlag, 2000. The book seems to reflect the political and social features of this time. A. LANGE points to the middle of the third century, BCE for the date (*In Diskussion mit dem Tempel*, p. 113, n. 4). In our judgment, Qoheleth may date shortly after the defeat of the Ptolemy V at the battle of Panium in 200 BCE by Antiochus III when there is a transition from the Ptolemaic to the Seleucid period (ca 200 BCE).

17. See J.J.G. GAMMIE and L.G. PERDUE (eds.), *The Sage in Israel and the Ancient Near East*, Winona Lake, IN, Eisenbrauns, 1990. The literary activities of the sages included the work of redacting sapiential and other texts (e.g., the headings of the seven collections of Proverbs; Qoh. 12,9-14; and the speeches of Job).

serve in the royal courts at home and abroad. The most detailed portrait of the sage, while late (ca 200-180 BCE), is painted by the brush of Jesus Ben Sirah (Sir 38,34–39,11). Indeed, this may even have been Ben Sirah's literary self-portrait in much the same fashion, though in a different artistic mode, of artists' self renderings in the Renaissance, and then in later periods of painting. According to this literary portrait, the sage is a counselor to kings and other people of prominence (39,4; cf. Prov 14,35; 25,15), one who travels to foreign countries and perhaps serves as a commissioned diplomat (31,1-31; 32,1-13; 39,1-4), a jurist, i.e. both a lawyer and a judge (38,34; cf. 10,1-5), a student and interpreter of the great literary culture of Israel and Judah (39,1-3), a cultivated person open to other cultures and their insights (see 1 Kings 5,9-14), one who is a person of great religious piety (Sir 18,27; 39,5; Prov 14,2; 15,29.33), one to whom secrets are entrusted (Sir 8,19; 9,18; Prov 10,19; 12,23), a moral man who controls his appetites, especially lust (Sir 31,12-21; 42,12-14; Prov 20,25-26; 23,26-28), and a generous person known for great charity (4,1-10; Prov 11,17.24-25). The more well-to-do scribes are among the social elite who had leisure, owned land (7,3.15.22) and slaves (7,20-21; 33,25-33; 42,5), and thus valued wealth (14,3-19; 30,21-25), and cultivated the social graces. Added to these is the emphasis that Ben Sirah placed on the reverence for and study of the Torah, which he identifies with divine wisdom, and on the temple cult and individual piety (6,37; 19,24; 22,27-23,6; 23,27; 24,23; 29,11-13; 39,1; 35,1-13; 36,1-22; and 50,1-21)[18].

In addition to serving in positions of prominence in royal courts, some of the traditional sages were teachers. Once again, Ben Sirah provides us important information for this sapiential role (51,23-30; cf. 39,8). The reference to students' lodging in his "house of instruction" (51,23-25) indicates that this sage may have operated a wisdom school for the children of the elite and for those who sought to become governmental and temple scribes and teachers. This school was closely affiliated with the temple and the religion of the Sadducees. What these sages taught consisted of moral teachings, grounded in the Torah, that were to be embodied and practiced by their students.

The theology of traditional wisdom is grounded in creation theology, while its moral teachings were undergirded by the theory of retribution

18. The Identification of wisdom with Torah in Ben Sirah is discussed by H. STADELMANN, *Ben Sira als Schriftgelehrter* (WUNT, II/6), Tübingen, J.C.B. Mohr (Paul Siebeck), 1980; and E.J. SCHNABEL, *Law and Wisdom from Ben Sira to Paul (*WUNT, II/16) Tübingen, J.C.B. Mohr (Paul Siebeck), 1985.

in Proverbs and Ben Sirah[19]. God is the creator of "heaven and earth" as well as of human beings. For the sages, knowledge was obtained through rational reflection on the cosmos, the sapiential tradition, and personal experience, but not through special revelation received in visions, dreams, or the casting of lots. Later, this knowledge also came through the revelation of Torah and/or dreams and visions.

Traditional Sages

The most commonly encountered thesis is that Qoheleth's opponents were the traditional sages of the post-exilic period, whose writings are found both in the later collections of Proverbs and then in the stream of thought that crystallized in the early second century, BCE, in the writings of Ben Sirah[20]. It may well be the case that either one of Ben Sirah's disciples, colleagues, or a precursor of the pre-Qumran apocalyptic sages took Qoheleth to task in their editing of the book (especially see 12, 9-14 in the Epilogue)[21], even as it appears that Qoheleth repudi-

19. For the teaching of retribution, see K. Koch, *Gibt es ein Vergeltungsdogma im Alten Testament?*, in *ZTK* 52 (1955) 1-42. The creation theology of wisdom literature is discussed by W. Zimmerli, *The Place and Limit of the Wisdom in the Framework of the Old Testament Theology*, in *SJT* 17 (1964) 146-158; and in detail in my book, L.G. Perdue, *Wisdom and Creation. The Theology of Wisdom Literature*, Nashville, TN, Abingdon, 1994.

20. This opposition to traditional teachings has led many scholars of the sages to argue that we have in Job and especially in Qoheleth a crisis of wisdom, since the teachings of the traditional sages usually did not hold true during periods of social and political turmoil. Indeed, von Rad even argued that it was this intellectual crisis of the sages that aided in shaping early apocalyptic thought. See F. Crüsemann, *The Unchangeable World: The 'Crisis of Wisdom' in Qoheleth*, in W. Schottroff and W. Stegemann (eds.), *God of the Lowly*, Maryknoll, NY, Orbis, 1984, pp. 55-77; H. Gese, *Die Krisis der Weisheit bei Koheleth*, in J. Leclant (ed.), *Les Sagesses du Proche-Orient Ancien*, Paris, Presses Universitaires de France, 1961, pp. 139-151; and A. Lauha, *Die Krise des Religiösen Glaubens bei Kohelet*, in M. Noth and D.W. Thomas (eds.), *Wisdom in Israel and in the Ancient Near East* (VTS, 3), Leiden, Brill, 1955, pp. 183-191.

21. In my view, the emphasis on "wisdom", "fear of God" and the "commandments" (= Torah) in 12,9-14 by a pious redactor, perhaps a colleague of Ben Sirah or a torah scribe who preceded them, is a direct criticism of Qoheleth (especially Sir 18,15-23, 27); see G.T. Sheppard, *The Epilogue to Qoheleth as Theological Commentary*, in *CBQ* 39 (1977) 182-189; Id., *Wisdom as a Hermeneutical Construct. A Study in the Sapientializing of the Old Testament* (BZAW, 151), Berlin, Walter de Gruyter, 1980; and N. Lohfink, *Les epilogues du livre de Qohelet et les debuts du canon*, in P. Bovati and R. Meynet (eds.) *Ouvrir les Écritures. Mélanges offerts à Paul Beauchamp* (LD, 162), Paris, Cerf, 1995, pp. 93-95. Apocalyptic sages from Qumran may also have been responsible for the editing of Qoheleth, including 12,13. See 1Q28b, I 1-2. However, F.J. Backhaus, *Qohelet und Sirach* (BN, 69), 1993, pp. 32-45; and J. Marböck, *Kohelet und Sirach. Eine vielschichtige Beziehung*, in L. Schwienhorst-Schoenenberger (ed.), *Das Buch Kohelet. Studien zur Struktur, Geschichte, Rezeption und Theologie* (BZAW, 254), Berlin, Walter de Gruyter, 1997, pp. 275-281, reject this argument. Torah ("command-

ated many of the teachings of these traditional sages[22]. The primary traditional teachings that Qoheleth opposed included revelation through divinely given wisdom, not what sages derived from experience and reason; the importance of wisdom in knowing how and when to act successfully as opposed to folly; the value of wealth, honor, and family who would enable one's memory to continue beyond death (2,14-16); a retributive system of justice in which a righteous God rewards the good and punishes the wicked; an earthly judgment of the righteous and wicked; the justice and goodness of God; and the importance of temple worship[23].

THE MANTIC SAGES

The practitioners of mantic wisdom have many similarities with the apocalyptic seers (see below), but preceded them and were found in particular in Babylonia. Mantic wisdom includes an emphasis on esoteric knowledge that is not simply revelatory through dreams and visions, but also has a cultic and magical dimension[24]. Thus, these sages are much like diviners in Mesopotamian religion who could read the entrails of animals, understand the meaning of flights of birds, and read other signs from nature that revealed the secrets of the gods. There are references to

ment[s]") is a dominant theme in Ben Sirah (6,37; 19,24; 23,27; 24,23; 29,11-13; and 39,1) and is found in other wisdom texts (Prov 4,4; 7,1f.; 19,16; cf. 1 Kings 2,43). Also see Sir 15,15; 32,22 [35,27] 37,12; 44,20; 1QH[a] XVI 13. 17; 1QSb I 1; CD II 18 ; etc.).

22. While Qoheleth and Ben Sirah had many themes in common, it is clear that Ben Sirah did not directly use Qoheleth. There is also little proof that Qoheleth specifically engaged this traditional sage: cf. T. MIDDENDORP, *Die Stellung Jesu ben Siras zwischen Judentum und Hellenismus,* Leiden, Brill, 1973, pp. 85-91.

23. Lange has made a strong case for the argument that the traditional sages who instructed their followers to participate in the temple worship taught a type of temple wisdom in the manner of Ben Sirah (see, *Weisheit und Torheit bei Kohelet*; cf. esp. 4,17-5,6). However, this heuristic model does not easily explain the coming together of temple and apocalyptic that, at least in the first half of the exilic period, represented very different approaches to reality.

24. See H.-P. MÜLLER, *Mantische Weisheit und Apokalyptik*, in H.-P. MÜLLER (ed.), *Mensch-Umwelt-Eigenwelt. Gesammelte Aufsätze zur Weisheit Israels*, Stuttgart, Calwer, 1992, pp. 194-219. Müller argues that this type of wisdom included Daniel. However, I would suggest that there is a more magical component to mantic wisdom than to apocalyptic. While overstating his case, Müller may be partially correct in arguing that mantic wisdom is one source for the development of apocalyptic. J. VANDERKAM, *The Prophetic-Sapiential Origins of Apocalyptic*, in J.R. MARTIN and P.R. DAVIES (eds.), A *Word in Season. Essays in Honor of William McKane* (JSOTSup, 42), Sheffield, JSOT, 1986, pp. 163-176, goes a step further. He argues that mantic knowledge, or divination, is found, not only in archaic wisdom, but also in prophecy. Yet this is not classical prophecy so much as it is a type of prophecy that was strongly akin to divination. According to VanderKam, this may have been the major stimulus for the development of apocalyptic.

mantic sages in biblical texts. Thus, one finds in Gen 41,8 a mention of the pharaoh's "sages" and "magicians". Jer 1,35ff. sets forth sages who are probably oracle priests (see Isa. 45,25). In Babylonia (cf. Isa 47,10ff.), the Hebrew Bible indicates there are several groups of mantic sages: those who observe the stars, those who understand the months, and counselors who are givers of advice. Then there are those who offer curses (Isa 19,11-13). Daniel's opponents are the sages of Babylon who are skilled in the occult sciences (2,27): אשׁפין (those who utters an oath), חרטמין (magicians), and גזרין (those who determine fortunes). Those who know the times are mantic sages at court (Wis 7,17f.), while there are those who have power over spirits (19f.). In Wis 8,8 the sages understand the use of language, solve riddles, possess foreknowledge of signs and wonders, are aware of the outcome of seasons and times, and know both the past and the future.

Probably after 587 BCE, the wise men of Judah came into contact with Babylonian sages, although their encounter with the Egyptian wise men could have gone back to the days of Solomon in the tenth century, BCE Israelite and Jewish sages were at home in foreign courts where they would have had mantic sages as their peers. Joseph is likely portrayed, at least partially, as an Egyptian mantic sage who has the gift of the interpretation of dreams. He himself is dressed in an Egyptian courtier's clothing in Gen 37-47. He is not so much a wise man of ancient Israel as he is a royal courtier of ancient Egypt who is the chief advisor to the king of Egypt, the administrator of the kingdom, and the interpreter of dreams. Daniel, on the other hand, is a Jewish youth living and being educated in the royal court in Babylon who becomes an interpreter of dreams and visions.

Apocalyptic Seers

A fourth thesis is that Qoheleth's opponents included early apocalyptic seers (cf. Prov 30,2-4)[25]. A major stimulus towards a more fully developed apocalyptic may be traced back to the transition from the Persian to the Hellenistic periods in Syro-Palestine (ca 334-300 BCE)[26].

25. See Fischer, *Kohelet und die Frühe Apokalyptik* (n. 1), pp. 339-356. The "Sayings of Agur" in Prov. 30,1-4 may have directed its criticism toward apocalyptic seers, since this text, often the subject of scholarly debates in terms of its translation and interpretation, rejects the heavenly ascent of a sage who later returns to the earth, presumably with a new revelation.

26. See J.J. Collins (ed.), *The Encyclopedia of Apocalypticism*, 1, New York, Continuum, 1998; *The Apocalyptic Imagination*, 2d ed., Grand Rapids, MI, Eerdmans, 1998; D.S. Russell, *The Message and Method of Apocalyptic*, Philadelphia, PA, Westminster, 1964; P. Hanson, *The Dawn of Apocalyptic*, Philadelphia, Fortress, 1975; D. Hellholm

Several books and sections of books integrated into prophetic literature prior to that time belong to proto-apocalyptic literature: Isaiah 24–27; Ezekiel 38–39; Joel; Zechariah 9–14; and Malachi[27]. However, more developed apocalyptic literature influenced by wisdom literary forms and thought includes 1 Enoch (the roots of which are in the early third century, BCE) and Daniel (third and second centuries, BCE), while the wisdom text of the Wisdom of Solomon (perhaps as early as the beginning of Imperial Rome circa. 30 BCE) is shaped by apocalyptic. Proto-apocalyptic began to emerge in the fifth century BCE[28]. These writers were not only prophets, but also seers who received special divine revelation about the future activities of God and the course of human and cosmic events, ranging from creation to the eschaton. They speak of hope in the intervention of God directly into human events in the establishment of a new world in which the nations would be ruled by the people of Yahweh. Emerging apocalyptic seers were primarily the successors of the classical prophets, only the seers' predictions were based on a view of cosmic history that was structured into eons.

More developed apocalyptic literature and thought are found in apocalypses that yet are also influenced by wisdom: 1 Enoch (the roots of which are third century, BCE) and Daniel (the Maccabean revolt in 168-164 BCE). The Wisdom of Solomon is a wisdom text written as early as the beginning of Imperial Rome (30 BCE) that was shaped by both Hellenistic popular philosophy and Jewish apocalyptic[29].

(ed.), *Apocalypticism in the Ancient Mediterranean World and the Near East*, Tübingen, J.C.B. Mohr (Paul Siebeck), 1989; and P. SACCHI, *Jewish Apocalyptic and Its History*, Sheffield, JSOT, 1996. G. VON RAD argued that wisdom, not late prophecy, was the source of apocalyptic *Theologie des Alten Testaments*, 2, 5th ed., Munich, C. Kaiser, 1968, pp. 316-328; and *Wisdom in Israel*, Nashville, TN, Abingdon, 1972. This thesis has been defended by H.-P. MÜLLER, *Mantische Weisheit*; and more recently A. LANGE, *Weisheit und Torheit bei Kohelet und in seiner Umwelt* (EHS. T., XIII/433), Frankfurt, Peter Lang, 1991.

27. This issue of prophetic and/or sapiential origins of apocalypticism has been examined judiciously by M.A. KNIBB, *Apocalyptic and Wisdom in 4 Ezra*, in *JSJ* 13 (1982) 56-62.

28. HANSON, *The Dawn of Apocalyptic* (n. 26).

29. J. COLLINS, *Cosmos and Salvation. Jewish Wisdom and Apocalypticism in the Hellenistic Age*, in *HTR* 17 (1977) 121-142; *Jewish Wisdom in the Hellenistic Age* (OTL), Louisville, KY, Westminister/John Knox, 1997; P. GRELOT, *L'eschatologie de la Sagesse et les apocalypses juives. À la rencontre de Dieu. Mémorial A. Gelin*, Le Puy, Mappus, 1961, pp. 165-178; M. KOLARCIK, in N. CALDUCH-BENAGES and J. VERMEYLEN (eds.), *Universalism and Justice in the Wisdom of Solomon. Treasures of Wisdom. Studies in Ben Sirah and the Book of Wisdom* (BETL, 143), Leuven, Peeters – University Press, 1999, pp. 289-301; C. LARCHER, *Études sur le Livre de la Sagesse* (EB), Paris, J. Gabalda, 1969; M. NOBILE, *La thématique eschatologique dans le Livre de la Sagesse en relation avec l'apocalyptique*, in *Universalism and Justice in the Wisdom of Solomon*, pp. 303-312; L.G. PERDUE, *Wisdom & Creation. The Theology of Wisdom Literature*, Nashville, TN, Abingdon, 1994; and G. ZIENER, *Die theologische Begriffssprache im Buche der Weisheit* (BBB, 11), Bonn, Hanstein, 1966.

The first complete portrait of apocalyptic seers is found in the Books of 1 Enoch and Daniel. These two wise men and seers composed texts during the Hellenistic period. Two segments of Enoch, "The Book of the Watchers" and "The Astronomical Book", are older than the final edition of the Book of Daniel. However, one notices the minor role of the primary literary forms and content of traditional wisdom (especially the instruction) and prophetic speeches in each of these texts.

The theology of apocalyptic, according to John J. Collins, differs from wisdom in several ways[30]. First, apocalyptic places "increased importance on the supernatural world and supernatural agents in human affairs". These include, not only God, but also angels and demons who were active in the world. Second, unlike wisdom, there is in apocalyptic "the expectation of eschatological judgment and reward or punishment beyond death". Third, in contrast to wisdom's largely optimistic view of the world, one finds in apocalyptic "the perception that something is fundamentally wrong with this world". Thus, there is a coming eschatological judgment that will result in the reward of the righteous and the punishment of the wicked. This divine action at the end of the age will set things right and bring about the restitution of a just order of reality, "a new heaven and a new earth", that will endure and enable the just to participate. The just dead will be resurrected to experience this new life. And fourth, unlike wisdom's emphasis on rational reflection on human experience, apocalyptic points to supernatural revelation as the primary means by which important knowledge was derived (this occurs in the divine gift of esoteric knowledge, dreams, and heavenly journeys).

The apocalypse is a literary genre, given classic definition by John J. Collins:

> a genre of revelatory literature with a narrative framework, in which a revelation is mediated by an otherworldly being to a human recipient, disclosing a transcendent reality which is both temporal, insofar as it envisages eschatological salvation, and spatial, insofar as it involves another supernatural world[31].

This is not to deny that individual texts had their own unique features. Many other texts were influenced by apocalyptic thought and language, though they are by no means placed in the form of an apocalypse. However, this definition does point to a common understanding of a literary form that became especially prominent in early Judaism and primitive

30. J.J. COLLINS, *Wisdom, Apocalypticism and Generic Compatibility*, in L.G. PERDUE, B.B. SCOTT, and W. J. WISEMAN (eds.), *In Search of Wisdom. Essays in Memory of John G. Gammie*, Louisville, KY, Westminster, 1993, pp. 165-185.

31. *The Jewish Apocalypses*, in J.J. COLLINS (ed.), *Apocalypse: The Morphology of a Genre*, in *Semeia* 14 (1979) 21-49.

Christianity. While there are those that focus on a heavenly journey of a seer (e.g., Enoch), most are historical in tracing the periods of human and especially Jewish history (e.g., Daniel). These two different apocalyptic texts both offered encouragement to a suffering people who looked to the future for a new world of justice and goodness. Righteous individuals will experience the glory of immortality with the angels. This suffering was brought about by the persecutions of Jews and, later on, Christians by foreign rulers (including first the Seleucids and later imperial Rome)[32].

The Book of Enoch (preserved in its entirety only in Ethiopic) is the oldest segment of the Enoch literature and the first real apocalypse[33]. Enoch is called both a scribe ("of righteousness", 12,3; and "of truth", 15,1) and a wise man (4Q203 8 4; 4Q206 2 2; 4Q530 2 ii = 6-12[?] 14) whose words and visions consist of "wisdom" (37,1-4; cf. Jub 4,17-25) that he is to teach to "men of old" and to his "children" (37,2; 81,6)[34]. Yet, he is also called a "seer", i.e., "one who sees", in particular visions (Book of Dreams) about the cosmos and what "has happened and will happen" (Jub 17-25). He has ascended into heaven (1 Enoch 39,3), journeyed to the mythical locations of the various dimensions of the universe and seen the astronomical features of the cosmos ((see the Astronomical Book)[35]. The only two sections of the book that are clearly apocalyptic visions in content and form are the "Book of Dreams" (1 Enoch 83-90) and the Apocalypse of Weeks (1 Enoch 93,1-10; 91,12-17), both of which pertain to the visions of the continuum of historical periods seen by Enoch.

Greek and Aramaic fragments of this text were discovered in Qumran. 4QMysteries and 4QInstruction are both apocalyptic and sapiential and

32. For a detailed look at the theology and literary characteristics of apocalyptic seers see J.J. COLLINS' *Apocalyptic Imagination*; and the collection of essays in the volume edited by J.J. COLLINS and J.H. CHARLESWORTH (eds.), *Mysteries and Revelations. Apocalyptic Studies Since the Uppsala Colloquium*, Sheffield, JSOT, 1991.

33. J.T. MILIK, *The Books of Enoch*, Oxford, Oxford University Press, 1976; J.C. VANDERKAM, *Enoch and the Growth of an Apocalyptic Tradition* (CBQMS, 16), Washington, DC, 1984; G.E. NICKELSBURG, *1 Enoch* (Hermeneia), Minneapolis, MN, Fortress Press, 2001; and the essay by M.A. KNIBB in this volume, *The Book of Enoch in the Light of the Qumran Wisdom Literature*. The Book of First Enoch and other pseudonymous books (Abraham, Moses, Daniel, Ezra, and Baruch) point to presumed "authors" whose experience is reflected in their teachings: e.g., Enoch and the mysteries of the heavens, Solomon and sapiential authority, and Moses and the Law.

34. See the work by R.A. ARGALL, *1 Enoch and Sirach. A Comparative Literary and Conceptual Analysis of the Themes of Revelation, Creation and Judgment* (Early Judaism and Its Literature, 8), Atlanta, GA, Scholars Press, 1995.

35. The distinction between heavenly ascents and cosmic journeys begins to disappear in later apocalyptic texts. See D. DIMANT, *Apocalyptic Texts at Qumran*, in E. ULRICH and J.C. VANDERKAM (eds.), *The Community of the Renewed Covenant*, Notre Dame, IN, University of Notre Dame, 1994, p. 183.

are similar in content to 1 Enoch. This text may be divided into five sections: the Book of the Watchers (1-36), the Similitudes (37-71), the Astronomical Book (72-82), the Book of Dreams (83-90), and the Epistle (91-105). All but the Similitudes date from the third to the early second centuries BCE. The Similitudes are much later and are usually dated somewhere in the first century BCE. The Astronomical Book and the Book of the Watchers are the two oldest parts of the Enoch literature and precede the final composition of the Book of Daniel. The first deals with the stars important for establishing a proper calendar, while the second speaks of the Watchers, i.e. fallen angels who offer forbidden knowledge to humans (see Gen 6 and the "sons of God"), and details Enoch's ascent to the heavens and journeys to the ends of the earth. The Book of the Watchers is composed by scribes for whom eschatology played an important theological role, and they engaged in a prediction of the future. This Book focuses on the problem of evil, the origins of which are attributed to fallen angels led by Asael and Shemihaza who slept with human women and taught them the secrets of heaven (see Gen 6,4), an eschatological judgment, and punishment or reward for human beings depending on their behavior and piety (thus a moral theology of retribution and an aspect of apocalyptic dualism). The Watchers are ultimately punished.

The Book of Daniel, another apocalypse, is comprised of two major parts: the narrative tales of Daniel and other pious men (chaps. 1-6) and the visions (chaps. 7-12). The tales more than likely come from the third century BCE, while the visions that are interpreted for Daniel by an angel date from the period of the Maccabean revolt (168-164 BCE). The pseudonymous author, Daniel, is also an apocalyptic sage whose name is associated with a legendary hero, Dan'el, of Ugaritic myth. In the tales of the Book of Daniel (chaps. 1-6), he is a pious hero, a sage, and, through the revelations from God and his angels, an interpreter of dreams and signs. In these tales, he is spoken about in the third person. The heroes, Daniel and his companions, are not the warriors, the Maccabees, but rather those who endure suffering for their religious faith and practice (chaps. 1, 3, and 6). Daniel is also an interpreter of dreams and signs (chapters 2, 4, and 5). The shift to the first person narrative style occurs in chapters 7-12. Here, Daniel is assisted in receiving the proper interpretations for his dreams and visions by angels.

This text, like parts of Enoch before it, begins to show some indication of the merging of apocalyptic and wisdom (the reference to sages [חכם], 2,21.27.48; Daniel as the ideal mantic sage and interpreter of dreams in chapters 4-5, especially 5,11; Daniel as the chief among the Babylonian sages, 2,12-14.18.24.27.48; 4,3.15; 5,7f.11; and Daniel as the chief interpreter of dreams and riddles, 2,19; 5,12). This mantic wisdom of Daniel is combined with the education at the Babylonian royal court (chapter 1). Qumran texts contain a number of fragments of Daniel: 1Q71-72, 4Q112-116, and 6Q7, suggesting that this biblical book was a popular one in the Qumran community and helped to shape their apocalyptic theology.

The Wisdom of Solomon is a Hellenistic-Roman Jewish text, written in Greek, that attempts to present Judaism in a Hellenistic guise that would be acceptable to pagan hosts of Jews of the Diaspora, especially those in Alexandria of Egypt, the probable setting for the origins of this book. The text dates somewhere between the first century BCE (the control of Egypt by Imperial Rome in 30 BCE) and the end of the first century CE. This text is not found in the literature of Qumran. The sapiential literary forms of Wisdom play a significant role in the Book as do apocalyptic themes[36]. The teacher who speaks is a teacher who sets forth an exhortatory speech or homily of persuasion (*logos protreptikos*) that points to the evils of idolatry, the spiritual nature of revelation that comes to the pious from the indwelling of divine wisdom, and the election of Israel. The apocalyptic themes deal with the origins of evil (the devil), the final judgment, the immortality of the soul of the righteous, the providential guidance of cosmos and history, and the salvation of God's chosen people who participate in the original exodus and typify those who are to experience future deliverance.

By contrast, Ben Sirah (ca 200 to 180 BCE) follows much more the tradition of the identification of Torah and wisdom. For Ben Sirah, it is the sage, not the apocalyptic seer, who, through the obtaining of wisdom and revealed knowledge, is the true interpreter of the Torah. Ben Sirah, as did Qoheleth before him, rejected apocalyptic thought, choosing, instead, a theology in which wisdom, the fear of God (religious piety and worship), the Torah, and salvation history come together in pointing to a type of realized eschatology in the temple cult of early second century Jerusalem.

These apocalyptic and sapiential texts result from the merging of a variety of streams of tradition from different sources: Canaanite myth, Persian dualism, ancient Near Eastern wisdom and divination, Israelite and Jewish prophecy, and Israelite and Jewish wisdom texts[37]. Thus, it

36. See J.J. COLLINS, *Cosmos and Salvation* (n. 29), pp. 121-142.

37. A. LANGE argues that Qoheleth engages in a criticism of a type of wisdom associated with the temple. This Torah wisdom is also found in the non-Essene wisdom texts in Qumran. See *In Diskussion mit dem Tempel* (n. 3), pp. 145-147. Elsewhere he has argued in much greater detail that Qoheleth contends not only with traditional wisdom, but also with the later merging of wisdom and Torah in the post-exilic period (*Weisheit und Torheit* [n. 26]).

becomes clear that the major stream of religious thought in post-exilic Judaism divides into a variety of tributaries that flow together again in various texts and times in different communities.

APOCALYPTIC SAGES

The most plausible theory for the interpretation of Qoheleth's opponents is that they were primarily apocalyptic sages who were active in the third century BCE and combined apocalyptic language and thought with traditional wisdom and the Torah. Their successors were present in communities like the one in Qumran[38].

These opponents who are actively in conflict with Qoheleth may be seen in the passages found in 2,1-26; 3,10-15.18-22; 4,1-5,19; 6,10–7,14; 9,1-10; and 11,1-9. In the language of Qoheleth, it is clear that he is in conversation with traditional wisdom and takes a critical stance toward it. But he also engages in conflict with a type of wisdom that included apocalyptic themes. One of the clearest cases of his criticism of this type of apocalyptic wisdom is 7,1-10. Michel, who argues that Qoheleth has a theological position that opposes other, contemporary theologies, suggests that the first six verses do not correspond with what he has elsewhere said about "joy", i.e. *carpe diem* (e.g., 2,24-26; 3,12-13; etc.)[39]. What earlier in 3,13 had been called the gift of God, i.e. eating, drinking, and taking pleasure from toil, is now understood as the actions of fools, i.e., those who lack insight and have hearts of stone. Michel suggests that the best explanation of these conflicting verses is that Qoheleth is citing and then arguing against a theology of despair over current human existence that derives from oppression and injustice. This theology of despair is best understood as a deep pessimism resulting from suffering, at times severe, that contrasts with traditional wisdom that is characterized by optimism and seeks to rule the world through wise and righteous actions and behavior[40]. This suggests that an

38. For the place of apocalypticism in Qumran, see H. STEGEMANN, *Die Bedeutung der Qumranfund für die Erforschung der Apokalyptik*, in D. HELLHOLM (ed.), *Apocalypticism* (n. 26), pp. 513-514; DIMANT, *Apocalyptic Texts at Qumran* (n. 35) pp. 175-191; F. GARCÍA MARTÍNEZ, *Qumran and Apocalyptic*, Leiden, Brill, 1992; as well as J.J. COLLINS, *Apocalypticism in the Dead Sea Scrolls*, London, Routledge, 1997; P. SACCHI, *Jewish Apocalyptic* (n. 26), and F. GARCÍA MARTÍNEZ, *Apocalypticism in the Dead Sea Scrolls*, in J. COLLINS (ed.), *The Encyclopedia of Apocalypticism* 1, pp. 162-192.

39. D. MICHEL, *Weisheit und Apokalyptik*, in A.S. VAN DER WOUDE (ed.), *The Book of Daniel in the Light of New Findings* (BETL, 106), Leuven, Peeters – University Press, 1993, pp. 413-434. See his detailed volume, *Untersuchungen zur Eigenart des Buches Qohelet* (BZAW, 183), Berlin, de Gruyter, 1989.

40. MICHEL, *Weisheit und Apokalyptik*, even argues that the traditional sages believed in life after death (see Psalms 37; 73; and Proverbs 2). This position is, in my estimation, not convincing.

apocalyptic view of despair over the present state of human existence characterizes the views of Qoheleth's opponents. In v. 10, the opponents' view that the "former days" were better than the present ones is rejected by Qoheleth who argues that this view does not result from "wisdom". The opponents apparently argued that reality was in a cosmic decline, with each passing eon being worse than the one before. For Qoheleth the end, i.e. death, is better than the beginning, since it is human destiny to be born to suffer in ignorance and darkness only to die in the blackness of oblivion and to be erased from human memory.

In 7,7-9 the discussion changes to Qoheleth's presentation of the views of traditional wisdom. The first is the observation that oppression makes the wise foolish (v. 7). Even more important, however, are the three wisdom sayings in vv. 8-9. Here, Qoheleth cites traditional wisdom in rejecting the pessimism of his opponents. The first two are "better" sayings that indicate that the conclusion of an event or matter is more important than its inception (v. 8a) and that the patient in spirit are better than the proud. The third saying (v. 9) rejects the attitude of "sorrow" (כעס), for this type of human emotion characterizes, not the sage, but the fool. In spite of the fact that humans do suffer in life, Qoheleth asserts the view that this pessimism about the present is not a proper attitude. Thus, the fact that death is better than birth is no cause for distress, since only fools harbor this feeling. The true sage is the one who patiently experiences the understanding of being born to suffer, a suffering that ends only when death comes. The one possible boon to human existence that may or may not come is the divine gift of joy. Thus, in 7,1-10 the opponents of Qoheleth assert that the present is worst than the past, that a wise person cannot rejoice in the world, and that a sage must be in the house of mourning with his thoughts, rather than in the house of rejoicing. Qoheleth views such a position as corruptive of true wisdom that enables one to make wise judgments. Qoheleth may agree with his opponents that one may live in a time of oppression, only for Qoheleth this is not an occasion for pessimism, but rather a time to do what one can in present circumstances to experience joy when and if it comes. The position of the opponents is odd even for the Book of Proverbs and thus seems to find its origins in the pessimism of apocalyptic about the present.

The key texts for identifying the opponents of Qoheleth include especially Qoheleth's teachings in 3,10-15 and 3,16.18-22. The disciples of these apocalyptic sages are also present, so one may argue, in the redaction of Qoheleth in 3,17, and 12,9-14. The reference to the "commandments" in the Epilogue suggests perhaps a second hand of one who, in the sapiential tradition of Ben Sirah, identified wisdom with the fear of God and Torah (12,13). These apocalyptic sages are primarily teachers who combine typical wisdom forms and teachings with apocalyptic thought and language. The apocalyptic features present in the content of the opponents of Qoheleth included in particular the stress placed on a final judgment of the righteous and wicked, the immortality of the righteous, the knowledge of God and divine action, and the holistic structure of time and events (Qoheleth 3). Qoheleth opposed their sapiential affirmations of the justice of God, earthly retribution, moral dualism (the wicked and the righteous), and the understanding of the correlation of time and event for a successful outcome. While Qoheleth is critical of the Torah's teaching concerning sacrificial worship in the temple and the making of vows, the redaction of Qoheleth found a place for the teachings of the priestly commandments (12,13b).

In the merging of traditions during the Hellenistic period, one finds the blending of wisdom and apocalyptic in the thought of some Jewish circles prior to the Essenes who founded the community of Qumran. This combination of what originally were two very different views of reality began as early as the third century, BCE. It is clear that apocalyptic sages were active in communities like the one in Qumran and likely before its founding[41]. It seems clear that at least some of the non-sectarian, pre-Qumran texts were written in a different social and religious context than that of the desert sectarians. Some texts, for example the Words of the Heavenly Luminaries (4Q504-506), the Mysteries of Creation (4Q304-305), and 4QInstruction (4Q416-18) have no known place of origin. These texts were taken by the Essenes into their own library to aid in shaping some of their instruction in theology and the moral life. 4QInstruction, a precursor to the Qumran community, demonstrates that wisdom and apocalyptic already had begun to come together in earlier Jewish thought from the third century BCE. The Qumran sectarians con-

41. T. ELGVIN, *Wisdom with and without Apocalyptic*, in D.K. FALK and F. GARCÍA MARTÍNEZ (eds.), *Sapiential, Liturgical and Poetical Texts from Qumran. Proceedings of the Third Meeting of the International Organization for Qumran Studies Oslo 1998*, Leiden, Brill, 2000, pp. 15-38. For the place of apocalypticism in Qumran, see H. STEGEMANN, pp. 513-514; DIMANT, pp. 175-191; F. GARCÍA MARTÍNEZ, *Qumran and Apocalyptic*; as well as J. COLLINS, *Apocalypticism in the Dead Sea Scrolls*; P. SACCHI, *Jewish Apocalyptic* (n. 26), and F. GARCÍA MARTÍNEZ, *Apocalypticism in the Dead Sea Scrolls*; J.J. COLLINS (ed.) *The Encyclopedia Of Apocalypticism 1*. For wisdom texts, see W.L. LIPSCOMB and J. A. SANDERS, *Wisdom at Qumran*, in J.G. GAMMIE (ed.), *Israelite Wisdom*, Missoula, MT, Scholars Press, 1978, pp. 277-285; C.A. NEWSOM, *The Sage in the Literature of Qumran. The Functions of the Maśkîl*, in J.G. GAMMIE and L.G. PERDUE, *The Sage in Israel and the Ancient Near East*, 373-382; D.J. HARRINGTON, *Wisdom Texts from Qumran* (The Literature of the Dead Sea scrolls), London, Routledge, 1996, and T. ELGVIN, *The Reconstruction of Sapiential Work A*, in *RQ* 16 (1995) 559-580.

sidered this combination in some of their own writings, including 1QS iii:13-iv:26. While these sectarians used sapiential language and thought, they came to interpret history apocalyptically.

Wisdom texts found in Qumran handle both the moral life and theological teaching. This may have been true even in the community's use of Qoheleth. The presence and use of Qoheleth at Qumran is indicated by the discovery of two fragments of Qoheleth manuscripts (4Q109 = 5,13-17, 6,3-8, 7,1-2, 4-9, 19-20; and 4Q110 = 1, 10-13, 1, 13f.), dating perhaps as early as the middle of the second century, BCE. One discovers the combination of wisdom and apocalyptic especially in 4QInstruction held a prominent place in the library, thought, and life of the Qumran community in the early part of the second century, BCE and informed sectarian thought. For example, 4QInstruction (4Q415-18, 4Q423), Enoch, and Daniel add to traditional wisdom teaching the eschatological themes of revelation through divine wisdom, eternal life, dualism, determinism, and judgment after death. The scrolls of the Qumran community are understood as indicating that the community that produced or, in certain cases, transmitted them is undergoing a period of persecution and is involved in an ongoing struggle between good and evil that would climax in a great war that would be won by God, the good angels, and the community of the righteous. Thus, study, piety, knowledge of sacred things, and moral behavior are the major categories of virtues taught to the participants in the community and most likely the larger sect, probably the Essenes, to whom the community likely belonged.

The sapiential texts of Qumran teach, in addition, that the final judgment is immanent[42]. Wisdom enables a person to escape destruction, both now and in the world to come. One finds that the wise and righteous as well as the wicked and foolish of Proverbs are categories now used to identify two different classifications of people: "those inside the sectarian fold and those outside, those chosen by God and those rejected, the 'children of light' and 'children of darkness'"[43]. One Mystery text

42. For the judgment of the wicked and the faithful, see 4Q416 frg. 1, D. For a study of wisdom in the Scrolls, in addition to HARRINGTON, *Wisdom Texts from Qumran* (n. 41), see J.I. KAMPEN, *Diverse Aspects of Wisdom*, in P.W. FLINT and J.C. VANDERKAM (eds.), *The Dead Sea Scrolls after Fifty Years 1*, Leiden, Brill, 1998, pp. 211-243; and C. HEMPEL, A. LANGE, and H. LICHTENBERGER (eds.), *The Wisdom Texts from Qumran and the Development of Sapiential Thought* (BETL, 159), Leuven, Peeters – University Press, 2002.

43. P.R. DAVIES, G.J. BROOKE and P.R. CALLAWAY (eds.), *The Complete World of the Dead Sea Scrolls*, London, Thames and Hudson, 2002. The teacher of righteousness is the *maśkîl* which represents a social rank of wise man instead of a leader of the community.

(4Q301), presented in a first person style, speaks of God's goodness to the elect and his punishment of the wicked. It is from the temple of the kingdom that God will establish cosmic justice. Other community texts speak of wisdom and creation, including the "Meditations on Creation" (4Q303-305). These three fragments speak of the reader's ability to discern divine wisdom in the acts of creation[44]. Still others speak of the design of God's creation, following the teachings of the community that lead to a life of virtue, meditation on the ages of the worlds, naming the faithful the "children of the dawn" (4Q298), and instruction of the members of the community to reflect on "the former years and contemplate the events of past generations". At Qumran wisdom is personified and plays a role in creation[45]. The "Hymn to the Creator" (in 11QPs[a]) brings together the language and thought of wisdom with creation theology[46]. However, the community's wisdom texts may have been more interested in the "future eschatological judgment as the horizon for ethical activity than in the past or the present of creation".

Wisdom, according to the apocalyptic sages, includes not only knowledge of the world through study and reflection on human experience, but also esoteric understanding of the cosmos, history, and divine world (e.g., 11QPs[a], see Psalm 154 in col. 18, v. 3). Esoteric knowledge comes from divine revelation that is given by God to a chosen group. Salvation comes from this knowledge and its embodiment in human life[47].

Dualism is an element of apocalyptic and wisdom that appears in Qumran, which includes both "cosmic-eschatological and "psychological ethical" dimensions[48]. In 1QS iii 13-iv 26 (see the Testament of the Twelve Patriarchs), one finds a list of virtues and vices. Thus, the apocalyptic sage(s) who composed this text uses biblical wisdom, particularly Proverbs, to divide humans into two groups active in the two spheres of good and evil. This dualism is present in the contrast between the wise-righteous and foolish-wicked (see especially Prov 10-15). This moralistic dualism between people is found in the redaction of the opponents of Qoheleth. For example, in the final judgment, the righteous and wicked will be judged by God (3,17). This verse also points to the presence in

44. *Ibid.*, p. 142.

45. See the *Hymn to the Creator* (11QPs[a] col. 26,9-15). Cf. Proverbs 8-9, Job 28, and Sirach 24.

46. D. HARRINGTON, *Wisdom Texts from Qumran* (n. 41); L.G. PERDUE, *Wisdom and Creation* (n. 29).

47. S. TANZER, *The Sages at Qumran. Wisdom in the Hodayot*, Dissertation Harvard University, 1987.

48. B. OTZEN, *Old Testament Wisdom Literature and Dualistic Thinking in Late Judaism*, in *Congress Volume: Edinburgh 1974* (VTSup, 28), Leiden, Brill, 1975, pp. 146-157; and M. HENGEL, *Judaism and Hellenism 1*, Philadelphia, PA, 1974, pp. 218-247.

Qoheleth of the cosmic-eschatological dimension of dualism in apocalyptic wisdom.

While much of the literature of Qumran was apocalyptic, there were also sapiential texts demonstrated by fragments of Proverbs (4Q102-103), Job (4Q99-101; Targums of Job 4Q and 11Q), Qoheleth (4Q109-110), and Ben Sirah (2Q18 and 11Q5) and by the presence of sapiential and apocalyptic-sapiential texts.

4Q184 and 185 are wisdom texts that present a literary personification of folly in the guise of the wicked woman (cf. the "strange woman" in Prov. 2,16-19; 5,1-23; 6,23-26; 7,1-27; and 9,13-18)[49]. 4Q185 also issues an instruction that, among various topics, sets forth the brevity of human life and the fear that results from the beholding of divine power. Here the sage warns his listeners against choosing the way of foolishness and exhorts them instead to take the path of wisdom and righteousness.

The six fragments of 4QInstruction found in Cave 4 are the most comprehensive sapiential text in Qumran and is similar to the Book of Enoch, in particular "The Book of Watchers" and the "Epistle of Enoch". The emphases of this text include creation, providence, wisdom, the revelation especially of esoteric knowledge to the elect, an eschatological understanding of history and the eons of time, and a final judgment[50]. 4QInstruction (see 4Q416, 417, 418; 1 Q26; 4Q415; and 4Q423) is an extremely popular text at Qumran, written in Herodian script of the late first century BCE or early first century CE. It is similar to other traditional wisdom texts, including Proverbs (especially 22, 17-24, 22), Ben Sirah, and late Egyptian texts, including Amenemopet and 'Onchsheshonq. This text combines wisdom teaching with the earlier sages' understanding of the cosmological order and a final eschatological judgment that would destroy the wicked and vindicate the righteous.

Other Qumran sapiential instructions include 4Q424 (those to avoid and those to seek out as friends in order to be successful) and 4Q420-21 (the traits of the righteous). Harrington indicates that other sapiential

49. T. TOBIN, *4Q185 and Jewish Wisdom Literature*, in H.W. ATTRIDGE, J.J. COLLINS, and T. TOBIN (eds.), *Of Scribes and Scrolls: Studies on the Hebrew Bible, Intertestamental Judaism, and Christian Origins. Presented to John Strugnell on the Occasion of His Sixtieth Birthday* (CTSRR, 5), Lanham, MD, University Press of America, pp. 145-152.

50. T. ELGVIN, *Wisdom, Revelation, and Eschatology in an Early Essene Writing*, in *SBL Seminar Papers* (1995) 440-463. For an overview of eschatology in the writings of Qumran, see J.J. COLLINS, *The Expectation of the End in the Dead Sea Scrolls*, in C.A. EVANS and P.W. FLINT (eds.), *Eschatology, Messianism, and the Dead Sea Scrolls*, Grand Rapids, MI, Eerdmans, 1997, pp. 74-90.

writings include 4Q413 that is the initial part of a hymn praising the obtaining of wisdom, 4Q298 that introduces an instruction by the *maśkîl* of the "sons of dawn", 4Q525 that lists five beatitudes as well as other materials too fragmentary to read, and the Book of Mysteries, 4Q299-301, the last text of which indicates the connection between wisdom and apocalyptic[51]. There is also in 4QBeatitudes a connection drawn between wisdom and the Torah (4Q525 4).

According to Harrington, the most important contribution of wisdom from Qumran texts is "...the insistence on wisdom as a gift from God and on the need for understanding the 'mystery that is to be/come'" or "a mystery that is coming into being" (רז נהיה)[52]. Wisdom is knowledge of a "mystery". This "mystery" is "a body of teaching that involves creation, ethical activity, and eschatology" (e.g., 4Q417 2 i 8-9)[53]. Creation and understanding of the cosmos is not simply eschatological, but also the order of reality and God's participation in human history. The "Mysteries" (1 Q27; 4Q299-300) belong to the wisdom texts and tell of "God's foreknowledge and predestination of all events and plans in history"[54]. Sadly, humans did not know this wisdom. Even so, wisdom's foundation is located in creation and provides practical moral counsel.

The merger of apocalyptic and sapiential texts forms the writings of apocalyptic sages. Qoheleth strongly opposed much of the teachings of the traditional sages, and he was strongly against the major themes of apocalyptic, including especially knowledge of divine character and activity, eschatological judgment of the righteous and the wicked, and life after death. It may well have been the case that Qoheleth was familiar with this type of apocalyptic wisdom in its early form during the Hellenistic period. As supported by the library at Qumran, along with other proto- and early apocalyptic texts, some of Qoheleth's opponents would have been sages who had some familiarity with apocalyptic literature and thought.

51. HARRINGTON, *Wisdom Texts from Qumran* (n. 41), pp. 60-74.
52. *Ibid.*, pp. 40-41.
53. *Ibid.*, p. 83.
54. P. DAVIES, G. BROOKE, and P. CALLAWAY (eds.), *The Complete World of the Dead Sea Scrolls* (n. 43), p. 141; L.H. SCHIFFMAN, *4QMysteries: A Preliminary Translation*, in *Proceedings of the Eleventh World Congress of Jewish Studies. Division A*, Jerusalem, World Union of Jewish Studies, 1994, pp. 199-206; ID., *4QMysteries^{b}, a Preliminary Edition*, in *RQ* 16 (1993) 203-223; and ID., *4QMysteries^{a}: A Preliminary Edition and Translation*, in Z. ZEVIT, S. GITIN and M. SOKOLOFF (eds.), *Solving Riddles and Untying Knots. Biblical, Epigraphic, and Semitic Studies in Honor of Jonas C. Greenfield*, Winona Lake, IN, Eisenbrauns, 1995, pp. 207-226.

QOHELETH 3,10-22 AND THE APOCALYPTIC SAGES

In 3,10-15[55], Qoheleth teaches:

> I have seen the business that God has given to humanity[56] with which to be busy. He has made everything appropriate for its time. Moreover, he has put the sense of the sense of mystery into their minds, without their discovering what he has done from the beginning to the end. I know that there is nothing better for them than to be happy and enjoy themselves as long as they live; in addition, it is God's gift that humanity should eat, drink, and take pleasure in all their toil. I know that whatever God does endures forever; nothing can be added to it, nor anything taken from it; God has done this, so that all should fear him. That which is, already has been before; that which is to be, already is; and God will search out that which has already vanished.

This section follows immediately the dualistic poem on time (3,1-8) and the resultant question (3,9) concerning the "gain, profit" that results from these human activities. Qoheleth 3,1-9 is a poem and a conclusion drawn on the correlation between time and action. Unlike the early apocalyptic sages who speak of a divine determinism of time and action known by the sages, there is no evidence for knowing both the structure of cosmic time and when certain actions are to occur to ensure their success and to profit from human toil. God himself is not only unknowable, even to the sages, but also hidden and distant. Indeed, for Qoheleth, God is the one who has determined the activity (ענין) of human beings (3,10; cf. 1,13b). This activity (ענין), earlier in the book described as "unfortunate" (1,13b, רע), is all-inclusive, for it is connected to the individual punctilious times (עת, 3,1-8,11) of the duality of actions and their opposites that may well be set within a (pre-determined?) cosmic order of time (זמן; see 3,1). For the apocalyptic sages, God has determined certain periods or eons that will result ultimately in an eschatological judgment and life beyond the tomb, and he determines when certain individual actions of human beings are to occur. However, for Qoheleth the particular times of human actions and their opposites have no overarching cosmic order of time and action open to human knowledge[57]. Thus, human activity (3,10), because it cannot be placed within a

55. K. GALLING, *Das Rätsel der Zeit*, in *ZTK* 58 (1961) 1-15.

56. A. SCHOORS notes that the expression, בני אדם, refers to humanity in Qoheleth (1,13; 2,3.8; 3,10.18.19.21; 8,11; 9,3.12) as does the word אדם with the definite article and those cases in when the syntax requires its elimination: *The Word* אדם *in Qoheleth*, in K. VAN LERBERGHE and A. SCHOORS (eds.), *Immigration and Emigration within the Ancient Near East* (Orientalia Lovaniensia Analecta, 65), Leuven, University Press – Peeters, 1998, pp. 339-356.

57. T. KRÜGER, *Die Rezeption der Tora im Buch Kohelet*, in L. SCHWIENHORST-SCHÖNBERGER (eds.), *Das Buch Kohelet* (n. 21), pp. 303-325. A. LANGE has argued that "Koh steht in drassen Widerspruch zum Weisheitsnomismus seiner Zeit: Die von Gott

cosmic order of time and action that allows one to know when and how to act in a successful manner is, according to 1,13 "unfortunate". Furthermore, the structure of time that includes divinely determined eons is not available to human knowledge. And, as we shall see later, there is for Qoheleth no evidence of any final judgment or life at the end of time. These secrets or mysteries result from the inability of sages and seers to know the nature and activity of the hidden God.

Some apocalyptic sages believed that human actions could influence their perpetrators' destiny, allowing them to belong to the chosen who would experience the coming salvation from oppression and death. Qoheleth, however, rejected the teaching that humans could influence their fate, even on the earth, through their behavior and the practice of wisdom (9,1-3). Ultimately, so he taught, the same fate awaited both the unrighteous wise and the wicked fool: the darkness of death and forgetfulness in collective human memory (2,14-16; 9,1-3). The apocalyptic seers argued that God has revealed the order of time and divine actions at least to a select few. However, Qoheleth denies that humans are able to know anything for sure, save for the fact that they will die (9,5). God has determined that human activity is to be without "profit", i.e. to lead to nothing that endures. This lack of permanency or continuation beyond death was ordained by God in order to "afflict" human beings.

In contrast to the apocalyptic sages, Qoheleth argues in 3,10-15 that all that God has "done" (עשׂה) as well as the creation (מעשׂה) he has made (עשׂה), including the time of its endurance, from the beginning (ראשׁ) to the end (סוף), are not open to human knowledge (v. 11; contra 4Q418 123 I-ii 3-4)[58]. Unlike the traditional sages before and after him,

gestiftete Ordnung, welche sich im Gesetz artikulierte, is für ihn zum Daemon geworden. Sie has ihren positiven Wert verloren. Ihre Alternative is die widergesetzliche Lebensfreude", *Weisheit und Torheit bei Kohelet* (n. 26), p. 177. According to Lange's careful study, Qoheleth not only enters into disputation with traditional wisdom, but also with a sapiential order articulated in the Torah (see M. WEINFELD, *Deuteronomy and the Deuteronomic School*, Oxford, University Press, 1972). Thus, one finds in Qoheleth the references to vows (5,3, see Deut 23,22-24) and sin sacrifice (4,7; see Leviticus 4-5; Num 15,22-31). In my view, it is true that Qoheleth is critical of the temple cult that is affirmed as valid by traditional sages (see my *Wisdom and Cult* [SBLDS, 30], Missoula, MT, Scholars Press, 1977). It is my view that the cult, including the emerging Torah in the exilic and post-exilic periods, is a part of the larger order of traditional wisdom thought. The merging of wisdom and the Torah is central to Ben Sirah and is found in some of the Qumran texts. Qoheleth's view of the lack of order has to do, not specifically with the inadequacy of the Torah, but rather with the fragmentation of the cosmos that was at the heart of earlier traditional wisdom's understanding of creation, social structure, moral and cultic behavior. Lange is correct in his argument that the "joy of life", regarded as foolishness in earlier wisdom, is for Qoheleth the central important value in human living that is in opposition to the dissolution of traditional wisdom.

58. See the comprehensive study of Qoheleth's view of creation in the study by M. SCHUBERT, *Schöpfungstheologie bei Qoheleth* (BEATAJ, 15), Frankfurt, Peter Lang, 1989.

Qoheleth rejects the understanding that the "data" of the world is open to human perception. This means that wisdom is no longer the ability to see a divine order in the cosmos that may be construed in the teachings of the wise[59]. In addition, divine activities and their consequent results will endure forever, unlike human activities that disappear and are quickly forgotten (1,11; 2,11). The creator knows and continues the past into the present and repeats all events that he chooses (3,15; contra "those who pursue knowledge" in 4Q299 8). He has made and maintains creation and acts decisively in order to demonstrate his unchallenged sovereignty before all human creatures who consequently "fear" (ירא) him (3,14)[60]. God does not reveal to anyone the inherent character, movement, and temporal nature of divine creation and events. Even if this revelation were offered, humans would possess neither the knowledge nor the power to add to or take away from what God has done (3,14).

Humans' inability to know God, the world, and the proper time to act is due to העלם that the creator has placed in the human mind (see 1,4, 10; 2,16; 3,14; 9,6; 12,5). This הָעֹלָם is a *crux interpretatum*, open to a variety of meanings: "the totality of time", "the world", but most likely, "mystery" or "concealment"[61]. Humans desire to know divine activity in ist past, present, and future forms ("from the beginning, ראש, to the end, סוף), a desire that the apocalyptic seers believed possible for a chosen few who received divine revelation in dreams and visions[62].

59. H. GESE, *Lehre und Wirklichkeit in der alten Weisheit*, Tübingen, J.C.B. Mohr (Paul Siebeck), 1958; and H.-H. SCHMID, *Gerechtigkeit als Weltordnung* (BHT, 40), Tübingen, J.C.B. Mohr (Paul Siebeck), 1968; LANGE, *In Diskussion mit dem Tempel* (n. 3), p. 119.

60. The "fear of God" (3,14; 5,6; 7,16-18; 8,10-13; 12,13 [redactional] in Qoheleth is discussed by E. PFEIFFER, *Die Gottesfurcht im Buche Kohelet*, in H. GRAF REVENTLOW (ed.), *Gottes Wort und Gottes Land*, Göttingen, Vandenhoeck & Ruprecht, 1965, pp.133-158; and H.-P. MÜLLER, *Wie sprach Qohälät von Gott,* in *VT* 18 (1968) 507-521. For a comprehensive study, see S. PLATH, *Furcht Gottes* (AzT, 2), Stuttgart, Calwer, 1962. For a detailed review of the "fear of God" in the Hebrew Bible, see J. BECKER, *Gottesfurcht im Alten Testament* (AnB, 25), Rome, Pontifical Biblical Institute, 1963.

61. "Mystery, secret thing, what is hidden" (עולם; see 12,14; Job 28,21; 42,3; Daniel 2 and 4). This would correlate to *raz nihyeh* (רז נהיה) in Qumran, meaning that Qoheleth has the inability to know the "history of creation" and "divine activity". See T. ELGVIN, *Wisdom, Revelation, and Eschatology* (n. 51).

62. In 4Q417 2 I 8-9, the cosmological theme that speaks of the mystery of divine creation is translated by Harrington: "For the God of knowledge is the foundation of truth, and by the *raz nihyeh* (רז נהיה) He has laid out its foundation, and its deeds He has prepared with (…) wisdom, and with all cunning He has fashioned it. And the domain of its deeds (…). And He expounded for their understanding every deed so that he could walk in the inclination of his understanding. And He expounded for hu(mankind …), and in purity of understanding were made known the secrets of his plan together with how he should walk perfect(ly in all his wo)rks. These things investigate always, and gain under-

This was not the case for Qoheleth who believed that divine actions, including those of predestination of the fate of human beings, remained shrouded in mystery (cf. Prov 16,9; 19,21; 20,24; 21,30-31; 27,1; and 30,2-4). Indeed, humans, even the wise, not only are incapable of knowing divine time and activity (3,15)[63], they are also unable to know the cosmological order of time and its associated divine and human actions due to the severe constraints of human knowledge decreed by God[64]. Thus, humans are incapable of understanding the past, present, and future actions of God, the nature of creation, or what he has predetermined (contrast 4Q299 3a ii-b, 5 and 6 I-ii; 4Q300 5[?]). While Qoheleth could affirm that God has created "everything (הכל) appropriate (יפה, which contrasts with "good" טוב in Gen 1,31; see 1,4ff.) for its time" (Qoh 3,10.12.18.21.24) and that there well may be a temporal cosmic order or law of time and action, this cannot be observed and understood by the sages. Thus, humans, even the sages, could not know when and how to act wisely and successfully. This is the "activity" God has given to humanity: the inability to know the correlation of times and actions. Nevertheless, Qoheleth still teaches the "appropriateness" of everything that exists in creation for its time. Thus, he rejects the apocalyptic belief that humans have so corrupted the present world that God is required to shape a new creation (Isaiah 65; "The Book of the Watchers", 1 Enoch 1-36)[65]. For Qoheleth, creation is complete in all of its features, although it is not largely accessible to human knowledge, even that of the sages.

According to Diethelm Michel, "this skepticism about human knowledge is doubtless directed against a form of wisdom that argued for the knowledge of the world and thus for the *yitrôn* that would result"[66]. Qoheleth denies there is any way to know time and events, including the hour of one's death, and he does not accept the apocalyptic teaching of a

standing (about a)ll their outcomes. And then you will know the glory of His might together with His marvelous mysteries and His mighty acts" (*Wisdom Texts from Qumran* [n. 41], p. 53). This *raz niyeh* is the "understanding of both past and future". See M. KNIBB, *The Book of Enoch in the Light of the Qumran Wisdom Literature* (in this volume, pp. 193-210).

63. "What already has been, is now, and will be" refers, not to human action "under the sun" (1:10), but rather to divine activity, from creation, to world maintenance, to the determination of the future, contra A. SCHOORS, *The Verb* hâyâ *in Qoheleth*, in D. PENCHANSKY and P. REDDITT (eds.), *Shall Not the Judge of All the Earth Do What is Right?*, Winona Lake, IN, Eisenbrauns, 2000, pp. 232-234.

64. H-P. MÜLLER, *Neige der althebraeischen 'Weisheit'. Zum Denken Qohäläts*, in *ZAW* 90 (1978) 238-268.

65. T. KRÜGER, *Alles Nichts? Zur Theologie des Buches Qohelet*, in *TZ* 57 (2001) 184-195.

66. *Untersuchungen zur Eigenart des Buches Qohelet*, p. 65.

future, probably eschatological, judgment (1,11; 9,10), for death and thus the elimination of the possibility of knowledge awaits everyone. An eschatological judgment is affirmed only in the redaction of the book (3,17; 11,9; and 12,13-14). Thus, one is to experience those moments of joy if and when they come (3,12-13)[67].

In 3,16-22, Qoheleth teaches:

> Moreover I saw under the sun that in the place of justice, there was wickedness, and in the place of righteousness there was wickedness. (I said in my heart, God will judge the righteous and the wicked, for he has appointed a time for every matter, and for every work). I said in my heart concerning humans that God is judging them to show that they are only animals. For the fate of human beings and the fate of animals is the same; as one dies, so dies the other. They all have the same spirit, and humans have no advantage over the animals, for all is vanity. All go to one place; all are from the dust, and all return to the dust. Who knows whether the human spirit goes upward, while that of animals goes downward to the earth? So I saw that there is nothing better than that all should enjoy their work for that is their lot; who can bring them to see what will be after them?

Qoheleth agrees with the apocalyptic sages that injustice prevails in the social reality of human existence. For him, this likely may be seen in the experiences that have occurred repeatedly during the rule of foreign governments over Judah. However, he disagrees with the apocalyptic sages that there will one day be an eschatological judgment that is based on human behavior. Thus, a later redactor inserted into verse 17 the statement, "God will judge the righteous and the wicked" (see also 11,9b; 12,14). These insertions likely result from the editorial activity of an apocalyptic sage who speaks of divine retribution in this life and who anticipates an eschatological judgment of either individuals or communities based on their actions (see 4QInstruction, including, e.g. 4Q416 1; and 1 Enoch)[68]. The apocalyptic sages speak of hope in the imminent future through divine intervention and action culminating in an eschatological judgment and new creation (see Deut 25,1; 1 Kings 8,13f.;

67. This joy does not result from the expectation of a new world that gave anticipation and hope to the apocalyptic seers (KRÜGER, *Alles Nichts?*, pp. 190-191).

68. See the clear and concise arguments for v. 17 as a redactional insertion by A.A. FISCHER, *Kohelet und die Frühe Apokalyptik* (n. 1), pp. 340-344. However, see the careful discussion of Schoors who discusses the implications of whether v. 17 and 11,9 are possibly original, and perhaps not redactional. If they are authentic, so he argues, then v. 17 probably suggests that both the righteous and the wicked are destined to die, since God has appointed this fate for everyone, while 11:9 indicates that there is a divine judgment of everything and everyone, though Qoheleth is not sure how; cf. A. SCHOORS, *Koheleth: A Perspective of Life after Death?*, in *ETL* 61 (1985) 295-303.

see 7,15; 8,10-14; 9,1-3; and numerous sapiential texts from Qumran)[69].

Unlike the apocalyptic sages and even earlier biblical writings (Gen 2,7), Qoheleth denies that there is a difference between the breath (רוח) of humans and animals (cf. Gen 2,7.19; 6,17; Ps 104,29-30; Job 34,14). Since both suffer the common fate of death and eventually go to one place, i.e. Sheol (3,20), human beings, like the animals, have nothing that remains. In their essence, both humans and animals are made from the dust of the earth, and at death both return to the dust (Gen 2,7; 3,19; Pss 104,29; 146,4; Job 1,21; 10,9; Qoh 12,7; and Sir 40,11). Indeed, Fischer is likely correct that לבר is a term of judgment from ברר ("separate out"). Thus, God is judging humanity in order to show them that all of them, including both wise and foolish and the righteous and the wicked, are the same as the cattle, for they all have the same fate (מקרה): death (see Psalm 49)[70].

Qoheleth's question, "Who knows whether the human spirit goes upward and the spirit of animals goes downward to the earth?" (against Daniel 12,3; 1 Enoch 104,2), is probably a rhetorical one, since it already seems to have been answered in his earlier conclusions that humans and animals at death go to the same place and that there is no distinction between them[71]. Humans and animals are both dust (see Gen 3,19; Ps 90,3; Job 10,9; and Sir 17,1). Besides, since humans do not enjoy divine revelation, the only other sphere of human knowledge, warped as it may be, is experience. Since humans die and go to Sheol where there is no memory, how would it be possible to know that there is any return of the human spirit, either at death (a Greek understanding of the immortal soul) or in a general resurrection in the end-time (Wis 2,1-9), to the creator who gave it? Most likely, Qoheleth is here engaged in a repudiation of apocalyptic sages who affirmed a life after death. Instead, for Qoheleth, the portion (חלק; 2,10.21; 5,17-18; 9,6; 9,9; 11,2) allotted to humans is to enjoy their activity if and when they can[72].

69. ELGVIN, *Wisdom, Revelation, and Eschatology* (n. 51), p. 442. He notes that 4QInstruction involves both eschatology and divine revelation to the elect. For eschatology in Qumran texts, see L.H. SCHIFFMAN, E. TOV and J.C. VANDERKAM (eds.), *Eschatological Wisdom in the Book of Qoheleth*, Jerusalem, 1997; and HARRINGTON, *Wisdom Texts from Qumran* (n. 41).

70. A.A. FISCHER, *Kohelet und die Frühe Apokalyptik* (n. 1), p. 346.

71. C.F. WHITLEY, *Koheleth. His Language and Thought* (BZAW, 148), Berlin, W. de Gruyter, 1979.

72. SCHOORS has concluded: "that 'life under the sun' is closed with death, which is final". In Sheol, "even the memory of man, so highly regarded by Sirach (chapter 44), vanishes.... To him, the disappointments with life on this earth are not compensated by the hope of a happy afterlife" (*Koheleth. A Perspective of Life after Death* [n. 69] pp. 302-303).

CONCLUSION

In conclusion, it is apparent that the library of Qumran and some of its texts demonstrate that several originally different theological and literary traditions (wisdom apocalyptic, and Torah) existed side by side and eventually began to influence each other and even at times merge together. This library, together with its texts that combined wisdom and apocalyptic, supports the view that the apocalyptic sages were most likely the major opponents of Qoheleth. The redactor, at least in 12,9-14, points to the merging of a third tradition that developed in the early second century, BCE. This editor places emphasis, not only on a final judgment and the viability of wisdom and retribution, but also on the authority of the commandments of the Torah[73].

Texas Christian University — Leo G. PERDUE
Brite Divinity School
P.O. Box 32923
Fort Worth TX 76129
USA

73. See M. GILBERT, *Qohelet et Ben Sirah*, in A. SCHOORS (ed.), *Qohelet in the Context of Wisdom* (n. 1), pp. 161-179. Gilbert discusses the issue of whether Qoh 12,13, "Fear God and keep his commandments", alludes to Sirach. Gilbert concludes that while both are dominant themes in Ben Sirah and that this redactional verse may result from the thought of Ben Sirah, there is lacking in this abbreviated statement the complexity of his thinking.

QOHÉLET ET LES SEPT REFRAINS SUR LE BONHEUR

Dans cette contribution, j'aimerais vous présenter une partie des résultats de ma thèse sur Qohélet, soutenue à Strasbourg en 2002, et publiée depuis[1]. Cette présentation ne concerne donc que le second des trois aspects de cette dialectique, le bien, et notamment une lecture suivie des sept refrains sur le bonheur qui ponctuent régulièrement le livre de Qohélet.

La première partie de ma recherche doctorale avait consisté en une exégèse exhaustive du terme רע et ses dérivés, qui, tout en comblant une lacune de la recherche, permit de dégager les conclusions suivantes: si tout est הבל, en revanche Qohélet ne dit pas הכל רע. Car si Qohélet constate de manière implacable et redoutable l'incontournable présence du mal en ce monde, non seulement il ne met pas Dieu en cause, mais encore il contrebalance existentiellement cette triste réalité par un appel pressant au bonheur, une invitation constante à profiter des joies que Dieu donne à l'homme dans son quotidien, en particulier dans une série de refrains dans lesquels la causalité divine est clairement mentionnée.

L'étude suivie de ces passages suit un cheminement ordonné, dont la progression se repère aisément dans leur agencement, chacun apportant un plus, par rapport au précédent, ainsi que l'a remarqué Whybray[2], dans son contenu et dans son mode. Une présentation ordonnée des sept refrains permet d'une part de repérer les *crescendos* qui les relient, et d'autre part de les mettre en rapport thématique avec les passages qui les précèdent. Cependant, dans le cadre de cette contribution, nous nous limiterons à donner les résultats de leur exégèse détaillée.

I. Premier refrain, Qo 2,24-26: les dons divins

S'il est vrai que le verset 1,2 (הֲבֵל הֲבָלִים הַכֹּל הָבֶל) forme une inclusion avec le verset conclusif du livre de Qohélet, il est tout aussi vrai qu'il entre en résonance avec le verdict de vanité qui ponctue le premier refrain (Qo 2,26). Ce premier jugement de vanité forme alors l'ouverture

1. *Le mal, le bien et le jugement de Dieu dans le livre de Qohélet* (OBO, 190), Fribourg, Éd. Universitaires, 2003.
2. Cf. R.N. Whybray, *Qoheleth Preacher of Joy*, in *JSOT* 23 (1982) 87-98.

de sa méditation, et il pourrait connoter lugubrement l'œuvre entière, s'il n'était suivi immédiatement d'une des questions essentielles que pose Qohélet: «Quel profit pour l'homme dans tout le travail dont il travaille sous le soleil?» (Qo 1,3).

Si la plupart des commentaires[3] constate d'emblée la place particulière de cette question en début de livre, rares sont ceux qui lui attribuent une valeur autre que rhétorique[4]. Pourtant ce questionnement initial semble bien le point de départ de la recherche de Qohélet, puisqu'il concerne l'un des points fondamentaux de toute vie humaine: quel profit l'homme a-t-il à travailler? Or, à cette première interrogation essentielle, Qohélet va associer deux autres questions fondamentales, situées elles aussi à des endroits stratégiques de ce premier passage. Les voici résumées substantiellement:

- Quel profit l'homme a-t-il à travailler? (Qo 1,3).
- Toute occupation est-elle mauvaise? (Qo 1,13).
- Que procure la joie? (Qo 2,2).

Lus à la suite l'un de l'autre ces trois versets font étonnamment sens, et paraissent concerner l'existence humaine toute entière, non seulement dans ce qui fait le quotidien vital de l'homme (le travail, la joie), mais aussi dans le sens profond qu'il attribue à la vie (que valent ses œuvres). Par ailleurs, ces trois questions acquièrent une profondeur surprenante si l'on considère les réponses que leur donne Qohélet au fil de sa méditation: commençant sa démarche par l'un des aspects existentiels les plus probants de toute vie humaine (la valeur intrinsèque du travail, dans sa fonction basique qui assure la survie, et dans sa fonction gratifiante qui procure la joie), Qohélet poursuit son questionnement en s'affrontant au problème du mal dans sa dimension humaine (Qo 1,13: les occupations de l'homme sont-elles toutes mauvaises?[5]), et le termine de manière fulgurante par le sens de la joie, dont il affirme qu'elle est un don de Dieu.

Ainsi le premier refrain clôt cette première partie (Qo 2,23-26), en appelant l'homme à apprécier les joies simples mais incontestables de la

3. Par exemple V. D'ALARIO, *Il libro del Qohelet. Struttura letteraria et retorica* (RivBib Sup., 27), Bologne, Dehoniane, 1993, p. 65, qui intitule ce verset 1,3 «L'interrogativo iniziale».

4. R. MURPHY, *Ecclesiastes* (WBC, 23 A), Dallas, TX, World Books, 1992, p. 7; J. VILCHEZ, *Ecclesiastés o Qohélet,* Estella, Verbo Divino, 1992, p. 148.

5. Cette compréhension suppose que l'on lise ce verset comme une question, avec N. LOHFINK, *Qoheleth 5:17-19: Revelation by Joy*, in *CBQ* 52 (1990) 625-635, et L. SCHWIENHORST-SCHÖNBERGER, *Nicht im Menschen gründet das Glück. Qohelet im Spannungsfeld jüdischer Weisheit und hellenistischer Philosophie* (Herders biblische Studien, 2), Fribourg-en Brisgau, Herder, 1996, p. 46, et non comme une affirmation sans appel.

vie, qui, en tout état de cause, sont des dons de Dieu. On peut cependant se demander ce qu'apporte ce premier refrain par rapport aux passages précédents où Qohélet / Salomon se réjouit de la vie (Qo 2,10). La réponse est inscrite dans deux versets du refrain: ces joies sont des *dons de Dieu* (Qo 2,24), et il est impossible de les vivre s'*Il ne le permet* (Qo 2,26)[6]. Ainsi le travail de l'homme n'est une garantie de bonheur que si Dieu permet d'en profiter; en revanche, accumuler des richesses ne procure aucun profit lorsque Dieu ne permet pas d'en jouir (Qo 6,2), et le travail dans les plaisirs fastueux ne procure aucun יתרון (Qo 2,11). Il convient alors de se réjouir dans l'instant des joies simples que Dieu donne.

II. Deuxième refrain, Qo 3,12-14: la crainte envers Dieu

La situation contextuelle de ce second refrain donne une indication très importante sur son contenu, qui semble en découler directement. Car le passage qui le précède (l'anthologie sur le temps, Qo 3,1-8) s'imbrique très étroitement avec le refrain, au point de faire corps avec lui et d'inclure les versets qui le suivent (Qo 3,9-15), et qui constituent l'un des passages théologiques les plus marquants de l'œuvre de Qohélet. En effet, si en Qo 1,13 Qohélet se demande si *toute* activité sous le ciel est mauvaise, en Qo 3,10 il répond de manière négative puisqu'il s'abstient soigneusement de qualifier cette activité humaine, évitant tout jugement prématuré, comme pour laisser le champ libre à l'agir de l'homme, qui le rendra bon ou mauvais pas ses diverses occupations. Encore une fois, Qohélet mentionne que cette activité est donnée par Dieu aux hommes, et ce don permet à ceux-ci de faire jouer, *dans une certaine mesure*, leur liberté d'agir[7].

Mais Qohélet se hâte aussitôt de fournir des limitations à cette liberté, puisqu'il précise que Dieu a fait toute chose belle en son temps et que l'homme n'a rien à y changer, car de toute façon il est dans l'incapacité de connaître son dessein (Qo 3,11)[8]. Si cette limite semble positive, l'œuvre divine étant belle (Qo 3,11) et éternelle (Qo 3,14), une seconde

6. WHYBRAY, *Qoheleth Preacher of Joy* (n. 1) écrit: «God may give joy and pleasure; man can not achieve it for himself, hoewer hard he may try».

7. Voir à ce sujet VILCHEZ, *Ecclesiastés o Qohélet* (n. 4), p. 238, qui écrit concernant le verset 3,11 de ce passage: «Dios da el *'olam* al hombre y lo da libre y soberanamente, sin condición alguna».

8. Au sujet de l'inconnaissance, voir T. KRÜGER, *Le livre de Qohélet dans le contexte de la littérature juive des III*[e] *et II*[e] *siècles avant Jésus Christ*, in *RTP* 131 (1999) 153-162; voir aussi N. LOHFINK, *Qohelet* (Die Neue Echter Bibel. Altes Testament), Brescia, Morcaelliana, 1997, p. 63.

limite, négative, a déjà été donnée par Qohélet: la mort met fin à toute activité, quelle que soit sa qualité (Qo 2,14-17). Quoiqu'il en soit, ces deux restrictions à la liberté de l'homme restent hors de la portée de celui-ci, et il n'est pas en son pouvoir d'agir sur elles, puisqu'aussi bien la mort que le plan divin font partie d'un ordre qui le dépasse. Et Qohélet insère dans ses constats théologiques son second refrain sur la joie, qui fait la part belle à l'immanence: les joies très simples et très gratifiantes de l'existence sont données par Dieu. Ce rappel de la proximité de Dieu dans le quotidien le plus humble de l'homme (boire, manger, être heureux dans son travail), ajouté à la transcendance et la beauté de son œuvre (Qo 3,11), doivent amener la créature à la crainte de son Créateur (Qo 3,14), qui est aussi reconnaissance. Cette crainte permet alors d'allier le respect de la transcendance à l'amour d'un Dieu proche et présent.

III. Troisième refrain, Qo 3,22: l'inconnaissance

Ce troisième refrain semble constituer la conclusion d'une péricope composée des versets 3,16-22, qui traite essentiellement du thème du jugement, et que nous pouvons résumer ainsi[9]: Dieu jugera le méchant, mais aussi le juste, là-bas (שָׁמָּה), devant son Tribunal (Qo 3,16.17)[10], dans tout ce qui constitue l'existence humaine (Qo 3,17). Puis Qohélet, après avoir constaté la similitude du sort corporel ultime de l'homme et de l'animal (Qo 3,18-20), s'interroge sur la destination du souffle de ce dernier. Et enfin le troisième refrain constitué du seul verset 3,22 vient clore le passage. Il est possible de comprendre ce verset en deux temps:

- Dans un premier temps, Qohélet réaffirme pour la troisième fois que le bonheur de l'homme se trouve dans son travail ou dans ses œuvres. Puis il ajoute que c'est là sa part (חֶלְקוֹ), comme l'avait déjà dit Qohélet / Salomon en Qo 2,10. Dans la pensée de Qohélet, חלק semble être synonyme de מַתַּת, et donc concerner ce qui est donné par Dieu à l'homme au cours de sa vie[11]. La similitude des sept refrains sur la joie atteste cette compréhension, et Qo 3,22 qui est moins prolixe que ses prédécesseurs, reste cependant de la même veine.

9. Pour une exégèse détaillée de ce passage, voir le chapitre troisième de notre livre.

10. Avec Schwienhorst-Schönberger, *Nicht im Menschen* (n. 5), p. 117, et D. Michel, *Untersuchungen zur Eigenart des Buches Qohelet* (BZAW, 183), Berlin, de Gruyter, 1989, p. 138.

11. Murphy, *Ecclesiastes* (n. 4), pp. 17, 37 et note 10a; voir aussie T. Zimmer, *Zwischen Tod und Lebensglück. Eine Untersuchung zur Anthropologie Kohelets* (BZAW, 286), Berlin, de Gruyter, 1999, p. 58.

- La seconde partie de ce verset conclusif est constituée d'une question rhétorique, qui apporte une seconde raison à l'homme pour se réjouir sur terre: outre le fait que les plaisirs de la vie sont des dons de Dieu, il est aussi nécessaire d'en profiter *présentement* puisque l'homme ne connaît pas «son après»[12]. Cette dernière information apporte un «plus» par rapport aux deux refrains précédents, mais n'empêche pas de se demander si Qohélet fait allusion à un avenir temporel ou à un avenir dans l'au-delà. Si l'on relie ce verset au contexte de la troisième partie, qui parle d'un jugement «là-bas», connotant un avenir *post mortem*, la seconde solution est sans aucun doute plus harmonieuse. Mais quel que soit l'avenir dont il est question, il demeure que Qohélet engage l'homme à se réjouir de la vie *maintenant*, sans se préoccuper d'un futur qu'il n'est pas donné à l'homme de connaître puisque, de toute façon, «Dieu a fait toute chose belle en son temps [...] sans que l'homme puisse découvrir l'œuvre que fait Dieu du début à la fin» (Qo 3,11).

IV. Quatrième refrain, Qo 5,17-19: la révélation de Dieu

Comme les refrains qui le précèdent, ce quatrième refrain semble en relation thématique avec ce qui le précède (Qo 4,1–5,16), au moins de manière ponctuelle. Ainsi, il est possible de suivre le fil du cheminement de la pensée de Qohélet, qui, dans une dialectique originale, apporte des réponses à ses trois questions inaugurales (Qo 1,3; 1,13; 2,1). Et ces réponses, qui n'apparaissent pas forcément dans un ordre logique, peuvent être regroupées en deux catégories:

- Oui, il y a des occupations mauvaises en ce monde, c'est-à-dire des cas particuliers de רע, ou des mauvaises occupations (toutes sortes de (וְעִנְיָן)[13].

- Mais l'homme peut trouver sa joie et son bonheur en suivant quelques conseils de vie, qui sont facilement accessibles, même si le bonheur ne trouve pas son origine dans l'homme mais en Dieu[14].

Enfin le refrain rappelle la joie de vivre et apporte à son tour un «plus» par rapport aux précédents, dans son dernier verset (Qo 5,19), où Dieu répond dans la joie du cœur de l'homme. Cette lecture implique que l'on lise le verbe ענה avec le sens de «répondre» avec Lohfink[15], qui

12. Whybray, *Qoheleth Preacher of Joy* (n. 1), p. 90 écrit: «it is because 'that is his lot' and because no one 'can let him know what will happen to him next' that man should set himself 'to enjoy his work'».

13. À ce sujet voir le premier chapitre de notre livre.

14. Voir le deuxième chapitre de notre livre.

15. Lohfink, *Qohelet* (n. 8), p. 86, qui écrit: «Nella traduzione adottata sopra ('perche Dio gli risponda con la gioia del suo cuore') l'estasi della felicità sarebbe data nel fenomeno psichico stesso della 'giogia' – in quanto questa sia cioè contemporaneamente 'riposta' divina, qualcosa di simile a una 'rivelazione'».

induit davantage que la connotation habituelle de «occuper». Car à la reconnaissance de la transcendance par l'acte créateur et donateur (qui donne la vie et la maintient), Qohélet ajoute l'immanence divine qui «répond» à l'homme. En effet, si Dieu donne à l'homme la vie et la possibilité de s'en réjouir, c'est aussi qu'il «se révèle» dans le cœur de l'homme par cette même joie[16]. Il reste à savoir en quoi consiste cette révélation.

Selon Lohfink[17], la pensée de Qohélet qui affleure dans ce verset est que la joie, qui est un don divin, permet à l'homme de ne pas penser à la mort, et donc de dépasser la «crainte de Dieu», en approchant par la joie, même fugace, quelque chose que seul Dieu voit normalement. Si nous acquiesçons à l'idée de Dieu qui se révèle dans la joie du cœur, nous pensons que le contenu de ce «message divin» est à la fois plus simple et plus immanent: à quoi peut bien faire allusion Qohélet dans ce verset 5,19 si ce n'est à ce qu'il a écrit précédemment (Qo 5,17-18), et qui est une reprise plus élaborée de ce qu'il a déjà dit dans ses trois premiers refrains? La joie de l'homme consiste dans les plaisirs qu'il éprouve lorsqu'il sait qu'ils viennent de Dieu. Et que peut lui dire Dieu à ce sujet si ce n'est d'en profiter pleinement, et de cette vie, et des joies qui vont avec, puisque c'est Lui le donateur? La «réponse» de Dieu serait alors la *révélation de son don,* dans cette joie dont il faut que l'homme profite maintenant, durant son existence terrestre[18]. Il est vrai que l'idée que l'on se fait habituellement de la théologie de Qohélet au sujet d'un Dieu lointain et inconnaissable ne tient plus avec cette compréhension du verset 5,19[19]. Par ailleurs, et dans le même ordre d'idée, Qohélet incite l'homme à préférer écouter (שמע) Dieu, plutôt que sacrifier (Qo 4,17).

V. Cinquième refrain, Qo 8,15: Qohélet fait l'éloge de la joie

Encore une fois il est possible de mettre ce refrain en rapport thématique avec certains passages qui le précèdent; on peut ainsi regrouper ces différents éléments en deux catégories usuelles chez Qohélet, en suivant la dialectique qui lui est chère: quelques cas particuliers de רע (Qo 7,25-

16. Pour cette idée voir Schwienhorst-Schönberger, *Nicht im Menschen* (n. 5), p. 149, notes 91 et 92, qui cite Lohfink, *Qoheleth 5:17-19: Revelation by Joy* (n. 5), p. 631.

17. Lohfink, *Qoheleth 5:17-19: Revelation by Joy* (n. 5), p. 634.

18. Voir à ce sujet A. Gianto, *Human Destiny in Emar and Qohelet,* in A. Schoors (ed.), *Qohelet in the Context of Wisdom* (BETL, 136), Leuven, Peeters – University Press, 1998, pp. 373-379.

19. Lohfink, *Qoheleth 5:17-19: Revelation by Joy* (n. 5), p. 635, qui conclut: «If the interpretation of Qoh 5,19 proposed is correct, it will not be possible to say that Qohelet is opposed to all the other books of the Bible by the fact that his God is 'an absolutely veiled and unrecognizable God'».

29; 8,9-14) et quelques conseils pour bien vivre (Qo 7,1-5). Le cinquième refrain offre alors une conclusion à cet ensemble, et il est consolidé par deux versets dont la thématique est similaire, l'un constitué d'une question (Qo 6,12: qui sait ce qui est bon pour l'homme durant sa vie?), et l'autre de sa réponse partielle (Qo 7,14: au jour de bonheur sois heureux, et au jour de malheur regarde). Et le cinquième refrain corrobore ce dernier conseil sous un angle très positif, où Qohélet fait explicitement l'éloge de la joie, comme en réponse à la révélation donnée par Dieu dans le précédent refrain (Qo 5,19). Cette réponse permet alors à l'homme de faire face à son destin, en se reconnaissant créature de Dieu, même s'il reste inutile et fatigant de chercher à percer son dessein (Qo 8,16-17). Le «plus» de ce refrain consiste alors dans l'éloge du bonheur, qui est l'acceptation reconnaissante de la révélation divine évoquée en Qo 5,17-19, dans la joie du cœur de l'homme, éloge qui est fait par Qohélet lui-même dans une sorte de *crescendo* quant à l'utilisation des modes.

VI. Sixième refrain, Qo 9,7-10: Qohélet exhorte l'homme à la joie

Dans ce sixième refrain Qohélet allonge notablement la liste des plaisirs de la vie et s'adresse directement à son destinataire. On ne peut manquer de remarquer le *crescendo* dans l'adresse des refrains, qui passe de l'impersonnel à l'exhortation par l'intermédiaire d'une implication de Qohélet lui-même: comment, en effet, Qohélet pourrait-il enjoindre le jeune homme ou le lecteur à se réjouir, s'il ne s'était lui-même porté garant de cette joie dont il fait l'éloge et qu'il conseille? Que Qohélet ait «testé» cette joie lui permet ensuite, et seulement ensuite, de convaincre le destinataire de son œuvre d'en profiter. Quel «plus» apporte alors le sixième refrain?

La réponse est donnée d'emblée par le verset 9,7 qui explique que Dieu a déjà apprécié les œuvres de l'homme. Le verbe רצה exprime la faveur divine, son acquiescement aux activités de l'homme[20]. Pourtant, dans le contexte immédiat de ce verset, il semble que ce terme désigne plutôt le fait que Dieu «permette» à l'homme de se réjouir de ses œuvres (Qo 9,7), ou de son travail (Qo 9,9). רצה pourrait alors signifier quelque chose de contraire au hiph'il de שלט en Qo 6,2, où Dieu *ne permet pas* à l'homme de profiter de ses biens. Ainsi on peut en déduire que si Dieu, en tant que donateur de la joie permet à l'homme de se réjouir, c'est qu'il a apprécié son travail, et en conséquence lui accorde la joie

20. Whybray, *Qoheleth Preacher of Joy* (n. 1), p. 92: «What good things God has given us are intended for our enjoyment, and in the giving of them he has shown his approval of our actions. To enjoy them is actually to do his will».

qui en découle. Or cela suppose en retour que l'homme accepte de profiter de cette joie qui lui est donnée.

VII. Septième refrain, Qo 11,9–12,1: le jugement de Dieu

Ce dernier refrain semble particulier, à la fois en raison de sa place dans le livre, et en raison de son contenu qui résume et achève les précédents. Par ailleurs, il entre aussi en résonance de manière ponctuelle avec quelques thèmes qui le précèdent ou le suivent.

Si par trois fois Qohélet rappelle l'incapacité foncière de l'homme à saisir son avenir et le dessein divin (Qo 9,11-12; 10,14; 11,5), il ne manque pourtant pas d'inviter l'homme à se réjouir durant les nombreuses années de sa vie, dans le verset 11,8 qui précède immédiatement le septième refrain. En formulant dans la foulée sa dernière exhortation à la joie, et en utilisant les deux expressions «chemins de ton cœur» et «regards de tes yeux» de manière non conventionnelle, Qohélet exprime à sa façon qu'aucune suspicion ne doit venir ternir la joie que procurent les biens de ce monde, quels qu'ils soient: le bonheur vient de Dieu, et doit donc être accueilli comme tel, et ainsi la joie dans son quotidien devient le chemin de l'expérience de Dieu[21].

Le dernier refrain sur le bonheur prend alors une place particulière dans ce passage et dans l'ouvrage tout entier. Précédant les derniers moments de l'homme, avant le retour de son souffle au Créateur (Qo 12,7), il se singularise aussi par sa forme: dernière exhortation, il s'adresse directement au jeune homme, insistant sur tout le temps de la vie qui précède l'extrême vieillesse et la mort, dont l'impuissance semble le trait dominant. Le vocabulaire de bonheur est ici plus dense que dans les autres refrains, comme l'est l'emploi de l'impératif: ce ne sont plus des conseils que Qohélet donne, mais presque des ordres, comme si le temps était compté. Et de fait, le *crescendo* arrive à son apogée, et l'œuvre de Qohélet à son terme. Il n'est plus temps de tergiverser, il faut agir, et bien agir: aimer la vie (Qo 11,9), et éviter le mal sous toutes ses formes (Qo 11,10). Il n'est plus utile de rappeler les plaisirs terrestres (boire, manger…), il faut maintenant insister sur tout autre chose, et qui est la raison ultime de l'urgence de cet appel au bonheur: Dieu jugera l'homme sur tout cela (Qo 11,9), c'est-à-dire sur sa capacité à accueillir le bonheur durant sa vie sur terre[22]. Et là se trouve le «plus» de ce dernier refrain, qui constitue en même temps l'élément essentiel de la dé-

21. Voir D. Dore, *Qohélet, Le Siracide* (Cahier Évangile, 91), Paris, Cerf, 1995, p. 31, qui exprime cette idée de manière similaire.

22. Schwienhorst-Schönberger, *Nicht im Menschen* (n. 5), p. 226.

marche de Qohélet. Pour quelle raison en effet Dieu se révélerait-il dans la joie du cœur de l'homme si ce n'était pour lui demander, *in fine*, ce qu'il en a fait? Là est la thématique du jugement de Dieu chez Qohélet, que nous avons développer dans le troisième chapitre de notre livre.

VIII. Conclusion

Arrivés au terme de cette contribution il reste possible de résumer la dialectique de Qohélet dans ses sept refrains de la manière suivante:

1) Les joies de la vie sont des dons de Dieu (Qo 2,24-25)
2) Qui doivent amener l'homme à la reconnaissance envers Dieu créateur et donateur (Qo 3,12-13.14)
3) Car l'homme ne connaît pas son avenir (Qo 3,22)
4) Mais Dieu se révèle dans la joie du cœur de l'homme (Qo 5,17-19)
5) Et Qohélet lui répond en faisant l'éloge de cette joie (Qo 8,15)
6) Puis exhorte l'homme à faire de même car Dieu permet ses œuvres (Qo 9,7-10)
7) Et le jugera sur sa capacité à avoir accueilli la joie (Qo 11,9–12,1), et sur son agir quotidien.

La joie semble bien le pivot de la réflexion de Qohélet: non seulement elle contrebalance existentiellement la présence du mal dans les mauvaises occupations humaines, mais encore elle est un don divin, qui concerne le quotidien de la vie. Et c'est sur cet accueil que l'homme réserve au don de Dieu dans son agir de tous les jours qu'il sera en fin de compte jugé. Certes les joies simples et authentiques dont parle Qohélet, et qui devraient être accessibles à tous les hommes, ne tiennent compte ni de la gloire ni de la puissance (comme les travaux fastueux de Qohélet/Salomon qui ne lui procurent pas de «profit», Qo 2,11). Mais Dieu ne se révèle pas à Elie dans l'ouragan, le tremblement de terre ou le feu, mais dans la douceur de la brise du soir (1 R 19, 11-13).

Pourquoi ne se révélerait-il pas à Qohélet, et à tout homme qui l'accueille, dans la douceur de la joie d'un cœur simple? Le Dieu de Qohélet est un Dieu bon et proche, qui donne la vie et la joie, et non le malheur. A l'homme de l'accepter, et de rendre bonnes par son agir quotidien les occupations que Dieu lui donne (Qo 1,13).

«Les solins»
F–71430 Saint-Aubin
France

Marie Maussion

WISDOM VERSUS APOCALYPTIC AND SCIENCE IN SIRACH 1,1-10

INTRODUCTION

How are the mysteries of heaven and earth revealed? Jewish contemporaries of Ben Sira would be able to look in three directions. First, they could follow the sage by contenting themselves with traditional Jewish wisdom, regarded as enshrined in the Law of Moses (Sir 24,23; cf. Deut 4,6). A second possibility would be to turn to the purported revelations contained in apocalyptic writings, particularly the early parts of 1 Enoch. A third possibility would be to investigate the inquiries of Greek philosophers and scientists such as Aristotle and Eratosthenes (perhaps with a visit to Alexandria). My reading of Sir 1,1-10 suggests that in the opening of his book Ben Sira wishes to defend traditional Hebrew wisdom against the twin challenges from Jewish apocalyptic and Greek science[1].

There is widespread agreement that Ben Sira may be classified as a wisdom book. The grandson's Greek translation employs the word σοφία ("wisdom") more than fifty times and the adjective σοφός ("wise") more than twenty-five times. Besides σοφία (1,1.4.6) and σοφός (1,8), Sir 1,1-10 uses other sapiential terminology, such as σύνεσις φρονήσεως ("prudent understanding", 1,4), πανουργεύματα (or πανουργήματα, "subtleties", 1,6), and γινώσκω ("know", 1,6). Hence, Sir 1,1-10 received treatment in studies of Ben Sira's sapiential theology undertaken by J. Marböck (1971) and O. Rickenbacher (1973), discussing the poem's use of earlier biblical themes and the way it fits into the sage's theological scheme[2].

Although sapiential and apocalyptic thinking have often been sharply distinguished, G. von Rad declared that wisdom was "the real matrix

1. Although I suggest many connections between Sir 1,1-10 and Jewish apocalyptic texts or Greek scientific writings, it is impossible to prove that Ben Sira had access to these works. In the case of a sapiential book such as Ben Sira, the problem is that we have only one side of the conversation. Hence the exegete needs to reconstruct Ben Sira's dialogue partners. Since Jewish apocalypticism was growing in third and second century BCE Palestine, while Greek science was developing at the same time in Alexandria, my hypothesis in this article is that Ben Sira was responding to these two important schools of thought.

2. J. MARBÖCK, *Weisheit im Wandel* (BBB, 37), Bonn, Hanstein, 1971; reprint (BZAW, 272), Berlin, de Gruyter, 1999, pp. 17-34, and O. RICKENBACHER, *Weisheitsperikopen bei Ben Sira* (OBO, 1), Göttingen, Vandenhoeck & Ruprecht, 1973, pp. 4-29.

from which apocalyptic literature originates"[3]. Although von Rad's view has not gained universal acceptance, many links between wisdom and apocalyptic can be discerned. In fact, my position is that Sir 1,1-10 may be read as a veiled critique of the early Enochic literature. Far from ignoring nascent Jewish apocalyptic, Ben Sira engages in a polemic against apocalypticism in Sir 1,1-10 and elsewhere in his book.

The 1976 publication of J.T. Milik's edition of the Qumran Aramaic fragments of 1 Enoch has enabled a reconsideration of links between 1 Enoch and Ben Sira[4]. An article by M.E. Stone (published in the same year) gathered "lists of revealed things" in 1 Enoch and Ben Sira, as well as in other Jewish works from the Second Temple period and its immediate aftermath[5]. In 1995, R.A. Argall published a study comparing 1 Enoch and Ben Sira on three theological themes[6]. Moreover, B.G. Wright (1997) has also viewed Ben Sira against the backdrop of apocalyptic writings such as 1 Enoch[7]. Since the opening poem employs the verb ἀποκαλύπτω ("reveal", Sir 1,6)[8] in the context of the mysteries of the divine wisdom, it seems worthwhile investigating whether Sir 1,1-10 may be presenting an alternative view to the approach of Jewish apocalyptists.

Another ingredient in Ben Sira's cultural world deserving consideration is the influence of Greek thought. A wide-ranging study of Jewish wisdom and apocalyptic in relation to Greek thought in second-century BCE Palestine is provided within M. Hengel's magisterial study, *Judaism and Hellenism*, which situates Ben Sira in the context of Hellenization in Syria-Palestine before the Maccabean period[9]. Although T. Middendorp's study (1973) may have overstated Ben Sira's dependence on themes from Greek literature, many of his suggested parallels

3. G. VON RAD, *Old Testament Theology*, I-II, Edinburgh, Oliver and Boyd, 1962-1965, II, p. 306.

4. J.T. MILIK, *The Books of Enoch: Aramaic Fragments of Qumrân Cave 4*, Oxford, Clarendon, 1976.

5. M.E. STONE, *Lists of Revealed Things in the Apocalyptic Literature*, in F.M. CROSS, W.E. LEMKE, P.D. MILLER (eds.), *Magnalia Dei: The Mighty Acts of God*, FS G.E. Wright, Garden City, NY, Doubleday, 1976, pp. 414-452.

6. R.A. ARGALL, *1 Enoch and Sirach: A Comparative Literary and Conceptual Analysis of the Themes of Revelation, Creation and Judgment* (SBL EJL, 8), Atlanta, GA, Scholars Press, 1995; on Sir 1,1-10, esp. pp. 155-156.

7. B.G. WRIGHT, "*Fear the Lord and Honor the Priest*" : *Ben Sira as Defender of the Jerusalem Priesthood*, in P.C. BEENTJES (ed.), *The Book of Ben Sira in Modern Research* (BZAW, 255), Berlin, de Gruyter, 1997, pp. 189-222.

8. The verb ἀποκαλύπτω occurs in an apocalyptic context in Theodotion Dan 10,1, for instance, while the cognate noun ἀποκάλυψις ("revelation") is present in Rev 1,1. To be sure, the noun and verb can also have a non-apocalyptic meaning, as in Sir 22,22 and 27,16.

9. M. HENGEL, *Judaism and Hellenism*, I-II, London, SCM, 1974; on Ben Sira see I, pp. 131-175 (esp. pp. 157-162 on Sir 1,1-10).

(especially to Theognis) are widely accepted[10]. Ben Sira's doctrine of paired opposites (Sir 33,14-15) echoes the view of the Greek Stoic philosopher Chrysippus (d. ca. 207 BCE)[11]. Moreover, the sage has other points of contact with Stoicism[12]. Hence it seems worthwhile also to consider whether Sir 1,1-10 may be offering a response to Greek philosophy, particularly in the area of scientific inquiry.

A brief word on the dating of sources is necessary. The almost universal view of scholars is that Ben Sira's book dates from 200-175 BCE and was written in Jerusalem[13]. My assumption is that he had access to most of the Hebrew scriptures, including at least the Torah, the Former and Latter Prophets, and Psalms, Proverbs, and Job[14]. The dating of 1 Enoch is more problematic. My postulate (on the evidence of Qumran paleography) is that the Book of the Watchers (1 Enoch 1-36) and most of the Astronomical Book (1 Enoch 72-82) were in existence by 200 BCE[15]. My supposition is that the Epistle of Enoch (1 Enoch 92-105) was in existence before 167 BCE, and thus probably in Ben Sira's lifetime[16]. Four famous Greek scientists predated Ben Sira: Aristotle

10. T. MIDDENDORP, *Die Stellung Jesu ben Siras zwischen Judentum und Hellenismus*, Leiden, Brill, 1973. This work has been critiqued by H.-V. KIEWELER, *Ben Sira zwischen Judentum und Hellenismus* (BEATAJ, 30), Frankfurt a.M., Lang, 1992. However, a number of Middendorp's suggestions are taken up in J.T. SANDERS, *Ben Sira and Demotic Wisdom* (SBL MS, 28), Chico, CA, Scholars Press, 1983, pp. 28-58; cf. P.W. SKEHAN and A.A. DI LELLA, *The Wisdom of Ben Sira* (AB, 39), New York, Doubleday, 1987, pp. 47-48.

11. J.J. COLLINS, *Jewish Wisdom in the Hellenistic Age*, Louisville, KY, Westminster John Knox, 1997, p. 85.

12. HENGEL, *Judaism and Hellenism* (n. 9), I, pp. 147-149; R. PAUTREL, *Ben Sira et le stoïcisme*, in *RSR* 51 (1963) 535-549; U. WICKE-REUTER, *Göttliche Providenz und menschliche Verantwortung bei Ben Sira und in der Frühen Stoa* (BZAW, 298), Berlin, de Gruyter, 2000, pp. 202-206 on Sir 1,1-10; D. WINSTON, *Theodicy in Ben Sira and Stoic Philosophy*, in R. LINK-SALINGER (ed.), *Of Scholars, Savants, and Their Texts*, New York, Lang, 1989, pp. 239-249. A critique of such proposed connections appears in S.L. MATTILA, *Ben Sira and the Stoics: A Reexamination of the Evidence*, in *JBL* 119 (2000) 473-501.

13. See, for instance, SKEHAN - DI LELLA, *The Wisdom of Ben Sira* (n. 10), p. 10; COLLINS, *Jewish Wisdom in the Hellenistic Age* (n. 11), p. 23; HENGEL, *Judaism and Hellenism* (n. 9), I, p. 131; J. CORLEY, *Ben Sira's Teaching on Friendship* (BJS, 316), Providence, RI, Brown University, 2002, p. 12.

14. SKEHAN - DI LELLA, *The Wisdom of Ben Sira* (n. 10), p. 41.

15. WRIGHT, *"Fear the Lord and Honor the Priest"* (n. 7), p. 191, n. 6; ARGALL, *1 Enoch and Sirach* (n. 6), p. 6. See also J.C. VANDERKAM, *Enoch and the Growth of an Apocalyptic Tradition* (CBQ MS, 16), Washington, DC, Catholic Biblical Association of America, 1984. According to VanderKam, most of the Astronomical Book (1 Enoch 72-79 and 82) is the oldest portion, dating before 200 BCE (pp. 79-88), while the next oldest is the Book of Watchers (1 Enoch 1-36), which is pre-Maccabean, and perhaps from the third century BCE (pp. 111-114).

16. F. GARCÍA MARTÍNEZ, *Qumran and Apocalyptic: Studies on the Aramaic Texts from Qumran* (STDJ, 9), Leiden, Brill, 1992, pp. 79-92; cf. ARGALL, *1 Enoch and Sirach* (n. 6), pp. 6-7. However, see VANDERKAM, *Enoch and the Growth* (n. 15), pp. 142-149, where the Epistle of Enoch is dated to 175-167 BCE.

(d. 322 BCE), Aristarchus (d. ca. 230 BCE), Archimedes (d. ca. 212 BCE), and Eratosthenes (d. ca. 194 BCE). My presumption is that most of their works in Greek existed in the huge library at Alexandria (where Eratosthenes worked).

The way Ben Sira opens his book may offer vital clues to his outlook[17]. To facilitate discussion, I begin by presenting my translation of the poem. In the absence of a Hebrew text, I follow the grandson's Greek version, except in 1,3b where I refer to the Old Latin[18].

> 1All wisdom is from the Lord,
> and is with him for ever.
> 2Sand of the seas and drops of rain
> and days of eternity – who can enumerate?
> 3Height of heaven and breadth of earth
> and depth of the deep[19] – who can fathom out?
> 4Before all things wisdom was created,
> and prudent understanding from eternity.
> 6The root of wisdom – to whom has it been revealed?
> And her subtleties – who has known?
> 8One is wise, greatly to be feared,
> sitting on his throne – the Lord.
> 9He himself created her, and saw and enumerated her,
> and poured her out upon all his works,
> 10Among all flesh in accordance with his giving,
> and he supplied her to those who love him[20].

17. Here I ignore the grandson's prologue, found in the Greek and Latin manuscripts of the book.

18. Unfortunately, the Hebrew text has not been found among the Dead Sea texts or the Cairo Geniza fragments. For the Greek see J. ZIEGLER, *Sapientia Iesu Filii Sirach* (Septuaginta 12/2), Göttingen, Vandenhoeck & Ruprecht, 1965; note that I ignore the glosses in the Origenic tradition (namely vv. 5. 7. 10cd); cf. SKEHAN – DI LELLA, *The Wisdom of Ben Sira* (n. 10), p. 136. For the Syriac see P.A. DE LAGARDE, *Libri veteris testamenti apocryphi syriace*, Leipzig, Brockhaus – London, Williams and Norgate, 1861. The Latin is taken from *Biblia Sacra iuxta latinam vulgatam versionem, 12: Sapientia Salomonis, Liber Hiesu filii Sirach*, Rome, Typis Polyglottis Vaticanis, 1964. Note that in this article all biblical translations are mine. For a comparison of the Greek and Syriac versions of Sir 1,1-10 see N. CALDUCH-BENAGES, *Traducir–interpretar: la versión siríaca de Sirácida 1*, in *EstBib* 55 (1997) 313-340, esp. pp. 321-322 (Syriac) and pp. 326-327 (Greek).

19. Here I adopt the Latin phrase "depth of the deep"; this reading is preferred by R. SMEND, *Die Weisheit des Jesus Sirach erklärt*, Berlin, Reimer, 1906, p. 6; so also MARBÖCK, *Weisheit im Wandel* (n. 2), p. 19; RICKENBACHER, *Weisheitsperikopen* (n. 2), pp. 7-8; SKEHAN - DI LELLA, *The Wisdom of Ben Sira* (n. 10), p. 137. Here instead, the Greek reads "the deep and wisdom", while the Syriac reads "the great deep".

20. The reading of the Syriac and some Lucianic Greek MSS ("those who fear him") is accepted by SMEND, *Sirach erklärt* (n. 19), p. 9; MARBÖCK, *Weisheit im Wandel* (n. 2), p. 21; RICKENBACHER, *Weisheitsperikopen*, (n. 2), p. 10. A recent advocate of this reading is M. GILBERT, *Voir ou craindre le Seigneur? Sir 1,10d*, in L. CAGNI (ed.), *Biblica et Semitica*, FS F. Vattioni, Naples, Istituto Universitario Orientale, 1999, pp. 247-252. However, as the Syriac reading provides a smoother introduction to the following pericope (1,11-30), it is the *lectio facilior* and probably a corruption. Note that in Sir 2,15 "those who fear the Lord" is in synonymous parallelism with "those who love him".

I. HEBREW LITERARY CONTEXT: BIBLICAL WISDOM

It is well known that Ben Sira often alludes to the thought and vocabulary of the earlier Hebrew scriptures[21]. Hence it is not surprising that the poem in Sir 1,1-10 echoes earlier biblical texts. The idea of a cosmic wisdom underlying creation is familiar from Prov 8,22-31. Thus the statement in Sir 1,4 ("Before all things wisdom was created, and prudent understanding from eternity") echoes wisdom's first-person declaration in Prov 8,22: "YHWH created me the first of his way, the beginning of his works from of old". Moreover, the question about "heaven ... earth ... the deep" in Sir 1,3 may reflect Prov 8,26-27: "When he had not made earth and fields, and the first of the dusts of the world; when he established the heavens, there was I, when he decreed a circle on the face of the deep".

Job's poem on the human search for wisdom (Job 28) also underlies Sir 1,1-10. In particular, an anticipation of Sir 1,6 occurs in the question of Job 28,20: "But wisdom – from where does she come? And what is the place of understanding?". Equally, an anticipation of Sir 1,8 occurs in the subsequent answer of Job 28,23: "God understands the way to her, and he knows her place". Moreover, a foreshadowing of Sir 1,2-3 appears in Job 28,24-26a:

> For he gazes to the ends of the earth;
>   beneath the whole heavens he sees,
> to make for the wind a weight,
>   and the waters he metes out in a measure,
> in his making a decree for the rain.

An additional anticipation of Sir 1,9 occurs in Job 28,27, describing God's establishing of wisdom: "Then he saw her and declared[22] her; he established her and also searched her out".

Further inspiration for the questions in Sir 1,2-3 may have come from a sapiential passage in Isa 40,12, which mentions waters (perhaps of the deep), then heaven, and then earth:

> Who has measured the waters in his hollow hand,
>   or measured out the heavens with a span,
> or contained in a measure the dust of the earth,
>   or weighed mountains in the scales, or hills in a balance?[23]

21. For examples, see SKEHAN - DI LELLA, *The Wisdom of Ben Sira* (n. 10), pp. 40-45.

22. This verb (piel of *spr*) may possibly mean "counted" or "enumerated" (cf. Ps 22,18[17]), as in Job 38,37: "Who can count the clouds by wisdom?" Note, incidentally, that Sir 1,11-30 includes an echo of Job 28,28 (see Sir 1,14).

23. The motif of divine weighing and measuring (in a somewhat different sense) occurs also in 4QInstruction: "With the scales of justice God measures all" (4Q418 126 ii 3; cf. 4Q418 127 6); see F. GARCÍA MARTÍNEZ, *The Dead Sea Scrolls Translated*, Leiden, Brill, 1994, p. 392.

Furthermore, Sir 1,2 recalls expressions for what is innumerable, taken from the Hebrew Bible. A frequent comparison (as in Sir 1,2) is to the sand on the seashore; for instance, Jacob recalls God's promise to Abraham: "I will make your descendants like the sand of the sea, which cannot be counted because of their number"(Gen 32,13[12])[24]. Another object of comparison (as in Sir 1,2) is to the eternal time-span of God's existence: "The number of his years is unfathomable" (Job 36,26). However, one interesting feature that is absent from Sir 1,2 is any mention of the stars, although a standard motif of Israelite tradition was that no human being could number the stars[25]. Against this background, it may perhaps be significant that Sir 1,2 does not refer to the stars. Indeed, this omission of the stars may reflect his desire to distance himself completely from astrology, which was found in Israel as well as in the surrounding pagan world[26]. Elsewhere, Ben Sira urges people to listen to the guidance of their heart rather than to astrologers (Sir 37,14), while Sir 42,15-43,33 passes from sun and moon (43,1-10) to meteorological phenomena (43,11-22) with only a brief mention of the stars (43,9)[27].

Space here prevents a more detailed examination of Ben Sira's echoes of other Hebrew biblical texts[28]. In fact, a more extensive survey of Hebrew Bible references underlying Sir 1,1-10 would show how Ben Sira was steeped in the traditions of biblical wisdom. Now, however, we will consider the poem as a response to two sorts of challenges to Israel's traditional faith, first the internal challenge of nascent apocalyptic ideas

24. Besides Gen 32,13[12], a similar comparison recalls the promise to Abraham in Gen 22,17; 1 Kings 4,20; Isa 10,22; 48,19; Jer 33,22; Hos 2,1[1,10]; Dan 3,36 LXX [= Prayer of Azariah v. 13]. Elsewhere the comparison with grains of sand expresses a vast number: Gen 41,49; Josh 11,4; Judg 7,12; 1 Sam 13,5; 2 Sam 17,11; 1 Kings 5,9[4,29]; Jer 15,8; Ps 78,27; 139,18; cf. Rev 20,8.

25. This motif often occurs, for instance, in God's promise to Abraham of a numberless progeny (Gen 15,5; 22,17; 26,4; Exod 32,13; Deut 1,10; 10,22; 28,62; Jer 33,22; 1 Chron 27,23; Neh 9,23; Dan 3,36 LXX [= Prayer of Azariah v. 13]). It also appears when a biblical author wishes to praise God as incomparable (Ps 147,4-5; cf. Isa 40,25-26; Bar 3,34-35).

26. On astrological thought in Israel see HENGEL, *Judaism and Hellenism* (n. 9), I, pp. 237-239. Note that Qumran literature includes some horoscopes (4Q186 and 561) as well as a brontologion (4Q318).

27. Besides 43,9, the only other Hebrew mention of "star" (*kôkāb*) in Ben Sira occurs at 50,6, in a simile describing the high priest's glory. Using the equivalent noun ἄστρον, the Greek has an additional instance (absent from the Hebrew and Syriac) in 44,21d, referring to God's promise to Abraham of offspring numerous as the stars (Gen 15,5; 22,17).

28. In Sir 1,1-10 there are further echoes of Prov 30,4; Job 11,7-9; 36,26-27; 38,4-5.16-18. For more details see MARBÖCK, *Weisheit im Wandel* (n. 2), pp. 30-34; RICKENBACHER, *Weisheitsperikopen* (n. 2), pp. 22-29; SKEHAN – DI LELLA, *The Wisdom of Ben Sira* (n. 10), pp. 137-139.

within Israel, and then the external challenge from the Greek scientific world view.

II. Jewish Apocalyptic Context: 1 Enoch

The important concept of divine revelation underlies Ben Sira's question in the middle of his opening poem (Sir 1,6a)[29]. For the sage, God's wisdom has been revealed in the form of the Mosaic Law; thus, Sir 24,23 (Greek) says of wisdom's utterances: "All these things are the book of the covenant of the Most High God, the Law which Moses commanded us" (cf. Sir 19,20). Ben Sira relies on the sentiment of Moses in Deut 29,28[29]: "The secret things are for YHWH our God, but the revealed things are for us and our children for ever, so as to do all the words of this law". This thought (combined with Ps 131,1) is at the basis of Sir 3,21-22 (Hebrew MS A):

> Do not seek marvels beyond you,
> and do not search out what is hidden from you.
> Consider what you were authorized,
> and you have no business with hidden things.

According to Skehan and Di Lella, here "Ben Sira cautions his readers about the futility of Greek learning", in particular "searching into the ultimate nature of the universe and of humankind"[30]. However, according to other scholars, Ben Sira's target is the hidden revelations of apocalyptic writings such as those found in 1 Enoch. Thus, Argall concludes that "Sirach 3,17-29 is not a polemic against Greek learning", but that "Ben Sira is responding to Jewish groups that propound esoteric teaching"[31]. In my understanding, Ben Sira is engaged in a two-pronged attack, directed at both the pretensions of Greek scientific learning and the mysteries of Jewish apocalyptic.

The monograph of R.A. Argall has shown the benefit of comparing and contrasting 1 Enoch with Ben Sira. Although 1 Enoch is generally classed as an apocalyptic work and Ben Sira as sapiential, 1 Enoch contains several wisdom passages and themes, while Ben Sira seems to be downplaying the role of Enoch and the apocalyptic speculation associ-

29. Cf. Rickenbacher, *Weisheitsperikopen* (n. 2), pp. 24-25. A thought comparable to Sir 1,6 occurs in Second-Isaiah's question in the Fourth Servant Song: "The arm [= strength] of YHWH – to whom has it been revealed?" (Isa 53,1).

30. Skehan – Di Lella, *The Wisdom of Ben Sira* (n. 10), p. 160.

31. Argall, *1 Enoch and Sirach* (n. 6), p. 78 (see pp. 73-78 on Sir 3,17-29); cf. Wright, *"Fear the Lord and Honor the Priest"* (n. 7), p. 209.

ated with him[32]. In a chapter on "The Created Order in Ben Sira's Book of Wisdom", within a subsection on "Hidden Aspects of the Creation", Argall discusses Sir 1,1-10 and 24,3-7[33]. The corresponding chapter on 1 Enoch also has a subsection on "Hidden Aspects of the Creation", treating 1 Enoch 12-36; 93,11-14; and 72-80 with 82,4-20. All of these Enoch passages are generally regarded as pre-Maccabean, so that Ben Sira could have known some form of the tradition in them[34].

Sir 1,6 asks: "The root of wisdom – to whom has it been revealed? And her subtleties – who has known?" Similarly, 1 Enoch 93,11-12 (according to 4Q212, completed with help from the Ethiopic) asks:

> [Who, among all men … ca]n understand the commandment of [(God. Or who)] can hear the words of the Holy One [without being upset or can visualise his thoughts?] Or who, among all men, [can consider all the works of the heavens or the] angular [columns] upon which they rest; [or who sees a soul or a spirit and can] go back to tell about [it? Or go up and see all their extremities and think or act like them?][35]

Sir 1,3 asks: "Height of heaven and breadth of earth and depth of the deep – who can fathom out?" The implied answer is: "No one [human]". According to the Qumran Aramaic text of 4Q212 (completed with help from the Ethiopic version) 1 Enoch 93,13-14 asks similar questions:

> Who [among the sons of men can know and measure what is] the length and breadth of all the earth? Or [to whom has all its (size) been shown] and its shape? Who, among all men, can [know what the extent of the heavens is, and what] their height is, or how they are supported, [or how large is the number of the stars?].

The implied answer to Enoch's questions has already been given in 1 Enoch 93,2 (Ethiopic): "I, Enoch … (will) let you know according to

32. Cf. ARGALL, *1 Enoch and Sirach* (n. 6), pp. 1-13. Although the Geniza Hebrew manuscript B of Sir 44,16 calls Enoch a "sign of knowledge", implying a revelatory role for him, the much-discussed verse appears to be a later gloss, as it is absent from the Masada Hebrew manuscript and the Syriac (while the Greek calls him an "example of repentance"). According to SKEHAN – DI LELLA, *The Wisdom of Ben Sira* (n. 10), p. 499, Enoch's "popularity in the last centuries B.C. as the custodian of ancient lore would seem to have prompted this expansion on Ben Sira's text". If Sir 44,16 is a gloss, then the sage has downplayed the role of Enoch by relegating this patriarch almost to the end of the Praise of the Ancestors (Sir 49,14). For different views see ARGALL, *1 Enoch and Sirach* (n. 6), pp. 9-11; T.R. LEE, *Studies in the Form of Sirach 44-50* (SBL DS, 75), Atlanta, GA, Scholars Press, 1986, pp. 230-232.

33. On "Hidden Aspects of the Creation" see ARGALL, *1 Enoch and Sirach* (n. 6), pp. 154-158 (Ben Sira) and pp. 112-133 (1 Enoch).

34. The sapiential nature poem in 93,11-14 occurs in 4Q212 (a mid-first century BCE MS), and may well be pre-Maccabean, even if (as some scholars assert) the Epistle of Enoch as a whole (92-105) dates from the end of the second century BCE.

35. For this and the following quotation from 4Q212 (1 Enoch 93), see GARCÍA MARTÍNEZ, *The Dead Sea Scrolls Translated* (n. 23), p. 259 (words added in Lacunae).

that which was revealed to me from the heavenly vision"[36]. We may also compare a text from the Book of the Watchers: "I, Enoch, saw the vision of the end of everything alone; and none among human beings will see as I have seen" (1 Enoch 19,3 [Ethiopic]). Indeed, already in the introduction to the composite work (1 Enoch 1,2 = 4Q201) the patriarch states: "[I heard] all the words of the Wat[chers] and of the Holy Ones [and because I heard it from them, I knew and understood everything]"[37]. In Ben Sira God reveals his wisdom through creation to "all flesh", but his revelation comes particularly to "those who love him", presumably Israel (Sir 1,10), whereas in 1 Enoch the ancient patriarch is the revealer of the divine mysteries. Indeed, whereas in Sir 1,9-10 God gives wisdom to all humanity, and especially to his chosen people, in 1 Enoch wisdom's gift is restricted to Enoch and his heirs (82,2), though in the end-time it is granted to the elect (5,8).

The similarity of the afore-mentioned sapiential passage in 1 Enoch 93,11-14 with verses 6 and 3 of Sirach 1 is remarkable[38]. Milik regards the Enoch nature poem as a "series of rhetorical questions which describe the transcendence of God in a way similar to that of the Book of Job and of several sapiential writings from Qumran". He also observes that "this passage constitutes a eulogy of Enoch (delivered by himself!) who had just accomplished things inaccessible to simple mortals", such as the journeys described in the Book of the Watchers. In a similar vein, D.C. Olson paraphrases the purpose of the passage: "Do not worry about what you do not and cannot understand. Who can bear to hear the voice of God? Who has been privileged to learn the deepest mysteries? (Who other than myself, that is. Your ignorance is best remedied by giving heed to me, the one person whose testimony about such matters may be presumed reliable)"[39]. In the Ethiopic text 93,11-14 appears to be out of place, since the Aramaic MSS of 4Q212 have a different text-order: 93,1-10; 91,11-17; 93,11-14. Such textual disruption suggests that 93,11-14 may have been a separate sapiential poem that has become an

36. E. ISAAC, *1 (Ethiopic Apocalypse of) Enoch*, in J.H. CHARLESWORTH (ed.), *The Old Testament Pseudepigrapha*, I-II, New York, Doubleday, 1983-1985, I, pp. 5-89, here p. 74. The next quotation is from p. 23.

37. GARCÍA MARTÍNEZ, *The Dead Sea Scrolls Translated* (n. 23), p. 246.

38. On 1 Enoch 93,11-14 see MILIK, *The Books of Enoch* (n. 4), pp. 270-272; STONE, *Lists of Revealed Things* (n. 5), pp. 423-426; ARGALL, *1 Enoch and Sirach* (n. 6), pp. 124-127; M. BLACK, *The Book of Enoch or 1 Enoch* (SVTP, 7), Leiden, Brill, 1985, pp. 286-287; D.C. OLSON, *Recovering the Original Sequence of 1 Enoch 91-93*, in *JSP* 11 (1993) 69-94, esp. pp. 82-85. The following two quotations in the main text come from MILIK, *The Books of Enoch*, p. 270.

39. OLSON, *Original Sequence* (n. 38), p. 84. Olson regards 1 Enoch 93,11-14 as having originally followed 1 Enoch 92,2 (see pp. 83-85).

"interpolated pericope" in 1 Enoch 93 (though Stone can justify the present arrangement)[40].

According to 1 Enoch, the patriarch gained his information by means of cosmic journeys during which he was able to see for himself the operations of heavenly and meteorological phenomena. Thus, in 1 Enoch 17,7 (Ethiopic) the patriarch states: "I saw the mountains of the dark storms of the rainy season and from where the waters of all the seas flow"[41], whereas Sir 24,5 asserts that this was a privilege of wisdom alone. One other text illustrates how Enoch acquired his cosmic knowledge: "I saw the ultimate ends of the earth which rests on the heaven. And the gates of heaven were open, and I saw how the stars of heaven come out; and I counted the gates out of which they exit" (1 Enoch 33,1-3 [Ethiopic]).

By means of his cosmic journeys, Enoch gained knowledge of the extent of heaven and earth and the deep. Hence, in 1 Enoch 18,9-11 according to the Qumran Aramaic text (4Q204, completed from the Ethiopic), the patriarch declares:

> [I saw a burning fire; beyond those mountains there is a place on the other side of the great earth,] and there [the heavens e]nd. [Then I was shown a great abyss between pillars of heavenly fire and I saw] in it pillars [of fire which go down to the bottom: its height and its depth were immeasurable][42].

Thus, whereas Sir 1,3 suggests that only God knows the cosmic dimensions, the Enochic Book of the Watchers (esp. 1 Enoch 18) attributes such knowledge to the patriarch[43].

Sir 1,2 inquires into who can count the grains of sand on the seashore. This motif was traditionally paired with the numbering of the stars of heaven (omitted by Ben Sira, perhaps out of a hostility to astrology)[44]. In

40. According to BLACK, *The Book of Enoch or 1 Enoch* (n. 38), p. 286, this is an "interpolated pericope", but an explanation for the present location is given by STONE, *Lists of Revealed Things* (n. 5), pp. 424-425.

41. ISAAC, *Enoch* (n. 36), p. 22. The following quotation of 1 Enoch 33 comes from p. 28.

42. GARCÍA MARTÍNEZ, *The Dead Sea Scrolls Translated* (n. 23), p. 252.

43. Cf. STONE, *Lists of Revealed Things* (n. 5), pp. 432-433; ARGALL, *1 Enoch and Sirach* (n. 6), p. 163. In addition, the later Book of Similitudes alludes to the revelatory work of angels, as explained to the patriarch: "These measurements shall reveal all the secrets of the depths of the earth" (1 Enoch 61,5); see ISAAC, *1 (Ethiopic Apocalypse of) Enoch* (n. 36), p. 42.

44. The motifs of sand and stars (regarded as innumerable items) are combined in Gen 22,17; Jer 33,22; Dan 3,36 LXX [= Prayer of Azariah v. 13]. A Greek parallel occurs in Plato's dialogue *Euthyd.* 294b, where Socrates asks his interlocutors: "Do you know things such as the numbers of the stars and of the sand?"; see B. JOWETT, *The Dialogues of Plato*, I-V, Oxford, Clarendon, 1875, here I, p. 220.

fact, 1 Enoch 93,14 asks whether any human being knows the number of the stars. The Astronomical Book (1 Enoch 72-82), presumably already existent in Ben Sira's lifetime, claims that such astronomical knowledge was revealed to Enoch. Thus, 4Q209 frag. 28 preserves part of 1 Enoch 82,9-13, listing constellations by name of their angelic masters[45].

Sir 1,2 also asks who can count the number of the raindrops. The Book of the Watchers regards the disposition of rain as indicating divine providence: "Notice the earth and scrutinise his works. ... And the indications of winter: how all the earth [is filled with water] and the clouds drip rain" (4Q201 ii 1-4 = 1 Enoch 2,2-3)[46]. Later in the Book of the Watchers (chapters 33-36), Enoch recounts his journey to the four ends of the earth, where he sees the open gates of heaven that produce rain and other meteorological phenomena. For instance, the patriarch reports what he saw at the extreme south: "[I] saw there three open gates of the heaven from where the south wind, dew, rain, and wind come forth" (1 Enoch 36,1 [Ethiopic])[47].

Mention of "days" in Sir 1,2 hints at a concern with the calendar, more prominent in 1 Enoch than in Ben Sira[48]. Sir 1,2 asks who can number "the days of eternity", with the implied answer: "No human being". By contrast, in 1 Enoch 72,1 (Ethiopic) the ancient patriarch is shown "the nature of the years of the world unto eternity". What Enoch claims to know is regarded by Ben Sira as a mystery known only to God.

Sir 1,6 asks to whom the "root of wisdom" has been revealed[49]. The image of wisdom's root, described as having branches in Sir 1,20, may

45. Cf. 1 Enoch 43,1-4; 60,12; 69,19-21 (from the Book of Similitudes). For postbiblical texts also dealing with listing the stars (e.g. 2 Enoch 40,2-3), see STONE, *Lists of Revealed Things* (n. 5), pp. 426-431.

46. GARCÍA MARTÍNEZ, *The Dead Sea Scrolls Translated* (n. 23), p. 246.

47. ISAAC, *Enoch* (n. 36), p. 29. The Astronomical Book also connects the origin of rain with the winds in 1 Enoch 76,6-13 (attested in fragmentary form in 4Q210 1 ii 5-9). The Enochic Book of Similitudes (probably composed after Ben Sira) describes Enoch being shown hidden meteorological phenomena, including the production of rain (1 Enoch 60,21-22 [Ethiopic]): "When the rain-wind becomes activated in its reservoir, the angels come and open the reservoir and let it out; and when it is sprayed over the whole earth, it becomes united with the water which is upon the earth ... So in this manner there is a measuring system for the rain given to the angels" (quotation from p. 41). STONE, *Lists of Revealed Things* (n. 5), pp. 431-434, notes other later texts concerned with the numbering of raindrops: 2 Bar 21,8; 59,5; 4 Ezra 5,36; 2 Enoch 40,8; 47,5.

48. For a comparison of 1 Enoch and Ben Sira on calendrical issues, see WRIGHT, "*Fear the Lord and Honor the Priest*" (n. 7), pp. 204-208. Note that a precise concern for the calendar occurs in various Qumran works, such as the Calendrical Documents (4Q320-330), while the calculation of jubilee years is a feature of 11QMelchizedek and the Book of Jubilees. The following quotation of 1 Enoch 72 comes from ISAAC, *Enoch* (n. 36), p. 50.

49. The phrase "root of wisdom" has been read in 4QMysteries[b]: "You did not look upon the root of wisdom" (4Q300 1 ii 3); see D.J. HARRINGTON, *Wisdom Texts from*

be an echo of the Tree of Knowledge in Gen 2,17. Such an echo of Genesis occurs more deliberately in 1 Enoch 32,3, where the patriarch says: "I saw … the Tree of Wisdom, whose fruit (the holy ones) eat and learn great wisdom"[50]. Thereafter, 1 Enoch 32,3-4 depicts the beauty of this tree, and the link with Gen 2,17 becomes explicit in 1 Enoch 32,6. Thus, in the context of 1 Enoch 32, the implied message of Sir 1,6 may be a denial that the root of wisdom (= Tree of Knowledge) has been revealed to Enoch.

III. Context of Greek Science

Much scholarship has considered Ben Sira's relation to Greek literature and philosophy (as noted above in the introduction to this article). For instance, T. Middendorp and H.-V. Kieweler have dealt with the sage's relation with Greek literature, while his links with Stoic thought have received treatment from M. Hengel and U. Wicke-Reuter[51]. This section focuses on his relationship with the Greek scientific enterprise, particularly from Aristotle to Eratosthenes.

A methodological question arises for us immediately. Did Ben Sira know any of the works of scientific authors such as Aristotle, Aristarchus, Archimedes, or Eratosthenes? There is no direct evidence that he did. Nevertheless, both Archimedes (ca. 287-212 BCE) and Eratosthenes (ca. 275-194 BCE) spent many years in Alexandria, the centre of the Ptolemaic empire, during the formative years of Ben Sira's life. The sage mentions that he had travelled extensively (Sir 34,12; cf. Sir 39,4)[52], and it is quite likely that he would have visited Alexandria. After all, it was the capital city of the Ptolemaic empire that ruled Palestine until 200 BCE, and it already had a substantial Jewish community. Some Jews who were fluent in both Hebrew and Greek evidently lived in that city during the third century BCE, since the Pentateuch was translated from Hebrew into Greek in Alexandria at that time[53]. Hence, in view of

Qumran, London, Routledge, 1997, p.71. However, a different reading is: "You have not seen the root of the vision"; so García Martínez, *The Dead Sea Scrolls Translated* (n. 23), p. 400. Note that Sir 1,20 equates the root of wisdom with fear of the Lord.

50. Translation of the Greek text in Argall, *1 Enoch and Sirach* (n. 6), p. 33. Argall also observes the similarity of 1 Enoch 32,3-4 with Sir 24,13-22 (see p. 93).

51. See n. 10 and n. 12 above.

52. See J.J. Lavoie, *Ben Sira le voyageur ou la difficile rencontre avec l'hellénisme*, in *Science et esprit* 52 (2000) 37-60; N. Calduch-Benages, *Elementos de inculturación helenista en el libro de Ben Sira: Los viajes*, in *EstBib* 54 (1996) 289-298.

53. The Greek Pentateuch "represents what Alexandrian Jewry of the third century B.C. thought their Hebrew Bible meant"; so J.W. Wevers, *Notes on the Greek Text of Exodus* (SBL SCS, 30), Atlanta, GA, Scholars Press, 1990, p. xvi. By the time of Ben

his great learning and his travels, it is conceivable that Ben Sira would have had some acquaintance, however indirect, with some of the currents of Greek science prevalent in third-century BCE Alexandria[54].

Ben Sira's questions in Sir 1,2-3 are about counting and measuring, which were concerns of Greek scientists. In his *Philebus* Plato (ca. 429-347 BCE) quotes a view that regards such techniques of exact science as superior to other crafts. Thus, in *Philebus* 55e Socrates declares: "If someone were to take away all counting, measuring, and weighing from the arts and crafts, the rest might be said to be worthless"[55]. Later (*Philebus* 57c-d) Protarchus asserts that although the exact sciences are more valuable than the imprecise crafts, philosophy is the highest form of inquiry: "Let it be said that these [exact] sciences are far superior to the other disciplines, but that those among them that are animated by the spirit of the true philosophers are infinitely superior yet in precision and truth in their use of measure and number". Moreover, Ben Sira would surely share Protarchus' faith in a rational principle at work behind the universe (*Philebus* 28e): "The only account that can do justice to the wonderful spectacle presented by the cosmic order of sun, moon, and stars and the revolution of the whole heaven, is that reason arranges it all"[56].

In Sir 1,2 the sage asks who can number the grains of sand on the seashore, or the raindrops, or the days of eternity[57]. Here the sage inquires about three forms of measurement: a dry measure (sand, reckoned by the Hebrew אפה or the Greek μέδιμνος), a liquid measure (water, reckoned by the Hebrew בת or the Greek μετρήτης), and a calendrical measure (time, reckoned by days). The Delphic priestess claimed to

Sira, there was "a flourishing Jewish literature in Greek in Alexandria", according to COLLINS, *Jewish Wisdom in the Hellenistic Age* (n. 11), p. 41. Moreover, the city is probably where the grandson translated Ben Sira's book; indeed, "the grandson learned a good deal from the Jewish community in Alexandria where he lived", according to SKEHAN – DI LELLA, *The Wisdom of Ben Sira* (n. 10), p. 134.

54. On the encounter between Israelite faith and Greek scientific thought see, for instance, S.L. JAKI, *Science and Creation*, Edinburgh, Scottish Academic Press, 1986, pp. 152-156; on Greek philosophy in Syria-Palestine see HENGEL, *Judaism and Hellenism* (n. 9), I, pp. 83-88. Greek cultural influence had reached Palestine by Ben Sira's time, according to COLLINS, *Jewish Wisdom in the Hellenistic Age* (n. 11), p. 24: "In Palestine alone there were some thirty Greek towns, mainly on the coast, around the Sea of Tiberias, and in Transjordan", though "there were no Greek settlements in Judea itself".

55. D. FREDE, *Plato: Philebus*, Indianapolis, IN, Hackett, 1993, p. 67. The following quotations are from pp. 69 and 27.

56. Compare the Hebrew text of Sir 42,21: "He has measured out the mighty deeds of his wisdom; he is one from eternity".

57. Cf. J.P. BROWN, *Israel and Hellas*, I (BZAW, 231), Berlin, de Gruyter, 1995, pp. 314-316 (on comparisons of number).

know the number of sand grains: "I count the grains of sand on the beach and measure the sea" (Herodotus, *Histories* 1,47,3)[58].

Employing a more scientific approach for counting the "sand of the seas", Archimedes (ca. 287-212 BCE) wrote a work called *The Sand-Reckoner* (or *Psammites*). This work aimed to measure the number of grains of sand that would fill the universe (even on Aristarchus' helio-centric model), and concluded that it was less than ten to the power of sixty-three (10^{63}). Archimedes begins his treatise with an address to the king (perhaps the ruler of Syracuse):

> There are some, king Gelon, who think that the number of grains of sand is infinite.... Others, indeed, do not assume that it is infinite, but they think that no such large expressible number exists that exceeds its multitude. It is clear that if those who hold this view imagined a volume of sand as large as would be the volume of the earth if all the seas and hollows in it were filled up to a height equal to that of the highest mountains, they would be even less inclined to believe that any number could be expressed which exceeds the number of grains of this sand. But I will try to show by means of geometrical proofs which you will be able to follow that the numbers named by us... include some which exceed not only the number of grains of the sand which, as stated, has a volume equal to that of the earth filled up in the way described, but also of the sand which has a volume equal to that of the cosmos[59].

Admittedly Archimedes uses sand as a convenient hypothetical means for measuring the volume of the universe, whereas Ben Sira refers to the real sand lying on the world's seashores. Nevertheless, the basic concept of trying to count grains of sand is similar. While Archimedes produces a huge figure as a mathematical approximation, Ben Sira considers that the actual number of grains of sand is beyond human computation.

When the sage goes on to mention the counting of days (Sir 1,2), he addresses a concern for the calendar that permeated the ancient world, whether Egypt or Greece or Babylonia. Indeed, Ben Sira's closeness to the Jerusalem temple (Sir 50,1-24) suggests that calendrical questions would have interested him. Perhaps it is no coincidence that, alongside days, Sir 1,2 also mentions both sand and raindrops, since sand and water were used in the ancient world to measure time. O.A.W. Dilke comments: "The sand-timer was no doubt the earliest timekeeper independent of the celestial bodies, but it is inefficient for measuring more than a

58. A. DE SÉLINCOURT (revised A.R. BURN), *Herodotus: The Histories*, Harmondsworth, Penguin, 1972, p. 58.

59. E. J. DIJKSTERHUIS, *Archimedes*, Copenhagen, Munksgaard, 1956, pp. 360-373, here p. 362. Cf. T.L. HEATH, *A Manual of Greek Mathematics*, Oxford, Clarendon, 1931, pp. 327-330.

limited duration. Hence attention turned at an early date to a simple form of water-clock"[60]. Almost a century before Ben Sira wrote his book, Ctesibius of Alexandria (who flourished around 270 BCE) devised the first reasonably accurate water-clock (clepsydra)[61].

When Sir 1,2 suggests the impossibility of calculating the "days of eternity", perhaps the sage is also reacting to the prevalent Greek idea of the recurring Great Year, a huge cosmic interval of time within which the world decays and comes to rebirth. The Great Year amounted to 36000 years according to Plato but 10800 years according to Heraclitus[62].

In Sir 1,3 the sage poses a question suggesting that no one except God can fathom the dimensions of the universe:

> Height of heaven and breadth of earth
> and depth of the deep – who can fathom out?

In view of the sage's awareness of other currents of Greek thinking, it seems probable that he is pointing to the limits of the Greek scientific enterprise, rather than simply being ignorant of it. A clear illustration of such scientific thought in Ben Sira's time is the case of Eratosthenes (ca. 275-194 BCE)[63]. G. Sarton notes that Eratosthenes' measurement of the earth was surprisingly accurate: "According to Aristotle the circumference of the Earth amounted to 400,000 stadia; according to Archimēdēs, 300,000 stadia; according to Eratosthenēs, 252,000 stadia"[64]. Sarton comments that by his calculation, Eratosthenes' result of 39,690 km was "almost unbelievably close to the real value (40,120 km)". As for trying to measure the "height of heaven", Aristarchus of Samos (ca. 310-230 BCE) wrote a work *On the Sizes and Distances of the Sun and Moon.*

60. O.A.W. DILKE, *Mathematics and Measurement* (Reading the Past, 2), London, British Museum, 1987, p. 44. He states: "Remains have been found of two types of Greek clepsydra, literally 'water-stealer'". Quoting Empedocles (ca. 493-433 BCE), Aristotle (384-322 BCE) mentions the clepsydra in the seventh chapter of his *De Respiratione* (473a15-474a6).

61. So Vitruvius, *De architectura* 9.8.4.

62. JAKI, *Science and Creation* (n. 53), p. 121; cf. HENGEL, *Judaism and Hellenism* (n. 9), I, pp. 191-192.

63. Eratosthenes combined great scientific achievement with a lingering belief in astrological systems. HENGEL, *Judaism and Hellenism*, I, p. 214, notes that Eratosthenes "reported an extensive journey of Hermes through heaven, in which he combined a modern scientific description of heaven and earth with the old Greek star sagas".

64. G. SARTON, *Hellenistic Science and Culture in the Last Three Centuries B.C.* (A History of Science, t. II), Cambridge, MA, Harvard University, 1959, p. 104. The following kilometre equivalent appears on p. 105. For Aristotle's estimate see *On the Heavens* 2,14 #298a; for Archimedes' reckoning (quoting the opinion of others, especially Dicaearchus of Messana) see *The Sand-Reckoner*, chapter 1; for Eratosthenes' figure see Strabo, *Geography* 2,5,7 (cf. 2,5,34).

However, although his theory was sound, he was unable to obtain accurate results[65].

Assuming that Ben Sira had some awareness of these intellectual developments in the great Ptolemaic capital city, the question arises why he opposed such scientific efforts to extend the bounds of human knowledge. The reasons are not entirely clear, but it appears that he thought the right human attitude before such apparent mysteries should be humility and reverence (cf. Sir 3,21-24). To attempt to calculate such things may have seemed to him like ὕβρις (cf. Sir 10,6-18). For instance, Sir 10,7a (Hebrew) asserts: "Hated by the Lord and human beings is pride", while Sir 10,9a (Hebrew) asks: "Why will dust and ashes be proud?" By contrast, the right human response towards the mysteries of creation, in Ben Sira's view, is surely to worship in awe (Sir 43,27-33).

Conclusion

Our investigation has attempted to situate Sir 1,1-10 in its cultural context. In the opening poem of his book, Ben Sira wishes to restate the biblical presupposition that all wisdom comes as a gift from the one God. Whereas Jewish apocalyptists claimed Enoch as the revealer of the secrets of the celestial bodies and meteorology, Ben Sira regards these matters as mysteries best left to God. Similarly, while Greek scientists attempted to calculate the number of sand grains on the seashore, or the height of the sun from the earth, Ben Sira sees these topics as mysteries known only to God.

His questions about the mysteries of the cosmos (Sir 1,2-3) serve a double purpose. On the one hand, to those attracted by the secret wisdom of the apocalyptic circles, he suggests that the cosmological mysteries remain unsolved, and have not been answered by any revelations from figures like Enoch. On the other hand, to those attracted by the claims of Greek science, he points to those same things in the universe that he believes are beyond fathoming by human science.

Whereas Jewish apocalyptists regarded Enoch as the revealer of heavenly wisdom, Ben Sira believed that all necessary wisdom had already been revealed to Israel in the Torah. While Greek scientists sought by human effort to uncover the mysteries of the cosmos, Ben Sira insisted that God had lavishly made known what humans need to know. Accord-

65. See T.L. HEATH, *Aristarchus of Samos, the Ancient Copernicus*, Oxford, Clarendon, 1913, esp. p. 330.

ing to the sage, God's people have been shown where true wisdom lies: "All wisdom is fear of the Lord, and in all wisdom is the fulfilment of the Law" (Sir 19,20).

Thus, Ben Sira directs the attention of his students, not to the "wisdom" supposedly revealed by Enoch (1 Enoch 82,2), nor to the "wisdom" claimed by Greek philosophy and science, but to the wisdom (cf. Deut 4,6-8) granted by God to those who love him, centred on the Torah given to Israel (Sir 19,20; 24,23; cf. Deut 29,28[29]). Such wisdom forms the subject of the rest of the sage's book.

To sum up: for the believer, all wisdom is from God. Human understanding is limited (Sir 18,4-7). True wisdom is not intellectual cleverness, but a respectful attitude towards God and the world – what Ben Sira will call in his next poem "the fear of the Lord".

Ushaw College
Durham, DH7 9RH
England

Jeremy CORLEY

THE MYSTERIES OF GOD
CREATION AND ESCHATOLOGY IN 4QINSTRUCTION
AND THE WISDOM OF SOLOMON

The Wisdom of Solomon is in many ways a different kind of book from the wisdom books of the Hebrew Bible or the teachings of Ben Sira. Unlike these older books, it was composed in Greek, and shows considerable acquaintance with Greek philosophy. It also departs rather sharply from the Hebrew wisdom tradition in its appraisal of life and death[1]. Qoheleth had famously questioned whether the spirit of humans goes upward while the spirit of animals goes downward to the earth, since all alike die[2]. Ben Sira, in the early second century BCE, still clung to the view that whether life is for ten or a hundred or a thousand years, there is no inquiry about it in Hades[3]. In the Wisdom of Solomon, those who think that humanity is doomed to Hades or Sheol are regarded as fools:

> Thus they reasoned, but they were led astray,
> for their wickedness blinded them
> and they did not know the mysteries of God (μυστήρια θεοῦ)
> nor hoped for the wages of holiness,
> nor discerned the prize for blameless souls;
> for God created man for incorruption
> and made him the image of his own eternity[4].
> By the envy of the devil death entered the world,
> and those who are of his lot experience it" (Wis 2,21-24).

The novelty of the worldview of the Wisdom of Solomon is commonly attributed to the influence of two factors: Hellenistic, Platonic, philosophy, and Jewish apocalyptic traditions[5]. It is widely agreed that

1. See my essay, *The Root of Immortality. Death in the Context of Jewish Wisdom*, in *Seers, Sibyls, and Sages in Hellenistic-Roman Judaism* (JSJS, 54), Leiden, Brill, 1997, pp. 351-367.

2. Qoh 3,19-21. On Qoheleth's treatment of death see S. BURKES, *Death in Qoheleth and Egyptian Biographies of the Late Period*, Atlanta, GA, Society of Biblical Literature, 1999, pp. 35-80.

3. Sir 41,4.

4. Or: his own proper being (reading ἰδιότητος instead of ἀϊδιότητος). See G. SCARPAT, *Libro della Sapienza*, Brescia, Paideia, 1989, 1, pp. 198-199.

5. The philosophical background is demonstrated throughout the commentary of D. WINSTON, *The Wisdom of Solomon* (AB, 43), New York, Doubleday, 1979. For the apocalyptic background see P. GRELOT, *L'Eschatologie de la Sagesse et les Apocalypses Juives*, in A. BARUCQ (ed.), *À la Rencontre de Dieu: Memorial Albert Gelin*, LePuy,

the author drew on an apocalyptic source in chapters 2 and 5[6]. The reference to mysteries becomes intelligible in this context. Traditional Hebrew wisdom teachers, such as Qoheleth and Ben Sira, relied on an empirical epistemology, and were wary of claims of revelation. In contrast, the apocalyptic literature claimed to disclose mysteries that were beyond the reach of normal human comprehension. Daniel succeeds where the Babylonian wise men fail because "there is a God in heaven who reveals mysteries" (Aramaic רז)[7]. In the Epistle of Enoch, the term mystery is used for the information that Enoch has learned from the tablets of heaven, and which is largely concerned with the fate of the righteous after death (1 Enoch 103,1)[8].

THE רז נהיה

The publication of the wisdom texts from Qumran, however, shows that the Wisdom of Solomon was not the first Jewish wisdom text to entertain the concept of "mystery". In 4QInstruction, the expression רז נהיה appears more than 20 times[9]. The phrase also occurs in some other

Mappus, 1961, pp. 165-78. On the combination of the two, see J.J. COLLINS, *Jewish Wisdom in the Hellenistic Age,* Louisville, KY, Westminster JohnKnox, 1997, pp. 183-187; ID., *Apocalyptic Eschatology in Philosophical Dress in the Wisdom of Solomon,* in J.L. KUGEL (ed.), *Shem in the Tents of Japheth* (JSJS, 76), Leiden, Brill, 2002, pp. 93-107.

6. See especially L. RUPPERT, *Der leidende Gerechte*, Würzburg, Katholisches Bibelwerk, 1972, pp. 70-105; ID., *Gerechte und Frevler (Gottlose) in Sap 1,1–6,21*, in H. HÜBNER (ed.), *Die Weisheit Salomos im Horizont Biblischer Theologie*, Neukirchen-Vluyn, Neukirchener Verlag, 1993, pp. 1-54. Ruppert argues that Wis 2,12-20 and 5,1-7 constitute a distinct source, which he calls a diptych, originally composed in Hebrew or Aramaic but translated into Greek before it was incorporated into the Wisdom of Solomon. It is unlikely that such a source can be isolated in Wisdom of Solomon. The material appears to be fully re-worked and integrated into its present context. Note also the parallels between Wisdom and the Books of Enoch highlighted by G.W.E. NICKELSBURG, *Resurrection, Immortality and Eternal Life in Intertestamental Judaism*, Cambridge, MA, Harvard University Press, 1972, pp. 76-78, 128-130; ID., *1 Enoch 1. A Commentary on the Book of 1 Enoch Chapters 1-36; 81-108* (Hermeneia), Minneapolis, MN, Fortress, 2001, pp. 78-79.

7. The only attestation of the word רז, mystery, in the Hebrew Bible is in the Aramaic part of the Book of Daniel, where it occurs 9 times. See further R.E. BROWN, *The Semitic Background of the Term 'Mystery' in the New Testament,* Philadelphia, PA, Fortress, 1968, who also surveys the use of "mystery" in the Dead Sea Scrolls that were available at that time.

8. The Aramaic of this passage is not extant. The word *raz* is used at 1 Enoch 106,19: "For I know the mysteries of the Lord that the holy ones have revealed and shown to me, and that I have read on the tablets of heaven" (4Q204 5 ii 26).

9. A closer parallel to the phrase in Wisdom of Solomon is found in the Instruction on the Two Spirits (1QS 3:23), which refers to רזי אל, the mysteries of God. The ability of the Angel of Darkness to corrupt even the righteous is ascribed to "the mysteries of God". Later in the Instruction, in 1QS 4,18, we are told that "God, in the mysteries of his knowledge and in the wisdom of his glory, has determined an end to the existence of injustice".

texts from Qumran: twice in the Book of Mysteries (1Q27 1 i 3,4 = 4Q300 3 4) and in 1QS 11,3-4. The word נהיה is a niphal participle of the verb to be. The exact connotation of this phrase is a matter of debate[10]. In biblical Hebrew, the niphal of the verb to be has the connotation "to be done". It is used of the utterance of a word: כי מאתי נהיה הדבר הזה (1 Kgs 12,24; cf. 2 Chron 11,4), or of an event that has (or has not) taken place: כמוהו לא נהיה מן העלם (Joel 2,2). In the Dead Sea Scrolls, it is often taken to refer to the future: the mystery that is to be, or that is to come. This understanding of the phrase was first suggested by the context in 1Q27 (the Book of Mysteries):

> And they do not know the רז נהיה nor understand ancient matters (קדמוניות). And they do not know what is going to happen to them, and they will not save themselves by the רז נהיה[11].

The editor, J. T. Milik, rendered the phrase as "le mystère future"[12]. The text goes on to speak of signs of what will happen. On Milik's interpretation, the future mystery complements the "ancient matters". A future sense is supported by Sir 42,19 and 48,25, where the plural נהיות is translated into Greek as τὰ ἐσσόμενα).

The verb to be is also used in the niphal in the Instruction on the Two Spirits (1QS 3,15: from the God of knowledge comes כול הויה ונהייה). This is commonly translated as "all that is and shall be", again on the assumption that the terms are complementary rather than synonymous. Again, in CD 2,9-10 לכל הוי עולמים ונהיות עד the נהיות עד is parallel to הוי עולמים – whatever has happened forever. Complementary parallelism gives excellent sense, but synonymous parallelism can not be ruled out. In 1QS 11,3-4 we read "from the source of his knowledge he has disclosed his light, and my eyes have observed his wonders, and the light of my heart the רז נהיה". Some scholars have given the phrase a more abstract translation, such as "the mystery of existence"[13] but נהיה is a ver-

10. A. LANGE, *Weisheit und Prädestination. Weisheitliche Urordnung und Prädestination in den Textfunden von Qumran* (STDJ, 18), Leiden, Brill, 1995, pp. 57-60; D.J. HARRINGTON, *The* Raz Nihyeh *in a Qumran Wisdom Text (1Q26, 4Q415-418, 4Q423)*, in *RQ* 17 (1996) 549-553; T. ELGVIN, *An Analysis of 4QInstruction* (Diss. Hebrew University, 1997), pp. 75-83; ID., *The Mystery to Come: Early Essene Theology of Revelation*, in F.H. CRYER – T.L. THOMPSON (eds.), *Qumran between the Old and New Testaments*, Sheffield, Sheffield Academic Press, 1998, pp. 113-150; M.J. GOFF, *The Worldly and Heavenly Wisdom of 4QInstruction* (Diss. University of Chicago, 2002), pp. 58-92.

11. The rebuke of the wicked for not knowing the mysteries is a striking parallel to Wis 2,21-24.

12. J.T. MILIK, *Livre des Mystères*, in D. BARTHÉLEMY – J.T. MILIK, *Qumran Cave 1* (DJD,1), Oxford, Clarendon, 1955, pp. 103-104.

13. R. EISENMAN – M. WISE, *The Dead Sea Scrolls Uncovered*, Rockport, Element, 1992, pp. 241-255, and F. GARCÍA MARTÍNEZ – E.J. TIGCHELAAR, *The Dead Sea Scrolls Study Edition*, Leiden, Brill, 1998, pp. 845-877, translate "the mystery of existence";

bal form, not an abstract noun[14]. Ultimately, the meaning of the phrase must be determined from the contexts in which it is used in 4QInstruction.

Many of those contexts are fragmentary, and the reference to the mystery is allusive in any case[15]. Typically, the addressee is told that his ear has been uncovered with respect to the mystery, or is told to gaze on it, or to seek it, or not be distracted from it. It is by the mystery that God has established the foundation of truth (4Q417 1 i 8-9). The mystery involves "all the paths of truth" and enables one to know what is good and bad (4Q416 2 iii 14-15; cf. 4Q418 9 15). It concerns "the birth times of salvation, and who is to inherit glory and iniquity" (4Q417 2 i 10-11)[16]. and enables the one who seeks it out to know his inheritance (4Q418 9 9). By contemplating the mystery, one can know the תולדות, which is variously understood as the generations or the nature and characteristics, of humanity (אדם), the judgment of human beings (אנוש) and the weight (evaluation?) of the periods[17]. It is clear from this contextual usage that the רז נהיה includes knowledge of eschatological reward and punishment, but it also includes the origin of the human and even the cosmic condition (תולדות). Harrington aptly notes that the range of material embraced by the mystery is similar to that covered in the Instruction on the Two Spirits: origin, ways in the world, and eschatological outcome[18]. Lange describes it as "eine Welt- und Schöpfungsordnung" which combines primeval, historical, eschatological and ethical elements[19]. Elgvin defines it as "a comprehensive word for God's mysterious plan for crea-

M. WISE – M. ABEGG – E. COOK, *The Dead Sea Scrolls. A New Translation*, San Francisco, CA, HarperSanFrancisco, 1996, pp. 378-390: "the secret of the way things are".

14. LANGE, *Weisheit und Prädestination* (n. 10), p. 57, captures the temporal dimension with "Geheimnis des Werdens". A. ROFÉ, *Revealed Wisdom: From the Bible to Qumran*, forthcoming in J.J. COLLINS – G. STERLING (eds.), *Sapiential Perspectives. Wisdom Literature in Light of the Dead Sea Scrolss*, Leiden, Brill, 2003, construes the word נהיה as a perfect rather than as a participle, and translates "the mystery of what happened, or what happens".

15. For a concise summary see D.J. HARRINGTON, *Mystery,* in L.H. SCHIFFMAN – J.C. VANDERKAM, (eds.), *The Encyclopedia of the Dead Sea Scrolls*, New York, Oxford University Press, 2000, pp. 588-591.

16. On the concept of the "birth times" see M. MORGENSTERN, *The Meaning of בית מולדים in the Qumran Wisdom Texts*, in *JJS* 51(2000) 141-144, who argues that the term refers to horoscopes at the time of birth. But see also the qualification of this view by E.J.C. TIGCHELAAR, *To Increase Learning for the Understanding Ones* (STDJ, 44), Leiden, Brill, 2002, p. 238. In this case, knowledge of the birth times of salvation enables one to know who is to be saved or damned. Strugnell and Harrington read עמל, toil, instead of עול, iniquity (DJD, 34, p. 173). See TIGCHELAAR, *To Increase Learning*, p. 56.

17. 4Q418 77. J. STRUGNELL – D. HARRINGTON, *Qumran Cave 4. XXIV. Sapiential Texts, Part 2. 4QInstruction* (DJD, 34), Oxford, Clarendon, 1999, p. 298. Compare the use of תולדות in the Instruction on the Two Spirits, 1QS 3,13.

18. HARRINGTON, *Mystery* (n. 15), p. 590.

19. LANGE, *Weisheit und Prädestination* (n. 10), p. 60.

tion and history … 'salvation history' in a wider meaning"[20]. This mystery provides a context for human action. By understanding it, one can walk in righteousness (4Q416 2 iii 9-10) and discern between good and evil (4Q417 1 i 6-8)[21].

There are some clear points of analogy between the רז נהיה in the text from Qumran and the mysteries of God in the Wisdom of Solomon. In both texts, understanding the mystery is the key to right behavior. This is so primarily because it discloses the ultimate outcome of righteous or wicked behavior – the reward of piety and the prize of blameless souls, in the idiom of Wisdom, or "who is to inherit glory and iniquity" in the phrase of 4Q Instruction. But this outcome is not arbitrary. It is grounded in the way in which God created humanity in the first case.

The Hope of the Righteous in Wisdom

It is generally recognized that the Wisdom of Solomon understands the afterlife in terms of the immortality of the soul[22]. The noun "immortality" (ἀθανασία) occurs 5 times in the book (3,4; 4,1; 8,13.17; 15,3) and the adjective "immortal" (ἀθάνατος) once (in 1,15, à propos of righteousness). In 4,1 and 8,13, immortality is associated with memory, and refers to an undying reputation. In 3,4 it is the hope of the righteous. In 3,4, we are told that the hope of the righteous is full of immortality. In 8,17, there is immortality in kinship with wisdom, and in 15,3 righteousness and the knowledge of God are the root of immortality. A related term, "incorruption" (ἀφθαρσία) appears 3 times (2,23; 6,18 and 6,19), and the adjective ἄφθαρτος twice (12,1 and 18,4). This term was associated with Epicurean philosophy[23]. The Epicureans explained the eternal life of the gods by saying that they consisted of incorruptible matter. According to Wisdom, humanity was created "for incorruptibility" (2,23). Incorruptibility is assured by keeping the laws of wisdom, and it causes one to be near to God (6,18-19). God's πνεῦμα is imperishable (12,1), as is the light of the law (18,4). According to Philo, "incorrup-

20. ELGVIN, *An Analysis of 4QInstruction* (n. 10), p. 80.

21. Formerly 4Q417 2, and cited in this way by HARRINGTON, *Mystery* (n. 15), p. 590.

22. See the discussion by WINSTON, *The Wisdom of Solomon* (n. 5), pp. 25-32, who notes that Wisdom modifies Platonic doctrine on this subject in significant ways. See also the discussion by C. LARCHER, *Études sur le Livre de la Sagesse,* Paris, Gabalda, 1969, pp. 236-327, who acknowledges the influence of Greek concepts but places greater weight on biblical influences. On the terminology see also J.M. REESE, *Hellenistic Influence on the Book of Wisdom and its Consequences* (Analecta Biblica, 41), Rome, Pontifical Biblical Institute, 1970, pp. 64-65.

23. WINSTON, *The Wisdom of Solomon* (n. 5), p. 121.

tion is akin to eternality"[24], and equally there seems to be no practical difference between immortality and incorruptibility in Wisdom. At no point does Wisdom speak of resurrection of the body, or even of resurrection of the spirit, in such a way as to imply that life is interrupted at death[25]. The righteous only seem to die (3,2), but are at peace. For Wisdom, as for Philo, the death that matters is the death of the soul, or spiritual death[26]. God did not make this death (1,13), and the righteous do not experience it. The wicked experience death, because they are worthy to be of its lot (1,16). Wisdom does not refer to any punishment of the wicked after death; it appears that they simply cease to exist. They lament that just as their wealth vanished like a shadow, "so we also, as soon as we were born, ceased to be, and we had no sign of virtue to show, but were consumed in our wickedness" (5,13). Their hope is like thistledown or smoke, dispersed in the wind[27].

Chrysostome Larcher raised the question whether bodily resurrection is not implied in Wis 3,7-8: "in the time of their visitation they will shine forth, and will run like sparks through the stubble", a passage that has often been understood in terms of astral immortality[28]. There is an obvious, parallel to Dan 12,3, where the משכלים shine like the brightness of the sky, and are like the stars forever[29]. But the idea of astral immortality was widespread in the Hellenistic world, as a form of immortality of the soul[30]. Throughout the Greco-Roman world, the soul was thought

24. *De Abr* 55.

25. Several authors have tried to find an implicit doctrine of bodily resurrection in Wisdom. See especially P. BEAUCHAMP, *Le salut corporel des justes et la conclusion du livre de la Sagesse*, in *Bib* 45 (1964) 491-526; É. PUECH, *La Croyance des Esséniens en la Vie Future: Immortalité, Résurrection, Vie Éternelle?*, Paris, Gabalda, 1993, pp. 92-98; ID., *Le Livre de la Sagesse et les manuscrits de la mer morte: un aperçu*, forthcoming in the proceedings of the 3° Convegno di Studi Biblici, *Il Libro della Sapienza. Tradizione Redazione Teologia*, Palermo, 2002, to be edited by A. PASSARO. Beauchamp points to the transformation of nature at the end of the book; Puech to the judgement scene in chapter 5. P. GRELOT, *L'Eschatologie de la Sagesse*, pp. 176-177, acknowledges that Wisdom does not speak of corporeal resurrection, but notes, correctly, that resurrection of the spirit is more typical of the apocalypses.

26. M. KOLARCIK, *The Ambiguity of Death in the Book of Wisdom 1-6* (Analecta Biblica, 127), Rome, Pontifical Biblical Institute, 1991, p. 180, and especially K.M. HOGAN, *The Exegetical Background of the 'Ambiguity of Death' in the Wisdom of Solomon*, in *JSJ* 30 (1999) 1-24.

27. Compare the fate of the Gentiles in 2 Bar 82,3-7.

28. C. LARCHER, *Le Livre de la Sagesse ou la Sagesse de Salomon*, Paris, Gabalda, 1983, 1. p. 285. The astral interpretation was argued most famously by A. DUPONT-SOMMER, *De l'immortalité astrale dans la Sagesse de Salomon*, in *REG* 62 (1949) 80-87, but he emended the text, to read "in the galaxy" rather than in the stubble.

29. Compare also 1 Enoch 38,4; 39,7; 104,2; 4 Ezra 7,97; 2 Bar 51,10, etc. WINSTON, *The Wisdom of Solomon* (n. 5), p. 128.

30. See A. SCOTT, *Origen and the Life of the Stars*, Oxford, Clarendon, 1991.

to consist of some kind of substance, be it air, fire, or πνεῦμα[31]. For the Stoics, all existence was physical. Even those who rejected the Stoic view, like Cicero, still considered the soul fiery or airy[32]. Philo says that the rational soul is "of the upper air (αἰθέρος)" a divine particle, the πνεῦμα breathed in by God[33]. It was precisely because the soul consisted of heavenly, fiery matter that it could ascend to the stars after death. In the Wisdom of Solomon, wisdom is conceived as a fine substance spread throughout creation[34], and it is not unlikely that the author conceived of the soul as a substance that could shine forth. But the analogy with sparks is obviously figurative, and such language should not be pressed. Again, the judgment scene in chapter 5, which portrays a post-mortem confrontation between the righteous and the wicked, is figurative speech to dramatize the contrast between the two ways of life, in the manner of Platonic myth[35]. The hope of the righteous in Wisdom is not resurrection, but immortality.

The objection is often raised that immortality in Wisdom does not derive from the inherent nature of the soul, as it does in Plato, but is a gift of God, and contingent on righteousness[36]. It is certainly true that Wisdom modifies Greek philosophy in light of Jewish belief at certain crucial points, as Philo also does[37]. There is no mention of metempsychosis, but it should be noted that this is also true of Cicero's *Tusculan Disputations* and *Dream of Scipio*, despite their Platonic inspiration[38]. There is a hint of the Platonic doctrine of the pre-existence of the soul in Wis 8,19-20: "I was indeed a child well-endowed, having had a noble soul fall to my lot, or rather being noble I entered an undefiled body". Such an idea

31. See D.B. MARTIN, *The Corinthian Body*, New Haven, CT, Yale, 1995, pp. 108-120.

32. *Tusculan Disputations* 1.17.41; 1.19.43; MARTIN, *The Corinthian Body* (n. 30), p. 115.

33. Philo, *Leg. Alleg.* 3. 161.

34. Wis 7,22-8,1. On this passage see LARCHER, *Le Livre de la Sagesse* (n. 28) 1, pp. 479-518; H. HÜBNER, *Die Sapientia Salomonis und die antike Philosophie*, in H. HÜBNER (ed.), *Die Weisheit Salomos im Horizont Biblischer Theologie* (n. 6), pp. 55-81; H. ENGEL, *'Was Weisheit ist, und wie sie entstand, will ich verkünden': Weish 7,22–8,1 innerhalb des* ἔγκωμιον τῆς σοφίας *(6,22-11,1) als Stärkung der Plausibilität des Judentums angesichts hellenistischer Philosophie und Religiosität*, in G. HENTSCHEL – E. ZENGER (eds.), *Lehrerin der Gerechtigkeit*, Leipzig, Benno, 1991, pp. 67-102.

35. On the interpretation of the judgement scene in the philosophical context of the book see COLLINS, *Apocalyptic Eschatology in Philosophical Dress* (n. 5).

36. So e.g. M.J. LAGRANGE, *Le livre de la Sagesse. Sa doctrine des fins dernières*, in *RB* 16 (1907) 94; PUECH, *La Croyance des Esséniens*, (n. 25), p. 93: "un don gratuit de Dieu comme récompense d'une bonne conduite".

37. See WINSTON, *The Wisdom of Solomon* (n. 5), pp. 25-32. Also REESE, *Hellenistic Influence* (n. 23), pp. 32-89.

38. See WINSTON, *The Wisdom of Solomon* (n. 5), pp. 28-29; J. DILLON, *The Middle Platonists*, London, Duckworth, 1977, pp. 96-102.

was not inconceivable in a Jewish context. Philo held that souls were pre-existent, and that "some, such as have earthward tendencies and material tastes, descend to be fast bound in mortal bodies"[39]. The vacillation between two formulations in Wisdom, however, shows that pre-existence was not important for the author's anthropology. The idea that immortality was contingent on righteousness was distinctively Jewish. Immortality was not strictly a reward for righteousness, however. It was the original design of the creator for all humanity.

Hope for the Afterlife in 4QInstruction

4QInstruction also entertains the hope for immortality. This includes the traditional hope for immortality by remembrance. 4Q416 2 iii 6-8 tells the addressee: "Let not thy spirit be corrupted by it (money?). And then thou shalt sleep in faithfulness, and at thy death thy memory will flow[er forev]er, and אחריתך will inherit joy". Strugnell and Harrington translate אחריתך as "your posterity"[40], but the word could be taken as "your hereafter". Other passages are less ambiguous. Some people, we are told, are to inherit glory, while others inherit toil (4Q417 2 i 11). 4Q418 126 ii 7-8 promises "to raise up the head of the poor... in glory everlasting and peace eternal".

As in the Wisdom of Solomon, the hope for the afterlife is formulated in terms of immortality rather than of resurrection: everlasting glory and peace (compare Wis 3,1-3). There is no clear reference to bodily resurrection in 4QInstruction. Torleif Elgvin, in his dissertation, claimed to find such a reference in 4Q418 69 ii 7: דורשי אמת יעורו למשפטי]: "the seekers of truth will wake up to the judgments [of God]"[41]. The final *yod* is only a trace, and Strugnell and Harrington read a *kaph*[42]. They translate "those who investigate the truth shall rouse themselves to judge y[ou". Puech accepts the same material reading, but still takes the passage to refer to resurrection: "les chercheurs fidèles seront réveillés pour votre jugement"[43]. The crucial questions here concern the identity of "those who investigate the truth", and the meaning of the verb יעורו (to wake or arouse). Elgvin and Puech take the investigators to be righteous human beings; Strugnell and Harrington take them to be angelic judges.

39. *De Somn* 1.138; cf. *De Plant* 11-14.
40. Strugnell – Harrington, in DJD, 34, p. 112.
41. Elgvin, *An Analysis* (n. 10), pp. 113-117.
42. So also Tigchelaar, *To Increase Learning* (n. 16), p. 210. This reading is now accepted also by Elgvin (oral communication).
43. Puech, *Le Livre de la Sagesse* (n. 25).

The immediate context reads as follows, in the translation of Strugnell and Harrington:

> 4. "And now, O you foolish-minded ones, what is good to a man who has not
> 5. [been created? And what] is tranquillity to a man who has not come into activity? And what is judgement to a man who has not been established? And what lament shall the dead make over their own death?
> 6. You were fashioned [by the power of G]od, but to the everlasting pit shall your return be. For it shall awaken [to condemn] you[r] sin, [and the creatures of]
> 7. its dark places [ ] shall cry out against your pleading, and all those who will endure forever, those who investigate the truth, shall rouse themselves to judge y[ou. And then]
> 8. will all the foolish-minded be destroyed. And the children of iniquity shall not be found any more, [and a]ll those who hold fast to wickedness shall wither [away. And then,]
> 9. at the passing of judgement upon you, the foundations of the firmament will cry out"[44].

The context, then, is an admonition to the wicked, which is followed after this passage by an exhortation to "the truly chosen ones". It should be noted that the pit is said to awaken, using the verb (קיץ) that is used in the context of resurrection in Daniel 12. The awakening of the pit, however, is not a matter of resurrection, but of arousal. The verb עור lends itself to a similar interpretation. (Compare Isa 51,9, where the arm of the Lord is addressed: עורי עורי). Puech cites 1QH 14,32 as an alleged use of the verb עור with reference to resurrection[45]. The passage reads: "then the sword of God will hasten in the era of judgment, and all the sons of his truth will arise to destroy [the sons of] wickedness". Here again it is by no means certain that the reference is to resurrection. It may rather be a matter of arousal for battle. Those who seek, or investigate, the truth are indentified as "those who will endure forever" כול נהיה עולם. Puech translates this phrase as "tous les destinés-à-l'éternité". But as we have seen, the niphal of the verb to be does not have an exclusively future sense. The phrase might be better translated simply as "those who endure forever", with reference to angelic beings rather than to resurrected humans. (The beings in question may be compared the "angels of destruction" who administer the punishment of the damned in CD 2,6 and 1QS 3,12)[46]. In all, then, it seems very doubtful that this

44. DJD, 34, p. 283.

45. The verse in question is numbered 14,29 in F. García Martínez – E.J. Tigchelaar, *The Dead Sea Scrolls Study Edition* (n. 13), 1, pp. 176-177.

46. C.H.T. Fletcher-Louis, *All the Glory of Adam. Liturgical Anthropology in the Dead Sea Scrolls* (STDJ, 42), Leiden, Brill, 2002, p. 118 argues that the verb דרש is not

passage can be taken as evidence for the idea of resurrection in 4QInstruction.

Of course the alternative to resurrection in the Hebrew wisdom text is not the Platonic idea of the immortality of the soul. The exhortation to the righteous that follows this passage in 4Q418 69 asks:

> As for the Sons of Heaven, whose lot is eternal life, will they truly say, 'we are weary of doing the works of Truth, and [we] have grown weary of them at all times'? Will [they] not walk in light everlasting ... glory and abundance of splendor ... in the council of the divine ones?[47]

It is disputed whether the primary reference of this passage is to angels (as maintained by the editors) or the human righteous[48]. In fact, the passage clearly supposes that the human righteous share the lot of the angels, and may hope for eternal life in the council of the divine ones. The idea that the righteous humans could be elevated to share the life of the angelic host is well attested in the last centuries before the common era. In the early apocalypses of Daniel and Enoch, this is the fate of the righteous after death. In the Hodayot from Qumran, the angelic state can be anticipated even in this life[49]. It does not seem to me that 4QInstruction envisions present exaltation to the degree that we find it in the Hodayot[50]. There is, nonetheless, a close association between the earthly righteous and the angelic host. If we assume, with the editors, that the primary reference in 4Q418 69 is to the angels, it is nonetheless clear that the person of understanding should aspire to a similar life. 4Q418 81 3-5 has been plausibly restored to read "among all the [God]ly [Ones] has he cast thy lot"[51]. The motif of fellowship with the angels as the eschatological reward of the righteous is also picked up in the Wisdom of Solomon. In the judgment scene, in Wis 5,5, the oppressors ask in astonishment when they see the righteous transformed: "Why have they been numbered among the children of God? And why is their lot among the holy ones?"

The association with the holy ones is a point of continuity between the wisdom texts and the early apocalypses of Daniel and Enoch. In Dan

used with angels as subjects in 4QInstruction or in the Scrolls in general, whereas it is commonly used of human beings. But neither are the human righteous ever said to rise to judge the wicked. The language of the passage is exceptional in any case.

47. On the angelic life, compare also 4Q418 55 (DJD, 34, pp. 265-266).

48. FLETCHER-LOUIS, *All the Glory of Adam* (n. 46), pp. 119-120.

49. See the classic study of H.-W. KUHN, *Enderwartung und gegenwärtiges Heil*, Göttingen, Vandenhoeck & Ruprecht, 1966; NICKELSBURG, *Resurrection* (n. 6), pp. 146-156; J.J. COLLINS, *Apocalypticism in the Dead Sea Scrolls*, London, Routledge, 1997, pp. 119-123.

50. See further my comments in *The Eschatologizing of Wisdom in the Dead Sea Scrolls*, forthcoming in COLLINS – STERLING (eds.), *Sapiential Perspectives* (n. 14).

51. DJD, 34, pp. 300, 302.

12,3, the resurrected משׂכילים shine like the stars. In 1 Enoch 104 the righteous are assured that they will "shine like the lights of heaven", "have great joy like the angels of heaven" and "become associates of the host of heaven". The wisdom texts differ from the apocalypses, however, insofar as they do not use the language of resurrection, but rather suggest that the life of the spirit is continuous. The language of 4QInstruction, with the motifs of light and everlasting glory, has a noteworthy parallel in the Instruction on the Two Spirits, where the visitation of the Sons of Light is described as "healing, plentiful peace in a long life, fruitful offspring with all everlasting blessings, and eternal joy in life without end, a crown of glory and a garment of majesty in unending light"[52]. Eternal life in such formulations, is not necessarily incorporeal. The "garment of majesty" may denote what St. Paul would call "a spiritual body" (1 Cor 15,44). As we have already seen, the immortal soul was commonly thought to consist of a heavenly substance (such as αἰθήρ or πνεῦμα) in Hellenistic-Roman thought. In Jewish sources, the idea seems to be a transformed or glorified נפש, which was not quite pure spirit in the Platonic sense. But there is no indication, either in 4QInstruction or in the Instruction on the Two Spirits, that eternal life involves a resurrected body of flesh and blood. As St. Paul would say, "flesh and blood cannot inherit the kingdom of God, nor does the perishable inherit the imperishable"[53]. Neither does it seem to involve a resurrection, in the sense that life is suspended for a time between death and glorification. While the texts are not as clear on the matter as we might wish, the view seems to be that the spirit simply lives on when the body dies. A similar view of the afterlife may be found in Jubilees 23,31, which says of the just that "their bones will rest in the earth, and their spirits will have much joy".

The idea of eternal life, as we find it in 4QInstruction or in the Instruction on the Two Spirits, does not appear to be influenced by Hellenistic philosophy. One possible source of such a hope in the biblical tradition lies in the cultic experience of the presence of God, as we find it expressed in the Psalms. In Ps 73,23-26, the psalmist says: "Nevertheless I am continually with you; you hold my right hand. You guide me with your counsel, and afterward you will receive me (תקחני) with honor ... My flesh and my heart may fail, but God is the strength of my heart and my portion forever". Similarly in Psalm 49,16 we read that "God

52. 1QS 4,6-8. There are numerous parallels between the Instruction on the Two Spirits and 4QInstruction. See LANGE, *Weisheit und Prädestination* (n. 10), pp. 126-130; TIGCHELAAR, *To Increase Learning* (n. 16), pp. 194-207.

53. 1 Cor 15,50.

will ransom my soul from the power of Sheol, for he will take me"[54]. Whether these psalms actually reflect a hope for eternal life on the part of the psalmist is disputed[55]. On the positive side, the use of the verb "to take" or "to receive" (לקח) recalls the assumption of Enoch (Gen 5,24). On the negative side is the predominant rejection of any such hope in the psalms. Even Psalm 49 affirms that the wise die together with the fool and the dolt (vs. 11) and twice declares that "humankind shall not live in glory" (vss. 13, 21, English 12, 20). In any case, this hope arises out of the sense that the presence of God is an experience that transcends time: "For a day in your courts is better than a thousand elsewhere" (Ps 84,10). The fellowship with the angels in the sectarian scrolls is also rooted in the context of worship, as can be seen, for example in the Songs of the Sabbath Sacrifice[56]. I am not persuaded that the few references to priestly matters in 4QInstruction require that that text originated in the milieu of the temple, as Armin Lange has argued[57], but it could be influenced by cultic traditions nonetheless. An alternative, or rather complementary, source for a hope for eternal life is found within the wisdom tradition itself. According to Prov 12,28: "in the paths of righteousness there is life, in walking its path there is no death". Wisdom claims that "whoever finds me finds life... all who hate me love death" (Prov 8,35-36)[58]. Here again there is debate as to whether such statements can be taken literally[59], but in any case they provide a biblical basis for the hope that the life nourished by wisdom will not be cut off by death. Both the cultic and the sapiential traditions, then, provide a basis

54. Compare also Ps 16,9-10.

55. For the positive view: M. DAHOOD, *Psalms III* (AB, 17A), New York, Doubleday, 1970, pp. XLI – LII; PUECH, *La Croyance* (n. 25), pp. 46-59. For the negative: B. VAWTER, *Intimations of Immortality and the Old Testament*, in *JBL* 91(1972) 158-171; reprinted in ID., *The Path of Wisdom*, Wilmington, DE, Glazier, 1986, pp. 140-160.

56. The cultic context of fellowship with the angels is emphasized by FLETCHER-LOUIS, *All the Glory of Adam* (n. 46), especially pp. 56-87. He speaks, however, of "angelomorphism" rather than fellowship, stressing the angelic nature of the human participants. Fletcher-Louis argues that the Songs of Sabbath Sacrifice refer primarily to "angelomorphic" humans rather than to angels. While much of his thesis is speculative, the connection between the angels and the cult is clear.

57. A. LANGE, *In Diskussion mit dem Tempel. Zur Auseinandersetzung zwischen Kohelet und weisheitlichen Kreisen am Jerusalemer Tempel,* in A. SCHOORS (ed.), *Qohelet in the Context of Wisdom* (BETL, 136), Leuven, University Press-Peeters, 1998, pp. 113-159. See especially 4Q418 81 and 4Q423 5. See the critique of Lange's position by T. ELGVIN, *Priestly Sages? The Milieus of Origin of 4QMysteries and 4QInstruction,* in COLLINS – STERLING (eds.), *Sapiential Perspectives* (n. 14).

58. See the classic article of G. VON RAD, *Life and Death in the OT*, in G. KITTEL (ed.), *Theological Dictionary of the New Testament*, 2, Grand Rapids, MI, Eerdmans, 1964, pp. 843-849.

59. PUECH, *La Croyance* (n. 25), pp. 59-65.

for a hope of immortality that does not use the more mythological language of resurrection.

Similarities in Eschatological Hope

There are, then, significant similarities between the eschatology of the Wisdom of Solomon and that of the older Hebrew 4QInstruction. Both speak of immortality or eternal life rather than resurrection[60]. Neither envisions a resurrection of the body of flesh and blood. Both speak of fellowship with the angels as the reward of the righteous, although this language is only used sparingly and figuratively in the Wisdom of Solomon. The Hellenistic book is also informed by Greek philosophical ideas of immortality, which modify the nature of the hope, even though it also adapts and modifies the philosophical doctrines in light of Jewish tradition. Nonetheless, it would seem that the author of Wisdom was familiar with traditions that were broadly similar to what we find in 4QInstruction. The biggest discrepancy in the eschatology is perhaps the fact that Wisdom does not envision the punishment of the damned after death, but only their disappearance.

Creation and Immortality

Both the Greek and the Hebrew wisdom texts seek to ground their view of humanity in their understanding of creation. According to Wis 2,23 God created the human being (ἄνθρωπος/Adam) for incorruption (ἐπ' ἀφθαρσίᾳ) and made him "the image of his own eternity". Immortality, then, is entailed by the creation of human beings in the image of God (Gen 1,27). Death, presumably the death of the soul, is not made by God, but enters the world through the envy of the devil (apparently a reference to the story of the Fall, although it has also been related to the story of Cain and Abel)[61].

60. M. Delcor, *L'immortalité de l'âme dans le livre de la Sagesse et dans les documents de Qumrân*, in *NRT* 77 (1955) 614-630, noted the affinity between Wisdom and the sectarian scrolls in this respect, but concluded that the milieu of Wisdom was not philosophical. The conclusion does not follow. Continuity with Hebraic wisdom does not mean that Wisdom has not reconceived its subject in philosophical categories.

61. For references, see Winston, *The Wisdom of Solomon* (n. 5), p. 121. If the reference is to Genesis 3, this is one of the earliest texts to identify the serpent as the devil. On the interpretation of Gen 1-3 in Wisdom see further M. Gilbert, *La relecture de Gn 1-3 dans le Livre de la Sagesse*, in L. Derousseaux (ed.), *La création dans l'Orient Ancien* (LD, 127), Paris, Cerf, 1987, pp. 323-344.

The association of immortality with creation in the image of God is widespread in Hellenistic Judaism[62]. Philo explains that the likeness is not a matter of bodily form: "No, it is in respect of the mind, the sovereign element of the soul, that the word 'image' is used"[63]. He also distinguishes between the man made in the image of God in Gen 1,27 and the man fashioned from clay in Gen 2,7. The latter "is an object of sense-perception, partaking already of such or such quality, consisting of body and soul, man or woman, by nature mortal; while he that was after the image was an idea or type or seal, an object of thought, incorporeal, neither male nor female by nature incorruptible (ἄφθαρτος)"[64]. It should be borne in mind that Philo is primarily interested in the allegorical meaning of Genesis as an account of universal psychological phenomena. The contrast is between two types or kinds of human being, rather than between two men. Philo also recognizes that the types can be mixed in individual cases:

> [The first man's] father was no mortal but the eternal God, whose image he was in a sense, in virtue of the ruling mind within the soul. Yet though he should have kept that image undefiled and followed as far as he could in the steps of his parent's virtues, when the opposites were set before him to choose or avoid, good and evil, honorable and base, true and false, he was quick to choose the false, the base and the evil and spurn the good and honorable and true, with the natural consequence that he exchanged immortality for mortality, forfeited his blessedness and happiness, and found an easy passage to a life of toil and misery[65].

Philo's interpretation of Genesis is complex, and draws on various exegetical traditions that are sometimes in tension with each other[66]. Our concern here is not with Philo, however, but the light his discussions of Genesis may shed on the Wisdom of Solomon. While Wisdom never expounds a doctrine of double creation, such as we find in Philo[67], there is some evidence that it associates the immortality of the soul with Gen 1,27 and the mortality of the body with Gen 2,7. In Wis 7,1, Solomon acknowledges that "I also am mortal, like everyone else, a descendant of

62. In addition to the references in Philo and Wisdom of Solomon, note Pseudo-Phocylides 106, and my essay, *Life after Death in Pseudo-Phocylides*, in F. GARCÍA MARTÍNEZ – G. P. LUTTIKHUIZEN (eds.), *Jerusalem, Alexandria, Roma. Studies in Ancient Cultural Interaction in Honour of A. Hilhorst* (JSJS, 82), Leiden, Brill, 2003, pp. 75-86.

63. *Op* 69.

64. *Op* 134

65. *Virt* 204-205.

66. For a nuanced exposition, see T.H. TOBIN, *The Creation of Man: Philo and the History of Interpretation* (CBQMS, 14), Washington, DC, Catholic Biblical Association, 1983.

67. *Ibid.*, pp. 102-134.

the first-formed child of earth". We may compare Philo's description of the "molded man" of Gen 2,7 as "by nature mortal"[68]. The earth symbolizes the material aspect of human existence, which, we are told in 9,15, "weighs down the soul". In contrast, the image of God is made for incorruptibility. Humanity became corrupted through "the envy of the devil". Adam, however, did not automatically suffer the full consequences of the Fall. According to Wis 10,1-2, Wisdom "delivered him from his transgression, and gave him strength to rule all things". Both immortality and spiritual death remain as possibilities for all human beings.

The creation of humanity in the image of God also plays a part in the understanding of the human condition in 4QInstruction. In a controversial passage in 4Q417 1 i 14-18 we are told that God gave the vision of Hagu, or book of rememberance, as an inheritance "to אנוש, with a spiritual people, for his fashioning is (or: He fashioned him)[69] according to the pattern of the holy ones" (כתבנית קדושים יצרו). In contrast, the Hagu was not given to the "the spirit of flesh" because it failed to distinguish between good and evil[70]. The allusions to Genesis are transparent[71]. אנושis not the patriarch Enosh[72], but the original human creature, as also in 1QS 3,17-18: והואה ברא אנוש לממשלת תבל. The pattern of the holy ones is a paraphrase of "in the image of God", בצלם אלוהים, in Gen 1,27[73]. The term אלוהים is often used in the DSS as a plural for angels or heavenly beings, and is taken as the plural "holy ones" here. Elgvin has drawn attention to an apt parallel in 1 Enoch 69,11: "For men were created no differently from the angels, that they might remain righteous and

68. *Op* 134; HOGAN, *The 'Ambiguity of Death'* (n. 26), p. 16.

69. Either translation is possible, and the sense is essentially the same in either case.

70. STRUGNELL – HARRINGTON, DJD, 34, pp. 151,155. On the Vision of Hagu, see ELGVIN, *An Analysis of 4QInstruction* (n. 10), pp. 92-94 and most recently C. WERMAN, *What is the Book of Hagu?*, in COLLINS – STERLING (eds.), *Sapiential Perspectives* (n. 14).

71. For full exposition of this passage, see my essay, *In the Likeness of the Holy Ones, The Creation of Humankind in a Wisdom Text from Qumran,* in D.W. PARRY – E. ULRICH (eds.), *The Provo International Conference on the Dead Sea Scrolls* (STDJ, 30), Leiden, Brill, 1999, pp. 609-618; also GOFF, *The Worldly and Heavenly Wisdom* (n. 10), pp. 94-144.

72. So LANGE, *Weisheit und Prädestination* (n. 10), p. 87; J. FREY, *The Notion of 'Flesh' in 4QInstruction and the Background of Pauline Usage*, in D.K. FALK – F. GARCÍA MARTÍNEZ – E.M. SCHULLER (eds.), *Sapiential, Liturgical and Poetical Texts from Qumran* (STDJ, 35), Leiden, Brill, 2000, p. 218. Strugnell and Harrington leave the reference open (DJD, 34, p. 164).

73. The allusion is recognized by Strugnell and Harrington, in DJD, 34, p. 165, and ELGVIN, *An Analysis of 4QInstruction* (n. 10), p. 90. The hesitation of FLETCHER-LOUIS, *All the Glory of Adam* (n. 46), pp. 115-116, is surprising in view of his own statement that "there can be no doubt that our passage is oriented to creation as it is originally intended".

pure, and death, which destroys everything, would not have touched them"[74].

The "people of spirit" who are fashioned in the likeness of the angels are contrasted with "the spirit of flesh" who fail to distinguish between good and evil. The latter phrase, "good and evil" brings to mind the second creation story in Genesis 2. This surely suggests that the two accounts of creation, Gen 1,27 and Gen 2,7, are being read as contrasting paradigms of humanity, just as they are in Philo, even if the conceptual framework in Philo is quite different. On this reading, 4QInstruction bears some resemblance to the more developed dualism of the Instruction on the Two Spirits, which says that when God created אנוש to rule the world (cf. Gen 1,28), he placed within him two spirits, so that they would know good and evil (1QS 4,26). While the formulation is significantly different, both texts would then see the distinction between two types of humanity as having its origin in creation[75].

Against this interpretation, Torleif Elgvin has argued that the use of יצר, fashion, in connection with "the pattern of the holy ones" shows that the two creation stories are being conflated, since this is the verb used in Gen 2,7[76]. On this reading, "4QInstruction sees only one Adam in the biblical text. Before he sinned, he shared angelic glory and wisdom; after his fall he shared the conditions of רוח בשׂר"[77]. Elgvin agrees that "Adam of the Urzeit is a type of the enlightened community of the Endzeit"[78]. This interpretation might shed some light on the formulation of 4Q417 1 i 19: ועוד לוא נתן הגוי לרוח בשר: but no more has Hagu been given to the spirit of flesh[79]. This would mean that the Vision of Hagu was initially given to Adam, but withdrawn when he failed to distinguish between good and evil. In this case, however, we might wonder why Adam failed to distinguish between good and evil in the first case, since he had been endowed with the vision of Hagu as his inheritance.

It is not clear to me, however, that 4QInstruction envisions a Fall, or a sin of Adam, at all. We find further echoes of Genesis 2-3 in the very

74. ELGVIN, *An Analysis of 4QInstruction* (n. 10), p 90.

75. Compare also the later rabbinic doctrine of two *yēṣers*, or inclinations. Midrash Rabbah 14,3; G.F. MOORE, *Judaism in the First Centuries of the Christian Era*, New York, Schocken, 1975, 1, pp. 474-496; E.E. URBACH, *The Sages: Their Concepts and Beliefs*, Jerusalem, Magnes, 1975, 1. pp. 471-83; G.H. COHEN STUART, *The Struggle in Man between Good and Evil: An Inquiry into the Origin of the Rabbinic Concept of Yeser hara*ᶜ, Kampen, Kok, 1984.

76. ELGVIN, *An Analysis of 4QInstruction* (n. 10), p 91.

77. *Ibid.*

78. *Ibid.*

79. Harrington and Strugnell translate "no more" (DJD, 34, p. 155). Elgvin translates "not before" (*An Analysis*, p. 85), but this would be problematic on his own interpretation, since the Hagu had been given to Adam.

fragmentary text 4Q423, which appears to take the garden as a metaphor for life, which may be either delightful or full of thorns depending on whether the gardener is faithful or not[80]. Even there, however, there is no clear reference to a primeval sin. Rather, Genesis is treated as a paradigmatic story that outlines two permanent possibilities in life. While much is unclear in 4QInstruction, because of the fragmentary state of the text, the contrast between the people of spirit, who are formed in the image of the holy ones, and the spirit of flesh, appears to be primordial. The fact that the verb "to fashion" is imported into the paraphrase of Genesis 1 does not necessarily mean that the two accounts are being fused into a single creation.

The context of the passage about the כתבנית קדושים in 4Q417 1 i concerns eschatological retribution. The addressee is told to meditate on the רז נהיה "and then you shall know truth and iniquity, wisdom [and foolish]ness you shall [recognize] every ac[t] in all their ways, together with their visitation (פקודתם) in all periods everlasting, and the eternal visitation. Then you shall discern between the [goo]d and [evil according to their deeds]". The visitations are already inscribed. The Vision of Hagu and book of remembrance contain the destiny of those who keep God's word, but also, presumably, the inscribed visitation of the sons of Sheth. So, while 4QInstruction does not say directly that immortality results from being in the image of God or the likeness of the Holy Ones, it clearly implies that there are contrasting destinies for the "people of spirit" and the "spirit of flesh". 4QInstruction closely resembles the Instruction on the Two Spirits at this point. Also, immortality is explicitly associated with the angelic state in 1 Enoch. The watchers are told that they had been "spiritual, holy, living an eternal life" before they had relations with human women (1 Enoch 15,3). According to 1 Enoch 69,11, death would not have touched humanity if they had not been corrupted by the Watchers, for they were created no different from the angels.

Similarities and Differences

The Wisdom of Solomon shares with 4QInstruction the view that it was the intention of the creator that humanity should be immortal. This view was grounded in the understanding of Gen 1,27, which says that Adam was created in the image of God. The two texts understand the meaning of the image somewhat differently. The Qumran text relates it

80. This passage is edited by Elgvin in DJD, 34, pp. 505-539. See also his comments in *An Analysis of 4QInstruction* (n. 10), pp. 71-75.

to the angels, while Wisdom speaks more abstractly of the eternity of God (or his proper being, if we read ἰδιότητος rather than ἀϊδιότητος in 2,23). In both cases, however, it entails immortality. Both texts draw a contrast, however indirectly, between the image of God, of Gen 1,27, and the creature born from the earth or the spirit of flesh, which is related to the story of Genesis 2. 4QInstruction relates this distinction to two kinds of people and two kinds of behavior. The Wisdom of Solomon, in contrast, draws the distinction between two aspects of the same human being. Solomon is mortal, as a descendant of Adam, with respect to his fleshly body, but he too is created for incorruption. There is a fundamental difference between the two books in their understanding of the flesh. The Hebrew book does not associate the flesh as such with corruption and mortality, in the manner of the Alexandrian authors. Flesh represents the weakness of unaided human nature, and sometimes it is regarded as sinful[81]. Those who share in the spirit of flesh, however, are no less immortal than the people of spirit. In contrast to Wisdom, where the wicked simply cease to exist, the wicked in 4QInstruction survive for punishment in the hereafter.

Conclusion

The editors of 4QInstruction described it as a "missing link" in the development of the Jewish wisdom literature, between the "secular" or common wisdom of Proverbs and the Torah-centered wisdom of Ben Sira[82]. I would suggest that it might better be described as a missing link between the older Hebrew wisdom and the Hellenistic Wisdom of Solomon. Some of the shifts in worldview that distinguish the Hellenistic book from Proverbs and Ben Sira are anticipated in 4QInstruction. These include the notion of a mystery, which concerns the comprehensive plan of God for humanity, and which involves an immortal destiny, grounded in creation in the divine image.

I do not wish to argue that the author of Wisdom was familiar with 4QInstruction, despite some intriguing parallels. For example, Wisdom repeatedly uses the word ἐπισκοπή, visitation[83], which is used in the LXX to translate the Hebrew פקודה. This Hebrew term occurs with disproportional frequency in 4QInstruction[84]. It seems to me that the re-

81. FREY, *The Notion of 'Flesh'* (n. 72), pp. 214-20.

82. STRUGNELL – HARRINGTON, in DJD, 34, p. 36.

83. Wis 2,20; 3,7.13; 4,15; 14,11; 19,15. See G. SCARPAT, *Libro della Sapienza* (n. 4), 1. pp. 195-66.

84. STRUGNELL – HARRINGTON, in DJD, 34, pp. 28. See TIGCHELAAR, *To Increase Learning* (n. 16), pp. 240-242. The term occurs 16 times in 4QInstruction and 6 or 7 times in the Instruction on the Two Spirits.

lation between the two books is of a more general sort. On one level, it involves exegetical traditions. Both books understand the opening chapters of Genesis typologically, and distinguish between the creation in the image of God in Genesis 1 and the creation of the fallible being in Genesis 2, although they understand these stories in somewhat different ways. On another level it involves the influence of common traditions. These may well include some apocalyptic texts, such as the Epistle of Enoch, but they also include the traditional wisdom literature, such as Proverbs, which spoke of life as a transcendent fruit of wisdom, without appeal to the language of resurrection. In the case of the Wisdom of Solomon, these common sources were filtered through a lens of Greek philosophy, of which there is no trace in the wisdom text from Qumran.

Perhaps the most important common element shared by 4QInstruction and the Wisdom of Solomon, however, was the concept of mystery. Both texts share the belief that right action follows from right understanding. This belief was integral to the Hebrew wisdom tradition, just as it was to Greek philosophy. But both these texts also shared the view that right knowledge was not available to everyone. According to the Hebrew text, it was a mystery that was only revealed to the elect, and apparently documented in the Vision of Hagu. The Hellenistic wisdom book does not use the language of revelation, but implies that the mystery is available to those who reason rightly. In both cases, however, right understanding involves a grasp of spiritual truths, of things unseen, and the true destiny of human beings concerns their fate after death, not their prosperity in this world.

Yale Divinity School
409 Prospect St.
New Haven CT 06337
USA

John J. COLLINS

SAGESSE 3,7-9; 5,15-23 ET L'APOCALYPTIQUE

Tous les commentateurs de la Sagesse de Salomon signalent que ce livre de la diaspora juive a des rapports avec l'apocalyptique, mais jusqu'à ce jour, aucune étude développée n'a été consacrée à ce sujet. Durant les premiers mois de cette année, deux biblistes sont encore revenus sur la question, Shannon Burkes[1] et John J. Collins[2], abordant l'un et l'autre les principaux thèmes de Sg qui renvoient à l'apocalyptique.

Dans ces quelques pages, je n'analyserai que deux textes, généralement retenus pour leur saveur apocalyptique; je chercherai à faire percevoir les problèmes qu'ils posent et les solutions qui ont été proposées.

Quel que soit le genre littéraire auquel on rattache les premiers chapitres de Sg, les deux textes auxquels je m'arrête font partie du même ensemble qui ouvre le livre par des perspectives eschatologiques.

SAGESSE 3,7-9

Après avoir donné la parole aux impies partisans d'un matérialisme jouisseur et agressif à l'encontre du juste (2,1-20), l'auteur a posé clairement sa thèse que ces impies se sont trompés: ils ont méconnu les secrets de Dieu et l'espérance d'une récompense pour la sainteté leur a manqué; en réalité, Dieu a créé l'homme incorruptible et l'auteur conclut par ces mots: ceux qui prennent le parti du diable font l'expérience de la mort (2,24b).

Vient alors le premier passage (3,1-9) dont la finale (3,7-9) nous intéresse. Il y est question du sort final des justes, mais le texte est difficile et son interprétation controversée. Pour tenter d'y voir plus clair, essayons de suivre la séquence des faits tels que l'auteur les présente par son emploi des temps verbaux, présent, passé ou futur, par rapport au moment où il écrit.

Δικαίων δὲ ψυχαὶ ἐν χειρὶ θεοῦ,
καὶ οὐ μὴ ἅψηται αὐτῶν βάσανος (3,1).

Aux impies persécuteurs l'auteur oppose «les âmes des justes». Cette expression doit signifier que ces justes sont décédés. En effet les autres

1. *Wisdom and Apocalypticism in the Wisdom of Solomon*, in *HThR* 95 (2002) 21-44.
2. *The Reinterpretation of Apocalyptic Traditions in the Wisdom of Solomon*, conférence donnée à Palerme le 23 mars 2002 au colloque sur *Il Libro della Sapienza* et en cours de publication.

emplois de ψυχή en 2,2c; 3,13; 4,11.14 viennent dans des contextes qui supposent un au-delà de la mort physique et c'est le sujet personnel qui survit. Dans ces quatre passages, il est question de personnes que l'on peut appeler justes. De plus, 3,1b: «aucun tourment ne les atteindra plus», confirme qu'il s'agit de trépassés; pour eux, les épreuves ne sont plus que du passé, sans avenir à redouter. D'autre part, pour notre auteur, l'âme est, de l'être humain, ce qui assure vie et personnalité (cf. 8,19-20); l'auteur peut donc parler aussi de la ψυχή des impies ici-bas (1,4.11d). Même s'il parle des âmes des justes, il s'agit, pour l'auteur, des justes eux-mêmes: le οἱ δέ, «mais eux», de 3,3b le prouve.

En raison du contraste que l'auteur établit entre ces derniers (3,1a) et les impies qui les persécutent (2,10-20.24), il me semble qu'il s'agit de justes souffrants, victimes d'avanies de la part des impies. Le «tourment» auquel ces impies voulaient les soumettre (2,19a: le «juste» est là une figure emblématique extrême) ne pourra plus les atteindre par delà la mort. Plus loin, en 3,5a.6, les termes employés supposent de fait que la vie terrestre de ces justes a connu de grandes souffrances. C'est pourquoi, malgré la Vulgate, dont le texte est ici peu sûr, il est vrai, le «tourment» n'est pas celui de la mort elle-même; ce n'est pas davantage l'ensemble des épreuves que comporte toute existence humaine sur terre et dont le décès délivrerait. Il s'agit plutôt, à mon sens, de ces justes qui ont souffert en raison de leur foi, comme celui auquel s'en prennent les impies dans leur discours programme de 2,12-20.

Ces justes sont à présent «dans la main de Dieu» (3,1b). Ce n'est pas qu'ils soient seulement soumis à son pouvoir (ainsi Jb 12,10; Qo 9,1; Si 10,4-5; Sg 7,16), mais plutôt, en raison du stique suivant affirmant que «nul tourment ne les atteindra plus», qu'ils sont désormais sous la protection de Dieu (cf. 5,16; 19,8).

Avec ces affirmations de 3,1, l'auteur est allé à l'essentiel. Les justes dans leur principe vital qu'est l'âme survivent à la mort physique et sont désormais protégés par Dieu lui-même de toute forme d'avanie et de persécution. Ce que l'auteur ne dit pas et même ne dira pas, c'est le lieu où se trouvent ces âmes des justes. Un tel silence peut étonner, mais il doit être respecté: l'auteur ne s'intéresse pas à ce lieu, mais à la relation des justes avec Dieu.

> ἔδοξαν ἐν ὀφθαλμοῖς ἀφρόνων τεθνάναι,
> καὶ ἐλογίσθη κάκωσις ἡ ἔξοδος αὐτῶν
> καὶ ἡ ἀφ' ἡμῶν πορεία σύντριμμα,
> οἱ δέ εἰσιν ἐν εἰρήνῃ (3,2-3).

Ces versets établissent un contraste entre les apparences et la réalité. Les apparences, c'est ce à quoi s'en tiennent les gens qui n'ont pas l'intelligence des «secrets de Dieu» (2,22a), ce sont des insensés. Qui sont-ils? Certainement des gens qui ne veulent s'appuyer que sur le témoignage de leurs sens, en particulier celui de la vue, sur laquelle l'auteur insiste en 3,2a.4a, et qui en tirent une conclusion trop rapide et par suite, dans le cas en question, erronée[3]. Une telle faiblesse intellectuelle est le fait des impies persécuteurs qui ne raisonnent pas correctement (2,1a.21a), mais aussi des impies en général (1,3b), voire, puisque notre auteur en 3,4a parle des humains, de ces foules sans intelligence devant le destin du juste (cf. 4,14c.17a [futur gnomique[4]]). Ce sont tous ceux qui ignorent les «secrets de Dieu» (2,22a).

Pour eux, ces justes décédés sont bien morts, en ce sens (infinitif parfait) que leur mort est définitive et surtout totale. Telle est leur opinion sur un fait qui, selon eux, réalise leurs idées sur la fin de la vie humaine (2,1b-5). C'est une κάκωσις, un σύντριμμα (3,2b.3a). Le premier mot peut avoir le sens actif de «sévices» ou le sens passif de «corruption», ou de «malheur», de «mauvaise fortune». Ces justes ont terminé leur existence terrestre dans le désastre. Le second mot signifie fondamentalement la mise en pièces irréparable, comme celle d'un vase. Les justes en mourant sont volés en éclats, sans aucune possibilité d'être recomposés. Mais, pour notre auteur, la mort physique des justes ne fut qu'une «sortie» de ce monde, une «migration», ils sont partis de chez nous, thème connu aussi bien de Platon[5] que de Cicéron[6].

A l'opinion des insensés, l'auteur oppose explicitement l'affirmation qu'en fait ces justes «sont en paix» (3,3b) ou peut-être mieux «demeurent en paix», car εἰσιν peut prendre le sens fort. Leur paix est une autre façon de dire leur survie sous la protection divine et sans plus aucun tourment. Leur sort n'est pas celui des trépassés dont les corps reposent en paix dans leur tombe (cf. Jb 3,13; Is 57,1-2). Eux sont sains et saufs, bien vivants, mais ailleurs.

> καὶ γὰρ ἐν ὄψει ἀνθρώπων ἐὰν κολασθῶσιν,
> ἡ ἐλπὶς αὐτῶν ἀθανασίας πλήρης·
> καὶ ὀλίγα παιδευθέντες μεγάλα εὐεργετηθήσονται (3,4-5a).

L'auteur explique 3,3b en 3,4-5a: «Car, même si, à vue humaine, ils étaient châtiés, leur espérance était pleine d'immortalité et, pour une légère correction reçue, ils seront grandement gratifiés».

3. La même erreur est signalée en Sg 13,1b.7b.

4. Ainsi C. LARCHER, *Le Livre de la Sagesse ou la Sagesse de Salomon*, II (ÉB NS, 3), Paris, 1984, p. 342.

5. *Phédon*, 107D.

6. *Tusculanes*, I, XII, 27.

Ce que le texte disait jusqu'en 3,3b, c'était que les justes, partis de ce monde, existaient sereinement. Non pas un lieu, mais simplement un état, une situation. En 3,4, l'auteur revient au passé terrestre des justes: si les gens ont considéré que les justes étaient châtiés, en fait l'espérance de ces derniers en l'immortalité était totale. Pour ceux qui s'en tiennent aux apparences, la mort dans la souffrance suffisait pour affirmer la culpabilité de ceux qui la subissaient. Mais les justes, en supportant la souffrance mortelle, étaient animés d'une espérance sans faille en l'immortalité: ils survivraient à cette mort physique tragique.

Pour notre auteur, la vérité ne s'arrête pas là. Ce que les justes avaient subi n'était pas un châtiment (3,4a), mais une correction bénigne que le Seigneur leur infligeait comme un père (cf. Pr 3,12, cité en Hb 12,6) pour les rendre meilleurs encore. En échange de quoi ces justes plus justes que jamais recevront de grands bienfaits. Le futur me paraît ici important: il annonce ceux de 3,7-9. Mais avant d'énumérer ces bienfaits, ainsi que le pense Pierre Grelot[7], l'auteur explicite le motif pour lequel ces justes en seront gratifiés par Dieu (3,5b-6).

ὅτι ὁ θεὸς ἐπείρασεν αὐτοὺς
καὶ εὗρεν αὐτοὺς ἀξίους ἑαυτοῦ·
ὡς χρυσὸν ἐν χωνευτηρίῳ ἐδοκίμασεν αὐτοὺς
καὶ ὡς ὁλοκάρπωμα θυσίας προσεδέξατο αὐτούς (3,5b-6).

L'auteur exprime sa pensée en trois étapes. La première: «Dieu en effet les a mis à l'épreuve et les a trouvés dignes de lui» (3,5bc). Les tourments que les justes ont subis n'étaient pas un châtiment (3,4a) comme le pensaient les gens à courte vue; c'étaient de légères corrections (3,5a), dont l'auteur précise maintenant qu'elles étaient en fait une mise à l'épreuve (3,5b) dont le résultat fut tout à fait probant: Dieu qui les testait les a trouvés dignes de lui (3,5c), c'est-à-dire, me semble-t-il, dignes de lui être associés, le détail n'étant pas donné ici mais en 3,7-9.

Puis viennent deux comparaisons selon le même schème: «comme l'or au creuset, il les a épurés; comme oblation consumée, il les a agréés» (3,6). L'épreuve par laquelle les justes sont passés est ici comparée au feu d'où sort de l'or estimé très pur ou au feu cultuel qui consume totalement l'offrande. Tels sont alors les justes aux yeux de Dieu: il les estime très précieux et il les agrée comme il agrée l'holocauste que les justes font de leur propre personne.

Ces versets 3,5b-6 montrent qu'en réalité, dans l'épreuve terrestre des justes, c'était Dieu qui était à l'œuvre, mais aussi les justes eux-mêmes.

7. *L'eschatologie de la Sagesse et les apocalypses juives*, in Id., *De la mort à la vie éternelle. Études de théologie biblique* (LeDiv, 67), Paris, 1971, p. 191.

Dieu les purifiait et eux faisaient le don total de leur personne; ils sont sortis de l'épreuve vraiment dignes de celui qui les y a fait passer. Cette explication de 3,5b-6 donne le sens profond des épreuves des justes du point de vue de Dieu qui y était l'acteur premier. Les justes se sont laissé purifier et consumer, animés qu'ils étaient de l'espérance en l'immortalité (3,4b).

Une telle attitude des justes recevra sa récompense (2,22c), c'est-à-dire des faveurs insignes sans commune mesure avec l'épreuve subie (cf. 3,5a; Rm 8,18; 2 Co 4,17). C'est en 3,7-9 que ces faveurs divines sont énumérées et le temps où elles leur seront octroyées est enfin indiqué: «au moment de la visite que leur rendra le Seigneur» (3,7a). L'auteur «envisage une nouvelle phase dans la condition des justes», note Chrysostome Larcher, qui ajoute: «les vbs sont maintenant au futur alors que les précédents revenaient (à l'aor.) sur la condition terrestre des justes ou sur leur mort même, ou bien évoquaient (au prés.) la condition qui suit la mort. Après une sorte de passivité ou de quiétude heureuse sous la protection divine, les justes entrent maintenant dans une phase glorieuse, active, triomphante, à la suite d'une intervention divine qu'évoque sans la préciser, le mot *episkopè*»[8].

καὶ ἐν καιρῷ ἐπισκοπῆς αὐτῶν ἀναλάμψουσιν
καὶ ὡς σπινθῆρες ἐν καλάμῃ διαδραμοῦνται·
κρινοῦσιν ἔθνη καὶ κρατήσουσιν λαῶν,
καὶ βασιλεύσει αὐτῶν κύριος εἰς τοὺς αἰῶνας.
οἱ πεποιθότες ἐπ' αὐτῷ συνήσουσιν ἀλήθειαν,
καὶ οἱ πιστοὶ ἐν ἀγάπῃ προσμενοῦσιν αὐτῷ (3,7-9b)

Comme dans les textes bibliques antérieurs, la «visite» est celle de Dieu qui apporte soit le salut aux justes (3,13; 4,15) soit le châtiment des impies (19,15) et de leurs œuvres (14,11). Mais à l'inverse de la plupart de ces textes antérieurs, elle a lieu, selon Sg comme en Is 24,22, au plan eschatologique et apocalyptique, non plus uniquement terrestre. Sur ce point, les commentateurs récents sont aujourd'hui unanimes. En 3,7a, cette visite, annoncée comme normalement pour le futur, se fera en faveur des justes dont les versets précédents ont parlé des épreuves passées et de la survie sereine à présent (3,3b). Il s'agit donc bien d'une nouvelle phase dont ils seront les bénéficiaires (cf. 3,5a) et qui a comme toujours une portée collective.

«Ils resplendiront»: les justes connaîtront une transformation qui les rendra étincelants comme les astres. Avec raison on renvoie le plus souvent à Dn 12,3 et à 1 Hénoch 104,2; 108,13, textes apocalyptiques, mais

8. *Le Livre de la Sagesse* (n. 4), p. 284.

notre auteur n'explicite pas davantage en quoi consistera cette transformation des justes. Dn 12,3 parle de résurrection et l'on sait la discrétion de notre auteur à ce sujet (ce qui ne veut pas dire qu'il n'y incline pas!). Cependant il ajoute (3,7b) que ces justes resplendissants «s'encourront comme étincelles dans le chaume». L'image, d'origine agricole, sert à décrire la destruction des impies chez Jl 2,5; Ab 18; Za 12,6; Ml 3,19 (4,1). Notre auteur, s'inspirant de ces textes, doit entendre, me semble-t-il, que les justes, désormais glorieux, détruiront les impies. Il y a d'ailleurs une certaine continuité entre le resplendissement des justes et le feu dévastateur qu'ils propagent.

Le problème est que cette action punitive est ici postérieure à la visite divine et à la glorification des justes qui l'accomplissent. Le combat eschatologique contre l'impiété aura-t-il lieu vraiment après l'une et l'autre? Le texte m'incite à le penser. Et où aura lieu ce combat? Sur terre où séviraient encore les impies? Je ne sais comment répondre à cette question qui agite bien des commentateurs. Il est vrai pourtant que 3,7-8 invitent à donner une réponse affirmative à la question.

Selon 3,8 cet incendie destructeur est en réalité un jugement apocalyptique des nations qui culmine dans la domination des peuples, comme déjà en Dn 7,26-27, mais le règne appartiendra à Dieu pour toujours et les sujets en seront précisément les justes: «le Seigneur sera leur roi pour l'éternité». On comprend alors que les justes participeront d'une certaine façon, par leur resplendissement (3,7a), à la gloire du Seigneur, sans qu'il faille voir en 3,8 autre chose que le succès du combat destructeur des justes de 3,7b.

Le verset suivant, 3,9ab donne une dernière dimension du triomphe des justes: eux qui ont mis leur confiance dans le Seigneur comprendront la vérité et demeureront auprès de lui. On a beaucoup discuté sur le sens de l'expression «ils comprendront la vérité». A mon sens, les justes, parce que, dans l'épreuve, ils ont témoigné de leur foi totale, découvriront qu'ils étaient dans le vrai. Dn 12,10 et 1 Hénoch 100,6 peuvent avoir préparé pareille affirmation. Celle-ci du reste confirme les dires du juste souffrant que les impies précisément lui reprochaient dans leur discours de 2,12-20.

ὅτι χάρις καὶ ἔλεος ἐν τοῖς ὁσίοις αὐτοῦ
καὶ ἐπισκοπὴ ἐν τοῖς ἐκλεκτοῖς αὐτοῦ (3,9cd)

On sait le problème textuel posé par ces deux stiques qui reparaissent presque identiques en 4,15. Ou bien on ne garde que le premier, 3,9c, avec le ms. Vaticanus et la Vieille latine-Vulgate: ainsi A. Rahlfs, *TOB*,

C. Larcher[9], A. Schmitt[10], G. Scarpat[11]; ou bien on conserve les deux stiques avec le Sinaiticus et l'Alexandrinus: ainsi J. Ziegler, D. Winston[12], J. Vílchez Líndez[13], H. Hübner[14].

De toute évidence, l'auteur conclut la péricope par une explication générale. Celle-ci ne porte pas seulement sur 3,9ab, me semble-t-il, mais sur l'ensemble de la péricope. Dans cette perspective, 3,9c: «grâce et miséricorde pour ses saints» ou «faveur et bonté fidèle pour ceux qui ont vécus saintement pour lui», vaut pour tout ce qui a été dit de ces derniers depuis 3,1; et 3,9d: «visite pour ses élus» ne se réfère qu'à l'exaltation des justes évoquée en 3,7a et à ce qui a suivi, 3,7b-9b.

Concluons. Quelles que soient les difficultés du texte ou ses silences, il faut le prendre tel qu'il est. Hormis M.-É. Boismard[15], je ne vois aucun commentateur récent refuser l'authenticité de ce texte dans son entièreté, le problème de 3,9d mis à part.

Sagesse 5,15-23

Le second texte auquel je m'arrête, 5,15-23, s'inscrit au terme d'une série d'affirmations de l'auteur sur le sort des impies.

Déjà en 3,10, en contraste avec le sort des justes, il écrit: «Les impies, par contre, recevront un châtiment conforme à leurs théories, eux qui ont négligé le juste (ou: ce qui est juste) et se sont éloignés du Seigneur». Plus avant, après avoir décrit l'enlèvement du juste avant son heure, l'auteur se fait plus précis. De ceux qui n'auront que mépris pour la mort prématurée du juste qui est aussi un sage, le Seigneur se rira (4,17-18) au terme de leur longue vie sur terre: «après quoi (cf. 2,2b), ils deviendront un cadavre qui ne mérite aucun honneur, un objet d'opprobre parmi les morts à jamais, car (le Seigneur) les abattra sans voix, tête en avant, il les arrachera de leurs fondements et ils seront définitivement stériles; ils seront en peine et leur souvenir périra» (4,19). Ces expressions très fortes décrivent la mort des impies: c'est le Seigneur qui les déracine et les jette au shéol, lieu de désolation et d'oubli. Telle est la situation des impies à leur mort.

9. *Le Livre de la Sagesse*, (n. 4), pp. 292-293.
10. *Das Buch der Weisheit. Ein Kommentar*, Würzburg, 1986, pp. 54-55.
11. *Libro della Sapienza*, I (Biblica, 1), Brescia, 1989, p. 239.
12. *The Wisdom of Solomon* (AncB, 43), Garden City, NY, 1979, p. 124.
13. *Sabiduría* (Nueva Biblia Española Sapienciales, 5), Estella, 1990, pp. 176 et 184.
14. *Die Weisheit Salomons. Liber Sapientiae Salomonis* (ATD Apokryphen, 4), Göttingen, 1999, p. 49.
15. *Faut-il encore parler de «résurrection»? Les données scripturaires* (Théologies), Paris, 1995, p. 100.

Pourtant l'auteur envisage une étape suivante qu'il décrit de 4,20 à 5,13. Quant ils auront à rendre compte de leurs péchés, ces impies viendront apeurés et leurs fautes les accuseront directement (4,20). Ils seront alors confrontés au juste qu'ils avaient méprisé et tourmenté. Mais ce juste, plein d'assurance, ne leur adressera plus la parole comme jadis (2,12); ils le verront, mais seront stupéfaits, car ils ne s'attendront pas à le voir sauvé (5,1-2). Ce salut dont bénéficiera alors ce juste est, par don de Dieu, la victoire de la vie sur la mort, l'immortalité au lieu de l'anéantissement dans la mort physique, comme le prévoyaient les impies.

De fait, le discours (5,4-13) qu'ils se diront à eux-mêmes, plein de remords et de gémissements (5,3), reprendra en ordre inverse celui qu'ils tenaient au temps de leur jactance sur terre (2,1-20), mais ce sera pour confesser l'effrayante réalité de leur sort qui correspondra dans l'au-delà à leurs théories sur la vie et la mort: leur vie impie n'aura eu aucune consistance et leur mort les aura réduits à néant. Cependant un tel aveu comportera aussi la reconnaissance explicite que le juste qu'ils bafouaient était dans le vrai: «Comment se fait-il qu'il ait été compté au nombre des fils de Dieu (cf. 2,18) et qu'il partage à présent le sort des saints?» se diront-ils (5,5). Qu'est-ce à dire?

Lors de leur reddition des comptes, les impies décédés auparavant reconnaîtront le juste qu'ils avaient persécuté sur terre et, plus encore, ils seront stupéfaits de le voir dans la situation qu'il prétendait être déjà la sienne sur terre (2,18). Autrement dit, lorsque les impies rendront compte de leurs péchés, le juste se trouvera déjà en compagnie des anges. C'est en effet dans ce sens qu'il convient de comprendre 5,5 et l'on peut renvoyer au Ps 88 LXX,6-8 et à de nombreux textes apocalyptiques bibliques, apocryphes et qumrâniens[16]. S'il en est ainsi, c'est que le juste aura déjà reçu la visite du Seigneur (cf. 2,20b; 3,7a) et que celle-ci aura eu pour effet son intégration à la cour céleste. L'exaltation céleste des justes précédera donc l'aveu des impies, ce que d'ailleurs l'aoriste de κατελογίσθη (5,5a) laisse entendre.

Il reste que le sort des impies, de leur propre aveu, semblera réglé. En reprenant la parole en 5,14, l'auteur le confirme: l'impie aura perdu tout espoir; sur terre son espérance était sans contenu (3,11b) et, lors des comptes, elle continuera d'être comme bale chassée par le vent, givre (ou écume?) et fumée qu'emporte la tempête; sans plus de consistance que le souvenir trop vague qu'on garderait d'un hôte qui n'a passé qu'un jour. Tel est bien le néant des impies par delà leur mort et même leur

16. Cf. LARCHER, *Le Livre de la Sagesse*, II (n. 4), p. 364.

reddition des comptes. Ils auront la monnaie de leur pièce. Il y a de la sorte une continuité entre les théories que les impies tenaient sur terre et la réalité qu'ils découvriront lors de leur reddition des comptes. Mais le jugement divin s'arrêtera-t-il là?

«Par contre, les justes vivent pour l'éternité et c'est dans le Seigneur que se trouve leur récompense, de même que le souci qu'on prend d'eux est le fait du Très-Haut» (5,15). En parlant ainsi, à quelle situation des justes l'auteur se réfère-t-il? Les avis sont partagés à ce propos. Pour les uns, l'auteur pense à la vie terrestre des justes (ainsi, parmi les commentateurs récents, C. Larcher[17], A. Sisti[18] et G. Scarpat[19]); d'autres considèrent qu'il est ici question du juste par delà la mort physique qu'il a subie (ainsi, implicitement, D. Winston[20] et A. Schmitt[21]; explicitement, J. Vílchez Líndez[22]); cependant que M. Kolarcik[23], H. Hübner[24] et M. McGlynn[25] ne se préoccupent pas du problème, Larcher[26] pensait en 1969 que «l'auteur semble avoir voulu, au v. 15, associer aux justes qui vivront encore sur terre, lors de l'exécution du grand jugement contre les impies, les justes déjà morts»; ou encore que «les justes vivent ici-bas dans l'espérance d'une vie immortelle, méritée par leur justice, et ils continuent de vivre, après leur mort, d'une vie qui doit être éternelle».

Je ferai ici deux remarques. La première est qu'il me semble y avoir une symétrie entre la façon de décrire l'impie en 5,14 et celle qui concerne les justes en 5,15. Selon 5,14, l'espoir de l'impie est balayé, pourrait-on dire, et il n'en reste rien: quand il était sur terre, cet espoir était vide et après la mort il s'évanouit définitivement. De même, en 5,15, l'auteur me paraît viser les justes à la fois durant leur existence terrestre et durant la tranquillité qu'ils connaissent dès après leur décès. Durant leur existence terrestre, ils proclamaient heureux le sort final des justes (2,16c), ils attendaient la visite du Seigneur en leur faveur (2,20b) et l'immortalité était l'objet sans faille de leur espérance (3,4b); immédia-

17. *Ibid.*, p. 381.

18. *Il Libro della Sapienza. Introduzione – Versione – Commento*, Assisi, 1992, p. 179.

19. *Libro della Sapienza* (n. 11), p. 307.

20. *The Wisdom of Solomon* (n. 12), p. 148, avec renvoi à PHILON, *Jos.*, 264.

21. *Das Buch der Weisheit* (n. 10), p. 73, avec renvoi à 2 M 7,9 et PHILON, *Jos.*, 264.

22. *Sabiduría* (n. 13), p. 218, n. 30.

23. *The Ambiguity of Death in the Book of Wisdom 1–6. A Study of Literary Structure and Interpretation* (AnBib, 127), Roma, 1991, p. 106.

24. *Die Weisheit Salomons* (n. 14), p. 77.

25. *Divine Judgement and Divine Benevolence in the Book of Wisdom* (WUNT, 2, 139), Tübingen, 2001, p. 86.

26. *Études sur le Livre de la Sagesse* (ÉB), Paris, 1969, p. 294.

tement après leur mort, ils survivent dans la paix sous la protection divine (3,1-3). Ceci revient à dire qu'en 5,15, l'auteur pourrait penser aussi bien aux justes sur terre qu'aux justes à peine décédés.

La seconde remarque concerne le rapport entre 5,15 et 5,16. Pour la clarté, voici le texte grec de 5,16:

> διὰ τοῦτο λήμψονται τὸ βασίλειον τῆς εὐπρεπείας
> καὶ τὸ διάδημα τοῦ κάλλους ἐκ χειρὸς κυρίου,
> ὅτι τῇ δεξιᾷ σκεπάσει αὐτοὺς
> καὶ τῷ βραχίονι ὑπερασπιεῖ αὐτῶν.

Ce que j'observe, c'est ceci. D'une part, selon 5,15b, «leur récompense est dans le Seigneur», tandis que l'accomplissement futur est indiqué en 5,16ab: «Ils recevront une couronne magnifique et un diadème de beauté». D'autre part, selon 5,15c, «le Seigneur se soucie d'eux», et cela se concrétisera également dans le futur: «ils les abritera de sa droite et les couvrira de son bras», comme le dit 5,16cd.

Toutefois reste le problème posé par διὰ τοῦτο... ὅτι...: quel rapport faut-il voir entre 5,16ab et 5,16cd? Les avis sont de nouveau partagés. Ou bien on n'en tient pas compte et on ne traduit pas ces mots; ainsi L. Alonso Schökel[27]. Ou bien on les traduit comme dans la Vulgate: «C'est pourquoi» il y aura couronnement, «parce que» il y aura protection; ainsi font la majorité des commentateurs, mais la cohérence est difficilement explicable, à moins de voir en 5,16cd un futur antérieur à celui de 5,16ab, comme le propose C. Larcher[28]: «le Seigneur les couronnera, car auparavant il les aura protégés». Ou bien encore on voit en διὰ τοῦτο une expression proleptique de ὅτι: «Voici pourquoi ils recevront la couronne: parce que le Seigneur les protégera»; ainsi font G. Scarpat[29] et A. Sisti[30], mais la logique ne me paraît pas plus claire.

Une chose est sûre, c'est que 5,16 envisage l'avenir eschatologique. Or, en 3,1, l'auteur disait que par delà la mort, les justes sont dans la main de Dieu, et 5,16cd pourrait se référer à cette première phase que vivront les justes après leur décès. Par conséquent, ou bien les futurs de 5,16cd sont de simples futurs et alors ils obligent de considérer les justes de 5,15 comme encore vivants en ce monde, ou bien, comme le propose C. Larcher, ce sont des futurs antérieurs et, dans ce cas, les justes de 5,15 sont ceux dont parle déjà 3,1, décédés et protégés, mais non encore glorifiés, c'est-à-dire avant la visite divine. Quant à leur couronnement

27. *Eclesiastes y Sabiduría* (Los Libros Sagrados, 17), Madrid, 1974, p. 109.
28. *Le Livre de la Sagesse*, II (n. 4), pp. 381 et 385.
29. *Libro della Sapienza*, I (n. 11), p. 337.
30. *Il Libro della Sapienza* (n. 18), p. 180.

(5,16ab), l'auteur y a déjà fait allusion en 3,8 et c'est la récompense que les justes recevront au temps de la visite. Compris de la sorte, 5,16 redit avec d'autres mots les deux étapes de 3,1-3 (dès après son décès, le juste est ou sera protégé par Dieu) et 3,7-9 (il aura sa récompense lors d'une étape ultérieure, celle de la visite divine). Je suis donc, pour 5,16, l'interprétation de C. Larcher.

Mais si l'on accepte cette opinion, il faut en déduire qu'en 5,14-16, l'auteur entend uniquement souligner une opposition très nette entre le sort eschatologique des deux catégories d'humains actuellement existants ou décédés, les impies et les justes. En outre, l'asyndète du verset suivant, 5,17, indique l'ouverture d'une nouvelle péricope qui aura sa propre logique: on assiste alors à la préparation et aux différentes phases du combat apocalyptique final au cours duquel le Très-Haut détruira les insensés.

Voyons donc comment s'organise le texte de 5,17-23.

Tous les verbes sont au futur. L'auteur postule donc une perspective d'avenir. Par ailleurs, jusqu'en 5,23a, les distiques et le tristique commencent en asyndète: 5,17a.18a.19.21a.22b.23a, 5,20b étant un monostique comme je le dirai. C'est là un procédé que l'auteur utilisera encore en 11,1-4 pour introduire son évocation de l'exode et en 19,19-21, hormis le γάρ initial, pour en rappeler les principaux épisodes.

λήμψεται πανοπλίαν τὸν ζῆλον αὐτοῦ
καὶ ὁπλοποιήσει τὴν κτίσιν εἰς ἄμυναν ἐχθρῶν (5,17).

Notre texte débute en 5,17 par une annonce de thème: d'une part, le Seigneur «saisira sa jalousie comme armement complet» et cet armement sera détaillé en 5,18-20a, tandis que, d'autre part, «il armera la création pour châtier (ou repousser) les ennemis», ce qui aura son effet en 5,20b-23b. Il va donc être question de préparatifs en vue d'un combat contre des ennemis qui seront qualifiés en 5,20b de «déraisonnables» et ce terme vise les impies.

ἐνδύσεται θώρακα δικαιοσύνην
καὶ περιθήσεται κόρυθα κρίσιν ἀνυπόκριτον·
λήμψεται ἀσπίδα ἀκαταμάχητον ὁσιότητα,
ὀξυνεῖ δὲ ἀπότομον ὀργὴν εἰς ῥομφαίαν (5,18-20a).

Ces deux distiques procèdent logiquement: tout d'abord l'armement qui couvre le corps du soldat – c'est la cuirasse – et la tête – voilà le casque –, ensuite l'armement que le soldat prend en mains soit pour se défendre – le bouclier – soit pour attaquer – l'épée. Mais chaque élément de cette «panoplie» n'est qu'une comparaison que l'auteur emprunte surtout à Is 59,17, texte à saveur apocalyptique, dont il suit de près le premier distique. Ce dont le Seigneur s'arme, c'est de justice, de jugement sans appel, de sainteté invincible et de colère implacable, cette dernière étant agressive comme une épée. Bref le Seigneur est prêt pour le combat.

συνεκπολεμήσει δὲ αὐτῷ ὁ κόσμος ἐπὶ τοὺς παράφρονας (5,20b).

Comme 5,17b l'annonçait, le Seigneur se donne le cosmos comme allié pour combattre contre des gens déraisonnables. En raison de son caractère général, le monostique 5,20b est une annonce de thème renouvelant celle de 5,17b et recevant son développement en 5,21a-23b:

πορεύσονται εὔστοχοι βολίδες ἀστραπῶν
καὶ ὡς ἀπὸ εὐκύκλου τόξου τῶν νεφῶν ἐπὶ σκοπὸν ἁλοῦνται,
καὶ ἐκ πετροβόλου θυμοῦ πλήρεις ῥιφήσονται χάλαζαι·
ἀγανακτήσει κατ' αὐτῶν ὕδωρ θαλάσσης,
ποταμοὶ δὲ συγκλύσουσιν ἀποτόμως·
ἀντιστήσεται αὐτοῖς πνεῦμα δυνάμεως
καὶ ὡς λαῖλαψ ἐκλικμήσει αὐτούς (5,21-23b)

L'auteur énumère trois types d'attaques, chacun d'eux commençant par une phrase en asyndète. Tout d'abord l'orage avec éclairs et grelons, puis le déchaînement des eaux de la mer et des fleuves, enfin le vent violent de l'ouragan. De la sorte, le feu, l'eau et l'air passent à l'attaque, sous l'impulsion du Seigneur.

καὶ ἐρημώσει πᾶσαν τὴν γῆν ἀνομία,
καὶ ἡ κακοπραγία περιτρέψει θρόνους δυναστῶν (5,23cd)

Le résultat est que la terre, le quatrième des éléments classiques, cette terre dont les impies entendaient profiter sans retenue (2,6-9), sera dévastée et les puissants qui pratiquaient l'iniquité seront détrônés. Tel est le châtiment des impies que le Dieu juste et justicier leur infligera en recourant aux forces cosmiques.

Ce tableau du combat apocalyptique demande quelques commentaires.

1. Les justes n'y participent pas. On ne peut trouver en 5,17-23 aucune trace de ce qu'on pense pouvoir lire en 3,7 sur la participation des justes à ce combat.

2. C'est la terre qui fait les frais de ce combat destructeur. Les attaquants sont le Seigneur qui se sert de certaines forces cosmiques – le feu, l'eau et l'air – rendues agressives et sans merci contre des gens déraisonnables, puissants iniques qui dominent la terre, et celle-ci sera réduite à un désert.

Pour notre auteur, ce combat est chose sûre et il le montrera lorsque dans la seconde moitié de son livre, dont on ne peut plus nier l'unité, il méditera sur l'exode et les événements cosmiques qui s'y sont produits pour châtier les gens du Pharaon et sauver les Hébreux: ces événements sont en effet pour notre auteur annonciateurs eschatologiques.

Il en résulte qu'il n'y a, de ce point de vue, aucune raison de considérer 5,17-23 comme un ajout intempestif, ainsi que le voudrait M.-É. Boismard[31].

3. Cependant comment faut-il situer ce combat apocalyptique? L'autonomie textuelle de 5,17-23, par rapport aux versets précédents, 5,14-16, qui opposent le sort des impies à celui des justes, me paraît importante. Si cela est vrai, C. Larcher[32] a raison d'écrire que «ce tableau [de 5,17-23] nous semble provenir d'une inspiration différente», car «il concerne plus immédiatement ceux qui vivent sur terre lors de la lutte suprême...». Dans son commentaire[33], C. Larcher a bien relevé que «l'auteur reprend successivement ou alternativement des motifs bibliques distincts qu'il plie à son propre dessein. (...) À ce titre aussi, le lien avec ce qui précède [c'est-à-dire avec la reddition des comptes des impies et leur confrontation avec le juste glorifié, en 4,20–5,13] n'est pas nécessairement aussi étroit qu'on le prétend».

En 5,17-23, les motifs bibliques auxquels Larcher[34] comme d'autres fait allusion sont bien connus. On les trouve en Is 13,5.9.11 (sur le châtiment de Babylone); 24,1.3.5.20-22 (sur l'intervention apocalyptique collective du Seigneur contre les impies); 59,17, mais aussi en Dn, où la destruction des empires terrestres précède la royauté des saints, ou encore en Ag 2,21-22, annonçant le renversement des trônes lors de l'ébranlement du ciel et de la terre.

4. Mais pour quelle raison notre auteur a-t-il placé ici ce combat apocalyptique final? Je crois que l'analyse de la structure littéraire de Sg 1–6, aujourd'hui très largement reconnue, peut éclairer notre question. Dans ces chapitres, l'auteur ne procède pas selon un ordre chronologique des événements eschatologiques. Son but est essentiellement de convaincre les princes de l'importance d'un gouvernement juste. Si les princes n'ont pas ce souci, ils risquent un châtiment (1,9c) qui sera implacable (6,3-8). L'auteur avait tout intérêt à décrire ce châtiment des princes

31. *Faut-il encore parler de «résurrection»?* (n. 15), pp. 98-100. Sh. BURKES, *Wisdom and Apocalypticism* (n. 1), p. 29, n. 32, laisse penser que J.J. COLLINS, *Jewish Wisdom in the Hellenistic Age* (OTL), Louisville, KY, 1997, p. 184, serait de la même opinion; en réalité Collins ne parle pas de Sg 5,17-23, mais de Sg 2,12-20; 5,1-7, selon la thèse de L. Ruppert.

32. *Études* (n. 26), p. 325.

33. *Le Livre de la Sagesse*, II (n. 4), pp. 380-381.

34. *Ibid.*, pp. 397-398.

déraisonnables (5,17-23) juste avant d'inviter très explicitement les gouvernants à ne pas le provoquer (6,3-8).

Notre auteur avait encore une autre raison de décrire le cataclysme final. Le discours programme des impies en 2,1-20 reçoit sa vérité eschatologique dans leur second discours que l'auteur imagine lors de leur reddition des comptes (5,4-13). Mais, dans ce second discours, l'auteur montre surtout que le juste persécuté sur terre sera exalté dans l'au-delà et que les impies récolteront ce qu'ils ont semé: à leurs yeux, la vie n'avait pas de sens au delà de la mort et, de fait, ils confesseront que pour eux elle n'en a plus aucun. Pourtant deux éléments de leur programme ne reçoivent aucun écho explicite dans leur second discours: 1. leur agressivité contre le juste n'est pas châtiée comme elle le mériterait; 2. leur méconnaissance de Dieu et leur abus des biens terrestres non plus. Or, c'est précisément ces deux éléments qui sont à la base de 5,17-23: d'agresseurs, ils deviendront agressés; ils voulaient la mort infamante du juste et, en retour, la mort fondra sur eux et détruira leurs œuvres; ils ignoraient Dieu et abusaient de la terre: Dieu le leur fera payer en se servant des forces de ce monde qui dévasteront l'objet de leurs plaisirs abusifs.

En poursuivant cette ligne d'interprétation, on observe que les premiers chapitres de Sg offrent quelques analogies avec les procès devant un tribunal. M. Kolarcik[35] l'a souligné. Il ne suffit pas en effet que le coupable reconnaisse sa faute (4,20–5,13), il faut encore, pour que justice soit rendue, que la sentence soit prononcée et exécutée. Sg 5,17-23 pourrait décrire l'exécution de la sentence, bien que les impies rendront compte de leurs crimes dans l'au-delà, alors que leur châtiment s'accomplira ici-bas.

Enfin, 5,17-23 montre à l'avance comment s'appliqueront aux temps eschatologiques les deux principes qui gouvernent les épisodes de l'exode tels que les comprend notre auteur. D'une part, l'instrument de la faute devient l'instrument du châtiment (11,16): les biens de ce monde ont servi aux impies pour leurs fêtes païennes et ce sont les forces de ce même monde qui les détruiront. D'autre part, ce qui est bienfait pour les uns est châtiment pour les autres (11,5): la mort dans la honte conduira les justes à leur glorification, mais elle anéantira les impies et leurs œuvres.

Ainsi compris, Sg 5,17-23 semble poser moins de problèmes. Après la confession des impies et l'exaltation du juste, rien n'est conclu tant que la défaite totale des impies n'a pas été mise en scène. C'est logique, sans que doive être respecté un ordre chronologique.

35. *The Ambiguity of Death* (n. 23), pp. 106-107.

CEPENDANT DES OBSCURITÉS DEMEURENT

Si l'on cherche à organiser les idées défendues par l'auteur de Sg, force est de constater que des questions demeurent sans réponse.

Tout d'abord au sujet des justes. Si l'interprétation de 3,7 retenue ici avec beaucoup de commentateurs est correcte, ce n'est qu'après leur glorification que les justes combattront les impies encore vivants sur terre. Mais cette lecture pose deux questions:

1. Le combat apocalyptique peut-il être envisagé après la glorification des justes? Émile Puech[36] l'affirme sur la base de 1QH XIV, 32-38 et Pierre Grelot[37] le reconnaît. Par contre, John J. Collins[38] le nie: à son avis, aucun texte apocalyptique ne prévoit de résurrection pour participer à la bataille eschatologique. De toute façon, Sg 3,7 ne parle pas explicitement de résurrection, mais il ne la nie pas, bien au contraire, me semble-t-il.
2. Comment se fait-il alors que 5,17-23 ne fasse pas participer les justes à ce combat apocalyptique? Je n'ai pas de réponse à cette question.

Ensuite au sujet des impies. Malgré les clarifications données ci-dessus à propos de 5,17-23, tout n'est pas clair, loin de là.

Peut-on penser que le combat apocalyptique qui anéantira ces impies sur terre précédera leur reddition des comptes dans l'au-delà (4,20–5,13)? L'ordre du texte va dans le sens inverse et j'ai essayé de dire pourquoi une certaine logique de l'exposé y conduisait l'auteur. Mais qui pose tout de même la question de l'ordre chronologique ne peut recevoir comme réponse que ceci: l'auteur de Sg n'est pas clair à ce propos, ou encore: c'est là une question qu'il ne s'est pas posée!

Concluons. Ces apories montrent que la doctrine eschatologique de l'auteur de Sg n'est pas totalement cohérente. En quelque sorte, il a fait flèche de tout bois, reprenant diverses traditions, utilisant chacune d'elles pour son propos immédiat, mais sans chercher à les harmoniser en une doctrine claire et cohérente. Je crois que la majorité des commentateurs seraient d'accord avec cette conclusion, aussi déroutante qu'elle soit.

Mais il ne s'ensuit pas que notre auteur n'affirme rien de clair sur l'au-delà. Bien au contraire. Pour lui, les justes y connaîtront le bonheur et vivront en communion avec leur Seigneur, tandis que les impies, dont

36. *La croyance des Esséniens en la vie future, II. Les données qumraniennes et classiques* (ÉB NS, 22), Paris, 1993, pp. 354-355.

37. Dans sa recension du livre d'É. PUECH, *La croyance des Esséniens* (n. 36), parue dans *RB* 102 (1995), spécialement p. 116.

38. Dans sa recension du même livre d'É. PUECH, parue dans *DSD* 1 (1994), spéc. p. 250.

le pouvoir sur terre n'est pas indéfini, seront châtiés pour les crimes qu'ils ont commis sur terre et pour lesquels par delà la mort ils se reconnaîtront responsables.

Enfin le clivage s'établit entre justes et impies, non plus, comme dans certains textes bibliques, entre Israël et les nations. C'est la justice qui est immortelle (1,15).

PIB, via della Pilotta, 25 Maurice GILBERT
I-00187 Roma

LAW AND WISDOM IN THE DEAD SEA SCROLLS WITH REFERENCE TO HELLENISTIC JUDAISM

1. Introduction

The role and function of the law of Moses in the inter-testamental/early Judaic period has not been researched exhaustively. This is true of the Septuagint and the Dead Sea Scrolls. Both corpora are nevertheless ready for such analyses. The publication programme of the LXX is expanding and many of the Qumran wisdom texts, that contain reflection on the law, have been published of lately[1].

Wisdom in its various forms during the inter-testamental period has also not been dealt with exhaustively. The most recent impressive analysis is that of Collins[2] who addresses the issues of Hebrew wisdom and wisdom in the Hellenistic diaspora. In the process he analyses Ben Sira, the Dead Sea Scrolls and a number of Hellenistic-Jewish wisdom writings, inter alia, the Wisdom of Solomon. He does, however, not deal with the important Septuagint version of the book of Proverbs. This is to be understood as the Septuagint has until quite recently been underestimated and practically avoided by the broader scholarly community. Fortunately the situation is rapidly changing[3].

There thus seems to me to be a lacuna in our knowledge of the entities of wisdom and law during the period under observance. In this contribution I intend to address these issues. This is but part of a more encompassing endeavour to fill this gap in our knowledge. I am currently en-

* I completed this contribution during the final stage of my stay at the K.U.Leuven as senior fellow. I am grateful to professors Marc Vervenne and Johan Lust who jointly invited me to their institution.

1. Cf. J.J. Collins, *Jewish Wisdom in the Hellenistic Age* (OTLibrary), Louisville, KY, 1997, pp. 112-131.

2. Cf. Collins, *Jewish Wisdom*.

3. The International Organization for Septuagint and Cognate Studies (IOSCS) is involved in major research projects. One is the New English Translation of the Septuagint (NETS) and another, related to this one, is an exegetical commentary on individual books. Cf. A. Pietersma, *A Proposed Commentary on the Septuagint*, in R. Sollamo & S. Sipilä (eds.), *Helsinki Perspectives on the Translation Technique of the Septuagint*, Göttingen, 2001, pp. 167-184 and J. Cook, *Towards a Computerised Exegetical Commentary on the Septuagint Version of Proverbs*, in Id. (ed.), *Bible and Computer – The Stellenbosch AIBI-6 Conference. Proceedings of the Association Internationale Bible et Informatique "From Alpha to Byte" University of Stellenbosch 17-21 July, 2000*, Leiden, 2002, pp. 417-430.

gaged in the writing of a monograph titled: *The torat Moshe as Wall and Well* in which I am addressing these phenomena in a chronological and thematical way. I concentrate on the law of Moses, but as is well-known there is a pertinent relationship between law and wisdom in most of the writings of the period under analysis which means that it will not be possible to focus exclusively on the torat Moshe. I will therefore address some aspects of wisdom during the mentioned period, however, without getting engaged in the role of wisdom in detail. In order to demarcate and restrict this study, therefore when dealing with wisdom I will concentrate on its relation with the law of Moses. I will firstly address the issues of wisdom and torah in specific writings of Hellenistic Judaism and then move on to wisdom and law in the Dead Sea Scrolls.

Since I have discovered significant ancient Jewish exegetical traditions that occur in LXX Proverbs, the Aristeas letter and the Damascus Document I plan to restrict my research to related writings. I will consequently commence with the Wisdom of Ben Sira, then deal with the first Hellenistic-Jewish philosopher, Aristobulus of Alexandria. Thereafter I will undertake further research on the Septuagint and more specifically LXX Proverbs, and, finally, the Letter of Aristeas. In the current contribution I will only deal with a small but representative number of these texts.

2. The Law of Moses During the Hellenistic Period

2.1 The Law of Moses in Ben Sira

As is well-known Ben Sira wrote this collection sometime during the first quarter of the second century BCE, probably before the hellenising attempts of Antiochus Epiphanes (175-164)[4]. This Semitic original was subsequently translated into Greek by his grandson during the last quarter of this century in Alexandria, during the reign of Ptolemy VII Euergetes II, sometime between 132-117 BCE.

A number of problems should naturally be kept in mind when endeavouring to understand this collection. Firstly, the transmission history of Ben Sira is extremely complicated. The Greek version is fully available but the Semitic original is only partly extant. Moreover the various versions (Syriac, Latin, etc.) have their own intricacies and problems[5]. Secondly, the prologue is a later addition by the grandson since it has no

4. P.W. Skehan – A.A. Di Lella (eds.), *The Wisdom of Ben Sira. A Translation with Notes* (AB, 39), New York, 1987, p. 9.

5. Cf. Collins, *Jewish Wisdom* (n. 1), p. 43.

Hebrew parent text. Thirdly, the relationship between the original Semitic and the later Greek remains a problematic one for the researcher. The grandson who translated the work did so in a different cultural context than the one where his grandfather operated. Finally, there seems to be no obvious order of subject matter.

Ben Sira was clearly a Jewish scribe, as can, inter alia, be infered from Chapter 39,1-11. He wrote in an era of fundamental change, however, seemingly before the devastating reforms of the Seleucid, Antiochus Epiphanes. Hence the anxious preoccupation with some cultural issues, significantly the torah, that is evident in later writings is not present in Ben Sira. Even though scholars differ as to the intention and the theme of this book[6], it is clear that the law of Moses was one of the fundamental themes in the mind of Ben Sira.

The noun νόμος occurs more than 30 times in Sirach. By far most of these occurrences can be related to the law of Moses. This is true of 2,16 (are filled with *his law*)[7]; 9,15 (your conversation be about the *Law of the Most High*); 11,15 (GII) (Wisdom and understanding and knowledge *of the Law*); 15,1; 19,17; 19,20; 21,11; 23,23; 24,23; 32,14 &15; 32,24; 33,2 & 3; 34,8; 35,1; 38,34; 39,8; 41,8; 42,2; 44,20; 45,3 & 5; 45,17; 46,14; 49,4.

These examples refer to the law of Moses. In a few instances νόμος does not refer to the law of Moses:

> 17,11 a law (νόμος) pledging life as their inheritance;
> 45,5 the law (νόμος) of life and understanding.

The law of life used in these contexts certainly does not fall outside of the semantic fields of the torat Moshe. However, it has more to do with wisdom and understanding – how to live a wise life. Perhaps one could deem the law of life as an indirect reference to the law of Moses.

There are also other Greek words that refer to the law of Moses. The noun ἐντολή is the most prominent: 1,26; 6,37; 15,15 (you can keep his commandment [ἐντολή]); 19,19; 23,27; 28,6; 29,1; 29,9; 32,23; 35,1; 35,7 (for all you offer is in fulfillment of a precept (ἐντολή)); 37,12; 39,31; 45,5; 45,17.

There can be no doubt that the torat Moshe plays an important role in Ben Sira. However, it is not immediately clear what the law of Moses meant to Ben Sira. For one, Sirach seems relatively uninterested in the legal side of the Torah. In Chapter 15,1 Sirach talks about the practice of the law, however, a contextual analysis immediately indicates that this has nothing to do with the cultic or legalistic side of the law.

6. *Ibid.*, p. 29 and SKEHAN – DI LELLA, *Wisdom of Ben Sira* (n. 4), p. 75.
7. I quote translations from SKEHAN – DI LELLA.

He who fears the Lord will do this;
he who practiced in the Law (νόμος) *will come to wisdom.*

The poem in this chapter is built up of two stanzas and describes the bliss of those who seek lady Wisdom[8]. Hence concepts such as bread of learning; water of understanding, trust, etc. appear abundantly.

The same is true of Chapter 21,11 where the keeping of the law is clarified by the context:

Whoever keeps the Law (νόμος) controls his impulses;
whoever is perfect in fear of the Lord has wisdom.

The first ten verses of this chapter address the transgressing son, but these sins are referred to only in general terms; as panic and pride; hating of rebukes; and crime. The second part of the poem again is filled with positive sapiential concepts: knowledge, counsel, the intelligent, the wise and the prudent, in contrast to the fool who has no knowledge; the wanton, the stupid, the arrogant, etc.

Even though Sira does not seem preoccupied with the detail of the law of Moses, this does not mean that the stipulations are insignificant to him. In Chapter 23,23 he refers to the adulterous wife which surely is an adaptation of Ex 20,14 and Deut 5,18[9]. Sirach even refers directly to the law of Moses and the book of the covenant of the Most high in Chapter 24,23. However, a glance at the immediate context reveals the sapiential content of this book, for states verse 25: "It is brimful, like the Pishon, with wisdom, like the Tigris at the time of the new crops".

There is a passage in Sirach that addresses the issue of true worship of God, Chapter 34,21-35. However, the references to the legal side of sacrifices are minimal. Here the social aspect of the sacrificial is stressed. Hence the number of references to the poor, the needy, etc. To be sure Sirach does mention issues of cultic sacrifices in this passage, verse 30:

If a person again touches a corpse after he has bathed,
What did he gain by the purification?

There are also references to the cultic law in Chapters 7,31 and 45,17. It would therefore be incorrect or at the least unsubtle to state that Sirach had no interest in things cultic. However, it should be clear that this is not his main interest. Collins also recognizes echoes of the social laws of Deut 15,7-11 as a background to Sir 4,1-6. However, he too acknowledges how little attention Sirach generally pays to the ritual commandments of Leviticus[10].

8. SKEHAN – DI LELLA, *Wisdom of Ben Sira* (n. 4), p. 263.
9. *Ibid.*, p. 325.
10. COLLINS, *Jewish Wisdom* (n. 1), p. 47.

A second characteristic of these passages is the prominence of the motif of the fear of the Lord (2,16; 15,1):

> 19,20 The whole of wisdom is fear of the Lord;
> Complete wisdom is the fulfillment of the Law (νόμος).

This verse is important since it refers to the fear of the Lord which is wisdom, on the one hand, and wisdom being the fulfillment of the law, on the other hand. Small wonder that Skehan & Di Lella quote this verse in an endevour to determine the theme of the collection[11]. Collins[12] thinks that there is practically an identification between wisdom and the fear of the Lord.

A third characteristic is the mentioning of the covenant of God:

> 24,23 All this is true of the book of the Most High's covenant,
> the Law (νόμος) which Moses enjoined on us
> as a heritage for the community of Jacob.

Chapter 39 even to some extend relates law and covenant, in a genitive construction.

> 39,8 He will show the wisdom of what he has learned
> and glory in the law (νόμος) of the Lord's covenant.

Probably the most significant characteristic of this collection is that Ben Sira seems to equate the keeping of the law and acquiring wisdom. This takes place in 1,26, as well as in 15,1:

> He who fears the Lord will do this;
> he who practiced in the Law (νόμος) will come to wisdom.

Even more explicit is 19,20:

> The whole of wisdom is fear of the Lord;
> Complete wisdom is the fulfillment of the Law (νόμος).

These passages have led to scholars talking about the identification of wisdom and law in Sirach. Schnabel[13], for example, claims that these entities have been completely identified in Ben Sira. Martin Hengel[14] argues that Ben Sira has identified wisdom and pious observance and that in practise wisdom and law are one and the same! Moreover, he thinks that in Sirach, contrary to Proverbs, torah is no longer instruction in gen-

11. SKEHAN – DI LELLA, *Wisdom of Ben Sira* (n. 4), p. 76.

12. COLLINS, *Jewish Wisdom* (n. 1), p. 46.

13. E.J. SCHNABEL, *Law and Wisdom from Ben Sira to Paul*, Tübingen, 1985, p. 45.

14. M. HENGEL, *Judaism and Hellenism. Studies in their Encounter in Palestine during the Early Hellenistic Period*, London, 1974, p. 138. "In practice, wisdom and the law have become one, and Ben Sira expresses this by putting the great hymn to wisdom (ch 24), in which this fusion is achieved, in the centre of his work" (p. 139).

eral but in particular the *torat Moshe*. This interpretation should off course be understood against the background of Hengel's specific view on the apologetical stance of Ben Sira against Hellenism[15].

Collins talks about the "eventual" identification of wisdom with the torah of Moses. However, he has a nuanced view in this regard: "When Sirach identifies wisdom and the law, he is in effect introducing the Torah of Moses into the wisdom school and thereby attempting to combine two educational traditions"[16].

Boccaccini[17] to the contrary argues that the relationship between these two traditions are actually asymmetrical. Rogers[18] agrees with this view. She is also sceptical of the anti-Hellenistic interpretation by Hengel[19].

It would therefore seem as if this relationship is more intricate than would seem at first glance. Firstly, it is clear that Ben Sira relates these concepts. However, he deems the law differently from, for example, Ezra. According to Lebram Ezra belonged to the purifying circles of the Hasidim, whereas Sirach belongs to the priestly circles[20]. To Sira not the cultic, nor the legalistic technical detail of the law of Moses is important, but the effects of the law. If you study the law of Moses you will become wise. One could therefore say that wisdom is clearly related to the law of Moses, but, contrary to Hengel, it is not identified with the *torat Moshe*. The *torat Moshe* is imperative for obtaining wisdom, but it is not identical to wisdom. I would therefore suggest that the term "association" (Collins) or "relation" be used but not "identification". Law and wisdom are clearly related but not identified with one another.

This perspective opens an important window on the attitude that Sira had towards the society in which he lived. To me it is evident that he was not as anxious about the law as was, for example, the Greek translator of Proverbs[21]. I will return again to this issue, however, suffice it to say at this stage that the chronological difference between Sirach and LXX Proverbs in my view is the reason for this conspicuous difference of approach. The latter came to be in the wake of the devastating reforms by Antiochus Epiphanes.

15. *Ibid.*, p. 138ff..

16. COLLINS, *Jewish Wisdom* (n. 1), p. 47.

17. Cf. G. BOCCACCINI, *Middle Judaism. Jewish Thought, 300 B.C.E. to 200 C.E.*, Minneapolis, MN, 1991, p. 81.

18. Cf. J.F. ROGERS, *Is Wisdom a Mediatrix in Sirach? A Study of the Wisdom Poems*. Unpublished Doctoral Dissertation, Stellenbosch, 2000, p. 135.

19. *Ibid.*, p. 135. COLLINS, *Jewish Wisdom* (n. 1), seems to share this scepticism: "Nowhere in Sirach do we find any explicit polemic against Greek wisdom".

20. Cf. J.C.H. LEBRAM, *Aspekte der alttestamentlichen Kanonbildung*, in *VT* 18 (1968), p. 189.

21. Cf. J. COOK, *The Law of Moses in Septuagint Proverbs*, in *VT* 49 (1999), p. 460.

2.2 *The Law of Moses in Aristobulus of Alexandria*

Aristobulus is called the first Jewish philosopher. He lived and worked in Alexandria in the first half of the second century BCE. He wrote his treatise to Ptolemy VI Philometor (181-145 BC) circa 174-170 BCE[22]. His intention was to present a correct understanding of the law of Moses. In Hengel's words: "To demonstrate that Jewish doctrine as presented in the Pentateuch, i.e. the Greek translation of the Mosaic law, represented the true 'philosophy' and did not contradict philosophically trained reason"[23]. In order to do this he made a selection of passages from the Pentateuch which he interpreted allegorically.

According to Clemens Alexandrinus (Strom. II 100, 3) Aristobulus was a "peripateticus". From the fragments that we received from Eusebius it is clear that he was actually an eclectic who was not influenced by any particular school of thought[24].

The relevance of Aristobulus for the current study is found in his allegorical interpretation of the creation and more specifically the combination of the resting of God on the seventh day and the creation of light on the first day with the pretemporal being of wisdom possibly according to Prov. 8,22 and certain philosophical notions[25]. This Pythagorean based speculation on the number 7 is found also in Philo of Alexandria. Aristobulus quotes a number of pentateuchal passages probably from the Septuagint, like Gen 1 and 2. The only possible point of contact between Aristobulus and LXX Proverbs, however, is his allegorical interpretation of Chapter 8,22ff. This, however, has nothing to do with the law of Moses, nevertheless, it does give us insight into the way Aristobulus interpreted this text.

An important issue in this regard is the question as to which text Aristobulus used for his interpretation. According to Walter it is probable that Aristobulus had the Greek text available[26]. From the passage quoted by him PE XIII, 12, 11a I do not see the immediate correspondence[27]:

22. Cf. N. WALTER, *Der Thoraausleger Aristobulos. Untersuchungen zu seinen Fragmenten und zu pseudepigraphischen Resten der jüdisch-hellenistischen Literatur* (Texte und Untersuchungen, 86), Berlin, 1964, p. 41. Cf. also C.R. HOLLADAY, *Fragments from Hellenistic Jewish Authors*, vol. III. *Aristobulus*, Atlanta, GA, 1995, p. 75.

23. Cf. HENGEL, *Judaism and Hellenism* (n. 14), p. 164.

24. *Ibid.*, p. 16 and WALTER, *Der Thoraausleger Aristobulos* (n. 22), p. 12.

25. HENGEL, *Judaism and Hellenism* (n. 14), p. 166.

26. WALTER, *Der Thoraausleger Aristobulos* (n. 22), p. 33.

27. K. MRAS, *Eusebius Werke* (Die Griechischen Christlichen Schriftsteller der ersten Jahrhunderte). Achter Band, Zweiter Teil, *Die Praeparatio Evangelica*, Berlin, 1956, p. 195.

σαφέστερον δὲ καὶ κάλλιον τῶν ἡμετέρων προγόνων τις εἶπε Σολομῶν πρὸ οὐρανοῦ καὶ γῆς ὑπάρχειν

But one of our forebears, Solomon, said more clearly and more beautifully that it (wisdom) was created before heaven and earth.

Firstly, the Greek words being used are quite different from those that appear in LXX Proverbs 8 verse 22: Κύριος ἔκτισέν με ἀρχὴν ὁδῶν αὐτοῦ εἰς ἔργα αὐτοῦ. The only real possible contact therefore is the reference to Solomon. This could at the most be an interpretation from memory, but it can not be taken as undisputed evidence of a quotation from the Septuagint. There must also be the possibility that Aristobulus had knowledge of the Hebrew text. Walter[28] deems it impossible.

There is another Hellenistic-Jewish author who used the LXX and testifies to the existence of the Pentateuch, the chronographer, Demetrius, who probably lived in Alexandria during the reign of Ptolemy IV (Philopater 222-205 BCE)[29]. He is the earliest witness for a Greek version of the Pentateuch, and thus is an important source for determining the origins of the LXX and determining its impact upon Hellenistic Judaism in Alexandria. However, the problem is that he has no reference to LXX Proverbs.

This issue has implications for the dating of LXX Proverbs and is therefore of great significance. A more important factor, however, is that there is no evidence of similar philosophical, allegorical speculations in the Septuagint of Proverbs[30]. The fact that this speculative treatise was written approximately at the time of the coming to be of LXX Proverbs[31] is no undisputable evidence that the translator of LXX Proverbs had the same understanding of the law of Moses. As a matter of fact the person responsible for this translation in my view had an anti-Greek philosophical perspective in this regard as will become evident in due course.

2.3 *The Law of Moses in LXX Proverbs*

The person(s) responsible for this translated unit had a rather systematic approach towards specific religious issues. For one, I demonstrated

28. WALTER, *Der Thoraausleger Aristobulos* (n. 22), p. 33.

29. C.R. HOLLADAY, *Fragments from Hellenistic Jewish Authors*, vol. I. *Historians*, Chico, CA, 1983, p. 51.

30. In my view this applies to LXX Genesis too. Cf. J. COOK, *Greek Philosophy and the Septuagint*, in *JNSL* 2/1 (1998) 177-191.

31. HENGEL, *Judaism and Hellenism* (n. 14), p. 163 puts it as follows: "The unknown translator of Proverbs is probably quite close in time to the first known Jewish 'philosopher', Aristobulus, about 170 BC, who refers to Prov 8.22ff. and perhaps presupposes that it has been translated".

that the various strange women in Chapters 1-9 are systematically interpreted in the Septuagint of Proverbs as a metaphor for foreign wisdom, namely the Hellenism of the day[32]. Another example is the question of contrasts/dualisms. The Greek version contains more dualisms than occur in the Hebrew. Hence in the *Festschrift* for Jim Sanders I spoke of this characteristic in LXX Proverbs as a translation technique[33]. I detected the same systematical approach toward the law of Moses. Firstly, various lexemes are used to describe the law of Moses. The Hebrew lexeme **תורה** occurs in 12 passages and is rendered differently: 1,8 (θεσμούς); 3,1 (νομιμών); 4,2 (νόμος); 6,20 (θεσμούς) and 23 (νόμος); 7,2 (λόγους); 13,14 (νόμος); 28,4 (νόμος), 7 (νόμος) and 9 (νόμος); 29,18 (νόμος) and 31,25 (ἐννόμως). The translator also distinguishes between parental instructions and the law of Moses. The latter is referred to in practically all the passages where νόμος acts as equivalent.

Secondly, in addition to these lexemes this Greek noun νόμος appears as pluses in comparison to the Hebrew in two passages; Prov 9,10 and 13,15 which are highly significant.

Proverbs 9,10

MT:

תְּחִלַּת חָכְמָה יִרְאַת יְהוָה וְדַעַת קְדֹשִׁים בִּינָה׃

The fear of the Lord is the beginning of wisdom, and the knowlegde of the holy one is insight.

LXX:

10 ἀρχὴ σοφίας φόβος κυρίου,
καὶ βουλὴ ἁγίων σύνεσις
[10] τὸ γὰρ γνῶναι νόμον διανοίας ἐστὶν ἀγαθῆς

The beginning of wisdom is the fear of the Lord
And the counsels of saints is understanding,
For to know the law is the sign of a sound mind,

Proverbs 13,15

MT:

שֵׂכֶל־טוֹב יִתֶּן־חֵן וְדֶרֶךְ בֹּגְדִים אֵיתָן׃

Good sense wins favour, but the way of the faithless is their ruin.

32. Cf. J. Cook, *אשה זרה (Prov 1-9 in the Septuagint) a Metaphor for Foreign Wisdom?*, in *ZAW* 106 (1994) 458-476.

33. Cf. J. Cook, *Contrasting as a Translation Technique in the LXX Proverbs*, in C.A. Evans – S. Talmon (eds.), *The Quest for Context and Meaning. Studies in Biblical Intertextuality in Honor of James A. Sanders* (Biblical Interpretation Series), Leiden, 1997, pp. 403-414.

LXX:

σύνεσις ἀγαθὴ δίδωσιν χάριν,
τὸ δὲ γνῶναι νόμον διανοίας ἐστὶν ἀγαθῆς,
ὁδοὶ δὲ καταφρονούντων ἐν ἀπωλείᾳ

Sound discretion gives favour,
And to know the law is the sign of a sound mind,
But the ways of scorners end in destruction.

Thus these passages have an identical addition (to know the law is the sign of a sound mind) which is part of the systematic application of exegetical perspectives by the translator. I have argued that it became necessary in the wake of a specific historical situation to stress the importance of the law of Moses. The translator namely warns the readers of the inherent "dangers" of foreign wisdom (the Hellenism of the day). One of these prominent dangers was the devaluation of the law of Moses[34].

Of special significance is the way the law of Moses is depicted in Chapter 28. It can be observed in the following translation of LXX Proverbs 28,4:

עֹזְבֵי תוֹרָה יְהַלְלוּ רָשָׁע וְשֹׁמְרֵי תוֹרָה יִתְגָּרוּ בָם׃

Those who forsake the law praise the wicked, but those who keep the law struggle against them.

οὕτως οἱ ἐγκαταλείποντες τὸν νόμον ἐγκωμιάζουσιν ἀσέβειαν,
οἱ δὲ ἀγαπῶντες τὸν νόμον περιβάλλουσιν ἑαυτοῖς τεῖχος

Likewise those who forsake the law and praise impious deeds;
However, those who love the law *build a wall around themselves.*

There seems to be no logical relationship beween the LXX and the Hebrew[35]. It is, nevertheless, possible that the Hebrew reading גור was deliberately understood as גדר (wall). Here the law has a protective function towards the righteous. This is markedly different from the view found in some later rabbinical writings, for example, the Mishna and in even later rabbinical writings such as Aboth I,1, according to which the torah must be protected! (The latter used to say three things: Be patient in justice, rear many disciples and *make a fence around the torah*).

I have located similar traditions in a number of Judaic sources, notably the Letter of Aristeas[36] and in the Dead Sea Scrolls.

34. Cf. COOK, *The Law of Moses* (n. 21), p. 457.
35. *Ibid.*, p. 457.
36. *Ibid.*, p. 459.

2.4 The Letter of Aristeas

In a legendary, probably ficticious letter by a seemingly burocrat of the reign of Ptolemy II Philadelphos named Aristeas, news of an important mission to the high priest in Jerusalem is provided. The background to the epistel is the request by Demetrius of Phaleron, the famous director of the Alexandrian library, to have a copy of the Jewish law added to the already encompassing list of originals. In reaction to a suggestion by Aristeas the king has a letter prepared to the high priest in Jerusalem in which, inter alia, he expresses his regret about the Jewish exiles who were brought forcibly to Alexandria in the past. A delegation, including Aristeas, from the king, is then sent to Jerusalem with the request to have a copy of the law of Moses prepared. After meeting the high priest the delegation returns to Alexandria with 72 translators in order to execute their task. "They were men who had not only acquired proficiency in Jewish literature, but had studied most carefully that of the Greeks as well (par. 121)"[37]. At their arrival they are entertained by Ptolemy at a banquet that lasts 7 days. During this time the king meets every translator and puts them all sorts of questions which all answer with great wisdom. Then the 72 translators (six from each Israelite tribe) are accommodated in a specially prepared house on the island of Pharos and after 72 days they complete their work. The translation is then read aloud to the Jewish community of Alexandria and the translations are perfectly concordant!

It is clear that this treatise belongs to the genre of Pseudepigraphon[38] and that it has an apologetical intention. Many scholars have argued that the main intention of this legend is to propagate a new translation of the Hebrew Pentateuch into Greek[39]. The situation is, however, more complicated. For one thing the letter is clearly to be dated much later than the proposed third century BCE[40]. Moreover, whereas De Lagarde argued that this letter is an apology for the original Greek translation, Brock[41] ingeniously demonstrated that it actually has to do with the later revisional activity in the Septuagint. Thus as a rejection of unnecessary

37. I use the translation by R.H. CHARLES, *The Apocrypha and Pseudepigrapha of the Old Testament in English*, vol. II, Oxford, 1913.

38. N. MEISNER, *Aristeasbrief*, in H. LICHTENBERGER (ed.), *Unterweisung in erzählender Form* (Jüdische Schriften aus hellenistisch-römischer Zeit, II/1-6), Gütersloh, 1999, p. 37.

39. Cf. the contributions in S. JELLICOE (ed.), *Studies in the Septuagint: Origins, Recensions, and Interpretations*, New York, 1974.

40. MEISNER, *Aristeasbrief* (n. 38), p. 43.

41. S.P. BROCK, *Aspects of Translation Technique in Antiquity*, in *GRBS* 20 (1979) 69-87; reprinted in ID., *Syriac Perspectives on Late Antiquity*, London, 1987.

tampering with the Greek translations, even though they differed from the Hebrew in many places.

However, the letter of Aristeas has more to offer than exclusively the acceptance of a new translation of the Pentateuch. It also provides insight into the Judaism of the day even though it is rather difficult to determine exactly where this epistel should be placed. Good arguments have been put forth as to the possible place of origin. The epistel itself proposes Alexandria as obvious place of origin. However, it is clear that the detail of the letter can not be trusted on face value. Meisner has creatively suggested the tempel of Leontopolis as possible origin of the letter[42]. He bases his arguments upon the dating of Bickermann of 127-118 BCE[43].

Be this as it may, what is clear is that this tendentious and legendary epistel was composed by someone in Egypt who perhaps has never been to Jerusalem but who needed the religious backing of the high priest for his propaganda. I will deal with these issues at a later stage, now I want to focus on the contents of the law of Moses in the Aristeas letter.

The law is called the godly law (θεῖος νόμος) in paragraph 3. It is also full of wisdom and free from all blemish (par. 31). The God who gave them their law is the Lord and Creator of the Universe who is called by different names, Zeus or Dis (par. 16). There is no doubt as to who this law belongs, it is the law of the Jews (τῶν Ἰουδαίων νόμινα) (par. 10). One of the main objects of the Aristeas letter was to assist the Jewish community obtaining a Greek translation of this law that has been written in the Hebrew characters and language and have been carelessly interpreted (par. 30).

The letter is seemingly infused with some Greek philosophical ideas. The author does not shy away from talking about God as Zeus or Dis (par. 15). However, the Jewishness of the epistel is unmistakeably present. The law to which is here referred is, inter alia, the cultic laws of the pentateuch.

In paragraph 139 the following statements are made:

> περίφραξεν ἡμᾶς ἀδιακόποις χάραξι καὶ σιδηροῖς τείχεσιν
>
> When therefore our lawgiver, equipped by God for insight into all things, has surveyed each particular, *he fenched us about with impregnable palisades and with walls of iron*, to the end that we should mingle in no way with any other nations, but remain pure in body and soul, free from all vain imaginations, worshipping the one Almighty God above the whole creation.

42. MEISNER, *Aristeasbrief* (n. 38), p. 43.
43. E. BICKERMANN, *Zur Datierung des Pseudo-Aristeas*, in *ZNW* 29 (1930) 280-296.

That this is indeed the cultic laws is clearly observed in par. 143: "Therefore lest we should be corrupted by any abomination, or our lives be perverted by evil communications, *he hedged us round on all sides by rules of purity*, affecting alike what we eat, or drink, or touch, or hear or see". Here we thus have an ancient exegetical tradition of the people of God being surrounded by the law in order to preserve them.

Thus the law referred to by Aristeas is the law of Moses but more specifically the cultic, Levitical laws that have the function of hedging the Jews about in order to preserve them from "un-Jewish" practises.

Aristeas also provides an interpretation of what the function of these laws are. Mentioning Moses by name he states: "For you must not fall into the degrading idea that it was out of regard to mice and weasels and other things that Moses drew up his laws with such exceeding care. All these ordinances were made for the sake of *righteousness to aid the quest for virtue and the perfecting of character* (par. 162)".

It is thus significant that this law of Moses is not unlogical nor irrational: "For our laws have not been drawn up at random or in accordance with the first casual thought that occurred in the mind, but with a view to truth and the indication of right reason (par. 161)". And in par. 168: "the whole system aims at righteousness and righteous relationships between man and man". The law of Moses has to do with cultic issues but it is aimed at wise conduct.

There are some motifs in Aristeas' views that appear also in the passages that I discussed earlier. Firstly, the motif of the law as surrounding hedge in LXX Proverbs and secondly the relationship between wisdom and the law. This brings me to the Dead Sea Scrolls.

3. The Torat Moshe in the Dead Sea Scrolls

The law of Moses plays a prominent role in the Dead Sea scrolls. Naturally one has to distinguish between individual documents. For the purpose of this paper I will concentrate on the so-called Damascus Document. The intricacies of this document that was discovered in the Cairo Geniza prior to the epochmaking discovery at Qumran, are well-known. Until recently the ground-breaking research of Davies[44] was the standard available work. Of lately aspects of this document has attracted the attention of an increasing number of scholars[45]. However, since I am

44. P.R. Davies, *The Damascus Document. An Interpretation of the "Damascus Document"*, Sheffield, 1982.

45. A congress was devoted to this all important document: J.M. Baumgarten, E.G. Chazon, A. Pinnick (eds.), *The Damascus Document: A Centennial of Discovery. Proceedings of the Third International Symposium of the Orion Center, 4-8 February 1998* (STDJ, 34), Leiden, 2000.

interested in the torat Moshe I need not get involved in the detail of these problems. Nevertheless, some issues should be accounted for. A prominent one is the question of diversity in CD. Davies[46] talks about Judaisms in this regard. Secondly the question of redactional reworking that CD has undergone and that different parts actually refer to different groups[47]. CD moreover distinguishes between the outsiders, which are Israel and which is subdivided into Israel and Aaron, on the one hand, and the priests, Levites, Israelites and *gerim*, on the other hand. The insiders are the true community of believers who "is constituted by scrupulous obedience to the *torah* as revealed in its own covenant"[48].

That this torah is not identical to the torat Moshe has been demonstrated by various scholars. Schiffman[49] is of the opinion that the "sect" distinguished between two categories of law; the revealed (נגלה) laws, that were known to the whole of Israel and the hidden (נסתר) laws which were exclusively known to the sect. The former should therefore be identified with the law of Moses whereas the latter is the new law for the new covenanters.

One thus needs to differentiate between the torat Moshe and the new torah in CD. It is not easy to do so. Some cases speak for themselves. For example, the noun תורה occurs 30 times in CD. In 5 instances (XV 2,9,12; XVI 2,5) it refers directly to the law of Moses (תורת משה). However, I am especially interested in the way this law functions in Chapters II, IV and VI since there I think we can find some allusions to the traditions that I have discussed above.

3.1 The Torat Moshe as Wall

The noun תורה appears in CD IV 8 in the statement "those who entered (the covenant) after them and who behave according to the details of the law (התורה)". Surely this is an explicit reference to the torat Moshe even though exactly what the contents of this law would have been to the addressees is not that evident. However, towards the end of this chapter it is stated that "there will be no (further) joining the House

46. DAVIES, *The Judaism(s) of the Damascus Document*, in *Centennial of Discovery*, pp. 27-43.

47. DAVIES, *The Damascus Document* (n. 44), p. 198f. Cf. also more recently C. HEMPEL, *The Laws of the Damascus Document. Sources, Tradition and Redaction* (STDJ, 29), Leiden, 1998, as well as ID., *The Laws of the Damascus Document and 4QMMT*, in *Centennial of Discovery*, pp. 69-84.

48. DAVIES, *The Judaism(s)* (n. 46), p. 33. I follow Davies' translation.

49. L.H. SCHIFFMAN, *Reclaiming the Dead Sea Scrolls. The History of Judaism, the Background of Christianity, the Lost Library of Qumran*, Philadelphia & Jerusalem, 1994, p. 247. Cf. also his *The Halakha at Qumran* (SJLA, 16), Leiden, 1975.

of Judah, but rather "each man must stand upon his watchtower: 'The wall is built, the boundary is extended'"[50]. On the face of it this could be an allusion to the torah. The notion of a wall being built to preserve the believing community in LXX Proverbs could be relayed to the Hebrew root גדר as I demonstrated above and which is also used here in CD. This quote is, moreover, part of a larger context where the 'faithful' Zadok is mentioned as well as the 'sons of Zadok' who are the chosen ones of Israel who are 'called by name' and who arise at the end of days.

Davies[51] proposes another interpretation of the building imagery. According to him it does not refer to a place from where the watcher looks out, but rather it is a flimsy building outside the city walls open to attack. I tend to agree with Swartz[52] that the wall is a symbol of separation between the insiders and the outsiders. This is borne out by the statement that the boundary is extended. This seems to be an allusion to Hosea 5,10-11. "The commanders of Judah have acted like shifters of field boundaries".

There is also a reference to "The builders of the wall (בוני החיץ)" in IV 19. In VIII 12 this image is developed further: "but all these things they do not understand, (these) builders of the wall and daubers of plaster, because a raiser of wind and spouter of lies spouted to them, against all of whose congregation the anger of God is aroused". The biblical context of the term בנה חיץ in Ezekiel 13,10 can provide some understanding of this phrase. The passage deals with a wall, which the people have built, and which false prophets daub with plaster. The prophet predicts that God will bring down the wall.

From this passage it is clear that the builders of the wall is seen as a negative grouping. This is also clear from the statement in IV 19: "the builders of the wall who have followed after Zaw (Hosea 5,11), the Zaw is a spouter". According to Davies and Stegemann the "builders of the wall" are the whole of Israel outside the Qumran community[53], those who violate the law of Moses. The 'builders of the wall' thus is a reference to a group of people who, metaphorically speaking, built a wall around the law of Moses in distinction to the new torah.

Schiffman[54] has a significant interpretation of the tradition concerning the builders of walls. According to him we can understand the legal the-

50. DAVIES, *The Damascus Document* (n. 44), p. 243. Prof. García Martínez referred me to this passage, as well as to the law as Well in CD.

51. *Ibid.*, p. 104.

52. O. SCHWARTZ, *Der erste Teil der Damascusschrifte und das AT*, Diest, 1965, pp. 139-140.

53. DAVIES, *The Damascus Document* (n. 44), p. 113.

54. SCHIFFMAN, *Reclaiming the Dead Sea Scrolls* (n. 49), p. 249.

ology of the Qumran sect from the scrolls, but we can also obtain from them information about the legal views of the Pharisees and Sadducees. So that what we learn about the Pharisees is derived indirectly from the sectarian polemics against their views.

According to Schiffman the builders of the wall are the villains. In his view in CD IV 19-20 the commanders of Judah are equated with Ephraim, a sectarian term for the Pharisees. They are the builders of the wall who follow the teachings of the commander. This same commander is the one who preaches improperly, hence defrauding his listeners. The sect regarded the Pharisees as preaching falsely and misleading their followers[55].

Schiffman[56] is moreover of the opinion that the designation "builders of the wall" derives from a concept found in the mishnaic tractate Avot, to which I have already refered: "Build a fence around the Torah" (M. Avot 1,1). "To build a fence refers to the Pharisaic-rabbinic concept of creating more stringent laws than those found in the Bible in order to safeguard biblical laws from violation. Although Talmudic sources consider this 'fence' (*siyyag* in Mishnaic Hebrew) a positive feature of rabbinic halakhah, the authors of the fragments oppose this approach, not only because they disagree with the specific laws that resulted but also because they did not accept expanding the law in this manner in the first place"[57].

In short then, Schiffman holds the opinion that the later Talmudic tradition concerning the wall surrounding the torah is already found in the CD, however, it is deemed a negative practise by the new covenanters. The point to make is off course that this tradition was already functioning much earlier than the Mishna.

Joseph Baumgarten[58] recently dealt with this tradition in the Damascus document. Referring to the שבות he makes the following statements: "The term שבות, which is used in rabbinic sources for rabbinic restrictions intended to preserve the non-secular character of the Sabbath, is not found in Qumran writings. It is, however, apparent that the Sabbath rules found in Jubilees and in the Damascus Document were not limited to those found in the Torah, but also embraced the שבות category of legal 'fences' designed to enhance the sanctity of the Sabbath".

According to Baumgarten Qumran law in effect carried out one of the principles attributed to the Men of the Great Assembly to which I re-

55. *Ibid.*, p. 249.
56. *Ibid.*
57. *Ibid.*
58. BAUMGARTEN, in *A Centennial of Discovery*, p. 22.

ferred to above: ועשׂו סיג לתורה, "And built a fence about the Torah" (m. Abot 1,1). He significantly differs from Schiffman[59] that the references in CD IV 19 and VIII 12 was particularly directed at the proto-rabbinic "fences" which served to protect the Law.

Be this as it may, what is important here is that there existed a tradition about the "law as a wall surrounding" in early Judaism, namely in the Septuagint; the Aristeas letter, as well as in the Dead Sea Scrolls. Clearly the differences between these traditions are prominent for in the former it is the righteous that are protected, whereas in Qumran and CD, and also in the Mishna, it is the law. However, as is well known the Damascus Document is not exclusively found at Qumran, for a copy of it was also discovered in Egypt, in the Cairo Genizah in 1929. This tradition must therefore have been known in both Egypt (CD, Aristeas and LXX Proverbs[60]) as well as in Palestine (Qumran & LXX Proverbs). I did not deal exhaustively with later traditions found in the Mishna and other Jewish exegetical writings such as Abot I,1. However, one of the implications of this study is that the tradition of a surrounding wall is not a late one, it occurs already in early rabbinic, Hellenistic times.

3.2 The Torat Moshe as Well

There are, however, also other traditions concerning the law of Moses in the Dead Sea scrolls, as a matter of fact in CD. CD VI 9 talks about the people (the nobles) who keep the law as being "well-diggers"! Again the immediate context is important: After referring to the detrimental influence of Belial, Jannes and his brother and those who prophesied falsely to turn Israel from God the following is said: "But God remembered the covenant of the fathers and he raised from Aaron men of understanding and from Israel men of wisdom, and he let them hear (his voice), and they dug the well, 'a well which princes dug, which nobles of the people dug with a staff'. The well is the law, and those who dug it are the 'captivity of Israel' who went out from the land of Judah and settled in the land of Damascus, all of whom God called 'princes' because they sought him and because their reknown was not denied by anyone. And the staff is the interpreter of the law of whom Isaiah spoke (when he said): 'He produces a tool for his work.' And the nobles of the people are those who have entered (the covenant) in order to dig the well with the staves (rules) which the staff (legislator) fashioned (legislated) to

59. SCHIFFMAN, *Reclaiming the Dead Sea Scrolls* (n. 49), p. 250.

60. Where this translation was actually conducted, Egypt or Palestine, is as yet uncertain.

walk during all the period of wickedness <and without them they will not succeed> until there shall arise one who will 'teach righteousness' at the end of the days".

This description is based upon the view that the well is the law (הבאר היא התורה) (verse 4). This well motif represents an interpretation of the song of the well in Numbers 21,17-18:

> Then Israel sang this song;
> Spring up, O well (באר) – sing to it –
> The well (באר) which the chieftains dug,
> which the nobles of the people started
> with mace (במחוקק), with their staves.

According to Fishbane the exegetical passage in CD transforms the biblical passage into a religious history of the new covenanters: "the באר in the desert has become a symbol for the Torah which the community and its leadership interprets according to their esoteric mode"[61]. This is therefore clear evidence of the torat Moshe as Well, yet again the contents of the torah seems different to that of the *torat Moshe*.

Finally, in the context of the statement הבאר היא התורה in verse 4 the following significant concept appears: המחוקק (verse 4). The Hebrew verb חקק (to inscribe) is used extensively in the pentateuch to describe the Torah. As a matter of fact two of the prominent words that refer to the law of Moses, or to certain precepts of the Torah, are related nouns חֹק and חֻקָּה. This is the case in Ex 12,14, 17 and 43. Deut 4,44 and 45 are also important in this regard, inasmuch as the law (התורה) is mentioned in verse 44 and its precepts (החקים) in verse 45. In Proverbs the root חקק is used a number of times. Prov 8,15 is one passage in which rulers who make just decrees are referred to. However, Prov 31,5 is the most instructive in this regard:

> פֶּן־יִשְׁתֶּה וְיִשְׁכַּח מְחֻקָּק וִישַׁנֶּה דִּין כָּל־בְּנֵי־עֹנִי
>
> lest they drink and forget what has been decreed,
> and pervert the rights of all the afflicted.
>
> ἵνα μὴ πιόντες ἐπιλάθωνται τῆς σοφίας
> καὶ ὀρθὰ κρῖναι οὐ μὴ δύνωνται τοὺς ἀσθενεῖς
>
> lest they drink and forget wisdom,
> and be not able to judge the poor rightly.

The Pual of חקק (מְחֻקָּק) appears only in this passage in the Hebrew Bible. McKane[62] is of the opinion that, in this context, the verb has to do

61. M. FISHBANE, *The Well of Living Water*, in M. FISHBANE – E. TOV (eds.), *"Sha'arei Talmon". Studies in the Bible, Qumran, and the Ancient Near East presented to Shemaryahu Talmon*, Winona Lake, IN, 1992, p. 7.

62. W. MCKANE, *Proverbs a New Approach*, London, 1974, p. 410.

with the civil law, emphasising the 'legal responsibility of the king'. The Greek translator, however, interprets rather freely in the opening verses of Chapter 31. First, the reference to king Lemuel is simply removed in verses 1 and 4. Secondly, σοφία is used as equivalent for מְחֻקָּק. The previous verses, especially in the LXX, emphasise the fact that responsible kings should 'do all things with counsel'. The book of Proverbs makes it clear that a ruler should govern wisely, and it is possible that the translator of 31,5 has actually interpreted wisdom in this broader sense. However, at least in the mind of the translator, the Hebrew term refers to the Torah. This is born out by the translation of verse 8:

פְּתַח־פִּיךָ לְאִלֵּם אֶל־דִּין כָּל־בְּנֵי חֲלוֹף׃

Open your mouth for the dumb,
for the rights of all who are left desolate.

ἄνοιγε σὸν στόμα λόγῳ θεοῦ
καὶ κρῖνε πάντας ὑγιῶς

Open your mouth with the word of God
and judge all fairly.

Although אִלֵּם in its unvocalized form could have been interpreted as a reference to deity, the whole phrase in Greek seems to refer to the Torah[63]. I would therefore argue that here is evidence of the association of law and wisdom in the LXX of Proverbs. This is true also of most of the passages that I discussed above.

4. CONCLUSION

The *torat Moshe* is described in various ways in early Judaism. The idea of it being a surrounding wall occurs early in the Septuagint and in the Aristeas letter. In these contexts it is the righteous who are protected. In later Talmudic times noteably in Abot I,1 the law is being protected from misinterpretations by means of a wall. This study has demonstrated that this tradition was already in use in the CD where the law of Moses was also surrounded.

Finally it is clear that there is some sort of interactive relationship between the law of Moses, on the one hand, and wisdom, on the other hand, in the passages that I analysed. In CD 6,2 it is said: "(God) raised men of understanding and men of wisdom in order 'to dig the well' ...

63. Cf. J. COOK, *The Septuagint of Proverbs Jewish and/or Hellenistic Proverbs. Concerning the Hellenistic Colouring of LXX Proverbs* (SVT, 69), Leiden, 1997, p. 301.

and they dug the well, 'a well which princes dug, which nobles of the people dug with a staff' (במחוקק)". This seems to be in line with LXX Proverbs chapter 31 as far as the relationship between law and wisdom is concerned. However, as I indicated there are also significant differences. The law as a well does not appear in the Jewish-Hellenistic literature that I have up to now studied. Moreover, the law of Moses is different from the new law of the covenanters. As I suggested these different exegetical traditions are the result of contextual differences.

Dept of Ancient Studies
University of Stellenbosch
South Africa

Johann Cook

WISDOM AND APOCALYPTIC IN 4QINSTRUCTION AND 4 EZRA

On the surface 4QInstruction (formerly known as Sapiential Work A) and 4 Ezra (also known as 2 Esdras 3–14) are very different texts. What separates them are their different life-settings, different understandings of wisdom and apocalyptic, and different ways of combining wisdom and apocalyptic. What links the two works together is the joining of sapiential and apocalyptic elements in two early Jewish writings from the land of Israel. Indeed, as Matthew Goff has remarked, the focus of 4QInstruction "on eschatological judgment and the angelic world...is more compatible with the apocalypticism of the late Second Temple period than with Proverbs or Ben Sira"[1].

In 4QInstruction we get a glimpse of a sometimes awkward attempt at presenting wisdom teachings in an apocalyptic framework and with motivations that include some basic concepts of apocalyptic thinking. In 4 Ezra the traditional concerns of ancient Near Eastern and biblical wisdom books have yielded to the profound theological questions raised by the destruction of the Second Temple and to the conviction that the only wisdom worth knowing must be obtained through divine revelation (apocalypse) given by God or by an angelic mediator.

The comparison that follows does not suggest a direct or dependent relationship between 4QInstruction and 4 Ezra. Rather, it uses the method of comparison primarily to show their fundamental differences and to let shine forth the distinctive character of each work, and so to contribute to the general issue of wisdom and apocalypticism.

The paper first examines how 4QInstruction interweaves wisdom and apocalyptic. Then it considers how 4 Ezra pushes aside conventional wisdom (while using some of its literary conventions) in favor of apocalyptic or revelation as the way to true wisdom. Finally it reflects on what these two books have in common, and where they differ. The central thesis of this paper is that 4QInstruction has a human instructor present *wisdom in an apocalyptic context*, while in 4 Ezra the angel of God (or God) reveals *apocalyptic wisdom.*

1. M. GOFF, Review of DJD 34 (see n. 2), in *Journal of Religion* 81 (2001) 276.

4QInstruction: Wisdom in an Apocalyptic Context

4QInstruction is the most extensive sapiential text discovered among the Dead Sea scrolls[2]. It appears in six (or seven [or more]) copies: 1Q26, 4Q415-418, and 4Q423. All the manuscripts are written in the Herodian script; that is, they are from the late first century B.C. or the early first century A.D. All the manuscripts are in Hebrew, which was undoubtedly the original language of composition.

The work is a wisdom instruction presented in small units, without much obvious concern for logical or thematic progression. In form and content it is like parts of the books of Proverbs (especially chaps. 1–9 and 22,17–24,22) and Sirach. The literary setting is typical for wisdom books: A senior sage is passing on wisdom to someone who seeks to understand. Since the person being instructed is often addressed as "O understanding one" (*'th mbyn*), he has been dubbed "the Maven". The translations that follow are taken from DJD 34, but the "King James" English has been modernized to make comprehension easier.

Although 4QInstruction shares some language with the more explicitly sectarian Qumran texts (1QS and 1QH), its instructions about business dealings, social relations, and wife and family presuppose a "secular" life-setting. The expression *raz nihyeh* ("the mystery that is to come") occurs at key points, and refers to a body of knowledge or perhaps a book that conveys wise teachings about creation, ethics, and eschatology[3]. Depending on how one views the history of the Qumran community, one can regard 4QInstruction as a book that influenced the language and theology of the Qumran group from the outside, as a witness to the broader Jewish movement that has come to light through the Qumran discoveries, or as evidence for the beliefs and practices of group- or sect-members (Essenes?) living in situations other than the isolated settlement by the Dead Sea.

The broad margin in fragment 4Q416 1 suggests that it came from the first column in the work. If this is so, then the initial section served the purpose of placing everything that follows in a cosmological and

2. J. Strugnell and D.J. Harrington (with T. Elgvin), *Qumran Cave 4. XXIV. Sapiential Texts, Part 2, 4QInstruction (Mûsār Lᵉ Mēvîn): 4Q415ff* (DJD, 34), Oxford, Clarendon Press, 1999. For a detailed restudy of the text, see E.J.C. Tigchelaar, *To Increase Learning for the Understanding Ones. Reading and Reconstructing the Fragmentary Early Jewish Sapiential Text 4QInstruction* (STDJ, 44), Leiden, Brill, 2001. For a general treatment of wisdom texts among the Qumran scrolls, see D.J. Harrington, *Wisdom Texts from Qumran*, London/New York, Routledge, 1996.

3. See D.J. Harrington, *The Raz Nihyeh in a Qumran Wisdom Text (1Q26, 4Q415-418, 423)*, in *RQ* 17 (1996) 549-553.

eschatological framework. Lines 1-10 describe God's orderly rule over the world, including the heavenly hosts and the luminaries. Then there is mention of God's judgment in which the wicked will be punished and the righteous will be rewarded (lines 10-11) and at which all creation will rejoice (lines 12-14). The column ends with references to discerning between good and evil and to the "inclination of flesh" (lines 15-17). The effect of this part of the preface to the work is to situate the more conventional sapiential instructions that follow in a highly theological context. The major apocalyptic element, of course, is the last judgment with its various rewards and punishments. Since only the Creator and Lord of the cosmos would be capable of such a definitive judgment, the apocalyptic link between *Urzeit* and *Endzeit* is quite natural.

Since 4Q417 1 i-ii continues the theological, cosmological, and eschatological line of thinking found in 4Q416 1, it too may have been part of (or at least near) the work's theological preface or framework. At three points (1 i 1, 14, 18) the speaker addresses the one who is being instructed as *'th mbyn* ("O understanding one"). The speaker seems to be a senior sage who gives instruction to a younger man who wants and/ or needs it. From this literary situation we derive the putative and descriptive title *Musar LeMebin* ("Instruction for a Maven")[4].

The first section (4Q417 1 i 1-13) features many calls for the Maven to apply himself to the "mystery that is to come" (*raz nihyeh*). Whether this expression refers to a book or to a body of oral traditions, or it is a way of talking about the divine plan (like "kingdom of God" in the Synoptic Gospels), is not clear. But we can get some idea of the content of the "mystery that is to come" by attending to what according to this passage it promises to reveal about ethics and eschatology: "then you shall know truth and iniquity, wisdom and foolishness ... together with their punishments in all ages everlasting". It also promises to impart important knowledge about God: "then you shall know the glory of His might, together with His marvelous mysteries and the mighty acts He has wrought". If apocalypticism purports to provide revelations about God, eschatology, and ethics, it appears that the "mystery that is to come" – which is the principal theological theme of 4QInstruction – qualifies as apocalyptic (though the work is not an apocalypse proper).

The second section beginning with "O understanding one" (4Q417 1 i 13-18a) reminds the Maven that the rewards and punishments are already written down in "a book of memorial" (see Mal 3,16). This

4. STRUGNELL and D.J. HARRINGTON in *DJD* 34, p. 3.

evokes the apocalyptic motif of the heavenly tablets as well as the apocalyptic determinism that is the presupposition for this motif. In the third section (4Q417 1 i 18b-24) the Maven is urged to "gaze on the mystery that is to come" from which he can expect to "know the paths of everyone that lives and the manner of his walking". As in most apocalyptic literature, knowledge about the future is expected to have an impact on how one lives in the present.

The "eschatology-and-ethics" theme is further developed at the end of column i in 4Q417 1 ("get understanding about all the mysteries concerning you") and what remains of column ii ("the mystery of what is to come"). The Maven is urged to bless God "despite every stroke" and to bear in mind that God "will punish all your ways". He is also counseled not to allow "the thought of an evil inclination" to mislead him. As in other Jewish apocalyptic writings the final judgment serves as the horizon for ethics, while due attention is given to the role of the "evil inclination" in human sin.

The conventional sapiential material is represented most fully in 4Q417 2 and 4Q416 2. Here the senior sage gives advice to the Maven about some standard wisdom topics. While there are many references to "the mystery that is to come", there is more wisdom instruction in these sections than there is apocalyptic. Nevertheless, the advice is generally set in a theological rather than a secular context.

4Q417 2 i 1-12a deals with forgiving and admonishing "the noble" in a modest way, choosing the right kinds of people as helpers and acquaintances, and striking a moderate course in all things. The motives for such behavior include the imitation of God ("He is a prince among princes") and the wisdom associated with "the mystery that is to come" (which is placed in parallelism with "the birth-times of salvation").

The next unit (4Q417 2 i 12b-17a) gives advice to the Maven about issuing judgments in legal matters and reminds him that the real judge is God: "And who will be declared righteous when He gives judgment?". Most of the rest of the column concerns financial matters. The senior sage urges both moderation and recognition of one's own poverty while acknowledging that God is the source of all good things (17b-21a). He also stresses the need to repay loans as quickly as possible, and adds a reminder about knowing "Him (= God) who has lent it to you". The part of the instruction preserved in 4Q417 2 i generally imparts wise advice along with motivations taken from theology (God as the true noble, the judge, and the source of all good things) and eschatology ("the mystery that is to come").

While 4Q416 2 overlaps with and continues the instruction begun in 4Q417 2 i-ii, there is less theology in general and less apocalyptic in particular as the discourse proceeds. The major topics are money, social relations, and family. Before these topics are treated, however, there are sections on not asking for food for oneself alone (4Q416 2 i 22 – ii 3) and on covering one's face at another's shame or folly (ii 3-4). For the first matter there is a theological motivation supplied: "For He (God) has unloosed His mercies... to give food to all that lives".

Financial matters and social relations predominate in 4Q416 2 ii. Here the Maven is told to pay back loans and to clear up financial obligations quickly, to recognize the value of his own "holy spirit," and to ingratiate himself with his "superior" through attentive service. Whether the superior is human or divine, is not clear. The advice about not humbling oneself before an "inferior" and not striking an inferior (ii 15b-16) is motivated by the typical sapiential concern with avoiding shame. The second column ends with a warning against selling oneself (into slavery?), a recommendation to seek moderation in everything, and an admonition against dishonoring the "vessel of your bosom" (presumably his wife, as in iv 13 and 1 Thess 4,4).

The third column in 4Q416 2 begins with further cautions about dealing with loans and the promise that such care will lead to a peaceful death and a form of immortality by memory: "at your death your memory will flower forever, and your posterity will inherit joy" (iii 7-8a). There is no explicit mention of immortality of the soul or of resurrection here. Next there is an exhortation to be content with one's poverty and to behave appropriately when one enjoys a sudden rise to good fortune. In both cases "the mystery that is to come" will enable one "to understand all the ways of truth and all the roots of iniquity". These sections are notable for their renewed emphasis on eschatology and ethics captured in the phrase "the mystery that it to come".

The remaining segments of 4Q416 2 iii and what can be read of column iv concern family relationships. Here the theological elements are more obviously related to Scripture texts than they have been in the instructions thus far. The biblical commandment to honor one's father and mother (Exod 20,12; Deut 5,16) is expanded to take account of the "low estate" of the one being instructed and compares the role of parents in a child's life to that of God. One reason why parents should be honored is because "they have uncovered your ear to the mystery that is to come" (iii 18).

It is expected that the Maven will marry in accordance with Gen 2,24: "Therefore a man leaves his father and his mother and clings to his wife, and they become one flesh". He is warned, however, not to allow his wife to distract him too much from "the mystery that is to come". Once he does marry, his wife is expected to obey her husband, desire him alone, and form "one flesh" with him. She is now under his authority, not that of her own parents (iv 2-6a). The husband's authority over his wife is illustrated in iv 6b-10 by a section based on Numbers 30 about his absolute power to annul her vows and votive offerings. While appeal to legal material in the Torah is unusual in this work (but see 4Q418 103 ii 7-9), it is of course frequent in the book of Sirach.

4Q418 55 emphasizes the need for humans to struggle in pursuing wisdom and the rewards associated with that pursuit. The fragment is distinctive for its "we" and "they" language in comparison with the "you" language that predominates in most of the book. There is a dualism here between the "foolish of heart" who fail to pursue knowledge and God's "elect ones" whose pursuit of wisdom will result in their honor and glory. But whether one can call the dualism in this fragment "apocalyptic" rather than merely "sapiential" is not clear.

The dualism in 4Q418 69, however, between the "foolish" and the "elect" does have a more apocalyptic dimension in that it concerns not only their respective ways of life in the present but also their eternal destinies in the future. The "foolish-minded ones" are warned that even though they "were fashioned by the power of God ... to the everlasting pit shall your return be" (69 6). On the contrary, the "truly chosen ones" join the angels in walking "in light everlasting ... glory and abundance of splendor with them" (69 14).

4Q418 81 is an instruction addressed to the Maven on what God has done on his behalf. After calling the Maven to bless God (lines 1-2), the senior sage recounts how God has exalted the Maven ("he is your portion and your inheritance ... He has appointed you as a Holy of Holies ... as a first-born") and calls on the Maven to love God and show zeal in return (3-8). The Maven is then reminded that God has opened up insight for him and placed him "in authority over His treasure" (9) and is urged to "get even more instruction from his teachers" (17). The idea is that by pursuing wisdom diligently in response to God's gifts the Maven will enjoy even greater happiness.

4Q418 103 is notable for its agricultural imagery ("plowman ... baskets ... barns") and for its appeal to the biblical laws about "mixed things" (see Deut 22,9-11 and Lev 19,19). There is nothing obviously apocalyptic about this fragment, though it is hard to know whether its content is to be taken literally (as real advice for farmers) or in some figurative sense.

There is some explicitly apocalyptic material in 4Q418 126 ii and 127. Fragment 126 ii describes God's judgment in which he will "repay vengeance to the masters of iniquity" (6) and "raise up the head of the poor ... in glory everlasting and peace eternal" (7-8). In fragment 127 there is a meditation on human mortality (1-4a) and on God's justice in the last judgment (4b-6): "For with righteous balances He has weighed out all their measurement". The poor state of these fragments' preservation makes it difficult to discern much more about their content.

4 EZRA: APOCALYPTIC WISDOM

The Jewish apocalypse known as 4 Ezra appears as chapters 3–14 of 2 Esdras[5]. In it Ezra serves as the spokesman for the exiled community in Babylon after the destruction of the First Temple. But as the visions of the Eagle and the Lion (chaps. 11–12) and the Man from the Sea (chap. 13) show, the historical setting for the work's composition must be the destruction of the Second Temple by the Roman armies in A.D. 70. The book was written in Hebrew around A.D. 100 and subsequently translated into Greek, Latin, and other languages. It explores the theological issues raised by the events of A.D. 70 and Israel's hopes for the future. As a classic apocalypse in line with the book of Daniel, it features dialogues, parables, dreams and visions, the angelic interpreter, forecasts of the future, signs and portents associated with the Day of the Lord, the distinction between "this age/world" and "the age/world to come," and so forth[6].

In the first dialogue (3,1-5,20) Ezra inquires about the present situation: "the desolation of Zion and the wealth of those who lived in Babylon" (3,2). While admitting Israel's sins, Ezra cannot understand why Babylon (a cipher for Rome), whose sins are far worse, should be prospering. In 3,31 he asks: "Are the deeds of Babylon better than those of Zion?". Associated with the sufferings of Zion are some deeper questions: Why has the "evil heart" (see 3,20-27) burdened Adam and his descendants? Why cannot Ezra understand the reasons for Israel's present sufferings? And when will these sufferings end? These questions go beyond the historical event of Zion's destruction, beyond the

5. The quotations are from the translation by B.M. METZGER, *The Fourth Book of Ezra*, in J.H. CHARLESWORTH (ed.), *The Old Testament Pseudepigrapha. Volume 1. Apocalyptic Literature and Testaments*, Garden City, NY, Doubleday, 1983, pp. 517-559.

6. For an introduction and commentary, see M.A. KNIBB (with R.J. COGGINS), *The First and Second Books of Esdras*, Cambridge, University Press, 1979; and M.E. STONE, *Fourth Ezra. A Commentary on the Book of Ezra* (Hermeneia), Minneapolis, MN, Fortress, 1990. See also the article by KNIBB, *Apocalyptic and Wisdom in 4 Ezra*, in *JSJ* 13 (1982) 56-74.

limits of human understanding, and beyond the conventional concerns of most wisdom literature.

The limits of human understanding are made clear to Ezra by the angel Uriel's challenge to "weigh for me the weight of fire, or measure for me a blast of wind, or call back for me the day that is past" (4,5). Since these are all matters in which Ezra has first-hand experience, he should theoretically be able to say something about them. But even these tasks are far beyond Ezra's ability. And so – and this is Uriel's point – a human being like Ezra should not imagine that he could understand on the basis of his own human wisdom the ways of God: "those who inhabit the earth can understand only what is on earth, and he who is above the heavens can understand what is above the height of the heavens" (4,21).

Nevertheless, Ezra can come to understand at least something about these issues by divine revelation. For this way to wisdom he is given Uriel as his angelic interpreter (though sometimes God speaks directly). Uriel ("God is my fire/light") answers Ezra's many questions and leads him along the path to understanding.

One device that Uriel uses repeatedly to bridge the gap between Ezra's limited human intelligence and the deep wisdom that he seeks to obtain is the parable – a literary form found frequently in both wisdom and apocalyptic writings. In 4,13-21, for example, Uriel tells the story about the forest of trees of the plain and the waves of the sea, gets Ezra to admit that each should stay in its proper territory, and applies the parable to the difference between understanding earthly matters and heavenly matters.

The answers to Ezra's hardest questions remain in the future, and so Ezra wants to know "When will these things be?" (4,33). After being cautioned to be patient with regard to the unfolding plan of God, Ezra then is assured that the time is near by means of similitudes or parables: The present time is like the smoke left over from a burning furnace, and like the last raindrops from a violent storm (4,48-49). Then Uriel reveals to Ezra the various signs that will precede the last day. One of those signs is the disappearance of wisdom: "then shall reason hide itself, and wisdom shall withdraw into its chamber, and it shall be sought by many but shall not be found" (5,9-10). In this time the only real guide is divine revelation such as is imparted by Uriel to Ezra.

The second dialogue (5,21–6,34) contains many of the same elements as the first one. In particular, Ezra wants to know why Israel as the elect people of God ("your only one among the many," 5,28) has been handed over to "those who opposed your promises" (5,29) rather than being punished directly by God. In general, Ezra seeks "to understand the way of the Most High and to search out some part of his judgment" (5,34).

The limits of Ezra's understanding are emphasized when he is presented with another series of impossible tasks: "Count up for me those who have not yet come, and gather for me the scattered raindrops, and make the withered flowers bloom again for me" (5,36). When Ezra describes himself as one "without wisdom" (5,39), God reminds Ezra that "you cannot discover my judgment, or the goal of the love that I have promised to my people" (5,40).

Here for the most part the interpreter is God ("the Most High ... sovereign Lord," 5,22-23). To explain what seems to Ezra to be the slowness in the unfolding of God's judgment, God compares his judgment to a circle where there is no first or last point (5,42) and to a woman's womb that must bear children not all at once but gradually and at intervals.

When Ezra is assured that the answers to his questions are in the future, God reminds Ezra that "the end shall come through me alone and not through another" (6,6). Then Ezra is presented with another series of "signs" (6,20) that will precede the last day. Finally God's salvation will be made manifest, faithfulness will flourish, and the truth shall be revealed, whereas "evil shall be blotted out, and deceit shall be quenched ... and corruption shall be overcome" (6,25-28). Ezra comes to know all these things through divine revelation, not through human reasoning or wisdom instruction.

In the third dialogue (6,35–9,25) the same basic pattern – what Ezra wants to know, the limits of human understanding, the means by which he can come to understand, and what he learns – appears again but at greater length. In particular, Ezra wants to know why the nation for whom God created this world (see 6,55) has been handed over to other nations. In general, Ezra wants to know whether God is just in rewarding the good and punishing the wicked (7,17-18), why God has allowed the "evil heart" to influence so many humans (7,45-48), what happens after death (7,75), why Adam was created at all or at least why he was not restrained from sinning (7,116-117), why we are born only to be destroyed so quickly (8,14), and why more people are to perish than be saved (9,14).

At various points in this long dialogue Ezra is reminded about the limits of his human understanding. He is criticized for not considering "what is to come, rather than what is now present" (7,16). Ezra himself suggests that humans might be better off without a mind (7,62-69), since then they would not be so concerned about sin, death, and what happens after death. The angelic interpreter (or God) helps Ezra to know something about what he wants to know by means of parables (see 7,3-9.52-58; 8,2-3.42-45; 9,14-22) and offers a forecast about the future (9,1-13). And Ezra comes to learn much about the intermediate period between death and eternal life (7,7-140), free will (7,127-131), and the character of God (7,132-140; 8,20-36).

The three visions (9,26–10,59; 11,1–12,51; 13,1-58) follow the pattern found previously in the book of Daniel. When the seer experiences a vision or dream, he seeks help in understanding it. Then the angelic interpreter (or God) explains in detail how the various elements in the vision contribute to clarifying the present and to forecasting the future course of history. In Daniel a vision constitutes a *raz* or "mystery", and its interpretation is a *pesher* or "solution". While these terms are not used explicitly in 4 Ezra, the dynamic of *raz/pesher* underlies its visions. This pattern implies that true wisdom is hidden or esoteric, and needs a divine revelation if humans are to understand it.

Ezra's vision of the Woman in Mourning (9,26–10,59) takes place in a field after he had been eating "the plants of the field for seven days". When Ezra encounters a woman lamenting the death of her only son on his wedding night, Ezra reminds her of the much greater disaster that has overtaken Zion, only to witness the remarkable transfiguration of the woman into a great city: "the woman was no longer visible to me, but a city was being built, and a place of huge foundations showed itself" (10,27). The woman's transformation marks Ezra's shift in focus from complaining about Zion's past and present to his interest in learning about the future of Israel and its foes. And yet at this moment Ezra is still in a state of "overpowering bewilderment" (10,28). He expresses his need for a revelation in this way: "For I have seen what I did not know, and I hear what I do not understand" (10,35). The interpretation of the vision (10,38-54) explains that he has been granted a vision of the New Jerusalem: "the woman whom you saw is Zion, which you now behold as a city being built" (10,44).

The remaining two "dream visions" (11–12; 13) concern "what the Most High will do to those who inhabit the earth in the last days" (10,59). In the vision of the Eagle and the Lion (11–12) the reign of the Eagle comes to an end with the judgment issued by the Lion. Between the vision (11,1–12,3a) and the interpretation (12,10-39) Ezra recognizes that the dream vision concerns "the end of the times and the last events of the times" (12,9). But he finds himself in great fear and even mental exhaustion until he can get a detailed explanation according to which the Eagle is Rome (12,11) and the Lion is the Messiah of Israel (12,32).

The vision of the Man from the Sea (13,1-58) takes place after Ezra has been eating flowers and plants for seven days. Between the vision (13,1-13a) and its interpretation (13,21-56), Ezra awakes in "great terror" (13,13b) and prays for an interpretation. The Man from the Sea is identified as "my Son" who will stand on Mount Zion and "reprove the assembled nations for their ungodliness" (13,37) and "gather to himself another multitude that was peaceable" (13,39). This interpretation is given to Ezra alone because "you have devoted your life to wisdom, and called understanding your mother" (13,55). But even Ezra needs a dream vision and its interpretation if he is to obtain wisdom about what is to come.

The narrative about Ezra the scribe (14,1-48) relates a vision granted to Ezra that is reminiscent of Moses' experience at the burning bush in Exodus 3–4. Reference is made to Moses having received revelations about "the secrets of the times" (14,5). Ezra asks God to "send the holy spirit" into him and volunteers to "write everything that has happened in the world from the beginning" (14,22). The result is that Ezra and his team of scribes are illumined by "the lamp of understanding" (14,25), and so they produce two sets of books: the twenty-four books of the Hebrew Bible which are to be made public, and the seventy books that are to be given only to "the wise". The so-called apocryphal books are said to contain "the spirit of understanding, the fountain of wisdom, and the river of knowledge" (14,47). The emphasis on divine inspiration and on hidden wisdom accessible only to "the wise" through revelation fits well with the basic theme of 4 Ezra that real wisdom belongs to God and humans gain access to it only through divine revelation.

4QINSTRUCTION AND 4 EZRA COMPARED

4QInstruction and 4 Ezra have some points in common. Both are early Jewish writings that were composed in Hebrew in the Land of Israel. Both texts are especially concerned with knowledge, and join together wisdom and apocalyptic in their own fashions. Both texts have come down to us by circuitous routes. We have 4QInstruction in a very fragmentary state and only by chance discovery after almost two-thousand years of oblivion. We have 4 Ezra in Latin and other languages through a complicated process of transmission in which the Hebrew original and most of the Greek version have been lost. The two works are very different, however, in their settings in life, approaches to wisdom and apocalyptic, and ways of combining wisdom and apocalyptic.

Settings in Life

The precise life-setting of 4QInstruction remains elusive, beyond the basic certainties about its composition in Hebrew presumably in the Land of Israel and in or before the first century B.C. The surviving fragments give us no clue about the precise situation in which the work was composed. Indeed, part of the convention of sapiential literature is to project a certain antiquity and even timelessness (as in Proverbs, Ecclesiastes, and Wisdom of Solomon). Moreover, the task of assigning a life-setting to 4QInstruction is further complicated by the problems associated with determining the character and history of the movement that gave us the Qumran library. By contrast, the life-setting of 4 Ezra – in apocalyptic circles in the Palestinian Jewish community after the destruction of the Second Temple in A.D. 70 – seems to be quite clear.

Approaches to Wisdom and Apocalyptic

The understanding of wisdom in 4QInstruction is to a large extent traditional in form and content. A senior sage imparts instructions to a neophyte ("O understanding one") about financial matters, social relations, and family life. But besides the usual appeals to common sense or self-interest and even to Scripture, there are many instances in which theological (statements about God) and eschatological (statements about the last judgment) motivations are attached to individual wisdom instructions. Moreover, what seems to have been the preface to the work and several other passages serve to place all the instructions in an apocalyptic context or framework.

By contrast, 4 Ezra is a classic apocalypse, a true descendant of the book of Daniel and a sibling of 2 Baruch. It shows little or no interest in the customary concerns of traditional Jewish wisdom literature. One gets the impression that the great crisis of A.D. 70 has rendered them otiose. The author of 4 Ezra is concerned with bigger theological questions about God's activity or lack of it, God's promises to Israel, suffering, life after death, and so forth. He insists that such questions cannot be fully answered by human reason or even by Scripture. What answers may be possible will become clear in the future when Israel's oppressors are defeated by the Lion (the Messiah) who is also the Man from the Sea ("my Son"). The enlightenment that Ezra receives in the present in response to his questions must come from Uriel the angelic interpreter or from God himself. Some of the most important information comes in the dream visions and their detailed interpretations. According to 4 Ezra human wisdom has virtually disappeared, and real knowledge is possible only through revelation or apocalyptic.

Their Ways of Combining Wisdom and Apocalyptic

The two works combine wisdom and apocalyptic in different ways. While 4QInstruction gives ample space to apocalyptic elements, this work remains a wisdom instruction with apocalyptic features. And at times the combination seems artificial or awkward. And while 4 Ezra uses some of the rhetorical techniques of wisdom literature (parables, riddles, etc.), it is clearly an apocalypse in both form and content and tends to ignore the traditional concerns of wisdom literature in favor of revelation. The fundamental difference is that 4QInstruction presents wisdom in an apocalyptic framework, whereas 4 Ezra presents apocalyptic or revealed wisdom.

Weston Jesuit School of Theology — Daniel J. HARRINGTON
3, Phillips Place
Cambridge, MA 02138
U.S.A.

DIE MESSIASERWARTUNG IN DEN HANDSCHRIFTEN VON QUMRAN

Am 7. Juli 2002 um 20.14 Uhr verbreitete das Israelische Außenministerium über seinen Mailer die Meldung „Water Stain on Western Wall Leads Some to Believe Redemption Near“ und „Some Jewish mystics believe it is a sign 'the wall is crying', signalising the coming of the Messiah“. Nach meinen langen Studien zum Thema „Messianismus“ verwundert es mich nicht, dass gläubige Juden gerade in diesen schweren Zeiten in Israel und Palästina ihre gegenwärtige Zeit als Endzeit interpretieren und folgerichtig die baldige Ankunft eines messianischen Erlösers erwarten. Hier können wir wieder einmal – wie so oft in der Antike – die historische Realisierung einer messianischen Idee im Judentum lokalisieren, aber nicht die Idee selbst[1].

Angesichts dieser aktuellen Problematik möchte ich wie folgt argumentieren: Ich gehe davon aus, dass die Erwartung einer eschatologischen Erlösergestalt allen großen Religionen vorgegeben ist. Die Messiaserwartung ist ein Signal für die Interpretation der Gegenwart als Endzeit, wie umgekehrt diese Interpretation Messiaserwartung generiert. Die Konturen der erwarteten Erlösergestalt, damit die Erlösergestalt selbst werden von der Erwartungsgemeinde (auch in Qumran) in der Regel als Kontrastbild zur jeweils real erlebten Gegenwart und ihrer Systeme entworfen. Die Traditionen spielen dabei eine verhältnismäßig geringe Rolle, insofern sie lediglich die „Idee“, d.h. Begriff und Bildmaterial liefern.

Meine These lautet: Trotz der Zeitgebundenheit der Messiaserwartung vermute ich eine Diachronie in ihrer Entwicklung, die bereits in der Vorgeschichte beginnt und in der Geschichte der Qumran-Bewegung folgerichtig fortentwickelt worden ist.

1. Die Fragestellung

Meines Wissens hat bereits 1963 Jean Starcky[2] zum ersten Mal in einem Aufsatz die Vermutung ausgesprochen, dass die Messiaserwartung

1. Zu dieser These vgl. G.S. Oegema, *Der Gesalbte und sein Volk. Untersuchungen zum Konzeptualisierungsprozeß der messianischen Erwartungen von den Makkabäern bis Bar Koziba* (Schriften des Institutum Judaicum Delitzschianum, 2), Göttingen, 1994, S. 305.

2. J. Starcky, *Les quatre étapes du messianisme à Qumrân*, in *RB* 70 (1963) 481-505.

in Qumran nicht aus dem unvermittelten synchronen Nebeneinander unterschiedlicher Vorstellungen besteht, sondern möglicherweise auf einer Diachronie basiert.

J.H. Charlesworth (1992) hat in vielen Stellungnahmen zum Messiasproblem bis in die jüngste Zeit hinein in etwa die Gegenposition zu Starcky bezogen, wenn er die Meinung vertritt, in der Messianologie sei von der Natur der Sache her keine Kohärenz möglich – weder in den Pseudepigraphen noch in Qumran – „the frequently contradictory messianic predictions prohibit anything approximating coherency in early Jewish messianology“[3].

F. García Martínez (1993) verzichtet in seiner ausführlichen Gesamtdarstellung bewusst auf eine Synthese, da er eine Diachronie der Belege im Sinne Starcky's nicht mehr für möglich hält.

Auch G.S Oegema (1994/98) resumiert, dass es weder eine „messianische Idee“ gegeben habe, noch von einem ideengeschichtlichen Verlauf der messianischen Erwartungen gesprochen werden könne; die jeweiligen Messias-Vorstellungen entwickelten sich vielmehr in direkter Auseinandersetzung mit den jeweiligen historischen Gegebenheiten.

1995 schrieb J.J. Collins in seinem Aufsatz zum Messianismus in Qumran: „I do not wish to deny the possibility of development during the life of the Qumran community, but I submit that in the matter of messianism the evidence does not permit us to trace it with any confidence“[4].

H. Stegemann hat 1996 in der Milik-Festschrift[5] die Frage einer Entwicklung in der Messiaserwartung wieder aufgenommen, die er anhand der schwierigen redaktionsgeschichtlichen Probleme von 1QS, 1QSa und 1QSb glaubt beantworten zu können. Dabei beobachtet er drei Stadien der Entwicklung, in denen sich Schritt für Schritt die qumranische Messiaserwartung artikulierte, um aktuelle Defizite zu kompensieren: Vor 150 v. Chr. findet er im Danielbuch, in der Grundschicht von 1QM (XI 6f.) und in 4Q491 als erste Form der Messiaserwartung eine kollektive Erwartung. Zwischen 150 und 110 v. Chr. habe sich – so aus 1QSa/1QSb zu ersehen – die Erwartung eines königlichen Messias herausgebildet, die möglicherweise von den Essenern selbst entwickelt worden sei als Antwort auf den nicht davidischen Makkabäer Jonathan und spä-

3. J.H. CHARLESWORTH, *From Messianology to Christology. Problems and Prospects*, in DERS. (Hg.), *The Messiah*, Minneapolis, MN, 1992, bes. S. 28.

4. J.J. COLLINS, *"He Shall not Judge by What his Eyes See". Messianic Authority in the Dead Sea Scrolls*, in *DSD* 2 (1995) 145-164, bes. S. 160.

5. H. STEGEMANN, *Some Remarks to 1QSa, to 1QSb, and to Qumran Messianism*, in F. GARCÍA MARTÍNEZ – É. PUECH (Hgg.), *Hommage à Józef T. Milik*, in *RQ* 17 (1996) 479-505, bes. S. 501-505.

ter auch in PsSal 17 zum Ausdruck gebracht werde. Die dritte Stufe schließlich artikulierte sich um 100 v. Chr. nach dem Tod des Lehrers der Gerechtigkeit in der Einfügung von 1QS VIII 15b-IX 11, in 4Q175 und in CD, wo mehrere messianische Gestalten nebeneinander genannt werden, wobei dem erwarteten messianischen Propheten insofern eine gewisse Sonderrolle zukommt, als seine Erwartung bereits in 1Makk 4 und 14 ausgesprochen wird und in Qumran nach dem Tod des Lehrers neue Aktualität gewann. In der Tat erscheint es sinnvoll, das Aufkommen bestimmter messianischer Erwartungen in Qumran im Zusammenhang mit dem Tod des Lehrers der Gerechtigkeit zu sehen[6].

Und schließlich hat Michael A. Knibb 1999 in seinem Aufsatz *Eschatology and Messianism in the Dead Sea Scrolls*[7] das Problem einer Chronologie in der Entwicklung dieser Erwartungen diskutiert. Den Ansatz von Stegemann nahm er zwar auf, versuchte aber die Eindeutigkeit Stegemanns wieder in eine Mehrdeutigkeit zurückzuführen, was wahrscheinlich dem schwierigen Charakter mancher Qumrantexte besser entspricht. Seine Zurückweisung einer kollektiv-messianischen Deutung von 4Q246 überzeugt mich jedoch nicht, da eine individuelle Deutung in jedem Fall dem Wortlaut des Textes widerspricht. Auch die Zurückweisung von Recht sprechenden und ausübenden Kollektiva als unzureichende Parallelen zum „Volk Gottes" erscheint mir übervorsichtig. Für Knibb ist jedenfalls klar, dass qumranische Messiaserwartungen vor 100 v. Chr. mehrdeutig, ab 100 v. Chr. jedoch deutlich auf einen kommenden Propheten und auf die Messiasse aus Israel und Aaron gerichtet waren. „No doubt messianic views at Qumran did change over time, but it may be wondered whether we will ever be in a position to reconstruct the evolution of these views in a series of stages in the way that Starcky felt able to do"[8].

Damit ist das Problem wieder offen bei gleichem Quellenmaterial. Scheinbar ohne Unterschiede sprechen die einen Qumrantexte von einem eschatologischen Priester (4Q541), andere vom davidischen Messias (4Q174), wieder andere erwarten offensichtlich einen doppelten Messias (4Q252). Wo fängt eigentlich was an? Wo liegen die eigentlichen Wurzeln für dieses Durcheinander, Nebeneinander oder vielleicht sogar Nacheinander? In der Tat spricht auch außerhalb von Qumran die Zeit-

6. So auch É. PUECH, *Messianism, Resurrection, and Eschatology*, in E. ULRICH – J.C. VANDERKAM (Hgg.), *Community of the Renewed Covenant: The Notre Dame Symposium on the Dead Sea Scrolls* (CJA, 10), Notre Dame, IN, 1994, S. 235-256, bes. S. 247.

7. In P.W. FLINT – J.C. VANDERKAM (Hgg.), *The Dead Sea Scrolls After Fifty Years II*, Leiden, 1999, S. 379-402.

8. M. KNIBB, *Eschatology* (n. 7), S. 400.

gebundenheit der unterschiedlichen Messiaserwartungen gegen eine Diachronie. Nach der neueren Judaistik (vgl. Jacob Neusner[9]) gab es sogar im Judentum nie eine zusammenhängende Messianologie, sondern je unterschiedliche Reaktionen auf unterschiedliche historische und gesellschaftliche Konstellationen, wobei die Erwartung eines Messias eine von mehreren Reaktionen war. Die Erwartungen divergierten (4Esra 11-12), konnten aber auch synthetisch zusammengeführt werden (äthHen 37-71). Offensichtlich haben wir auch in den Handschriften von Qumran ganz disparate Messiasvorstellungen und -erwartungen vor uns. Entsprechend der Vorgabe Neusners möchte ich darin also Reaktionen der Gemeinschaft oder verschiedener Gemeinschaften auf je verschiedene historische und gesellschaftliche Konstellationen sehen.

Meine eigene Feststellung: „Letztendlich bleibt der Versuch einer Rekonstruktion der Diachronie der Messiaserwartungen unbefriedigend“[10] soll mich nicht daran hindern, hier erneut nach einer Diachronie zu fragen. Dank der fortgeschrittenen Forschung (z.B. A. Lange) wird die Datierung der Texte aus Qumran immer präziser, so dass sich eine vermutete Diachronie genauer darstellen lässt.

2. Überblick über die Forschungsgeschichte

Die Literatur zum Thema „Messianismus“ ist inzwischen nicht mehr zu überblicken. Gerade die Handschriften von Qumran haben einen Boom ausgelöst, der jetzt schon seit mehr als einem Jahrzehnt unvermindert anhält.

Das grundlegende Werk zum Messianismus in Qumran wurde bereits 1957 geschaffen von A.S. van der Woude[11]. Seinen Gedanken und Anstößen haben wir es zu verdanken, dass wir uns auch heute wieder mit dem Thema „Messias“ beschäftigen.

F. García Martínez[12] griff 1993 diese Anstöße auf und bietet seitdem die klassische Darstellung der Belege aus den Handschriften von Qumran. Er nahm die klassische Einteilung vor in 1.) Texte, die nur eine einzige messianische Gestalt kennen (davidischer und priesterlicher

9. Vgl. J. Neusner – W. Scott Green – E.S. Frerichs (Hgg.), *Judaisms and Their Messiahs at the Turn of the Christian Era*, Cambridge-New York, 1987.

10. H.-J. Fabry – K. Scholtissek, *Der Messias. Perspektiven des Alten und Neuen Testamentes* (NEB-Themen, 5), Würzburg, 2002, S. 37.

11. A.S. van der Woude, *Die messianischen Vorstellungen der Gemeinde von Qumran*, Assen, 1957.

12. F. García Martínez, *Messianische Erwartungen in den Qumrantexten*, in *JBTh* 8 (1993) 171-208.

Messianismus; neu ist dabei die Kategorie des „himmlischen Messias", die er in 4Q246 – „einen endzeitlichen Befreier himmlischer Natur"[13] – vorfinden will). Es folgen 2.) Texte mit mehreren messianischen Gestalten („Messiasse Aarons und Israels"; „Fürst der Gemeinde" und „Ausleger der Tora", der „himmlische Messias" und der „endzeitliche Prophet"; und schließlich 3.) Texte mit drei Messiassen.

G.S. Oegema[14] deutete in seinen Werken den „Messias" als eine priesterliche, königliche oder andere Figur, die eine befreiende Rolle in der Endzeit spielt. Bei seiner Analyse der messianischen Erwartungen der ausgehenden alttestamentlichen Zeit stellte er die auch für mich entscheidende These auf, dass die Messias-Konzeptionen *„meistens"*[15] in einer Kontrast-Analogie zu den „negativen" Vorbildern der politisch-religiösen Machtverhältnisse stehen. Was aber ist zu tun, wenn in unterschiedlichen Situationen einander ähnliche, in gleichen Situationen z.T. gegensätzliche Messiasvorstellungen generiert werden? Ist tatsächlich jede messianische Konzeption geschichtlich bedingt, oder im Sinne von Oegema: *nur* geschichtlich bedingt? Trotzdem scheint mir die These im Prinzip zutreffend zu sein, aber von Oegema wird noch nicht ausreichend erfasst, was denn zu diesen die messianischen Erwartungen generierenden „historischen Gegebenheiten" zählt. Gehören dazu nicht auch dominierende Auslegungen bestimmter theologischer Inhalte, z.B. die Rolle von Sünde und Buße[16]?

James C. VanderKam veröffentlichte das Heft 2/1995 der *Dead Sea Discoveries* zum Thema „Messianism" mit den bedeutenden Beiträgen von Martin G. Abegg[17], John J. Collins[18], Michael A. Knibb[19], Craig A. Evans[20] und Richard Bauckham[21].

13. *Ibid.*, S. 192.

14. G.S. OEGEMA, *Der Gesalbte* (Anm. 1); DERS., *The Annointed and His People. Messianic Expectations from the Maccabees to Bar Kochba* (JPS Suppl. Ser, 227), Sheffield, 1998; DERS. *Messianic Expectations in the Qumran Writings: Theses on their Development*, in J.H. CHARLESWORTH – H. LICHTENBERGER – G.S. OEGEMA, *Qumran Messianism. Studies on the Messianic Expectations in the Dead Sea Scrolls*, Tübingen, 1998, S. 53-82.

15. *Der Gesalbte* (Anm. 1), S. 102.

16. Vgl. die Rezension von B. EGO, in *ThR* 94 (1998) 164-167.

17. M.G. ABEGG, *The Messiah at Qumran: Are We Still Seeing Double?*, in *DSD* 2 (1995) 125-144.

18. J.J. COLLINS, *"He Shall not Judge by what his Eyes See"* (Anm. 5), S. 145-164.

19. M.A. KNIBB, *Messianism in the Pseudepigrapha in the Light of the Scrolls*, in *DSD* 2 (1995) 165-184.

20. C.A. EVANS, *A Note on the "First-Born Son" of 4Q369*, in *DSD* 2 (1995) 185-201.

21. R. BAUCKHAM, *The Messianic Interpretation of Isa. 10:34 in the Dead Sea Scrolls, 2 Baruch and the Preaching of John the Baptist*, in *DSD* 2 (1995) 202-216.

M.G. Abegg geht von den vier Belegen des „Messias aus Aaron und Israel" in CD XII 23-XIII 1; XIV 18-19; XIX 10-11 und XX 1 aus und fragt nach der Möglichkeit eines doppelten Messias, wie sie dann in 1QS IX 9-11 explizit vorliege. Aus der Geschehensabfolge beim eschatologischen Gemeinschaftsmahl (1QSa II) erschließt er, dass es sich im Grunde um die Erwartung eines messianischen Königs handelt, dem ein gesalbter priesterlicher Begleiter beigegeben ist. Hier aber muß er sich fragen lassen, wie er dann die stereotype Aufzählung „Messias aus Aaron und Israel" mit der deutlichen *Vorordnung* der priesterlichen Gestalt interpretieren will.

J.J. Collins versteht den Messias[22] als einen „göttlichen Agenten in der Endzeit", derer er aber in Qumran drei vorfindet: den königlich-davidischen Messias aus Israel, den priesterlich-aaronidischen Messias = den „Interpreten der Tora" und schließlich einen prophetischen Messias. Für ihn ist die Annahme einer Mehrzahl messianischer Figuren in Qumran nicht zu leugnen, auch wenn der entscheidende Beleg in 1QS IX möglicherweise eine sekundäre Überarbeitung darstelle. Obwohl die kanonischen Texte des AT genügend Hinweise enthalten, entstand die Messiaserwartung recht spät im Nachgang zum Aufstieg der Hasmonäer, die bekanntlich ihre Monarchie nicht auf David zurückführen konnten. In diese Zeit datiert der älteste Beleg (aus Pharisäerkreisen?) aus PsSal 17f. Alexander Jannai hatte sich als erster auf Münzen als König bezeichnet. Aber bereits seit Simon Makkabäus hatten die Hasmonäer das Hohepriestertum mit der staatlichen Regentschaft verbunden, ein Zustand, der leicht die Forderung nach einer Trennung der Funktionen auf zwei Messiasse generieren konnte. Nun standen die Qumraner aber den Hasmonäern zumindest zeitweise positiv gegenüber, wenn man 4Q448 mit Collins als vorsichtige Parteinahme für den „Pharisäerschlächter" Alexander Jannai[23] deuten kann[24]. Daneben konnte selbstverständlich eine messianische Erwartung artikuliert werden, die sich auf eine Restauration der davidischen und der aaronidischen (zadokidischen) Traditionslinie richtete, von denen doch keine einzige von den Hasmonäern nachgewiesen werden konnte. Auch hatte man möglicherweise schon ein bestimmtes Datum vor Augen: der Text

22. Dazu vgl. J.J. COLLINS, *Messiahs in Context. Method in the Study of Messianism*, in M.O. WISE – N. GOLB – J.J. COLLINS – D. PARDEE (Hgg.), *Methods of Investigation of the Dead Sea Scrolls and the Khirbet Qumran Site: Present Realities and Future Prospects*, New York, Academy of Sciences, 1994, S. 213-227 und DERS., *The Scepter and the Star. Messianism in Light of the Dead Sea Scrolls*, New York, 1995.

23. JOSEPHUS FLAVIUS, *Antiquitates XIII*, 327-383.

24. Man beachte aber auch die häufig vorgetragene Deutung auf den Makkabäer Jonathan!

4Q175(4QTest) enthält neben seinen messianischen alttestamentlichen Bezügen zum Abschluß völlig unmessianisch den Fluch über den Wiedererbauer von Jericho (Jos 6,26), was sich im Tod des Johannes Hyrkan und seiner Söhne Antigonus und Aristobul I. (103 v. Chr.) realisiert habe. Ob damit der Weg für die messianischen Gestalten frei war?

Collins entnimmt nun aus der Tempelrolle die Zeichnung des idealen Königs, die ebenfalls dem Hohenpriester eine starke Weisungsbefugnis gegenüber dem König zuspricht (TR LVI 12-LIX 21). Davon ausgehend deutet er – zu meiner Überraschung – den aramäischen „Sohn-Gottes-Text" (4Q246) als einen Text, der sich (wegen Anklänge an 2Sam 7 und Ps 2) auf den davidischen Messias beziehe. Das halte ich für völlig ausgeschlossen. Hier geschieht dann aber eine entscheidende Weichenstellung für den Blick auf die qumranische Messianologie.

Nun ist seit der Veröffentlichung von 1QS der priesterliche Messias, der „Messias aus Aaron" literarisch offenkundig. Aber ist neben der übermächtigen Person eines davidischen Messias solches überhaupt denkbar? In 1QSa, 1QSb, 1QM; 4Q161; 4Q285 u.ö. ist die priesterliche Gestalt so übermächtig, dass eine „bifurcation of authority in the messianic era"[25] angezeigt ist. Talmon[26] und auch Fabry haben mehrfach darauf hingewiesen, dass solches nur mit den politischen Idealen der damaligen Zeit zusammengesehen werden kann, bes. in der Rezeptionsgeschichte von Sach 4,14. Aber auch die geringe Rezeption dieses Textes – wohl nur in 4Q252 – ist als Reaktion auf die Hasmonäer zu sehen. Der priesterliche Messias sollte für die Sünden des Volkes sühnen (CD XIV 19), vor allem aber war er ein Lehrer (4QTest)[27]. Für Collins ist – wie für G.J. Brooke – klar, dass damit die historische Gestalt des „Lehrers der Gerechtigkeit" und die des endzeitlichen „Interpreten der Tora" in den Blick kommt. Die Gemeinschaft denkt sich den definitiven, eschatologischen Hohenpriester im Bild des historischen Lehrers. Das heißt aber auch ganz eindeutig, dass für ihn der priesterliche Messias die dominierende Gestalt der Endzeit ist.

M.A. Knibb befasste sich mit dem Messianismus in pseudepigraphischen Schriften, allen voran mit PsSal 17f., wo explizit ein davidischer Messias erwartet wird. In diesem Sinne deutet er auch 4Q246, der eine auf einen davidischen Messias zu beziehende Terminologie enthält.

25. J.J. COLLINS, *"He Shall not Judge by what his Eyes See"* (Anm. 5), S. 157.

26. S. TALMON, *Waiting for the Messiah at Qumran*, in *Judaisms and Their Messiahs* (Anm. 9), S. 290ff.

27. Zur lehrenden Aufgabe der Priester in Qumran vgl. noch 1QSb III 23f.; IV 27f.; 4Q541.

Antti Laato legte 1997 mit seinem Buch *A Star is Rising*[28] sicher keine umfassende Messianologie vor und hat sich durch eigenartige methodische Ansichten nicht viele Freunde gemacht. Man wird seiner These, dass die Hoffnung auf einen davidischen Messias nicht erst in hasmonäischer Zeit oder im Exil geboren worden sei, sondern bereits die gesamte Geschichte Israels durchziehe, nicht mehr ernsthaft diskutieren wollen. Seine Arbeit hat aber gezeigt, dass es nötig ist, dass die Messianologie sich wieder mehr mit der alttestamentlichen Königsideologie – und ich würde hinzufügen: auch mehr mit dem alttestamentlichen Königsrecht – auseinandersetzen muß, um der Messianologie auch der rabbinischen Zeit, die ja grundsätzlich den nicht-biblischen Terminus „der König Messias" (*hammælæk hammašîaḥ*)[29] verwendet und damit eine eigene Vorstellung signalisiert, gerecht zu werden.

Im Jahr 1998 erschien die Publikation von J.H. Charlesworth - H. Lichtenberger - G.S. Oegema (Hgg.), *Qumran-Messianism. Studies on the Messianic Expectations in the Dead Sea Scrolls*, Tübingen, 1998, mit Beiträgen u.a. von den Herausgebern, von J.J. Collins, F. Dexinger, M.G. Abegg, C.A. Evans und J. Zimmermann aus den SNTS-Seminaren der Jahre 1995 und 1996. Dem hervorragenden Querschnitt durch die gegenwärtige Forschung ist ein Verzeichnis aller Belege der Begriffe, die man für messianisch hält („messianic passages")[30], beigegeben. Aber der Weg über die Terminologie scheint mir nur so lange gangbar, so lange noch keine sichere Kriteriologie messianischer Texte vorliegt.

Johannes Zimmermann[31] geht es in seiner Tübinger Dissertation[32] bei Hengel darum, ein breit angelegtes zeitgenössisches Messiasbewusstsein aufzuzeigen, das nach ihm in Qumran vorliege. Er sieht mit Collins im „Gesalbten Aarons und Israels" eine „bifurcation of authority in the messianic era", zieht in einem weiteren Kapitel die weiteren messianischen Titel „Fürst der ganzen Gemeinde", „Sproß Davids", „Sohn Gottes" und „der Erwählte" (4Q534) heran und deutet in diesem Zusammenhang den Text 4Q246 im Blick auf Lk 1,32 messianisch (!). Zimmermann untersucht die priesterlichen, dann die prophetischen Messiasvorstellungen, in die er auch den qumranischen Melchisedek-Text

28. A. LAATO, *A Star Is Rising. The Historical Development of the Old Testament Royal Ideology and the Rise of the Jewish Messianic Expectations*, Atlanta, GA, 1997.

29. Mündlicher Hinweis von J. MAIER.

30. M.G. ABEGG – C.A. EVANS, *Messianic Passages in the Dead Sea Scrolls*, in *Qumran Messianism* (Anm. 14), S. 191-203.

31. J. ZIMMERMANN, *Messianische Texte aus Qumran. Königliche, priesterliche und prophetische Messiasvorstellungen in den Schriftfunden von Qumran* (WUNT, 2/104), Tübingen, 1998.

32. Vgl. meine ausführliche Besprechung in *OLZ* 95/6 (2000) 625-630.

(11QMelch) einordnet. In der Synthese beobachtet er die bekannte Dreiteilung der qumranischen Messianologie; er glaubt, eine Entwicklung der Messiaserwartungen beobachten zu können, deren einzelne Stufen er – so schon Schiffman – mit unterschiedlichen Gruppeninteressen verbinden möchte. Es gelingt Zimmermann nicht so recht, weder das synchrone noch das diachrone Verhältnis der drei Zweige der Messiaserwartung zueinander in Beziehung zu setzen. Trotzdem kann man seinen Beobachtungen zustimmen, in vorqumranischen Handschriften eine diffuse, in den Regelwerken des ausgehenden 2. Jh. v. Chr. eine doppelte, und in den Pesharim eine davidische Messiaserwartung vorzufinden.

Michael A. Knibb hat 1999 ein zweites Mal in die Diskussion eingegriffen. In seinem Aufsatz *Eschatology and Messianism in the Dead Sea Scrolls*[33] hat er als erstes eine Kriteriologie für eschatologisch-messianische Texte entwickelt. Danach stellt er die bekannten Grundmuster der Messiaserwartung in Qumran vor.

Craig A. Evans hat im Jahr 2000 in seinem Artikel *Messiahs*[34] eine ausgezeichnete Zusammenstellung aller relevanten Termini und Belege vorgelegt. Dabei legt er sein Hauptgewicht auf die Sichtung der biblischen Wurzeln, die er in den Belegen Gen 49,10; Num 24,17 und Jes 11,1-6 (mehr nicht!) gegeben sieht. Er zeigt die vollständige Rezeptionsgeschichte dieser Belege bis hin zu den Targumen und zu den Kirchenvätern auf. Einem messianischen Proprium Qumrans erteilt er eine klare Absage, eine mögliche Diachronie diskutiert er nicht einmal.

Schließlich hat sich James H. Charlesworth im Jahr 2001 noch einmal zum Messianismus in Qumran geäußert in einem umfangreichen Beitrag für *Histoire du Christianisme*[35].

3. Terminologie

Es ist Konsens, dass man die Messianologie des Alten Testamentes und Qumrans über die Terminologie kaum adäquat erfassen kann, denn *mašîaḥ* o.ä. beziehen sich nach Johann Maier[36] fast ausschließlich auf unmessianische, gesalbte Menschen (König, Priester, Propheten). Jeder messianische Bezug muß eigens nachgewiesen werden. Den alttestamentlichen Vorstellungen – so disparat sie sein mögen – eignet ein ex-

33. S.a. Anm. 7.

34. *EDDS* I, Oxford, 2000, S. 537-542.

35. J.H. Charlesworth, *Les Grandes Croyances des Juifs II, Le Messianisme*, in F. Laplanche (Hg.), *Anamnèsis* (Histoire du Christianisme), Paris, 2001, S. 485-551.

36. J. Maier, *Messias oder Gesalbter? Zu einem Übersetzungs- und Deutungsproblem in den Qumrantexten*, in *Hommage à Józef T. Milik* (Anm. 5), S. 585-612.

klusives Verhältnis des Gesalbten zu JHWH. Diese privilegierte Gottesbeziehung wurde zum Paradigma für die Konzeption des Typos eines von Gott auserwählten Menschen und zum Inbegriff des Menschseins überhaupt bis hin zur Konzeption der Vorstellung von der Gottebenbildlichkeit. Ein absoluter determinierter Gebrauch, etwa *hammašîaḥ*, ist im AT nicht belegt. Der früheste Beleg begegnet erst in Qumran (1QSa II 12). Sicher wird *mašîaḥ* / χριστός erst in den Psalmen Salomos und im Neuen Testament Bezeichnung für den „Messias".

Die Bezeichnung „Menschensohn"[37] fungierte in apokalyptischen Zusammenhängen als *terminus technicus*, wurde bereits in vorchristlicher Zeit als Titel gebraucht und hatte von Hause aus nichts mit Messiasvorstellungen zu tun. Nach Dan 7 wird der Menschensohn von Gott mit der Weltherrschaft betraut und scheint damit eine Transformation der davidischen Messiasvorstellung darzustellen[38]. Fraglich ist eine Identifizierung des „Menschensohnes" von Dan 7 mit dem „Sohn Gottes" des nahezu zeitgleich entstandenen apokalyptischen Flugblattes 4Q246.

Der Titel „Sohn Gottes" ist seit Ps 2,7; 2 Sam 7,14 eine Bezeichnung für den König. Die Sohn-Terminologie begegnet in Qumran 7mal[39], wobei messianische Konnotationen jedoch umstritten sind. Häufig wird die Bezeichnung „Sohn Gottes ... Sohn des Höchsten" in 4Q246 II 1 mit der Gestalt des „Menschensohnes" von Dan 7,13 verbunden und auf einen Repräsentanten des Volkes Gottes und messianischen Heilsbringer hin gedeutet. Nach dieser Vorstellung übe dann der „Menschensohn" vom himmlischen Bereich her die Herrschaft und das Gericht aus, während der „Sohn Gottes" die Gottesherrschaft gegen alle chaotischen Mächte auf der Erde durchsetzt.

Als messianischer Titel begegnet „Sohn Davids" in vorchristlicher Zeit wohl nur in PsSal 17,21, später dann auch in den jüdischen Überlieferungen. Qumran kennt diesen Titel nicht und spricht stattdessen vom „Spross Davids"[40], der vielleicht auf Jer 23,5; 33,15 zurückgeht. Die seltene Verwendung des Titels ist damit zu begründen, dass die David-

37. In der Septuaginta kann auch ἄνθρωπος „Mensch" im messianischen Sinne verstanden werden (z.B. in Ps 87[86],5, wo die Aussage des MT „Jeder Mann ist dort [sc. am Zion] geboren" messianisch umgedeutet wird zur Aussage, dass „ein Mensch vom Zion hervorgehen wird"); dazu vgl. J. SCHAPER, *Der Septuaginta-Psalter als Dokument jüdischer Eschatologie*, in M. HENGEL – A.M. SCHWEMER (Hgg.), *Die Septuaginta zwischen Judentum und Christentum* (WUNT, 72), Tübingen, 1994, S. 38-61, bes. S. 52f.

38. H. GESE, *Der Messias*, in DERS., *Zur biblischen Theologie. Alttestamentliche Vorträge* (BEvTh, 78), München, 1977, S. 128-151, bes. S. 140.

39. Z.B. 4Q174 1-3 I 11; 4Q246 II 1; 4Q254 4,2; 4Q369 1 II 6.

40. 4Q161, 7-10 III 22; 4Q174 III 11; 4Q252 (PatrBless) V 3f.; 4Q285, 5,3f; Offb 5,5.

sohnschaft politische Züge trägt. Er wurde erst im Rahmen der messianischen Deutung der sonstigen Titel auf den Messias übertragen und damit Signum der davidischen Erwählung und Heilsverheißungen, zugleich Betonung seiner Innerweltlichkeit und Innerzeitlichkeit, im NT auch Betonung seiner Menschlichkeit und Niedrigkeit.

Der „Erstgeborene" (4Q369 1 II 6) ist wegen des fragmentarischen Kontextes nicht eindeutig als messianische Größe zu bestimmen.

„Stern und Szepter" aus Num 24,17 werden fast durchgehend[41] auf den Messias bezogen. Die Identifikation des „Stern" mit dem *dôreš hattôrah* in CD VII 18 hat dann auch diese zentrale Gestalt der qumranischen Ekklesiologie messianisch konnotiert.

4. Die qumranischen Messiaserwartungen in ihrem Umfeld

Es besteht Konsens darüber, dass die Handschriften von Qumran Einblick in Traditionen gewähren, die im AT „angedacht" worden sind, aber erst in nach-alttestamentlicher Zeit zur Entfaltung gelangten. Dies trifft auch für die messianischen Erwartungen zu. Der allenthalben notierte „pluralism of ideas"[42] der qumranischen Messias-Vorstellungen und -erwartungen ist bisher zwar immer beschrieben, aber noch nicht überzeugend erklärt worden. In der synchronen Sicht erscheinen sie jedenfalls als völlig uneinheitlich. Die messianologischen Differenzen werden in der Regel erklärt als Reaktionen auf bestimmte Zeiterscheinungen, als Produkte unterschiedlicher Trägergruppen oder gruppen-interner Fluktuationen[43] und schließlich auch noch aus der unterschiedlichen Interpretation biblischer Vorgaben. In dieser Hinsicht scheint es zuzutreffen, „that the messianism of the Dead Sea Scrolls coheres with what can be ascertained from other Jewish sources from this period" und „it would appear that in most of the major points Qumran messianism is not much different from that of other pious, hopeful Jews"[44]. Aber trotzdem greift diese Ansicht von C.A. Evans entschieden zu kurz.

Gehen wir von der heuristischen Vermutung aus, dass Krisenzeiten Messiaserwartungen produzieren, dann kämen in etwa folgende Zeiträume mit ihren historischen Ereignisfeldern in Frage:

– die Auseinandersetzung mit dem Hellenismus nach Alexander;
– der Kulturkampf unter Antiochus IV. und dem Hohenpriester Menelaos;

41. CD VII 20; 1QSb V 27-28; 1QM XI 4-9; 4Q175, 1,9-13.

42. Vgl. L. Schiffman, *Messianic Figures and Ideas in the Qumran Scrolls*, in *The Messiah* (Anm. 3), S. 116-129.

43. G. Stemberger, in *TRE* 22 (1992), S. 622-630, bes. S. 623.

44. C.A. Evans, *Messiahs*, in *EDSS* I (2000), S. 537-542, bes. S. 539.

– der Makkabäeraufstand und die anschließende makkabäisch-hasmonäische Restauration;
– die antisadduzäischen Wirren unter Johannes Hyrkan;
– die Tyrannei des Alexander Jannai;
– der Bürgerkrieg zwischen Hyrkan II. und Aristobul;
– die Eroberung Jerusalems durch Pompejus (63 v. Chr.).

Da die Gemeinschaft von Qumran den Termin für die Äonenwende 100 Jahre nach der Ermordung des Hohenpriesters Onias III. (170 v. Chr.) ansetzte, dürfte ihre Messiaserwartung spätestens mit dem Einmarsch der Römer ihren Höhepunkt (und Abschluß?) erreicht haben, was nicht ausschließt, dass es auch vorher schon zu Hochspannungen kommen konnte.

4.1. Die Messiaserwartungen in der voressenischen Zeit

Die Erwartung eines priesterlichen Messias setzt in der voressenischen Zeit ein und ist angeregt durch die Leuchtervision Sach 4. Die beiden Moses-Apokryphen 4Q375 und 4Q376 aus vielleicht persischer Zeit[45] gehören zu Pseudo-Moses-Texten[46], hinter denen eine spätdtr Priestergruppe steht, die priesterliche Sondertraditionen bewahrt hat. Der „gesalbte Priester, über dessen Haupt das Öl der Salbung ausgegossen wurde" (4Q375 1 I 9; vgl. 4Q376 1,1)[47], scheint in der Zeit der Bedrängnis die höchste Beurteilungskompetenz wahrer oder falscher Propheten zu haben; zugleich obliegt ihm die Einholung von Orakeln. Der historische Bezug beider Texte ist jedoch unklar.

Der voressenische Text 4Q541 (4QApocLevi^{b})[48] steht der Apokalyptik nahe und stellt den endzeitlichen Priester – den Terminus „Gesalbter" verwendet er nicht – in einen Zusammenhang von Sühne, Widerstand und Verfolgung. Die starke Formelhaftigkeit des Textes zeigt ihn als Relecture des Gottesknechtsliedes Jes 53. Aus der Retrospektive kann man den Text als Beispiel vorchristlicher messianischer (?) Interpretation von Jes 53[49] verstehen.

45. Vgl. M. BROSHI, in J. STRUGNELL, DJD, 19, Oxford, 1995, S. 130f.

46. Vgl. noch 1Q22; 1Q29.

47. Vgl. Lev 21,10.

48. Vgl. dazu G.J. BROOKE, *4QTestament of Levi^{d}(?) and the Messianic Servant High Priest*, in M.C. DE BOER (Hg.), *From Jesus to John. Essays on Jesus and New Testament Christology in Honour of Marinus de Jonge* (JSNT SS, 84), Sheffield, 1993, S. 83-100, bes. S. 95. Paläographisch ist die Handschrift als hasmonäisch zu datieren; vgl. M.E. STONE – J.C. GREENFIELD, *The Third and Fourth Manuscripts of Aramaic Levi Document from Qumran (4QLevi^{c} Aram and 4QLevi^{d} Aram)*, in *Le Muséon* 109 (1996) 245-259, bes. S. 251.

49. In der targumischen Auslegung wird der Gottesknecht als „König Messias" betitelt, der den Tempel aufbaut, die Vergebung der Sünden Israels erwirkt und ein Friedens-

Fazit: Es überrascht, dass die Erwartung eines *nur* priesterlichen Messias ausschließlich in Schriften der vorqumranischen Zeit formuliert wird. Die in der Qumrangemeinde selbst verfaßten Schriften vertreten diese Messianologie nicht.

4.2. Die Messiaserwartung in der essenischen – vorqumranischen Zeit

Seit dem ausgehenden 3. Jh. v. Chr. (Danielbuch) beherrschte die Vorstellung einer Weltkatastrophe die apokalyptischen Schriften. Sie entstand aus der szenischen Ausgestaltung des kosmischen Dualismus, der in äthHen 6ff.15ff. auf den Mythos vom Engelsturz zurückgeführt wurde. Spätestens in dieser Zeit werden die alttestamentlichen Ankündigungen von Rettergestalten aufgenommen und in die jeweilige Erwartungsszenerie hinein umgesetzt. Offensichtlich haben solche Erwartungen zuerst kollektive Konturen, die in spätalttestamentlichen Vorstellungen vom „Rest" und vom „Volk Gottes" ihre Wurzeln haben.

Kollektive Auslegungen alttestamentlicher Heilserwartungen sind ab dem ausgehenden 3. Jh. v. Chr. üblich, so auch die kollektive Deutung des Menschensohnes (Dan 7) im Nachgang zur kollektiven Deutung der Königspsalmen. Es gab also bereits in der vor- und frühessenischen Phase Erwartungen, die auf die Gemeinden selbst in ihrer Reinheit, Heiligkeit und Identität mit der Gottesgemeinschaft (der *'elîm*) als die eschatologische Heilsbringer-Gestalt zielten.

Eine historische Anbindung kann nur ganz vorsichtig vorgeschlagen werden: Das ausgehende 3. Jh. war geprägt vom 4. und 5. Syrisch-ägyptischen Krieg, vom kriegerischen Wechselspiel zwischen Seleukiden und Ptolemäern mit dem seleukidischen Sieg bei Raphia (217 v. Chr.) und den anschließenden proptolemäischen Aufwiegelungen unter Onias II. und Hyrkan gegen den Hohenpriester Simon und der Familie des Joseph[50]. Nach dem seleukidischen Sieg bei Banjas (200 v. Chr.) kam es sogar zu einem Exodus proptolemäischer jüdischer Gruppen. Nach Josephus, Ant XII, 145f. und CD I muß „im Zuge dieses Herrschaftswechsels in Jerusalem eine konservativ-zadokidische Linie mit strikten Reinheits- und Heiligkeitsauffassungen" zum Zuge gekommen sein[51].

Um 175 v. Chr. ist nach weitgehender Überzeugung der „Sohn-Gottes"-Text 4Q246 anzusetzen. Er steht dem Danielbuch nahe und stammt aus vorqumranischer Zeit. In einem (fiktiven?) Gespräch zwischen Daniel und dem König wird folgendes Szenarium entwickelt: Mächtige

reich errichten wird. Zum TgJes 53 vgl. J. ZIMMERMANN, *Messianische Texte aus Qumran* (Anm. 31), S. 270.

50. JOSEPHUS, *Ant XII*,186.224.228f.

51. Vgl. J. MAIER, *Die Qumran-Essener: Die Texte vom Toten Meer III* (UTB, 1916), München, 1996, S. 26.

Könige haben auf der Erde eine katastrophale Situation herbeigeführt, die von Kriegen und Nöten gekennzeichnet ist. Ein neuer König tritt auf, mit dem die anderen Könige Frieden schließen (müssen). „'Sohn des großen Herrn' nennt er sich ... 'Sohn Gottes' sagt man von ihm und 'Sohn des Allerhöchsten' wird er gerufen". Diese Titulatur entstammt gängiger Königsideologie. Impliziert sie aber auch eine messianische Identifikation[52] und wer ist gemeint? Da die Herrschaft dieses Königs zum Zertreten der Völker untereinander führen wird, „bis sich das Volk erhebt und alles vor dem Schwert ruht.... Sein Königtum ist ein ewiges Königtum, und alle seine Wege sind Wahrheit" (4Q246 II 4-9), kann er kaum der Messias sein, da die eigentliche messianische Periode erst auf diesen König folgen wird. Der als „Sohn Gottes" Titulierte ist demnach nicht der Messias, sondern ein eher königlicher Amtsträger, der sich selbst als Messias ausgeben möchte. Als „Sohn des großen Königs" (I 9) erinnert er an den Seleukiden Antiochus IV. Epiphanes. Dieser nutzte offensichtlich die Möglichkeiten der apokalyptischen Literatur[53] und bot sich selbst den Juden als messianischer König an[54]. Erst nach ihm wird das Volk Gottes als Heilsgestalt der abschließenden Epoche auftreten (vgl. Dan 7,13). Der Text bietet also trotz seiner Kürze eine gängige Form der Messiaserwartung und lehnt nicht sie ab, sondern den, der sie abgöttisch auf sich bezieht, und projiziert sie auf ein Kollektiv. Diese Kritik der Ansprüche des Seleukiden könnte zusammenhängen mit der Gestalt des erstmals (?) auftretenden „Anweisers der Tora" um 177 v. Chr. (390 + 20 Jahre nach der Zerstörung Jerusalems nach CD I 5-10), dem es natürlich darum gehen musste, das Selbstbewusstsein seiner Gemeinde aufzubauen.

52. Es wurde argumentiert, dass eine solche Bezeichnung niemals einem heidnischen Herrscher beigegeben wurde (vgl. jedoch Kyros), also eine israelitisch-jüdische Heilsbringer-Gestalt gemeint sein müsse, etwa Alexander Balas (150-145 v.Chr.) „Theopator" (bzw. *Deo Patre natus*), der in Aussicht genommene Thronfolger des regierenden Königs oder der Antichrist. Erwogen wurde auch eine messianische Identifikation mit dem Erzengel Michael, mit Melchisedek, einem endzeitlichen Befreier (ähnlich dem Menschensohn in Dan 7) oder schließlich explizit mit einem davidischen Messias. Die von J. ZIMMERMANN beobachtete textliche Nähe zu Lk 1,32 ist sicherlich auffällig, auch sein Vorschlag, die passivischen Verbformen als *passivum divinum* zu erklären und hier – wie in Ps 2 – eine göttliche Adoption des messianischen Königs vorzufinden, ist beachtlich, kann aber letztlich den zeitlichen Abstand von 4Q246 und Lk 1 (ca. 300 Jahre) nicht erklären.

53. Vgl. H.-J. FABRY, *Die frühjüdische Apokalyptik als Reaktion auf Fremdherrschaft. Zur Funktion von 4Q246*, in B. KOLLMANN – W. REINBOLD – A. STEUDEL (Hgg.), *Antikes Judentum und Frühes Christentum*. FS H. Stegemann (BZNW, 97), Berlin, 1999, S. 84-98.

54. Das ist das Phänomen der „Führer-Literatur". Der Versuch des Antiochus IV., sich als Messias anerkennen zu lassen, mußte schief gehen, da er als Seleukide weder eine davidische Abstammung hatte, noch über eine priesterliche Linie reüssieren konnte.

Auch in der weiteren Geschichte Qumrans sind solche kollektiven Deutungen vorzufinden, auch wenn sie kaum messianischen Charakter haben: So bezeichnet sich die Gemeinde als „Wunderrat" (aus Jes 9,5)[55] oder bezieht die Bezeichnung „Gesalbter" (Ps 2,2) auf das Volk Israel[56]. Diese Texte stimmen darin überein, dass das jeweilige „Ich" sich als zur himmlischen Engelsgemeinschaft zugehörig versteht, wobei jedoch eine individuelle (Lehrer, Weiser, Priester, Erzengel Michael) oder eine kollektive Deutung (Gemeinde) möglich ist.

Fazit: Es waren primär schwierige historische Ereignisse, die zur Ausbildung einer kollektiven Messianologie führten, in der sich die Gemeinde selbst als reines und heiliges Gottesvolk verstand, dem dann auch als entscheidendes Werkzeug Gottes in der Endzeit bald kriegerische Züge zukamen (1QM; 4Q491; 4Q471b; 4Q427)[57].

4.3. Die Messiaserwartung in der frühqumranischen Zeit

Noch in vorqumranischer Zeit wurde die kollektive Deutung von einer eher individuell geprägten Messiaserwartung überlagert, die priesterliche und königliche Funktionen voneinander trennte, um eine Gegenkonzeption zur Personalunion der Hasmonäer zu präsentieren. Aus der Leuchtervision des Sacharja (Sach 4,14) wurde eine doppelte Messiaserwartung mit einer Gleichgewichtung der Ämter und Funktionen der beiden Gesalbten entwickelt. Die Benennung „Gesalbte/Messiasse Aarons und Israels" (nur 1QS V 1–IX 26 [150-100 v. Chr.]) zeigt einerseits diese Doppelung eindeutig und kann sich dabei auch auf gute alttestamentliche Vorgaben berufen[58]. Zugleich impliziert sie aber eine Vorordnung des priesterlichen Gesalbten. Auch die Qumrangemeinde im engeren Sinne sah in der „Regel für die Versammlung Israels am Ende der Tage" eine Nachordnung des laikalen „Messias Israels" nach Oberpriester und Priester (Aaroniden) vor (1QSa II 11-22 [nach 150 v. Chr.]). Die Funktionslosigkeit beider Messiasse ist auffällig; es interessiert nur das Faktum ihres Kommens und ihrer Anwesenheit – in der Gemeinde von Qumran!

Eine zeitliche Fixierung solcher Aussagen will nicht so recht gelingen. Bedenkenswert erscheint mir ein zeitlicher Zusammenhang einer

55. 1QH III 9f.; vgl. CD VII 16f.
56. 4Q174 III 18f.
57. Vgl. J. ZIMMERMANN, *Messianische Texte aus Qumran* (Anm. 31), S. 285-311.
58. Vgl. die Zusammenstellung bei EVANS, *Messiahs* (Anm. 44), S. 539: Parallelisierung von Aaron und Israel in Ex 16,9; 18,12; 34,30; Lev 17,2; 21,24; 22,18; Num 13,26; Ps 114,12; 135,19; vgl. vor allem die gleichzeitige Salbung von Salomo und Zadok 1Chr 19,22.

solchen doppelten Messiaserwartung als Reaktion auf den Träger der makkabäischen Revolte Judas, mit dem das tora-treue Volk große Hoffnungen verband. Nach einer merkwürdigen Notiz bei Josephus[59] hatte Judas vor seinem Tod (162 v. Chr.) noch drei Jahre das Amt des Hohenpriesters (gegen Alkimus) inne. Möglicherweise hatte diese Doppelfunktion – die aber letztlich nicht sonderlich effektiv war – eine entsprechende messianische Erwartung generiert.

Diese „bifurcation of authority in the messianic era“[60] blieb in der Folgezeit[61] noch weiter als messianisches Modell erhalten. Aber bereits CD VII 18-21(um 100 v. Chr.) führte sie singularisierend eng zum „Messias Aarons und Israels“. Nach CD XII 23-XIII 1 galten für die Gemeinden Interimsvorschriften „bis zum Auftreten des Messias Aarons und Israels“. Apostaten durfte bis zur Ankunft des „Messias *aus* Aaron und *aus* Israel“ keine Rekonziliation gewährt werden (CD XIX 33-XX 1). Dem Messias oblag die Rechtsentscheidung in Fällen der Apostasie. Er bildete die höchste Rechtsinstanz und löste damit den „Anweiser der Tora“ ab (CD XIX 7-11).

Fazit: Im Blick auf den makkabäischen Aufstand – näherhin vielleicht auf Judas Makkabäus – entstand die Erwartung eines doppelten Messias mit deutlicher Präponderanz des priesterlichen Parts. Im ausgehenden 2. Jh. v. Chr. sprechen die Formulierungen in CD für eine fortschreitende Singularisierung der Messiaserwartung der „Gemeinde des Neuen Bundes im Lande Damaskus“. Diese Fusion der zwei Messiasgestalten war vielleicht eine Folge der bewährten zurückliegenden Personalunionen eines Jonatan (152-143 v. Chr.), eines Simon (143-134 v. Chr.) oder der dem Schreiber eher gegenwärtigen Personalunion des Johannes Hyrkan I. (134-105 v. Chr.). Vielleicht hatten diese Formen sich als ein für die Damaskusgemeinde tragbares Modell erwiesen[62].

4.4. Das „munus triplex“ zur Zeit der Gründung Qumrans

Etwa zeitgleich zeigte sich sogar die Erwartung eines dreifachen Messias aus dem Hause Davids, dem Geschlecht Aarons und eines Vorläufer-Propheten, wobei das Bild eines Idealstaates mit seinen drei zentra-

59. *Ant XII*, 434.

60. J.J. COLLINS, *The Scepter and the Star* (Anm. 22), S. 76.

61. 4Q161; 4Q174; 4Q285.

62. JOSEPHUS FLAVIUS, *Ant XIII*, 10 berichtet, ein Pharisäer habe dem Hyrkan nahe gelegt, auf das Hohepriester-Amt zu verzichten, worauf es zu heftigen Auseinandersetzungen gekommen sei. Die Qumran-Essener waren grundsätzlich anti-pharisäisch eingestellt, so dass sie möglicherweise die Personalunion Hyrkans tolerierten.

len Institutionen als Basis gedient haben könnte (TestRub 6,7.10 [2. Jh. v. Chr.]; 1Makk 14,41 [um 100 v. Chr.]).

In Qumran ist 1QS IX 11 (150-100 v. Chr.) locus classicus für die messianische Trias. Seit Beginn der Messiasforschung in den Handschriften von Qumran wird dieser Beleg heftig diskutiert vor allem auch deshalb, weil in der Kopie 4Q259(4QS^{e}) 1 III 6 (um 100 v. Chr.) dieser Abschnitt der Gemeinderegel fehlt. Ein Blick in DJD XXVI gibt darüber Auskunft, dass die Kol. III aus 2 Fragmenten zusammengesetzt ist[63]. Der für uns in Frage kommende Text der Zeile 6 befindet sich mitten auf dem Fragment 3b: dort folgt auf den Text 1QS VIII 15 nach einem normalen Spatium unmittelbar der Text 1QS IX 12. Damit ist der Erklärungsvorschlag von L.H. Schiffman, die Fragmente seien falsch zusammengesetzt, vom Tisch.

Wie nun soll man das Fehlen von 1QS IX 11 in 4QS^{e} erklären? Nach den Vorarbeiten von S. Metso[64] wird meistens angenommen, 4QS^{e} enthalte die ältere[65] Texttradition und kenne noch keine messianische Trias. Dagegen steht die Meinung, 1QS enthalte die ältere Textstufe[66] und 4QS^{e} sei Zeugnis für eine spätere Messianologie ohne Trias. Dann kam der Gedanke auf, sowohl 1QS wie auch 4QS^{e} haben ursprünglich diese Trias nicht gekannt, 1QS IX 10ff. sei deshalb als eine sekundäre Fortschreibung[67] im Text zu werten, stelle also ein noch jüngeres Stadium der Entwicklung der Messiaserwartungen in Qumran dar. Dem letzteren steht entgegen, dass 1QS von allen S-Handschriften die älteste ist, also kaum Spielraum für diese Lösung bietet.

Schließlich besteht auch die Möglichkeit, dass beide Handschriften die messianische Trias gekannt haben, in 4QS^{e} aber ein Textausfall vorliegt. Das deutet M.G. Abegg[68] an, wenn er darauf hinweist, dass der Schreiber von 4QS^{e} nicht nur unsere Messiasaussage, sondern sogar eine ganze Kolumne mit 24 Zeilen ausgelassen hat. Ein solcher Textausfall lässt sich tatsächlich erklären: Der Text bietet nämlich den singulären

63. Plate XV beziffert sie als Fragmente 3a und 3b.

64. S. METSO, *The Textual Development of the Qumran Community Rule* (STDJ, 21), Leiden, 1997, S. 147.152f.

65. J. POUILLY, *La Règle de la Communité de Qumrân: son évolution littéraire* (Cahiers de la Revue Biblique, 17), Paris, 1976; vgl. G.J. BROOKE, *Isaiah 40:3 and the Wilderness Community*, in DERS. – F. GARCÍA MARTÍNEZ (Hgg.), *New Qumran Texts and Studies* (STDJ, 15), Leiden, 1994, S. 117-132, bes. 128: "1QS, with the most recent form of the text, may well be the oldest manuscript copy".

66. A. LANGE – H. LICHTENBERGER, in *TRE* 28 (1997), S. 58.

67. So noch J.T. Milik und P. Wernberg-Møller. Vgl. auch S. METSO, *The Primary Results of the Reconstruction of 4QS^{e}*, in *JJS* 44 (1993) 303-308, bes. S. 304: „I am going to suggest, however, that the whole passage of 1QS VIII,15-IX,11 is a secondary insertion".

68. M.G. ABEGG, *The Messiah at Qumran* (Anm. 17), S. 131.

Fall, dass zwei Überschriften[69] aufeinanderstoßen: „Das ist der Midrasch der Tora, die von Moses befohlen wurde“ und „Das sind die Bestimmungen für den *maśkîl*“. Dieser harsche Kontext ändert sich nicht wesentlich, wenn man erstere als Unterschrift (Abschlussformulierung) und die zweite als Überschrift versteht. Da sich diese doppelte Titulatur literarkritisch nicht lösen lässt, bleibt nur noch die Erklärung als Abschreibefehler. Der Abschreiber hat tatsächlich infolge einer aberratio oculi eine ganze Kolumne seiner Vorlage übersprungen. Das spricht dafür, dass der Abschnitt mit dem munus triplex auch dem Schreiber von 4QS^{e} real vorgelegen haben konnte, zu seiner Zeit also die Erwartung einer messianischen Trias in der Gemeinderegel verankert war. Wann aber war das?

Die paläographische Datierung von 4QS^{e} an den Beginn des 1. Jh. v. Chr. haben die offiziellen Herausgeber P. Alexander und G. Vermes[70] nicht übernommen, wenn sie die Handschrift mit Cross in frühherodianische Zeit (50-25 v. Chr.) datieren. Lange/Lichtenberger nennen sie eine „relativ junge Handschrift“[71], auch wenn sie alte S-Traditionen enthält.

Die historische Anbindung einer triadischen Messiaserwartung ist nicht leicht; aber trotzdem bietet sich ein Hintergrund an: Im Umkreis der Neueinweihung des Tempels nach dem Makkabäischen Aufstand am 25. Kislew 165/64 spricht 1Makk 4,46 das Problem der entweihten Altarsteine an: Die gesetzestreuen Priester rissen den Altar ab und deponierten die Steine auf dem Tempelberg an einem geeigneten Ort, „*bis ein Prophet aufstehen*“ und sie anweisen würde, was damit zu geschehen habe. Es ist spekuliert worden, ob diese Aussage auf eine Vakanz des Amtes des *dôreš hattôrah* (vgl. CD I) zur Zeit der Tempelweihe hinweise. Vielleicht hatten ihn die Makkabäer entmachtet, was die langandauernde Gegnerschaft der Qumraner gegenüber den Hasmonäern begründen könnte. Ein zweites Mal begegnet diese Unabdingbarkeit des prophetischen Amtes bei der Einsetzung des Makkabäers Simon als Hegemon und Hoherpriester „für immer bis zum Auftreten eines verlässlichen Propheten“ im Jahr 143 v. Chr. (1Makk 14,41ff.). Weil diese doppelte Zeitangabe „für immer“ und „bis zum Auftreten…“ sehr störend wirkt, kann sie nur durch einen gezielten Eingriff in den Text entstanden sein in einer Zeit, in der eben die Ankunft eines Propheten mit Entscheidungskompetenz zum unabdingbaren Erwartungsgut gehörte.

69. Auch im Buch Deuteronomium liegt ein doppeltes Überschriftensystem vor, das sich nur mit Hilfe literarkritischer Operationen deuten lässt.

70. DJD, 26, 1998, S. 133.

71. LANGE – LICHTENBERGER (Anm. 66), S. 58.

Der „geborene" historische Ort für das munus triplex ist jedoch das Dreifachamt des Johannes Hyrkan als Archont, Hoherpriester und (Weissage-)Prophet sowie sein demonstrativer Parteiwechsel vom Pharisäismus zu den hasmonäerfreundlichen Sadduzäern[72] (um 120 v. Chr.), was in der Qumrangruppe eine Kontrasterwartung generiert haben könnte. Man wird davon ausgehen können, dass zu dieser Zeit der Lehrer der Gerechtigkeit bereits gestorben war, so dass sich auch aus einer gemeinde-internen Notlage heraus die Erwartung einer messianischen Trias erklären würde: Die aus der Tradition bekannte Notwendigkeit eines Propheten wurde nun mit der doppelten Messiaserwartung verknüpft.

Fazit: Man kann also nicht umhin, die messianische Trias für einen ursprünglichen Bestandteil von S zu erachten, der auch noch späteren Abschreibern vorlag. Das bedeutet, dass in der Zeit des ausgehenden 2. Jh. v. Chr., also zur Zeit der Gründung Qumrans dem Messias ein munus triplex zugesprochen wurde. Als historische Anbindung bietet sich die Erinnerung an die Amtseinsetzung des Simon Makkabäus an, als Anlaß der Tod des Lehrers der Gerechtigkeit.

4.5. Melchisedek als messianische Gestalt in Qumran

Nach TestLevi 18 (200-174 v. Chr.) wird Gott einen neuen Priester erwecken, der ein „Gericht der Wahrheit" auf der Erde halten und den Frieden bringen wird. Da er dezidiert „keinen Nachfolger haben" wird, eignet ihm ein Ewigkeitsaspekt. Der in TestJuda 24 genannte königliche Messias ist ihm gegenüber deutlich zweitrangig. Es gibt also außerhalb Qumrans schon recht früh die Erwartung *eines* priesterlichen Messias. In Qumran selbst ist diese Erwartung zum ersten Mal wahrscheinlich mit der Person des Melchisedek verbunden worden.

Melchisedek und das von ihm repräsentierte Herrschaftsideal waren wegen ihrer Verbindung von Königtum und Priestertum in Personalunion (Gen 14,18-20) für Qumran natürlich interessant. Melchisedek verkörperte die kanaanäische Dynastie Jerusalems und zugleich eine Jerusalemer Priester-Linie. Das AT hat diese Priester-Linie vorerst nicht weiter verfolgt. Es muß sich aber schon bald eine Sondertradition entwickelt haben, die im AT nur noch in Ps 110,4 greifbar wird. Mit der Thronbesteigung übernahm der König auch das alte jebusitische Stadtkönigtum und eine priesterliche Amtswürde. Im AT war diese Kombination bekannt (2Sam 6,13-18; 24,17; 1Kön 8,14.56), aber nie explizit genannt. Erst Simon Makkabäus wurde zum „Herrscher *und* Hohepriester

72. JOSEPHUS, *Ant XIII*, 293ff.299ff.

für immer" bestellt (1Makk 14,41). Von einer Personalunion bei Judas Makkabäus (s.o.) weiß das AT nichts.

Der apokalyptisch orientierte[73] Midrasch (11Q13[Melch]) aus der Hasmonäerzeit[74] (paläographisch: späthasmonäisch: 1. Jh. v. Chr.) sah Melchisedek als *'elôhîm* „göttliches Wesen" im endzeitlichen Geschehen involviert. Im letzten Erlaßjahr (vgl. Lev 25) fungiert Melchisedek als Priester, König und Richter (vgl. Ps 82,1); er tritt als Anführer der himmlischen Heerscharen auf, kämpft gegen Belial und führt damit den Anbruch der Heilszeit herbei (Aufnahme von Jes 49,8; 52,7). Dieser Anbruch der Heilszeit wird von einem gesalbten Propheten (*mašîaḥ haruaḥ*) angesagt. Sein Auftreten erinnert dabei an den *mašîaḥ* in Jes 61,1-3 und seine Funktionen machen ihn mit dem Erzengel Michael vergleichbar, mit dem er gelegentlich sogar identifiziert wird[75]. Als Engelwesen empfängt er jedoch keine Salbung, so dass ihm zumindest terminologisch der Gesalbtentitel[76] vorenthalten bleibt. Als Priester vollzieht er am eschatologischen Versöhnungstag die Sühneriten im Himmel. Seine Funktionen erinnern an die des „neuen Priesters" in TestLevi 18,1, der allerdings auf der Erde tätig ist. Da Melchisedek eine himmlische Gestalt ist und im himmlischen Bereich agiert, fehlt ihm der für den Messias wesentliche Bezug zur Menschenwelt. Sein heilbringendes Handeln vermittelt der Menschheit deshalb der in 11Q13 genannte „Gesalbte des Geistes" (vgl. Jes 52,7; 61,1; Lk 4,17ff.). Insofern ist 11Q13 Zeugnis für das Auftreten eines Propheten, der einer priesterlichen messianischen Figur assistiert und im Rückgriff auf die Verheißung der Sendung eines „Propheten wie Moses" (Dtn 18,15ff.) zur bevollmächtigten Auslegung heiliger Schriften berufen ist.

Fazit: Jede historische Anbindung muß mangels literarischer Zeugnisse hypothetisch bleiben. Möglicherweise haben die Hasmonäer die Doppelfunktion des Melchisedek aus Gen 14 zur Legitimation ihrer königlichen *und* priesterlichen Ansprüche mißbraucht. Dem hat Qumran einen Kontrastentwurf entgegengesetzt und Melchisedek konsequent als himmlisches Engelwesen gezeichnet[77], bei dem aber – entsprechend dem

73. A. STEUDEL, אחרית הימים *in the Texts from Qumran*, in *RQ* 16 (1994) 225-247.

74. E. PUECH, *Notes sur le manuscrit de XIQMelkîsédeq*, in *RQ* 12 (1985-87) 483-513, bes. S. 507ff.

75. A.S. VAN DER WOUDE, *Melchisedek als himmlische Erlösergestalt in den neugefundenen eschatologischen Midraschim aus Qumran Höhle XI*, in *OTS* 14 (1965) 354-373, bes. S. 367.372.

76. F. GARCÍA MARTÍNEZ, *Messianische Erwartungen in den Qumrantexten* (Anm. 12), S. 202.

77. Vgl. H.W. HERTZBERG, *Die Melchisedek-Traditionen*, in DERS., *Beiträge zur Traditionsgeschichte und Theologie des Alten Testamentes*, Göttingen, 1962, S. 36-44.

zadokidischen Selbstbewusstsein der Gemeinde von Qumran – die priesterliche Amtsausstattung dominiert. Es muß zugleich beachtet werden, dass die Artikulation dieser priesterlichen Messiaserwartung ganz ohne aaronidische Komponente geschieht.

4.6. Die Messiaserwartung zu Beginn des 1. Jh. v. Chr.

Durch Erneuerung des Davidbundes (1QSb V,20ff.) wird der „Fürst der Gemeinde" in die Sukzession der großen Verheißungen gestellt. CD VII 18-21 schließlich greift die Verheißung von „Stern und Szepter" aus Num 24,17 auf und bezieht sie auf den „Anweiser der Tora" und auf den erwarteten „Fürsten der ganzen Gemeinde", dem jedoch der Titel „König" vorenthalten wird. Die stringente Davidisierung des königlichen Messias geschieht in der qumranischen Gemeinde selbst. Der eschatologische Midrasch 4Q174 (nach 70 v. Chr.) schildert die Zeit unmittelbar vor dem Eschaton, in der der „Sproß Davids" auftreten und Belial besiegen wird. Die qumranische Naherwartung verdichtete sich im 1. Quartal des 1. Jh. v. Chr. In dem Pesher zum Buch Genesis 4Q252(pGen^{a})[78] findet sich eine messianische Auslegung des Juda-Segens Gen 49,10: „Wenn Israel die Herrschaft hat, wird nicht ausgerottet werden, der auf dem Thron für David sitzt, denn der Herrscherstab ist der Bund der Königsherrschaft, [und die Geschlechter] Israels, sie sind die Fahnen. – Bis zum Kommen des Gesalbten der Gerechtigkeit, des Sprosses Davids, denn ihm und seinem Samen ist gegeben der Bund der Königsherrschaft seines Volkes bis zu ewigen Geschlechtern" (4Q252 1 V 1-4)[79].

Jes 11,1-5 wird als Hinweis auf die eschatologische Ankunft eines Davididen gedeutet (4Q161[pJes^{a}; um 100 v. Chr.]). „Der Sproß] Davids wird aufstehen am En[de der Tage … Gott wird ihn stützen … alle

Das zwischentestamentliche Judentum, die Samaritaner (EUSEBIUS, *PraepEv IX*, 17,2-9) und Qumran kannten diese Tradition (vgl. auch die Theodotianer [„Melchisedekianer"] des 2. Jh. n. Chr.). Im Hebräerbrief wurde Melchisedek als Vorausbild Jesu gedeutet (Hebr 5,6.10; 6,20; 7,1. 3.10.11.15.17). Nach PHILO (*All III*, 79-82) repräsentierte Melchisedek als Logos den transzendenten Gott. JOSEPHUS (*Ant XVI*, 6) sah in ihm den Gründer Jerusalems und den Urpriester. Da seine Herkunft und Abstammung unbekannt waren, zog er bald die Attribute Präexistenz und Ewigkeit, vom Namen her dann auch Gerechtigkeit und Frieden an sich. Damit wurde Melchisedek zum messianischen Prototyp.

78. Die frühere Bezeichnung lautet: „4QPatriarchal Blessings". Die Literatur zu dieser Handschrift ist gegenwärtig nicht mehr überschaubar. Nach Meinung von G.J. BROOKE, *The Genre of 4Q252: From Poetry to Pesher*, in *DSD* 1 (1994) 160-179 handelt es sich um einen Kommentar zu den Kapiteln des Genesisbuches, die im Land spielen, eine Mischform mit den Elementen eines Pesher und eines Midrasch. Die Herkunft aus der Gemeinde von Qumran ist gesichert.

79. Nach J. ZIMMERMANN, *Messianische Texte aus Qumran* (Anm. 31), S. 114.

Völker (?) wird er beherrschen" (Fragm. 8-10 III 18-21). Er wird Recht sprechen, allerdings nach der Weisung der Priester. Diese Bindung des messianischen Heilsbringers an priesterliche Weisung überrascht, scheint aber durch priesterliche Prärogative bedingt. Die königlich-davidische Messiaserwartung richtete sich entsprechend der Hauptbedürfnisse in der apokalyptisch geprägten Zeit auf einen endzeitlichen Militärführer (1QM V 1f. [ca. 30 v. Chr.]), dem die eschatologische Kriegsführung, die Herbeiführung einer Segenszeit sowie die Präsentation der Gegenwart Gottes (4Q285 [ca. 30 v. Chr.]) obliegen sollten.

Dieser Text ist neben PsSal 17-18 das älteste Zeugnis für die explizite Bezeichnung des erwarteten davidischen Königs als „Gesalbter" und will den Fortbestand der David-Sukzession angesichts ausländischer Usurpatoren in Juda betonen[80]. Der 18. Psalm schaut auf die Einnahme Jerusalems durch den Römer Pompeius zurück und „rekapituliert ein Bild, das seinen eigenen Vorstellungen von einem idealen Israel strikt widerspricht und erst durch die Herrschaft des Gesalbten überwunden werden kann"[81]. Im Rückgriff auf die alten Verheißungen wird der erwartete König ein „Sohn Davids" sein, Kritik an der Herrschaft der Hasmonäer und Römer[82]. Ihm obliegt die Bestrafung der Gegner, die Reinigung Jerusalems von den Heiden, die Niederschlagung der Feinde Judas (vgl. äthHen 85-90) und die Vernichtung der gesetzlosen Völker mit seinem machtvollen Wort. Er wird das heilige Volk sammeln und ihm Recht sprechen, die soziale Gerechtigkeit wiederherstellen, das Land an die Stämme neu verteilen und die Fremden ausweisen. Dann wird er Jerusalem auf die eschatologische Völkerwallfahrt vorbereiten. Für die erfolgreiche Durchführung dieser Großtaten wird er von Gott mit Weisheit, Stärke, Gerechtigkeit und Gottesfurcht ausgestattet werden.

Natürlich hat dieses eschatologisch-messianische Konzept alttestamentliche Traditionen aufgenommen, vor allem interessanterweise aus

80. D.R. SCHWARTZ, *The Messianic Departure from Judah (4Q Patriarchal Blessings)*, in *TZ* 37 (1981) 257-266, bes. S. 263. Es wurde auch vorgeschlagen, in diesem Text eine Betonung der wahren Daviddynastie gegenüber den regierenden Herodianern zu sehen. Das impliziert natürlich eine recht späte Ansetzung dieses Textes, so M. KARRER, *Der Gesalbte. Die Grundlagen des Christustitels* (FRLANT, 151), Göttingen, 1990, S. 255; zur Diskussion vgl. J. ZIMMERMANN, *Messianische Texte aus Qumran* (Anm. 31), S. 120.

81. S.H. BRANDENBURGER, *Der „Gesalbte des Herrn" in Psalm Salomo 17*, in DERS. – T. HIEKE (Hgg.), *Wenn drei das Gleiche sagen. Studien zu den ersten drei Evangelien* (Theologie, 14), Münster, 1998, S. 217-236, bes. S. 220.

82. Gelegentlich wird erwogen, diese pharisäische Kritik richte sich gegen Herodes; vgl. K. ATKINSON, *On the Herodian Origin of Militant Davidic Messianism at Qumran: New Light from Psalm of Solomon 17*, in *JBL* 118 (1999) 435-460. Diese Ansetzung scheint mir jedoch zu spät zu sein. Die Vorstellung vom kriegerischen Messias ist wohl hergeleitet von Jes 11,4 „Er schlägt den Gewalttätigen mit dem Stock seines Wortes" und findet sich noch in 4Q161; 4Q285 und Offb 19,11-21, bes. v.13.

der Frühzeit Israels (Aufenthalt in der Wüste, Verteilung des Landes an die Stämme Israels). Entsprechend trägt der König die alte Titulatur des Hirten, der seine Herde in Treue und Gerechtigkeit weidet. Dieser Messias war das Gegenstück zu den Hasmonäern und Römern, die ihr Volk unterdrückten und identitätslos auseinanderlaufen ließen.

Versucht man eine historische Verknüpfung dieser boomenden davidisch geprägten Messiaserwartung im Qumran des 1. Jh. v. Chr., dann wird man an die wirrenreiche Zeit des Alexander Jannai (103-76 v. Chr.) denken können. Das blutrünstige Pontifikat eines Aristobul I. hatte wohl vielen den Gedanken an einen priesterlichen Messias verleidet. Das berühmte Pogrom am Laubhüttenfest (Ant XIII 372f.) mit den 6000 Toten, die Kreuzigung von 800 Pharisäern und der Bürgerkrieg in den Jahren 95-83 v. Chr. ließen im Volk den Wunsch nach einem politisch starken Messias aufkommen. Sicher war das Maß voll, als Königin Salome Alexandra (76-67 v. Chr.) mit ihrer propharisäischen Politik ein für viele untragbares Frauenregime betrieb, das keinerlei Stabilisierung bedeutete, sondern das Volk erst recht in einen neuen Bruderkrieg hineintrieb.

Fazit: Die davidische Messianologie ist in Qumran konsequent unter Aufnahme alttestamentlicher Vorgaben ausformuliert worden und ist als Kritik zu verstehen an den hohepriesterlichen Ansprüchen auf königliche Kompetenzen, der Ämterkumulation durch die Hasmonäer und schließlich als Gegenentwurf zu den Wirren um Salome Alexandra. Diese davidische Messiaserwartung ließ sich in der Folgezeit gut rezipieren als Kritik gegenüber den Fremdherren (Römer) und später den Nichtjudäern (Herodes) auf dem Jerusalemer Thron. Es fällt auf, dass die entscheidende Ausformulierung im Rahmen der unmittelbaren Auslegung biblischer Texte erfolgte, die Gemeinde von Qumran ihre Messianologie also biblisch fundiert und nicht aus irgendwelchen Spekulationen hergeleitet hat.

4.7. Die Erwartung des endzeitlichen Propheten im 1. Jh. v. Chr.

Die Messiaserwartung wurde bereits in präqumranischen Texten gelegentlich um die Erwartung eines endzeitlichen Propheten erweitert. Den Vorläufer-Propheten hat der fragmentarische Text 4Q558 aus voressenischer Zeit im Blick, wenn er von der Sendung des Elija spricht. Der Text ist „zwar nicht sicher, aber mit einiger Wahrscheinlichkeit ein Beleg für die Erwartung des wiederkommenden Elia in vorchristlicher Zeit“[83].

83. J. ZIMMERMANN, *Messianische Texte aus Qumran* (Anm. 31), S. 415.

Der aus hasmonäischer Zeit stammende Text 4Q521 wurde vom Herausgeber als „messianische Apokalypse“[84] bezeichnet[85]. Die 2. Kolumne beginnt mit dem Satz: „Himmel und Erde werden auf seine/n Gesalbten hören und alles, was in ihnen ist, wird nicht abweichen von den Geboten der Heiligen“. Die Frage nach der Identität dieses/dieser Gesalbten ist ungelöst. Der Text spricht die neue Heilszeit an, denn es werden die Wunder und Zeichen genannt, die (vgl. Mt 11,2; par. Lk 7,19) das klassische Repertoire der messianischen Großtaten (ἔργα τοῦ χριστοῦ) bilden: Befreiung der Gefangenen, Heilung der Blinden und Aufrichtung der Gebeugten (vgl. Ps 146,7f.; Jes 35,5), Heilung der Geschlagenen, Wiederbelebung der Toten und die Verkündigung der frohen Botschaft (vgl. Jes 61,1). Das eigentlich handelnde Subjekt hinter diesen Großtaten bleibt unklar, aber die Verkündigung der frohen Botschaft ist Aufgabe des gesalbten Propheten. Damit legt sich nahe, dass an die Großtaten eines prophetischen Messias gedacht ist, wobei die Bezüge zu Elijas Totenerweckung (1Kön 17; vgl. Sir 48,3) offensichtlich sind. Die Kombination der beiden Jesaja-Zitate in Qumran hat mit dem NT das Textplus der Wiederbelebung der Toten gemeinsam.

Nach 11Q13(Melch) soll Melchisedek die Freilassung verkünden, die Herrschaft des Rechtes errichten, die Rache Gottes an den Frevlern durchführen, den in Jes 52,7 angekündigten eschatologischen Frieden durchsetzen und die Trauernden trösten: „Und der Freudenbote, er ist der Gesalbte des Geistes, von dem Daniel gesprochen hat … und der Bote des Heiles, der die Rettung verkündet …“ (II 9-19). Die meist verhandelte Frage, ob dieser „Gesalbte des Geistes“ eine menschliche Gestalt, den Vorläufer-Prophet, einen inspirierten Ausleger prophetischer Botschaft, den Prophet Daniel selbst oder den prophetisch verstandenen Messias meine, läßt sich nicht beantworten.

Zur eigentlichen Ausprägung der prophetischen Messiaserwartung kommt es jedoch erst später in der Hochphase der apokalyptischen Naherwartung. Der eschatologische Midrasch 4Q174 (nach 71 v. Chr.) erwartet den prophetischen „Anweiser der Tora“ zusammen mit dem „Sproß Davids“. 4Q175 denkt wie 1QS IX 11 an eine prophetische Gestalt, die Gottes Wort vermitteln soll. Dann springt der Text zur doppelten Messiaserwartung („Stern und Szepter“, nach Num 24,15-17) und zum Zitat des Levi-Segens aus Dtn 33,8-11, das als Ankündigung eines

84. E. PUECH, *Une Apocalypse messianique (4Q521)*, in *RQ* 15 (1992) 475-522; DERS., DJD, 25, 1998, S. 1-38.

85. Dagegen z.B. M. BECKER, *4Q521 und die Gesalbten*, in *RQ* 18 (1997) 73-96. Er hält dafür, dass dieser Text sich nicht von den qumranischen Messiasvorstellungen her erklären läßt, wohl aber ein prophetisches Gesalbtenverständnis hier weiterhelfen kann.

priesterlichen Messias zu deuten ist. Jedenfalls scheint dieser Text den endzeitlichen Propheten selbst nicht als messianische Gestalt verstanden zu haben[86]. Die mehrfach gebrauchte Titulatur „Gesalbter des heiligen Geistes" (CD II 12; 1QM XI 7; 4Q270[4QD^{e}], Fragm. 2 II [frühherodianisch]) könnte eine prophetische Gestalt meinen, über eine messianische Funktion wird jedoch nichts gesagt. Das gilt auch für „seinen Gesalbten Mose", der in einer apokryphen Darstellung der Sinai-Theophanie (4Q377, Fragm. 2)[87] genannt wird.

Fazit: Damit ist der Titel „Gesalbter" für prophetische Gestalten in Qumran gut bezeugt, auch für endzeitlich erwartete prophetische Boten, die die Ankunft des eigentlichen Messias ansagen. Auffällig ist die zentrale Bedeutung der Ankündigung der Entsendung eines „Propheten wie Mose" (Dtn 18,15.18) und die Betonung von Geistbesitz und Salbung (Jes 61,1). Der in Qumran bekannte „Anweiser der Tora" ist – obwohl geschichtlich – zugleich auch eine Gestalt, deren Auftreten für die Endzeit erwartet wird. Das Auftreten dieses Amtsinhabers wird mit den eschatologischen Prophetengestalten verbunden (4Q174). Da er in der Gemeinschaft selbst eine entscheidende Rolle spielt (1QS VI 6; CD VI 2-11), ist die Erwartung seines Auftretens auch in der Endzeit zugleich Äußerung der endzeitlichen Kontinuität der Gemeinschaft als Wirkungsort dieser Autorität.

4.8. 11QPs^{a} – Das Gebetbuch des Messias

Die wohl in der 2. Hälfte des 2. Jh. v. Chr. entstandene Psalmenrolle – die erhaltene Kopie 11Q5 stammt aus der Zeit 30-50 n. Chr. – nimmt den „politischen Messias" aus 1QSa auf und identifiziert ihn als David redivivus. Solche Messianisierungen des Davidbildes wurden jetzt von U. Dahmen[88] aufgewiesen durch Vergleich des Textes der Psalmenrolle mit dem masoretischen Psalmentext. Nur einige Beispiele sollen dies verdeutlichen.

Eine Analyse der Textvarianten zeigt einige Tendenzen auf: So werden die pluralischen „Throne des Hauses David" in Ps 122,5 (MT) als Ausdruck demokratisierter kollektiver Erwartung (vgl. 1QM XI 6f;

86. F. García Martínez, *Messianische Erwartungen* (Anm. 12), S. 204, betrachtet die drei parallelen Zitate aus Dtn 18; Num 24 und Dtn 33 als gleichrangig und erschließt daraus auch für den Propheten einen messianischen Rang. Diese Argumentation ist nicht beweiskräftig.

87. Alter unbestimmt, paläographisch: herodianisch.

88. U. Dahmen, *Psalmen- und Psalter-Rezeption im Frühjudentum. Rekonstruktion, Textbestand, Struktur und Pragmatik der Psalmenrolle 11QPs^{a} aus Qumran* (STDJ, 49), Leiden, 2003.

4Q491 11 I 12-19) nun auf einen einzigen Thron individualisiert (vgl. 1QSa II 12.14.20; 1QSb V 20-29). – Nach Ps 132,11f. sollen die Söhne Davids für immer „auf dem Thron sitzen". 11Q5 macht daraus einen Neuanfang, wenn der Text jetzt davon spricht, dass der Nachkomme David „den Thron besteigen" wird. Das setzt eine davidische Sedisvakanz voraus und kann sich deshalb nur auf den davidischen Messias beziehen. – Ps 151A,5 ist gegenüber dem LXX-Text im Blick auf 1 Sam 16,1-13 präziser, wenn nun die Sendung Samuels ausdrücklich als „zu salben und groß zu machen" beschrieben wird. Damit werden die „messianischen Elemente" der Salbung und Größe Davids in den Text eingebracht. – Ps 151B wird durch Motivanleihe an Jes 11,2 (*g^e^bûrah* „Stärke") zum Auftakt der messianischen Zeit des davidischen Messias umgedeutet.

Ein Vergleich der Komposition des masoretischen Psalters mit der der Psalmenrolle zeigt, dass auch die Gesamtkomposition der Psalmenrolle davidisch-messianisch zu verstehen ist: Schon durch die Rahmung durch Ps 101 und 2 Sam 23,1-7 („Davids letzte Worte") wird der gesamte Text der Rolle als Vermächtnis des historischen David und als das persönliche Gebetbuch des messianischen David verstanden. – Durch die Abfolge der Gebete wird das Wirken des davidischen Messias als zwar politisch, aber nicht herrschaftspolitisch charakterisiert. Er ist der Vermittler der Gottesnähe. Nach Ps 146 strebt er kein weltliches Herrschertum an, sondern sein Programm angesichts der Königsherrschaft Gottes ist das Gotteslob. Entsprechend wird in 11QPs^{a} der Titel „König" grundsätzlich nur Gott vorbehalten[89]. – Der Schluß des Wallfahrtspsalters (Ps 120-134) wird tendenziell neu gebildet und zurückgebunden an die von Ps 101 herkommende messianische Programmatik. Die Wallfahrt ist nun auf den erwarteten eschatologisch erneuerten Tempel ausgerichtet. – Mit dem „Lob in der Gemeinde der Frommen" (Ps 149) beginnt die Schlusskomposition der Rolle, die das messianische Gebetbuch ganz in die Hand der Gemeinde der Frommen gibt, die nun mit diesem neuen Psalterium die Ankunft des davidischen Messias erwartet. „Sie betrachtet sich bedrängt... sowohl von ihren jüdischen Glaubensbrüdern (vgl. die ‚Brüder' in Ps 151A) in Jerusalem als auch von den heidnisch-hellenistischen Mächten ihrer Umwelt... Aber sie sind gewiß, als gottlobende messianische Gemeinde den Kampf mit den Söhnen der Finsternis siegreich zu bestehen"[90].

89. M. KLEER, *„Der liebliche Sänger der Psalmen Israels". Untersuchungen zu David als Dichter und Beter der Psalmen* (BBB, 108), Bonn, 1996, S. 273f. 308.
90. *Ibid.*, S. 316.

5. Zusammenfassung

Der Nachweis einer diachronen Entwicklung der Messiaserwartungen in Qumran scheint zu gelingen, bleibt aber nach wie vor so schwierig und hypothetisch, wie die einzelnen beigezogenen Texte schwierig und hypothetisch zu deuten sind.

Als sicher kann gelten, dass die priesterlich und königlich geprägte Erwartung aus der Spätzeit der alttestamentlichen Prophetie zu allen Zeiten im Schrifttum von Qumran nachgewirkt hat. Diese Nachwirkungen geschahen aber mit unterschiedlicher Intensität.

1. In Texten aus der *vorqumranisch-voressenischen* Zeit finden sich erste Messiaserwartungen, die eindeutig priesterlich geprägt sind. Damit ist bereits eine Einspurung erfolgt, die nie mehr aus dem Blick geraten wird.

2. In Texten aus der *vorqumranisch-essenischen* Zeit setzt man nun – zeitgeschichtlich bedingt – auf ein messianisches Kollektiv, auf das „Volk Gottes“ als die endzeitliche Größe, die den heidnischen Machenschaften der Seleukiden entgegen stehen. Auch diese Vorstellung blieb in der späteren Qumrangemeinde latent präsent und wurde zum tragenden Pfeiler qumranischer Ekklesiologie.

3. In *frühqumranischer* Zeit entwickelte die sich konstituierende Gemeinde eine Gegenkonzeption gegen die hasmonäische Personalunion, die Erwartung eines doppelten Messias, in der jedoch entsprechend der Zusammensetzung der Gemeinde die priesterliche Komponente dominierte. Die etwa zeitgleiche Gemeinde von Damaskus konzentriert dieses Doppelamt auf eine einzelne Person.

4. Gegen *Ende des 2. Jh. v. Chr.* kam es zur Ausbildung des messianischen munus triplex. Wohl aus Anlaß des Todes des Lehrers der Gerechtigkeit wurde aus der Tradition die Erwartung eines endzeitlichen Propheten rezipiert und in Reminiszenz an die triplexe Amtseinführung des makkabäischen Hohenpriesters mit der bereits vorhandenen doppelten Messiaserwartung zum munus triplex verbunden.

5. Wohl eine messianologische Seitenlinie entstand in der Pflege der Melchisedek-Tradition, aus der das traditionelle Doppelamt nun auf die priesterliche Komponente enggeführt wurde unter konsequenter Unterlassung jeder aaronidischen Anspielung.

6. Im *1. Jh. v. Chr.* wurde die alleinige königliche Messiaserwartung dominierend (vgl. auch PsSal 17f.) als Ruf nach einer starken Hand gegen die Wirren unter Aristobul und Salome Alexandra.

7. Latent im marginalen Bereich verblieb die Erwartung eines messianischen Propheten, die wohl als eine eigenständige Sonderentwicklung verstanden werden muß und erst nach dem Tod des Lehrers der Gerechtigkeit auch für Qumran wichtig wurde.

8. Die große Psalmenrolle schließlich bezeugt für die *frühchristliche Zeit* das Ineinander der davidischen Messiaserwartung und des messianischen Selbstverständnisses der Gemeinde von Qumran, womit sich der Kreis zu den frühen Ausprägungen der messianischen Erwartungen schließt.

Turmfalkenweg 15 Heinz-Josef FABRY
D-53127 Bonn

ECSTATIC WORSHIP IN THE SELF-GLORIFICATION HYMN (4Q471B, 4Q427, 4Q491C)

Implications for the Understanding of an Ancient Jewish and Early Christian Phenomenon

John, the Seer of the Book of Revelation describes the scenario before the throne of God and the worship in the heavens. After ascending to the heavens in trance (4,1), John beheld the throne of God and the heavenly beings – the *hayyot*, the elders and the angels – worshipping[1]. But in the following visions multitudes of human beings are also seen singing praises in the heavens, as we can read in chapter 7.

After the presentation of the suffering Christians in chap. 6 (those who are waiting for judgement under the altar v. 9-11) we find a multitude praising in chapter 7,9

> After this I beheld, and, lo, a great multitude, which no man could number, of all nations, and kindreds, and people, and tongues, stood before the throne, and before the Lamb, *clothed with white robes*, and palms in their hands.

These are shown here as a multitude of exalted worshippers in the heavens. And before the throne of God, these Christians who have been lifted up to heaven are singing and worshipping:

> And they cried with a loud voice, saying, Salvation to our God which sitteth upon the throne, and unto the Lamb (7,10).

They have come through the "great tribulation" (7,14-15). They are singing in front of God's throne (7,15). This is the same tribulation which John says that he and his "companions" (συνκοινώνοι) are facing in 1,9. In spite of attempts in modern exegesis to differentiate between images of Christians who were still alive and martyrs (those executed in a supposedly widespread Roman persecution), we must also understand that they are shown in an ambiguous way: they are suffering persecution (or are about to suffer persecution), but due to their fidelity in the present they are *already singing* before the throne of God[2]. There-

1. Cf. P.A. DE S. NOGUEIRA, *Êxtase visionário e culto no Apocalipse de João. Uma análise de Apocalipse 4 e 5 em comparação com viagens celestiais da Apocalíptica,* in *Revista de Interpretação Bíblica Latino-Americana* 34 (2000) 41-64.

2. We find that kind of temporal dualism also in chapter 12, where the acclamations of chapter 12,9 or the summon to praise of 12,12 is exalting the victory of Michael – with the help of the Christians, of the "word of their witness" – against the Dragon in a time when the eschatological woes are just about to begin with the Dragon's fall down to the earth.

fore only in 7,15b can we find the use of the future tense: "the seated on the throne *will camp* among them" and also in 7,17 that the lamb "*will herd* them".

It is my view that the description of celestial worship in chap. 7 is not exclusively a vision of martyrs in heaven, but of the *entire Johannine community*[3] which, through practicing resistance during a period of tension in the sphere of their social relationships, believes that it has access to the heavenly sphere, and has the expectation that in the present, in their services, they will experience the same complete union with God. In Revelation we have a clear picture of Christians who experience their religiosity by means of ecstatic worship, believing that in some way they ascend to the heavens in order to take part in the angelic worship. I think that most of the consciousness of the irruption of the eschatological expectations of Revelation arises from experiences of this kind of power.

We have further evidence in Early Christian Literature of belief in the ascension to the heavens in worship, as in the case of Hebrews 12,22-24:

> But ye are come unto mount Sion, and unto the city of the living God, the heavenly Jerusalem, and to an innumerable company of angels, to the general assembly and church of the firstborn, which are written in heaven, and to God the Judge of all, and to the spirits of just men made perfect, and to Jesus the mediator of the new covenant…

This is also the case of the experience of Paul in the ambiguous account of 2 Corinthians 12 that may indicate some relationship between the ecstatic worship of his communities (1 Cor 12-14) and this type of experience. Morton Smith acutely observed that the First Christians were "constantly oriented towards ascent to the heavens"[4]. Our specific concern here is to understand this type of practice – of being lifted up to the heavens – during ecstatic Early Christian worship.

We encounter some difficulty when investigating the origins of this type of religious experience. There are some pseudepigraphic texts that show visionaries ascending to the heavens and taking part or watching the heavenly service before the throne of God. This is the case in the

3. The context of heavenly worship at which John is present in chapter 4 continued in chapter 7. The credential of those who are singing praises in 7,14 are also similar to those of faithful Christians in the letter to the communities of the Apocalypse: "and have washed their robes, and made them white in the blood of the Lamb" (like 3,5: "he same shall be clothed in white raiment" and 6,11: "white robes"). In the beginning of the paragraph they are presented as the "clothed with white robes" (7,9).

4. *Ascent to the Heavens and the Beginning of Christianity*, in S.J.D. COHEN (ed.), *The Cult of Yahweh, vol. 2, New Testament, Early Christianity and Magic*, Leiden, Brill, 1996, p. 58.

Apocalypse of Abraham, the Ladder of Jacob and the Ascension of Isaiah, just to mention a few examples[5]. Despite the witness of these pseudepigraphic texts (and we could quote many others) there is a problem that we cannot resolve: the fact that the seer is always an important figure of the past. Even in accounts that show details of the trance, as in the case of the Ascension of Isaiah, we cannot know whether they are simply part of pseudepigraphic fiction. Can we, from these accounts, draw information about the patterns of religious experience of the readers? Were the visionary trance, communion with the angels and participation in the heavenly worship only a literary *topos* for the legitimization of the antiquity of the revelation? Or were the paradigmatic visionary experiences of Enoch, Abraham, Isaiah, etc. performed in Jewish communities? Our skepticism regarding this kind of account contributes to the belief that this kind of experience does not have any type of historic relationship to Jewish religion.

The theme of communion with angels and of the visionary ecstasy in Qumran has been treated above all in recent research. But it has not diminished the frustration of New Testament scholars once the majority of the studies try to elucidate the relationship of that phenomenon with Jewish mysticism of the second century CE, know as hekhalot mysticism. In this paper we would like to ask if the Dead Sea Scrolls can be helpful to a better understanding of this Early Christian phenomenon.

The first Qumran text that comes to mind when we think of heavenly worship, communion with angels and mysticism are The Songs of the Sabbath Sacrifice (*shirot 'olat hashabbat*)[6]. In the 12th song, for example, there are explicit references to the heavenly *merkavah*. Though they intend to be a liturgical instruction[7], the contents of the *Shirot* seem to have originated in visionary experience. We have signs of this in the structure of its language. For example, the emphatic repetition of adjectives, as though human language has reached its limits. The *Shirot* also presupposes the parallelism between heavenly and earthly worship, where the latter is an imperfect copy of the former. Carol Newsom has

5. NOGUEIRA, *Êxtase visionário e culto* (n. 1), pp. 41-64.

6. F. GARCÍA MARTÍNEZ and E.J.C. TIGCHELAAR, *The Dead Sea Scrolls. Study Edition*, vol. 2, *4Q274-11Q31*, Brill, Leiden, 1998, pp. 805-837. See also C. NEWSOM, *Songs of the Sabbath Sacrifice: A Critical Edition* (Harvard Semitic Studies), Atlanta, GA, Scholars Press, 1985, and E. ESHEL *et al.* (eds.), *Qumran Cave 4, VI, Poetical and Liturgical Texts, Part 1, Discoveries in the Judean Desert, XI* (DJD, 11), Oxford, Clarendon Press, 1998, pp. 173-401.

7. This text is an instruction for the Sabbath sacrifice directed to the instructor (למשכיל). It contains thirteen songs introduced by the formula "For the Instructor. Song for the Sacrifice of the first (etc) sabbath" plus the imperative "praise", followed by descriptions of the celestial worship performed by the angels.

suggested the hypothesis that the songs could have the aim of provoking communion with angelic beings:

> Both the highly descriptive content and the carefully crafted rhetoric direct the worshipper who hears the songs recited toward a particular kind of religious experience, a sense of being in the heavenly sanctuary and in the presence of the angelic priests and worshippers. That this experience is intended as a communal experience of the human worshipping community is made clear by the first person plural which appear in 4Q400 2 6-8 (probably from the second Sabbath song): "our priesthood;" "the offering of our mortal tongue;" "How shall we be considered [among] them?"; "let us exalt." Even though the *Sabbath Shirot* do not appear to have been designed as vehicles for the incubation of visions or of mystical ascent by individuals, the sophisticated manipulation of religious emotion in the songs would seem to have increased the possibility of ecstatic experience among some worshippers[8].

The Songs of the Sabbath Sacrifice can be considered to display the same religious framework (heavenly worship parallel to the earthly one, the *merkavah* imagery) which Early Christian communities may have used to imagine the whole community praising in the heavens.

But even so, we need to point out the limits of that contribution to the discussion. The *Shirot* provides the frame of what is imagined, the worship of heavenly beings before the *merkavah*, but they do not say anything about the context of the community that conceived it[9]. The text describes the contents of a vision, but not how and in which context it was experienced. The numinous aspect of the language presupposes ecstasy, but – possibly due to the literary form of the *Shirot* – does not provide any detailed information. It can lead to interpretations such as that the *Shirot* are concerned with a representation of alternative sacrifices in Qumran, without any heavenly ascent[10]. They are not texts that remit us to the world of a seer and his ecstatic experience.

8. NEWSOM, *Songs of the Sabbath Sacrifice* (n. 6), p. 17. See a new but quite different interpretation of the *shirot* by C.H.T. FLETCHER-LOUIS, *All the Glory of Adam: Liturgical Anthropology in the Dead Sea Scrolls* (STDJ, 42), Leiden, Brill, 2002, pp. 252-394. His main thesis is that the Songs represent instructions for the sacrifice sabbath worship led by the priests of the Qumran community. The community members – and above all their priests – understood themselves in an angelomorphic way. Fletcher-Louis rejects the idea of a heavenly worship parallel to the earthly.

9. Despite its being possible deduce from texts like 4Q400 2 ("to praise your glory wondrously with the divinities of knowledge, and the praises of your kingship with the m[ost] holy ones") that it is a call to praise and communion between angels and humans in its praise. E. CHAZON, *Liturgical Communion with the Angels at Qumran*, in D.K. FALK, F. GARCÍA MARTÍNEZ, E.M. SCHULLER (eds.), *Sapiential, Liturgical and Poetical Texts from Qumran* (STDJ, 35), Leiden, Brill, 2000, p. 98.

10. FLETCHER-LOUIS, *All the Glory of Adam* (n. 8), p. 393. He points out differences with the merkavah mysticism and the heavenly ascent: "… unlike the stories of ascent in

In the *Self-Glorification Hymn*, recension A (4QH[a] 7,1, 4Q471b, 1QH[a]) and B (4Q491c)[11], we have a liturgical piece in which someone claims to have been lifted up to the heavens, where he experienced communion with angels and some type of exaltation. While communion with angels has been documented in many places in Qumran (4QBerakot, War Scroll and Hodayot) the way it is described in this hymn is in some ways quite special.

Here I would like to point out some important semantic fields of the Self-glorification Hymn.

I

The most important of them for our analysis is the one that refers to communion with angels and to proximity with God, a theme common to the two recensions:

In 4Q427 7, 1+9 (= 1QH[a] XXVI) we find: "I am friend of the kin]g, companion of the holy ones... with the Gods is [my] position (12) and my glory is with the sons of the king". We can read the same in 4Q471b: "I am (7) friend of the king, companion of the holy ones". These expressions do not leave any doubt that the speaker intended to communicate some type of unusual intimacy with the angels (the אלים, the "holy ones") and with God (the "king").

In recension B the expressions are much more emphatic because they not only refer to proximity with the angels and with God, but also to a type of enthroning of the speaker: "... a mighty throne in the congregation of the gods above with none of the kings of the East shall sit ... my glory is in{comparable} and besides me no one is exalted, nor comes to me, for I reside in the heavens, and there is no [...] ... I am counted among the gods and my dwelling is in the holy congregation; [my] desire is not according to the flesh, [but] all that is precious to me is in (the) glory (of) [...] the holy [dwel]ling" (5-8). And, finally, "[friend of the king, companion of the holy ones... incomparable, f]or among the gods is my posi[tion, and] my glory is with the sons of the king" (11).

It is important to observe that however emphatic these expressions are, they do not supply the items required above. In the Self-glorification Hymn there is no reference to visions or to the scenario

the apocalypses and techniques of ecstasy in the Hekhalot literature, in the Sabbath Songs ascent is a ritualized and communal experience, not one for lone patriarchs or the shamanic altered states of consciousness of the adept" (392).

11. E. ESHEL, *4Q471b: A Self-Glorification Hymn*, in *RQ* 17 (1996) 176-203.

of worship of the *merkavah*, with images that are close to the *Shirot*. We also do not find explicit references to ascension and visionary experience. They are only presupposed. But notwithstanding that limitation – since religious texts are not written in order to fulfil expectations of modern exegetical demands – we find here a set of surprising expressions of a human being who claims to have entered in communion with angels, dwelling in the heavens, being exalted and, according 4Q491c, enthroned.

Are we dealing with a text that is isolated from the rest of the Qumran library? The information seems to provide explicit expressions of the Hodayot regarding communion with heavenly beings[12]. 1QH XXVI is a parallel to 4Q427 7, so that it is possible to reconstruct the first from the second. There is no lack of references to the presence of the speakers of the Hodayot in the "holy council" (XV 10) or statements like "the depraved spirit you have purified from great offence so that he can take a place with the host of the holy ones, and can enter in communion with the congregation of the sons of heaven" (XI 21-22). The Self-glorification Hymn is not – through its specific features – an aberration among the liturgical texts of the sect.

Problems of interpretation emerge when we consider the expressions of exaltation above other aspects of the text. The expressions of glorification, exaltation and enthronement have to be considered together with the following ones.

II

One of them is the set of expressions regarding *distinctive speaking*, which in the text is characterized as superior "teaching" and "instruction" ("I have been instructed, and there is no teaching comparable [to my teaching…]", 4Q491c i 9-10), but also as "what issues from my lips" (ומזל שפתי) in 4Q491c 10, 4Q71b 6 and 4Q427 9, "tongue" in 4Q427 6, 4Q471 9 (in 4Q491c 10 "open my mouth"). Finally, these words are explained as משפט, "judgment". These expressions regarding distinctive speaking always have a polemic tone, challenging comparison with those of the adversaries. The stress on the doctrinal features of such speaking (הריה) has led to conclusions that the speaker would be

12. See more about the relationship of the Self-glorification Hymn with the Hodayot in the excursus: Parallels in the Hodayot in J.J. Collins, *The Scepter and the Star. The Messiahs of the Dead Sea Scrolls and Other Ancient Literature*, New York, Doubleday, 1995, p. 138 and Eshel, *4Q471b* (n. 11), pp. 191-194.

the Teacher of Righteousness or a High Priest of Qumran, since they were responsible for teaching in the יחד[13].

In the Hodayot we observe the "wonderful mysteries" (רזי פלא) as the object of the instruction (1QH[a] XIX 4 and 9-10). In the context of 1QH[a] XIX the expressions referring to "being taught" and "being instructed" are inserted in a hymn with references to communion with the angels and calls to worship. Since the context of these expressions referring to the "teaching" is not of doctrinal instruction or interpretation of the Scripture, we can interpret them in a broader context, as the distinctive religious knowledge of that Jewish sect.

III

The expressions of exaltation of the speaker also cannot be separated from those that express suffering. They are also presented in the first person in the form of a rhetorical question: "Who bea[rs all] sorrows like me? And who [suffe]rs evil like me?" (4Q491 9 and also in 4Q471 2). It is interesting to note that these boastings of being able to bear suffering are located between expressions of dwelling among the angels in 4Q471 as well as in 4Q491c.

This information has been also attributed to the biography of the Teacher of Righteousness. But they can also be related to the social life of the community if we associate them with the few but important references to the poor in the hymn. At the top of 4Q491c we read about the "council of the poor for an eternal congregation" (4). We should also observe that 4Q427 7 I+9 is followed by column II – in its place in the Hodayot of the Cave 4 – where we read: "Great is the God [who works wonders] for he brings down the arrogant spirit without even a remnant;

13. We are trying to give alternatives to the identification of the author of the Self-glorification Hymn with the Teacher of Righteousness or with a Qumran Priest. FLETCHER-LOUIS, *All the Glory of Adam* (n. 8), p. 205, suggests that the author was a High Priest because of his teaching work. ESHEL, *4Q471b* (n. 11), p. 201, and COLLINS, *The Scepter and the Star* (n. 12), pp. 146-149, ascribe the Hymn to an eschatological figure. Eshel thinks that he is an eschatological High Priest. In an unpublished article, *Amazing Grace. The Transformation of the Thanksgiving Hymn at Qumran*, read at the conference "*Up with a Shout: The Psalms in Jewish and Christian, Religious, Artistic and Intellectual Traditions*" at Yale, Jan 20-23, 2001, p. 7, J.J. Collins admits that there is "an affinity between the congregation and the individual speaker", that the exaltation experience of the speaker be shared by the congregation. M. WISE, *מי כמוני באלים. A Study of 4Q491c, 4Q471b, 4Q427 7 and 1QH[a] 25:35-26:10*, in *DSD* 7 (2000) 131-52, p. 218, defends the interpretation of the Teacher of Righteousness authorship, but he admits: "each individual believer could make them [the statements of the Hymn] true for himself or herself by partaking in the charisma of the Teacher".

and he raises the poor from the dust to [...] and up to the clouds he extols him in stature and together with the gods in the congregation of the community" (8-9).

These three semantic fields – referring to exaltation, suffering and to distinctive religious knowledge – must be interpreted together as central expressions of the religious identity of that group. This is why we find the rhetorical question concerning the three themes: a) "who is comparable to me in my glory?", b) "who suffers evil like me?", c) "Who can endure the flow of my lips?"

But the specific context where the religious identity of that group emerges in the Self-glorification Hymn is worship. This is made evident through liturgical expressions and summons to praise that follow both versions of the text. In A: "sing" (2x), "rejoice", "exult", "ascribe greatness", "sanctify his name", "raise your voices", "unceasingly bow down", "bless" and in the recension B: "exult" (2x), "rejoice", "sing", "proclaim", "jubilation". They show that the Self-glorification Hymn was inserted as the summit of praise to the community. And the summoned people should not only be expectant of the glory of the speaker, on the contrary, they have to join with him in the heavenly realm, as evident in 4Q491c 13-18: " rejoice *in the united assem]bly of God*, exult in the tent of salvation, praise *in the [holy] residence*, [*e*]*xalt together with the eternal host* ... unceasingly bow down *in the united assembly*". If we identify the "assembly of God", the "holy residence" and the "eternal host" as the angelic assembly in the heavens and assume that the audience is challenged to join them, then we can consider the possibility that the experience of this hymn is not exclusive to the speaker but also interchangeable.

Our hypothesis is that the Self-glorification Hymn reflects the context of an ecstatic worship which involves the whole community once the speaker summons all his hearers to take part in heavenly worship. That can be deduced from the imperatives to praise and to join the celestial assembly. This hymn also presents the religious identity of the group with all its ambiguities: at the same time they are exalted among the heavenly beings, possess a distinctive discourse that differentiates them from the context, and possibly suffer some degree of persecution and poverty.

Their self-identity, in terms of the suffering that they are facing and fidelity to the discourse that separates them from society, became marks required for their religious experience of ascending to the heavens, joining with the angels and – possibly – sitting on thrones.

We can grant that this religious experience could be experienced by their leaders, but not exclusively by them, as the summons to join the praise in heaven as the two recensions have shown. It is not absurd to imagine that this kind of exaltation was accessible to more people in the *yahad*. In religions of trance this type of experience and competence is not restricted to the leaders. This is not what we can observe in modern analogies, such as third world Pentecostal churches or Afro-Cuban and Afro-Brazilian *orissa* religions, where almost the whole community is possessed by the experience of trance. That these skills are required of the leaders does not imply that they are limited to them.

In the New Testament Paul boasts of having ascended to the third heaven and of speaking more in tongues than anyone in the Corinthian community, though many other people possessed that ability in Corinth.

In Revelation the democratization of the trance seems to be more evident, since people characterized as ideal members of the community are expected to take part in the heavenly liturgies. It is also possible to see analogies between the skills required of the readers of Revelation and the speaker of the Self-glorification Hymn: they are people submitted to a situation of suffering and social segregation, they bear witness (also a kind of distinctive speaking), and their true identities manifests themselves in their communion with angels in the heavenly worship.

Even if the Teacher of Righteousness (or an important priest from Qumran) is the author of the Self-Glorification Hymn – a thesis with which we do not agree – his experience of cultic exaltation, in the parameters we are proposing here, would represent no more than the tip of the iceberg in the spirituality of the members of the *yahad*.

Universidade Metodista de São Paulo
R. do Sacramento, 495 Ap. 112-VI
BR-09640-000 SBC-SP

Paolo Augusto DE SOUZA NOGUEIRA

MAKARISMEN IN DEN QUMRANTEXTEN UND IM NEUEN TESTAMENT

I. Einleitung

Bei dem Gesamttext von 4Q525 handelt es sich um einen Weisheitstext, der insgesamt eine große Nähe zu Prov hat. Er ist erhalten in ca. 50 Fragmenten, abgeschrieben am Übergang von späthasmonäischer zu frühherodianischer Schrift, also ca. in der ersten Hälfte des ersten Jahrhunderts v.Chr. Der Name Béatitudes beschreibt sachgerecht lediglich Kolumne 2 der Fragmente 2 und 3, und diese 10 Zeilen waren es auch, die seit der Vorankündigung von J. Starcky[1] die Diskussion beherrschten. In dieser Reihe von vier vollständig erhaltenen und einem weiteren aufgrund von Ps 15,2f relativ sicher zu rekonstruierenden Makarismus (vor Zeile 1) war die nächste Analogie zu den Makarismenreihungen der Bergpredigt bzw. der Feldrede gegeben. Es ist darum nicht verwunderlich, daß dieser Bezug die Arbeit an diesem Text bestimmte, und zwar sowohl was die formale (Form und Zahl der Makarismen) als auch was die inhaltliche Seite (ethische und eschatologische Ausrichtung) betrifft; freilich hat man dabei nicht immer die notwendige methodische Sorgfalt walten lassen. Dies bezieht sich m.E. insbesondere auf E. Puechs wiederholt geäußertes Postulat, man könne in Analogie zu Mt 5,3-12 bzw. dem von ihm rekonstruierten Makarismus 1QH^{a} VI 13-15 über die belegten 4+1 Makarismen von 7 bzw. 8+1 ausgehen.

Hier ist zu bedenken, daß Mt einerseits ca. 200 Jahre später als die Entstehung (nicht Abschrift) von 4Q525 ist, andererseits die mt Fassung der Makarismen gegenüber Lk (bzw. Q) sekundär ist. Nach einem weitgehenden Konsens hat Lk nicht nur die ursprüngliche Zahl (3+1), sondern auch mit der Anrede in der 2. Pers. Pl. die wahrscheinlichere Form erhalten. Die Ausgestaltung mit 8+1 bei Mt ist demgegenüber als mt Erweiterung zu betrachten, die sich weitgehend schriftgelehrter Exegese bzw. einer ethisch-paränetischen Ausrichtung verdankt; dazu gehört auch der Wechsel in die 3. Person, die einerseits alttestamentlich ist, andererseits in der späteren rabbinischen Verwendung bevorzugt wird. Die

1. *Le travail d'édition des fragments manuscrits de Qumrân*, in *RB* 63 (1956), S. 67: „Un manuscrit de caractère sapientiel contient une série de macarismes pour ceux qui accomplissent les commandements [...אשרי] et la description des tourments qui attendent les impies“ (zitiert nach É. Puech, DJD, 25, S. 115 Anm. 1).

Weherufe bei Lukas ihrerseits könnten lukanisches Werk sein. Es ist daher methodisch bedenklich, aufgrund der mt Endgestalt auf die ursprüngliche Zahl der Makarismen in 4Q525 zu schließen. Formal gesehen gibt es eine wichtige Gemeinsamkeit zwischen Mt/Lk und 4Q525 im Achtergewicht des letzten Makarismus: 4Q525 bietet ein ungewöhnliches Beispiel für die paränetische Ausgestaltung des letzten Gliedes (Z. 3-10), wie sie auch in Mt 5,11f/Lk 6,23f begegnet – darauf hat Heinz-Josef Fabry[2] besonders hingewiesen –, aber auch z.B. in slHen 42,14 vorliegt:

> Selig sind, welche jedes von Gott gemachte Werk des Herrn begreifen und es preisen. Denn die Werke des Herrn sind gerecht, aber die Werke des Menschen – die einen sind gut, die anderen aber sind böse. Und an den Werken werden die Lästerlügner erkannt.

Für die Achtzahl Sir 14,20-27 zu bemühen (so É. Puech), ist methodisch unzulässig, da dort keine Wiederaufnahme von אשרי erscheint. Offenbar wiederholen sich an jedem Text die methodischen Fehler, die von Anfang an die Erfassung des Verhältnisses von Qumran zum Neuen Testament belasteten.

II. Zur Vorgeschichte der alttestamentlichen Gattung

Die Vorgeschichte der Sprachform des Makarismus ist – wie mir scheint – nicht sicher geklärt. „In der Keilschrift-Literatur gibt es keine befriedigenden Parallelen“[3]. Dort finden sich Wendungen, die die Psalmensprache vorbereiten: „Möge er glücklich sein“[4]. Die Belege weisen eher nach Ägypten (J. Dupont). Bei Petosiris (2. Jh. v. Chr.) finden sich ganz enge Berührungen: „Glücklich der Mann, der sein Herz auf den Weg des Lebens führt“, „Glücklich der, der Gott liebt“, „Glücklich der, den sein Herz auf den Weg der Treue führt“. Aber auch schon 1000 Jahre früher (Ramses II) begegnet die Form: „Glücklich, wer dich versteht, Amon“[5]. Von Ägypten her legte sich für die alttestamentlichen Makarismen eine Herkunft aus der Weisheit nahe. Dies ist nach wie vor umstritten: K. Koch[6] hält einen kultischen Ursprung für plausi-

2. H.-J. Fabry, *Die Seligpreisungen in der Bibel und in Qumran*, in Ch. Hempel – A. Lange – H. Lichtenberger (Hgg.), *The Wisdom Texts from Qumran and the Development of Sapiential Thought* (BETL, 159), Leuven, 2002, S. 189-200, hier S. 195.
3. H. Cazelles, in *ThWAT*, I, S. 483.
4. *ANET*, S. 387.
5. Nach Cazelles, S. 483.
6. K. Koch, *Was ist Formgeschichte? Methoden der Bibelexegese*, Neukirchen, [5]1989, S. 21 A1a.

bel, da sich 60% der alttestamentlichen Makarismen in den Psalmen finden; ein weisheitlicher Gebrauch wäre demgegenüber sekundär. Gerade im Blick auf den Psalter widerspricht hier E. Zenger[7], der den Sitz im Leben im staatlich-politischen Bereich und in der Weisheitsschule ansetzt. Die Frage wäre dann, ob es überhaupt einen kultischen Bezug außerhalb der Sammlung (welcher?) des Psalters gibt. Für unsere Fragestellung kann diese Problematik zunächst auf sich beruhen, da hier der weisheitliche Kontext evident ist, aber wir müssen wieder darauf zurückkommen.

III. Die Form der Makarismen

Wenn wir bisher von Seligpreisungen oder Makarismen gesprochen haben, so geschah das relativ unreflektiert, was aber gemeint war, ist eindeutig: eine bestimmte Form der Rede, die zunächst einmal ganz einfach dadurch charakterisiert war, daß sie mit אשרי bzw. μακάριος/μακάριοι eingeleitet wird. Wir gehen noch einen Schritt weiter und fügen eine zweite Beobachtung hinzu: 4Q525 bietet eine Reihung von Makarismen.

1. Einzelne Makarismen

Makarismen sind der Antike insgesamt eigen. Für das Verständnis des Psalters ist von weitreichender Bedeutung der Beginn mit Ps 1,1: ... אשרי האיש. Doch auch in der griechischen Welt war der Makarismus zu Hause. Wir achten auf Semantik des Wortes und auf die Form des Makarismus. μακάριοι sind eigentlich Götter, im Gegensatz zu den Menschen, Homer, Od 5,7: „glückselige Götter, die unsterblich (= immer) sind". Wenn es dann bei Hesiod von Menschen gebraucht wird, so in bezug auf den seligen, göttergleichen Zustand im Jenseits auf den Inseln der Seligen. μακάριοι beschreibt also „den glücklichen Zustand der über irdische Leiden und Mühen erhabenen Götter und geht über das bloße εὐδαίμων hinaus"[8]. Seit Aristophanes (5./4. Jh.) geht es in die Alltagssprache über und bezeichnet das angenehme Leben der Reichen. Aristoteles differenziert wieder: Die Götter haben die vollkommene Glückseligkeit (die μακαριότης, den Menschen kommt nur εὐδαιμονία zu). Es findet sich auch die feste Form des Makarismus, bezogen auf irdisches Glück. Homer, Od 24,191f: „Glücklicher ... Odysseus, wahr-

7. E. Zenger, in F.-L. Hossfeld – E. Zenger, *Die Psalmen I*, Würzburg, 1993, S. 45.
8. F. Hauck, in *ThWNT*, IV, S. 365.

lich, dir ward eine Frau von großer Tugend beschieden". Oder in Bezug auf Eltern wohlgeratener Kinder; ich zitiere ein lateinisches Beispiel, Petronius, Satyricon 94,1: „Glücklich deine Mutter, die einen Sohn wie dich geboren hat". Auch die Wohlhabenden werden glücklich gepriesen, ebenso der, der Ruhm, Ehre und Tugend erworben hat. Freilich ist auch der Tote, der der Eitelkeit der Welt entkommen ist, μακάριος – von hier leitet sich auch der Sprachgebrauch der 'Seligen' als den Toten ab[9].

Jemand, der in einer Notlage ist, könnte dagegen niemals als אשרי bezeichnet werden. Dies gilt auch für das AT: „Eine Seligpreisung des Verfolgten aber sucht man im Alten Testament vergeblich"[10], denn[11] das den alttestamentlichen Seligpreisungen zugrundeliegende אשרי kommt von dem Verbum אשר, das 'glücklich preisen' heißt.

Neben dem Gebrauch mit Suffix wird der Satz oft mit einem Nomen weitergeführt, z.B. Ps 32,2: „Wohl dem Menschen, dem der Herr die Schuld nicht zurechnet, in dessen Geist kein Falsch ist".

Die alttestamentlichen Seligpreisungen wird man am ehesten als „prädikative(n) Heilsspruch (...) verstehen, der einen Menschen (oder eine Personengruppe) aufgrund seines beglückenden Heilszustandes lobend hervorhebt und als exemplarisch – insofern ermahnend – hinstellt, und der vor allem im weisheitlichen, dann aber auch im engeren religiösen Interesse ergangen sein dürfte"[12]. Besonders in weisheitlichen Kontexten bezieht sich der Makarismus auf Besitz von Kindern, Schönheit und Ehre, aber auch das Finden der Weisheit. Der wird als glücklich gepriesen, der auf Gott vertraut, der auf ihn baut, ihn fürchtet und liebt: Ps 2,12: ... אשרי „Wohl denen, die auf ihn trauen!" und Prov 28,14 „Glückselig der Mensch/Mann, der allezeit in der Furcht Gottes bleibt". Gottes Volk wird glückselig gepriesen: Dtn 33,29 (beachte hier, anders als in den Beispielen zuvor, die 2. Person!) אשריך ישראל. אשרי ist, wem die Sünden vergeben sind (Ps 32,1-2) oder der vor Sünde bewahrt wurde.

Schließlich kann im 4. Makk 7 der Märtyrer μακάριος genannt werden und die Hoffnung auf die ewige Seligkeit 'glückseliges Leben'. „O, welch glückseliges Greisenalter, welch ehrfurchtgebietendes Silberhaar, welch gesetzestreues Leben, das im Tod das Siegel der Glaubwürdigkeit und seiner Vollendung fand" (7,15). Am deutlichsten schließlich in

9. Christlich erst nachkonstantinisch; auf jüdischen Grabinschriften nur einmal μακάριος, *CIJ* II, S. 1175; wenn ich recht sehe, findet sich auf keinem antiken jüdischen Grabstein ein ausgeführter Makarismus.

10. W. ZIMMERLI, *Die Seligpreisungen der Bergpredigt und das AT*, in E. BAMMEL u.a. (Hgg.), *Donum Gentilicium*. FS D. Daube, Oxford, 1978, S. 8-26, hier 16.

11. Cf. CAZELLES, in *ThWAT*, I, S. 481-485.

12. M. SABØ, *THAT*, I, S. 259.

äthHen 58,2: „Selig seid ihr Gerechten und Auserwählten, denn herrlich wird euer Los sein".

Damit haben wir auch einen Übergang geschaffen von weisheitlichen zu apokalyptischen Makarismen.

Wie bei den weisheitlichen gibt es hier häufig eine Begründung: slavHen 42,11: „Selig ist, wer den Samen der Gerechtigkeit ausstreut, denn er erntet siebenfältig". Oft stehen solche Makarismen am Abschluß einer weisheitlichen oder eschatologischen Belehrung (zu weiteren eschatologisch ausgerichteten Makarismen siehe bei den Reihungen).

Zusammenfassung

In der alttestamentlich-jüdischen Überlieferung finden wir den Makarismus besonders in weisheitlichen und apokalyptischen Kontexten. Er ist ein Heilsspruch über einen glücklichen, gesegneten Menschen bzw. eine Gruppe, Israel. Er begegnet vorherrschend in der 3. Person: „Glückselig der Mann der...", jedoch auch in der 2. Person: „Glückselig bist du, Israel...".

2. *Makarismenreihungen*

Makarismenreihungen begegnen uns in der alttestamentlich-jüdischen Überlieferung sowohl in weisheitlichen wie in apokalyptischen Texten:

Weisheitlich z.B. Sir 25,7-11:

> Neun Erkenntnisse preise ich glücklich im Herzen
> und das Zehnte spreche ich aus mit meiner Zunge:
> Ein Mensch, der fröhlich ist über seine Kinder,
> wer zu Lebzeiten sieht den Fall der Feinde.
> Glückselig ist, wer mit einer verständigen Frau zusammenlebt,
> und der mit seiner Zunge keine Übertretung verübt
> und der nicht Diener eines Menschen sein muß, der seiner unwürdig ist.
> Glückselig ist der, der Einsicht findet,
> und der, der sie ausspricht vor den Ohren derer, die zuhören.
> Wie groß ist der, der Wahrheit findet!
> Aber keiner überragt den, der den Herrn findet[13].

Apokalyptisch slavHen 42,6ff:

> Ich aber sage euch, meine Kinder:
> Selig ist, wer den Namen des Herrn fürchtet und im-
> mer vor seinem Angesicht dient, und die Gaben aufrichtig ordnet mit Furcht in diesem Leben, und in diesem Leben gerecht lebt und stirbt.

13. Übers. G. SAUER, *Jesus Sirach*, JSHRZ, III,5, S. 567.

Selig ist, wer ein gerechtes Gericht hält, nicht um eines Lohnes, sondern um der Gerechtigkeit willen, ohne danach irgendwelche Dinge zu erhoffen. Schließlich wird ihm ein Gericht ohne Ansehen der Person folgen.
Selig ist, wer die Nackten mit einem Gewand bekleidet und dem Hungrigen sein Brot gibt.
Selig ist, wer ein gerechtes Gericht für die Waise und die Witwe richtet und jedem Gekränkten hilft.
Selig ist, wer sich abwendet vom zeitlichen Weg dieser nichtigen Welt und wandelt auf dem rechten Weg, der in jenes endlose Leben führt.
Selig ist, wer gerechten Samen sät, denn er wird siebenfach ernten.
Selig ist, in welchem die Wahrheit ist, damit er auch die Wahrheit zu seinem Nächsten redet.
Selig ist, wer Barmherzigkeit in seinem Munde hat und Sanftmut im Herzen.
Selig sind, welche jedes von Gott gemachte Werk des Herrn begreifen und es preisen. Denn die Werke des Herrn sind gerecht, aber die Werke des Menschen – die einen sind gut, die anderen aber sind böse. Und an den Werken werden die Lästerlügner erkannt[14].

Antithetisch können 'Wehe' und 'Glückselig' einander gegenüberstehen: „Wehe dir, Land, dessen König ein Kind ist und dessen Fürsten am Morgen schon schwelgen.

Wohl dir, Land, dessen König ein Edler ist und dessen Fürsten zur rechten Zeit essen, als Männer und nicht als Zecher“ (Koh 10,16f).

Heilsaussage und Unheilsaussage, Selig und Weh begegnen auch nebeneinander bzw. parallel. Diese Reihen von Seligpreisungen können zusammenstehen mit Verfluchungen. Hier wieder ein Beispiel aus dem pseudepigraphischen Schrifttum, wobei besonders die Parallelität von Heilsaussage und Unheilsaussage zu beachten ist:

slavHen 52:

Selig ist der Mensch, der seinen Mund öffnet zum Lob des Gottes Sabaoth und den Herrn lobt mit seinem ganzen Herzen.
Verflucht ist jeder Mensch, der sein Herz öffnet zur Schmähung und den Armen schmäht und den Nächsten verleumdet, denn dieser schmäht Gott.
Selig ist, wer seinen Mund öffnet, um Gott zu rühmen und zu preisen.
Verflucht ist, wer seinen Mund öffnet für Flüche und für Lästerung vor dem Angesicht des Herrn alle seine Tage.
Selig ist, wer alle Werke des Herrn rühmt.
Verflucht ist, wer alle Geschöpfe des Herrn schmäht.
Selig ist, wer darauf sieht, die Arbeiten seiner Hände aufzurichten.
Verflucht ist, wer schaut und eifert, das Fremde zu verderben.
Selig ist, wer die Fundamente seiner Väter, die von Anbeginn an sind, bewahrt.
Verflucht ist, wer die Festsetzungen seiner Vorfahren und Väter zerstört.

14. Ch. Böttrich, *Das slavische Henochbuch,* JSHRZ, V,7, S. 955-957.

> Selig ist, wer den Frieden der Liebe pflanzt.
> Verflucht ist, wer die aus Liebe Friedfertigen zugrunde richtet.
> Selig ist, wer auch wenn er mit der Zunge nicht Frieden sagt, [dennoch] in seinem Herzen Frieden zu allen hat.
> Verflucht ist, wer mit seiner Zunge Frieden sagt, aber in seinem Herzen keinen Frieden hat, sondern ein Schwert.
> Dies alles wird aufgedeckt werden auf Waagen und in Büchern am Tag des großen Gerichts[15].

In dem vorstehenden Beispiel finden wir Heilsaussage und Unheilsaussage jeweils parallel zugeordnet; Heilsaussage in einer Reihe, einer Reihe von Unheilsaussagen gegenüber begegnen häufiger Segens- und Fluchreihen. Vorgreifend zitiere ich ein Beispiel aus den Qumrantexten: 1QM XIII 2ff.

> Gepriesen ist der Gott Israels in seinem gesamten heiligen Plan und den Werken seiner Wahrheit und gepriesen sind alle, die ihm in Gerechtigkeit dienen, die ihn in Treue erkennen.
> Aber verflucht ist Belial im Plan seiner Feindschaft, und verwünscht ist er in der Herrschaft seiner Schuld.
> Und verflucht sind alle Geister seines Loses in ihrem ruchlosen Plan, und verwünscht sind sie in allem Dienst ihrer abscheulichen Unreinheit.
> Denn sie sind das Los der Finsternis, aber Gottes Los gehört zum ewigen Licht[16].

Ein rabbinisches Beispiel für die gegensätzliche Parallelität bBer 61b:

> Heil dir, Rabbi Aqiba, daß du festgenommen worden bist wegen Worten der Tora; wehe aber dem Papos, der festgenommen worden ist wegen eitler Dinge.

Frühchristliche Seligpreisungen außerhalb des NT greifen Evangelienüberlieferung auf, so EvThom 54:

> Jesus sprach:
> „Selig sind die Armen, denn euer ist das Reich der Himmel",

oder 68-69:

> Jesus sprach:
> „Ihr seid selig, wenn sie euch hassen und verfolgen, und sie werden keinen Platz finden an dem Ort, an dem sie euch verfolgten!
> Selig sind die, welche verfolgt werden in ihrem Herzen! Jene sind es, die den Vater in Wahrheit erkannt haben.
> Selig sind die Hungernden, denn man wird den Leib dessen füllen, der wünscht"[17].

15. *Ibid.*, S. 975-977.
16. Übers. nach E. LOHSE, *Die Texte aus Qumran,* München, 1964, S. 209-211 (Änderungen H. L.).
17. Übers. E. HAENCHEN, in K. ALAND, *Synopsis Quattuor Evangeliorum,* Stuttgart, ^{3}1988, S. 524.526.

Eine ausführliche Makarismenreihe findet sich in den ActPaul 5-6: (Paulus spricht):

> Selig sind, die reinen Herzens sind, denn sie werden Gott schauen.
> Selig sind, die ihr Fleisch rein bewahrt haben, denn sie werden ein Tempel Gottes werden.
> Selig sind die Enthaltsamen, denn Gott wird zu ihnen reden.
> Selig sind, die dieser Welt entsagt haben, denn sie werden Gott wohlgefallen.
> Selig sind, die Frauen haben, als hätten sie nicht, denn sie werden Gott beerben.
> Selig sind, die Gottesfurcht haben, denn sie werden Engel Gottes werden.
> Selig sind, die vor den Worten Gottes zittern, denn sie werden getröstet werden.
> Selig sind, die die Weisheit Jesu ergriffen haben, denn sie werden Söhne des Höchsten heißen.
> Selig sind, die die Taufe bewahrt haben, denn sie werden bei dem Vater und dem Sohn ausruhen.
> Selig sind, die das Verständnis Jesu Christi erfaßt haben, denn sie werden im Lichte sein.
> Selig sind, die um der Liebe Gottes willen das weltliche Wesen verlassen haben, denn sie werden Engel richten und zur Rechten des Vaters gesegnet werden.
> Selig sind die Barmherzigen, denn sie werden Barmherzigkeit erlangen, und den bitteren Tag des Gerichts werden sie nicht sehen.
> Selig sind die Leiber der Jungfrauen, denn sie werden Gott wohlgefallen und sie werden den Lohn ihrer Keuschheit nicht verlieren.
> Denn das Wort des Vaters wird ihnen zum Werk der Rettung auf den Tag des Sohnes werden, und sie werden Ruhe finden in alle Ewigkeit[18].

D.h. eine Reihe von dreizehn Seligpreisungen, die Gut der Seligpreisungen der Evangelien und anderes Gut der Jesusüberlieferung aufnimmt und in den Dienst der besonderen Tugend- und Keuschheitspredigt der Paulusakten stellt.

Zusammenfassung

1. Die beiden Formen, die Seligpreisung in der 3. Person: „Glückselig ist der Mann", „ist wer... /sind die...", und die in der 2. Person: „Glückselig bist du, seid ihr...", sind in der alttestamentlich-jüdischen und neutestamentlichen Überlieferung verbreitet. Dabei ist die 3. Person häufiger.
2. Desgleichen finden wir dort Reihungen von Seligpreisungen und auch parallel Reihungen von Verwünschungen/Verfluchungen.

18. Übers. W. SCHNEEMELCHER, in DERS., *Neutestamentliche Apokryphen II. Apostolisches, Apokalypsen und Verwandtes*, Tübingen, ^{5}1989, S. 216f.

3. Während der weisheitliche Makarismus einen gegenwärtigen Glücks- oder Heilszustand eines Menschen/Volkes/einer Gruppe anspricht, hat der apokalyptische Makarismus, ausgehend von der Seligpreisung einer Person, deren Tun, Eigenschaft o.ä., das endzeitliche Ergehen im Blick: „Selig seid ihr Gerechten und Auserwählten, denn euer Los wird herrlich sein" (äthHen 58,2). Die Seligpreisungen der Bergpredigt und Feldrede sowie die Weherufe der Feldrede gehören zur apokalyptischen Gruppe.

IV. Makarismen im rabbinischen Judentum

Blickt man in die gängigen Lexika, so scheint sich das Urteil K. Kochs[19] zu bestätigen, in rabbinischen Texten tauchten Makarismen „auffallend selten" auf. So bietet ThWNT[20] einen Beleg (bHag 14b), ThWAT[21] verweist lediglich auf Billerbeck und behauptet darüber hinaus, in Qumran käme אשרי nicht vor. G. Strecker in EWNT[22] nennt keinen einzigen Beleg, auch nicht in seinem Bergpredigtkommentar[23]. Der Vernachlässigung des rabbinischen Materials hat M. Hengel abgeholfen und eine umfassende Sammlung von Makarismen zusammengestellt[24]. Nur drei Phänomene sollen hervorgehoben werden:
(1) Das Überwiegen der Anrede 2. Pers. sing/pl in Mischna und Tosephta; in späteren Texten dagegen eher die 3. Pers. sing/pl.
(2) Auch in der rabbinischen Literatur wird die Makarismenreihung verwendet, dabei werden drei Glieder selten überschritten, am bekanntesten bHag 14b, R. Johanan ben Zakkai zu zweien seiner Schüler:

Heil euch und
Heil euren Müttern!
Heil auch meinen Augen, die das gesehen haben.

(3) Es findet sich auch antithetische Struktur heil-wehe, z.B. bJoma 86a in einer Baraita, die Dtn 6,5 auslegt[25].

Der Name des Himmels soll durch dich beliebt werden (vgl. Mt 5,16). Wenn jemand (die Schrift) liest, (die Tora) studiert und Gelehrtenschüler

19. *Formgeschichte* (Anm. 6), S. 9, Anm. 8; s. M. Hengel, *Zur matthäischen Bergpredigt und ihrem jüdischen Hintergrund,* in *ThR* 52 (1987) 327-400; jetzt in Ders., *Judaica, Hellenistica et Christiana, Kleine Schriften II,* Tübingen, 1999, S. 219-292.
20. G. Bertram, *ThWNT*, IV, S. 369.
21. Cazelles, *ThWAT,* I, S. 484.
22. G. Strecker, *EWNT*, II, S. 925-932.
23. G. Strecker, *Die Bergpredigt, Ein exegetischer Kommentar*, Göttingen, ²1985.
24. Hengel, *Zur matthäischen Bergpredigt* (Anm. 19), S. 332-341.
25. *Ibid.*, S. 337.

bedient und im Verkehr mit Menschen freundlich ist, was sprechen die Leute über ihn? „*Heil* seinem Vater, der ihn die Tora lehrte, *heil* seinem Lehrer; *wehe* den Leuten, die die Tora nicht gelernt haben…“. Wenn einer Tora studiert, aber im Handel nicht gewissenhaft und im Gespräch mit Menschen nicht freundlich ist, was sagen die Menschen über ihn? „*Wehe* dem, der ihn Tora lehrte, *wehe* seinem Vater, der ihn Tora lehrte, *wehe* seinem Lehrer, der ihn Tora lehrte“.

Die rabbinischen Belege machen deutlich, daß die biblische Sprachform des Makarismus über Jahrhunderte hin gepflegt wurde, und daß sie eindeutig im nichtkultischen Bereich zuhause ist. Darum ist es nicht verwunderlich, daß Seligpreisungen auch in den Qumranfunden erhalten sind, erstaunlich jedoch ist ihre geringe Zahl.

V. 4Q185: Eine weisheitliche Mahnrede mit Seligpreisungen

Fünf Jahre nach dem Erscheinen von DJD, 5[26] hat H. Cazelles[27] die irrtümliche Behauptung aufgestellt, אשרי sei in den Qumranfunden nicht belegt[28]. Der wegen seines beklagenswerten Erhaltungszustandes und seiner schwierigen Lesbarkeit wenig beachtete Text 4Q185 bietet gleich zwei Belege in einem eindeutig weisheitlichen Kontext[29].

Der Text ist leider nicht nur in seinen erhaltenen Partien sehr stark zerstört, auch das Vorliegende ist nur das Bruchstück eines größeren Textes. Er ist fragmentarisch auf 3 Kolumnen sowie einer Anzahl von Fragmenten erhalten, hat aber aufgrund der äußeren Gegebenheiten gewiß aus mehr Kolumnen als den vorliegenden bestanden.

Die Mahnrede ruft dazu auf, sich dem göttlichen Willen nicht zu verschließen, sondern aus seiner Befolgung Heil und Leben zu empfangen. Doch in welcher Weise tritt der Gotteswille in Erscheinung? Diese Fragestellung führt mitten in das Problem des Textes: J. Strugnell[30] hat bereits darauf hingewiesen, daß sich die Suffixe der 3. Person fem. Sing.

26. J.M. Allegro, *Qumrân Cave 4*, DJD, 5, Oxford, 1968.
27. *ThWAT*, I, S. 484.
28. Siehe H.-J. Fabry, *Der Makarismus, mehr als nur eine weisheitliche Lehrform. Gedanken zu dem neu-edierten Text 4Q525*, in J. Hausmann – H.-J. Zobel (Hgg.), *Alttestamentlicher Glaube und Biblische Theologie*. FS H. D. Preuß, Stuttgart, 1992, S. 362-371, hier S. 365.
29. Siehe zum folgenden H. Lichtenberger, *Eine weisheitliche Mahnrede in den Qumranfunden (4Q185)*, in M. Delcor (ed.), *Qumrân. Sa piété, sa théologie et son milieu*, Paris-Leuven, 1978, S. 151-162; Ders., *Der Weisheitstext 4Q185 – eine neue Edition*, in *The Wisdom Texts from Qumran* (Anm. 2), S. 127-150.
30. J. Strugnell, *Notes en marge du volume V des ‚Discoveries in the Judaean Desert of Jordan'*, in *RQ* 7 (1970) 161-276, zu 4Q185: S. 269-273.

auf die Weisheit oder das Gesetz beziehen können. Diese Auffassung erscheint uns sachgemäß, und man sollte zwischen den beiden Größen keine Alternative aufstellen: die sich an Dtn 4,6 anlehnende Identifikation von Weisheit und Gesetz ist auch hier vollzogen, und die Gaben, die in der Tora für das Tun des von Gott gebotenen Weges gegeben werden, sind eben die, die in weisheitlichen Texten die Gaben der Weisheit sind. Das besondere Spezifikum dieses Textes beruht aber darauf, daß hier nicht allein Israel angeredet wird, sondern sich deutliche Hinweise finden (leider hindert der schlechte Erhaltungszustand an ganz sicheren Aussagen), daß auch die Völker in bezug auf die Weisheit/das Gesetz angesprochen sind. Vielleicht hat gerade das in Dtn 4,6 genannte Staunen der Völker dazu geführt, nun auch diesen Israels Weisheit anzubieten.

Mit wechselnden Motiven, Gattungselementen und Redeformen wird die Mahnrede entfaltet:

In der Sprache und Topik der Ankündigung vom Kommen Jahwes (vgl. Nah 1) bzw. von Jahwes Boten (vgl. Mal 3) wird die Unmöglichkeit betont, vor Gottes Engeln und seinen Richtern zu bestehen (1-2 I 7-9); siehe auch Jes 66,14-16. Die Unfähigkeit, Bestand zu haben, ist begründet in der Nichtigkeit und Vergänglichkeit des Menschen. Nach einer Lehr-Eröffnungsformel ואתם בני „aber ihr, meine Söhne" (1-2 I 9) wird in einer Vergänglichkeitsklage das Geschick des Menschen dargelegt, unter deutlicher Verwendung von Jes 40,6-8; Ps 90,5-6; 103,15-16; Hiob 14,1.

> Denn siehe, wie Gras sproßt er,
> und (was) seine Schönheit (betrifft), (so) blüht er wie eine Blume;
> (doch) seine Anmut – weh[t] sein (scil. Gottes) Wind [darüber],
> dann vertrocknet sein Wurzelstock
> und seine Blüte nimmt der Wind weg,
> so daß [an seiner Ste]lle [gar] nichts mehr ist,
> und es ist nichts mehr da außer (dem) Wind.
> Man sucht ihn,
> aber man findet ihn nicht,
> und er hat keine Hoffnung,
> und seine Tage sind wie ein Schatten auf der Er[de].

Angesichts der Nichtigkeit des Menschen ermahnt ein erneuter Aufruf, „mein Volk" (1-2 I 13-14) zur Einsicht: „Toren kommen um vor der Macht unseres Gottes" (1-2 I 14). Die Taten Gottes an Ägypten sollen zur Warnung dienen: „so daß euer Herz aus Furcht vor ihm erschrecke" (1-2 I 15). Konsequenz daraus kann nur der Wandel entsprechend der göttlichen Weisung sein (1-2 II 1-4). Wer ihr folgt, erfährt täglich ihre reichen Güter und kommt durch Gefährdungen nicht mehr vom rechten Weg ab.

Nach einem Makarismus: ... אשרי אדם נתנה לו בן אד[ם „Glückselig ist der Mann, dem sie gegeben ist, der Mensch [...]" folgt der Einwand eines Frevlers 1-2 II 9-11.

Nachdem zuvor der glückselig gepriesen wurde (אדם נתנה לו), dem sie gegeben ist (1-2 II 8), wird in einem weiteren Makarismus der אשרי genannt, der sie erwirbt (1-2 II 13 אדם יעשנה) und sie, wie sie seinen Vätern gegeben wurde, in Besitz nimmt und an seine Nachkommen weitergibt (1-2 II 13-15).

Gattungsmäßig läßt sich der Text im weiteren Sinne zur Gruppe weisheitlicher Mahnreden stellen. Wir finden aber innerhalb dieser Rahmengattung verschiedene Gattungselemente, die dem Text in ihrer Folge eine starke Bewegtheit geben, z.B. Belehrung mit Lehr-Eröffnungsanruf, Elemente der Vergänglichkeitsklage, Erinnerung an Geschichte, Imperativreihen, Einrede von Frevlern und Makarismen.

Der Text kann trotz seines Fundes in Qumran und trotz einer Reihe von Parallelen nicht als ein typisches Beispiel für die Qumranschriften gelten, er reicht seiner Entstehung nach wahrscheinlich in vorqumranische Zeit[31].

VI. Eine Seligpreisung in 1QH VI 13-16?

É. Puech[32] glaubt im Zuge der Reorganisation der Handschrift 1QH[a33] für VI 13-16 eine Seligpreisung entdeckt zu haben:

13 אשרי] אנשי אמת ובחורי צדק דורשי
14 שכל ומבקשי בינה בונ[י (?) שלום (?)
ואו[הבי רחמים וענוי רוח מזוקקי
15 עוני וברורי מצרף רחומ[י סליחות (?)
ותמימי דרר (?)] מתאפקים עד קץ משפטיכה
16 וצופים לישועתך

31. Folgende Gründe sind dafür namhaft zu machen: 1. Es findet sich ein auffälliger Gebrauch der Defektivschreibung. 2. Der Text bietet eine Anzahl von Wörtern, die zum erstenmal in dem durch die Qumranfunde verfügbaren Schrifttum auftauchen, was aber hauptsächlich durch den besonderen Gegenstand bedingt sein wird. 3. Sprachlich auffällig ist die große Nähe zu späten Schriften des Alten Testaments und besonders zur Weisheitsliteratur. 4. Ein besonders wichtiges Argument für die frühe Entstehung des Textes liegt in der freien, d.h. außerhalb eines Bibelzitates vorkommenden Verwendung von יהוה (1-2 II 3) und אלהים (1-2 I 14). Die genannten Argumente können dafür sprechen, daß der Text vorqumranisch ist. Der Fund innerhalb des Komplexes der Qumrantexte belegt, daß er aber in Qumran in Gebrauch war; die späthasmonäische Handschrift bezeugt möglicherweise, daß er in der Qumrangemeinde kopiert wurde.

32. *Un hymne essénien en partie retrouvé et les Béatitudes. 1QH V 12-VI 18 [=col XIII-XIV 7] et 4QBéat*, in *RQ* 13 (1988) 59-88.

33. Vgl. H. Stegemann, *Rekonstruktion der Hodajot. Ursprüngliche Gestalt und kritisch bearbeiteter Text der Hymnenrolle aus Höhle 1 von Qumran*, Diss. phil. Heidelberg, 1963.

13 Selig,] die Männer der Wahrheit und die Erwählten der Gerechtigkeit, die suchen
14 nach Wissen und streben nach Einsicht, die Er[bauer des Friedens (?) und die] Vergebung lieben, die Armen des Geistes, die Gereinigten
15 von den (?) Sünden und die Reinen aus der Läuterung, die Erbarmten [der Verzeihungen und die, die auf dem richtigen Weg sind (?)], die sich zusammennehmen bis (zum Ende?) zur Zeit deines Gerichtes,
16 und die nach deiner Rettung Ausschau halten[34].

Wenn wir sicher sein könnten – das entscheidende אשרי ist ergänzt –, daß es sich um einen Makarismus handelt, würde er sich sehr gut in den weisheitlichen Kontext einfügen und darüber hinaus durch die enthaltenen eschatologischen Elemente belegen, daß weisheitliche und eschatologische Ausrichtung keineswegs einen Gegensatz darstellen.

VII. Wir ziehen eine Zwischenbilanz

Nicht erst durch das Bekanntwerden von 4Q525 ist evident, daß Seligpreisungen in den Qumranfunden erhalten sind. Das Grundproblem bleibt einerseits die spärliche Zahl der Belege, andererseits eine mögliche qumran-essenische Herkunft. Für 4Q185 erscheint mir eine voressenische Entstehung sicher; ist 1QH[a] VI ein Makarismus (אשרי ist ergänzt), wäre dies ein qumran-essenischer Beleg. Zu prüfen ist, ob 4Q525 qumran-essenischer Herkunft ist. Die starken Verbindungen zur späteren alttestamentlichen Weisheitsliteratur deuten eher auf eine voressenische Entstehung. Andererseits wird konsequent das Tetragramm vermieden. É. Puech verweist auf die sprachlichen Bezüge zu qumran-essenischen Texten wie S, H, M, CD[35]. Hier besteht weiterer Klärungsbedarf.

Ungeachtet einer Entscheidung über die qumran-essenische Entstehung von 4Q525 ist der Befund auffällig:

1. Das faktische Fehlen von Seligpreisungen in Texten der Qumrangemeinde, und
2. Eine Zahl von Segen- und Fluch-Reihen ארור ארורים//ברוך/ברוכים bzw. זעום/זעומים und eine starke Verbreitung der Segen- und Fluch-Terminologie.

Oben wurde vorgreifend 1QM XIII 2ff. zitiert; es sei an den bekanntesten Text aus 1QS II 1ff, der Adaption des aaronitischen Segens, erinnert:

34. Text und Übersetzung nach Fabry, *Der Makarismus* (Anm. 28), S. 336.
35. Puech, DJD, 25, S. 119.

Und die Priester sollen segnen alle Männer des Loses Gottes, die vollkommen wandeln in all seinen Wegen, und sie sollen sprechen:
„Er segne dich mit allem Guten,
und er behüte dich vor allem Bösen,
und er erleuchte dein Herz mit Erkenntnis des Lebens,
und er sei dir gnädig mit ewiger Erkenntnis,
und er erhebe das Angesicht seiner Gnaden über dich zum ewigen Frieden".
Und die Leviten sollen verfluchen alle Männer des Loses Belials und anheben und sprechen:
„Verflucht bist du in all den frevlerischen Werken deiner Verschuldung;
es gebe dir Gott Schrecken durch alle, die Rache rächen;
und er suche dich heim (mit) Vernichtung durch alle, die heimzahlen Vergeltung.
Verflucht bist du ohne Erbarmen entsprechend der Finsternis deiner Taten,
und verwünscht bist du in der Finsternis ewigen Feuers.
Nicht sei dir Gott gnädig, wenn du (zu ihm) rufst,
und nicht erbarme er sich, deine Sünden zu sühnen;
er erhebe sein zorniges Angesicht zur Rache über dich,
und nicht sei dir Friede durch alle, die Fürsprache einlegen".
Und alle, die in den Bund eintreten, (sollen) sprechen nach den Segnenden und den Verfluchenden:
„Amen, amen"[36].

Zu vergleichen sind die Flüche in 4Q280; 5Q14; 4Q509 u.a.; in den Gesamtkontext gehören auch die Beschwörungen in 11Q11 (PsAp[a]), die jedoch wohl voressenisch sind.

Ich ziehe wieder eine Zwischenbilanz:

Dem (fast?) völligen Fehlen von Seligpreisungen (und Wehe) steht ein deutliches Übergewicht von Segen- und Fluch-Formularen sowie überhaupt der Segen- und Fluch-Terminologie gegenüber. Die beiden (voressenischen) Texte, in denen Seligpreisungen belegt sind, sind eindeutig weisheitliche Texte. Dies führt zu der oben diskutierten Frage nach dem Sitz im Leben zurück: *Seligpreisungen* im weisheitlichen, lehrorientierten, 'laizistischen' Bereich; *Segen und Fluch* im kultischen Bereich.

Hier ist eine Zwischenbemerkung notwendig: Natürlich hat Segen und Segnen im AT auch in der Familie (z.B. Sterbesegen) und in der alltäglichen Kommunikation (Begrüßung; Abschied) seinen Ort. Aber die ritualisierte Form verweist auf den priesterlich/levitischen, also kultischen Bereich. Zu diesem eher privaten Bereich gehört im NT der Ab-

36. Übers. H. LICHTENBERGER, in J.H. CHARLESWORTH (Hg.), *The Dead Sea Scrolls: Rule of The Community. Photographic Multi-Language Edition*, Philadelphia, PA, 1996, S. 120f.

schiedssegen des Auferstandenen Lk 24,50: „er erhob die Hände und segnete sie; und es geschah, als er sie segnete, schied er von ihnen und fuhr auf gen Himmel“[37].

VIII. Eine Skizze des neutestamentlichen Befundes

Dem faktischen Fehlen der Seligpreisungen in Qumran steht ein eindeutiges Übergewicht in der Jesusüberlieferung gegenüber und ein programmatischer Gebrauch am Anfang der Bergpredigt. Wir nehmen darum noch einmal die Makarismen der Bergpredigt auf. Mit der Jesusüberlieferung kommen wir zugestandenermaßen nicht hinter Q zurück. Wie ich das Verhältnis der matthäischen und lukanischen Makarismen zu Q sehe, wurde oben erläutert.

Matthäus (bzw. z.T. ihm bereits vorliegend) hat in schriftgelehrter Weise neue Makarismen geschaffen, z.B.:
- die Sanftmütigen, die die Erde besitzen werden, verdanken sich Ps 37,11;
- die reinen Herzens sind Ps 24,4.

Daneben hat er eigene theologische Grundgedanken eingetragen:
- für ihn ist δικαιοσύνη von entscheidender Bedeutung; das Hungern und Dürsten nach Gerechtigkeit ist in seinem Sinn der ‘Rechttat’ zu verstehen,
- er selbst hat mit Hilfe der βασιλεία τῶν οὐρανῶν die erste und achte (!) seiner Makarismen gerahmt, bevor er entsprechend Q in die 2. pers.pl. übergeht: „Glückselig seid ihr, wenn sie euch schmähen“ etc.

Er schafft so einen Zyklus von 8+1 gegenüber dem lukanischen aus Q stammenden 3+1.

Der matthäischen Fassung einen ausschließlich paränetischen und demgegenüber der lukanischen einen deklaratorischen oder gar performativen Charakter zuzuschreiben, halte ich im Gesamtkontext der Bergpredigt für nicht angemessen. Denn Matthäus fährt fort:

> Ihr *seid* das Salz der Erde...
> Ihr *seid* das Licht der Welt....

Der matthäische Gesamtkontext ist die angebrochene und doch zukünftige βασιλεία: das zeigen auch die vorwiegend fut. passiv-Formen

37. Siehe jetzt die Tübinger Habilitationsschrift von U. HECKEL, *Der Segen im Neuen Testament. Begriff, Formeln* (2001/2).

in den ὅτι-Sätzen. Lk hat den Gegensatz von leidvoller Gegenwart und künftigem Heil durch νῦν geradezu verstärkt, vgl. Lk 16,25; der reiche Mann hat sein Gutes schon empfangen, Lazarus auf Erden nicht, darum wird er *jetzt* getröstet.

Das NT übermittelt in der Jesusüberlieferung zwar 'Weherufe' – das Pendant zu Seligpreisungen (cf. Lk), aber kein ἐπικατάρατος.

- Ausnahme: Verfluchung des Feigenbaumes Mk 11,21.

D.h. Jesus hat *nicht* die kultisch-priesterliche Sprachform des Fluches übernommen, wohl aber ihr Pendant: den Segen.

- Evident in Lk 6,28: „segnet, die euch verfluchen".
- Oder in der Aufnahme der Jesusüberlieferung bei Paulus:
- εὐλογεῖτε καὶ μὴ καταρᾶσθε „segnet, und verflucht nicht", Röm 12,14.

Wo die Jesusüberlieferung negative Aussagen über Menschen, Gruppen oder ganze Städte macht, gebraucht sie nicht ἐπικατάρατος, sondern οὐαί, das wir schon aus den lk. Weherufen (Lk 6,24-26 in Parallelität zu den lk Seligpreisungen) kennen. Dieses 'Wehe' findet sich reichlich (über die genannten der Feldrede hinaus).

Beispiele – über Chorazin und Bethsaida Mt 11,21

- in Mt 23 wiederholt über die Schriftgelehrten und Pharisäer
- bei Lk über die Gesetzeslehrer (νομικοί)
- über den, durch den σκάνδαλα entstehen Mt 18,7 bzw. der Mensch, durch den der Menschensohn ausgeliefert wird Mk 14,21 par Mt 26,24; Lk 22,22.

Zu vergleichen – aber darauf soll nur hingewiesen werden – wären auch die 'Wehe' in der JohApk, besonders die drei 'Wehe' in 9,12 („Das erste Wehe ist vorüber; siehe, es kommen danach noch zwei Wehe"). In JohApk findet sich auch das doppelte 'Wehe' οὐαὶ οὐαί 18,10.16.19 (über die große Stadt).

Neben Apg 23,14 ist Paulus der einzige Autor im NT, der ἀνάθεμα verwendet:

- er selbst möchte um des Heils Israels willen (lieber) ἀνάθεμα ... ἀπὸ τοῦ Χριστοῦ sein, Röm 9,3;
- keiner, der im Geist Gottes redet, kann sagen: ἀνάθεμα Ἰησοῦς, 1Kor 12,3;
- wer den Herrn nicht liebt, sei ἀνάθεμα 1Kor 16,22;

- wer immer (ihr oder ein Engel Gottes) ein anderes Evangelium verkündigt, sei ἀνάθεμα, Gal 1,8f.

IX. Schluss: Der Versuch einer Deutung

Diesem Fehlen der eigentlichen Fluchterminologie in der Jesusüberlieferung und der Seltenheit im übrigen NT (ἀνάθημα nur bei Paulus; s. weiter Apg 23,14) steht eine frappierende Häufigkeit in den (authentischen) Qumranfunden gegenüber. Das hat seinen Grund nicht darin, daß Qumran eben mehr vom Unheil redete, Jesus dagegen allein Verkündiger des Heils wäre. Eine solche Sicht würde die Befunde für beide Bereiche unzulässig und klischeehaft verkürzen. Die Qumrantexte stellen durchweg neben die Fluchaussagen die Segens- und Heilsaussage, wie in der Jesusverkündigung bzw. Jesusüberlieferung neben die μακάριος/μακάριοι-Wendungen die οὐαί-Aussagen treten.

Die Antwort muß auf einer anderen Ebene gesucht werden, die m.E. historisch, traditionsgeschichtlich-soziologisch zu bestimmen ist: Die Segen- und Fluchformulare in Qumran leiten sich aus der geschichtlichen Herkunft der Qumran-Essener aus einer priesterlichen, vom Tempel kommenden Gruppe her, und bekunden die fortdauernde Dominanz priesterlichen Denkens und Handelns in Qumran.

Jesus und die Jesusbewegung verwenden die weisheitlicher und 'laizistischer' Tradition entstammenden Makarismen und Weherufe und greifen auch dort, wo sie Segensbegrifflichkeit verwenden, auf diese zurück (z.B. im Abschiedssegen).

Der Unterschied ist also nicht in einem Mehr oder Weniger an Heilszusage begründet, sondern in unterschiedlichen historischen, traditionsgeschichtlichen und soziologischen Faktoren. Die Unterschiede dürfen nicht zu einer Wertung führen, sondern zu einer präziseren Erfassung der beiden Bereiche: Qumran und Neues Testament.

Universität Tübingen
Liebermeisterstrasse 12
D-72076 Tübingen

Hermann Lichtenberger

BÉATITUDES DE QUMRÂN ET BÉATITUDES ÉVANGÉLIQUES ANTÉRIORITÉ DE MATTHIEU SUR LUC?

Le problème de l'antériorité des béatitudes de Lc 6,20-23 par rapport à celles de Mt 5,3-12 avait été résolu, du moins le croyait-on, par les ouvrages magistraux de Jacques Dupont[1]. À la fin de son premier volume, il résumait ainsi sa pensée:

> D'une manière générale, le texte de Matthieu reproduit plus exactement le texte de base, mais il l'explicite et élargit sa portée dans un sens spirituel et moral en y insérant divers compléments. La rédaction de Luc se montre souvent assez libre à l'égard du vocabulaire et elle n'hésite pas à retoucher le style des sentences. En revanche, elle n'ajoute rien d'important à la source quand elle la suit; c'est seulement après l'avoir reproduite qu'elle ajoute les malédictions[2].

1. La position de Jacques Dupont

On pourrait résumer comme suit les principaux points acquis par l'auteur:

1. Luc a conservé la teneur générale des trois premières béatitudes, celles qu'on peut attribuer à Jésus lui-même. On y reconnaît le centre de sa prédication et de son action: le royaume de Dieu arrive de manière imminente et il est promis aux pauvres et aux opprimés.
2. Matthieu a mieux conservé le style des béatitudes et certains mots spécifiques empruntés à Is 61,1-3. À titre d'exemple, citons l'emploi de la 3e personne plus courante que la 2e dans l'Ancien Testament et le judaïsme dans le genre littéraire des béatitudes. Le mot 'les affligés' ou littéralement 'les endeuillés' (πενθοῦντες, Mt 5,4) qui provient d'Is 61,1-3 est plus probable que 'ceux qui pleurent' (κλαίοντες) de Lc 6,21b[3]. D'autre part, l'addition de l'adverbe νῦν (maintenant) dans le premier stique des 2e et 3e béatitudes de Luc est

1. J. Dupont, *Les Béatitudes,* Tome 1, *Le problème littéraire. Les deux versions du Sermon sur la montagne et des béatitudes,* Louvain, Nauwelaerts, 1952; Tome 2, *La Bonne Nouvelle*, Paris, Gabalda, 1969; Tome 3, *Les Évangélistes*, Paris, Gabalda, 1973. Un résumé pratique dans *Le message des béatitudes* (Cahiers Évangile, 24), Paris, Le Cerf, 1978.

2. J. Dupont, *Les Béatitudes,* t. 2, p. 344.

3. Luc connaît, par ailleurs, la racine πενθέω (affligé, endeuillé) qu'il emploie dans sa 3e malédiction (Lc 6, 25b). C'est un argument supplémentaire en faveur de l'originalité des 'endeuillés'. D'autre part, la racine πενθέω revient trois fois dans Is 61, 1-3 LXX.

une caractéristique propre de son style et devait être absent du texte primitif[4].

3. Le texte de base, proche de celui prononcé par Jésus, et qu'on attribue à la source Q, devait être à peu près le suivant:

Matthieu 5	Luc 6	Quelle
3 Heureux les pauvres en esprit car c'est à eux qu'est le Royaume des cieux.	20 Heureux vous les pauvres car c'est à vous qu'est le Royaume de Dieu.	Heureux les pauvres car à eux est le Royaume de Dieu.
4 Heureux ceux qui sont affligés (= endeuillés) car eux seront consolés.	21b Heureux vous qui pleurez maintenant car vous rirez.	Heureux ceux qui sont affligés (= endeuillés) car ils seront consolés.
6 Heureux ceux qui ont faim et soif de la justice, car eux seront rassasiés.	21a Heureux vous qui avez faim maintenant car vous serez rassasiés	Heureux ceux qui ont faim car ils seront rassasiés.

4. La béatitude des doux (Mt 5,5) est un doublet de celle des pauvres en esprit (Mt 5,3 avec le même mot hébreu de base ענוים). Les béatitudes des cœurs purs et des artisans de paix (Mt 5,7-9) ne se trouvaient pas non plus dans la source Q. Si Luc avait connu ces béatitudes matthéennes particulières ils ne les aurait omises en aucun cas, d'autant plus qu'elles correspondent parfaitement à sa théologie personnelle[5]. D'autre part, il est généralement admis que c'est Matthieu qui a ajouté τῷ πνεύματι aux 'pauvres' de Mt 5,3 et τὴν δικαιοσύνην à 'ceux qui ont faim et soif' (Mt 5, 6)[6].

Ces quatre points qui apparaissent évidents à beaucoup d'exégètes ont été récemment remis en question par le Père Émile Puech dans un livre magistral et trois articles importants qui ont complètement renouvelé le débat[7].

4. À la suite de J. Dupont, Marcel DUMAIS, *Le Sermon sur la Montagne. État de la recherche, interprétation, bibliographie*, Paris, Letouzey et Ané, 1995, p. 124.

5. J. DUPONT, *Les Béatitudes*, t. 1, pp. 344-345.

6. J. DUPONT, *Les Béatitudes*, t. 3, pp. 382-384 et 469-471.

7. É. PUECH, *La croyance des Esséniens en la vie future: immortalité, résurrection, vie éternelle?* (ÉB 21-22), Paris, Gabalda, 1993; ID., *Un hymne essénien en partie retrouvé et les Béatitudes. 1QH V 12-VI 18 (col. XIII-XIV 7) et 4QBéat.*, in *RQ* 13 (1988) 59-88; ID., *4Q525 et la péricope des Béatitudes en Ben Sira et Matthieu*, in *RB* 98 (1991) 80-106; ID., *The Collection of Beatitudes in Hebrew and in Greek (4Q525, 1-4 and Mt 5, 3-12)*, in F. MANNS – E. ALLIATA (eds.), *Early Christianity in Context*, Jérusalem, Franciscan Printing Press, 1993, pp. 353-368.

2. La remise en cause d'Émile Puech

Plusieurs textes de Qumrân ont des affinités évidentes avec les béatitudes de Mt 5,3-12. Du point de vue de la forme, le texte de 4Q525 contient au moins 5 béatitudes qui fournissent un parallèle littéraire intéressant au texte des 9 béatitudes de Matthieu. Du point de vue du contenu, le texte restauré des Hymnes (1QH VI 13-16) fournit au moins deux expressions caractéristiques des béatitudes de Matthieu: עניי רוח (les pauvres en esprit) אהבי רחמים (ceux qui aiment la miséricorde). Ces deux textes, et surtout celui des Hymnes présentent un parallèle si proche de Matthieu qu'ils nous obligent à nous poser de nouvelles questions. Si les rapprochements proposés s'avèrent réels, ne serait-ce pas Matthieu qui aurait conservé au mieux le texte original des béatitudes, et pourquoi pas, les *ipsissima verba* de Jésus?

Le texte de 4Q525 II 1-6 contient 4 béatitudes bien conservées, avec la quasi certitude de pouvoir reconstituer un premier macarisme en amont: אשרי, ce qui fait 5 béatitudes assurées. Le passage qui précède étant lacuneux, on peut raisonnablement supposer 2 ou 3 béatitudes antécédentes supplémentaires. Nous obtiendrions d'après Puech une séquence de 7 macarismes, c'est-à-dire de 3 + 4 béatitudes courtes + une longue, ou peut-être même, une séquence de 8 macarismes, c'est-à-dire de 4 + 4 béatitudes courtes + une longue. Dans ce dernier cas de figure, nous arriverions au nombre exact de Mt 5,3-12: 2 strophes de 4 béatitudes courtes + 1 béatitude longue[8].

Voici le texte:

4Q525

(Heureux celui qui dit la vérité) avec un cœur pur,
et ne calomnie pas avec sa langue.
Heureux ceux qui s'attachent à ses décrets,
et ne s'attachent pas à des voies de perversité.
Heureux ceux qui se réjouissent grâce à elle,
et ne se répandent pas dans des voies de folie.
Heureux celui qui la cherche avec des mains pures,
et ne la recherche pas avec un cœur fourbe.

Heureux l'homme qui a atteint la Sagesse,
qui marche dans la Loi du Très-Haut,
et applique son cœur à ses voies,
qui s'attache à ses leçons
et dans ses corrections toujours se plaît,

8. Puech, *4Q525*, pp. 87-89; Id., *Qumrân grotte 4. Tome 18: Textes hébreux (4Q521-528, 4Q576-579)* (DJD, 25), Oxford, Clarendon, 1998, pp. 126-128.

mais qui ne la repousse pas dans l'affliction de (ses malheurs),
et au temps de la détresse ne l'abandonne pas,
qui ne l'oublie pas (aux jours) d'effroi,
et dans l'humilité de son âme ne (la) réprouve pas.

Dans son état actuel, le texte présente d'abord 4 béatitudes courtes introduites par אשרי et qui présentent chacune deux hémistiches, l'un positif et l'autre négatif. La 5e béatitude est beaucoup plus longue et présente d'abord un hémistiche positif de type sapiential suivi par 4 hémistiches positifs de structure parallèle, suivis eux-mêmes par 4 hémistiches négatifs de structure également parallèle.

Ce texte peut être comparé utilement avec deux autres. D'abord avec le Psaume 15, un beau poème sapiential de type didactique qui décrit la montée au Temple (dont la 'tente' du v.1 constitue une désignation archaïque) et le dialogue qui s'établit ensuite entre les pèlerins et les prêtres. Une introduction et une conclusion de 2 hémistiches très courts enserrent 2 strophes centrales qui contenaient chacune 6 hémistiches. Chacune des 2 strophes centrales est divisée en 3 hémistiches positifs et négatifs[9].

Ensuite, la comparaison formelle s'établit aussi avec le Siracide 14,20-27, petit poème qui commence par un macarisme sapiential: «Heureux l'homme qui médite sur la sagesse». L'auteur décrit l'avidité de la recherche de la sagesse sous les traits habituels de la littérature sapientiale: l'image du chasseur qui poursuit son gibier ou du nomade qui dresse sa tente près d'une belle demeure et qui cherche un abri contre la chaleur à l'ombre d'un grand arbre. Les doubles hémistiches commencent souvent par un participe situé au début du premier et se terminent à la fin du second hémistiche par un verbe à l'inaccompli, comme c'était le cas, par ailleurs, pour le Psaume 15 et 4Q525[10].

Venons en maintenant à la comparaison essentielle, à celle qui porte sur le contenu. Il s'agit de l'hymne 1QH VI 13-16 qui avait été publié sous le numéro XIV par E.L. Sukenik en 1954-1955[11]. Ce texte a été remis en ordre, complété et considérablement restauré par É. Puech en 1988[12].

9. Pour une division stichométrique du Psaume 15, voir PUECH, *The Collection of Beatitudes* (n. 7), pp. 356-357.

10. PUECH, *The Collection of Beatitudes* (n. 7), pp. 358-359; ID., *4Q525* (n. 7), pp. 91-94.

11. E.L. SUKENIK, *'Oçar ha-Megillôt ha-Genuzôt,* Jérusalem, 1954; ID., *The Dead Sea Scrolls of the Hebrew University*, prepared by N. AVIGAD et J. LICHT, *Hodayôt*, Jérusalem, 1955.

12. PUECH, *Un hymne essénien* (n. 7), pp. 59-88; ID., *4Q525*, p. 90 (texte présenté en 7 fois 2 hémistiches).

L'hymne comporte 14 hémistiches dont les 12 premiers sont constitués de participes ou de substantifs à l'état construit et les deux derniers d'un participe à l'état absolu suivi d'une préposition et d'un substantif avec suffixe de la deuxième personne du masculin singulier.

1QH VI 13-16

13 1. (Heureux) les hommes de vérité	et les élus de j(ustice)
2. les chercheurs[14] de sagesse	et les quêteurs d'intelligence
3. les bâtisseurs (Puech: de paix) (*bôney shalôm*)	et les... de...
4. (ceux qui ai)ment la miséricorde (*'ôhabey raḥamim*)	et les pauvres en esprit (*'anwey rûaḥ*)
5. les épurés[15] de la pauvreté	et les purifiés de l'épreuve
6. les miséricordieux (Puech: de pardons)...	(Puech: et les parfaits de conduite)
7. les tempérants jusqu'à la fin de tes jugements	16 et les guetteurs de ton salut.

Ce texte étonnant de proximité avec les béatitudes de Matthieu appelle trois remarques:

1. L'expression ענוי רוח (littéralement 'les pauvres de l'esprit') qui constitue le premier hémistiche de Mt 5, 3 ('les pauvres en esprit') résume en quelque sorte les autres béatitudes de Matthieu. Elle se trouve en huitième position des hémistiches de 1QH VI 13-16. Elle apparaît ailleurs en 1QM XIV 7 (Règle de la guerre) et dans son parallèle de 4Q491 8-10 I 5. Cette expression rappelle celle de la Règle de la communauté רוח ענוה ('l'esprit de pauvreté' ou 'l'esprit d'humilité') en 1QS III 8 et IV 3. Elle rappelle aussi l'Apocalypse messianique 4Q521 2 II 6: «Et sur les pauvres planera son Esprit», qui emploie le verbe רחף (planer) comme en Gen 1, 2. Elle rappelle surtout Is 61,1ab: «L'esprit du Seigneur Yahvé est sur moi, parce que Yahvé m'a oint. Il m'a envoyé porter la bonne nouvelle aux pauvres» (לבשׂר ענוים)[13].
2. L'expression אוהבי רחמים ('ceux qui aiment la miséricorde') est certaine et évoque inévitablement la 5e béatitude de Mt 5,7: 'Heureux les miséricordieux'.
3. L'expression בוני [שלום] («les bâtisseurs [de paix]») évoque la 7e béatitude de Mt 5,9 («Heureux les artisans de paix»). Le problème ici vient de l'absence du mot *shalôm* dans le texte. Suffit-il d'évoquer Prov 10,10 et 2 Hén 52,6-7 ainsi que le texte de Fl. Josèphe, *Bell* 2,

13. PUECH, *La croyance des Esséniens* (n. 7), pp. 413-414 et 636-637; ID., *The Collection of Beatitudes* (n. 7), pp. 362-363.

135, qui parle des Esséniens comme εἰρήνης ὑπουργοί (serviteurs de la paix) pour combler une lacune du texte? C'est possible, mais ce n'est pas évident[14].

Un autre hymne consacré à la fontaine de sagesse contient trois expressions qui ont un rapport direct avec le texte d'Isaïe 61, 1-3 et deux d'entre elles ont un rapport direct avec les béatitudes de Matthieu. Nous citons la partie du texte qui intéresse notre propos[15]:

1QH XXIII 13-16 (*partim*)

13. Et tu as ouvert (une) fontaine…
15. pour (consa)crer selon ta vérité le messager (de la bonne nouvelle) (*l*[mšḥ] *k'mtkh mbśr*),
(et pour racon)ter) ta bonté,
pour annoncer une bonne nouvelle aux pauvres (*lbśr ʿnwym*) selon l'abondance de tes miséricordes (*lrwb rḥmykh*)
16. (et pour ra)ssasier depuis la fontaine de sa(ges)se
(et pour consoler les con)trits d'esprit ([wlnḥm nk]*'y rwḥ*) et les endeuillés (*w'blym*)
en vue de la joie éternelle.

Quelques remarques:

1. L'expression «pour consacrer selon ta vérité le messager de la bonne nouvelle» (*mšḥ mbśr*) est une allusion claire à Is 61, 1ab.
2. Pour annoncer une bonne nouvelle aux pauvres» est une allusion directe à Is 61,1b «pour porter la bonne nouvelle aux pauvres, il m'a envoyé». C'est aussi une allusion indirecte au fond commun de la première béatitude de Matthieu et Luc. Le rapprochement avec le mot 'pauvres' est évident. Le rapprochement entre 'la bonne nouvelle' et 'le royaume de Dieu' est indirect. Le thème de la bonne nouvelle et celui du royaume s'appellent l'un l'autre dans la pensée de Jésus. Les pauvres sont proclamés heureux, parce qu'ils sont les destinataires privilégiés du royaume de Dieu (perspective théologique) et aussi de la bonne nouvelle annoncée par Jésus en leur faveur (perspective christologique)[16].

14. PUECH, *Un hymne essénien* (n. 7), p. 79. À l'opposé, DUPONT, *Les Béatitudes*, t. 3 (n.1), pp. 634-635 et 641-643. L'A. refuse ces parallèles et renvoie à la rédaction de Matthieu. Il conclut pp. 665-666: «Le point de vue n'est plus celui d'une annonce de l'intervention de Dieu en faveur des déshérités pour leur procurer un bonheur qu'ils ne devront qu'à sa miséricorde entièrement gratuite; l'accent se place maintenant sur les conditions à remplir pour avoir part au bonheur promis».

15. PUECH, *Un hymne essénien* (n. 7), pp. 83-84; ID., *4Q525*, (n. 7), p. 102; ID., *La croyance des Esséniens* (n. 7), pp. 666-667.

16. J. DUPONT, *Jésus annonce la bonne nouvelle aux pauvres* (1978) et *Jésus, Messie des pauvres, Messie pauvre* (1984), in ID., *Études sur les Évangiles synoptiques* (BETL, 70), t. 1, Leuven, Peeters, 1985, pp. 63-65 et 98-99.

3. L'expression 'et consoler les contrits d'esprit' (*[wlnḥm nk]'y rwḥ*) est une citation d'Is 66,2 d'après le manuscrit d'Isaïe de Qumrân (1QIsa), avec *nk'y* au pluriel. L'expression 'les endeuillés' (*'blym*) revient deux fois dans Is 61,1-3 TM et trois fois dans Is 61,1-3 LXX avec la mention des πενθοῦντες[17].

3. Utilisation d'Is 61,1-3 dans les Béatitudes et la prédication de Jésus

«Porter la bonne nouvelle aux pauvres» (Is 61,1-6) consiste à leur porter la bonne nouvelle du royaume de Dieu; ce royaume qui est précisément promis aux pauvres par Mt 5,3 et Lc 6,20b.

Examinons d'abord les points de contact entre Is 61,1-3 et le texte des béatitudes. Ensuite, nous étudierons le rapport d'Is 61,1-3 avec les deux seuls textes des Évangiles où il est cité explicitement: la prédication de Jésus à Nazareth (Lc 4,18-19) et l'ambassade de Jean-Baptiste (Mt 11,5-6; Lc 7,22).

1. Les Béatitudes

Jésus s'identifie avec le messager dont parle Is 61, avec l'oint consacré par Dieu, sur qui repose l'Esprit. Cette mission de Jésus consiste à porter la bonne nouvelle aux pauvres: «Heureux les pauvres (*'anawim* ou πτωχοί?) car le Royaume de Dieu est à eux».

La référence à Is 61,1-3 dans les béatitudes est quasi certaine:

1. Emploi commun du mot πτωχοῖς.
2. Porter la bonne nouvelle aux pauvres (Is 61,1b), c'est annoncer la venue du Jour de Yahvé ou du Règne de Dieu et cela équivaut dans les béatitudes de l'Évangile à annoncer le Royaume de Dieu promis aux pauvres[18].
3. Les pauvres dont parle Is 61,1b sont associés aux 'affligés' ou 'endeuillés': deux fois dans le TM (*'blym)* et trois fois dans la LXX (racine πενθέω). Ce sont précisément ces 'endeuillés' qui sont les destinataires de la 2e béatitude (Mt 5,4)[19].

17. D. Flusser, *Blessed are the Poor in Spirit ...*, in *IEJ* 10 (1960) 1-13; article repris dans Id., *Judaism and the Origins of Christianity*, Jérusalem, Magness Press, 1988, pp. 102-114.

18. Dupont, *Les Béatitudes*, t. 2 (n. 1), p. 97: «Le 'Royaume' que Jésus promet aux pauvres correspond au 'Règne' de Yahweh dont le prophète 'annonce la bonne nouvelle'».

19. Quelques manuscrits minoritaires de Matthieu placent le v. 5 (les doux) avant le v. 4 (les endeuillés). Nous suivons B.M. Metzger, *A Textual Commentary of the Greek of the New Testament*, Londres et New York, United Bible Societies, 1971, p. 12: «If verses

Nous reviendrons plus loin sur la première béatitude et sa relation à Is 61,1b.

2. La prédication inaugurale de Jésus à Nazareth (Lc 4, 18-21)

L'expression 'les pauvres sont évangélisés' ne se trouve que deux fois dans le Nouveau Testament:

- en Lc 4,18: εὐαγγελίσασθαι πτωχοῖς (propre à Luc)
- en Mt 11,5 et Lc 7,22: πτωχοὶ εὐαγγελίζονται (texte Q)

Etudions le premier texte et comparons-le à Is 61,1-3 LXX:

Lc 4,18-19

18 a. L'Esprit du Seigneur est sur moi parce qu'il m'a oint;
b. il m'a envoyé porter la bonne nouvelle aux pauvres,
c. proclamer aux captifs la délivrance (ἄφεσιν)
d. et aux aveugles le recouvrement de la vue (τυφλοῖς ἀνάβλεψιν)
e. renvoyer les opprimés en liberté (ἐν ἄφεσιν)
19 proclamer une année de grâce (δεκτόν) du Seigneur.

Is 61,1-3 LXX

1 a. L'Esprit du Seigneur est sur moi parce qu'il m'a oint;
b. pour porter la bonne nouvelle aux pauvres (εὐαγγελίσασθαι πτωχοῖς), il m'a envoyé,
c. pour guérir ceux qui sont brisés de coeur,
d. pour proclamer aux captifs la liberté (ἄφεσιν),
e. et aux aveugles le recouvrement de la vue (τυφλοῖς ἀνάβλεψιν)
2 a. pour annoncer une année de grâce (δεκτόν) du Seigneur et un jour de rétribution,
b. pour consoler tous les endeuillés (παρακαλέσαι πάντας τοὺς πενθοῦντας),
3 a. pour donner aux endeuillés de Sion la gloire au lieu de la cendre (τοῖς πενθοῦσιν)
b. une huile d'allégresse pour les endeuillés (τοῖς πενθοῦσιν), un vêtement de gloire à la place d'un esprit d'abattement.

La citation de Lc 4,18 = conflation de Is 61,1a.b.d; 58,6d; 61,2a.
Omission de Lc 4,18 - de Is 61,1c «guérir ceux qui ont le cœur brisé»
- de Is 61,2a (= LXX) «un jour de rétribution»
(= TM) «le jour de vengeance de notre Dieu»
Le texte d'Is 61,1e LXX = τυφλοῖς ἀνάβλεψιν «et aux aveugles le recouvrement de la vue» (= Lc 4,18d) est différent du TM au même endroit (Is 61, 1e: «et aux prisonniers l'ouverture de la prison», פקח קוח).

3 and 5 had originally stood together, with their rhetorical antithesis of heaven and earth, it is unlikely that any scribe would have thrust v.4 between them. On the other hand, as early as the second century, copyists reversed the order of the two beatitudes so as to produce such an antithesis and to bring ptôchoi and praeis into closer connexion».

Cet hapax est rendu:

- par τυφλοῖς ἀνάβλεψιν dans la LXX («aux aveugles le recouvrement de la vue»);
- par *clausis apertionem* dans la Vulgate («ouverture aux reclus [de la prison]»);
- par *vinctis apertionem* dans Vetus Latina («l'ouverture pour les enchaînés»).

Le TM est bien attesté par les traductions latines (Vulgate et Vet. lat.). D'où vient l'interprétation de la LXX dans le sens du recouvrement de la vue? On peut penser à une démarche métaphorique semblable à celle du Targum d'Isaïe, qui traduit l'expression par un verbe à l'impératif: *'itgelû lenêhôr* («apparaissez à la lumière»). Pour des prisonniers, l'ouverture de la prison signifie l'apparition de la lumière et le retour à la vision[20].

- Is 61,1d LXX («pour proclamer aux captifs la liberté») a été repris exactement par Lc 4,18c et complété ensuite en Lc 4, 18e par «renvoyer les opprimés en liberté», qui provient d'Is 58,6d LXX ἀπόστελλε τεθραυσμένους ἐν ἀφέσει. Is 61,1d utilisait aussi le mot-crochet ἀφέσει mais à propos des αἰχμαλωθοί (les captifs) qui sont proches par le sens du mot 'opprimés' d'Is 58,6d.
- Is 61, 2a «pour annoncer une année favorable (δεκτός) du Seigneur» qui rend l'hébreu *raçôn* du TM. Il n'est pas évident que Lc 4, 19 ait pensé ici à l'année du Jubilé (Lév 25), en employant le mot δεκτός. De même, la double mention du mot ἄφεσις (hébreu *derôr*) en Is 61,1d et en Is 58,6d ne suffit pas non plus à évoquer l'année jubilaire aux yeux de Luc[21]. La situation est évidemment très différente dans les textes de Qumrân concernant Melkisédeq[22].

Lc 4,21 va préciser que c'est 'aujourd'hui' (σήμερον) que cette écriture s'est accomplie 'à vos oreilles'. Ce que le prophète Isaïe envisageait pour l'avenir se réalise dans le présent de l'activité thaumaturgique de Jésus. L'oracle d'Is 61,1b s'accomplit 'aujourd'hui' et 'aux oreilles' des auditeurs de Jésus (Lc 4,21). C'est exactement la définition du *pesher*, genre littéraire fréquent à Qumrân et dont l'hymne cité de 1QH XXIII 13-16 nous fournit un exemple excellent.

20. L'explication de J.A. SANDERS, *Luke and Scripture*, in C.A. EVANS et J.A. SANDERS, Minneapolis, MN, Fortress Press, 1993, p. 49, qui s'appuie surtout sur le parallèle de Is 42, 7 ἀνοῖξαι ὀφθαλμοὺς τυφλῶν («pour ouvrir les yeux des aveugles») me semble assez loin de l'expression originale d'Is 61, 1e et Lc 4, 18d.

21. J.-M. VAN CANGH, *Le Jubilé Biblique: un temps marqué ouvrant un temps neuf*, in *Science et Esprit* 53 (2001) 63-92 (ici pp. 88-89).

22. PUECH, *La croyance des Esséniens* (n. 7), t. 2, pp. 515-562.

Le messager de l'hymne de Qumrân XXIII 15-16 trouve dans l'oracle d'Is 61 la définition de sa propre mission auprès des pauvres. De même, Jésus en accomplissant les miracles prédits par Is 61 se présente comme l'envoyé de Dieu qui réalise le salut des pauvres de son peuple.

3. L'ambassade de Jean-Baptiste (Mt 11,5-6; Lc 7,22)

Citons le texte de Mt 11,5-6:

Les aveugles recouvrent la vue et les estropiés marchent
Les lépreux sont purifiés et les sourds entendent
Les morts se lèvent et la bonne nouvelle est annoncée aux pauvres
Et heureux celui qui ne se scandalisera pas à mon sujet.

La seule différence entre la version de Mt 11,5-6 et Lc 7,22 est l'emploi de la conjonction καί. Matthieu en a 4 et répartit les 6 signes en 3 groupes de 2; Luc n'en a qu'1, au milieu de la liste, qui est divisée ainsi en 2 groupes de 3 signes.

Le texte de Mt 11,5-6 et Lc 7,22 contient deux éléments repris à Is 61,1-3:

1. «La bonne nouvelle annoncée aux pauvres» occupe la 6e et dernière place dans l'énumération de Jésus comme le sommet d'un *crescendo* alors qu'elle occupe la 1re place en Is 61,1-3 LXX.
2. «Les aveugles recouvrent la vue» occupe la 1re place dans le texte évangélique et la 4e dans le texte d'Is 61,1-3 LXX (τυφλοῖς ἀνάβλεψιν), alors qu'il est absent dans Is 61,2 TM et remplacé par l'expression פקח קוח («et aux prisonniers l'ouverture de la prison»).

Pour expliquer la présence des autres termes de l'énumération des six signes, il faut recourir à d'autres textes d'Isaïe: 26,19; 29,18-19; et surtout 35,5-6:

> Alors les yeux des aveugles s'ouvriront et les oreilles des sourds entendront,
> Alors l'estropié bondira comme un cerf et la langue des bègues sera claire.

Pour la mention de la résurrection des morts, on la trouve dans Is 29,18-19. La purification des lépreux, en revanche, est absente d'Isaïe.

23. H.E. TÖDT, *Der Menschensohn in der synoptischen Überlieferung*, Gütersloh, 1959, pp. 234-235.

La finale de Mt 11,6 (par. Lc 7,23) attire l'attention sur la personne de Jésus. C'est l'attitude de chaque homme à son égard qui détermine le sort de chacun (*logion* dont le sens est proche de Lc 12,8-9)[23].

La bonne nouvelle annoncée aux pauvres (reprise d'Is 61,1b) suppose un messager divin distinct de Dieu lui-même. Dans l'Évangile, c'est Jésus lui-même, avec ses miracles en faveur des pauvres, qui réalise la prophétie d'Isaïe. La perspective est nettement christologique comme dans la prédication inaugurale à Nazareth (Lc 4,18-19). L'annonce de la bonne nouvelle aux pauvres résume tous les bienfaits accordés par Jésus dans ses miracles. Le fait que les malades sont guéris devient une bonne nouvelle pour tous les pauvres de tout genre et est le début de la réalisation de la promesse eschatologique en leur faveur («le Royaume de Dieu est pour eux!»).

On comprend le scandale de Jean-Baptiste (Mt 5,6 et Lc 7,23). Jésus le renvoie aux oracles d'Isaïe uniquement positifs qui décrivent son activité bienfaisante en faveur des malheureux. Il supprime tous les traits négatifs des prophéties d'Isaïe, à commencer par Is 61,2 TM: «un jour de vengeance pour notre Dieu» (LXX: «un jour de rétribution»). Avec Jésus, on est loin du message terrible du Baptiste, avec la description du justicier qui «tient en sa main la pelle à vanner» (Mt 3,12; Lc 3,17) et dont «la cognée se trouve déjà à la racine des arbres» (Mt 3,10; Lc 3,9)[24].

En Lc 4,18, Luc mentionne par fidélité à sa source vétéro-testamentaire (Is 61,1-2 et l'ajout de Is 58,6 LXX), en plus des miracles habituels, la libération des prisonniers et des opprimés, qui sont absents du ministère de Jésus. En Mt 11,5 et Lc 7,22, il s'agit uniquement de la liste bien réelle des principaux miracles de Jésus.

La différence essentielle dans l'utilisation de la citation d'Is 61dans les deux premières béatitudes concernant les pauvres et les endeuillés, c'est que ces dernières ne sont pas d'abord christologiques, elles ne définissent pas d'abord la mission de Jésus comme celle du messager de Dieu qui opère des miracles en faveur des pauvres de toutes sortes. Les béatitudes sont d'abord théologiques. C'est Dieu lui-même qui va établir son Règne en mettant un terme à la souffrance des pauvres. Heureux les pauvres, les affligés et les affamés, parce que Dieu est sur le point d'inaugurer son Royaume pour eux. Et cela signifie la fin de leurs misères, de la même manière que la bonne nouvelle apportée aux pauvres d'Is 61 signifiait la fin de leurs souffrances par l'arrivée du Règne de

24. J. Dupont, *L'ambassade de Jean-Baptiste (Matthieu 11, 2-6; Luc 7, 18-23)*, in *NRT* 83 (1961) 805-821 et 943-959 (ici pp. 955-958).

Yahvé. Il y a un parallèle évident entre les deux messagers et l'établissement du Royaume de Dieu sur terre.

4. Antériorité des pauvres tout court

Nous nous trouvons devant un paradoxe. Jésus ne recourt que deux fois à l'expression vétéro-testamentaire si caractéristique de son message: «Il m'a envoyé porter la bonne nouvelle aux pauvres». Cette citation d'Is 61,1b est reprise littéralement en Mt 11,5 par. Lc 7,22 dans l'ambassade de Jean-Baptiste et en Lc 4,18 dans la prédication inaugurale à Nazareth et uniquement dans ces deux seuls textes des évangiles. Le texte hébreu utilise le mot ענוים qui signifie 'les courbés, les humbles'. Le texte grec de la LXX et des évangiles utilise le mot πτωχός qui signifie 'pauvre, indigent, celui qui manque du nécessaire et ne peut l'acquérir par lui-même'[25]. Il y a un glissement évident entre le sens spirituel du mot 'pauvre' en hébreu (proche de Matthieu) et le sens réaliste du mot en grec (suivi par Luc et dont l'origine est à rechercher dans la prédication et l'activité de Jésus). Chaque fois, les pauvres sont entourés des aveugles, des sourds, des boiteux, des lépreux, bref de tous les hommes misérables dont s'occupe Jésus (Mt 11,5; Lc 4,18). Et c'est clairement ce sens commun du mot 'pauvre' qui est visé par Jésus.

Sur 24 emplois du mot πτωχός dans les Évangiles, 23 emplois signifient 'pauvre' dans le sens matériel et réaliste du mot. Jésus l'a donc employé dans ce sens-là, comme le prouve la liste des malheureux cités dans les deux seuls textes (Mt 11,5 par. Lc 7,22 et Lc 4,18) qui reprennent explicitement Is 61, 1-3. La seule exception est le texte de Mt 5,3: «Heureux les pauvres en esprit». C'est un ajout de Matthieu au texte de la source Q[26]. On ne peut pas bâtir une théorie sur un cas unique et il est clair que Jésus visait les pauvres de toutes sortes, sans exclure pour autant le sens spirituel de Matthieu.

Le premier évangéliste a-t-il trouvé cette expression (*'anwey rûaḥ*) à Qumrân dans un texte semblable à 1QH VI 14? C'est possible, mais on ne peut pas le prouver. Sur ce point, É. Puech a raison de noter la grande similitude entre les béatitudes de Matthieu et celles de l'hymne qumranienne. Mais Jésus n'est pas Matthieu. Il ne promet pas le Royaume aux seuls pauvres en esprit, mais à tous les pauvres de la terre. Et peu importe le genre de malheur dont ils sont atteints.

25. Dupont, *Les Béatitudes,* t. 1 (n. 1), pp. 19-34; Id., *Jésus, Messie des pauvres* (n. 16), pp. 92-93.

26. Dupont, *Les Béatitudes*, t. 2 (n. 1), pp. 214-217.

Conclusion

Nous avons noté l'extension du message de Jésus aux pauvres tout court et pas seulement aux pauvres spirituels. Une des nouveautés de sa prédication, c'est précisément de sortir de la morale de la rétribution juive. Ce qui est en jeu ici, ce ne sont pas les mérites ou les vertus des pauvres, ni même leurs bonnes dispositions spirituelles. Ce qui est en cause ici, ce sont les dispositions royales de Dieu. Dieu, tout simplement parce qu'il est Dieu, a décidé de rétablir la justice en faveur des pauvres, des petits et des faibles, de ceux qu'on exploite et qu'on opprime. Dieu a pris le parti des pauvres!

Nous touchons ici à une différence essentielle entre la communauté des parfaits de Qumrân et celle de Jésus. Qu'on relise, par exemple, la Règle annexe (1QSa II 3-9) qui exclut de l'assemblée sainte les paralysés, les boiteux, les aveugles, les sourds, les muets, les tarés et les vieillards qui vacillent [27]. On est aux antipodes de la position de Jésus!

Avenue du Ciseau 8/202
B–1348 Louvain-la-Neuve

Jean-Marie VAN CANGH

27. A comparer avec la Règle de la Guerre (1QM VII 4-6) et le Rouleau du Temple XLV 7-18, où l'on trouve d'autres exclusions du même genre. Voir, par exemple, dans *La Bible. Écrits Intertestamentaires* (Bibliothèque de la Pléiade), Paris, 1987, pp. 51; 103-104 et 204-205.

THE FATE OF THE RIGHTEOUS AND THE CURSED AT QUMRAN AND IN THE GOSPEL OF MATTHEW

Over the years research on the Scrolls has developed into a relatively autonomous discipline ("Qumranology") with its own problems, methodology, and specialized journals and monograph series. Fortunately, this evolution did not result in a complete separation of "Qumran" studies from other fields of biblical studies, including the New Testament[1].

1. For recent surveys on "Qumran and the New Testament" in general, see, e.g., É. PUECH, *Les manuscrits de la mer Morte et le Nouveau Testament*, in É.-M. LAPERROUSAZ (ed.), *Qoumrân et les manuscrits de la mer Morte*, Paris, Cerf, 1997, pp. 253-313. J. FREY, *Die Bedeutung der Qumranfunde für das Verständnis des Neuen Testaments*, in M. FIEGER *et al.* (eds.), *Qumran – Die Schriftrollen vom Toten Meer. Vorträge des St Galler Qumran-Symposiums vom 2./3. Juli 1999* (NTOA, 47), Freiburg, Universitätsverlag – Göttingen, Vandenhoeck & Ruprecht, 2001, pp. 129-208. G.J. BROOKE, *The Scrolls and the Study of the New Testament*, in R.A. KUYLER – E.M. SCHULLER (eds.), *The Dead Sea Scrolls at Fifty. Proceedings of the 1997 Society of Biblical Literature Qumran Section Meetings* (Early Judaism and Its Literature, 15), Atlanta, GA, SBL, 1999, pp. 61-76. Cf. also some of the contributions in the section "The Scrolls and Early Christianity" in the jubilee volumes edited by P.W. FLINT – J.C. VANDERKAM (eds.), *The Dead Sea Scrolls After Fifty Years. A Comprehensive Assessment*, Leiden, Brill, 1999, II, pp. 573-598 (C.A. Evans, on Jesus), 599-621 (J.A. Fitzmyer, on Paul), 622-648 (D.E. Aune, on the Book of Revelation); and by L.H. SCHIFFMAN – E. TOV – J.C. VANDERKAM (eds.), *The Dead Sea Scrolls. Fifty Years After Their Discovery. Proceedings of the Jerusalem Congress, July 20-25, 1997*, Jerusalem, IES, 2000, pp. 116-132 (J.H. Charlesworth), 133-138 (J.J. Collins, on apocalypticism), 157-169 (J. Kampen, *The Significance of the Scrolls for the Study of the Book of Matthew*). Note also the collection of studies by J.A. FITZMYER, *The Dead Sea Scrolls and Christian Origins* (Studies in the Dead Sea Scrolls and Related Literature), Grand Rapids, MI – Cambridge, Eerdmans, 2001, esp. pp. 1-17 (on methodology).

Specifically with regard to the Gospel of Matthew, several studies have been published in recent years on legal matters (divorce), Wisdom texts (the Beatitudes and the antitheses), and the structure and organisation of the community and communal discipline in Qumran (CD) and in Mt (ch. 18). See, a.o., J. KAMPEN, *The Matthean Divorce Texts Reexamined*, in G.J. BROOKE – F. GARCÍA MARTÍNEZ (eds.), *New Qumran Texts and Studies* (STDJ, 15), Leiden, Brill, 1994, pp. 149-168; *Aspects of Wisdom in the Gospel of Matthew in Light of the New Qumran Evidence*, in D.K. FALK *et al.* (eds.), *Sapiential, Liturgical, and Poetical Texts from Qumran Published in Memory of Maurice Baillet* (STDJ, 35), Leiden, Brill, 2000, pp. 227-239; *The Sectarian Form of the Antitheses Within the Social World of the Matthean Community*, in *DSD* 1 (1994) 338-363; *"Righteousness" in Matthew and the Legal Texts from Qumran*, in M.J. BERNSTEIN *et al.* (eds.), *Legal Texts and Legal Issues*. FS J.M. Baumgarten (STDJ, 23), Leiden, Brill, 1997, pp. 481-487. On Mt 18, see, e.g., J. GNILKA, *Die Kirche des Matthäus und die Gemeinde von Qumrân*, in *BZ* 7 (1963) 43-63. G.N. STANTON, *A Gospel for a New People. Studies in Matthew*, Edinburgh, T&T Clark, 1992, pp. 85-107. A. ITO, *Matthew and the Community of the Dead Sea Scrolls*, in *JSNT* 48 (1992) 23-42. D.C. ALLISON, *Scriptural Allusions in the New Testament. Light from the Dead Sea Scrolls* (The Dead Sea Scrolls & Christian Origins Library, 5), North Richland Hills, TX, BIBAL Press, 2000, pp. 31-36.

The Gospel of Matthew uses a wide range of images to describe the destiny of the righteous and of the wicked at the last judgement. Often this is presented in such a way that the destiny of the respective groups is juxtaposed in clear contrast. There are those who will be in the kingdom of the Father (13,42) and those who will be gathered out of it by His angels (13,43), like the bad part of the catch (13,48), and who "will be thrown in the furnace of fire" (13,42, quoting Dan 3,6, and 13,50) like the weeds of the field (13,42). There are those who will be reclining "with Abraham, Isaac, and Jacob in the kingdom of heaven" (8,11), or will be attending the marriage feast (22,11, and again 25,10), or will be set over much (25,21.23), and those who "will be thrown into the outer darkness" (8,12; cf. 22,13 and 25,30), or whom the master-bridegroom will not recognize and let in (25,10-12; cf. 7,23). There are those who "shall enter the kingdom of heaven" (7,21), and those who will be sent away as "evildoers" (7,23). And there are those who "will enter life" (18,8.9), and those who "will be thrown into the eternal fire" (18,8), or "into the hell of fire" (18,9), or will "go into hell" (5,30; cf. v. 29). In the judgement scene of Mt 25,31-46 a contrast is made between those who "will inherit the kingdom" (v. 34), and those who are cursed and will have "to depart into the eternal fire" (v. 41). The latter "will go away into eternal punishment, but the righteous into eternal life" (v. 46 καὶ ἀπελεύσονται οὗτοι εἰς κόλασιν αἰώνιον, οἱ δὲ δίκαιοι εἰς ζωὴν αἰώνιον)[2].

1. Parallels to Mt 25,46

In the following I will deal with this last verse. Two texts are often quoted in the literature as parallels, or as the source, of 25,46. The first is

2. On judgement in Mt and on Mt 25,31-46 in particular, see, a.o., J.H. Friedrich, *Gott im Bruder? Eine methodenkritische Untersuchung von Redaktion, Überlieferung und Traditionen in Mt 25,31-46* (Calwer theologische Monographien, A7), Stuttgart, Calwer, 1977, pp. 271-297. E. Brandenburger, *Das Recht des Weltenrichters. Untersuchung zu Matthäus 25,31-46* (SBS, 99), Stuttgart, KBW, 1980. D. Marguerat, *Le jugement dans l'évangile de Matthieu* (Le Monde de la Bible), Genève, Labor et Fides, 1981, [2]1995. M. Reiser, *Die Gerichtspredigt Jesu. Eine Untersuchung zur eschatologischen Verkündigung Jesu und ihrem frühjüdischen Hintergrund* (NTAbh, 23), Münster, Aschendorff, 1990. Stanton, *A Gospel for a New People* (n. 1), pp. 207-231. U. Luz, *The Final Judgment (Matt 25:31-46). An Exercise in "History of Influence" Exegesis*, in D.R. Bauer – M.A. Powell (eds.), *Treasures New and Old. Recent Contributions to Matthean Studies* (SBL Symposium Series, 1), Atlanta, GA, Scholars, 1996, pp. 271-310. D.C. Sim, *Apocalyptic Eschatology in the Gospel of Matthew* (SNTS MS, 88), Cambridge, UP, 1996, pp. 110-128. C. Riniker, *Die Gerichtsverkündigung Jesu* (EHS, 23/653), Bern, P. Lang, 1999, pp. 438-456.

Dan 12,2. The N^{26-27} edition no longer prints parts of 25,46 in bold (or italic) as this was still the case in N^{25} to indicate that it is a citation from or allusion to the OT, but it has obviously retained the reference to Dan 12,2 in the margin of the text. Not a few scholars have argued that this verse from Dan is indeed Matthew's primary source in v. 46. The Hebrew and the LXX version of Dan 12,2 differ somewhat in the second half of the verse, with the former reading "many of those who sleep in the dust of the earth will wake, some to everlasting life and some to the reproach of eternal abhorrence" (NEB), and the latter καὶ πολλοὶ τῶν καθευδόντων ἐν τῷ πλάτει τῆς γῆς ἀναστήσονται, οἱ μὲν εἰς ζωὴν αἰώνιον, οἱ δὲ εἰς ὀνειδισμόν, οἱ δὲ εἰς διασπορὰν καὶ αἰσχύνην αἰώνιον[3]. Matthew has reversed the order of punishment and reward, thus creating a chiasm with the preceding (vv. 34 and 41), but he uses the same expression for the latter (ζωὴν αἰώνιον), and he also retained the qualification αἰώνιον for the punishment. It is well possible that his οὗτοι ... οἱ δὲ δίκαιοι was also taken from the same context in Dan. In 12,3 MT reads, "The *wise leaders* (המשׂכלים) shall shine like the bright vault of heaven, and *those who have guided* (מצדיקי) the people in the true path shall be like the stars for ever and ever". In the conclusion of his explanation of the Parable of the Weeds in 13,43, Matthew is probably alluding to this verse from Dan when writing τότε οἱ δίκαιοι ἐκλάμψουσιν ὡς ὁ ἥλιος ..., thus replacing "the wise leaders" by οἱ δίκαιοι, "either as a free adaptation of מצדיקי or in agreement with Theodotion", as R.H. Gundry has noted[4]. If this is true also for 25,46, Matthew has anticipated this vocabulary already in v. 37 (οἱ δίκαιοι) and maybe in v. 44 (a mere αὐτοί for those who will be condemned). Gundry rightly concludes that the allusion to Dan 12 at the end of the apocalyptic discourse of Mt 24–25 does not come as a surprise, but that it rather "shows the inner connection of the latter part, peculiar to Mt, with that which Mt has in common with Mk, where allusions to Dan 11 and 12 abound"[5]. On the other hand, however, one should also note that Mt did not merely reproduce the text of Dan 12,2. Most importantly, he left out the explicit reference to the resurrection of the dead, which is replaced by ἀπελεύσονται.

3. Theodotion is closer to the Hebrew: καὶ πολλοὶ τῶν καθευδόντων ἐν γῆς χώματι ἐξεγερθήσονται, οὗτοι εἰς ζωὴν αἰώνιον καὶ οὗτοι εἰς ὀνειδισμὸν καὶ εἰς αἰσχύνην αἰώνιον.

4. R.H. GUNDRY, *The Use of the Old Testament in St. Matthew's Gospel. With Special Reference to the Messianic Hope* (SupplNT, 18), Leiden, Brill, 1967, p. 138.

5. *Ibid.*, p. 143. More debatable is "the similar horticultural connotation" Gundry claims to discover between Mt's κόλασις, "from κολάζειν, 'to prune off'", and MT חרפות, "from חרפ, 'to pluck off (fruit)'".

J. Friedrich, in his monograph on Mt 25,31-46, is critical of the Dan hypothesis[6]. The expression "eternal life", and its counterpart "eternal punishment", can be found in other writings too. Most significant for Friedrich are the occurrences in "the Book of the Parables" and in other sections of 1 Enoch, which he considers to be the primary source of Matthew in 25,31-46. While several motifs and expressions certainly have a close parallel in 1 Enoch (see esp. the complex of the Son of Man coming in glory, sitting on his throne for an eschatological judgement), one should note that Friedrich cites only passages that speak of "eternal life" but not of a contrast between reward and punishment as this is the case in Mt 25,46. 1 En 58,3 ("And the righteous will be in the light of the sun, and the chosen in the light of eternal life") is clearly influenced by Dan 12,2-3[7]. In 37,4, it is Enoch himself who is granted this reward ("in accordance with the wish of the Lord of Spirits by whom the lot of eternal life has been given to me"), whereas in 40,9 it is used to describe the responsibility of the angel Phanuel ("who is in charge of the repentance leading to hope of those who will inherit eternal life"). Friedrich also cites some other passages from 1 Enoch that do not have the expression "eternal life" as such but a synonym. In two of these the fate of the blessed is contrasted to that of the wicked. In 62,11-16 it is said that the righteous "will dwell, and eat, and lie down, and rise up for ever and ever" (v. 14), that they will put on "the garment of life" (v. 15), that "their garments will not wear out" (v. 16), and that "they will never see the face of the sinners and the lawless from then on" (v. 13), but the destiny of the latter is not described for itself. Perhaps the best parallel to Mt 25,46 does not come from the judgement scenes in chs. 62-63, but from the beginning of the book. In 5,5-9 it is announced to those who have not persevered in the observance of the Law that "the eternal curse will increase, and you will not receive mercy" (v. 5, cf. v. 6)[8]. This curse is contrasted to the promise to "the chosen" in v. 7 ("there will be light and joy and peace, and they will inherit the earth. But for you, the impious, there will be a curse") who "will all live" (v. 8) and whose "life will grow in peace, and the years of their joy will increase in gladness and in eternal peace all the days of their life" (v. 9)[9]. The motifs of the

6. FRIEDRICH, *Gott im Bruder* (n. 2), p. 161: "M.E. liegt aber in Mt 25,41 [46?] gar kein bewusster Bezug auf Dan 12,2 vor".

7. Citations of 1 Enoch are from M.A. Knibb's translation in H.F.D. SPARKS (ed.), *The Apocryphal Old Testament*, Oxford, Clarendon, 1984, pp. 169-319.

8. The Greek adds "or peace" to "mercy", which can be compared to 1 En 12,5.6 (cf. also 5,4: "you will not have peace").

9. Friedrich cites this passage to illustrate the destiny of both groups (p. 161), but he does not emphasize the contrast itself.

curse and the inheritance are of course also mentioned in Mt 25,31-46 (vv. 41 and 34), but it seems judgement is described rather differently as what will come upon the cursed and the blessed in this life (cf. v. 5: "And because of this you will curse your days, and the years of your life you will destroy", and v. 9 cited above)[10].

Occasionally one also finds a reference to one or another text from the Qumran library in connection with Mt 25,41.46. Long ago, H. Braun pointed out that the concept of punishment by eternal fire (25,41), as well as by being left behind "in the dark" (cf. 25,30), was known in Qumran (and in Judaism in general)[11]. This conclusion was nuanced by J. Gnilka when noting that the texts refer to punishment by fire, but not by "eternal fire"[12]. As a matter of fact, of the texts that are cited by Braun, 1QS IV 13 speaks of "permanent terror and shame *13* without end with the humiliation of destruction by the fire of the dark regions"[13], whereas 1QpHab X 5.13 reads, "*5* And in their midst he will proclaim him guilty and will punish him with sulphurous fire. ... so that *13* those who derided and insulted God's chosen will go to the punishment of fire (יבואו למשפטי אש)"[14], and CD II 5, "strength and power and a great anger with flames of fire"[15].

Overall, however, Braun himself rather emphasized the differences between Matthew's judgement scene and the evidence from Qumran. For the Qumran community the separation that Matthew expects to take place at the final judgement has already been realized[16]. Moreover, the identification of the Judge with "the little ones" would go far beyond

10. Cf. G.W.E. NICKELSBURG, *1 Enoch. A Commentary on the Book of 1 Enoch, Chapters 1-36; 81-108* (Hermeneia), Minneapolis, MN, Fortress, 2001, pp. 159-164: "The two major passages describing curse and blessing (5:5-6c; 5:8-9) are to a large extent structured by contrasting emphases on the shortened life of the sinners and the longevity of the righteous" (p. 160).

11. H. BRAUN, *Qumran und das Neue Testament*, Tübingen, Mohr, 1966, I, p. 53; with reference to his *Spätjüdisch-häretischer und frühchristlicher Radikalismus. Jesus von Nazareth und die essenische Qumransekte* (BHT, 24), Tübingen, Mohr, 1957, II, p. 46 n. 1 and to J. DANIÉLOU, *Eschatologie sadocite et eschatologie chrétienne*, in *Les manuscrits de la Mer Morte. Colloque de Strasbourg*, Paris, PUF, 1957, pp. 111-125, esp. 116.

12. J. GNILKA, *Das Matthäusevangelium* (HTK NT, 1/2), Freiburg, Herder, 1988, p. 377 n. 44: "Das ewige Feuer (noch 18,8) ist eine dem Mt eigene Formulierung. Qumran kennt sie nicht. Gegen Braun, Qumran I 53. Dort ist aber die Sache bekannt".

13. Translation from F. GARCÍA MARTÍNEZ – E.J.C. TIGCHELAAR, *The Dead Sea Scrolls. Study Edition*, Leiden, Brill – Grand Rapids, MI, Eerdmans, 2000, I, pp. 76/77 (Henceforth: *Study Edition*)

14. *Ibid.*, I, pp. 18/19.

15. *Ibid.*, I, pp. 552/553; cf. 4Q266 2 II 5 (I, pp. 582/583).

16. So, e.g., J. CARMIGNAC, *Le docteur de justice et Jésus-Christ*, Paris, Éd. De l'Orante, 1957, pp. 103-104.

the more exclusivistic ethics of the commandments in the community's Rule[17]. To this should be added that, of the texts cited above, 1QpHab X does not speak of the righteous, but only of those that are lost, and that CD II contrasts the (future) destruction of the wicked (II 5-6) with the (present) situation of the remnant that are left behind, "in order to fill *12* the face of the world with their offspring". In 1QS IV the future fate of "the sons of justice" and of "the sons of deceit" (III 20-21) is described in a much more elaborate way than in Mt 25,46, juxtaposing a large number of images, some of which can be compared with Mt, though none of them occurs in the gospel in the same combination as in 1QS IV[18]. Thus Mt nowhere mentions "the humiliation of destruction by the fire of the dark regions" or "the bitter weeping and harsh evils in the abysses of darkness" (both in IV 13). Perhaps the closest parallel is in Mt 13,42.50, where the punishment of "being thrown in the furnace of fire" is followed by ἐκεῖ ἔσται ὁ κλαυθμὸς καὶ ὁ βρυγμὸς τῶν ὀδόντων that Matthew uses elsewhere in combination with the punishment of being thrown out into the darkness (see 8,12 par. Lk 13,28; 22,13; 25,30), which may seem slightly more appropriate, but also with διχοτομήσει αὐτὸν καὶ τὸ μέρος αὐτοῦ μετὰ τῶν ἀποκριτῶν θήσει (24,51, added to Q 12,46)[19]. The expression seems to have become a standard formula for Mt, very much like "for many are called, but few are chosen" or "he who has ears, let him hear", which are in fact combined with the saying about weeping and gnashing of teeth in Mt 22,13-14 and 13,42-43.

In dealing with the Mechizedek traditions in Qumran and in the New Testament, P.J. Kobelski has drawn attention to the presentation in

17. Thus BRAUN, *Qumran*, I, p. 53. Cf. also his *Radikalismus*, II, p. 60 n. 3 and 94 n. 2. See, e.g., the characterisation of "the sons of truth" in 1QS IV,5 as being "of generous compassion with all the sons of truth" (*Study Edition*, I, pp. 76/77).

18. Braun's comment might yield the wrong impression that this would be the case in Mt 25,30.41 when he writes: "das Gericht bringe ... in vielen Qumrantexten das Feuer als Strafmittel (Daniélou) und den Weltenbrand (... s. zu Mt 25,41 ...), gelegentlich auch das Schwefelfeuer ..., womit die Finsternis als Strafmodus Hand in Hand gehen könne (s. zu Mt 25,30)" (*Qumran*, II, p. 270).

19. O. Betz has interpreted this verse in a context of excommunication as evidenced in 1QS II 16-17. This view is now criticized by K. Weber who does however point out that 24,51b may be compared to the curses that are mentioned in 1 QS II 11-18. See O. BETZ, *The Dichotomized Servant and the End of Judas Iscariot (Light on the Dark Passages: Matthew 24,51 and Parallel; Acts 1,18)*, in *RQ* 5 (1964) 43-58. K. WEBER, *Is There a Qumran Parallel to Matthew 24,51 // Luke 12,46?*, in *RQ* 16 (1995) 657-663. On Mt 24,51 see most recently, T. FRIEDRICHSEN, *A Note on καὶ διχοτομήσει αὐτόν (Luke 12:46 and the Parallel in Matthew 24:51)*, in *CBQ* 63 (2001) 258-264. D.C. SIM, *The Dissection of the Wicked Servant in Matthew 24:51*, in *Hervormde Teologiese Studies* 58 (2002) 172-184 (comparing with the Story of Ahiqar).

11QMelch (11Q13) as "the prime pre-NT example" of how an historical person was turned into a heavenly royal figure executing judgement with the assistance of God's angels[20]. Kobelski further specifically pointed out parallels with Mt for such details as the sounding of the trumpet (24,31 and 11QMelch II 25) and the destruction by fire (13,42 and 25,41, and 11Q Melch III 7)[21]. Indirectly this text plays a role in the interpretation of the fragment that will be discussed below (p. 445), and the motif of Belial being devoured by the fire might well be compared to Mt 25,41, but there is no parallel here to v. 46.

The concept of "the devil and his angels" in 25,41 reminds Davies and Allison of "the dualism in Zechariah 3 and the Dead Sea Scrolls"[22], whereas that of "eternal punishment" in 25,46 is compared to "the related Hebrew expression" (לכלת עולם (עולמים[23] that is found in several passages from the Scrolls[24]. Davies and Allison do not offer a parallel, however, for the kind of juxtaposition of the destinies of the righteous and the damned as in Mt 25,46, and no such parallel can be found in the texts that are listed by them, except perhaps for 4Q427 7 II 10, but there is a lacuna here, and for 1QM I 5, but the scenery of an eschatological war in which the sons of light take an active part in the downfall of Belial and his lot is hardly comparable to that of Mt 25,31-46.

2. The Parallel in 4Q548 (4QVisions of ʿAmram F?)

A better, and in any case stylistically much closer, parallel for the pointed contrast between the fate of those that are saved and those that are lost that is characteristic for Mt 25,46, and one, moreover, that uses the same verb "to go" for both sides, can be found in a fragmentary text in Aramaic that is currently listed as 4Q548.

20. P.J. Kobelski, *Melchizedek and Melchirešaʿ* (CBQ MS, 10), Washington, DC, CBAA, 1981, p. 135.

21. *Ibid.*, p. 136.

22. *A Critical and Exegetical Commentary on The Gospel According to Saint Matthew* (ICC), Edinburgh, T&T Clark, 1997, III, p. 431.

23. *Ibid.*, p. 432 n. 71.

24. See 1QS II 15 ("May God's anger and the wrath of his verdicts consume him for everlasting destruction"); 1QS V 12-13 ("in order to administer fierce punishments for everlasting annihilation without there being any remnant"); 1QM I 5 ("And th]is is a time of salvation for the nation of God and a period of rule for all the men of his lot, and of everlasting destruction for all the lot of Belial"); 1QM IX 5-6 ("All these shall pursue the enemy to exterminate them in God's battle for eternal destruction"); 4Q510 (4QShir[a]) I 7-8 ("And you have been placed in the era of the rul[e of] wickedness and in the periods of humiliation of the sons of lig[ht], in the guilty periods of [those] defiled by iniquities; not for an everlasting destruction [but ra]ther for the era of the humiliation of sin"); and 4Q427 (4QH[a]) 7 II 10 ("and wrath for eternal destruction"). In addition Davies and Allison also mention TestReuben 5,5 and TestGad 7,5 and 2 Clem 6,7.

The identification, reconstruction, and interpretation of this text remains debated. It can be reconstructed with some certainty on the basis of the context and the contrast between light and darkness that dominates the whole. J.T. Milik, who in 1972 first published a part of it, including the passage that is of interest to us, reconstructed and translated the relevant lines as follows:

12 ארי כל כסל ורש[ע חשיכי]ן וכל [של]ם וקשוט נהיר[ין ארי כל בני נהורא]
13 לנהורא לשמח[ת עלמא ולח]דות[א יהכו]ן וכל בני חש[וכא לחשוכא למותא]
14 ולאבדנא יהכון[...]

12 Car toute folie et ini[quité sont sombres], mais toute [paix] et vérité sont lumineuses. [Car tous les fils de la lumière *13* iron]t vers la lumière, vers la joie [éternelle] et [vers la ré]jouissance, tandis que tous les fils des ténè[bres] iront [vers les ténèbres, vers la mort] *14* et vers la perdition. […][25].

"Sons of darkness" occurs in l. 11 and probably also in l. 10 ("… darkness"). "Death and p[erdition]" offers a most plausible reconstruction at l. 4. Milik did not give an explanation for the rest of his reconstruction. The first occurrence of the verb "to go" (l. 13) is obviously completed on the basis of l. 14.

K. Beyer (1984) proposed to read ורשיע, "Frevler", instead of ורשע, "foolishness", and [הכי]ם, "wise", instead of [של]ם, "peace", at l. 12 (so Milik, Fitzmyer-Harrington, and Kobelski), reconstructed l. 13 as לנהורא לשמא[לא ול...ול... יהכו]ן ("werden zum Licht nach Norden [und zum … und zum … gehen]"), and allowed for another word beginning with ל between לחשוכא and ולמותא ("zur Finsternis nach … und zum Tode") at the end of l. 13[26]. García Martínez and Tigchelaar also read "wise" at l. 12, and, more correctly, סכל (so already Eisenmann-Wise, 1984) for כסל (so Milik and Beyer), but otherwise keep to the reconstruction of Milik: "*12* For all foolish and ev[il are dark,] and all [wi]se and truthful are brilliant. [This is why the sons of light] *13* [will go] to the light, to [everlasting] happiness [and to re]joicing; and all the sons of dark[ness] will go [to the shades, to death] *14* and to annihilation"[27]. In his *Ergänzungsband* of 1994, Beyer proposes two rather drastic changes at l. 13: "und zur Wärme [und zum wahren] Recht" (ולחמ[י]מ[ו]תא ול[ד]ין [קשטא) for "to [everlasting] happiness [and to re]joicing", and accordingly "und

25. J.T. MILIK, *4Q Visions de 'Amram et une citation d'Origène*, in *RB* 79 (1972) 77-97, p. 90 (part of [ ] added by me in accordance with Milik's reconstruction of the Aramaic). Milik was followed by Fitzmyer-Harrington and by Kobelski for this part of the fragment (not for l. 9). For a survey of the reconstructions and translations that are cited or referred to in the following, see the Appendix below, pp. 450-452.

26. K. BEYER, *Die aramäischen Texte vom Toten Meer*, Göttingen, Vandenhoeck & Ruprecht, 1984, p. 213.

27. *Study Edition*, II, pp. 1094/1095.

zur Kälte" (ולקרא) instead of "to death" as the second of the punishments[28].

In his monograph on the resurrection of 1993, É. Puech likewise reads "wise", but proposes a rather different reading for the first half of l. 13: *lnhwr' lśmḥ [wlšlm' b]dyn[' rb' yhkw]n*, "à la lumière, à la joie [et à la paix, lors du grand] jugement (?) [ils iro]nt"[29]. Puech argues that this reading would better account for what remains of some of the letters and for the lacuna between]דינ[and יהכו]ן. There is not enough space for two words between]לשמח and]דינ[, as Beyer assumed (1984; above), and the reading with "rejoicing", לח[דות]א, is uncertain (so already Milik, who nevertheless opted for it) and a duplicate after לשמח]א, and would leave an unexplainable blank before יהכו]ן. In 2001 Puech has published the official edition of the fragment in DJD 31[30]. I quote here ll. 12-14a:

12 ארי כל סכל ורש[יע חשי]ך וכל[חכי]ם וקשיט נהיר[ארו כל בני נהורא]
13 לנהורא ל{תמימותא} <נעימתא>[ולשלמא ב]דינ[א רבא יהכו]ן וכל בני חש[וכא
לחשוכא למותא]
14 ולאבדנא יהכון[...

12 Car tout insensé et méch[ant (sera) enténé]bré et tout[sag]e et juste (sera) illuminé.[Car tous les fils de lumière] *13* à la lumière, à la {perfection} <suavité>[et à la paix, lors du grand] jugement [ils iron]t, et tous les fils de ténè[bres aux ténèbres, à la mort] *14* et à l'Abaddon ils iront.

He now proposes to read on l. 12 ורש[יע (not ורשע), and חשי]ך and נהיר in the singular (cf. already Beyer, 1994)[31]. More important to our purpose, however, is the reconstruction he proposes for the first half of l. 13. The reading לח[דות]א (Milik; *Study Edition*), "au *taw* impossible", is again rejected for ב[דינ]א, as in Beyer, but the latter's קשטא, "(zum) wahren (Recht)", is said to be too long for the lacuna and is replaced with רבא. Puech now also rejects the reading לשמחא ("à la joie"), which went uncontested in 1993, and thinks one should read instead לנעימתא ("à la suavité"), which he suspects to be a correction of an original לתמימותא, "perfection" (clearly inspired by Beyer's לחמימותא)[32].

28. *Die aramäischen Texte vom Toten Meer. Ergänzungsband*, Göttingen, Vandenhoeck & Ruprecht, 1994, p. 88. At l. 12 he now also accepts סכל and opts for the sg. חשי]ך and נהיר.

29. É. PUECH, *La croyance des Esséniens en la vie future: Immortalité, résurrection, vie éternelle? Histoire d'une croyance dans le judaïsme ancien* (ÉB, 21-22), Paris, Gabalda, 1993, p. 539.

30. É. PUECH, *Qumrân Grotte 4. XXII. Textes araméens. Première Partie. 4Q 529-549* (DJD, 31), Oxford, Clarendon, 2001, pp. 391-398 (henceforth *DJD 31*).

31. *Ibid.*, p. 395: "tête de *kaph* final (*nun* final exclu)" and p. 397 n. 5: *kaph* "est de lecture certaine".

32. *Ibid.*, p. 397: "La *lecture prima manu* paraît devoir être … 'la perfection' corrigé en 'la suavité'".

There can be little or no doubt that a contrastive parallelism was intended between the destinies of the sons of light and the sons of darkness. That their fate was described in a threefold way is a most plausible hypothesis because it would match the length of the lacunas after "to the light" at the beginning of l. 13 and after "sons of dark[ness]" at the end of it[33]. It is also generally accepted that the verb "to go", which occurs in l. 14, should be reconstructed in l. 13 too, and that the fragmentary "sons of dark[ness]" in l. 13 is sufficient reason to conjecture a reading with "sons of light" at the end of l. 12, even though still other titles are used in the fragment[34]. The major problem, however, lies with the reconstruction of the punishments and the rewards, especially the latter. Only the first element of the first half and the last of the second have been preserved intactly, which has led some not to attempt a reconstruction[35]. Others, however, have tried to reconstruct the lists of rewards and punishments, and with some good results. An expression such as "to the shades/dark" is a most natural counterpart of "to the light". The contrast is attested already in ll. 9-10. The reading "to death" as the second in the series of punishments fits the lacuna[36]. It is based on l. 4, which reads "from death and from [...]" (מן מותא ומן א]) and of which the defective word is thought to be "Abaddon". Lines 13-14 would be a repetition of this same expression. "Abaddon" may also have figured in l. 11, which Puech in 1993 reconstructed as "[et dans l'Abaddôn ils seront enchaînés (?)]"[37]. In the edition he leaves it open, but in the notes he conjectures as a possible reading ובאבדנא יאבדון לעלמין[38].

The reconstruction of the second and third reward constitutes a far greater difficulty. The reading לח]דות[א, "to re[joicing]" (Milik; *Study Edition*, *et al.*), though lacunous and difficult to decipher, could be defended on the basis of l. 7, where García Martínez (and Puech 1993) read חדא בי, "rejoice in me", but this is now rejected by Puech in the edition in favour of חרא בי, "brûle en moi", though he is not absolutely

33. An exception is G. Vermes who retains only two punishments ("towards death] and perdition") against three rewards.

34. "Sons of light" is attested once (l. 16), besides "sons of the blessing" (l. 5) and, less clearly, "sons of ri[ghteousness]" (l. 7) and "son[s of truth]" (l. 8, in contrast to "sons of lie").

35. See J. Maier (1995) and Wise-Abegg (1996) in the Appendix below.

36. The reconstruction of "sons of dark[ness] to the shades, to death" at the end of l. 13 reckons with a lacuna of fourteen letters, which corresponds well with the thirteen letters of "That is why the sons of light" at the end of l. 12.

37. *Croyance* (n. 29), p. 539 and n. 58: "bien attesté par d'autres textes qumrâniens et extra-qumrâniens".

38. *DJD 31* (n. 30), p. 397: "La fin de la ligne 11 devait continuer le thème de la perdition dans le shéol ou les ténèbres, par exemple ...".

certain about it[39]. The combination of "[eternal] happiness and re[joicing]" (so Milik, Fitzmyer-Harrington, and *Study Edition*) sounds somewhat redundant indeed, as Puech remarks[40], but the same is true for some of the elements in one of the texts with similar lists of rewards that are cited by Puech in reconstructing this part of 4Q548[41]. He reads instead ב]דינ[א רבא, "lors du grand jugement", because of the lacuna and the trace of the last letter of]דינ[which he assures cannot be a *taw*[42]. Since almost nothing is left of the third letter, his confidence on this point is rather surprising[43]. As to the lacuna, Puech's]דינ[א רבא יהכו[ן counts twelve letters which would have to correspond to the nine letters of וכל]חכי[ם וק (וק from וקשיט) in l. 12[44]. The mention of "great judgement" would introduce an element that has no direct parallel in the second half. But perhaps this is not really a problem since it would apply to both halves (but so does the verb "to go", and yet it is repeated), or should one take [ביומא דנה] that follows on l. 14[45] together with the preceding ("… and to perdition on that day") instead of with the following[46]? A greater difficulty might be that the expression, for which Puech

39. *Ibid*., p. 395: "*res* (difficilement *dalet*)".

40. *Croyance* (n. 29), and *DJD 31* (n. 30), p. 397.

41. *Croyance*, p. 540 n. 60. The references need some correction (only the last three are repeated in *DJD 31*, p. 397):
1QM XII 12 "joie et lumière"; cf. *Study Edition*: כבוד ("glory") … ברכה ("blessing"); 1QM XIII 5-6 "la lumière"; *Study Edition:* לאור]עולמ[ים ("everlasting light"); 1QM XIII 15-16 "lumière et joie"; *Study Edition*: להשגיל חושך ולהגביר אור ול … ושמחה ("to humiliate darkness and strengthen light … and happiness"); 1QM XVII 6-7 "lumière, joie, paix et bénédiction"; *Study Edition*: באור עולמים להאיר בשמחה ... שלום וברכה לגורל אל ("in everlasting light, to illuminate with joy … peace and blessing to God's lot"); 1QS IV 6-8 "guérison, paix, longueur de jours, fécondité, bénédiction perpétuelle, joie éternelle, vie sans fin, gloire, éclat et lumière éternelle"; *Study Edition*: ופקודת כול הולכי בה למרפא ורוב שלום באורך ימים ופרות זרע עם כול ברכות עד ושמחת עולמים בחיי נצח וכליל כבוד עמ מדת הדר באור עולמים ("And the reward of all those who walk in it will be healing, plentiful peace in a long life, fruitful offspring with all everlasting blessings, eternal enjoyment with endless life, and a crown of glory with majestic raiment in eternal light"); 1QH[a] V 23: "gloire éternelle, délices, joie perpétuelle" and V 34-35 (!) "délices, paix éternelle, longueur de jours", which should probably be taken together as one passage (1QH[a] V 23-25); *Study Edition*: בהדרך תפארני ותמשילה]ו בר[וב עדנים עם שלום עולם ואורך ימימו ("You embellish him with your splendour, you install [him over an ab]undance of pleasures, with everlasting peace and length of days"). As for somewhat redundant expressions, note esp. כבוד עם מדת הדר באור עולמים in 1QS IV 7-8.

42. See the comment quoted above p. 435.

43. He is certain about the ד (*DJD 31*, p. 395), but does not comment on the י, and perhaps rightly so, for from what is left of the letter it is impossible to decide whether one should read a י or a ו. Both letters are almost identical in the last word of l. 14 (ואחוי or ואחיו); see below n. 69.

44. As can be seen on the plates (*DJD 31*, pl. XXII), the ד of]דינ[is right under the ו of וכל, and the ן of יהכו]ן right under the ק of קשיט. See further below.

45. So Puech in *DJD 31* (n. 30), diff. *Croyance* (n. 29), p. 539: *'rw 'nh*.

46. So Puech in *DJD 31*, p. 396: "[*Ce jour-là briller*]*a* …".

cites 1 En 22,4 and 91,15 (both attested in Qumran)[47], does not occur in the passages to which he refers for reconstructing the list of rewards (see above).

In the edition Puech now also rejects the reading לשמחא ("à la joie"), which he still accepted in 1993, and suggests לנעימתא ("à la suavité") supplanting an original לתמימותא ("à la perfection"). The manuscript is lacunous and almost completely erased for the part that is preserved, and so all reconstructions are more or less speculative. For the third element which fits in the place that is left by rejecting the reconstruction [עלמא] after לשמחא, Puech proposes ולשלמא ("and to peace"), because it fits the lacuna and makes sense in combination with לנעימתא[48]. In 1993 he had hesitated between שלמא and שמחא as possible readings at the end of l. 5[49], and he also remained undecided about whether these words were to be read on the same level as the preceding בני ברכתא, or as a second qualification of בני: "les fils de la bénédiction et (*de*?) la p[aix]/ j[oie] (?)"[50]. In the edition he now also suggests a reconstruction for the lacuna in the first half of l. 5: שלמא להוה עליכון, "la paix sera s]ur vous", and opts for ושמחא] at the end of the line ("et [la] j[oie]"). If this would be the correct reading of l. 5, and if ולשלמא is accepted as the third reward in l. 13, it would leave לנעימתא the only word in the parallel of ll. 12-14 that is not attested in the rest of the fragment, and indeed in none of the passages that were cited by Puech in 1993 where its closest equivalent seems to be עדנים (see above)[51]. Yet it is given preference over another word ("happiness") that is accepted in the reconstruction of the end of l. 5 and that is also well attested in the parallels mentioned above (1QM XIII 16 and XVII 7, and 1QS IV 7). The reading שלמא at the beginning of l. 5 is defended "comme le propre des fils de la bénédiction"[52]. The same should then probably be said of שמחא. Puech now translates as "la paix sera s]ur vous, les fils de la bénédiction, et [la] j[oie]", and no longer seems to hesitate about the connection between שמחא and בני. He points to the contrast between שלמא and אבדן[53]. But one should also observe that the combination שלמא / שמחא of l. 5 is preceded by א]בדנא / מותא in l. 4. What reason would there have been not to take up this contrast again in ll. 12-14? So perhaps one should stick with

47. *Croyance* (n. 29), p. 540 (there also 1 En 10,6) and *DJD 31* (n. 30), p. 397.

48. *DJD 31*, p. 397: "Après לנהורא לנעימתא], on attend pour l'espace et le sens ולשלמא au sens de 'paix et salut'".

49. *Croyance* (n. 29), p. 537 and 538 n. 55.

50. *Ibid.*, p. 538; cf. n. 55.

51. The same problem arises with the reconstruction of Beyer ("Wärme ... Kälte") quoted above.

52. *DJD 31*, p. 397; with reference to 1QM XVII 7, 1QS IV 6-8, 1QH^a V 34.

53. *Ibid.*: "s'opposerait bien".

לשמחא (instead of לנעימתא), with or without עולמא[54], as the second of the rewards. As for the third element, while "peace" is possibly attested at the beginning of l. 5[55], and in several of the texts that are cited by Puech (he esp. stresses the fact that it occurs there no less than three times[56]), there may be a problem with the total length of the reconstruction he proposes. The reading [ולשלמא ב] <לנעימתא> (so Puech) contains fourteen letters to correspond with the twelve of סכל ורש[יע חשי]ך of the previous line[57]. This is not impossible, but when the two lacunas on l. 13 are taken together (from לנעימתא to יהכו]ן), Puech's reconstruction contains twenty-six letters (fourteen and twelve), and a total of fifty-four for l. 13, which would make it the longest line in the fragment of all those that can be reconstructed (against forty-eight on l. 9, fifty-one on l. 10, and forty-six on l. 12). The reading with לשמח]ת עלמא ולח[דות]א יהכו]ן (so Milik) numbers twenty-one letters (twelve and nine) for a total of forty-nine letters (or twenty-two and a total of fifty if one reads לשלמא for עלמא), and would be identical to the number of letters for the corresponding section סכל to וק(שיט) on l. 12:

12 ארו כל //סכל ורשיע חשיך (12) //כל חכים וק(9)//שיט נהיר ארו כל בני נהורא

13 לנהורא//לנעימתא ולשלמא ב(14)//דינא רבא יהכון (12)// וכל בני חשוכא לחשוכא למותא (Puech)

13 לנהורא //לשמחת עלמא ולח(12)//דותא יהכון (9)// וכל בני חשוכא לחשוכא למותא (Milik)

3. 4Q548 AND MT 25,46

None of the rewards (light – happiness or sweetness/perfection – peace or rejoicing) or punishments (shades – death – annihilation) occurs as such in Mt 25,31-46, but the parallels in Mt, in 1 Enoch, or in the other Qumran texts that have been cited show a great creativity and a great diversity (in number and content) in describing these rewards and punishments. If one should read שמחא עלמא 4Q548 would at least

54. If one does not retain עלמא, one is forced to accept the reading with "the great judgement" and to conjecture a third element in place of עלמא which could be שלמא (see the order of 1QM XVII 16-17 cited above). When reading עלמא with "happiness", one of the rewards receives a qualification that was perhaps not needed in the list of punishments (though "eternal shades" would have made sense), but is in any case lacking in the second half. It is also to be noted that in four of the six passages mentioned above one or another of the rewards bears this qualification (1QM XIII 5-6 and XVII 16-17, 1QH[a] V 23-25, and "eternal happiness" in 1QS IV 7).

55. Milik and Fitzmyer-Harrington read it also in l. 12 instead of "the wise" (see above).

56. *Croyance* (n. 29), p. 540 n. 60.

57. According to the plates, traces of the ל can be detected somewhat to the right of the beginning of סכל, and the כ of חשיך stands more or less right above where one has to suspect the ב on l. 13.

contain the same qualification as Mt 25,46. If, on the other hand, one accepts as authentic the reading with "the great judgement", 4Q548 contains a clear reference to a judgement scene, as is the case in Mt 25,31-46, even though the noun κρίσις or the verb κρίνω are absent. Matthew mentions only one reward and one punishment in v. 46 against the threefold series of 4Q548. But in v. 41 it is said that the cursed will be given to the fire, which should perhaps be distinguished from the κόλασις of v. 46, and in v. 34 the blessed are promised to inherit the kingdom, which in Mt is also connected with joy and happiness (13,44; 22,2.11; 25,10; or its opposite for those that are excluded from it: 8,11; 13,50; 22,13), as well as with righteousness (5,50; 6,33; cf. 4Q548 l. 7) and healing (4,23 and 9,35; 10,7; cf. 4Q548 l. 3?). Thus Matthew too could be referring to more than one reward/punishment. He also combines the motif of destruction (v. 41) with that of perpetual torture (v. 46), as this is the case in 4Q548 ("shades", and "death and annihilation"). Moreover, it is not so evident whether 4Q548 speaks of three rewards/punishments, or of only one that is further explicitated with two more qualifications. Beyer (1984 and 1993) and Eisenmann-Wise (1992) connect the various elements with an "and"[58]. Milik, the *Study Edition*, and Puech take a more neutral position ("to the shades, to death and to annihilation"). But in the Dutch translation of García Martínez and van der Woude (1995), "happiness and rejoicing" and "death and annihilation" further explain "the light" and "the shades"[59]. Finally, it should also be noted that it is not impossible that at ll. 15 ff. of 4Q548 the list of rewards and punishments is repeated in somewhat the same form as in Mt (one reward against one punishment). At least that is how Puech in 1993 reconstructed the last line and a half of the fragment: "car tous [les fils de lumière (?) (*seront dans la joie*?) et tous] *16* les fils de [ténèbres (*seront châtiés dans le feu*?)] et tous les fils de lumière[..."[60]. In the edition Puech no longer proposes a reconstruction of the reward/punishment itself in his presentation of the text, but he keeps the alternation "all [the sons of light ... and all] *16* the sons of [darkness ...] and all the sons of light[...", and in the notes he comments, "L. 15-16 L'opposition des fils de lumière et de ténèbres continue dans ces lignes"[61].

Perhaps most remarkable is the fact that in both Mt 25,46 and 4Q548 the contrast between the destiny of the "righteous" (vv. 34 and 46; cf.

58. Beyer (1994): "zur Finsternis und zur Kälte und zum Tode"; Eisenmann-Wise: "for Darkness and death and destruction".

59. García Martínez – van der Woude: "naar het licht tot [eeuwige] vreugde [en blijdschap] ... [naar de duisternis tot dood] en tot verderf".

60. *Croyance* (n. 29), p. 540 and n. 62: "16 *bny [ḥšwk'* ..., peut-être en opposition, qui seront châtiés dans le feu de l'Abaddôn".

61. *DJD 31* (n. 30), p. 398.

4Q548 l. 7: "sons of right[teousness]") and the cursed is expressed most acutely, in one and the same clause and in an almost dualistic way[62], and with the rather "plain" verb "to go". Mt 25,46 stands out among other verses in the gospel referring to the judgement because it uses the same verb to describe its outcome for both parties. Instead of expressing the contrast by using different verbs for the fate of the good and the bad as in 18,8-9 (εἰσελθεῖν εἰς / βληθῆναι εἰς), 8,11-12 (ἀνακλιθήσονται μετά / βληθήσονται εἰς), 13,42-43 (βαλοῦσιν εἰς / ἐκλάμψουσιν), or 13,48 (συνέλεξαν / ἔξω ἔβαλον), Matthew now has only one verb, ἀπελεύσονται εἰς ("And they will go away into"). This feature seems to have escaped the attention of the commentators, and the reason why Matthew may have written here ἀπέρχομαι is usually not discussed. Gundry is an exception when he notes in his commentary, "We might have expected Matthew to write βληθήσονται, 'will be thrown'; but the switch from πῦρ, with which he regularly uses that verb (see 3:10; 7:19; 13:42, 50; 18:8[bis]), to κόλασιν leads him to a verb that will double for eternal punishment and eternal life – viz., ἀπελεύσονται. The parallel between eternal punishment and eternal life forestalls any weakening of the former"[63]. I wonder whether it is really the "switch" to κόλασιν that occasioned the use of ἀπέρχομαι. Mt could as well have used a verb of the stem κολαζ- as in 26,67 (κολαφίζω par. Mk 14,65), or any other verb denoting punishment or destruction. The "switch" had already been prepared in 25,41 where he wrote, πορεύεσθε ἀπ' ἐμοῦ ... εἰς τὸ πῦρ τὸ αἰώνιον.

'Απέρχομαι is a favourite of Mt, and he uses the verb to describe the execution of a judgement in 5,30 (εἰς γέενναν ἀπέλθῃ par. Mk 9,43), 13,28 (θέλεις οὖν ἀπελθόντες συλλέξωμεν αὐτά), 18,30 (ἀπελθὼν ἔβαλεν αὐτὸν εἰς φυλακήν), and 27,5 (καὶ ἀπελθὼν ἀπήγξατο)[64], as he also once writes ἀποχωρεῖτε ἀπ' ἐμοῦ (7,23)[65]. Dan 12,1LXX has παρελεύσεται Μιχαηλ (Theod. ἀναστήσεται; MT "shall appear"), but the verb does not denote the judgement itself. In Dan 12,2 the same verb (ἀναστήσονται εἰς) refers to the fate of both sides, as in Mt 25,46, but Matthew preferred a different verb and in so far he has significantly weakened the parallel[66].

62. On the "cosmic dualism" of 4Q544, see J. Frey, *Different Patterns of Dualistic Thought in the Qumran Library. Reflections on Their Background and History*, in Bernstein, *Legal Texts* (n. 1), pp. 275-335, here 320-322.

63. *Matthew. A Commentary on His Literary and Theological Art*, Grand Rapids, MI, Eerdmans, 1982, p. 516.

64. See also Mk 6,28 καὶ ἀπελθὼν ἀπεκεφάλισεν, par. Mt om. ἀπελθών.

65. For πορεύομαι, see Mt 22,15.

66. Jn 5,29 ἐκπορεύσονται ... εἰς ἀνάστασιν ζωῆς, ... εἰς ἀνάστασιν κρίσεως is closer to Dan, but the choice for ἐκπορεύσονται might reflect the influence of the way Mt has formulated it in 25,46.

The use of the *verba eundi* in Mt 25,31-46 may be intentional. It is the Son of Man, who will come in glory (v. 31), who will invite to come with him or send away those who are to be judged. First a contrast is created between the invitational δεῦτε οἱ εὐλογημένοι τοῦ πατρός μου in v. 34 and the condemning πορεύεσθε ἀπ' ἐμοῦ οἱ κατηραμένοι in v. 41[67]. In v. 46 this contrast of reward and punishment is then repeated, but while now using the same verb ἀπέρχομαι in both halves to indicate the execution of the verdict. The use of יהכון in ll. 13-14 of 4Q548 is probably no less intentional and certainly equally striking within the extended contrastive parallelism of ll. 9-14.

In 1993 Puech had discussed 4Q548 as an attestation of the belief in the resurrection in the Qumran community. He did this on the basis of l. 14 which he read as, *ʾrw ʾnh mnh]r lʿmʾ nhyrwtʾ wʾḥyw l[ʿlmyn bny nhwrʾ (?)]*, "*[Car, moi, je ferai brill]er / Ce jour-là s'illumi]ne[ra]* pour le peuple l'illumination et seront ressuscités p[our toujours les fils de la lumière]"[68]. He prefers to read ואחיו ("seront ressuscités"), instead of ואחוי ("je [leur] montrerai", "make known", sg.)[69], because of the plural וא[ו]דעו ("et ils ont été informés") on the next line, and he opts for the meaning "resurrect", though admitting that the verb can also mean "to live"[70]. Puech has repeated his views in a contribution of 1997[71], in discussion with J.J. Collins, who in a review of Puech's monograph had contested his reading of l. 14 as "questionable", and in a more recent publication observes that, "While the text is very clear about eternal reward and punishment, however, the notion of resurrection is at best implicit"[72]. In the edition Puech has now given up the interpretation of l. 14: "Il faut reconnaître que la première proposition [i.e., ואחיו, as proposed by Milik in 1972, who translated, however, as "on fera vivre", and not "resurrect"], pour tentante qu'elle soit, reste difficile qui suppose un *waw* conversif en araméen. Aussi devrait-on retenir la deuxième lecture [ואחוי]"[73]. The reference to resurrection is indeed implicit at most, and in so far Mt is closer to 4Q548 than to, e.g., Dan 12,2.

It is not clear who is the subject of אחוי. It must be the same character who is referring to himself in the first person in l. 7 ("brûle en moi" /

67. Cf. also *venite/discedite* in Vg.

68. *Croyance* (n. 29), p. 537 and 539-540 (comment).

69. As the י and the ו in this particular word is almost identical it is difficult to decide on the sole basis of the orthography.

70. *Ibid.*, p. 540 n. 61.

71. *Les esséniens croyaient-ils à la résurrection?*, in LAPERROUSAZ, *Qoumrân* (n. 1), pp. 409-440, esp. 428 n. 43.

72. *Apocalypticism in the Dead Sea Scrolls* (The Literature of the Dead Sea Scrolls), London – New York, Routledge, 1997, p. 126. Cf. his review of Puech, in *DSD* 1 (1994) 246-252, here 252.

73. *DJD 31* (n. 30), p. 397.

"rejoice in me") and in l. 9 ("I will [tea]ch you ..., I would let [you] know"), and who is instructing the sons of light/darkness about their destiny. Milik had cited part of 4Q548 in an article dealing with a text describing a vision of someone whose life is disputed by two "watchers", one of which is called Melchiresa. This fragment (4Q544) contains some overlaps with three other fragmentary texts (4Q543, 545, 546). In two of these one reads the following passage (probably the title or the beginning of the work): "Copy of [the writing of the words of the vision](s) of ʿAmram, son of [Qahat, son of Levi"[74]. Milik therefore identified the various fragments as remnants of several copies of a pseudepigraphical writing which he gave the title "Vision" or "Testament of ʿAmram" (VA). No other textual evidence is known to exist besides that attested in the Scrolls[75]. Though 4Q548 contains no such overlaps with the other fragments, Milik nevertheless argued that it also stemmed from the same "Testament"[76] and was in fact a comment by ʿAmram on the meaning of the dispute of the watchers/angels: "Ici, le patriarche aura expliqué à ses enfants plus en détail la signification générique et humaine de sa vision des deux anges"[77]. By the time of the Leuven Qumran conference of 1976, Milik had changed his mind and now identified 4Q548 as part of a pseudepigraphical "Testament (or Vision) of Levi"[78]. The same identification was accepted with much reserve by Puech in 1992[79], but in his edition he now returns to Milik's original proposal, because of the motif of light and darkness that is

74. 4Q543 1 and 545 1. The text of 544 can be reconstructed by combining the two fragments. See the survey of overlaps and parallels in 4Q543-547 by E.J.C. TIGCHELAAR, *Annotated List of Overlaps and Parallels in the Non-Biblical Texts from Qumran and Masada*, in E. TOV (ed.), *The Texts from the Judaean Desert* (DJD, 39), Oxford, Clarendon, 2002, pp. 285-322, here 317. On the chronology of ʿAmram's life as mentioned in 4Q543 and 545, see P. GRELOT, *Quatre cents trente ans (Ex 12,40). Notes sur les Testaments de Lévi et de ʿAmram*, in L. ALVAREZ VERDES – E.J ALONSO HERNANDEZ (eds.), *Miscelanea de Estudios Biblicos y Hebraico. Homaje a Juan Prado*, Madrid, CSIC, 1975, pp. 559-570. PUECH, *DJD 31* (n. 30), p. 286.

75. See P.W. SKEHAN, *Littérature de Qumrân: B) Apocryphes de l'Ancien Testament*, in *DBSuppl* 9 (1978) 822-828, esp. cc. 826-827. A.-M. DENIS, *Introduction à la littérature religieuse judéo-hellénistique*, Turnhout, Brepols, 2000, pp. 287-289.

76. *4Q Visions* (n. 25), p. 90: "un autre exemplaire".

77. *Ibid.*

78. *Écrits préesséniens de Qumrân: d'Hénoch à Amram*, in M. DELCOR (ed.), *Qumrân. Sa piété, sa théologie et son milieu* (BETL, 46), Paris-Gembloux, Duculot, 1978, pp. 91-106, here 95.

79. *Fragments d' un apocryphe de Lévi et le personnage eschatologique 4QTest Lévi $^{c-d}$ (?) et 4QAJa*, in J. TREBOLLE BARRERA – L. VEGAS MONTANER (eds.), *The Madrid Qumran Congress* (STDJ, 11), Leiden, Brill, 1992, pp. 449-501, esp. 491 n. 48. For criticism, see, a.o., M. DE JONGE, *Levi in Aramaic Levi and in the Testament of Levi*, in E.G. CHAZON – M. STONE (eds.), *Pseudepigraphic Perspectives. The Apocrypha and Pseudepigrapha in Light of the Dead Sea Scrolls* (STDJ, 31), Leiden, Brill, 1999, pp. 71-89, esp. 77-78 and 84.

present also in the fragments that bear the same name (title) "Vision(s) of ʿAmram": "On peut ... revenir à un exemplaire des Visions de ʿAmram, mais sans certitude en l'absence de recoupement avec les autres exemplaires, tout en relevant l'importance qu'occupe le dualisme lumière et ténèbres dans cette composition. Serait-il recommandé de donner le sigle 4QVisions ʿAmram ^{f} (?)?"[80].

In 4Q544, the fragment with which Milik was concerned in 1972, ʿAmram, speaking in the first person, asks one of the watchers about their name. In reply the watcher reveals, first, that the other has three names, of which only the last one is preserved in the text (Melchiresa) and that this watcher "rules over all darkness" and he himself "over all that is bright" (II 5), and then adds that he too has three names, none of which is preserved. On the basis of the sole name of Melchiresa, Milik quite convincingly suggested the following reconstruction: "Belial, Prince of darkness, Melchiresa", to which corresponds as his counterpart, "Michael, Prince of light, Melchizedek"[81]. This identification has been generally accepted[82], and it also figures in Puech's edition of 4Q544[83].

80. *DJD 31* (n. 30), p. 392; cf. p. 283: "hypothèse de travail". It should be remarked that in recent editions and translations as a rule no attempt is made to situate 4Q548 within the whole of VA. See earlier, T. GASTER, *The Dead Sea Scriptures*, Garden City, NY, Doubleday, ³1976, pp. 512-513.

81. The identification of Melchizedek/Michael is based on 11QMelch and was first suggested for this text by A.S. VAN DER WOUDE, *Melchisedek als himmlische Erlösergestalt in den neugefundenen eschatologischen Midraschim aus Qumran Höhle XI*, in *Oudtestamentische Studiën* 14 (1965) 354-373, here pp. 370-372. It was further commented upon in M. DE JONGE – A.S. VAN DER WOUDE, *11Q Melchizedek and the New Testament*, in *NTS* 12 (1966) 301-326, here p. 305. Milik built on it for reconstructing 4Q544; see the arguments in *4Q Visions* (n. 25), pp. 85-86. This passage is of course also briefly mentioned in Milik's survey of the Melchizedek traditions: *Milkî-ṣedeq et Milkî-rešaʿ dans les anciens écrits juifs et chrétiens*, in *JJS* 23 (1972) 96-144, esp. pp. 126-127.

82. See KOBELSKI, *Melchizedek* (n. 20), p. 28. F. GARCÍA MARTÍNEZ, *4QʿAmram BI, 14: Melki-rešaʿ o Melki-ṣedeq?*, in *RQ* 12 (1985) 111-114. É.-M. PUECH, *Notes sur le manuscrit de 11QMelkîsédeq*, in *RQ* 12 (1987) 483-513, esp. pp. 510-511. ID., *Croyance* (n. 29), p. 536. See also the literature on Michael and/or Melchizedek traditions in general: F.C. HORTON, Jr., *The Melchizedek Tradition. A Critical Examination of the Sources to the Fifth Century A.D. and in the Epistle to the Hebrews* (SNTS MS, 30), Cambridge, UP, 1976, pp. 67-82 (11QMelch). C. GIANOTTO, *Melchisedek e la sua tipologia. Tradizioni giudaiche, cristiane e gnostiche* (SupplRivBib, 12), Brescia, Paideia, 1984, pp. 75-79 and 84-86. M.J. DAVIDSON, *Angels at Qumran. A Comparative Study of 1 Enoch 1-36, 72-108 and Sectarian Writings from Qumran* (JSP SS, 11), Sheffield, JSOT, 1992, pp. 264-268. F. MANZI, *Melchisedek e l'angelologia nell'Epistola agli Ebrei e a Qumran* (AnBib, 136), Roma, PIB, 1997, pp. 32-39, 279-280, 285-287. D.D. HANNAH, *Michael and Christ. Michael Traditions and Angel Christology in Early Christianity* (WUNT, 2/109), Tübingen, Mohr, 1999, pp. 72-73, with the concluding observation: "This [Milik's] is a possible reconstruction, but rather than confirming the ... reading of 11QMelch, it depends upon it". García Martínez proposes an interesting correction at l. 14 by reading הענכן ("smiling") instead of חענכן (Milik: "un vipère"), which has been taken over by Beyer and Maier. Cf. also C. MARTONE, *A proposito di un passo di 4Q Visioni di ʿAmram in alcune interpretazioni recenti*, in *RSLR* 33 (1997) 615-621, esp. pp. 619-621.

83. *DJD 31* (n. 30), pp. 327-329.

If 4Q548 can be connected with 4Q544 and the other fragments from the ʿAmram pseudepigraphon, the one who is speaking in the first person at l. 14 as the guide of the people ("I will show [them]", cf. also ll. 7 and 9) could be identified with Michael, as Puech argues. In 1993 he builds on it, and on the possible allusion to Dan 12,1-2 that this identification together with the reference to "the people" would entail, for considering the reading "they will resurrect" as the authentic one[84]. But the identification also holds without this latter implication as he shows in the comment in his edition[85]. Matthew does not mention any of the three names, but instead speaks of the Son of Man with all his angels (25,31). However, this difference should perhaps not be overemphasized. After all, Matthew's Son of Man coming in glory sitting on his (God's) throne and executing God's judgement takes upon him very much the same task as "the one like a son of man" who is mentioned in Dan 7,13 and who has been identified by a number of scholars with the archangel Michael[86], and as does Melchizedek in 11QMelch II 9-13. In so far, early Christian tradition, and Matthew in particular, may have continued a line of interpretation in which an historical figure (Melchizedek, Jesus) returns as an heavenly judge. Or as Kobelski has put it, more generally, in line with many others, "The more-than-human, 'heavenly' aspect of the NT concept has been provided by the phrase 'one like a son of man' in Dan 7:13 – and its probable reference there to the angel Michael – and by 11QMelch, which portrays Melchizedek as the heavenly leader of the forces of light, identical with the angel Michael, whose exalted role in the heavenly assembly alongside God is that of the executor of God's final judgement"[87]. In light of such a conclusion, it may be worth observing that in Mt 25,34 and 41 (and only here in the Synoptic gospels[88]) the Son of Man of v. 31 is addressed as "King", and in vv. 37 and 44 as "Lord", as is Michael/Melchizedek in 4Q544 II 3 ("And I said: 'My Lord' ...")[89], and that those who are saved are twice called "the righteous" (vv. 37 and 46). The motif of "Satan and his angels" of v. 41, on the other hand, recalls that of Belial

84. *Croyance* (n. 29), p. 540 n. 61

85. *DJD 31* (n. 30), p. 397: "Dans ce contexte avec l'ange de lumière/Michel/Melkîsedeq comme interlocuteur de ʿAmram (?), עמא devrait correspondre aux emplois de עמך en Dn 12:1".

86. Cf. KOBELSKI, *Melchizedek* (n. 20), pp. 130-137 and J.J. COLLINS, *Daniel* (Hermeneia), Minneapolis, MN, Fortress, 1993, pp. 304-310, and *Apocalypticism* (n. 72), p. 75.

87. KOBELSKI, *Melchizedek*, p. 137; cf. 130 n. 3. See above n. 20.

88. The only other instance of such an association that is somewhat comparable is in Jn 1,49-51.

89. *Ibid.*, p. 33 n. 15.

and his lot in 11QMelch, but also of Melchiresa who "rules over all darkness" according to 4Q544 II 5.

4. The Vision of ʿAmram and Later Tradition

4Q548 is dated by Puech in the second half of the first century BC[90]. But the "Testament" / "Vision" is certainly older. Milik suggested a date for 4Q544 in the (early) second century BC[91], whereas Puech opts for the second half of that century[92]. He adds, however, that the language points to a date for the original in the third century or at least in the first part of the second, i.e., VA was composed some time before the Qumran community came into existence. That it was accepted and read in Qumran should not come as a surprise in light of its dualistic tendency and its interest in predestination, "dont le milieu sadocite qumranien a pu et dû hériter"[93].

There is also some evidence that the work was likewise known outside Qumran. Puech agrees with Milik that the author of the Book of Jubilees (which he dates ca. 160 BC) made use of it for the information about how the Israelites transferred the bones of Jacob's children (except Joseph's) out of Egypt to be buried in Hebron where some, ʿAmram was among them, had to stay since they could not return to Egypt because of the war with Canaan (Jub 46,9-11 and 4Q544 I 1-9)[94]. According to Milik, Josephus once must have read VA and profited from it in decribing the birth of Moses in AJ 1,210-216[95]. VA most probably even circulated in certain early Christian communities. Milik argued that the motif of Michael contending with the devil over the body of Moses that is found in Jude 9 was not borrowed from AssMos, as Clement of Alexandria and Origen thought, but directly from VA which was also the source of AssMos[96]. His comment is repeated almost literally by Puech[97]. K. Berger, on the other hand, has nuanced Milik's hypothesis of direct literary dependence, and concludes that Jude 9 has in mind AssMos, which itself was possibly inspired by VA. "Das wäre dann eine

90. *DJD 31* (n. 30), p. 393.

91. *4Q Visions* (n. 25), p. 78: "Ce manuscrit fort archaïque – certainement du IIe siècle avant notre ère, peut-être même de sa première moitié".

92. *DJD 31* (n. 30), p. 285.

93. *Ibid.*, p. 287.

94. *4Q Visions* (n. 25), p. 97 (who extends the parallel to Jub 46,9-47,9 and also cites 45,16) and Puech, *DJD 31* (n. 30), pp. 285-286, cf. also 258 n. 3.

95. *4Q Visions* (n. 25), p. 95.

96. *Ibid.*

97. *DJD 31* (n. 30), p. 288.

etwas weniger direkte Form von literarischen Abhängigkeit"[98]. Milik also traced back to (the influence of) VA the motif of the burial of Jacob and the fathers at Shechem that is mentioned by Stephen in Acts 7,15-16, but this does not seem to have caught the eyes of recent commentators of Acts[99]. In later tradition VA is possibly mentioned in the Apostolic Constitutions when referring to an apocryphon τῶν τριῶν πατριαρχῶν among the βίβλια ἀπόκρυφα ... φθοροποιὰ καὶ τῆς ἀληθείας ἐχθρά (6,16,3), which Milik took for a general title covering the Testaments of Levi, Qahat, and ʿAmram [100]. The work may also have figured in other and later catalogues[101], but it is difficult to ascertain that these still had access to all the works they mention. Milik was convinced that VA (in its Greek version) must have inspired almost the whole of the early Christian literature dealing with Melchizedek, from the Epistle of the Hebrews and Hermas (*Sim.* 8), over gnostic authors such as Theodotus, to several of the writings of Nag Hammadi. As for the latter, he mentioned in particular *Pistis Sophia* 139-140, but was confident that the treatise on Melchizedek "fournira sans doute d'autres parallèles frappants"[102].

Some more solid evidence can perhaps be found in Origen's homily on Lk 12,58-59, as Milik has argued[103]. In commenting upon the identity of the various characters that are mentioned by Luke, Origen refers to an apocryphon where one can read how the angels of justice and the angels of iniquity fight over the body of Abraham: "Legimus – si tamen cui placet huiuscemodi scripturam recipere – iustitiae et iniquitatis angelos

98. *Der Streit des guten und des bösen Engels um die Seele. Beobachtungen zu 4Q ʿAmr^{b} und Judas 9*, in *JSJ* 4 (1973) 1-18, p. 12. He also refers (pp. 13-14) to a passage from the "Palaea Historica" that may have been taken from a Jewish-hellenistic writing and likewise speaks of a fight over the body of Moses between Michael and an adversary who is called "Samuel" (for Samael?).

99. *Écrits préesséniens* (n. 78), pp. 101 and 106; PUECH, *DJD 31* (n. 30), p. 287.

100. *4Q Visions* (n. 25), pp. 96-97; cf. PUECH, *DJD 31* (n. 30), p. 288.

101. *Milkî-ṣedeq* (n. 81), p. 103; *DJD 31* (n. 30), p. 288.

102. *4Q Visions* (n. 25), p. 95. On PSophia 1-3 and 4, see HORTON, *Melchizedek* (n. 82), pp. 135-151; GIANOTTO, *Melchisedek* (n. 82), pp. 223-233. Gianotto also discusses the evidence in the "Melchizedek" treatise of Nag Hammadi (pp. 193-216). Cf. J. HELDERMAN, *Melchisedeks Wirkung. Eine traditionsgeschichtliche Untersuchung eines Motivkomplexes in NHC IX, 1,1-27,10 (Melchisedek)*, in J.-M. SEVRIN (ed.), *The New Testament in Early Christianity* (BETL, 86), Leuven, UP – Peeters, 1989, pp. 335-362, esp. 339-347, and most recently Gianotto's commentary in W.P. FUNK *et al.*, *Melchisédek (NH IX,1). Oblation, baptême et vision dans la gnose séthienne* (Bibliothèque copte de Nag Hammadi. Section "Textes", 30), Laval, UP – Leuven, Peeters, 2001, pp. 115-165 (reference to 11QMelch on p. 163, but no mention of VA).

103. *4Q Visions* (n. 25), p. 95. Earlier, A. HARNACK, *Geschichte der altchristlichen Litteratur bis Eusebius*, Leipzig, Hinrichs, 1893, I,2, pp. 857-858, thought of an apocryphal work on Abraham.

super Abrahae salute et interitu disceptantes, dum utraeque turmae suo eum volunt coetui vindicare"[104]. Milik took this for a reference to a passage from VA that is preserved in 4Q544 (with overlaps in 4Q543 and 546). The shift from ʿAmram to Abraham is easily understandable and is documented in the textual tradition of the OT[105]. Milik has ingenuously conjectured that "utraeque turmae" might be a corruption for an original δύο ειρειν (the transcription in Greek of עירין, "watchers", as in 4Q544 II 2), which was taken over in the Latin (**eirein*) and then changed into **tirme* and so into "turmae", because the word made no sense to the copyists[106]. The reference to the Pastor (Mand 6,2,1) that follows in Origen ("ad volumen, quod titulo Pastoris inscribitur, et inveniet cuncto hominis duos abesse angelos ..."), while perhaps not fully appropriate since it does not speak of the presence of these angels at the moment of one's death[107], nevertheless shows that Origen must have thought of two individuals rather than of two groups[108]. Puech accepts Milik's identification of the apocryphon without reserve: "Origène fait une allusion explicite à un livre apocryphe qui paraît bien être les 'Visions d' ʿAmram'"[109]. Berger is again more critical and points to several other Christian texts, of a later date, that contain the motif of a fight between two (groups of) angels: "4QAmr[b] und Origenes, Homilie 35 (dürfen) nicht isoliert konfrontiert werden – vielmehr ist eine direkte literarische Abhängigkeit nicht das Wahrscheinlichste"[110]. While this may be so for (most of) the other texts[111], it should be noted that Origen is the only one who explicitly refers for it to an apocryphal written source ("legimus").

Matthew does not mention ʿAmram, but then he does not mention Enoch either. Those who can accept that he may nevertheless have been

104. *Hom.* 35 (GCS 35, 1930, p. 207; GCS 49, ²1959, pp. 197-198). The Greek text that is printed in parallel to this passage differs from the Latin and may contain an echo of Mt 13,42-43 (ἀφορισθείς).

105. *4Q Visions* (n. 25), pp. 91-92.

106. DAVIDSON, *Angels at Qumran* (n. 82), p. 265, is critical of this reading in 4Q544 II 2 and II 1: "In view of the uncertainty of the reading, nothing should be made to depend on the matter. If watchers are mentioned here, they will be watchers in the general sense of leading angels".

107. So BERGER, *Streit* (n. 98), p. 1.

108. *4Q Visions* (n. 25), pp. 86-89. In the GCS edition of Origen's homilies, the editor (M. Rauer) also refers to Tertullian, *de anima*, 39.

109. *DJD 31* (n. 30), p. 287.

110. BERGER, *Streit* (n. 98), p. 16. MARTONE, *4Q Visioni* (n. 82), who is also critical of Milik's suggestion, refers to a similar scene of two angels fighting in *TestAbr* A, 12, but he must admit that Abraham "è solo spettatore della scena" (p. 618).

111. These are the "Testament of Mary" in the "Koimesis" of John of Saloniki, the various versions of the Apocalypse of Paul, the Ethiopic Apocalypse of Mary and the Apocalypse of Gorgios, an homily of Ephrem Syrus, and the Ethiopic "Book of the Angels".

influenced by the Book of Enoch can probably also accept that he may have been acquainted with other but similar traditions. Perhaps that could do, and it is not necessary to argue for (direct) literary dependence. That others at least may have had in mind VA when reading Mt 25,31-46, and specifically the verses on the destiny of the righteous and the cursed, can perhaps be shown from Origen's comments upon v. 41: "*ignem* autem *aeternum* non illis, quibus dicitur *discedite a me maledicti, paratum* ostendit, sicut regnum iustis, sed *diabolo et angelis eius*, quia (quantum ad se) homines non ad perditionem creavit sed ad vitam et gaudium, peccantes autem coniugunt se diabolo. et sicut qui salvantur sanctis angelis coaequantur et fiunt 'filii resurrectionis' et 'filii dei' et angeli, sic qui pereunt diaboli angelis coaequantur et fiunt angeli eius"[112]. The combination of "ad perditionem" (אבדנא?)[113] and "ad vitam et gaudium" (שמחא ?) is most striking indeed, as is the emphasis on becoming part of the lot of Satan ("coniugunt se diabolo", cf. 4Q544 and "Melchiresa ruling over all that is dark") that is further explained with reference to Lk 20,36[114]. Do we have here another echo in Origen of VA, this one a combination of motifs that are attested in 4Q544 and in 4Q548?

A. Thierylaan 32 Joseph VERHEYDEN
B-3001 Leuven

112. *CommSer.* 72 (GCS 38, 1933, p. 172).

113. In v. 46 Origen has "poenam aeternam" for κόλασιν αἰώνιον.

114. The motif of "darkness" shows up quite unexpectedly at the end of the comment on the Parable of the Talents. Origen explicitly connects this Parable with the Parable of the Last Judgement. In the comment on Mt 25,31-46 he compares the reward of those at the right hand and the punishment of those at the left with that of the servant with the one and the ten talents (*CommSer.* 70, p. 167: "tale est et quod dicit apud Lucam: [19,24-26]"). In commenting upon Mt 25,25 he refers forward to the Parable of the Judgement when he adds the punishment for the one who hid his talent in the ground: "quasi inutilis mittitur in tenebros exteriores, ubi nulla inluminatio est forsitan" (*CommSer.* 69, p. 163). This he further explains with a reference to an anonymous author who had commented on this "abyss of darkness" ("legimus aliquem qui fuit ante nos exponentem de tenebris abyssi") and who may be Philo (so E. Klostermann in his edition of *CommSer.*, p. 183 n. 3: *de Opificio mundi*, §32).

APPENDIX

Reconstructions and Translations of 4Q548 (4QVisions of ʿAmram[f]?), ll. 12-14a

J.T. MILIK (above, n. 25), p. 90

12 ארי כל כסל ורש[ע חשיכי]ן וכל [של]ם וקשוט נהיר[ין ארי כל בני נהורא]
13 לנהורא לשמח[ת עלמא ולח]דות[א יהכו]ן וכל בני חש[וכא לחשוכא למותא]
14 ולאבדנא יהכון[...

12 Car toute folie et ini[quité sont sombres], mais toute [paix] et vérité sont lumineuses. [Car tous les fils de la lumière *13* iron]t vers la lumière, vers la joie [éternelle] et [vers la ré]jouissance, tandis que tous les fils des ténè[bres] iront [vers les ténèbres, vers la mort] *14* et vers la perdition. [...]

T.H. GASTER (above, n. 80), p. 513
that, (since) all folly and wicked[ness] are things of [darkness], while all [probi]ty and truth [are] things of light, [all the sons of light will go (hereafter)] into light, into joy [everlasting and into] renewal, while all the sons of dark[ness] will go [into darkness, hell (and)] perdition; ...

J.A. FITZMYER – D.J. HARRINGTON, *A Manual of Palestinian Aramaic Texts (Second Century B.C. – Second Century A.D.)* (Biblica et Orientalia, 34), Roma, PIB, 1978, pp. 96-97 (reconstruction as in Milik)
12 for all foolishness and wicked[ness are dar]kened, and all [pea]ce and truth are illumi[ned; for all the sons of light] *13* wi[ll go] to the light, to [eternal] happine[ss, and to j]o[y;] and all the sons of dar[kness to darkness, to death,] *14* and to perdition will go; [...]

P.J. KOBELSKI (above, n. 20), p. 35 (reconstruction as in Milik)
12 For all stupidity and wicke[dness are dark]ened, but all [pea]ce and truth are illumi[ned. For all the sons of light] *13* [g]o to the light, to [eternal] joy, [and to re]joicing; but all the sons of da[rk, to darkness, to death,] *14* and to destruction, they go. [...]

K. BEYER (above, n. 26), p. 213

12 ארי כל כסל ורש[יע השיכי]ן וכל [חכי]ם וקשיט נהיר[ין .. .. כל בני נהורא]
13 לנהורא לשמא[לא ול..ול.. יהכי]ן וכל בני חש[וכא לחשוכא ל .. ולמותא]
14 ולאבדנא יהכון [...

12 Denn jeder Tor und Frevler sind [finster], und jeder Weise und Wahrhaftige sind hell. [... Alle Söhne des Lichtes] *13* werden zum Licht nach Norden [und zum ... und zum ... gehen]. Und alle Söhne der Finsternis werden [zur Finsternis nach ... und zum Tode] *14* und zum Untergang gehen. [...]

K. BEYER (above, n. 28), p. 88

12 ארי כל סכל ורש[יע חשי]ך וכל [חכי]ם וקשיט נהיר[... כל בני נהורא]
13 לנהורא ולחמ[י]מ[ותא ול]דין [קשטא יהכי]ן וכל בני חש[וכא לחשוכא ולקרא ולמותא]
14 ולאבדנא יהכון [...

12 Denn jeder Tor und Frevler ist finster, und jeder Weise und Wahrhaftige ist hell. [... Alle Söhne des Lichtes] *13* werden zum Licht und zur Wärme [und zum wahren] Recht gehen. Und alle Söhne [der] Finsternis werden [zur Finsternis und zur Kälte und zum Tode] *14* und zum Untergang gehen. [...]

G. VERMES, *The Dead Sea Scrolls in English*, London, Penguin, 1962, [3]1987, p. 263
12 For all folly and wicked[ness are dar]k, and all [pea]ce and truth are brigh[t. For all the Sons of Light g]o towards the light, towards [eternal] jo[y and re]joicin[g], and all the Sons of Dar[kness go towards death] and perdition ...

R.H. EISENMANN – M. WISE, *The Dead Sea Scrolls Uncovered*, Shaftesbury, Element, 1992, pp. 154-155, 156 (reconstruction as in Milik, but with סכל instead of כסל and השו]וכה להשוכה in l. 13)
12 For all foolishness and Evi[l will be darken]ed, while all [pea]ce and Truth will be made Ligh[t. All the sons of Light] *13* [are destin]ed for Light and [eternal j]oy (and) [re]joic[ing.] All the sons of Dark[ness] are destined for [Darkness and death] *14* and destruction ...

F. GARCÍA MARTÍNEZ, *Textos de Qumrán*, Madrid, Trotta, 1992, p. 322
12 Porque toda locura y maldad son tenebrosas, y toda paz y verdad son luminosas. [Por eso todos los hijos de la luz] *13* irán a la luz, a la alegría eterna, al regocijo; y todos los hijos de las tinie[blas irán a las sombras, a la muerte] *14* y a la perdición. [...]

É. PUECH (above, n. 29), pp. 537-539
12 'rw kl skl wrš[' ḥšyky]n wkl[ḥky]m wqšyṭ nhyr[yn 'rw kl bny nhwr'] 13 lnhwr' lśmḥ' [wlšlm' b]dyn[' rb' yhkw]n wkl bny ḥš[wk' lḥšwk' lmwt'] 14 wl'bdn' yhkwn[...
12 Car tous, fou et imp[ie, sont ténébreu]x, et tous, [sa]ge et véridique, sont lumin[eux, car tous les fils de lumière,] *13* à la lumière, à la joie [et à la paix, lors du grand] jugement (?) [ils iro]nt, mais tous les fils de ténè[bres, aux ténèbres, à la mort] *14* et à l'Abaddôn ils iront. ...

F. GARCÍA MARTÍNEZ, *The Dead Sea Scrolls Translated. The Qumran Texts in English*, Leiden, Brill, 1994, p. 275
12 For all senselessness and ev[il are dark,] and all [pea]ce and truth are brilliant. [This is why the sons of light] *13* will go to the light, to [everlasting] happiness, [to rejoicing;] and all the sons of dark[ness will go to the shades, to death] *14* and to annihilation. [...]

F. GARCÍA MARTÍNEZ – A.S. VAN DER WOUDE, *De Rollen van de Dode Zee*, Kampen, Kok, 1995, pp. 402-403
12 Want alle dwaasheid en goddeloos[heid zijn duister], maar alle [vre]de en waarheid zijn stralend. [Alle kinderen des lichts] *13* [zullen gaa]n naar het licht tot [eeuwige] vreugde [en blijdschap], maar alle kinderen der dui[sternis zullen naar de duisternis tot dood] *14* en tot verderf gaan [...]

J. MAIER, *Die Qumran-Essener. Die Texte vom Toten Meer*, II (UTB, 1863), München, Reinhardt, 1995, p. 723
12 Denn jeder Tor und Fr[evler –]. Und j[eder Wei]se (?) und Wahrhaftige helleuchtend [–] *13* für das Licht und für ... [–]..[.........]. Alle Söhne der Finst[ernis –] *14* und zum Verderben gehen sie hin [–]

M. WISE, M. ABEGG, JR., E. COOK, *The Dead Sea Scrolls. A New Translation*, San Francisco, Harper, 1996, p. 436
12 Indeed every fool and wicked man [is dark] and every [wise] and honest man is light [… all the Children of Light] *13* are destined for light and […] and [shall receive a just] judgment while all the children of dark[ness are destined] for darkness […] *14* and shall go to destruction […]

F. GARCÍA MARTÍNEZ – E.J.C. TIGCHELAAR (above, n. 13), pp. 1094-1095

12 ארי כל סכל ורש[ע חשיכי]ן וכל [חכי]ם וקשיט נהיר[ין ארי כל בני נהורא]
13 לנהורא לשמח[ת עלמא ולח]דות[א יהכו]ן וכל בני חש[וכה לחשוכה למותא]
14 ולאבדנא יהכון [...

12 For all foolish and ev[il are dark,] and all [wi]se and truthful are brilliant. [This is why the sons of light] *13* [will go] to the light, to [everlasting] happiness [and to re]joicing; and all the sons of dark[ness] will go [to the shades, to death] *14* and to annihilation. […]

A. CAQUOT, *Les Testaments qoumrâniens des Pères du sacerdoce*, in *RHPR* 78 (1998), p. 24
12 car tout (homme) sot et tout (homme) méchant sera enténébré et tout (homme) sage, tout (homme) véridique sera illu[miné … tous les enfants de lumière] *13* [iront] à la lumière et à la jo[ie? …] et tous les enfants des ténèbres iront aux tén[èbres, à la mort] *14* à la perdition […]

É. PUECH (above, n. 30), p. 394, 396

12 ארי כל סכל ורש[יע חשי]ך וכל[חכי]ם וקשיט נהיר[ארו כל בני נהורא]
13 לנהורא ל{תמימותא} <נעימתא[> ולשלמא ב]דינ[א רבא יהכו]ן וכל בני חש[וכא
לחשוכא למותא]
14 ולאבדנא יהכון[...

12 Car tout insensé et méch[ant (sera) enténé]bré et tout[sag]e et juste (sera) illuminé.[Car tous les fils de lumière] *13* à la lumière, à la {perfection} <suavité>[et à la paix, lors du grand] jugement [ils iron]t, et tous les fils de ténè[bres aux ténèbres, à la mort] *14* et à l'Abaddon ils iront…

INDEX OF AUTHORS

INDEX OF REFERENCES

HEBREW BIBLE

EARLY JEWISH LITERATURE (EXCEPT QUMRAN)

QUMRAN

NEW TESTAMENT

GREEK AND LATIN LITERATURE

BIBLIOTHECA EPHEMERIDUM THEOLOGICARUM LOVANIENSIUM

Series I

* = Out of print

*1. *Miscellanea dogmatica in honorem Eximii Domini J. Bittremieux,* 1947.
*2-3. *Miscellanea moralia in honorem Eximii Domini A. Janssen,* 1948.
*4. G. Philips, *La grâce des justes de l'Ancien Testament,* 1948.
*5. G. Philips, *De ratione instituendi tractatum de gratia nostrae sanctificationis,* 1953.
6-7. *Recueil Lucien Cerfaux. Études d'exégèse et d'histoire religieuse,* 1954. 504 et 577 p. Cf. *infra,* nos 18 et 71 (t. III). 25 € par tome
8. G. Thils, *Histoire doctrinale du mouvement œcuménique,* 1955. Nouvelle édition, 1963. 338 p. 4 €
*9. *Études sur l'Immaculée Conception,* 1955.
*10. J.A. O'Donohoe, *Tridentine Seminary Legislation,* 1957.
*11. G. Thils, *Orientations de la théologie,* 1958.
*12-13. J. Coppens, A. Descamps, É. Massaux (ed.), *Sacra Pagina. Miscellanea Biblica Congressus Internationalis Catholici de Re Biblica,* 1959.
*14. *Adrien VI, le premier Pape de la contre-réforme,* 1959.
*15. F. Claeys Bouuaert, *Les déclarations et serments imposés par la loi civile aux membres du clergé belge sous le Directoire (1795-1801),* 1960.
*16. G. Thils, *La «Théologie œcuménique». Notion-Formes-Démarches,* 1960.
17. G. Thils, *Primauté pontificale et prérogatives épiscopales. «Potestas ordinaria» au Concile du Vatican,* 1961. 103 p. 2 €
*18. *Recueil Lucien Cerfaux,* t. III, 1962. Cf. *infra,* n° 71.
*19. *Foi et réflexion philosophique. Mélanges F. Grégoire,* 1961.
*20. *Mélanges G. Ryckmans,* 1963.
21. G. Thils, *L'infaillibilité du peuple chrétien «in credendo»,* 1963. 67 p. 2 €
*22. J. Férin & L. Janssens, *Progestogènes et morale conjugale,* 1963.
*23. *Collectanea Moralia in honorem Eximii Domini A. Janssen,* 1964.
24. H. Cazelles (ed.), *De Mari à Qumrân. L'Ancien Testament. Son milieu. Ses écrits. Ses relectures juives* (Hommage J. Coppens, I), 1969. 158*-370 p. 23 €
*25. I. de la Potterie (ed.), *De Jésus aux évangiles. Tradition et rédaction dans les évangiles synoptiques* (Hommage J. Coppens, II), 1967.
26. G. Thils & R.E. Brown (ed.), *Exégèse et théologie* (Hommage J. Coppens, III), 1968. 328 p. 18 €
*27. J. Coppens (ed.), *Ecclesia a Spiritu sancto edocta. Hommage à Mgr G. Philips,* 1970. 640 p.
28. J. Coppens (ed.), *Sacerdoce et célibat. Études historiques et théologiques,* 1971. 740 p. 18 €

29. M. DIDIER (ed.), *L'évangile selon Matthieu. Rédaction et théologie,* 1972. 432 p. 25 €
*30. J. KEMPENEERS, *Le Cardinal van Roey en son temps,* 1971.

SERIES II

31. F. NEIRYNCK, *Duality in Mark. Contributions to the Study of the Markan Redaction,* 1972. Revised edition with Supplementary Notes, 1988. 252 p. 30 €
32. F. NEIRYNCK (ed.), *L'évangile de Luc. Problèmes littéraires et théologiques,* 1973. *L'évangile de Luc – The Gospel of Luke.* Revised and enlarged edition, 1989. x-590 p. 55 €
33. C. BREKELMANS (ed.), *Questions disputées d'Ancien Testament. Méthode et théologie,* 1974. *Continuing Questions in Old Testament Method and Theology.* Revised and enlarged edition by M. VERVENNE, 1989. 245 p. 30 €
34. M. SABBE (ed.), *L'évangile selon Marc. Tradition et rédaction,* 1974. Nouvelle édition augmentée, 1988. 601 p. 60 €
35. B. WILLAERT (ed.), *Philosophie de la religion – Godsdienstfilosofie. Miscellanea Albert Dondeyne,* 1974. Nouvelle édition, 1987. 458 p. 60 €
36. G. PHILIPS, *L'union personnelle avec le Dieu vivant. Essai sur l'origine et le sens de la grâce créée,* 1974. Édition révisée, 1989. 299 p. 25 €
37. F. NEIRYNCK, in collaboration with T. HANSEN and F. VAN SEGBROECK, *The Minor Agreements of Matthew and Luke against Mark with a Cumulative List,* 1974. 330 p. 23 €
38. J. COPPENS, *Le messianisme et sa relève prophétique. Les anticipations vétérotestamentaires. Leur accomplissement en Jésus,* 1974. Édition révisée, 1989. XIII-265 p. 25 €
39. D. SENIOR, *The Passion Narrative according to Matthew. A Redactional Study,* 1975. New impression, 1982. 440 p. 25 €
40. J. DUPONT (ed.), *Jésus aux origines de la christologie,* 1975. Nouvelle édition augmentée, 1989. 458 p. 38 €
41. J. COPPENS (ed.), *La notion biblique de Dieu,* 1976. Réimpression, 1985. 519 p. 40 €
42. J. LINDEMANS & H. DEMEESTER (ed.), *Liber Amicorum Monseigneur W. Onclin,* 1976. XXII-396 p. 25 €
43. R.E. HOECKMAN (ed.), *Pluralisme et œcuménisme en recherches théologiques. Mélanges offerts au R.P. Dockx, O.P.,* 1976. 316 p. 25 €
44. M. DE JONGE (ed.), *L'évangile de Jean. Sources, rédaction, théologie,* 1977. Réimpression, 1987. 416 p. 38 €
45. E.J.M. VAN EIJL (ed.), *Facultas S. Theologiae Lovaniensis 1432-1797. Bijdragen tot haar geschiedenis. Contributions to its History. Contributions à son histoire,* 1977. 570 p. 43 €
46. M. DELCOR (ed.), *Qumrân. Sa piété, sa théologie et son milieu,* 1978. 432 p. 43 €
47. M. CAUDRON (ed.), *Faith and Society. Foi et société. Geloof en maatschappij. Acta Congressus Internationalis Theologici Lovaniensis 1976,* 1978. 304 p. 29 €

*48. J. KREMER (ed.), *Les Actes des Apôtres. Traditions, rédaction, théologie,* 1979. 590 p.

49. F. NEIRYNCK, avec la collaboration de J. DELOBEL, T. SNOY, G. VAN BELLE, F. VAN SEGBROECK, *Jean et les Synoptiques. Examen critique de l'exégèse de M.-É. Boismard,* 1979. XII-428 p. 25 €

50. J. COPPENS, *La relève apocalyptique du messianisme royal. I. La royauté – Le règne – Le royaume de Dieu. Cadre de la relève apocalyptique,* 1979. 325 p. 25 €

51. M. GILBERT (ed.), *La Sagesse de l'Ancien Testament,* 1979. Nouvelle édition mise à jour, 1990. 455 p. 38 €

52. B. DEHANDSCHUTTER, *Martyrium Polycarpi. Een literair-kritische studie,* 1979. 296 p. 25 €

53. J. LAMBRECHT (ed.), *L'Apocalypse johannique et l'Apocalyptique dans le Nouveau Testament,* 1980. 458 p. 35 €

54. P.-M. BOGAERT (ed.), *Le livre de Jérémie. Le prophète et son milieu. Les oracles et leur transmission,* 1981. *Nouvelle édition mise à jour,* 1997. 448 p. 45 €

55. J. COPPENS, *La relève apocalyptique du messianisme royal. III. Le Fils de l'homme néotestamentaire.* Édition posthume par F. NEIRYNCK, 1981. XIV-192 p. 20 €

56. J. VAN BAVEL & M. SCHRAMA (ed.), *Jansénius et le Jansénisme dans les Pays-Bas. Mélanges Lucien Ceyssens,* 1982. 247 p. 25 €

57. J.H. WALGRAVE, *Selected Writings – Thematische geschriften. Thomas Aquinas, J.H. Newman, Theologia Fundamentalis.* Edited by G. DE SCHRIJVER & J.J. KELLY, 1982. XLIII-425 p. 25 €

58. F. NEIRYNCK & F. VAN SEGBROECK, avec la collaboration de E. MANNING, *Ephemerides Theologicae Lovanienses 1924-1981. Tables générales. (Bibliotheca Ephemeridum Theologicarum Lovaniensium 1947-1981),* 1982. 400 p. 40 €

59. J. DELOBEL (ed.), *Logia. Les paroles de Jésus – The Sayings of Jesus. Mémorial Joseph Coppens,* 1982. 647 p. 50 €

60. F. NEIRYNCK, *Evangelica. Gospel Studies – Études d'évangile. Collected Essays.* Edited by F. VAN SEGBROECK, 1982. XIX-1036 p. 50 €

61. J. COPPENS, *La relève apocalyptique du messianisme royal. II. Le Fils d'homme vétéro- et intertestamentaire.* Édition posthume par J. LUST, 1983. XVII-272 p. 25 €

62. J.J. KELLY, *Baron Friedrich von Hügel's Philosophy of Religion,* 1983. 232 p. 38 €

63. G. DE SCHRIJVER, *Le merveilleux accord de l'homme et de Dieu. Étude de l'analogie de l'être chez Hans Urs von Balthasar,* 1983. 344 p. 38 €

64. J. GROOTAERS & J.A. SELLING, *The 1980 Synod of Bishops: «On the Role of the Family». An Exposition of the Event and an Analysis of its Texts.* Preface by Prof. emeritus L. JANSSENS, 1983. 375 p. 38 €

65. F. NEIRYNCK & F. VAN SEGBROECK, *New Testament Vocabulary. A Companion Volume to the Concordance,* 1984. XVI-494 p. 50 €

66. R.F. COLLINS, *Studies on the First Letter to the Thessalonians,* 1984. XI-415 p. 38 €

67. A. PLUMMER, *Conversations with Dr. Döllinger 1870-1890.* Edited with Introduction and Notes by R. BOUDENS, with the collaboration of L. KENIS, 1985. LIV-360 p. 45 €

68. N. LOHFINK (ed.), *Das Deuteronomium. Entstehung, Gestalt und Botschaft / Deuteronomy: Origin, Form and Message,* 1985. XI-382 p. 50 €
69. P.F. FRANSEN, *Hermeneutics of the Councils and Other Studies.* Collected by H.E. MERTENS & F. DE GRAEVE, 1985. 543 p. 45 €
70. J. DUPONT, *Études sur les Évangiles synoptiques.* Présentées par F. NEIRYNCK, 1985. 2 tomes, XXI-IX-1210 p. 70 €
71. *Recueil Lucien Cerfaux,* t. III, 1962. Nouvelle édition revue et complétée, 1985. LXXX-458 p. 40 €
72. J. GROOTAERS, *Primauté et collégialité. Le dossier de Gérard Philips sur la Nota Explicativa Praevia (Lumen gentium, Chap. III).* Présenté avec introduction historique, annotations et annexes. Préface de G. THILS, 1986. 222 p. 25 €
73. A. VANHOYE (ed.), *L'apôtre Paul. Personnalité, style et conception du ministère,* 1986. XIII-470 p. 65 €
74. J. LUST (ed.), *Ezekiel and His Book. Textual and Literary Criticism and their Interrelation,* 1986. X-387 p. 68 €
75. É. MASSAUX, *Influence de l'Évangile de saint Matthieu sur la littérature chrétienne avant saint Irénée.* Réimpression anastatique présentée par F. NEIRYNCK. *Supplément: Bibliographie 1950-1985,* par B. DEHANDSCHUTTER, 1986. XXVII-850 p. 63 €
76. L. CEYSSENS & J.A.G. TANS, *Autour de l'Unigenitus. Recherches sur la genèse de la Constitution,* 1987. XXVI-845 p. 63 €
77. A. DESCAMPS, *Jésus et l'Église. Études d'exégèse et de théologie.* Préface de Mgr A. HOUSSIAU, 1987. XLV-641 p. 63 €
78. J. DUPLACY, *Études de critique textuelle du Nouveau Testament.* Présentées par J. DELOBEL, 1987. XXVII-431 p. 45 €
79. E.J.M. VAN EIJL (ed.), *L'image de C. Jansénius jusqu'à la fin du XVIII*e *siècle,* 1987. 258 p. 32 €
80. E. BRITO, *La Création selon Schelling. Universum,* 1987. XXXV-646 p. 75 €
81. J. VERMEYLEN (ed.), *The Book of Isaiah – Le livre d'Isaïe. Les oracles et leurs relectures. Unité et complexité de l'ouvrage,* 1989. X-472 p. 68 €
82. G. VAN BELLE, *Johannine Bibliography 1966-1985. A Cumulative Bibliography on the Fourth Gospel,* 1988. XVII-563 p. 68 €
83. J.A. SELLING (ed.), *Personalist Morals. Essays in Honor of Professor Louis Janssens,* 1988. VIII-344 p. 30 €
84. M.-É. BOISMARD, *Moïse ou Jésus. Essai de christologie johannique,* 1988. XVI-241 p. 25 €
84A. M.-É. BOISMARD, *Moses or Jesus: An Essay in Johannine Christology.* Translated by B.T. VIVIANO, 1993, XVI-144 p. 25 €
85. J.A. DICK, *The Malines Conversations Revisited,* 1989. 278 p. 38 €
86. J.-M. SEVRIN (ed.), *The New Testament in Early Christianity – La réception des écrits néotestamentaires dans le christianisme primitif,* 1989. XVI-406 p. 63 €
87. R.F. COLLINS (ed.), *The Thessalonian Correspondence,* 1990. XV-546 p. 75 €
88. F. VAN SEGBROECK, *The Gospel of Luke. A Cumulative Bibliography 1973-1988,* 1989. 241 p. 30 €

89. G. THILS, *Primauté et infaillibilité du Pontife Romain à Vatican I et autres études d'ecclésiologie*, 1989. XI-422 p. 47 €
90. A. VERGOTE, *Explorations de l'espace théologique. Études de théologie et de philosophie de la religion*, 1990. XVI-709 p. 50 €
*91. J.C. DE MOOR, *The Rise of Yahwism: The Roots of Israelite Monotheism*, 1990. *Revised and Enlarged Edition*, 1997. XV-445 p.
92. B. BRUNING, M. LAMBERIGTS & J. VAN HOUTEM (eds.), *Collectanea Augustiniana. Mélanges T.J. van Bavel*, 1990. 2 tomes, XXXVIII-VIII-1074 p. 75 €
93. A. DE HALLEUX, *Patrologie et œcuménisme. Recueil d'études*, 1990. XVI-887 p. 75 €
94. C. BREKELMANS & J. LUST (eds.), *Pentateuchal and Deuteronomistic Studies: Papers Read at the XIIIth IOSOT Congress Leuven 1989*, 1990. 307 p. 38 €
95. D.L. DUNGAN (ed.), *The Interrelations of the Gospels. A Symposium Led by M.-É. Boismard – W.R. Farmer – F. Neirynck, Jerusalem 1984*, 1990. XXXI-672 p. 75 €
96. G.D. KILPATRICK, *The Principles and Practice of New Testament Textual Criticism. Collected Essays*. Edited by J.K. ELLIOTT, 1990. XXXVIII-489 p. 75 €
97. G. ALBERIGO (ed.), *Christian Unity. The Council of Ferrara-Florence: 1438/39 – 1989*, 1991. X-681 p. 75 €
98. M. SABBE, *Studia Neotestamentica. Collected Essays*, 1991. XVI-573 p. 50 €
99. F. NEIRYNCK, *Evangelica II: 1982-1991. Collected Essays*. Edited by F. VAN SEGBROECK, 1991. XIX-874 p. 70 €
100. F. VAN SEGBROECK, C.M. TUCKETT, G. VAN BELLE & J. VERHEYDEN (eds.), *The Four Gospels 1992. Festschrift Frans Neirynck*, 1992. 3 volumes, XVII-X-X-2668 p. 125 €

SERIES III

101. A. DENAUX (ed.), *John and the Synoptics*, 1992. XXII-696 p. 75 €
102. F. NEIRYNCK, J. VERHEYDEN, F. VAN SEGBROECK, G. VAN OYEN & R. CORSTJENS, *The Gospel of Mark. A Cumulative Bibliography: 1950-1990*, 1992. XII-717 p. 68 €
103. M. SIMON, *Un catéchisme universel pour l'Église catholique. Du Concile de Trente à nos jours*, 1992. XIV-461 p. 55 €
104. L. CEYSSENS, *Le sort de la bulle Unigenitus. Recueil d'études offert à Lucien Ceyssens à l'occasion de son 90e anniversaire*. Présenté par M. LAMBERIGTS, 1992. XXVI-641 p. 50 €
105. R.J. DALY (ed.), *Origeniana Quinta. Papers of the 5th International Origen Congress, Boston College, 14-18 August 1989*, 1992. XVII-635 p. 68 €
106. A.S. VAN DER WOUDE (ed.), *The Book of Daniel in the Light of New Findings*, 1993. XVIII-574 p. 75 €
107. J. FAMERÉE, *L'ecclésiologie d'Yves Congar avant Vatican II: Histoire et Église. Analyse et reprise critique*, 1992. 497 p. 65 €

108. C. BEGG, *Josephus' Account of the Early Divided Monarchy (AJ 8, 212-420). Rewriting the Bible*, 1993. IX-377 p. 60 €
109. J. BULCKENS & H. LOMBAERTS (eds.), *L'enseignement de la religion catholique à l'école secondaire. Enjeux pour la nouvelle Europe*, 1993. XII-264 p. 32 €
110. C. FOCANT (ed.), *The Synoptic Gospels. Source Criticism and the New Literary Criticism*, 1993. XXXIX-670 p. 75 €
111. M. LAMBERIGTS (ed.), avec la collaboration de L. KENIS, *L'augustinisme à l'ancienne Faculté de théologie de Louvain*, 1994. VII-455 p. 60 €
112. R. BIERINGER & J. LAMBRECHT, *Studies on 2 Corinthians*, 1994. XX-632 p. 75 €
113. E. BRITO, *La pneumatologie de Schleiermacher*, 1994. XII-649 p. 75 €
114. W.A.M. BEUKEN (ed.), *The Book of Job*, 1994. X-462 p. 60 €
115. J. LAMBRECHT, *Pauline Studies: Collected Essays*, 1994. XIV-465 p. 63 €
116. G. VAN BELLE, *The Signs Source in the Fourth Gospel: Historical Survey and Critical Evaluation of the Semeia Hypothesis*, 1994. XIV-503 p. 63 €
117. M. LAMBERIGTS & P. VAN DEUN (eds.), *Martyrium in Multidisciplinary Perspective. Memorial L. Reekmans*, 1995. X-435 p. 75 €
118. G. DORIVAL & A. LE BOULLUEC (eds.), *Origeniana Sexta. Origène et la Bible/Origen and the Bible. Actes du Colloquium Origenianum Sextum, Chantilly, 30 août – 3 septembre 1993*, 1995. XII-865 p. 98 €
119. É. GAZIAUX, *Morale de la foi et morale autonome. Confrontation entre P. Delhaye et J. Fuchs*, 1995. XXII-545 p. 68 €
120. T.A. SALZMAN, *Deontology and Teleology: An Investigation of the Normative Debate in Roman Catholic Moral Theology*, 1995. XVII-555 p. 68 €.
121. G.R. EVANS & M. GOURGUES (eds.), *Communion et Réunion. Mélanges Jean-Marie Roger Tillard*, 1995. XI-431 p. 60 €
122. H.T. FLEDDERMANN, *Mark and Q: A Study of the Overlap Texts.* With an *Assessment* by F. NEIRYNCK, 1995. XI-307 p. 45 €
123. R. BOUDENS, *Two Cardinals: John Henry Newman, Désiré-Joseph Mercier.* Edited by L. GEVERS with the collaboration of B. DOYLE, 1995. 362 p. 45 €
124. A. THOMASSET, *Paul Ricœur. Une poétique de la morale. Aux fondements d'une éthique herméneutique et narrative dans une perspective chrétienne*, 1996. XVI-706 p. 75 €
125. R. BIERINGER (ed.), *The Corinthian Correspondence*, 1996. XXVII-793 p. 60 €
126. M. VERVENNE (ed.), *Studies in the Book of Exodus: Redaction – Reception – Interpretation*, 1996. XI-660 p. 60 €
127. A. VANNESTE, *Nature et grâce dans la théologie occidentale. Dialogue avec H. de Lubac*, 1996. 312 p. 45 €
128. A. CURTIS & T. RÖMER (eds.), *The Book of Jeremiah and its Reception – Le livre de Jérémie et sa réception*, 1997. 331 p. 60 €
129. E. LANNE, *Tradition et Communion des Églises. Recueil d'études*, 1997. XXV-703 p. 75 €

130. A. DENAUX & J.A. DICK (eds.), *From Malines to ARCIC. The Malines Conversations Commemorated*, 1997. IX-317 p. 45 €
131. C.M. TUCKETT (ed.), *The Scriptures in the Gospels*, 1997. XXIV-721 p. 60 €
132. J. VAN RUITEN & M. VERVENNE (eds.), *Studies in the Book of Isaiah. Festschrift Willem A.M. Beuken*, 1997. XX-540 p. 75 €
133. M. VERVENNE & J. LUST (eds.), *Deuteronomy and Deuteronomic Literature. Festschrift C.H.W. Brekelmans*, 1997. XI-637 p. 75 €
134. G. VAN BELLE (ed.), *Index Generalis ETL / BETL 1982-1997*, 1999. IX-337 p. 40 €
135. G. DE SCHRIJVER, *Liberation Theologies on Shifting Grounds. A Clash of Socio-Economic and Cultural Paradigms*, 1998. XI-453 p. 53 €
136. A. SCHOORS (ed.), *Qohelet in the Context of Wisdom*, 1998. XI-528 p. 60 €
137. W.A. BIENERT & U. KÜHNEWEG (eds.), *Origeniana Septima. Origenes in den Auseinandersetzungen des 4. Jahrhunderts,* 1999. XXV-848 p. 95 €
138. É. GAZIAUX, *L'autonomie en morale: au croisement de la philosophie et de la théologie*, 1998. XVI-760 p. 75 €
139. J. GROOTAERS, *Actes et acteurs à Vatican II*, 1998. XXIV-602 p. 75 €
140. F. NEIRYNCK, J. VERHEYDEN & R. CORSTJENS, *The Gospel of Matthew and the Sayings Source Q: A Cumulative Bibliography 1950-1995*, 1998. 2 vols., VII-1000-420* p. 95 €
141. E. BRITO, *Heidegger et l'hymne du sacré*, 1999. XV-800 p. 90 €
142. J. VERHEYDEN (ed.), *The Unity of Luke-Acts*, 1999. XXV-828 p. 60 €
143. N. CALDUCH-BENAGES & J. VERMEYLEN (eds.), *Treasures of Wisdom. Studies in Ben Sira and the Book of Wisdom. Festschrift M. Gilbert*, 1999. XXVII-463 p. 75 €
144. J.-M. AUWERS & A. WÉNIN (eds.), *Lectures et relectures de la Bible. Festschrift P.-M. Bogaert*, 1999. XLII-482 p. 75 €
145. C. BEGG, *Josephus' Story of the Later Monarchy (*AJ *9,1–10,185)*, 2000. X-650 p. 75 €
146. J.M. ASGEIRSSON, K. DE TROYER & M.W. MEYER (eds.), *From Quest to Q. Festschrift James M. Robinson*, 2000. XLIV-346 p. 60 €
147. T. RÖMER (ed.), *The Future of the Deuteronomistic History*, 2000. XII-265 p. 75 €
148. F.D. VANSINA, *Paul Ricœur: Bibliographie primaire et secondaire - Primary and Secondary Bibliography 1935-2000*, 2000. XXVI-544 p. 75 €
149. G.J. BROOKE & J.D. KAESTLI (eds.), *Narrativity in Biblical and Related Texts*, 2000. XXI-307 p. 75 €
150. F. NEIRYNCK, *Evangelica III: 1992-2000. Collected Essays*, 2001. XVII-666 p. 60 €
151. B. DOYLE, *The Apocalypse of Isaiah Metaphorically Speaking. A Study of the Use, Function and Significance of Metaphors in Isaiah 24-27*, 2000. XII-453 p. 75 €
152. T. MERRIGAN & J. HAERS (eds.), *The Myriad Christ. Plurality and the Quest for Unity in Contemporary Christology*, 2000. XIV-593 p. 75 €
153. M. SIMON, *Le catéchisme de Jean-Paul II. Genèse et évaluation de son commentaire du Symbole des apôtres*, 2000. XVI-688 p. 75 €

154. J. VERMEYLEN, *La loi du plus fort. Histoire de la rédaction des récits davidiques de 1 Samuel 8 à 1 Rois 2*, 2000. XIII-746 p. 80 €
155. A. WÉNIN (ed.), *Studies in the Book of Genesis. Literature, Redaction and History*, 2001. XXX-643 p. 60 €
156. F. LEDEGANG, *Mysterium Ecclesiae. Images of the Church and its Members in Origen*, 2001. XVII-848 p. 84 €
157. J.S. BOSWELL, F.P. MCHUGH & J. VERSTRAETEN (eds.), *Catholic Social Thought: Twilight of Renaissance*, 2000. XXII-307 p. 60 €
158. A. LINDEMANN (ed.), *The Sayings Source Q and the Historical Jesus*, 2001. XXII-776 p. 60 €
159. C. HEMPEL, A. LANGE & H. LICHTENBERGER (eds.), *The Wisdom Texts from Qumran and the Development of Sapiential Thought*, 2002. XII-502 p. 80 €
160. L. BOEVE & L. LEIJSSEN (eds.), *Sacramental Presence in a Postmodern Context*, 2001. XVI-382 p. 60 €
161. A. DENAUX (ed.), *New Testament Textual Criticism and Exegesis. Festschrift J. Delobel*, 2002. XVIII-391 p. 60 €
162. U. BUSSE, *Das Johannesevangelium. Bildlichkeit, Diskurs und Ritual. Mit einer Bibliographie über den Zeitraum 1986-1998*, 2002. XIII-572 p. 70 €
163. J.-M. AUWERS & H.J. DE JONGE (eds.), *The Biblical Canons*, 2003. LXXXVIII-718 p. 60 €
164. L. PERRONE (ed.), *Origeniana Octava. Origen and the Alexandrian Tradition*, 2003. Forthcoming.
165. R. BIERINGER, V. KOPERSKI & B. LATAIRE (eds.), *Resurrection in the New Testament. Festschrift J. Lambrecht*, 2002. XXXI-551 p. 70 €
166. M. LAMBERIGTS & L. KENIS (eds.), *Vatican II and Its Legacy*, 2002. XII-512 p. 65 €
167. P. DIEUDONNÉ, *La Paix clémentine. Défaite et victoire du premier jansénisme français sous le pontificat de Clément IX (1667-1669)*, 2003. XXXIX-302 p. 70 €

PRINTED ON PERMANENT PAPER • IMPRIME SUR PAPIER PERMANENT • GEDRUKT OP DUURZAAM PAPIER - ISO 9706
N.V. PEETERS S.A., WAROTSTRAAT 50, B-3020 HERENT

WISDOM AND APOCALYPTICISM
IN THE DEAD SEA SCROLLS
AND IN THE BIBLICAL TRADITION